Frommer's

Colorado

Here's what the critics say about Frommer's:

"Amazingly easy to use. Very portable, very complete."
—*Booklist*

♦

"The only mainstream guide to list specific prices. The Walter Cronkite of guidebooks—with all that implies."
—*Travel & Leisure*

♦

"Complete, concise, and filled wih useful information."
—*New York Daily News*

♦

"Hotel information is close to encyclopedic."
—*Des Moines Sunday Register*

Other Great Guides for Your Trip:

Frommer's Denver, Boulder & Colorado

Frommer's National Parks of the American West

Frommer's Arizona

Frommer's Utah

Frommer's®

5th
Edition

Colorado

by Don & Barbara Laine

MACMILLAN • USA

ABOUT THE AUTHORS

Residents of northern New Mexico for more than 25 years, **Don and Barbara Laine** have traveled extensively throughout the Rocky Mountains and the Southwest. In addition to *Frommer's Colorado,* they are the authors of *Frommer's Denver, Boulder & Colorado Springs, Frommer's Utah,* and *Frommer's Zion & Bryce Canyon National Parks,* and have contributed to *Frommer's USA* and *Frommer's National Parks of the American West.* The Laines have also written *New Mexico & Arizona State Parks* (The Mountaineers Books).

MACMILLAN TRAVEL

A Simon & Schuster Macmillan Company
1633 Broadway
New York, NY 10019

Find us online at **www.frommers.com**

ISBN 0-02-862611-7
ISSN 1053-2463
Editor: Leslie Shen
Production Editor: Mark Enochs
Photo Editor: Richard Fox
Design: Michele Laseau
Digital Cartography: Barbara Laine and Ortelius Design
Page creation by Ellen Considine, Sean Monkhouse, and Linda Quigley
Back Cover Photo: Dallas Divide, Mt. Sneffels Range

SPECIAL SALES

Bulk purchases (10+ copies) of Frommer's and selected Macmillan travel guides are available to corporations, organizations, mail-order catalogs, institutions, and charities at special discounts, and can be customized to suit individual needs. For more information write to Special Sales, Macmillan General Reference, 1633 Broadway, New York, NY 10019.

Manufactured in the United States of America

Contents

12 The Western Slope 303

13 Southwestern Colorado 334

14 The Southern Rockies 369

15 Southeastern Colorado 393

Appendix: Useful Toll-Free Numbers & Web Sites 409

List of Maps

AN INVITATION TO THE READER

In researching this book, we discovered many wonderful places—hotels, restaurants, shops, and more. We're sure you'll find others. Please tell us about them, so we can share the information with your fellow travelers in upcoming editions. If you were disappointed with a recommendation, we'd love to know that, too. Please write to:

Frommer's Colorado, 5th Edition
Macmillan Travel
1633 Broadway
New York, NY 10019

AN ADDITIONAL NOTE

Please be advised that travel information is subject to change at any time—and this is especially true of prices. We therefore suggest that you write or call ahead for confirmation when making your travel plans. The authors, editors, and publisher cannot be held responsible for the experiences of readers while traveling. Your safety is important to us, however, so we encourage you to stay alert and be aware of your surroundings. Keep a close eye on cameras, purses, and wallets, all favorite targets of thieves and pickpockets.

WHAT THE SYMBOLS MEAN

✪ Frommer's Favorites

Our favorite places and experiences—outstanding for quality, value, or both.

The following abbreviations are used for credit cards:

AE	American Express	EU	Eurocard
CB	Carte Blanche	JCB	Japan Credit Bank
DC	Diners Club	MC	MasterCard
DISC	Discover	V	Visa
ER	EnRoute		

FIND FROMMER'S ONLINE

Arthur Frommer's Budget Travel Online (www.frommers.com) offers more than 6,000 pages of up-to-the-minute travel information—including the latest bargains and candid, personal articles updated daily by Arthur Frommer himself. No other Web site offers such comprehensive and timely coverage of the world of travel.

The Best of Colorado

The old and the new, the rustic and the sophisticated, the wild and the refined—all of these experiences exist practically side by side in Colorado, amid what is arguably the most breathtaking mountain scenery in America.

Colorado's booming cities—Boulder, Colorado Springs, and Denver—and its admittedly somewhat glitzy resorts—especially Vail and Aspen—offer excellent dining and some of the finest jazz, rock, blues, and film festivals around. Throughout the state, you'll also find testaments to another time, when life was simpler but rougher, and only the strong survived: historic Victorian mansions, working turn-of-the-century steam trains, old gold mines, thousand-year-old adobe-and-stone villages, and authentic Old West towns complete with false-fronted saloons, dusty streets, and boardwalks.

Colorado truly comes alive for the visitor who ventures into the outdoors—among the towering peaks of the Rocky Mountains, the mesas of the western plateaus, and the broad plains in the east. You'll discover what inspired Katharine Lee Bates to pen the lyrics to "America the Beautiful" here in 1893 after you experience the view from the top of Pikes Peak. Go horseback riding, hiking, mountain biking, skiing, snowboarding, four-wheeling, rafting, or rock climbing—or simply sit in the sun and gaze at the mountains. Whatever you do, though, don't stay indoors. Enos Mills, an early-20th-century environmentalist and one of the driving forces behind the creation of Rocky Mountain National Park, said that a knowledge of nature is the basis of wisdom. In other words, get out and get smart. For many, that's the essence of Colorado.

Most visitors to Colorado combine a variety of activities, exploring historic sites as well as hiking trails, and possibly including a concert, a night in a handsome historic hotel, and a meal in one of the state's top restaurants. Following are the experiences we consider Colorado's very best, an overview of the state's highlights that will help you begin planning your trip.

1 The Best Ski Resorts

- **Aspen:** Not only do Aspen and its affiliated mountains have predictably superior ski terrain that ranges from some of the most fantastic expert skiing in Colorado to what *Ski* magazine has called the best mountain in America for those just learning to ski

(Buttermilk), but it is also one of the most fun, genuinely historic ski towns in Colorado. Although the town might come off at first as somewhat glitzy and certainly expensive, Aspen is still a real town, with longtime, year-round residents and a history that goes beyond the slopes. All of these reasons make it among our top picks to spend a week. See chapter 11.

- **Breckenridge:** The lure of Breckenridge, somewhat like Aspen, lies in its fabulous skiing for skiers of all abilities, its location in an old gold-prospecting settlement, and its abundance of ski-in/ski-out lodging. Breckenridge is also less expensive than Aspen and more down-home in feel. It's especially attractive to families because of its welcoming attitude toward snowboarders and variety of après-ski activities. You can easily keep yourself fully occupied here for a week. See chapter 11.
- **Vail:** This is it, the big one, America's most popular ski resort as well as its largest, with 4,644 acres of skiable terrain, 174 trails, and 10 high-speed quad lifts. Every serious skier needs to ski Vail at least once, and it would be very easy to spend a week here and rarely cross the same path twice. Vail is probably the easiest major resort to get around; everything's convenient via the resort's free bus system. But be prepared for steep prices, and don't look for Victorian charm—all you'll find are rows of condominiums. See chapter 11.
- **Purgatory:** One of Colorado's best-kept skiing secrets, this resort in the state's southwest corner is known for its beautiful sunny days, heavy annual snowfall, and exceptionally friendly and easy-going atmosphere. More than $4 million in trail and facilities improvements recently helped bring Purgatory into the major leagues of Colorado skiing. See chapter 13.

2 The Best Active Vacations

- **Cowpunching on a Cattle Drive:** To really step back into the West of the 1800s, join working cowboys on a genuine cattle drive. **Broken Skull Cattle Company** near Steamboat Springs (☎ 970/879-0090) offers a 9-day drive with a herd of longhorns; you'll ride horseback, help with the wrangling chores, eat chuckwagon meals, and sleep in tents. See chapter 11.
- **Skiing the San Juan Hut System:** Ambitious cross-country skiers who want to put a few miles behind them and ski among 14,000-foot alpine peaks love the San Juan Hut System's trail and series of shelters between Telluride and Moab, Utah. Designed for those of intermediate ability, skiers can tackle small sections or the entire trail, staying overnight at the huts, which are equipped with bunks, a propane cook stove, a wood stove, and kitchen equipment. See chapter 13.
- **Rafting with a String Quartet:** Lots of companies offer rafting trips, but how many take along an ensemble of professional musicians? **Dvorak's Kayak and Rafting Expeditions** (☎ 800/824-3795 or 719/539-6851) does just that. You won't get a lot of white-water excitement on this trip, but your full week on the Dolores or Green Rivers won't be boring either, as plenty of time is set aside for listening to the musicians perform in the riverside sandstone canyons. You can explore the canyons and forests, or just loaf in the sun. See chapter 14.

3 The Best Hiking Trails

- **The Buttes Trail at Pawnee Buttes:** This easy day-hike lets you see some of the "other" Colorado: the prairie on the state's eastern plains. A 1½-mile trail leads to Pawnee Buttes, the Rattlesnake Buttes made famous in James Michener's

Centennial. It's also a good trail for spotting coyotes, a variety of birds, and other wildlife, and has colorful wildflowers in the spring. See chapter 10.

- **The Colorado Trail at Kenosha Pass:** This easy section of the Colorado Trail near Breckenridge is a fun day's walk or can be the starting point for a serious backpacking trip. Off U.S. 285 (some 60 miles southwest of Denver), pick up the trail where the highway crosses 10,001-foot Kenosha Pass. This access point provides opportunities for short or long hikes through the aspen and bristlecone forest. See chapter 11.

- **The Bear Creek Canyon Trail:** Just south of Ouray, this national forest trail is particularly noted for its lush open meadows loaded with wildflowers in spring, as well as its old mine shafts, buildings, and equipment. Allow a full day. See chapter 13.

- **Hiking the Dunes in Great Sand Dunes National Monument:** This isn't a trail at all, but an opportunity to don your best French Foreign Legion hat and set out into the shifting sands in search of dramatic views from the top of a 750-foot dune. See chapter 14.

4 The Best Mountain Biking

- **Colorado State Forest Park:** Located in the mountains some 75 miles west of Fort Collins, this beautifully rugged country offers miles and miles of trails, as well as strategically located shelters for those on multi-day treks. You may find that you're not alone on the trails, though; the resident moose sometimes use them, too. See chapter 10.

- **Tipperary Creek Trail:** Considered by many to be Colorado's very best mountain-biking trail, this 30-mile ride from Fraser to Winter Park runs through dense forest and wildflower-covered meadows, offering views of rugged snowcapped peaks. It is strenuous, rising from an 8,600-foot elevation to more than 10,000 feet. See chapter 11.

- **Zephyr Express (Winter Park):** A chairlift for skiers in winter, the Zephyr Express hauls mountain bikers to several exciting trails from early June to Labor Day. Ambitious bikers can tackle the Roof of the Rockies Trail, which takes them to 11,200-foot Lunch Rock, or the easier Long Trail, which meanders some 6 miles down and around the mountain. See chapter 11.

- **Crested Butte:** Crested Butte vies with Winter Park for the title of mountain-biking capital of Colorado. The highly skilled will want to try Trail 401, a strenuous single-track loop that combines scenic beauty with steep grades and rough terrain. The less ambitious will be more interested in the Cement Creek Trail, a dirt road that follows Cement Creek, with many side trails to explore higher terrain. See chapter 14.

5 The Best Wilderness Experiences

- **Hiking the Colorado Trail:** For some 500 miles, this trail winds from Denver to Durango, through some of the state's most spectacular—and rugged—terrain, crossing the Continental Divide, eight mountain ranges, and six wilderness areas. Just to the west of Leadville, the trail passes through the Collegiate Peaks Wilderness with a view of some of Colorado's most prominent fourteeners (mountains more than 14,000 feet in elevation) and fields of wildflowers. The more hardy might take a side trip to the top of Mount Elbert, the state's tallest peak at 14,433 feet. See chapters 5 and 11.

- **Hiking the Mills Lake Trail in Rocky Mountain National Park:** Although it's packed at first, it usually becomes much less crowded after you've logged a few miles. At trail's end (elevation 10,000 feet), there's a gorgeous mountain lake ringed by towering peaks. The trailhead is easily accessible from Estes Park. See chapter 11.
- **Rafting Glenwood Canyon:** Running the rapids of the Colorado River is one of the best and surely most exciting ways to see one of the most beautiful canyons in the West. Although a bit too popular to provide a genuine wilderness experience, this stretch of river has sections rated for experts during the high spring runoff as well as quieter areas appropriate for everyone. See chapter 12.

6 The Best Places to Discover American Indian Culture

- **The Manitou Cliff Dwellings:** These easily accessible cliff dwellings, moved by preservationists at the turn of the century to protect them from marauding treasure seekers, accurately depict how the people of the Southwest lived some 900 years ago. See chapter 8.
- **Ute Indian Museum (Montrose):** One of Colorado's few museums dedicated to an existing Indian tribe, this excellent collection, run by the Colorado Historical Society, shows how Utes lived in the 19th century, as they were being forced to reconcile their way of life with that of the invading white pioneers. There's a particularly good exhibit of Ute ceremonial items. See chapter 12.
- **Mesa Verde National Park:** Home to the most impressive prehistoric cliff dwellings in the Southwest, Mesa Verde (Spanish for "green table") overwhelms you with its size and complexity. The first national park set aside to preserve works created by humans, it is located just outside Cortez and is spread over some 52,000 acres. Among the most compelling sites are Spruce Tree House and Square Tower House. Be sure to take the short guided hike to the Cliff Palace, the park's most famous attraction, a perfectly preserved, four-story, apartment-style dwelling. See chapter 13.
- **Ute Mountain Tribal Park:** What makes this group of ruins different from others in southwest Colorado is its location on the Ute Mountain Indian Reservation. The only way to see it is on a guided tour conducted by members of the Ute tribe. You'll see ruins and petroglyphs similar to those in Mesa Verde, but with an informed personal guide and without the crowds. See chapter 13.

7 The Best Places to Recapture the Old West

- **Old Town (Burlington):** On Colorado's eastern plains, right next door to Kansas, is this living-history museum, containing two dozen buildings (many from the 1880s). You can see a can-can show, a melodrama, or a gunfight, all in a setting that's much more reminiscent of Dodge City than Colorado's Victorian mountain towns. See chapter 10.
- **Creede, Lake City, Leadville, and Other Genuine Old Mining Towns:** With their extensive historic districts, stone jails, and false-fronted buildings, these mountain towns transport you back 100 years to the time when Butch Cassidy, Doc Holliday, Wyatt Earp, and other infamous characters stalked the saloons in search of the next card game. See chapter 11 for Leadville and chapter 14 for Creede and Lake City.

- **Bent's Old Fort National Historic Site (La Junta):** Reconstructed to the way it appeared in the 1830s and 1840s, this adobe fort shows life as it really was, when pioneers spent their time either trading peaceably with or fighting off plains warriors. Keep in mind that this is a reconstruction—not an original—but it's a faithfully rendered one at that. See chapter 15.

8 The Most Scenic Views

- **Garden of the Gods:** There's nothing like sunrise at Garden of the Gods in Colorado Springs, with its fantastic and sometimes fanciful red-sandstone formations sculpted by wind and water over hundreds of thousands of years. Although you can see a great deal from the marked view points, it's worth spending some time and foot-power to get away from the crowds on one of the park's many trails, to listen to the wind, and imagine the gods cavorting among the formations. See chapter 8.
- **The Black Canyon of the Gunnison:** Among the steepest and most narrow canyons in North America, the Black Canyon of the Gunnison, near Montrose, offers breathtaking and sometimes eerie views into the darkness below or, for ambitious hikers, from the canyon depths to the daylight above. The sheerness of its 2,500-foot-high walls, the narrowness of its 40-foot-wide base, and the resulting darkness at its core evoke a somber, almost religious mood. See chapter 12.
- **Colorado National Monument:** Located just west of Grand Junction, this national monument provides stunning distant views across its red-rock canyons and sandstone monoliths. The 23-mile Rim Rock Drive offers incredible views, and a series of short walks and backcountry trails provide additional vistas and a lot more solitude. The best light is either early in the morning or late in the afternoon, when the rocks are deep red and shadows dance among the stone sculptures. See chapter 12.
- **The San Juan Skyway:** This 238-mile circle drive that passes through the towns of Durango, Telluride, and Ouray is among the most beautiful scenic drives in America, crossing five mountain passes and leading past historic mining camps, fields of wildflowers, stately forests, snowcapped peaks, and cascading waterfalls. It's a thrilling drive but not advisable for those who have difficulty with high elevation (Red Mountain Pass is 11,008 feet above sea level) or steep, winding roads. Except in summer, it's wise to check first to see if the passes are closed due to snow. See chapter 13.

9 The Best Family Vacations

- **Panning for Gold and Other Adventures in Idaho Springs:** This excursion from Denver offers kids and adults alike the chance to pan for gold, explore a gold mine, take home an ore sample, and visit a mill and museum. The Argo Express is a half-scale replica of an old-time steam train, providing rides at the Argo Mill. While in the area, you can take a drive to the summit of 14,260-foot Mount Evans, or go horseback or pony riding. See chapter 7.
- **Ropin' Dogies at Sylvan Dale Guest Ranch:** Nestled in the mountains outside Loveland, this is a real cattle-and-horse ranch where guests are encouraged to pitch in with chores when they're not horseback riding, swimming, fishing, or busy loafing. There's an outdoor pool, tennis and volleyball courts, an indoor recreation room, and a kids' play area. Guided nature hikes, square dancing, and hayrides are popular. See chapter 10.

- **Riding the Durango & Silverton Narrow Gauge Railroad:** Based in Durango, this 1880s steam-train excursion is a trip into the past, complete with smoke in your eyes and cinders in your hair. In addition, it's an exciting way to see the beautiful San Juan mountains, just as travelers here saw them 100 years ago. See chapter 13.
- **Exploring Great Sand Dunes National Monument:** There's no ocean, but this gigantic beach, about 40 miles northeast of Alamosa, is a great place to explore, camp, hike, or just play in the 700-foot-tall dunes. Rangers provide guided nature walks and campfire programs during summer, and a hiking/off-road-vehicle trail leads out the back of the monument into the national forest. See chapter 14.

10 The Most Unusual Travel Experiences

- **United States Mint (Denver):** This is where all that money comes from—at least the coins. If you've ever wondered just how those heavy chunks of metal actually become legal tender, this is your opportunity to find out as you watch the stamping of some of the five billion coins produced here each year. But let's be honest—the real reason to visit the mint is simply to be surrounded by all that cold, hard cash. See chapter 7.
- **Hakushika Sake USA:** Located in Golden, just outside Denver, this brewery produces the unofficial national drink of Japan. Sake is created much like beer, and the brewery has been designed to give visitors an excellent view of the process. There's also an exhibit of brewing techniques from past centuries. A bonus is the exquisite display of Japanese art. See chapter 7.
- **The San Luis Valley Alligator Farm:** Alamosa, one of the coldest spots in America, is not where you'd expect to find alligators, but geothermal wells apparently make conditions just right for breeding the not-so-friendly beasts, who share the site with a fish hatchery. See chapter 14.
- **The Colorado Territorial Prison Museum and Park (Cañon City):** Located in a former women's prison, this museum may be a bit too macabre for some. It contains an actual gas chamber, the last hangman's noose used legally in Colorado, and other reminders of what became of some of those Old West outlaws we've heard so much about. See chapter 15.

11 The Best Luxury Hotels

- **The Brown Palace Hotel** (Denver; ☎ **800/321-2599** or 303/297-3111 in North America; 800/228-2917 in Colorado): Denver's finest hotel, the Brown Palace has been open continuously since 1892, serving high society and celebrities—from President Dwight Eisenhower to the Beatles—with elegance and charm. Although most of the rooms are Victorian in decor, with Tiffany lamps and other accoutrements, our favorites are the art-deco rooms, with an undeniable feel of the 1920s and 1930s. See chapter 6.
- **The Broadmoor** (Colorado Springs; ☎ **800/634-7711** or 719/634-7711): Colorado's top-rated resort hotel has it all—excellent dining, golf courses, pools, tennis courts, exercise facilities, and shopping, plus extraordinary service—in a fascinating historic building with extensive and well-kept grounds. Although some might consider the Broadmoor a bit pretentious, it certainly knows how to pamper its guests. See chapter 8.

- **Hyatt Regency Beaver Creek** (Avon; ☎ **800/233-1234** or 970/949-4164): This plush ski-in/ski-out resort at the foot of the Beaver Creek lifts combines a casual, comfortable atmosphere with superb service in a handsome, elegant building. The rooms' decor is a quirky combination of Old West and French country that works. See chapter 11.
- **The St. Regis Aspen** (Aspen; ☎ **970/920-3300**): At the base of Aspen Mountain, the St. Regis offers great views of the mountains or town, impeccable service, splendid rooms, and all the services and amenities you'd expect in a fine hotel. Although a bit pricey, especially over the Christmas holidays, the hotel is supremely elegant in a comfortable, cozy way. See chapter 11.

12 The Best Moderately Priced Accommodations

- **Hearthstone Inn** (Colorado Springs; ☎ **800/521-1885** or 719/473-4413): This Colorado Springs gem, situated in two adjoining historic Victorian homes, is perfect for those who like the charm and amenities of a bed-and-breakfast but the privacy of a hotel. All rooms are different, but each has antiques, collectibles, and brass beds. A definite plus here is the breakfast, which is included. See chapter 8.
- **Days Inn Boulder** (Boulder; ☎ **303/499-4422**): Perhaps the best managed chain motel we've ever seen, this four-story Days Inn is quiet and handsomely appointed, and the upper floors offer great views of the mountains. What's surprising is the better-than-average continental breakfast, included in the room rate. See chapter 9.
- **Baldpate Inn** (Estes Park; ☎ **970/586-6151**): This small inn near Rocky Mountain National Park is open only in summer, and most units share bathrooms, but it has personality galore: handmade quilts, early-20th-century furnishings, and a large stone fireplace in the living room. Named for the novel *Seven Keys to Baldpate,* the inn takes its theme seriously, inviting guests to add their own keys to a collection that now exceeds 20,000. It also offers an excellent soup-and-salad buffet dinner. See chapter 11.
- **Mid-Town Motel** (La Junta; ☎ **719/384-7741**): Those looking for a clean, quiet mom-and-pop motel at extremely good rates will do no better than the Mid-Town in La Junta. Solo travelers get rooms with recliners, and pets are welcome. See chapter 15.

13 The Best Bed-and-Breakfasts

- **Holden House 1902 Bed & Breakfast Inn** (Colorado Springs; ☎ **719/471-3980**): When you picture a storybook Victorian home, filled with family heirlooms and antiques, this Colorado Springs B&B is it. Of course, there are so many objects around, it's sometimes hard to find a place to put down your suitcase—but you gladly will. Homey touches include the two resident cats, who will happily curl up on your bed if you leave the door open. See chapter 8.
- **The Alps** (Boulder; ☎ **800/414-2577** or 303/444-5445): This historic log lodge on a mountainside west of Boulder is a perfect country bed-and-breakfast inn. It has spacious rooms, all with lots of wood, working Victorian fireplaces, British antiques, and views of the mountains and forests. Although only a few minutes from downtown Boulder, the inn is secluded and very quiet—a great getaway spot. See chapter 9.

- **The Cottonwood Inn & Gallery** (Alamosa; ☎ **800/955-2623** or 719/589-3882): Decorated with regional art, this 1908 bungalow in Alamosa has a variety of rooms, each unique, including one that is great for small families, complete with stuffed animals and children's books. Another unit contains a fascinating combination of southwestern and art-deco furnishings. See chapter 14.

Getting to Know Colorado 2

The Rocky Mountains are the backbone of North America, and Colorado is their heart, with more than 50 peaks that soar above 14,000 feet. The Rockies—with their evergreen and aspen forests, racing streams and rivers, and wealth of wildlife—are perfect for recreation throughout the year, from summer hiking and rafting to winter skiing through deep powder snow.

But Colorado isn't just mountains. It is also the wheat and corn fields of the vast eastern prairies, the high plateau country of the west, and the modern, sophisticated cities of the Front Range.

Take the time to see the sights of cosmopolitan Denver, the "Mile High City"; Colorado Springs, home of the U.S. Air Force Academy and U.S. Olympic Training Center; and the university towns of Boulder and Fort Collins. Indulge in luxury hotels, gourmet cuisine, and year-round recreation at thriving resort communities such as Aspen, Vail, and Steamboat Springs. Ride narrow-gauge steam trains and relive the mining-boom days in historic towns such as Durango, Georgetown, and Creede—straight out of the Old West yet alive with 20th-century verve. Immerse yourself in the natural and man-made wonders of national parks and monuments such as Mesa Verde, Rocky Mountain, Great Sand Dunes, Dinosaur, Black Canyon of the Gunnison, and Bent's Old Fort, each with its own unique appeal.

1 The Natural Environment

First-time visitors to Colorado are often awed by the looming wall of the Rocky Mountains, which come into sight a good 100 miles away, soon after drivers cross the line from Kansas. East of the Rockies, a 5,000-foot peak is considered high—yet Colorado has 1,143 mountains above 10,000 feet, including 54 over 14,000 feet! Highest of all is Mount Elbert at 14,433 feet, southwest of Leadville.

The Rockies were formed some 65 million years ago by pressures that forced hard Precambrian rock to the earth's surface, breaking through and pushing layers of earlier rock up on end. Then millions of years of erosion eliminated the soft surface material, producing the magnificent Rockies of calendar fame.

An almost-perfect rectangle, Colorado measures some 385 miles east to west, and 275 miles north to south. The ridge of the

Continental Divide zigzags more or less through the center of the 104,247-square-mile state, eighth largest in the nation.

2 The Regions in Brief

Colorado's basic topography can be visualized by dividing the state into vertical thirds: The eastern part is plains; the midsection is high mountains; and the western third is mesa land.

That's a broad simplification, of course. The central Rockies, though they cover six times the mountain area of Switzerland, are not a single vast highland but a series of high ranges running roughly north–south. East of the Continental Divide, the primary river systems are the South Platte, Arkansas, and Rio Grande, all flowing toward the Gulf of Mexico. The westward-flowing Colorado River system dominates the western part of the state, with tributary networks including the Gunnison, Dolores, and Yampa-Green Rivers. In most cases, these rivers are not broad bodies of water like the Ohio or Mississippi, but streams heavy with spring and summer snowmelt, which are reduced to mere trickles during much of the year by the demands of farm and ranch irrigation. Besides agricultural use, they provide life-giving water to wildlife and offer wonderful opportunities for rafting and fishing.

The forested mountains are essential to retaining precious water for the lowlands. Eleven national forests comprise 15 million acres of land, and there are eight million acres controlled by the Bureau of Land Management, also open for public recreation. Another half million acres are within national parks, monuments, and recreation areas under the administration of the National Park Service. In addition to all this, the state operates more than 40 state parks.

Colorado's name, Spanish for "red," derives from the state's red soil and rocks. Some of the sandstone agglomerates have become attractions in their own right, such as Red Rocks Amphitheater west of Denver and the startling Garden of the Gods in Colorado Springs.

Of Colorado's 3.8 million people, some 80% live along the Front Range, the I-25 corridor, where the plains meet the mountains. Denver, the state capital, has a population just over 500,000, with another million in the metropolitan area. Colorado Springs has the second largest population, with just over 300,000 residents, followed by Pueblo (99,000) and Boulder (84,000).

3 Colorado Today

Ask any seasoned Coloradan what makes the state unique, and the response most likely will be its mountains. It is almost impossible to overemphasize the spectacular beauty here, or the influence it has had on the development and present-day character of the state. Colorado has been a prime tourist destination practically since the day the first pioneers arrived. Particularly in the 19th century, but also in the first half of the 20th century, those attracted to this rugged land tended to be independent types—sometimes downright ornery and antisocial—who sought wide-open spaces, untamed wilderness, and plenty of elbow room. Of course, the dream of riches from gold and silver mines helped, too.

These early transplants established the state's image as the domain of rugged individualists—solitary cowboys, prospectors, and others—who just wanted to be left alone. Much of that feeling still survives, and today's Coloradans have a deserved reputation as a feisty, independent lot. Colorado has the distinction of being home

Colorado

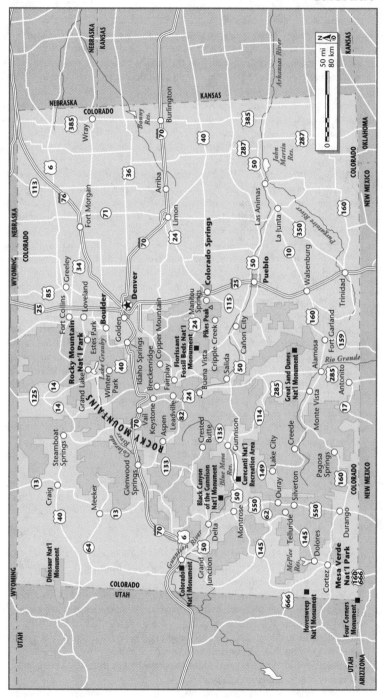

to some of the most politically active liberals and conservatives in the country. They don't follow trends; they make them. It's where some of the country's first municipal gay-rights ordinances were passed; yet it's also home to the vanguard of the family values movement: Focus on the Family, one of the most powerful lobbying organizations for the Christian right's political agenda, is based in Colorado Springs.

Somewhat understandably, such a diversity of political perspectives doesn't exactly engender accord. In the early 1990s, the rest of the country got a quick lesson in Colorado-style politics during the controversy surrounding Amendment 2, a state constitutional amendment aimed at prohibiting certain antidiscrimination laws.

Although the successful 1992 ballot measure was vaguely worded, its intent was clear: to eliminate local gay-rights ordinances that Aspen, Boulder, and Denver had passed, and to prevent other communities, or the state legislature, from creating laws that would specifically protect gays and lesbians from discrimination in employment and housing.

A high-profile nationwide boycott of the state was launched in 1993, and although it scared off some convention business and kept a few tourists away, the end result was a bit of a wash, and the 1992–1993 ski season was among the best in the state's history. The boycott was called off when the amendment was declared unconstitutional by the state Supreme Court later that year. The state appealed, but the ruling was upheld by the U.S. Supreme Court in the spring of 1996.

After the controversy died down, further proof of Colorado's maverick streak came just a few months later, when former three-term governor Richard Lamm—known as "Governor Gloom" for his philosophy of fiscal conservatism and individual sacrifice—announced he would seek the presidential nomination from Ross Perot's Reform Party, virtually ensuring a showdown with the megalomaniacal Perot, but also broadening the appeal of Perot's creation. Not surprisingly, he lost to Perot, but in true Colorado spirit, he went down fighting. Lamm described the toe-to-toe experience with Perot as akin to drinking water out of a fire hydrant, but also admitted he wouldn't have missed it for the world.

An issue on which almost all Coloradans agree, pretty much regardless of other differences, is the need to control tourism. While the industry's financial benefits to the state are well understood, it's generally acknowledged that if tourism is allowed to grow unchecked, the cost to the state's natural resources will be tremendous.

To that end, town officials in Vail reached an agreement with resort management in 1995 to limit the number of skiers on the mountain and alleviate other aspects of overcrowding in the village. The word from Vail and other high-profile Colorado tourist destinations is that visitors will be given incentives, such as discounts, to visit at off-peak times. Ski area officials also have not ruled out turning away skiers after a set number of passes are sold.

Conflicts between environmentalists and the ski industry came to a head in October 1998, when militant environmental activists set fires at a Vail resort that caused more than $12 million in damage. A group called Earth Liberation Front claimed credit for the arson, although investigators said they could not prove the group was responsible. The organization wanted to halt an expansion project at Vail that it said would harm a potential habitat for the lynx, a threatened member of the cat family that is similar to a bobcat.

In addition to overcrowded ski resorts, many in the state are concerned about the increasing popularity of Rocky Mountain National Park. In autumn, during the elk-rutting season, hundreds of people make their way to the Moraine Park and

Horseshoe Park areas every evening. National park officials say that motor vehicle noise is starting to affect the experience and disturb the animals' routines. Disappointed visitors are asking where they can go to find the quiet serenity they had hoped to experience there.

Another issue that has wide support across the state is controlling growth. The rugged mountains and scenic beauty that lure tourists and outdoor recreation enthusiasts have also fueled an influx of transplants—a 1990s version of the gold-seekers and pioneers who settled the state. Since 1990, Colorado has gained new residents at the staggering rate of three times the national average. According to recently released figures from the Census Bureau, 11 of the nation's 30 fastest-growing counties in the first half of the 1990s were in Colorado. Six are within 75 miles of Denver, including the two fastest growing, the wealthy southern suburbs of Douglas and Elbert.

Many of these new residents are active, outdoorsy types who relish the idea of riding their bikes to work and escaping the pollution, crime, and overcrowding of the coasts. But perhaps inevitably, many native and long-term Coloradans have begun to complain that these newcomers are changing the character of the state, and bringing with them the very problems from which they sought escape.

The challenge for Coloradans as the 21st century dawns is to solve the twin riddles of tourism and growth that are plaguing much of the American West: How do we achieve a balance between preserving a state's unique character and spectacular natural resources for future generations, while still enjoying all it has to offer today?

4 History 101

To explore Colorado today is to step back into its history, from its dinosaur graveyards, impressive stone and mud cities of the ancestral Puebloans (also known as the Anasazi), reminders of the Wild West of Bat Masterson and Doc Holliday, and elegant Victorian mansions, to today's science and technology. The history of Colorado is a testimony to the human ability to adapt and flourish in a difficult environment.

The earliest people in Colorado are believed to have been nomadic hunters, who arrived some 12,000 to 20,000 years ago via the Bering Strait, following the tracks of the now-extinct woolly mammoth and bison. Then, about 2,000 years ago, the ancestors of today's Pueblo people arrived, living in shallow caves in the Four Corners area, where the borders of Colorado, Utah, Arizona, and New Mexico meet.

Originally hunters, they gradually learned farming, and basket making, pottery making, and the construction of pit houses. Eventually they built complex villages, such as can be seen at Mesa Verde National Park. For some unknown reason, possibly drought, they deserted the area around the end of the 13th century, probably moving southward into present-day New Mexico and Arizona.

Although the ancestral Puebloans were gone by

Dateline

- **12,000 B.C.** First inhabitants of Colorado include Folsom Man.
- **3000 B.C.** Prehistoric farming communities appear.
- **A.D. 1000** Ancestral Puebloan cliff-dweller culture peaks in Four Corners region.
- **Late 1500s** Spanish explore upper Rio Grande Valley, colonize Santa Fe and Taos, New Mexico, and make forays into what is now southern Colorado.
- **1776** U.S. declares independence from England.
- **1803** The Louisiana Purchase includes most of modern Colorado.
- **1805** The Lewis and Clark expedition sights the Rocky Mountains.
- **1806–07** Captain Zebulon Pike leads first U.S. expedition into Colorado Rockies.

continues

- **1822** William Becknell establishes Santa Fe Trail.
- **1842–44** Lieutenant John C. Frémont and Kit Carson explore Colorado and American West.
- **1848** Treaty of Guadalupe-Hidalgo ends Mexican War, adds American Southwest to the United States.
- **1858** Gold discovered in modern Denver.
- **1859** General William Larimer founds Denver. Major gold strikes in nearby Rockies.
- **1861** Colorado Territory proclaimed.
- **1862** Colorado cavalry wins major Civil War battle at Glorieta Pass, New Mexico. Homestead Act is passed.
- **1863–68** Ute tribe obtains treaties guaranteeing 16 million acres of western Colorado land.
- **1864** Hundreds of Cheyenne killed in Sand Creek Massacre. University of Denver becomes Colorado's first institution of higher education.
- **1870** Kansas City–Denver rail line completed. Agricultural commune of Greeley established by newspaperman Nathan Meeker. Colorado State University opens in Fort Collins.
- **1871** General William Palmer founds Colorado Springs.
- **1876** Colorado becomes 38th state.
- **1877** University of Colorado opens in Boulder.
- **1878** Little Pittsburg silver strike launches Leadville's mining boom, Colorado's greatest.
- **1879** Milk Creek Massacre by Ute warriors leads to tribe's removal to reservations.

continues

the time Spanish conquistadors arrived in the mid–16th century, in their place were two nomadic cultures: the mountain dwellers of the west, primarily Ute; and the plains tribes of the east, principally Arapahoe, Cheyenne, and Comanche.

EXPLORATION & SETTLEMENT   Spanish colonists, having established settlements at Santa Fe, Taos, and other upper Rio Grande locations in the 16th and 17th centuries, didn't immediately find southern Colorado attractive for colonization. Not only was there a lack of financial and military support from the Spanish crown, but the freedom-loving, sometimes-fierce Comanche and Ute also made it clear that they would rather be left alone.

Nevertheless, Spain still held title to southern and western Colorado in 1803, when U.S. President Thomas Jefferson paid $15 million for the vast Louisiana Territory, which included the lion's share of modern Colorado. Two years later the Lewis and Clark expedition passed by, but the first official exploration by the U.S. government occurred when Jefferson sent Capt. Zebulon Pike to the territory. Pikes Peak, Colorado's landmark mountain and a top tourist attraction near Colorado Springs, was named for the explorer.

As the West began to open up in the 1820s, the Santa Fe Trail was established, cutting through Colorado's southeast corner. Bent's Fort was built on the Arkansas River between 1828 and 1832, and you can visit the reconstructed fort, a national historic site, near La Junta.

Much of eastern Colorado, including what would become Denver, Boulder, and Colorado Springs, was then part of the Kansas Territory. It was populated almost exclusively by plains tribes until 1858, when gold-seekers discovered flakes of the precious metal near the junction of Cherry Creek and the South Platte, and the city of Denver was established, named for Kansas governor James Denver.

The Cherry Creek strike was literally a flash in the gold-seeker's pan, but two strikes in the mountains just west of Denver in early 1859 were more significant: Clear Creek, near what would become Idaho Springs; and in a quartz vein at Gregory Gulch, which led to the founding of Central City.

THE TERRITORY   Abraham Lincoln was elected president of the United States in November 1860, and Congress created the Colorado Territory three months later. The new territory absorbed neighboring sections from Utah, Nebraska, and New Mexico to form the boundaries that comprise the state today. Lincoln's Homestead Act of 1862 brought much of the public domain into private ownership, and led to the platting of Front Range townships, starting with Denver in 1861.

Controlling the American Indian peoples was a priority of the territorial government. A treaty negotiated in 1851 had guaranteed the entire Pikes Peak region to the nomadic plains tribes, but that had been made moot by the arrival of settlers in the late 1850s. The Fort Wise Treaty of 1861 exchanged the Pikes Peak territory for five million fertile acres of Arkansas Valley land, north of modern La Junta. But when the Arapaho and Cheyenne continued to roam their old hunting grounds, conflict became inevitable. Frequent rumors and rare instances of hostility against settlers led the Colorado cavalry to attack a peaceful settlement of Indians—who were flying Old Glory and a white flag—on November 29, 1864. More than 150 Cheyenne and Arapaho, two-thirds of them women and children, were killed in what has become known as the Sand Creek Massacre.

Vowing revenge, the Cheyenne and Arapaho launched a campaign to drive whites from their ancient hunting grounds. Their biggest triumph was the destruction of the northeast Colorado town of Julesburg in 1865, but the cavalry, bolstered by returning Civil War veterans, managed to force the two tribes onto reservations in Indian Territory, in what is now Oklahoma—a barren area that whites thought they would never want.

Also in 1865, a smelter was built in Black Hawk, just west of Denver, setting the stage for the large-scale spread of mining throughout Colorado in years to come. When the first transcontinental railroad was completed in 1869, the Union Pacific went through Cheyenne, Wyoming, 100 miles north of Denver, but four years later the line was linked to Denver by the Kansas City–Denver Railroad.

STATEHOOD Colorado politicians had begun pressing for statehood during the Civil War, but it wasn't until August 1, 1876, that Colorado became the 38th state. Occurring less than a month after the United States' 100th birthday, it was natural that Colorado would become known as "the Centennial State."

- **1890** Sherman Silver Purchase Act boosts price of silver. Gold discovered at Cripple Creek, leading to state's biggest gold rush.
- **1893** Women win right to vote. Silver industry collapses following repeal of Sherman Silver Purchase Act.
- **1901–07** President Theodore Roosevelt sets aside 16 million acres of national forest land in Colorado.
- **1906** U.S. Mint built in Denver.
- **1913** Wolf Creek Pass highway is first to cross Continental Divide in Colorado.
- **1915** Rocky Mountain National Park established.
- **1934** Direct Denver–San Francisco rail travel begins. Taylor Grazing Act ends homesteading.
- **1941–45** World War II establishes Colorado as military center.
- **1947** Aspen's first chairlift begins operation.
- **1948–58** Uranium "rush" sweeps western slope.
- **1955** Environmentalists prevent construction of Echo Park Dam in Dinosaur National Monument.
- **1967** Colorado legalizes medically necessary abortions.
- **1972** Colorado voters reject a chance to host the 1976 Winter Olympics.
- **1988** Senator Gary Hart, a front-runner for the Democratic presidential nomination, withdraws from race after a scandal.
- **1992** Colorado voters approve Amendment 2, a controversial constitutional amendment banning laws that protect gays and lesbians from discrimination.

continues

- **1993** Denver becomes 15th U.S. city with three major professional sports teams with the acquisition of the Rockies, a new major-league baseball franchise.
- **1995** The $4.2-billion state-of-the-art Denver International Airport and $2.16-million Coors Field baseball stadium open. Denver goes sports-crazy with its fourth major professional sports team, the Avalanche, a member of the National Hockey League.
- **1996** The U.S. Supreme Court strikes down Amendment 2, saying it denies gays and lesbians constitutional rights afforded all Americans.
- **1996** The Avalanche win the Stanley Cup, giving Colorado its first championship in any major league.
- **1997** Weather wreaks havoc across the state. First, a summer rainstorm turns a small creek that runs through Fort Collins into a roaring river that floods parts of the town, killing five residents and causing some $200 million in damage. Then, in late October, a 24-hour blizzard, the worst October storm in Denver since 1923, piles snow across the Front Range, virtually shutting down I-25 from Wyoming to New Mexico and stranding thousands of passengers at Denver International Airport.
- **1997** Gary Lee Davis, convicted of the 1986 abduction and murder of a Colorado farm wife, is executed by lethal injection, the state's first execution in 30 years.

continues

The state's new constitution gave the vote to blacks, but not to women, despite the strong efforts of the Colorado Women's Suffrage Association. Women finally succeeded in winning the vote in 1893, three years after Wyoming became the first state to offer universal suffrage.

At the time of statehood, most of Colorado's vast western region was still occupied by some 3,500 mountain and plateau dwellers of a half dozen Ute tribes. Unlike the plains tribes, their early relations with white explorers and settlers had been peaceful. Chief Ouray, leader of the Uncompahgre Utes, had negotiated treaties in 1863 and 1868 that guaranteed them 16 million acres—most of western Colorado. In 1873, Ouray agreed to sell the United States one-fourth of that acreage in the mineral-rich San Juan Mountains in exchange for hunting rights and $25,000 in annuities.

But a mining boom that began in 1878 led to a flurry of intrusions into Ute territory and stirred up a "Utes Must Go!" sentiment. Two years later the Utes were forced onto small reserves in southwestern Colorado and Utah, and their lands opened to white settlement in 1882.

THE MINING BOOM Colorado's real mining boom began on April 28, 1878, when August Rische and George Hook hit a vein of silver carbonate 27 feet deep on Fryer Hill in Leadville. Perhaps the strike wouldn't have caused such excitement had not Rische and Hook, eight days earlier, traded one-third interest in whatever they found for a basket of groceries from storekeeper Horace Tabor, the mayor of Leadville and a sharp businessman. Tabor was well acquainted with the Colorado "law of apex," which said that if an ore-bearing vein surfaced on a man's claim, he could follow it wherever it led, even out of his claim and through the claims of others.

Tabor, a legend in Colorado, typifies the "rags-to-riches" success story of a common working-class man. A native of Vermont, he had mortgaged his Kansas homestead in 1859 and moved west to the mountains, where he worked as a postmaster and storekeeper in several towns before moving to Leadville. He was 46 when the silver strike was made. By age 50, he was the state's richest man and its Republican lieutenant governor. His love affair with and marriage to Elizabeth "Baby Doe" McCourt, a young divorcée for whom he left his wife, Augusta, became both a national scandal, the subject of numerous books, and even an opera. Today the town of Leadville is among the best places to relive the West's mining days.

Although the silver market collapsed in 1893, gold was there to take its place. In the fall of 1890, a cowboy named Bob Womack found gold in Cripple Creek, on the southwestern slope of Pikes Peak, west of Colorado Springs. He sold his claim to Winfield Scott Stratton, a carpenter and amateur geologist, and Stratton's mine earned a tidy profit of $6 million by 1899, when he sold it to an English company for another $11 million. Cripple Creek turned out to be the richest gold field ever discovered, ultimately producing $500 million in gold.

Unlike the flamboyant Tabor, Stratton was an introvert and a neurotic. His fortune was twice the size of Tabor's, and it grew daily as the deflation of silver's value boosted that of gold. But he invested most of it back in Cripple Creek, searching for a fabulous mother lode that he never found. By the early 1900s, like silver, the overproduction of gold began to drive the price of the metal down.

■ 1998 The Denver Broncos win the Super Bowl, defeating the Green Bay Packers (the defending champs) 31 to 24. The stunning victory saves the Broncos the indignity of becoming the first team to lose five Super Bowls. Militant environmental activists set fires that caused more than $12 million in damage in an effort to stop expansion at a Vail resort.

ENVIRONMENTALISM & TOURISM   Another turning point for Colorado occurred just after the beginning of the 20th century. Theodore Roosevelt had visited the state in September 1900 as the Republican vice-presidential nominee. Soon after he acceded to the presidency in September 1901 (following the assassination of President McKinley), he began to declare large chunks of the Rockies as forest reserves. By 1907, when an act of Congress forbade the president from creating any new reserves by proclamation, nearly one-fourth of Colorado was national forest land—16 million acres in 18 forests. Another project that reached fruition during the Roosevelt administration was the establishment in 1906 of Mesa Verde National Park, the first national park to preserve the works of humans.

Tourism grew hand-in-hand with the setting aside of public lands. Easterners had been visiting Colorado since the 1870s, when General William J. Palmer founded a Colorado Springs resort and made the mountains accessible via his Denver & Rio Grande Railroad.

Estes Park, northwest of Boulder, was among the first resort towns to emerge in the 20th century, spurred by a visit in 1903 by Freelan Stanley. With his brother, Francis, Freelan had invented the Stanley Steamer, a steam-powered automobile, in Boston in 1899. Freelan Stanley shipped one of his steamers to Denver and drove the 40 miles to Estes Park in less than two hours, a remarkable speed for the day. Finding the climate conducive to his recovery from tuberculosis, he returned in 1907 with a dozen Stanley Steamers and established a shuttle service from Denver to Estes Park. Two years later he built the luxurious Stanley Hotel, still a hilltop landmark today.

Stanley developed a friendship with Enos Mills, a young innkeeper whose property was more a workshop for students of wildlife than a business. A devotee of conservationist John Muir, Mills believed tourists should spend their Colorado vacations in the natural environment, camping and hiking. As Mills gained national stature as a nature writer and lecturer, he urged that the national forest land around Longs Peak, outside Estes Park, be designated a national park. In January 1915, the 400-square-mile Rocky Mountain National Park was created by President Woodrow Wilson, and today it is one of America's leading tourist attractions, with more than two million visitors each year.

The 1920s saw the growth of highways and the completion of the Moffat Tunnel, a 6.2-mile passageway beneath the Continental Divide that (in 1934) led to the long-sought direct Denver–San Francisco rail connection. Of more tragic note was the worst flood in Colorado history. The city of Pueblo, south of Colorado Springs, was devastated when the Arkansas River overflowed its banks on June 1, 1921; 100 people were killed, and the damage exceeded $16 million. The Great Depression of the 1930s was a difficult time for many Coloradans, but it had positive consequences. The federal government raised the price of gold from $20 to $35 an ounce, reviving Cripple Creek and other stagnant mining towns.

World War II and the subsequent Cold War were responsible for many of the defense installations that are now an integral part of the Colorado economy, particularly in the Colorado Springs area. The war also indirectly caused the other single greatest boon to Colorado's late-20th-century economy: the ski industry. Soldiers in the 10th Mountain Division, on leave from Camp Hale before heading off to fight in Europe, often crossed Independence Pass to relax in the lower altitude and milder climate of the 19th-century silver-mining village of Aspen. They tested their skiing skills, needed in the Italian Alps, against the slopes of Ajax Mountain.

In 1945, Walter and Elizabeth Paepcke—he the founder of the Container Corporation of America, she an ardent conservationist—moved to Aspen and established the Aspen Company as a property investment firm. Skiing was already popular in New England and the Midwest, but had few devotees in the Rockies. Paepcke bought a 3-mile chairlift, the longest and fastest in the world at the time, and had it ready for operation by January 1947. Soon, Easterners and Europeans were flocking to Aspen—and the rest is ski history.

THE MODERN ERA   Colorado continued steady growth in the 1950s, aided by tourism and the federal government. The $200-million U.S. Air Force Academy, authorized by Congress in 1954 and opened to cadets in 1958, is Colorado Springs' top tourist attraction today. There was a brief oil boom in the 1970s, followed by increasing high-tech development and even more tourism.

Weapons plants, which had seemed to be a good idea when they were constructed during World War II, began to haunt Denver and the state in the 1970s and 1980s. Rocky Mountain Arsenal, originally built to produce chemical weapons, was found to be creating hazardous conditions at home, contaminating the land with deadly chemicals. A massive cleanup was begun in the early 1980s, and by the 1990s the arsenal was well on its way to accomplishing its goal of converting the 27-square-mile site into a national wildlife refuge.

The story of Rocky Flats, a postwar nuclear weapons facility spurred on by the Cold War, is not so happy. Massive efforts to figure out what to do about contamination caused by nuclear waste have been largely unsuccessful. Although state and federal officials announced early in 1996 that they had reached agreement on the means of removing some 14 tons of plutonium, their immediate plan calls for keeping it in Denver until at least the year 2010, and Department of Energy officials don't know what they'll do with it then. In the meantime, plans are under way to build storage containers that will safely hold the plutonium for up to 50 years.

In 1992, Colorado voters approved a constitutional amendment banning current laws that protected gays and lesbians, and preventing the enactment of new gay-rights legislation. In May 1996, the U.S. Supreme Court struck down the measure, saying that it denied constitutional rights to homosexuals.

As the state approaches the 21st century, thoughts have turned to controlling growth. With a growth rate in the early 1990s of three times the national average, residents and government leaders are questioning how this unabated influx of outsiders can continue without doing serious harm to the state's air, water, and general quality of life.

5 Recommended Books & Videos

Travelers planning Colorado vacations have a number of sources available for background on the state and its major cities. A good place to start is the short, easy-to-read *Colorado: A History,* by Marshall Sprague. *A Lady's Life in the Rocky Mountains* is a fascinating compilation of Isabella L. Bird's letters to her sister; they were written in the late 1800s as she traveled alone through the Rockies, usually on horseback. For another trip back in time, check out Muriel S. Wolle's *Stampede to Timberline: The Ghost Towns and Mining Camps of Colorado,* or David Lavender's *Bent's Fort,* a history that makes the old Santa Fe Trail come alive.

Those who enjoy lengthy novels will want to get their hands on a copy of James Michener's 1,000-page *Centennial,* inspired by the northeastern plains of Colorado. For a more bohemian point of view, look no further than Jack Kerouac's classic, *On the Road.* And readers of fiction are sure to be engrossed by Wallace Stegner's Pulitzer Prize–winning 1971 novel, *Angle of Repose.*

Travelers interested in seeing wildlife will likely be successful with help from the *Colorado Wildlife Viewing Guide,* by Mary Taylor Gray.

An excellent video introduction to the state is *Explore Colorado,* a 55-minute video tour that touches on most of the state's scenic and historic highlights.

Books are available mail order from the state's largest bookstore, a tourist attraction in its own right, the **Tattered Cover,** 2955 East First Ave., Denver, CO 80206 (☎ **800/833-9327** or 303/322-7727; www.tatteredcover.com). Another good source for Colorado books is the smaller, and somewhat more personal, **Chinook Bookstore,** 210 N. Tejon St., Colorado Springs, CO 80903 (☎ **800/999-1195** or 719/635-1195). Videos, in both VHS and PAL formats, as well as interactive CD-ROMs, can be obtained from **Interpark,** P.O. Box 10427, Prescott, AZ 86304 (☎ **800/687-5967**).

3

Planning a Trip to Colorado

The beauty of a vacation here is that there's truly something for everyone. Depending on where you choose to go, you can have an affordable and fun time, or you can spend a bit more and have a truly world-class experience. The more expensive resorts—Vail, Aspen, Steamboat, and Telluride—tend to fill up quickly, especially during ski season. You'll want to book as far in advance as possible to stay there. The same is true for the state's most popular attractions, such as the national parks—especially over busy school vacation periods. This chapter gives you the information you need to get started.

1 Visitor Information & Money

VISITOR INFORMATION

Start by contacting **Colorado Travel and Tourism Authority,** P.O. Box 3524, Englewood, CO 80155 (☎ **800/COLORADO** or 303/296-3384; www.colorado.com), for a free copy of the official state vacation guide, which includes a state map and describes attractions, activities, and lodgings throughout Colorado. Another good source for Colorado information is the website of the *Denver Post,* the state's major daily newspaper, at **www.denverpost.com**.

The **Colorado Hotel and Lodging Association,** 999 18th St., Suite 1240, Denver, CO 80202 (☎ **303/297-8335;** www.coloradolodging.com), offers a free guide to lodging across the state. The nonprofit **Bed and Breakfast Innkeepers of Colorado,** P.O. Box 38416, Colorado Springs, CO 80937-8416 (☎ **800/265-7696;** www.innsofcolorado.org), has prepared a directory describing the group's more than 170 member B&Bs, including a number of historic inns. Another source of information for those seeking unique lodging is **Historic Hotels of the Rockies** (☎ **303/546-9040;** www.historic-hotels.com). The association's free brochure describes more than a dozen historic hotels in Colorado and other Rocky Mountain states.

Hostelling International–American Youth Hostels has a computerized system for making reservations in hostels worldwide, including those in Colorado. For complete information, see "For Students" under "Tips for Travelers with Special Needs," later in this chapter.

A free copy of *Colorado State Parks,* which contains details on the state's 40 parks, is available from state park offices at 1313 Sherman St., Suite 618, Denver, CO 80203 (☎ **303/866-3437;** www.dnr.state.co.us/parks). State park offices can also provide information on boating and snowmobiling.

The **Colorado Agency of Camping, Cabins, & Lodges,** 5101 Pennsylvania Ave., Boulder, CO 80303-2799 (☎ **888/222-4641** or 303/499-9343; fax 303/499-9333; www.coloradodirectory.com; e-mail: info@coloradodirectory.com), will send you a free booklet that describes commercial campgrounds, cabin facilities, resorts, country B&Bs, and fun things to do throughout the state.

If it's a ranch vacation you're after, contact the **Colorado Dude & Guest Ranch Association,** P.O. Box 300V, Tabernash, CO 80478 (☎ **970/887-3128;** www. coloradoranch.com; e-mail: 103104.1071@compuserve.com), which has information on more than three dozen dude and guest ranches in the state.

MONEY

American Express cardholders can write a personal check, guaranteed against the card, for up to $1,000 in cash at any American Express office. The Denver branch is at 555 17th St., Qwest Tower, Denver (☎ **303/298-7100**). It's open Monday through Friday from 8:30am to 5pm. To report a lost card, call ☎ **800/528-4800.** To report lost traveler's checks, call ☎ **800/221-7282.**

U.S. dollar traveler's checks and credit cards are accepted in most hotels, restaurants, shops, and attractions, plus many grocery stores; they can be exchanged for cash at banks and most check-issuing offices. However, be aware that smaller businesses may not be able to cash traveler's checks or even American currency in large denominations (over $50). ATMs (automatic teller machines) for all the major national networks are practically everywhere, including many supermarkets.

2 When to Go

Colorado has essentially two tourist seasons: warm and cold. Those who want to see the state's parks and other scenic wonders, or hike, mountain bike, or raft, will usually visit between May through October; those who prefer skiing, snowboarding, and snowmobiling will obviously have to wait for winter, usually from late November through March or April, depending on snow levels. Although you can visit most major museums year-round, some, especially those in smaller communities, close in winter.

The best way to avoid crowds at the more popular destinations, such as Rocky Mountain National Park, Garden of the Gods, and Pikes Peak, is to try to visit during the shoulder seasons of March through May and October through mid-December. Generally, those traveling without children will want to avoid visiting during school vacations.

To hear Coloradans tell it, the state has perfect weather all the time. Although they may be exaggerating just a bit, the weather here is usually quite pleasant, with an abundance of sun and relatively mild temperatures in most places—just avoid those winter snowstorms.

Along the Front Range, where Denver and Colorado Springs are located, summers are hot and dry, evenings pleasantly mild. Relative humidity is low, and temperatures seldom rise above the 90s. Evenings start to get cooler by mid-September, but even as late as November the days are often warm. Surprisingly, winters here are warmer and less snowy than those of the Great Lakes or New England.

Most of Colorado is considered semi-arid, and overall the state has an average of 296 sunny days a year—more sunshine than San Diego or Miami Beach. The prairies average about 16 inches of precipitation annually; the Front Range, 14 inches; the western slope, only about 8 inches. Rain, when it falls, is commonly a short deluge—a summer afternoon thunderstorm. However, if you want to see snow, simply head to the mountains, where snowfall is measured in feet rather than inches, and mountain peaks may still be white in July. Mountain temperatures can be bitterly cold, especially if it's windy—but even at the higher elevations of some of the nation's top ski resorts, you'll find plenty of sunshine.

Average Monthly High/Low Temperatures (°F) & Precipitation (inches)

		Jan	Feb	Mar	Apr	May	June	July	Aug	Sept	Oct	Nov	Dec
Denver	Temp. (°F)	43/16	47/20	52/26	62/35	71/44	81/52	88/59	86/57	77/48	66/36	53/25	45/17
elev. 5,280'	Precip. (in.)	0.5	0.6	1.3	1.7	2.4	1.8	1.9	1.5	1.2	1.0	0.9	0.6
Grand Junction	Temp. (°F)	36/15	45/24	56/32	66/38	76/48	88/57	94/64	91/62	81/54	68/42	51/39	66/40
elev. 4,586'	Precip. (in.)	0.6	0.5	0.9	0.8	0.9	0.5	0.7	0.8	0.8	1.0	0.7	0.6
Col. Springs	Temp. (°F)	41/16	45/20	49/24	60/33	69/43	80/52	85/57	82/56	75/47	66/37	50/25	44/19
elev. 6,035'	Precip. (in.)	0.3	0.4	0.9	1.2	2.2	2.3	2.9	3.0	1.3	0.8	0.5	0.5

COLORADO CALENDAR OF EVENTS

January

- **International Snow Sculpture Championships,** Breckenridge. Four-person teams transform 20-ton blocks of snow into works of art. Call ☎ **970/ 453-6018.** Second week in January.
- **Cowboy Downhill,** Steamboat Springs. Professional rodeo cowboys tame a slalom course, lasso a resort employee, and saddle a horse before crossing the finish line. Call ☎ **970/879-0880.** Mid-January.
- ✪ **National Western Stock Show and Rodeo,** Denver. World's largest livestock show and indoor rodeo. Call ☎ **303/297-1166** for details. Second and third weeks in January.
- **Colorado Indian Market,** Denver. Members of more than 90 tribes display, sell, and demonstrate arts and crafts and perform traditional dances. Call ☎ **303/892-1112.** Second and third weeks in January.
- **Ullrfest,** Breckenridge. A week-long festival honors Ullr, Norse god of snow, with ski competitions, a torchlight display, fireworks, and parade. Call ☎ **970/453-6018.** Third week in January.
- ✪ **Aspen/Snowmass Winterskol,** Aspen. A 5-day event that includes a parade, fireworks, and torchlight descent. Call ☎ **970/925-1940.** Third week in January.
- **Boulder Bach Festival,** Boulder. A celebration of the master baroque composer. Call ☎ **303/494-3159.** Last weekend in January.
- **Colorado MahlerFest,** Boulder. The only festival in the world devoted to the music of Gustav Mahler, with performances, films, discussions, and seminars. Call ☎ **303/494-1632.** January.

February

- **Steamboat Springs Winter Carnival,** Steamboat Springs. Festivities include races, jumping, broomball, and skijoring street events. Call ☎ **970/879-0880.** First full week in February.
- **Loveland Valentine Remailing Program,** Loveland. Over 250,000 valentines are remailed from Loveland. Call ☎ **970/667-6311.** Early February.

- **Buffalo Bill's Birthday Celebration,** Golden. Commemoration of the life of the legendary scout and entertainer. Call ☎ **303/526-0744.** Last weekend in February.

March

- **Crystal Carnival,** Leadville. A celebration of winter, with a parade of lights, snowmobile races, and hot-air balloon rides. Call ☎ **719/486-3900.** Early March.
- **Pow Wow,** Denver. More than 700 American Indians, representing some 70 tribes, perform traditional music and dances. Call ☎ **303/455-4575.** Mid-March.

April

○ **Easter Sunrise Service,** Colorado Springs. Worshippers watch the rising sun highlight red sandstone formations in the Garden of the Gods. Call ☎ **719/594-6602.** Easter Sunday.

May

○ **Boulder Kinetic Fest,** Boulder. In this wacky, crowd-pleasing event, some 70 teams race over land and water in a variety of imaginative human-powered conveyances. Activities include a parade, concerts, kite flying, and the kinetic ball. Call ☎ **303/444-5600.** Early May.
- **Bolder Boulder,** Boulder. A 10-kilometer (6.2-mile) race that attracts some 40,000 walkers, joggers, and runners. Call ☎ **303/444-7223.** Memorial Day.
- **Iron Horse Bicycle Classic,** Durango. Mountain bikers race a steam train from Durango to Silverton. Call ☎ **800/525-8855.** Memorial Day weekend.

June

- **FIBArk Festival,** Salida. North America's longest and oldest downriver kayak race highlights this festival, which includes carnival rides, a parade, foot races, and live entertainment. Call ☎ **719/539-2068.** Mid-June.
- **Strawberry Days,** Glenwood Springs. One of Colorado's oldest civic celebrations, with a rodeo, talent show, music, dancing, an arts-and-crafts fair, parade, carnival, and foot races. Call ☎ **970/945-6589.** Mid-June.
- **Greeley Independence Stampede,** Greeley. One of the West's biggest rodeos, with top national entertainers. Call ☎ **800/982-2855.** Mid-June to early July.
- **Colorado Music Festival,** Boulder. The single largest arts event in Boulder features world-renowned musicians in symphony orchestra and chamber music performances. Call ☎ **303/449-1397.** Mid-June to early August.
○ **Aspen Music Festival and School,** Aspen. Considered one of the finest summer music festivals in the country, featuring world-renowned artists in classical, chamber, and opera performances. Call ☎ **970/925-9042.** Mid-June to mid-August.
○ **Telluride Bluegrass Festival,** Telluride. An event featuring bluegrass and country music. Call ☎ **800/624-2422.** Late June.
○ **Colorado Shakespeare Festival,** Boulder. Among the top Shakespeare festivals in the country, performed in an outdoor theater. Call ☎ **303/492-0554.** Late June to mid-August.

July

- **Pikes Peak Auto Hill Climb,** Colorado Springs. This "race to the clouds," held annually since 1916, takes drivers to the top of 14,110-foot Pikes Peak. Call ☎**719/685-4400.** July 4.

- **Colorado State Mining Championship,** Creede. Entrants from six states compete in old-style hand steeling, hand mucking, spike driving, and newer methods of machine drilling and machine mucking. Call ☎ **800/327-2102.** July 4 weekend.
- **Brush Rodeo,** Brush. Billed as the world's largest open rodeo, with more than 400 participants, it offers traditional rodeo events, wild-cow milking, a parade, footrace, dance, and fireworks. Call ☎ **800/354-8659.** Early July.
- **Strings in the Mountains Festival of Music,** Steamboat Springs. Top-notch classical and jazz musicians perform. Call ☎ **970/879-5056.** Early July to mid-August.
- **Genuine Jazz in July,** Breckenridge. A showcase of Colorado jazz groups—from Dixieland to bebop. Call ☎ **970/453-6018.** Second weekend in July.
- **Denver Black Arts Festival,** Denver. Features the work of black artists and entertainers, plus a parade. Call ☎ **303/329-3976.** Mid-July.
- **Pikes Peak Highland Games & Celtic Festival,** Colorado Springs. Sponsored by the Scottish Society of the Pikes Peak Region, with the caber toss and other traditional games, a Highland dance competition, and Scottish foods. Call ☎ **719/481-4597.** Third Saturday in July.
- **Colorado Dance Festival,** Boulder. Balletomanes from around the world flock to this event, offering classes, lectures, film screenings, and panel discussions. Call ☎ **303/442-7666.** All month.

August

- **Pikes Peak or Bust Rodeo,** Colorado Springs. Largest outdoor rodeo in the state. Call ☎ **719/635-3547.** Early August.
- **Boom Days,** Leadville. Events include a parade, carnival, street fair, mine-drilling competition, and 22-mile pack-burro race. Call ☎ **719/486-3900.** First weekend in August.
- ✪ **Rocky Mountain Wine and Food Festival,** Winter Park. Colorado's finest chefs and many of America's best-known vintners offer their creations to benefit the National Sports Center for the Disabled. Call ☎ **970/726-5514.** First weekend in August.
- **Sculpture in the Park,** Loveland. Show and sale of sculpture, with demonstrations and an auction. Call ☎ **970/663-2940.** Mid-August.
- **Colorado State Fair,** Pueblo. There's a national professional rodeo, carnival rides, food booths, industrial displays, horse shows, animal exhibits, and entertainment by top-name performers. Call ☎ **800/876-4567.** Mid-August to Labor Day.

September

- **A Taste Of Colorado,** Denver. Billed as "a festival of mountain and plain," with crafts exhibits, free concerts, and specialties from local restaurants. Call ☎ **303/892-7004.** Labor Day weekend.
- **Steamboat Vintage Auto Race & Concours d'Elégance,** Steamboat Springs. More than 200 classic cars on a mountain course, plus a vintage aircraft fly-in and rodeo series finals. Call ☎ **970/879-0880.** Labor Day weekend.
- ✪ **Telluride Film Festival,** Telluride. An influential festival within the film industry that has premiered some of the finest independent films. Call ☎ **603/643-1255.** Labor Day weekend.
- **Vail Fest,** Vail. An Oktoberfest-style weekend with street entertainment, yodeling contest, 5- and 10-kilometer (3.1- and 6.2-mile) runs, dancing, games, and sing-alongs. Call ☎ **800/525-3875.** Second weekend in September.

October

- **Oktoberfest,** Ouray. Polkas, food, crafts, and an antique auto show. Call ☎ **800/ 228-1876.** Early October.
- **Cowboy Gathering,** Durango. Cowboy poetry, western art, films, historical lectures, and demonstrations. Call ☎ **800/525-8855.** Early October.
- **Great American Beer Festival,** Denver. Considered the largest and most prestigious beer event in the United States, with hundreds of American beers for sampling, plus seminars. Call ☎ **303/447-0816.** Early October.
- **Colorado Performing Arts Festival,** Denver. A celebration of performing arts, offering dance, music, theater, and storytelling. Call ☎ **303/640-2678.** Early October.
- **Vintage Six Wine Tasting,** Denver. Annual benefit for the Denver public television station. Call ☎ **303/620-5700.** Mid-October.

November

- **Colorado Ski Expo,** Denver. Skiers and snowboarders gather at the Colorado Convention Center to check out the newest equipment and get information on the state's resorts. Call ☎ **303/837-0793.** Early November.
- **Christmas Mountain USA,** Salida. More than 3,000 lights outline a huge tree; also a parade of lights and a visit from Santa Claus. Call ☎ **719/539-2068.** Day after Thanksgiving.

December

- **Parade of Lights,** Denver. A holiday parade winds its way through downtown Denver, with floats, balloons, and marching bands. Call ☎ **303/534-6161.** Early December.
- **Christmas in Old Town,** Burlington. Victorian carolers and Christmas music, plus other Victorian Christmas activities. Call ☎ **800/288-1334.** Early December.
- Holiday Home Tour, Colorado Springs. A tour of bed-and-breakfast inns, decorated for the holidays, with proceeds to benefit the Old Colorado City Historical Society. Call ☎ **719/632-9194.** Early December.
- **World's Largest Christmas Lighting Display,** Denver. The Denver City and County Building is illuminated by some 40,000 colored floodlights. All month.

3 Health, Safety & Insurance

HEALTH

Colorado's high elevation—about two-thirds of the state is more than a mile above sea level—means there's less oxygen and lower humidity than elsewhere in the West. Those in generally good health need not take any special precautions but can ease the transition to a higher elevation by changing altitude gradually. For instance, spend a night or two in Burlington (elevation 4,163 feet) before going to Denver (elevation 5,280 feet); or spend at least two or three nights in Colorado Springs (elevation 6,012 feet) before driving or taking the cog railway to the top of Pikes Peak (elevation 14,110 feet).

Those not used to higher elevations should get sufficient rest, avoid large meals, and drink plenty of nonalcoholic fluids, especially water. Lowlanders can also help their bodies adjust to higher elevations by taking it easy for their first few days in the mountains, cutting down on cigarettes and alcohol, and avoiding sleeping pills and other drugs. The drug Diamox, available by prescription only, can be taken to help prevent altitude problems and relieve the symptoms if they occur; consult a medical professional about its use. Individuals with heart or respiratory problems should consult their home physician before planning trips to the Colorado mountains.

Because the sun's rays are more direct in the thinner atmosphere, sunburn occurs more quickly. The potential for skin damage increases when the sun is reflected off snow or water. A good sunblock is strongly recommended, as are good-quality, ultraviolet-blocking sunglasses and a brimmed hat.

If you plan to hike in the mountains, be sure to take plenty of water—at least one gallon per person, per day. Don't overexert, as that makes you susceptible to acute mountain sickness, characterized in its early stages by headaches, shortness of breath, appetite loss and/or nausea, tingling in the fingers or toes, and lethargy or insomnia. Ordinarily, it requires no medical treatment, and can be alleviated by an aspirin and a slower pace. If it persists or worsens, descend to a lower altitude.

Less common but more serious is high altitude pulmonary edema, whose symptoms include a congested cough and shortness of breath. It looks and feels a lot like pneumonia. If you think you may have it, consult a doctor immediately.

Finally, there's Hantavirus, a rare but often fatal respiratory disease. First recognized in 1993, about half of the country's 100-plus confirmed cases have been reported in the Four Corners states of Colorado, New Mexico, Arizona, and Utah. The disease is believed to be spread by the urine and droppings of deer mice and other rodents. Campers should avoid areas with evidence of rodent droppings and thoroughly air out tents or cabins before use, especially if they've been unused for a period of time. Early symptoms are similar to those of flu, but quickly lead to breathing difficulties and shock.

SAFETY

While there are many reasons to visit Colorado, the two cited most often are its historic sites and magnificent outdoor activities. However, both can lead to accidents.

When visiting ghost towns, gold mines, and railroads, keep in mind that they were probably built more than 100 years ago, at a time when safety standards were extremely lax, to say the least. Never enter abandoned buildings, mines, or railroad equipment on your own. When you're visiting commercially operated historic tourist attractions, use common sense and don't be afraid to ask questions.

Walkways in mines are often uneven, poorly lit, and sometimes slippery, caused by seeping groundwater that can also stain your clothing with its high mineral content. When entering old buildings, be prepared for steep, narrow stairways, creaky floors, and low ceilings and doorways. Steam trains are a wonderful experience as long as you remember that steam is hot, and oil and grease can ruin your clothing.

When heading into the great outdoors, keep in mind that injuries often occur when people fail to follow instructions. Pay attention when the experts tell you to stay on established ski trails, hike only in designated areas and carry rain gear, and wear a life jacket when rafting. Mountain weather can be fickle, and many of the most beautiful spots are in remote areas. Be prepared for extreme changes in temperature at any time of year, and watch out for those sudden summer afternoon thunderstorms that can leave you drenched and shivering.

INSURANCE

Before starting out, check your medical insurance policy to be certain you're covered away from home; if not, purchase a special traveler's policy, available from travel agents, insurance agents, and travel clubs. It's useful to carry a medical-insurance identification card with you at all times.

Besides being prepared for medical emergencies, it's wise to carry insurance to cover you in case of an accident, loss of personal possessions such as luggage and cameras (this may be included in your homeowner's or renter's policy), or trip cancellation (especially if you've prepaid a large portion of your vacation expenses). If you are a motorist, be sure to carry proof of automobile liability insurance, and be certain that your policy includes protection from uninsured motorists. If you're planning to drive in Colorado, see "By Car" under "Getting Around," below.

4 Tips for Travelers with Special Needs

FOR TRAVELERS WITH DISABILITIES

Travelers with physical disabilities should find Colorado relatively easy to get around. Some small towns aren't wheelchair-accessible, but the Front Range cities, and most major parks and historical monuments, are. To be safe, it's best to call ahead to make sure facilities are suitable.

If you're planning to visit Colorado's national parks and monuments, you can get the National Park Service's **Golden Access Passport,** available at all visitor centers. This lifetime pass is issued to any U.S. citizen or permanent resident who is medically certified as disabled or blind. The pass permits free entry and gives a 50% discount on park-service campgrounds and activities (but not on those offered by private concessions).

Mobility International USA, P.O. Box 10767, Eugene, OR 97440 (☎ **541/ 343-1284** voice and TDD), is a national nonprofit member organization that provides travel information and referrals, plus other services for those with disabilities.

With 24-hour notice, **Amtrak** (☎ **800/USA-RAIL**) will provide porter service, special seating, and a discount on most runs. If you're traveling with a companion, **Greyhound** (☎ **800/231-2222**) will carry you both for a single fare.

FOR GAY & LESBIAN TRAVELERS

In general, gay and lesbian travelers will find they are treated just like any other visitors in Colorado. Even cities such as Colorado Springs, home of Focus on the Family and other conservative groups, have become somewhat more open-minded about alternative lifestyles recently. Those with specific concerns can contact **Gay, Lesbian, and Bisexual Community Services of Colorado** (☎ **303/831-6268**) in Denver; the organization can also provide information on events and venues of interest to gay and lesbian visitors.

FOR SENIORS

Many Colorado hotels and motels offer discounts to senior citizens, and an increasing number of restaurants, attractions, and public transportation systems do so as well. **Train travelers** 62 and older receive a 15% discount on most Amtrak fares. You can save sightseeing dollars if you are 62 or over by picking up a **Golden Age Passport** from any federally operated park, recreation area, or monument. There is a one-time fee of $10 that entitles holders to free admission to parks and other federally managed fee areas plus a 50% savings on camping fees.

Membership in the **American Association of Retired Persons (AARP),** 601 E St. NW, Washington, DC 20049 (☎ **800/424-3410** or 202/434-2277), entitles you to discounts at numerous places; the organization can help with specifics on motels, cruise lines, and car rentals.

FOR TRAVELERS WITH PETS

Many of us wouldn't dream of going on vacation without our pets. Under the right circumstances, bringing your pet along can be a wonderful experience for both you and your animals. Dogs and cats are accepted at many motels around the state, but not as universally in resorts and at the more expensive hotels. Throughout this book, we've tried to consistently note those lodgings that take pets. Some properties require you to pay a fee or damage deposit in advance, and most insist they be notified at check-in that you have a pet.

Be aware, however, that national parks and monuments and other federal lands administered by the National Park Service are not pet-friendly. Dogs are prohibited on all hiking trails, must always be leashed, and in some cases cannot be taken more than 100 feet from established roads. On the other hand, U.S. Forest Service and Bureau of Land Management areas, as well as most state parks, are pro-pet, allowing dogs on trails and just about everywhere except inside buildings. State parks require that dogs be leashed; regulations in national forests and BLM lands are generally looser.

Aside from regulations, though, you need to be concerned with your pet's well-being. Just as people need extra water in Colorado's dry climate, so do pets. And keep in mind that many trails are rough, and jagged rocks can cut the pads on your dog's feet.

One final note on pets: There is no punishment too severe for the human who leaves a dog or cat inside a closed car parked in the sun. The car heats up more quickly than you'd think—so don't do it, even for a minute.

FOR STUDENTS

You can use your high school or college ID to obtain an **International Student Identity Card,** available for $20 at colleges and other locations throughout the United States, including about a dozen locations in Colorado. It entitles you to various student discounts, including transportation, lodging, and cultural attractions, although not as many as in foreign countries. It also includes basic accident insurance to cover you while traveling outside the United States. Teacher IDs ($20) and cards for anyone under 26 years old ($20) are also available. To obtain cards by mail or for the nearest location to purchase one in person, contact the **Council on International Educational Exchange (CIEE),** 205 E. 42nd St., New York, NY 10017 (☎ **888/268-6245**). For inexpensive accommodations, as well as the opportunity to meet other traveling students, join **Hostelling International–American Youth Hostels,** Box 37613, Washington, DC 20013-7613 (☎ **202/783-6161**). For $3, or free with membership, they'll send a directory of all U.S. hostels. Twelve-month membership costs $25 for those ages 18 to 54 and $10 for those 17 and under. In Colorado you can contact **American Youth Hostels Rocky Mountain Council** at P.O. Box 2370, Boulder, CO 80306 (☎ **303/442-1166**).

5 Getting There

BY PLANE

The state's two major airports are Denver International Airport (DIA) and Colorado Springs Airport; with direct flights from many cities in the United States and Canada. Both airports offer car rentals and shuttle services to their city's hotels.

Denver International Airport is 23 miles northeast of downtown Denver, about a 35- to 45-minute drive. It has five runways and averages 1,300 flights each day. An information line (☎ **800/AIR-2-DEN**) provides data on flight schedules and connections, parking, ground transportation, current weather conditions, and local accommodations. The local airport switchboard number is ☎ **303/342-2000.** Airlines serving Denver include **Air Canada** (☎ 800/776-3000; www.aircanada.ca); **American** (☎ 800/433-7300; www.americanair.com); **America West** (☎ 800/235-9292; www.americawest.com); **Aspen Mountain Air** (☎ 800/877-3932; www.aspenmountainair.com); **British Airways** (☎ 800/247-9297; www.britishairways.com); **Continental** (☎ 800/525-0280; www.flycontinental.com); **Delta** (☎ 800/221-1212; www.delta-air.com); **Frontier** (☎ 800/432-1359; www.frontierairlines.com); **Korean Air** (☎ 800/438-5000; www.koreanair.com); **Martinair** (☎ 800/366-4655; www.martinair.com); **Mexicana** (☎ 800/531-7921; www.mexicana.com); **Midwest Express** (☎ 800/452-2022; www.midwestexpress.com); **Northwest** (☎ 800/225-2525; www.nwa.com); **Reno Air** (☎ 800/ 736-6247; www.renoair.com); **Sun Country** (☎ 800/359-5786; www.suncountry.com); **TWA** (☎ 800/221-2000; www.twa.com); **United and United Express** (☎ 800/241-6522; www.ual.com); **US Airways** (☎ 800/428-4322; www.usair.com); and **Vanguard** (☎ 800/826-4827; www.flyvanguard.com).

Colorado Springs Airport has more than 100 flights each day, with connections to most major U.S. cities. The airport's main phone is ☎ **719/550-1900.** In the southeast corner of Colorado Springs, the airport is served by **American** (☎ 800/433-7300; www.americanair.com); **America West** (☎ 800/235-9292; www.americawest.com); **Continental** (☎ 800/525-0280; www.flycontinental.com); **Delta** (☎ 800/221-1212; www.delta-air.com); **Mesa** (☎ 800/637-2247; www.mesa-air.com); **Northwest** (☎ 800/225-2525 domestic or 800/447-4747 international; www.nwa.com); **Reno Air** (☎ 800/736-6247; www.renoair.com); **TWA** (☎ 800/ 221-2000; www.twa.com); and **United** (☎ 800/241-6522; www.ual.com).

BY CAR

Some 1,000 miles of interstate highways form a star on the map of Colorado, with its center at Denver. **I-25** crosses the state from south to north, extending from New Mexico to Wyoming; over its 300 miles, it goes through nearly every major city of the Front Range, including Pueblo, Colorado Springs, Denver, and Fort Collins.

I-70 crosses from west to east, extending from Utah to Kansas, a distance of about 450 miles; it enters Colorado near Grand Junction, passes through Glenwood Springs, Vail, and Denver, and exits just east of Burlington. **I-76** is an additional 190-mile spur that begins in Denver and extends northeast to Nebraska, joining **I-80** just beyond Julesburg.

Visitors entering Colorado from the southwest may take **U.S. 160** (from Flagstaff, AZ) or **U.S. 550** (from Farmington, NM). Both routes enter the state near Durango.

If you aren't already a member, it's a good idea to join the **American Automobile Association (AAA)** (☎ 800/336-4357), which has hundreds of offices nationwide. Members can get excellent maps, information on road construction, and emergency road service; they'll even help you plan an exact itinerary.

BY TRAIN

Amtrak (☎ 800/USA-RAIL; www.amtrak.com) has two routes through Colorado. One, linking San Francisco and Chicago, passes through Grand Junction,

Glenwood Springs, Granby, Winter Park, Denver, and Fort Morgan en route to Omaha, Nebraska. Another, which runs between Los Angeles and Chicago, travels from Albuquerque, New Mexico, via Trinidad, La Junta, and Lamar before crossing the southeastern Colorado border into Kansas.

BY BUS

Greyhound (☎ **800/231-2222;** www.greyhound.com) has an extensive network that reaches nearly every corner of the state, with daily connections practically everywhere. Parts of southern Colorado are also served by **TNM&O Coaches** (Texas, New Mexico & Oklahoma Coaches), which can be booked through Greyhound.

6 Getting Around

BY CAR

Driving is an excellent way to see Colorado. Roads are well maintained and well marked, and a car is often the most economical and convenient way to get somewhere; in fact, if you plan to explore beyond the Denver, Boulder, or Colorado Springs areas, it's practically the only way to get to some places. However, visitors who drive their own cars will find that steep mountain roads can put a severe strain on their vehicles, particularly the cooling and braking systems. If you're planning to travel in winter, make sure you add plenty of antifreeze to your engine—most residents make sure there's enough to protect their cars to –35°F—temperatures can get well below zero in the mountains. Tires rated for mud and snow are needed in most areas in winter and are required on roads leading to most ski areas from November to March.

CAR & R.V. RENTALS   National rental agencies readily available in Colorado include **Advantage** (☎ 800/777-5500; www.arac.com); **Alamo** (☎ 800/327-9633; www.goalamo.com); **Avis** (☎ 800/331-1212; www.avis.com); **Budget** (☎ 800/527-0700; www.budgetrentacar.com); **Dollar** (☎ 800/800-4000; www.dollarcar.com); **Enterprise** (☎ 800/325-8007; www.pickenterprise.com); **Hertz** (☎ 800/654-3131; www.hertz.com); **Kemwel Holiday Auto (KHA)** (☎ 800/678-0678; www.kemwel.com); **National** (☎ 800/227-7368; www.nationalcar.com); and **Thrifty** (☎ 800/FOR-CARS; www.thrifty.com). Campers, travel trailers, and motor homes are available in Denver from **Cruise America** (☎ 800/327-7778); motorcycles can be rented in the Denver area at **North American Motorcycle Tours, Inc.** (☎ 303/692-1051).

DRIVING RULES   Colorado law requires all drivers to carry proof of insurance, as well as a valid driver's license. Safety belts are required for drivers and all front-seat passengers; restraints are required for everyone aged 15 and younger, regardless of where they're sitting. You must be 16 to drive in Colorado, period—even if you have a valid license from another state. The maximum speed limit on interstate highways is 75 miles per hour; 65 miles per hour on non-interstates, unless otherwise posted. Radar detectors are permitted. A driver will be considered intoxicated with a minimum blood-alcohol content of 0.10%. Colorado law allows drivers to make a right turn at a red signal after coming to a complete stop, unless posted otherwise.

MAPS   A state highway map can be obtained from any state Welcome Center or by mail (see "Visitor Information," at the beginning of this chapter). Otherwise,

Colorado Driving Times & Distances

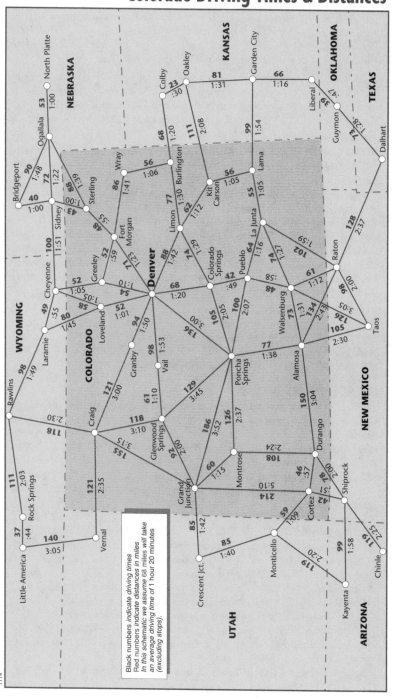

Black numbers indicate driving times
Red numbers indicate distances in miles
In this schematic we assume 68 miles will take
an average driving time of 1 hour 20 minutes
(excluding stops).

31

maps can be purchased at bookstores, gas stations, and most supermarkets and discount stores. Maps are available free to members of the American Automobile Association. An excellent source for all kinds of maps and road atlases is **Maps Unlimited** in Denver (☎ **800/456-8703** or 303/623-4299).

INSURANCE   Be sure to carry proof of automobile liability insurance, and be certain that your policy includes protection from uninsured motorists. If you're renting a car, check your credit cards to see if any of them include a collision-damage waiver (CDW) when you rent with their card; it may save you as much as $12 a day on the cost of your rental.

ROAD CONDITIONS & WINTER CLOSINGS   A recorded **24-hour hot line** (☎ **303/639-1111** or 303/639-1234) provides information on road conditions statewide.

Two notable Colorado highways are closed in winter: U.S. 34 (the Trail Ridge Road through Rocky Mountain National Park) and Colo. 82 (over Independence Pass east of Aspen, the main route between Denver and Aspen in summer). In addition, the Mount Evans Road (Colo. 103 and Colo. 5) from Idaho Springs to the summit of Mount Evans is open from June to September only. The Eisenhower Tunnel through Loveland Pass (along I-70) is sometimes closed due to winter storms, but only for short periods. Snow tires or chains are often required when roads are snow-covered or icy.

ROADSIDE ASSISTANCE   In case of an accident or road emergency, contact the state patrol. American Automobile Association members can get free emergency road service by calling **AAA's emergency number** (☎ **800/AAA-HELP**). In Colorado, AAA headquarters is at 4100 E. Arkansas Ave., Denver, CO 80222-3491 (☎ **800/283-5222** or 303/753-8800; www.aaacolo.com).

PACKAGE TOURS

Travelers who want to avoid the hassles of planning, making reservations, renting cars, and the rest have some good options among package tours, including a few unique choices. A compromise between doing your own thing and joining an organized tour is to work with **Colorado Reservation Service** (☎ **800/777-6880**), who will make reservations for lodging statewide, air and ground transportation, and ski, golf, and other outdoor activity packages.

Among the better companies that offer specialized tours to and within Colorado are the following.

Discover Colorado Tours, 2401 East St., Suite 204, Golden, CO 80401 (☎ **800/641-0129** or 303/277-0129), offers personalized half-day, full-day, or multi-day tours, for individuals and groups, throughout Colorado, including trips to gold mines, ghost towns, Rocky Mountain National Park, Pikes Peak, Mesa Verde, and the U.S. Air Force Academy.

Gray Line, 5855 E. 56th Ave. (P.O. Box 17527), Denver, CO 80217-0527 (☎ **303/289-2841**), provides traditional bus and van tours to the U.S. Air Force Academy, Pikes Peak, Rocky Mountain National Park, and other areas.

Maupintour, 1515 St. Andrews Dr., Lawrence, KS 66047 (☎ **800/255-4266**), offers well-planned multi-day tours that include Rocky Mountain National Park and other scenic and historic areas.

Sample Colorado Travel Club, P.O. Box 621906, Littleton, CO 80162-1906 (☎ **303/904-2376**), offers scheduled and custom tours with a historic theme throughout the state—both day trips from Denver and multi-day excursions.

For those who enjoy train travel, **American Orient Express Railway Company,** 2025 First Ave., Suite 830, Seattle, WA 98121 (☎ **888/759-3944** or 206/ 441-2725), has vintage rail cars outfitted in polished mahogany and brass, and dining cars decked out with china, silver, crystal, and linen, and a cuisine to match. One of its offerings is a 10-day trip to national parks of the West, including stops at Rocky Mountain National Park and Denver.

FAST FACTS: Colorado

Area Codes   Colorado uses four telephone area codes. Area codes in the imme- diate Denver and Boulder area are **303** and **720**. To make local calls in these cities, you will have to dial all 10 digits, starting with 303 or 720. The south- central and southeastern parts of the state, including Colorado Springs, use area code **719**; and the rest (west and north) use **970.** In 719 and 970 areas, local calls are reached by using only the seven-digit number. Long distance calls in all areas of the state require dialing 1 plus the area code plus the seven-digit number.

Business Hours   Banks are typically open weekdays from 9am to 5pm, occa- sionally later on Friday, and sometimes for several hours on Saturday. Most branches have automatic teller machines that are available 24 hours a day. Gen- erally, stores are open six days a week, with many open on Sunday, too; depart- ment stores usually stay open until 9pm at least one evening a week. Discount stores and supermarkets are often open later than other stores, and some super- markets in major cities are open 24 hours a day.

Car Rentals   See "Getting Around," above.

Climate   See "When to Go," above.

Drugstores   See "Pharmacies," below.

Embassies and Consulates   See chapter 4, "For Foreign Visitors."

Emergencies   For any emergency, dial ☎ **911.** Coins are not required at pay phones. In some rural areas, you must dial "0" (zero) for the operator.

Liquor Laws   The legal drinking age is 21. Except for 3.2% beer (sold in super- markets and convenience stores seven days a week from 5am to midnight), alco- holic beverages must be purchased in liquor stores. These are open Monday through Saturday from 8am to midnight. Beverages may be served in licensed restaurants, lounges, and bars Monday through Saturday from 7am to 2am, Sunday from 8am to 2am, and Christmas Day from 8am to midnight, with the proper licenses. Incidentally, 3.2% beer, which is sold only in Colorado, Utah, Oklahoma, and Kansas, does have less alcohol than beer sold elsewhere, despite what some storekeepers may tell you. According to the Budweiser people, 3.2% beer has about 4% alcohol by volume (which is equivalent to 3.2% alcohol by weight), while full-strength American beers have about 5% alcohol by volume.

Newspapers/Magazines   The state's largest daily newspaper is the *Denver Post,* which is published in Denver and distributed statewide. Other cities and large towns, especially regional hubs, have daily newspapers, and many smaller towns publish weeklies. National newspapers such as *USA Today* and the *Wall Street Journal* can be purchased in cities and major hotels, and you can find practically any newspaper or magazine you want (at least the Sunday edition) at **Tattered Cover Bookstore,** 2955 E. First Ave., Denver (☎ **800/833-9327** or 303/ 322-7727).

Pharmacies   You'll find 24-hour prescription services available at selected Walgreens Drug Stores around the state. For locations, call ☎ **800/WALGREENS.** Many supermarkets and discount stores also have pharmacies.

Taxes   Combined city and state sales taxes vary from place to place but are usually between 6% and 9% for purchases, and 9% to 13% for lodging.

Time   Colorado is on mountain standard time (7 hours behind Greenwich mean time), which is 1 hour ahead of the West Coast and 2 hours behind the East Coast. Daylight savings time is in effect from April to October.

For Foreign Visitors 4

American fads and fashions have spread across other parts of the world to such a degree that the United States may seem like familiar territory before your arrival. But there are still many peculiarities and uniquely American situations that any foreign visitor may find confusing or perplexing. This chapter will provide some specifics about getting to the United States as economically and effortlessly as possible, plus some helpful information about how things are done in Colorado—from receiving mail to making a local or long-distance telephone call.

1 Preparing for Your Trip

ENTRY REQUIREMENTS

DOCUMENT REGULATIONS Canadian nationals need only proof of Canadian residency to visit the United States. Citizens of the United Kingdom and Japan need only a current passport. Citizens of other countries, including Australia and New Zealand, usually need two documents: a valid passport with an expiration date at least six months later than the scheduled end of their visit to the United States, and a tourist visa, available at no charge from a U.S. embassy or consulate.

To get a tourist or business visa to enter the United States, contact the nearest American embassy or consulate in your country; if there is none, you will have to apply in person in a country where there is a U.S. embassy or consulate. Present your passport, a passport-size photo of yourself, and a completed application, which is available through the embassy or consulate. You may be asked to provide information about how you plan to finance your trip or show a letter of invitation from a friend with whom you plan to stay. Those applying for a business visa may be asked to show evidence that they will not receive a salary in the United States. Be sure to check the length of stay on your visa; usually it is six months. If you want to stay longer, you may file for an extension with the Immigration and Naturalization Service once you are in the country. If permission to stay is granted, a new visa is not required unless you leave the United States and want to reenter.

MEDICAL REQUIREMENTS No inoculations are needed to enter the United States unless you are coming from, or have stopped over in, areas known to be suffering from epidemics, particularly cholera or yellow fever.

If you have a disease requiring treatment with medications containing narcotics or drugs requiring a syringe, carry a valid, signed generic prescription from your physician to allay any suspicions that you are smuggling drugs. The prescription brands you are accustomed to buying in your country may not be available in the United States.

CUSTOMS REQUIREMENTS   Every adult visitor may bring into the United States, for their own personal use, free of duty: 1 liter of wine or hard liquor; 200 cigarettes or 100 cigars (but no cigars from Cuba) or 1 pound of smoking tobacco; and $100 worth of gifts. These exemptions are offered to travelers who spend at least 72 hours in the United States and who have not claimed them within the preceding six months. It is altogether forbidden to bring into the country foodstuffs (particularly cheese, fruit, cooked meats, and canned goods) and plants (vegetables, seeds, tropical plants, and so on). Foreign tourists may bring in or take out up to $10,000 in U.S. or foreign currency with no formalities; larger sums must be declared to Customs on entering or leaving.

INSURANCE

Unlike most other countries, the United States does not have a national health system. Because the cost of medical care is extremely high, we strongly advise all travelers to secure health coverage before setting out.

You may want to take out a comprehensive travel policy that covers (for a relatively low premium) sickness or injury costs (medical, surgical, and hospital); loss or theft of your baggage; trip-cancellation costs; guarantee of bail in case you are arrested; costs of accident, repatriation, or death. Such packages (for example, "Europ Assistance" in Europe) are sold by automobile clubs at attractive rates, as well as by insurance companies and travel agencies and at some airports.

MONEY

The U.S. monetary system has a decimal base: One American **dollar** ($1) = 100 cents (100¢). Dollar bills commonly come in $1 (a "buck"), $5, $10, $20, $50, and $100 denominations (the last two are not welcome when paying for small purchases and are usually not accepted in taxis or at subway ticket booths). There are six coin denominations: 1¢ (one cent or a "penny"), 5¢ (five cents or a "nickel"), 10¢ (ten cents or a "dime"), 25¢ (twenty-five cents or a "quarter"), 50¢ (fifty cents or a "half dollar"), and the $1 pieces (both the older, large silver dollar and the newer, small Susan B. Anthony coin).

Traveler's checks in U.S. dollars are accepted at most hotels, motels, restaurants, and large stores. Sometimes photo identification is required. American Express, Thomas Cook, and Barclay's Bank traveler's checks are readily accepted in the United States.

Credit cards are the method of payment most widely used: Visa (BarclayCard in Britain), MasterCard (EuroCard in Europe, Access in Britain, Diamond in Japan), American Express, Discover, Diners Club, and Carte Blanche, in descending order of acceptance. You can save yourself trouble by using "plastic" rather than cash or traveler's checks in 95% of all hotels, motels, restaurants, and retail stores. A credit card can also serve as a deposit for renting a car, as proof of identity, or as a "cash card," enabling you to draw money from automatic teller machines (ATMs) that accept them.

If you plan to travel for several weeks or more in the United States, you may want to deposit enough money into your credit-card account to cover anticipated expenses and avoid finance charges in your absence. This also reduces the likelihood of your receiving an unwelcome big bill on your return.

You can telegraph money, or have it telegraphed to you very quickly, by using the **Western Union** system (☎ **800/325-6000**).

SAFETY

Although foreign tourists in Colorado have not been subject to much crime, its cities are generally not as safe as those in Europe or Japan. This is particularly true in certain sections of Denver. It would be wise to ask local visitor information centers or your hotel concierge or desk clerk if you're not sure about the safety of certain neighborhoods. Avoid deserted areas, especially at night. Generally speaking, you can feel safe in areas where there are lots of people and many open establishments.

Be especially careful in national parks and other popular public lands. Recent years have seen an increase in crime at parks and national monuments, particularly thefts from campsites and parked vehicles.

Remember also that hotels are open to the public, and in a large hotel, security may not be able to screen everyone entering. Always lock your room door—don't assume that once inside your hotel, you are automatically safe and no longer need to be aware of your surroundings.

DRIVING   Safety while driving is particularly important. Question your rental agency about personal safety, or ask for a brochure of traveler safety tips when you pick up your car. Obtain written directions, or a map with the route marked in red, from the agency showing how to get to your destination. And, if possible, arrive and depart during daylight hours.

Recently more and more crime has involved cars and drivers. If you leave the highway and drive into a doubtful neighborhood, leave the area as quickly as possible. If you have an accident, even on the highway, stay in your car with the doors locked until you assess the situation or until the police arrive. If you are bumped from behind on the street or are involved in a minor accident with no injuries and the situation appears to be suspicious, motion to the other driver to follow you. Never get out of your car in such situations, but drive to the nearest police station, well-lighted service station, or all-night store.

If you see someone on the road who indicates a need for help, do not stop. Take note of the location, drive on to a well-lighted area, and telephone the police by dialing 911.

Park in well-lighted, well-traveled areas if possible. Always keep your car doors locked, whether attended or unattended. Never leave any packages or valuables in sight. If someone attempts to rob you or steal your car, do not try to resist the thief/carjacker—report the incident to the police department immediately.

2 Getting to the U.S.

Travelers from overseas can take advantage of the APEX (Advance Purchase Excursion) fares offered by all the major U.S. and European carriers. Aside from these, attractive values are offered by Virgin Atlantic Airways from London to New York/Newark.

Among international cities with nonstop flights to and from Denver are Amsterdam, Calgary, London, Mazatlan, San Jose del Cabo, Toronto, Vancouver, and Zacatecas. International travelers can also take flights to international airports in Chicago, Los Angeles, and New York, and then take connecting flights to Denver or Colorado Springs.

Visitors arriving by air, no matter what the port of entry, should cultivate patience and resignation before setting foot on U.S. soil. Getting through Immigration Control may take as long as two hours on some days, especially summer weekends, so have your guidebook or something else to read handy. Add the time it takes to clear Customs, and you'll see that you should allow extra time for delays when planning connections between international and domestic flights—an average of two to three hours at least.

In contrast, travelers arriving by car or by rail from Canada will find border-crossing formalities streamlined to the vanishing point. And air travelers from Canada, Bermuda, and some places in the Caribbean can sometimes go through Customs and Immigration at the point of departure, which is much quicker.

3 Getting Around the U.S.

BY PLANE   On their trans-Atlantic or trans-Pacific flights, some large U.S. airlines offer special discount tickets for any of their U.S. destinations (American Airlines' Visit USA program and Delta's Discover America program, for example). These tickets are not on sale in the United States and must, therefore, be purchased before you leave your foreign point of departure. This program is the best, easiest, and fastest way to see the United States at low cost. You should obtain information well in advance from your travel agent or the office of the airline concerned, because the conditions attached to these discount tickets can be changed without advance notice.

BY RAIL   Amtrak (☎ 800/USA-RAIL; www.amtrak.com) connects Colorado to both the East and West Coasts. International visitors can buy a **USA Railpass,** good for 15 or 30 days of unlimited travel on Amtrak, available through many foreign travel agents. Prices in 1998 for a 15-day pass were $260 off-peak, $375 peak; a 30-day pass costs $350 off-peak, $480 peak (off-peak is August 21 to June 16). With a foreign passport, you can also buy passes at some Amtrak offices in the United States, including those in San Francisco, Los Angeles, Chicago, New York, Miami, Boston, and Washington, D.C.

Amtrak also frequently has low-cost passes available for anyone, covering certain regions of the country. Reservations are generally required for train travel and should be made for each part of your trip as early as possible.

Visitors should also be aware of the limitations of long-distance rail travel in the United States. With a few notable exceptions, service is rarely up to European standards: Delays are common, routes are limited and often infrequently served, and fares are rarely significantly lower than discount airfares. Thus, cross-country train travel should be approached with caution.

BY BUS   The cheapest way to travel the United States is by bus. **Greyhound/Trailways** (☎ 800/231-2222; www.greyhound.com), the sole nationwide bus line, offers an **Ameripass** (☎ 888/454-7277) for unlimited nationwide travel for 7 days (for $199), 15 days (for $299), 30 days (for $409), and 60 days (for $599). Be aware that bus travel in the United States can be both slow and uncomfortable, so this option isn't for everyone. In addition, bus stations are often located in undesirable neighborhoods.

BY CAR   Because much of Colorado is rural, with limited or nonexistent public transportation, the best way to explore the state is by car. Many car-rental companies (see city listings) offer unlimited-mileage weekly specials that can be quite affordable.

FAST FACTS: For the Foreign Traveler

Automobile Organizations   Auto clubs will supply maps, suggested routes, guidebooks, accident and bail-bond insurance, and emergency road service. The major auto club in the United States is the **American Automobile Association (AAA),** with close to 1,000 offices nationwide, including offices in the Denver metro area, Boulder, Colorado Springs, Pueblo, Grand Junction, Fort Collins, and Greeley. Members of some foreign auto clubs have reciprocal arrangements with the AAA and enjoy its services at no charge. If you belong to an auto club, inquire about AAA reciprocity before you leave home. The AAA can provide you with an **International Driving Permit** validating your foreign license. You may be able to join AAA even if you are not a member of a reciprocal club. For AAA emergency road service, call ☎ **800/222-4357.** In addition, some automobile-rental agencies now provide these services; ask about their availability when you rent your car.

Automobile Rentals   To rent a car, you need a major credit card. A valid driver's license is required, and you usually need to be at least 25 years old. Some companies do rent to younger people but add a daily surcharge. Be sure to return your car with the same amount of gas you started with; rental companies charge excessive prices for gasoline. See "Getting Around" in chapter 3.

Business Hours   See "Fast Facts" in chapter 3.

Climate   See "When to Go" in chapter 3.

Currency   See "Money" in "Preparing for Your Trip," above.

Currency Exchange   The "foreign-exchange bureaus" so common in Europe are rare in the United States. They're at major international airports, and there are a few in most major cities, but they're nonexistent in medium-size cities and small towns. Try to avoid having to change foreign money, or traveler's checks denominated other than in U.S. dollars, at small-town banks, or even at branches in a big city; in fact, leave any currency other than U.S. dollars at home (except the cash you need for the taxi or bus ride home when you return to your own country)—otherwise, your own currency may prove more nuisance to you than it's worth.

In Denver, **Thomas Cook Currency Services** is located downtown in the World Trade Center, at 1625 Broadway; and at Cherry Creek North, 299 Detroit St. There's also a currency-exchange booth at Denver International Airport, and you can call ☎ **800/CURRENCY** for locations of other Thomas Cook offices.

In Boulder, currency-exchange services are available at **First World–American Express Travel,** 1113 Spruce St. (☎ **303/234-1551** for information). In Colorado Springs, go to **Bank One,** 30 E. Pikes Peak Blvd. (☎ **719/471-5000**).

Drinking Laws   See "Liquor Laws" in chapter 3.

Electricity   The United States uses 110–120 volts, 60 cycles, compared to 220–240 volts, 50 cycles, as in most of Europe. In addition to a 100-volt converter, small appliances of non-American manufacture, such as hair dryers or shavers, will require a plug adapter, with two flat, parallel pins.

Embassies/Consulates   All embassies are located in the nation's capital, Washington, D.C.; some consulates are located in major cities; and most nations have a mission to the United Nations in New York City. Foreign visitors can obtain telephone numbers for their embassies and consulates by calling "Directory

Assistance" in Washington, D.C. (☎ 202/555-1212). The following countries have consulates in the Denver area: **Australia,** 999 18th St. (☎ 303/297-1200); **Denmark,** 5353 W. Dartmouth Ave., Lakewood (☎ 303/980-9100); **France,** 1420 Ogden St. (☎ 303/831-8616); **Germany,** 350 Indiana St. (☎ 303/279-1551); **Italy,** 16613 W. Archer Ave., Golden (☎ 303/271-1429); **Korea,** 1600 Broadway (☎ 303/830-0500); **Mexico,** 48 Steele St. (☎ 303/331-1110); **Netherlands,** 5560 S. Chester Court, Greenwood Village (☎ 303/770-7747); **Norway,** 370 17th St. (☎ 303/592-5930); **Sweden** (☎ 303/758-0999); **Switzerland,** 2810 Iliff St., Boulder (☎ 303/499-5641); and **Thailand,** 3980 Quebec St. (☎ 303/320-4029).

Emergencies   Call ☎ **911** for fire, police, and ambulance. If you encounter such traveler's problems as sickness, accident, or lost or stolen baggage, call Traveler's Aid, an organization that specializes in helping distressed travelers. (Check local directories for the location nearest you.) Most U.S. hospitals have emergency rooms, with a special entrance where you will be admitted for quick medical attention.

Gasoline (Petrol)   One U.S. gallon equals 3.75 liters, while 1.2 U.S. gallons equals 1 Imperial gallon. You'll notice there are several grades (and price levels) of gasoline available at most gas stations and that their names change from company to company. Unleaded gasoline with the highest octane is the most expensive, but most rental cars will run fine with the least expensive "regular" unleaded.

Holidays   On the following legal U.S. national holidays, banks, government offices, post offices, and some government-run attractions are closed: January 1 (New Year's Day); third Monday in January (Martin Luther King, Jr. Day); third Monday in February (Presidents' Day); last Monday in May (Memorial Day); July 4 (Independence Day); first Monday in September (Labor Day); second Monday in October (Columbus Day); November 11 (Veterans' Day/Armistice Day); fourth Thursday in November (Thanksgiving Day); and December 25 (Christmas). The Tuesday following the first Monday in November is Election Day and is a legal holiday in presidential-election years.

Stores and some restaurants often close only for New Year's Day, Easter, and Christmas.

Languages   Major hotels sometimes have multilingual employees, with Spanish and German being the most common foreign languages spoken in Colorado.

Legal Aid   The foreign tourist, unless positively identified as a member of organized crime or a drug ring, will probably never become involved with the American legal system. If you are stopped for a minor infraction, such as speeding or some other traffic violation, never attempt to pay the fine directly to a police officer; you may be arrested on the much more serious charge of attempted bribery. Pay fines by mail or directly to the clerk of the court. If you are accused of a more serious offense, it's wise to say and do nothing before consulting a lawyer. Under U.S. law, an arrested person is allowed one telephone call to a party of his or her choice; call your embassy or consulate.

Mail   If you want your mail to follow you on your vacation and you aren't sure of your address, your mail can be sent to you, in your name, **c/o General Delivery** at the main post office of the city or region where you expect to be. The addressee must pick it up in person and produce proof of identity (driver's license, passport, and so on). For post office locations and hours throughout Colorado, call the **U.S. Postal Service** (☎ **800/275-8777**).

Mailboxes are blue with a blue-and-white eagle logo, and carry the inscription UNITED STATES POSTAL SERVICE.

If your mail is addressed to a U.S. destination, don't forget to add the five-figure postal code, or **ZIP Code,** after the two-letter abbreviation of the state to which the mail is addressed (CO for Colorado, CA for California, UT for Utah, FL for Florida, NY for New York, and so on).

Newspapers/Magazines   National newspapers generally available in Colorado include the *New York Times, USA Today,* and the *Wall Street Journal.* National news magazines include *Newsweek, Time,* and *U.S. News & World Report.* The state's major daily newspaper is the *Denver Post.* Some 70 foreign newspapers, mostly Sunday editions, are available at the Tattered Cover bookstore, 2955 E. First Ave., opposite Cherry Creek Shopping Center in Denver (☎ **800/ 833-9327** or 303/322-7727). These include, from the United Kingdom, *The Times of London, Independent, The Mail, Manchester Guardian, Observer, Express, Mirror, Telegram,* and *The Times Literary Supplement.* The store also carries major newspapers from Canada, Australia, New Zealand, Ireland, Switzerland, Germany, Norway, Finland, Denmark, Sweden, France, Italy, Spain, Russia, Japan, China, Greece, Israel, Colombia, Brazil, Chile, Mexico, and North Africa.

Post   See "Mail" above.

Radio/Television   Six coast-to-coast networks—ABC, CBS, NBC, PBS (Public Broadcasting Service), Fox, and CNN (Cable Network News)—play a major part in American life. In Colorado, television viewers usually have a choice of at least a dozen channels via cable or satellite. PBS and the cable channel Arts and Entertainment (A&E) broadcast a number of British programs. You'll also find a wide choice of local radio stations, each broadcasting particular kinds of talk shows and/or music—classical, country, jazz, pop—punctuated by news broadcasts and frequent commercials.

Safety   See "Safety" in "Preparing for Your Trip" above.

Taxes   In the United States, there is no VAT (value-added tax) or other indirect tax at a national level. Every state, as well as each city, has the right to levy its own local tax on all purchases, including hotel and restaurant checks, airline tickets, and so on. Sales tax is levied on goods and services by state and local governments, however, and is not included in the price tags you'll see on merchandise. These taxes are not refundable. Sales taxes in Colorado vary but usually total from 6% to 9%. An exception is the tax on lodging, which often runs 9% to 13%, and is also not usually included in the quoted rate but will certainly be added to your bill.

There is also a $10 Customs tax, payable on entry to the United States, and a $6 departure tax.

Telephone, Fax & Telegraph   The telephone system in the United States is run by private corporations, so rates, especially for long-distance service, can vary widely even on calls made from public telephones. Local calls in the United States usually cost 25¢ or 35¢ from pay telephones.

In the past few years, many American companies and government offices have installed voice-mail systems, so be prepared to deal with a machine instead of a human if calling a business number, attraction, or government office.

For **long-distance** or **international calls,** it's most economical to charge the call to a telephone charge card or a credit card, or you can use a lot of change. The pay phone will instruct you how much to deposit and when to deposit it into the slot at the top of the telephone box.

For long-distance calls in the United States, dial 1 followed by the area code and number you want. For direct overseas calls, first dial 011, followed by the country code (Australia, 61; Republic of Ireland, 353; New Zealand, 64; United Kingdom, 44; and so on), and then by the city code (for example, 71 or 81 for London, 21 for Birmingham, 1 for Dublin) and the number of the person you wish to call.

Before calling from a hotel room, always ask the hotel phone operator if there are any telephone surcharges. There almost always are, especially in full service hotels, and they often are as much as 75¢ or $1, even for a local call. These charges can sometimes be avoided by calling collect or using a telephone charge card, or finding a public phone to make your calls.

For **reversed-charge** or **collect calls,** and for **person-to-person calls,** dial "0" (zero, *not* the letter "O") followed by the area code and number you want; an operator will then come on the line, and you should specify that you are calling collect, or person-to-person, or both. If your operator-assisted call is international, immediately ask to speak with an overseas operator.

For local **directory assistance** (information), dial 1-411; for **long-distance information,** dial 1, then the appropriate area code and 555-1212.

Fax facilities are readily available in many hotels, motels, and even small bed-and-breakfasts, and 24-hour service is available at numerous copy centers, including Kinko's outlets, in larger cities.

Like the telephone system, **telegraph** services are provided by private corporations such as ITT, MCI, and, above all, **Western Union.** You can bring your telegram in to the nearest Western Union office (there are hundreds across the country), or dictate it over the phone (☎ **800/325-6000**). You can also telegraph money, or have it telegraphed to you, very quickly over the Western Union system.

Time   The continental United States is divided into four **time zones** (six, including Alaska and Hawaii). From east to west, these are: eastern standard time (EST), central standard time (CST), mountain standard time (MST; which includes all of Colorado), Pacific standard time (PST), Alaska standard time (AST), and Hawaii standard time (HST). Always keep time zones in mind if you are traveling (or even telephoning) long distances in the United States. For example, noon in New York City (EST) is 11am in Chicago (CST), 10am in Denver (MST), 9am in Los Angeles (PST), 8am in Anchorage (AST), and 7am in Honolulu (HST).

Daylight saving time (DST) is in effect in Colorado and most of the country, from the first Sunday in April through the last Saturday in October (actually, the change is made at 2am on Sunday). Daylight saving time moves the clock one hour ahead of standard time. Note that Arizona (except for the Navajo Nation), Hawaii, part of Indiana, and Puerto Rico do not observe DST.

Tipping   Some rules of thumb: Tip bartenders 10% to 15% of the check; bell-hops, at least 50¢ per bag, or $2 to $3 for a lot of luggage; cab drivers, 10% of the fare; chambermaids, $1 per day; checkroom attendants, $1 per garment; hairdressers and barbers, 15% to 20%; waiters and waitresses, 15% to 20% of the check; valet parking attendants, $1. You are not expected to tip theater ushers, gas-station attendants, or employees at cafeterias and fast-food restaurants.

Toilets   Foreign visitors often complain that public toilets are hard to find in most U.S. cities. There are few on the streets, but you can usually find a clean one in a visitor information center, shopping mall, restaurant, hotel, museum, department or discount store, or service station (although service-station facilities often leave much to be desired). Note, however, a growing practice in some restaurants is to display a sign: TOILETS ARE FOR PATRONS ONLY. You can just ignore this sign or, better yet, avoid arguments by paying for a cup of coffee or soft drink, which will qualify you as a patron.

5 The Active Vacation Planner

The variety and sheer number of active sports and recreational activities Colorado has to offer is staggering. It's a place where you can easily arrange a week-long, hard-core mountaineering expedition, but it's also a place where you can just as easily take one of the most scenic 2-hour bike rides of your life—right in downtown Boulder—not to mention the superb winter activities, from skiing to snowmobiling. This chapter outlines your choices and offers a few tips for planning everything from a guided, multi-sport vacation to an afternoon's outing.

1 Preparing for Your Active Vacation

Once you've picked the sport or activities you want to pursue, ask yourself a few questions: How physically fit am I really? How much skill in this particular activity do I have? How dangerous is this activity? How much money am I willing to spend? Answering these questions honestly can make the difference between a successful vacation and an unmitigated disaster. Some activities, such as cattle drives, require an outfitter, while others, such as biking, camping, or hiking, you can easily do on your own. Obviously, if you're attempting a dangerous sport in which you're inexperienced, such as rock climbing, it's best to go with someone who literally knows the ropes.

If cost is an issue, prearranged escorted tour packages that include virtually everything can often save you money. On the other hand, you'll be with a group, with limited freedom and flexibility to strike out on your own. Some people enjoy the company of their fellow tour members and the convenience of having everything set up for them; others can't stand it. It's your choice.

Most outfitters and many tour operators keep their group size small and offer trips of different lengths and varying levels of ability. The best outfitters run well-organized trips and are willing to answer any and all questions, promptly and fully. They should have well-maintained equipment, possess appropriate land-use permits, and be fully insured. If you have any doubts, ask for the name and phone number of a satisfied former customer, and call that person and ask about their experience.

Several government agencies and other organizations provide maps and information that can be extremely useful for a variety of activities. These include **Colorado State Parks** (for state park, boating, RV, and snowmobile regulations), 1313 Sherman St., no. 618, Denver, CO 80203 (☎ **303/866-3437;** www.parks.state.co.us); the **Colorado Outfitters Association** (for a list of licensed guides and outfitters in the state), P.O. Box 440021, Aurora, CO 80044-0021 (☎ **303/368-4731**); the **U.S. Bureau of Land Management** (for maps and information on activities on the vast amount of BLM land in the state), 2850 Youngfield St., Lakewood, CO 80215 (☎ **303/239-3600;** www.co.blm.gov); the **U.S. Forest Service** (for maps and information about activities and facilities in national forests), Rocky Mountain Region, P.O. Box 25127, Lakewood, CO 80225 (☎ **303/236-9431;** www.fs.fed.us/r2); the **U.S. Geological Survey** (for topographical maps), Box 25286, Denver, CO 80225 (☎ **303/202-4200;** www.usgs.gov); and the **U.S. National Park Service** (for information on national parks, monuments, and recreation areas), P.O. Box 25287, Denver, CO 80225 (☎ **303/969-2000;** www.nps.gov).

On the Internet, the Colorado section of **GORP** (Great Outdoor Recreation Page), at **www.gorp.com/gorp/location/co/co.htm,** provides detailed information about hiking trails, fishing accesses, water sports, and other activities on Colorado's public lands, with links to related sites.

Those looking to buy or rent equipment will find shops practically everywhere in the state, particularly in resort towns. A convenient, statewide resource is **Gart Brothers,** the state's largest sporting-goods chain. For the location of the store nearest you, contact the **Gart Sports Castle,** a huge sales, repair, and rental facility, at 1000 Broadway in Denver (☎ **303/861-1122;** www.gartsports.com).

2 Visiting Colorado's National Parks & Monuments

Some of the most beautiful parts of Colorado have been preserved within the federal government's national park and monument system.

Rocky Mountain National Park, easily the most popular of the state's national parks in terms of number of visitors, is also the most spectacular. Because photos of its magnificent snowcapped peaks have graced so many calendars and coffee-table books, people often envision Rocky Mountain National Park when they think of Colorado. The state's other national park, Mesa Verde, is entirely different. Its reason for being is its history, with the best-preserved ancient cliff dwellings in the Southwest.

The state's national monuments—Colorado, Black Canyon of the Gunnison, and Dinosaur—may not compare with Rocky Mountain National Park in terms of overall beauty, but each has its own charm and is well worth a visit. Colorado National Monument is similar to the national parks of southern Utah—somewhat barren, with incredible red-rock formations. Dinosaur National Monument should really be two parks: a scenic but arid canyonlands section in Colorado and its namesake dinosaur quarry just across the border in Utah. And Black Canyon of the Gunnison is an extremely narrow, rocky river canyon that's wild and beautiful, but difficult to explore because of its steep canyon walls.

To get the most from your visit, try to avoid school vacation periods and the dead of winter, when the high country of Rocky Mountain National Park and parts of Mesa Verde are inaccessible. Although the parks are beautiful under a frosting of snow, you won't be able to see as much.

If you can, take a hike. Most park visitors tend to stay on the beaten track, stopping at the same scenic vistas before rushing to the next one. If you can spend even an hour or two on the trail, it's often possible to simply walk away from the crowds.

American parks and monuments are some of the biggest travel bargains in the world. If you plan to visit a number of national parks and monuments within a year, a **Golden Eagle Pass** for $50 will save you a bundle. It allows the bearer, plus everyone traveling with him or her in the same vehicle, free admission to all national parks and monuments (camping fees are extra) for 12 months. The **Golden Age Passport,** for those 62 and older, has a one-time fee of $10 and provides free admission to all national parks and monuments, plus a 50% discount on camping fees. Finally, there's the **Golden Access Passport,** free for blind or permanently disabled U.S. citizens, with the same benefits as the Golden Age Passport. All passes can be purchased at park entrances.

3 Outdoor Activities A to Z

BALLOONING   You can take a hot-air balloon ride virtually anywhere in the state, but the most awe-inspiring scenery is in the mountains. Generally, you can book a ballooning trip a few days in advance, although at peak times such as holidays, make your reservations as far ahead as possible. Hot-air ballooning is expensive, and it's one sport where you don't want to cut corners. Choose an experienced and well-established balloon company, and if you have any qualms, ask about their safety record. As with most Colorado activities, you'll pay the highest rates at resorts. Prices are usually reasonable in Colorado Springs and Boulder, but somewhat higher in Denver.

BICYCLING   Bicycling is popular throughout Colorado, but especially in Boulder, which has more bikes than people; even in Fort Collins, public buses have bike racks. Most larger cities are bike-friendly, with established bike paths, but bicyclists will still occasionally find themselves surrounded by cars, or blocked by parked cars where they expected to find a bike path. Our favorite city bike path is the **Boulder Creek Path,** which meanders through 10 miles of Boulder parklands, with no cross streets or motor vehicle intrusion of any kind.

To plan a bike trip, pick up the annual magazine *Bicycle Colorado* (for a free copy, call ☎ 800/997-2453). It details the best spots for cycling in the state and provides other useful tips as well.

BOATING   Those who take their powerboats along on their visit to Colorado will find lakes scattered across the state. Most have boat ramps, some have fuel and supplies, and some of the larger lakes offer boat rentals. Popular choices include Bonny Lake near Burlington (known for water-skiing), Pueblo Reservoir, and Trinidad Lake. Navajo State Park in the Durango area offers a 35-mile-long reservoir straddling the New Mexico border, with a variety of boats available for rent, including fully equipped houseboats.

CAMPING   With so many acres of public land, Colorado offers practically unlimited opportunities for camping, especially in the mountains. There are over 400 public campgrounds in the national forests alone, plus sites in Bureau of Land Management areas, national parks, national monuments, and state parks. In addition, most communities have commercially operated campgrounds with RV hookups. If you plan to drive an RV in Colorado, a word of advice: have the mechanical system checked out thoroughly first, as there are some extremely steep grades in the mountains.

One of the best places to camp in the state is Rocky Mountain National Park, but it can be crowded, especially in summer. Visit in late September or early October, if possible. Backpackers will find numerous camping opportunities along the Colorado Trail and in Colorado State Forest Park west of Fort Collins. Mueller State Park, west of Colorado Springs, is tops for RV camping.

The **Colorado Agency of Camping, Cabins, & Lodges,** 5101 Pennsylvania Ave., Boulder, CO 80303-2799 (☎ **888/222-4641** or 303/499-9343; fax 303/499-9333; www.coloradodirectory.com), publishes a free annual booklet that describes commercial campgrounds, cabin facilities, and resorts throughout the state. A free copy of *Colorado State Parks,* which contains details on the state's 40-plus parks, is available from state park offices (see above). A nationwide directory of Kampgrounds of America (KOA) franchise campgrounds is available free at any KOA, or by mail for $3 from **Kampgrounds of America, Inc.,** Executive Offices, Billings, MT 59114-0558 (☎ **406/248-7444;** www.koakampgrounds.com); and members of the American Automobile Association can request the club's free *Southwestern CampBook,* which includes campgrounds and RV parks in Colorado. Several massive campground directories can be purchased in major bookstores, including *Trailer Life Campground, R.V. Park & Services Directory,* published annually by TL Enterprises, Inc., P.O. Box 6060, Camarillo, CA 93011 (www.camping.tl.com).

CATTLE DRIVES   As elsewhere in the West, opportunities abound for city slickers to play cowboy, riding and roping cattle on actual drives that last from a day to a week or more. Each drive is different, so ask very specific questions about food, sleeping arrangements, and other conditions before plunking down your money. It's also a good idea to book your trip as early as possible. The best places for joining a cattle drive are Steamboat Springs and Aspen, with their beautiful mountain scenery and fun towns—perfect for relaxing at the end of the trail.

CROSS-COUNTRY SKIING   Practically every major ski area also offers cross-country skiing, and there are thousands of miles of trails throughout Colorado's national forests—often old mining and logging roads—that are perfect for cross-country skiing, and free. Among the state's top destinations are Breckenridge, with a series of trails that wind through open meadows and a spruce forest, and the beautiful San Juan Mountains at Purgatory Resort near Durango and in Telluride.

A free directory of nordic centers, hut systems, guides, and guest ranches that cater to cross-country skiers is available from the **Colorado Cross Country Ski Association,** Box 1292, Kremmling, CO 80459 (☎ **800/869-4560;** www.colorado-xc.org). Also contact the **U.S. Forest Service** (see above).

DOGSLEDDING   If your fantasy is to be a Canadian Mountie mushing across the frozen Yukon, save the airfare and head to the mountains of Colorado instead. Dogsled rides are offered at several ski resorts, but we like Aspen best, where dog-power takes you far from the crowds into the rugged backcountry. Some rides end with a fancy dinner. Incidentally, those movies you've seen are wrong: The dogs almost never bark while running, just before and after.

FISHING   Many cold-water species of fish live in the state's mountains, lakes, and streams, including seven kinds of trout (native cutthroat, rainbow, brown, brook, lake, kokanee, and whitefish), walleye, yellow perch, northern pike, tiger muskie, and bluegill. Warm-water sport fish (especially in eastern Colorado and in large rivers) include catfish, crappie, and bass: largemouth, smallmouth, white, and wiper.

The fishing season is year-round, except in certain specified waters. A 1-year license costs $40.25 for an adult nonresident (ages 15 and over), $20.25 for a resident; 5-day licenses are $18.25, and 1-day licenses are $5.25, for nonresidents and residents alike. Children under 15 are restricted to half the daily bag limit without a license.

4×4 = Four-Season Four-Wheeling

For years, experienced skiers have known that four-wheel-drive vehicles make getting to and from the slopes much easier in the dead of winter. Now that luxury sport-utility vehicles and 4×4 trucks have virtually eclipsed cars in popularity, more and more travelers are choosing to see Colorado by four-wheel-drive vehicle year-round.

If you own a 4×4 and plan to drive it into the state, consider contacting the **Colorado Association of Four-Wheel-Drive Clubs** before you leave home, at P.O. Box 1413, Wheat Ridge, CO 80034 (☎ **303/343-0646**). The association sells books of maps of four-wheel-drive roads throughout Colorado and can direct you to local off-road clubs that welcome visitors on their trips. Another good source of information is the **Colorado Off Highway Vehicle Coalition,** P.O. Box 620523, Littleton, CO 80162 (☎ **800/318-3395** or 303/744-1435; www.cohvco.org).

Southwestern Colorado is an excellent place for off-roading; the San Juan Mountains offer scores of old mining trails that are just right for this kind of backcountry exploring. Ouray has two outfitters that lead 4×4 tours into the high country: **Switzerland of America,** 226 Seventh Ave. (☎ **800/432-5337** or 970/325-4484; www.soajeep.com), and **San Juan Scenic Jeep Tours,** 480 Main St.(☎ **877/325-4385** or 970/325-4444). Independent travelers can also rent their own four-wheeler upon arrival in the state from most major car-rental companies.

The **Colorado Division of Wildlife,** 6060 Broadway, Denver, CO 80216 (☎ **303/297-1192** or 303/291-7529), offers anglers several handy recorded messages. For **general information** on fishing, call ☎ **303/291-7533;** for a list of **fishing regulations,** call ☎ **303/291-7299;** for **fishing reports** from April through September, call ☎ **303/291-7534.**

GOLF   Clear blue skies and beautiful scenery are hallmarks of Colorado golf courses, but don't think they're merely pretty faces; these courses can be as challenging as any in the country. Balls travel farther here than at sea level, and golfers tend to tire more quickly, at least until they've adapted to the higher elevation. Be prepared for cool mornings and afternoon thunderstorms even at the height of summer. Courses at lower elevations, such as along the western slope, in the southwest corner, and around Denver, are often open year-round, however.

Good golf resorts can be found in Crested Butte, Winter Park, Pueblo, and Alamosa; for high-altitude putting, try Leadville; and for the top resort, go to the Broadmoor in Colorado Springs. For a directory of the state's major golf courses, contact the **Colorado Golf Resort Association,** 2110 S. Ash St., Denver, CO 80222 (☎ **303/699-4653**). Information is also available from the **Colorado Golf Association,** 5655 S. Yosemite St., Suite 101, Englewood, CO 80111 (☎ **303/779-4653**). The **American Lung Association of Colorado,** 1600 Race St., Denver, CO 80206 (☎ **303/388-4327**), offers a golf discount card with free or reduced greens fees at more than 700 courses in the western United States and British Columbia, including several dozen in Colorado. The cost is $25 per person.

HIKING, BACKPACKING & MOUNTAINEERING   Colorado is literally crisscrossed with hiking trails and dotted with mountains begging to be climbed. The best opportunities, particularly for scenic beauty, are probably in Rocky Mountain

National Park, but park hiking trails are among the most crowded in the state, especially in July and August. It's possible to get away from the crowds by taking longer hikes on lesser-used trails (ask rangers for suggestions), or by joining a climbing expedition. The highly respected **Colorado Mountain School,** P.O. Box 2062, Estes Park, CO 80517 (☎ **970/586-5758**), leads climbs up Longs Peak in the national park and can also provide advice on mountaineering in other parts of the state.

The 500-mile **Colorado Trail,** which winds from Denver to Durango, crosses seven national forests and six designated wilderness areas. Scenery and terrain are varied, from grassy plains to snowcapped mountains. Although the entire trail can be hiked by those in excellent physical condition in 6 to 8 weeks, most hikers prefer excursions of a week or less, and many enjoy day hikes. Most of the trail is above 10,000 feet elevation (the highest point is at 13,334 feet), and hikes of more than a day or two will inevitably include some steep climbs. However, most of the trail has grades of no more than 10%. You'll find the easiest sections of the trail in the first 90 miles from Denver, but other sections, such as one 20-mile stretch near Salida, are also easy to moderate. In the Breckenridge and Winter Park areas, the trail is fairly rugged, and most sections below U.S. 50 are mountainous and at least somewhat strenuous.

The Colorado Trail's most crowded sections are near major population centers. There is much less trail use south of U.S. 50, where the trail winds through the San Juan Mountains. It's serenely peaceful here, but there are also fewer services, and if you're injured, it could be a long wait for help. If you're really looking for serenity, consider climbing one of the fourteeners—peaks over 14,000-feet elevation—just off the Colorado Trail. Among the easiest is the climb to the summit of 14,420-foot Mount Harvard, the state's third-highest peak. The trail branches off the Colorado Trail about 8 miles north of Buena Vista.

Those planning multi-day hikes on the Colorado Trail should carry maps or the official guidebook, which includes maps and details of the entire trail—elevation changes, trail conditions, vehicle access points, closest services, and general descriptions. Contact the **Colorado Trail Foundation,** American Mountaineering Center, 710 10th St. #210, Golden, CO 80401 (☎ **303/526-0809** or 303/384-3729, ext. 113; fax 303/384-3743; www.coloradotrail.org). The **Friends of the Colorado Trail,** at the same address, offers supported treks and accredited courses on the trail.

Although the Colorado Trail may be the state's most famous hike, there are plenty of other opportunities. We particularly like the hike to **Long Lake** in the **Routt National Forest** outside Steamboat Springs, a moderately difficult 12-mile round-trip hike that leads through a forest and past several waterfalls to a peaceful, pristine alpine lake. Although hikers in the Denver area often head out on the Colorado Trail, another pleasant hike is the easy 9-mile walk around **Barr Lake,** 18 miles northeast of the city, which offers excellent viewing of wildlife and birds. For the best city hike, try the **Boulder Creek Path,** a 10-mile trail that leads from downtown Boulder into the nearby mountains, offering wildlife and bird watching and good views of the mountains and city. Those in Colorado Springs can hike among the beautiful red sandstone formations in **Garden of the Gods,** or head west about 30 miles to **Mueller State Park,** with its 90 miles of trails through mountain scenery much like you'll find at Rocky Mountain National Park.

HORSEBACK RIDING   It's fun to see the Old West the way the pioneers of 100 years ago did: from a horse's saddle. Plenty of stables and outfitters lead rides lasting from 1 hour to several days, but we recommend those near Estes Park, Steamboat Springs, Grand Junction, and Telluride. If you'd like to spend your entire vacation on horseback, the **Sylvan Dale Guest Ranch** (☎ **970/667-3915;** fax 970/ 635-9336; www.sylvandale.com; e-mail: ranch@sylvandale.com) just outside of Loveland is highly regarded. You'll find stables in Denver and Colorado Springs, but the best are in Colorado Springs, where you can explore the Garden of the Gods on horseback.

ICE CLIMBING   Among the top spots in the state for this dizzying sport is Steamboat Springs.

MOUNTAIN BIKING   The town of Crested Butte claims to be the mountain-biking capital of Colorado, but Telluride and Vail are also popular spots for fat-tire explorations. Those planning to go mountain biking in western Colorado can receive a free trail map by sending a stamped, self-addressed envelope to **Colorado Plateau Mountain Bike Trail Association,** P.O. Box 4602, Grand Junction, CO 81502.

The **Colorado Trail,** which runs some 500 miles from Denver to Durango, is also open to mountain bikers. Riding all the way across it is easily the state's top mountain bike adventure. It'll take at least 4 weeks, but you'll be traveling through Colorado's most scenic and rugged country: deep forests and high plains. You'll share the trail with hikers and horseback riders (bikers yield to both), and those with bikes must take detours around designated wilderness areas. Mountain bikers looking for a shorter trip can join or leave the trail at almost any point. One easily accessible stretch runs 24 miles from Copper Mountain Ski Resort to Tennessee Pass, crossing 12,280-foot Elk Ridge and descending into the ghost town of Camp Hale. For information, contact the **Colorado Trail Foundation** (see "Hiking, Backpacking & Mountaineering," above).

There are also numerous trails on public lands. Our favorites are the many trails around Crested Butte and Winter Park, and Colorado State Forest Park, west of Fort Collins. These areas offer a variety of terrain, with trails for all levels of skill and physical condition.

RAFTING & KAYAKING   Rivers swollen with melted snow lure rafters and kayakers from spring through midsummer, when rivers are at their fullest. Salida has become a famous rafting center; other popular destinations include Fort Collins, Estes Park, Grand Junction, and Glenwood Springs.

Rivers are classified from I to VI, depending on the roughness of their rapids. Class I is an easy float trip, practically calm; class II has some rapids but is mostly calm; class III has some difficult rapids, with waves and boulders, and can be narrow in spots; class IV is considered very difficult, with long stretches of rough raft-flipping rapids; class V is extremely difficult with violent rapids and steep drops; and class VI is considered unrunnable in any type of raft or kayak. Rivers vary, though, so it is not unusual to float through a calm class I section and just around the bend find an exciting class III section. The Arkansas River near Salida offers a variety from easy to almost unrunnable, and the Colorado River through Glenwood Canyon is a particularly scenic class II–III river, wild enough for some thrills but with enough calm stretches to let you catch your breath and enjoy the view.

You'll find a variety of trips from numerous reliable outfitters, including **Dvorak's Kayak & Rafting Expeditions** (☎ **800/824-3795;** www.vtinet. com/ dvorak) and **Four Corners Rafting** (☎ **800/332-7238;** www.pikes-peak.com/ fourcorners). For a free directory of licensed river outfitters and tips on choosing a rafting company, contact the **Colorado River Outfitters Association,** P.O. Box 1662, Buena Vista, CO 81211 (☎ **303/369-4632;** www.croa.org).

ROCK CLIMBING   Although rock climbing is not as big here as in other parts of the West, such as Zion National Park in Utah, Colorado does attract its share of climbers. One of the best spots is the spectacular Glenwood Canyon in Glenwood Springs, but it is far too popular with rafters and sightseers to offer anything near a wilderness experience. Somewhat more secluded and just as pretty is the Black Canyon of the Gunnison near Montrose, an extremely narrow canyon that sees very little daylight; there are also several good spots near Durango.

ROCKHOUNDING & GOLD-PANNING   The state's mining heritage continues in many areas among rock hounders, who search for semiprecious gemstones, petrified woods, and agatized fossil bones. Gold is found in most major mining areas, and gold-panning is a popular pastime. The Salida area has some of the best rockhounding opportunities in the state. Those who want to try their hands at gold-panning will enjoy Idaho Springs (near Denver) and Breckenridge, where they can receive instructions and rent pans. Contact the **Colorado Geological Survey,** 1313 Sherman St., no. 715, Denver, CO 80203 (☎ **303/866-2611,** or 303/866-3340 for the publications office), for information on rock collecting, geology, fossils, and a list of rockhounding locations, as well as detailed guides and maps to rockhounding and gold-panning locations.

SKIING & SNOWBOARDING   The most popular winter sport in Colorado is, of course, downhill skiing. Since the state's first resort (Howelsen Hill in Steamboat Springs) opened in 1914, Colorado has been virtually synonymous with skiing in the western United States. The state attracts more skiers per day than any other state, and its major resorts continue to win accolades from ski-magazine editors and readers.

The snowboarding craze has hit Colorado just as hard as it has other wintersports destinations, and after some initial resistance, it's been welcomed with open arms. Many resorts have opened snowboarding parks and offer lessons and rentals.

For **current ski conditions** and general information, call **Colorado Ski Country USA,** 1560 Broadway, Suite 1440, Denver, CO 80202 (☎ **303/ 837-0793;** www. skicolorado.org). *Ski* magazine's website (**www. skinet.com/ ski/ reports**) is another useful tool. In addition to posting its annual reader resort survey, in which North America's top ski resorts are rated by the magazine's readers on such factors as conditions, terrain, challenge, accessibility, food, and the après-ski scene, it offers a resort finder service that helps you select the ski area or resort that best fits your interests and budget.

The slopes are most crowded over Christmas and New Year's, and on the Martin Luther King, Jr. and Presidents' Day holiday weekends, when lodging rates are at their highest. Those who can ski midweek will find more elbow room on the slopes, and the beginning and end of the season are the best times to avoid crowds—assuming snow conditions are good.

Colorado's ski areas range from predominately day-use areas, with little beyond a mountain with trails and a few lifts, to full-fledged resorts, with a variety of accommodations, restaurants, and nightlife all within a half-hour of the slopes. The overview that follows describes the key mountains at these ski areas and resorts.

Arapahoe Basin (Summit County)   Arapahoe Basin, called "A-Basin" by its loyal fans, is the highest ski area in the state, and one of the oldest. Because of its elevation, it gets a bit more snow than elsewhere, so some prefer to ski it during spring's warmer temperatures.

Aspen Highlands (Aspen)   An intense mountain for only the most skilled and athletic of skiers. The views from the top are stupendous.

A Word about Rates & Statistics

In the write-ups for each ski area in the regional chapters, we give exact daily lift-ticket rates. Although handy for comparison, few people actually pay these prices. Most skiers buy packages that often include lift tickets for a certain number of days, but might also include rental equipment, lessons, lodging and/or meals, transportation, and lift tickets for other nearby ski areas. The possibilities are practically unlimited.

Although official lift-ticket prices don't change much throughout the season, discounts are offered at slow times, and when combined with lodging, transportation, and other costs, choosing a less popular time to visit can save a bundle. Without a doubt, the most expensive time to ski is between December 20 and January 1, followed by the Martin Luther King, Jr. and Presidents' Day holiday weekends. February to March is the next most expensive time to ski; January is generally cheaper; and the least expensive is from Thanksgiving until mid-December and April until ski areas close. We prefer the last few weeks of the season; the snow's still great, the weather's nice, and the slopes are less crowded, because most skiers have turned their thoughts to golf and tennis by that time.

Aspen Mountain (Aspen)   With more than 100 restaurants and bars, Aspen is one of Colorado's most sophisticated resorts. Aspen Mountain was designed for advanced skiers and is the second most challenging of Aspen's four slopes.

Beaver Creek (Vail)   Once considered Vail's sister resort, Beaver Creek has come into its own. It's now probably the most refined ski community in Colorado. The mountain has a good mix of runs for everyone but the super-expert, and lift lines are usually shorter than at Vail Mountain, especially on weekends.

Berthoud Pass (Winter Park)   Berthoud Pass is small but historically significant: It had the first rope tow in Colorado (1937), the first double chairlift (1940s), and was the first ski area to welcome snowboarders. Most of its 65 runs are for experts.

Breckenridge (Summit County)   Colorado's second most popular resort, Breckenridge is the crown jewel of Summit County's four ski areas. There's something for all levels of skiers, and it makes a great base camp for those who want to ski a different Summit County mountain every day.

Buttermilk (Aspen)   The last of Aspen's four mountains, the usually uncrowded Buttermilk is a great place for affluent novices to practice their moves. It's located just outside the main village; there's a great ski school here.

Copper Mountain (Summit County)   With its four superb bowls and variety of trails for all levels, Copper is a fun place to ski. The village is less expensive than nearby Breckenridge, with fewer amenities and less charm—but it's planning a $400-million reconstruction to correct the lack.

Crested Butte (Crested Butte)   Dependable snow, good beginner and intermediate trails, and lots of extreme skiing, but very little expert terrain mark this area.

Cuchara Mountain Resort (Trinidad)   This family-oriented resort has more than two dozen runs covering some 230 acres, and claims to never have a lift line.

Eldora (Nederland)   Just 21 miles from Boulder, Eldora is one of the state's smaller resorts, but has a good mix of terrain and is the closest ski area to the Denver–Boulder metropolitan area.

Keystone (Summit County)   Of the four ski areas in Summit County, Keystone is the closest to Denver, about 90 miles west of the airport. Its three separate mountains make it a good place for cruising, night skiing draws locals from miles around, and it's developing a new base area, with a planned completion date of 2002.

Loveland (North of Denver)   Less than an hour from Denver by car, Loveland is an old-fashioned day-ski area: no village, but enough beginner and advanced trails to satisfy the average skier. If you're staying in Denver in winter, give it a whirl.

Monarch (Salida)   This family-oriented resort in southern Colorado has among the lowest rates, with good terrain and fewer crowds.

Powderhorn (Grand Junction)   This is a good mountain for groups of varying abilities, with half its slopes intermediate, and another 30% advanced or expert.

Purgatory (Durango)   This small, low-key ski area offers mostly intermediate, narrow, hilly trails meandering through the trees amid the breathtakingly beautiful San Juan Mountains.

Silver Creek (Winter Park)   Geared to beginners and intermediates (but with some black diamond trails), Silver Creek is great for families; it's nearly impossible to lose someone, as all trails end at the same base area. There's also an excellent nursery and child-care center, plus a children's ski park.

Ski Cooper (Leadville)   A small, inexpensive resort at a high elevation, Ski Cooper is known for its all-natural snow and beautiful mountain scenery.

Ski Sunlight (Glenwood Springs)   Ski Sunlight is family oriented, geared to intermediate skiers, and very affordable.

Snowmass (Aspen)   The highlight of Aspen, with plenty of wide-open spaces and trails for absolutely every level of ability. This is, by far, the largest mountain at Aspen. The base village has plenty of beds, but not much nightlife—most night owls hop the free shuttle bus to Aspen, 20 minutes down the road.

Steamboat (Steamboat Springs)   One of Colorado's three largest mountains (the other two are Vail and Snowmass), Steamboat offers near-perfect skiing. It's well laid out and has gorgeous valley views, and the base village offers a wide choice of accommodations and restaurants. Another draw is the authentic old ranching town of Steamboat Springs, just a few miles away.

Telluride (Telluride)   Set at the top of a lovely box canyon, Telluride caters mainly to intermediate skiers, but also has novice trails some 2½ miles long and a number of steep expert trails.

Vail (Vail Valley)   Colorado's most popular resort, Vail mountain has a top-notch ski school and trails for everyone. The completely self-contained village at its base was created for skiers and is serviced by free shuttle buses.

Winter Park (Winter Park)   Owned by the city of Denver, Winter Park is unique—the focus is on value, with a variety of trails for all levels, plus well-regarded programs for children and skiers with disabilities. Young and athletic in spirit, it's adding a base village, Phase I of which should be completed by the 1999–2000 season.

Wolf Creek (Near Pagosa Springs)   One of the state's oldest ski areas, Wolf Creek is famous for consistently having the most snow in the state—an annual average of 465 inches (almost 39 feet). There is terrain for skiers of all ability levels, but especially intermediates.

Ski Packages & Tours

While many skiers enjoy planning their trips, others prefer making one phone call or sending one e-mail, and then letting someone else take care of all the details. Packages not only save time, but they're also sometimes cheaper than doing it yourself. The key is to make sure you get all the features you want, without paying for things you don't want. Packages often include air and ground transportation, lodging, and lift tickets, and sometimes include trip-cancellation insurance and some meals.

A good first step is to check with a ski club in your home town. These nonprofit organizations often offer some of the best deals if they happen to be planning a trip to where you want to ski at a time you want to go. Many travel agents can arrange ski vacations, and the central reservations service for a particular resort and the reservations desks of nearby lodgings can give you the scoop on the latest packages.

SNOWMOBILING   If you've never been snowmobiling, the best places for a guided snowmobile tour are Vail, Aspen, Keystone, and Steamboat Springs.

If you're an experienced snowmobiler and you plan to bring your rig with you, national forest trails are prime snowmobiling spots. Some of the state's best and most scenic rides are in Roosevelt National Forest, about 50 miles west of Fort Collins (via U.S. 287 and Colo. 14) at Chambers Lake. Because many of these trails are multi-use, snowmobilers should watch out for cross-country skiers and snowshoers, and slow down when passing them.

Colorado's light, dry snow is usually suitable for snowmobiling all winter long, although warm spring days can result in sticky snow, especially at lower elevations, that can gum up the works and make the going rough.

A free, comprehensive list of national forest trails open to snowmobilers is available from the **Colorado Snowmobile Association,** P.O. Box 1260, Grand Lake, CO 80447 (☎ **800/235-4480**).

WILDLIFE & BIRD WATCHING   There are numerous locations in Colorado to see animals and birds in the wild, including some that are close to the state's major cities. The South Platte River Greenway near Denver is a good spot to see ducks and other waterfowl, songbirds, deer, and beaver; and the U.S. Air Force Academy grounds in Colorado Springs offer opportunities to see deer, an occasional elk, peregrine falcons, and golden eagles. Other top spots to see wildlife include Durango, Glenwood Springs, Fort Collins, Vail, Rocky Mountain National Park, and Colorado National Monument.

Settling into Denver 6

It's no accident that Denver is called "the Mile High City." When you climb up to the State Capitol, you're precisely 5,280 feet above sea level when you reach the fifteenth step. The fact that Denver happens to be at this altitude was purely coincidental; you see, Denver is one of the few cities that was not built on an ocean, lake, or navigable river, or even on an existing road or railroad.

In the summer of 1858, a few flecks of gold were discovered by eager Georgia prospectors where Cherry Creek empties into the shallow South Platte River. A tent camp quickly sprang up on the site (the first permanent structure was a saloon). When militia Gen. William H. Larimer arrived in 1859, he claim-jumped the land on the east side of the Platte, laid out a city, and, hoping to gain political favors, named it after James Denver, governor of the Kansas Territory, to which this land belonged. Larimer didn't know that Denver had recently resigned.

Larimer's was one of several settlements on the South Platte. Three others also sought recognition, but Larimer, a shrewd man, had a solution. For the price of a barrel of whiskey, he bought out the other would-be town fathers, and the name Denver caught on.

Although the gold found in Denver was but a teaser for much larger strikes in the nearby mountains, the community grew as a shipping and trade center, in part because it had a milder climate than the mining towns it served. A devastating fire in 1863, a deadly flash flood in 1864, and American Indian tribal hostilities in the late 1860s created many hardships. But the establishment of rail links to the east and the influx of silver from the rich mines to the west kept Denver going. Silver from Leadville and gold from Cripple Creek made Denver a showcase city in the late 19th and early 20th centuries. The U.S. Mint, built in 1906, established Denver as a banking and financial center.

In the years following World War II, Denver mushroomed to become the largest city between the Great Plains and Pacific Coast, with about 500,000 residents within the city limits and more than 1.8 million in the metropolitan area. Today, it's a sprawling city, extending from the Rocky Mountain foothills on the west, far into the plains to the south and east. It's also a major destination for both tourists and business travelers, and the late 1990s are seeing a lodging boom, with 7,000 rooms either planned or under construction in summer 1998. Denver is noted for its dozens of tree-lined boulevards; 200 city parks comprising more than 20,000 acres; and its architecture, from Victorian to sleek contemporary.

1   Orientation

ARRIVING

BY PLANE   Denver International Airport, which opened in February 1995, is 23 miles northeast of downtown, usually a 35- to 45-minute drive. Covering 53 square miles (twice the size of Manhattan), DIA has 94 gates and five full-service runways, and can handle around 33 million passengers annually.

   Major national airlines serving Denver include American, America West, Continental, Delta, Frontier, Northwest, Sun Country, TWA, United, and US Airways. **International airlines** include Air Canada, British Airways, Korean Air, Martinair Holland, and Mexicana de Aviacion. **Regional** and **commuter airlines,** connecting Denver with other points in the Rockies and Southwest, include Aspen Air, Mountain Air Express, and three United Express airlines: Air Wisconsin, Great Lakes Aviation, and Mesa.

   For airlines' national reservations phone numbers and websites, see "Getting There" in chapter 3. For other information, call the Denver International Airport **information** line ☎ **800/AIR-2-DEN** (TDD 800/688-1333) or 303/342-2000 (TDD 303/299-6089). Other important airport phone numbers include: administration ☎ 303/342-2200; ground transportation ☎ 303/342-4059; vehicle assistance, including emergency car start ☎ 303/342-4650; paging ☎ 303/342-2300; and parking ☎ 303/342-4096.

Getting to & from the Airport   Bus, taxi, and limousine services shuttle travelers between the airport and downtown, and most major car-rental companies have outlets at the airport. Because many major hotels are some distance from the airport, travelers should check on the availability and cost of hotel shuttle services when making reservations.

   The cost of a **city bus** ride from the airport to downtown Denver is $6; from the airport to Boulder and suburban Park-n-Ride lots, it is about $8. The **Denver Airport Shuttle** (☎ 800/525-3177 or 303/342-5454) provides transportation to and from a number of hotels downtown and in the Denver Tech Center. Fares vary and may be paid in part or completely by the hotel. The **SuperShuttle** (☎ 303/370-1300) has frequent scheduled service between the airport and downtown hotels for $17 one-way, $30 round-trip; door-to-door service is also available. **Taxi** companies (see "Getting Around," below) are another option, with fares generally in the $30 to $50 range, and you can often share a cab and split the fare by calling the cab company ahead of time. For instance, **Yellow Cab** (☎ 303/777-7777) will take up to five people from DIA to most downtown hotels for a flat rate of $43.

   Those who prefer a bit of luxury may prefer the ride provided by **Mile Hi City Limousine** (☎ 800/910-7433 or 303/355-5002; www.whitedovelimo.com). Rates to different parts of the Denver metro area vary, but one-way fares between the airport and downtown Denver are as follows: sedan limousine for up to three people, $77; six-passenger stretch limo, $113; eight-passenger stretch limo, $125; 10-passenger stretch limo, $155; 12-passenger stretch limo, $185. Charter services are also available.

BY CAR   The principal highway routes into Denver are **I-25** from the north (Fort Collins, 65 miles; Cheyenne, 100 miles) and south (Colorado Springs, 70 miles; Albuquerque, 440 miles); **I-70** from the east (Burlington, 165 miles; Kansas City, 610 miles) and west (Grand Junction, 260 miles); and **I-76** from the northeast

(Sterling, 120 miles). If you're driving into Denver from Boulder, take **U.S. 36;** from Salida and southwest, take **U.S. 285.**

BY TRAIN   Amtrak serves Union Station, 17th and Wynkoop Streets (☎ **800/ USA-RAIL** or 303/825-2583), in the lower downtown historic district.

BY BUS   Greyhound, 19th and Arapahoe Streets (☎ **800/231-2222**), is the major bus service in Colorado, with about 60 daily arrivals and departures to communities both in and out of the state.

VISITOR INFORMATION

The **Denver Metro Convention and Visitors Bureau** operates a visitor center at 1668 Larimer St. (☎ **303/892-1112**), just off the 16th Street Mall, open Monday through Friday from 8am to 5pm and Saturday from 9am to 1pm. Visitor information is also available in Tabor and Cherry Creek Shopping Centers, and at the Colorado State Capitol and Denver International Airport. Ask for the *Official Visitors Guide,* an impressive 150-plus-page full-color booklet with a comprehensive listing of accommodations, restaurants, and other visitor services in Denver and surrounding areas.

For advance information, contact the Denver Metro Convention and Visitors Bureau, 1555 California St., Suite 300, Denver, CO 80202-4264 (☎ **800/ 645-3446;** www.denver.org). Another good resource is **www.denver.sidewalk. com**.

CITY LAYOUT

You can never truly get lost in Denver, as long as you remember that the mountains, nearly always visible, are to the west. All the same, it can be perplexing to get around a city of half a million people. One element of confusion is that Denver has both an older grid system, which is oriented northeast–southwest to parallel the South Platte River, and a newer north–south grid system that surrounds the older one.

There's a good Denver map in the *Official Visitors Guide,* available free of charge from the Convention and Visitors Bureau (see "Visitor Information," above).

MAIN ARTERIES & STREETS   It's probably easiest to get your bearings from Civic Center Park. From here, Colfax Avenue (U.S. 40) extends east and west as far as the eye can see. The same is true for Broadway, which reaches north and south.

North of Colfax and west of Broadway is the center of **downtown Denver,** where the streets follow the old grid pattern. A mile-long pedestrian mall, **16th Street,** cuts northwest off Broadway just above this intersection. (The numbered streets parallel 16th to the northeast, extending all the way to 44th; and to the southwest, as far as Fifth.) Intersecting the numbered streets at right angles are **Lawrence Street** (which runs one-way northeast) and **Larimer Street** (which runs one-way southwest), 12 and 13 blocks, respectively, from the Colfax–Broadway intersection.

I-25 skirts downtown Denver to the west, with access from Colfax or **Speer Boulevard,** which winds diagonally along Cherry Creek past Larimer Square.

Outside the downtown sector, the pattern is a little less confusing. But keep in mind that the numbered *avenues* that parallel Colfax to the north and south (Colfax is equivalent to 15th Avenue) have nothing in common with the numbered *streets* of the downtown grid. In fact, any byway labeled an "avenue" runs east–west, never north–south.

FINDING AN ADDRESS   North–South Arteries   The thoroughfare that divides avenues into "east" and "west" is **Broadway,** which runs one-way south between 19th Street and I-25. Each block east or west adds 100 to the avenue address; thus, if you wanted to find 2115 E. 17th Ave., it would be a little more than 21 blocks east of Broadway, just beyond Vine Street.

Main thoroughfares that parallel Broadway to the east include Downing Street (1200 block), York Street (2300 block; it becomes University Boulevard south of Sixth), Colorado Boulevard (4000 block), Monaco Parkway (6500 block), and Quebec Street (7300 block). **Colorado Boulevard** (Colo. 2) is the most significant artery, intersecting I-25 on the south and I-70 on the north. North–south streets that parallel Broadway to the west include Santa Fe Drive (U.S. 85; 1000 block); west of I-25 are Federal Boulevard (U.S. 287 North, site of several sports arenas; 3000 block), and Sheridan Boulevard (Colo. 95; 5200 block), the boundary between Denver and Lakewood.

East–West Arteries   Denver streets are divided into "north" and "south" at **Ellsworth Avenue,** about 1½ miles south of Colfax. Ellsworth is a relatively minor street, but it's a convenient dividing point because it's just a block south of First Avenue. With building numbers increasing by 100 each block, that puts an address like 1710 Downing St. at the corner of East 17th Avenue. First, Sixth, Colfax (1500 block), and 26th Avenues, and Martin Luther King, Jr., Boulevard (3200 block) are the principal east–west thoroughfares. There are no numbered avenues south of Ellsworth. Major east–west byways south of Ellsworth are Alameda (Colo. 26; 300 block), Mississippi (1100 block), Florida (1500 block), Evans (2100 block), Yale (2700 block), and Hampden Avenues (U.S. 285; 3500 block).

NEIGHBORHOODS IN BRIEF

LOWER DOWNTOWN   Downtown Denver can be divided into three subdistricts. Lower Downtown ("LoDo") is the oldest part of the city. It extends northwest from Lawrence Street to Union Station and from the shops of Tivoli Student Union northeast to 19th Street. Coors Field, the baseball stadium built for the Colorado Rockies, opened here in 1995 and revitalized the area. Since then, numerous restaurants and shops have opened in historic buildings, bringing new excitement to the area. No skyscrapers are permitted in LoDo, most of which dates from the late 19th century.

CENTRAL BUSINESS DISTRICT   This extends along 16th, 17th, and 18th Streets between Lawrence Street and Broadway. Here, the ban on skyscrapers certainly does not apply.

CIVIC CENTER PARK   This area is at the southeast end of 15th Street, where Broadway and Colfax Avenue meet. The two-square-block oasis of green is surrounded by state and city government buildings, the Denver Art Museum, Colorado History Museum, U.S. Mint, and the public library. The State Capitol Building is lodged at the east end of the park.

CAPITOL HILL   This area is located just southeast of downtown and extends roughly from the State Capitol (Colfax and Lincoln) past the Governor's Mansion to East Sixth Avenue, and from Broadway to Cheesman Park (on Franklin Street). Here you'll find a great many Victorian mansions from the mining-boom days of the late 19th and early 20th centuries, including the Molly Brown House (see chapter 7). But you'll see no old wooden buildings: After the disastrous fire of 1863, the government forbade the construction of wooden structures until after World War II.

CHERRY CREEK   Home of the Cherry Creek Shopping Center and Denver Country Club, this area extends north from East First Avenue to East Eighth Avenue, and from Downing Street east to Steele Street. You'll find huge, ostentatious stone mansions, especially around Circle Drive (southwest of Sixth and University), where many of Denver's wealthiest families have lived for generations.

HISTORIC DISTRICTS   Among the 17 recognized historic districts in Denver are Capitol Hill, the Clements District (around 21st Street and Tremont Street, just east of downtown), and Ninth Street Park in Auraria (off Ninth Street and West Colfax Avenue). Historic Denver, 821 17th St., Suite 500 (☎ **303/296-9887**), offers walking-tour maps of several of these areas.

GLENDALE   Denver fully surrounds Glendale, an incorporated city in its own right. The center of a lively entertainment district, Glendale straddles Cherry Creek on South Colorado Boulevard south of East Alameda Avenue.

TECH CENTER   At the southern end of the metropolitan area is the Denver Tech Center, along I-25 between Belleview Avenue and Arapahoe Road. In this district, about a 25-minute drive from downtown, you'll find the headquarters of several international and national companies, high-tech businesses, and a handful of upscale hotels heavily oriented toward business travelers.

2 Getting Around

BY PUBLIC TRANSPORTATION

The **Regional Transportation District (RTD)** (☎ **800/366-7433** or 303/299-6000, or TDD 303/299-6089 for route and schedule information, 303/299-6700 for other business; www.rtd-denver.com) calls itself "The Ride" for its bus routes and light-rail system, with transfer tickets available free. It provides good service within Denver and its suburbs and outlying communities (including Boulder, Longmont, and Evergreen), as well as free parking at 50 Park-n-Ride locations throughout the Denver–Boulder metropolitan area. The light-rail service is designed to get buses and cars out of congested downtown Denver; many of the bus routes from outlying areas deliver passengers to light-rail stations rather than downtown.

The local fare is $1.25 during peak hours (Monday through Friday from 6 to 9am and 4 to 6pm) and 75¢ during off-peak hours. Regional fares vary (for example, it costs $2.50 between Denver and Boulder). Seniors and passengers with disabilities pay only 25¢ off-peak, and children ages 5 and under travel free. Exact change is required for buses, and train tickets can be purchased at vending machines beneath light-rail station awnings.

Each route has its own schedule, including departure time of the last bus or train (which varies from 9pm to 1am). Maps for all routes are available at any time at the RTD Civic Center Station, 16th Street and Broadway; and the Market Street Station, at Market and 16th Streets. RTD also provides special service to Colorado Rockies home baseball and Broncos home football games. All RTD buses and trains are completely wheelchair accessible.

Free buses run up and down the 16th Street Mall between the Civic Center and Market Street every 90 seconds during peak hours (less frequently at other times), daily from 6am to 1am.

Visitors particularly enjoy the **Cultural Connection Trolley** (☎ **303/299-6000**), which runs daily every 30 minutes between 9:30am and 7:30pm, with stops at Denver's most popular tourist attractions, including the State Capitol, Denver Botanic Gardens, Denver Zoo, U.S. Mint, and most major downtown museums. A full-day pass costs $3 (children 5 and under ride free); detailed route information is available at the Denver Visitors Center on Larimer Street. The trolley ticket is also good on RTD buses and light rail.

From June through August you can ride the open-air **Platte Valley Trolley** (☎ 303/458-6255). Between 11am and 4pm daily there's a half-hour "Seeing Denver" ride ($2 adults, $1 seniors and children), which operates from 15th Street at Confluence Park, south to Decatur Street along the west bank of the Platte River. Another excursion leaves at noon Monday through Friday, and 2pm Saturday and Sunday ($4 adults, $3 seniors, $2 children). This one-hour trip takes visitors west of Decatur Street, following a portion of a historic tram line that ran to Golden until 1950. During April, May, September, and October, the trolley runs, weather permitting, Tuesday through Sunday between 11am and 3pm; in winter it operates only on weekends, 11am to 3pm, also weather permitting. Special charter trips can be arranged in off hours; call for details.

BY TAXI

The main companies are **Yellow Cab** (☎ 303/777-7777), **Zone Cab** (☎ 303/444-8888), and **Metro Taxi** (☎ 303/333-3333). Taxis can be hailed on the street, though it's preferable to telephone for a taxi or wait for one at a taxi stand outside a major hotel.

BY CAR

Because cars are not really necessary downtown, visitors can save the rental cost and parking fees (some downtown hotels charge up to $17 per night) by arranging to stay downtown the first few nights, and then renting a car when planning to leave the area.

The Denver office of the **American Automobile Association (AAA)** is at 4100 E. Arkansas Ave., Denver, CO 80222-3491 (☎ **800/283-5222** or 303/753-8800); there are several other locations in the Denver area.

CAR RENTALS   Most major car-rental agencies have outlets in or near downtown Denver, as well as at Denver International Airport. These include **Alamo,** 24530 East 78th Ave. (☎ 800/327-9633 or 303/342-7373); **Avis,** 1900 Broadway (☎ 800/831-2847 or 303/839-1280; 303/342-5500 at DIA); **Budget,** 1980 Broadway (☎ 800/527-0700 or 303/341-2277); **Dollar,** 7939 E. Arapahoe Rd., Denver Tech Center (☎ 800/800-4000 or 303/790-0970; 303/342-9099 at DIA); **Enterprise,** 5179 South Broadway (☎ 800/325-8007 or 303/794-3333); **Hertz,** 2001 Welton (☎ 800/654-3131 or 303/297-9400; 303/342-3800 at DIA); **National,** at Denver International Airport (☎ 800/227-7368 or 303/342-0717); and **Thrifty,** in the Sheraton Hotel in the Denver Tech Center (☎ 800/367-2277 or 303/985-7756; 303/342-9400 at DIA). You can rent campers, travel trailers, motor homes, and motorcycles from **Cruise America,** 7450 E. 29th Ave. (☎ 800/327-7778 or 303/426-6699; www.cruiseamerica.com).

Per-day rentals for mid-size cars range from $30 to $50, although AAA and other discounts are often available, and weekend and multi-day rates can also save money. Four-wheel-drive vehicles, trucks, and campers cost more.

For the traveler seeking true luxury, Denver has several limousine services, including **Admiral Limousines,** 4400 Garfield St. (☎ 800/828-8680 or 303/296-2003); **Colorado Limousine Service,** 1304 Ogden St. (☎ 800/628-6655 or 303/832-7155); and **Parker Suburban Limousine** in Commerce City (☎ 888/271-1305 or 303/288-1305), with four-wheel-drive Suburbans and front-wheel-drive Caravans.

PARKING   Downtown parking-lot rates vary from 75¢ per half hour to $10 per full day. Rates are higher in the vicinity of the 16th Street Mall and the central business district. Keep a handful of quarters if you plan to use on-street parking meters.

FAST FACTS: Denver

American Express   The American Express Travel Agency is located at 555 17th St. (☎ **303/298-7100**); it's open Monday through Friday from 8:30am to 5pm. Full member services and currency exchange are offered. To report a lost card, call ☎ **800/528-4800;** to report lost traveler's checks, call ☎ **800/221-7282.**

Area Code   Area codes are **303** and **720,** and local calls require 10-digit dialing. See the "Telephone, Fax & Telegraph" section under "Fast Facts: For the Foreign Traveler" in chapter 4.

Baby-sitters   Front desks at major hotels can often arrange baby-sitters for their guests.

Business Hours   Banks are usually open weekdays from 9am to 5pm, occasionally a bit later on Friday, and sometimes on Saturday. There's 24-hour access to the automatic teller machines (ATMs) at most banks, plus in many shopping centers and other outlets.

Generally, business offices are open weekdays from 9am to 5pm, and government offices are open from 8am until 4:30 or 5pm. Stores are open six days a week, with some open on Sunday, too; department stores usually stay open until 9pm at least one day a week. Discount stores and supermarkets are often open later than other stores, and some supermarkets are open 24 hours a day.

Car Rentals   See "Getting Around," earlier in this chapter.

Doctors/Dentists   Doctor and dentist referrals are available by calling **1-800-Doctor** (☎ 800/362-8677 or 303/443-2584). **Centura Health** (☎ 800/327-6877 or 303/777-6877) provides free physician referrals and answers health questions; the **Parent Smart Line** (☎ 303/861-0123) specializes in referrals to children's doctors and dentists, and also has staff on hand to provide advice.

Drugstores   Throughout the metropolitan area, you will find Walgreens and Payless pharmacies, as well as Safeway and King Soopers grocery stores (which also have drugstores). The **Walgreens** at 2000 E. Colfax Ave. is open 24 hours a day (☎ 303/331-0917). For the locations of other Walgreens, call ☎ **800/WALGREENS**. For an old-fashioned, family owned drugstore (complete with soda fountain), there is **Watson's,** 900 Lincoln St. (☎ 303/837-1366), open Monday through Thursday from 8am to 9pm, Friday from 8am to 10pm, and Saturday from 10am to 10pm.

Emergencies   For the **Poison Control Center,** call ☎ 303/739-1123. For the **Rape Crisis Hotline,** call ☎ 303/892-8900.

Eyeglasses   One-hour replacements and repairs are usually available at **Pearle Vision,** 2720 S. Colorado Blvd. at Yale Avenue (☎ 303/758-1292), and **Lenscrafters,** in Cherry Creek Shopping Center (☎ 303/321-8331).

Hospitals   Among Denver-area hospitals are **St. Joseph's,** 1835 Franklin St. (☎ 303/837-7111), just east of downtown, and **Children's Hospital,** 1056 E. 19th Ave. (☎ 303/861-8888).

Maps   Denver's largest map store, **Maps Unlimited by Pierson Graphics,** 800 Lincoln St., Denver, 80203 (☎ 800/456-8703 or 303/623-4299), offers USGS and recreation maps, state maps and travel guides, raised relief maps, and globes.

Newspapers/Magazines   The morning *Denver Post* (www.denverpost.com) is Colorado's largest daily newspaper. The afternoon *Rocky Mountain News* (www.rockymountainnews.com) also covers the metropolitan area. A widely read free weekly, *Westword* (www.westword.com), is known as much for its controversial jibes at local politicians as for its entertainment listings. National newspapers such as *USA Today* and the *Wall Street Journal* can be purchased at newsstands and at major hotels.

Photographic Needs   For photographic supplies, equipment, 45-minute photo processing, and repairs, visit **Robert Waxman Camera and Video** at one of its dozen Denver locations; its downtown branch, at 1545 California St. (☎ 800/525-6113 or 303/623-1155), is among the biggest camera stores in the world. One-hour processing and printing is available from **CPI Photo/Fox Photo** (☎ 800/366-3655 or 303/363-6801), which has about a dozen Denver outlets, including locations on the 16th Street Mall and in Cherry Creek Mall. The television section in Sunday's *Denver Post* often includes discount coupons for CPI photo.

Post Office   The main downtown post office is at 951 20th St., open Monday through Friday from 7am to 6pm, Saturday from 9am to 1pm. For full 24-hour postal service, go to the General Mail Facility, 7500 E. 53rd Place. For other post office locations and hours, call the U.S. Postal Service (☎ **800/275-8777**).

Radio/TV   A large variety of music, news, sports, and entertainment is presented on some four dozen AM and FM radio stations in the Denver area, including KOA (850 AM) for news and talk; KKFN (950 AM) for all sports; KPOF (910 AM) for Christian and classical music; KEZW (1430 AM) for big band and nostalgia; KWBI (91.1 FM) for Christian ministry and music; KIMN (100.3 FM) for adult hits; KRFX (103.5 FM) for classic rock; KXPK (96.5 FM) for rock alternative; KBCO (97.3 FM) for alternative music; KYGO (98.5 FM and 1600 AM) for new and classic country, respectively; KUVO (89.3 FM) for Latin, jazz, and blues music and news; and KVOD (92.5 FM) for classical music.

Denver has 14 television stations, including KCNC (Channel 4), the CBS affiliate; KMGH (Channel 7), the ABC affiliate; KUSA (Channel 9), the NBC affiliate; and KDVR (Channel 31), the Fox affiliate. Other major stations include KWGN (Channel 2), an independent; and KRMA (Channel 6), the PBS affiliate. Cable or satellite service is available at most hotels.

Safety   Although Denver is a relatively safe city, it is not crime free. The 16th Street Mall is seldom a problem, but even streetwise Denverites avoid late-night walks along certain sections of East Colfax Avenue, just several blocks away. If you are unsure of the safety of a particular area you want to visit, ask your hotel concierge or desk clerk.

Taxes   State and local sales tax in Denver is about 7% (it varies slightly in neighboring counties and suburbs).

Useful Telephone Numbers   For a weather report, time, and temperature, call ☎ **303/337-2500.** Statewide road condition reports are available by calling ☎ **303/639-1111.** For information on possible road construction delays in the Denver area and statewide, call ☎ **303/573-ROAD** (ext. **7623**).

3 Accommodations

Although most hotels and motels in the Denver area do not have seasonal rates (as you'll find in many other parts of Colorado), hotels that cater to business travelers, such as the Brown Palace and The Warwick (see below), offer substantial discounts on weekends, sometimes as much as 50% off the regular rates.

The lodging industry is still trying to catch up with the construction of Denver International Airport several years ago, and you'll find that many of the major chains and franchises have built or are in the process of constructing facilities near the new airport. Among those now open near the airport are **Courtyard by Marriott at DIA,** 6900 Tower Rd., Denver, CO 80249 (☎ 800/321-2211 or 303/371-0300), with rates of $92 for two; **Fairfield Inn–DIA,** 6851 Tower Rd., Denver, CO 80249 (☎ 800/228-2800 or 303/576-9640), which charges $75 to $99 double; and **Hampton Inn DIA,** 6290 Tower Rd., Denver CO 80249 (☎ 800/426-7866 or 303/371-0200), with rates for two of $95 to $99.

Those in the downtown area include **Comfort Inn,** 401 17th St., Denver, CO 80202 (☎ 800/237-7431 or 303/296-0400), with a convenient location and rates of $109 to $172 double; **La Quinta Inn Downtown,** 3500 Park Ave. W. (at I-25 exit 213), Denver, CO 80216 (☎ 800/531-5900 or 303/458-1222), charging $58 to $77 double; **Ramada Inn–Mile High Stadium,** 1975 Bryant St. (at I-25 exit 210B), Denver, CO 80204 (☎ 800/272-6232 or 303/433-8331), with rates of $82 to $92 double; and **Super 8,** 2601 Zuni St. (at I-25 exit 212B for Speer Boulevard), Denver, CO 80211 (☎ 800/800-8000 or 303/433-6677), which charges $40 to $47 double.

Outside downtown, chain lodgings include **Hampton Inn,** 4685 Quebec St., Denver, CO 80216 (☎ 800/HAMPTON or 303/388-8100), with rates of $79 to $89 double; **Quality Inn Denver South,** 6300 E. Hampden Ave., Denver, CO 80222 (☎ 800/647-1986 or 303/758-2211), with rates of $68 to $99 double (see "Family-Friendly Hotels," below); and **Motel 6,** 480 Wadsworth Blvd., Lakewood, CO 80226 (☎ 800/466-8356 or 303/232-4924), charging $40 to $46 double. Among the four Best Westerns in the metro area is **Best Western Denver West,** 11595 W. Sixth Ave., Lakewood, CO 80215 (☎ 800/528-1234 or 303/238-7751), which has rates for two from $69 to $89.

These official, or "rack," rates, do not take into consideration any discounts, such as those offered to members of AAA or AARP. Be sure to ask if you qualify for a reduced rate. Because a chain hotel's national reservations service may not be able to offer discounts, your best bet might be to call the hotel directly.

Another way to save money on lodging and activities in the Denver area is to call the **Mile Hi Adventure Club and Mile Hi Lights** (☎ 800/489-4888). You can get discounted rates at more than 30 hotels, plus discounts on such activities as fishing, golf, skiing, hot-air ballooning, rafting, sporting events, theaters, and concerts.

In the following listings, rates do not include the 12% tax that is added to all accommodation bills.

DOWNTOWN
VERY EXPENSIVE

Adam's Mark Denver. 1550 Court Pl., Denver, CO 80202. ☎ **800/444-2326** or 303/893-3333. Fax 303/626-2542. www.adamsmark.com. E-mail: sales@denver.adamsmark.com. 1,317 units. A/C TV TEL. $185–$300 double; $375–$1,200 suite. AE, CB, DC, DISC, MC, V. Underground valet parking, $15 per day or $19 overnight; self-parking, $2 per half hour up to $12, or $15 overnight; 7 ft. 4 in. height limit. Pets accepted with a deposit.

The largest hotel in Colorado, this former Hilton has been completely remodeled. There are two buildings: the 22-floor Tower Building on the east side of Court Place and the Plaza Building across the street (a pedestrian bridge on the second floor connects the two). From the upper floors of the Tower, the west-facing rooms have marvelous views of the Front Range.

The classic decor puts an emphasis on brass, marble, and solid woods such as oak and mahogany. Colors are muted and restful. Terrific weekend packages are available starting at $79, and theater packages can be arranged.

Downtown Denver Accommodations

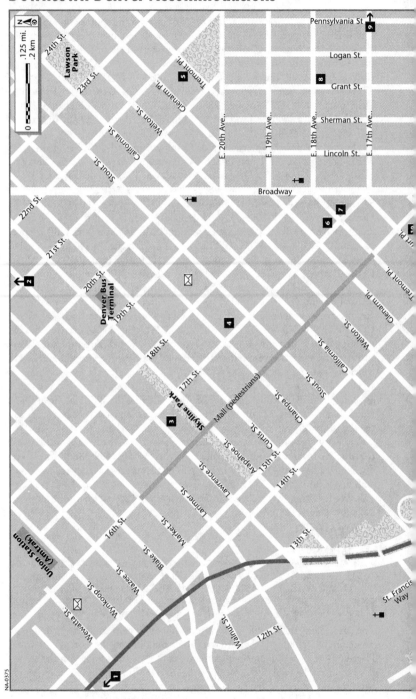

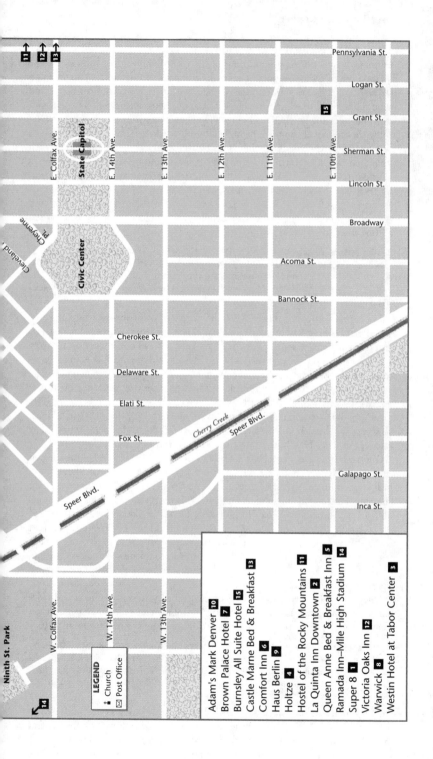

LEGEND
✝ Church
⊠ Post Office

Adam's Mark Denver 10
Brown Palace Hotel 7
Burnsley All Suite Hotel 15
Castle Marne Bed & Breakfast 13
Comfort Inn 6
Haus Berlin 9
Holtze 4
Hostel of the Rocky Mountains 11
La Quinta Inn Downtown 2
Queen Anne Bed & Breakfast Inn 5
Ramada Inn–Mile High Stadium 14
Super 8 1
Victoria Oaks Inn 12
Warwick 8
Westin Hotel at Tabor Center 3

Pennsylvania St.
Logan St.
Grant St.
Sherman St.
Lincoln St.
Broadway
Acoma St.
Bannock St.
Cherokee St.
Delaware St.
Elati St.
Fox St.
Galapago St.
Inca St.

E. Colfax Ave.
E. 14th Ave.
E. 13th Ave.
E. 12th Ave.
E. 11th Ave.
E. 10th Ave.

State Capitol
Civic Center
Cleveland Pl.
Cheyenne Pl.

Cherry Creek
Speer Blvd.
Speer Blvd.

Ninth St. Park
W. Colfax Ave.
W. 14th Ave.
W. 13th Ave.

Dining/Diversions: For fine Italian food, head for Bravo! Ristorante (see "Dining," below) on the ground floor of the Plaza Building; just behind it is the Tiffany Rose, a lounge offering light snacks, live piano music most evenings, and a jazz combo on Friday and Saturday nights. Trattoria Colorado offers buffet and menu dining at all three meals daily. The Capitol Bar is an elegant cigar bar with light fare. The Tower Building houses Players, a sports bar with big-screen TVs, sandwiches and salads from 11am, and coffee service daily from 6 to 10am; and the Supreme Court Cafe & Nightclub (see "Denver After Dark," in chapter 7), with happy hour weekdays from 4 to 7pm and live music most evenings.

Amenities: Laundry (including self-serve), dry cleaning, and shoe shine; executive level with concierge and business services, full breakfast, local and national newspapers, happy hour with hors d'oeuvres, coffee and desserts; health club with sauna, weight room, cardiovascular machines, and outdoor pool; business center; meeting space for up to 4,500; florist; gift shop.

✪ **Brown Palace Hotel.** 321 17th St., Denver, CO 80202. ☎ **800/228-2917** or 303/297-3111 in Colorado; 800/321-2599 elsewhere in North America. Fax 303/312-5900. www.brownpalace.com. E-mail: marketing@brownpalace.com. 230 units. A/C TV TEL. $195–$275 double; $275–$775 suite. Weekend rates start at $125. AE, CB, DC, MC, V. Valet parking $15 overnight.

For more than 100 years, this has been the place to stay for anyone who is anyone. A National Historic Landmark, the Brown Palace opened in August 1892 and has been operating continuously ever since. Designed with an odd triangular shape by architect Frank Edbrooke, it was built of Colorado red granite and Arizona sandstone. The lobby's walls are paneled with Mexican onyx, and the floor is white marble. Elaborate cast-iron grillwork surrounds six tiers of balconies up to the stained-glass ceiling high above the lobby.

Guest rooms are uniquely decorated in either Victorian or art-deco style. Each has a desk, TV hidden in an armoire, and its own heating and cooling control. The water's great here: The Brown Palace has its own artesian wells!

Dining/Diversions: Excellent international cuisine is served in the elegant Palace Arms (jacket and tie required at dinner). Ellyngton's (smoke-free) serves breakfast and lunch (light grills and pastas), and a champagne brunch on Sunday. The Ship Tavern, the hotel's oldest restaurant, is open daily for drinks and casual dining. The Churchill Bar (see "Denver After Dark," in chapter 7), a sophisticated cigar bar with a library atmosphere, occupies founder Henry C. Brown's office, next to the Palace Arms. Afternoon tea and cocktails are available in the lobby daily. Reservations are recommended for the English tea, complete with sandwiches and pastries from the Brown Palace bakery. The Brown Palace Club serves lunch for private members and hotel guests only.

Amenities: 24-hour room service, concierge, dual voice-modem lines and voice mail in all rooms, turndown, robes, laundry, in-room massage (extra charge); fitness center, business center, boutiques, beauty salon, meeting facilities for up to 750.

Westin Hotel at Tabor Center. 1672 Lawrence St., Denver, CO 80202. ☎ **800/228-3000** or 303/572-9100. Fax 303/572-7288. www.westin.com. 420 units. A/C MINIBAR TV TEL. $118–$195 single or double; $244–$1,200 suite; call for weekend rates and packages. Children under 18 stay free in parents' room. AE, CB, DC, DISC, MC, V. Parking $13–$15 per day.

The focal point of the two-square-block Tabor Center shopping-and-office complex, the 19-story Westin bridges the gap between the central business district and lower downtown, and is conveniently located near Coors Field. Its contemporary design incorporates architectural elements of nearby Victorian-era structures. The elegant second-floor lobby features three-dimensional murals and modern fountains. Personnel are very friendly and helpful.

The spacious guest rooms, many of which have king-size beds, are beautifully appointed with modern, European-style furnishings. Every unit is equipped with a TV/VCR, coffeemaker, stocked minibar, and hair dryer. The Executive Club on the hotel's top three floors provides upgraded features and amenities, including in-room wet bar, continental breakfast, afternoon cocktails, and a resident concierge.

Dining: The award-winning Augusta still serves breakfast daily but is reserved for private parties only for lunch and dinner. The Palm, located in the lower lobby, serves lunch and dinner (see "Dining," below).

Amenities: Room service; valet laundry; health club with indoor/outdoor pool, hot tub, sauna, exercise and weight room, and racquetball courts; business center, meeting space for 400; beauty salon and shopping arcade.

EXPENSIVE

The Burnsley All Suite Hotel. 1000 Grant St. (at E. 10th Ave.), Denver, CO 80203. ☎ **800/231-3915** or 303/830-1000. Fax 303/830-7676. 80 suites. A/C TV TEL. $109–$169 single or double. Rates include buffet breakfast. Weekend rates available. AE, CB, DC, MC, V. Free covered parking.

This small, elegant hotel offers suites with private balconies and fully stocked kitchen areas. The units are handsomely furnished, with the recently renovated 24 upper-level suites featuring a rich color scheme, marble entrance floors, and antiques. Renovation of the remaining suites will be completed by the end of 1999.

The restaurant serves breakfast and dinner daily plus lunch on weekdays. The menu features fresh salmon, Colorado game plate, and vegetarian dishes. Amenities include room service (6:30am to 10:30pm), self-serve laundry, a pool, business center, conference rooms, and access to a nearby health club. The hotel is convenient to the Cherry Creek shopping areas and only five blocks from downtown.

Castle Marne Bed & Breakfast. 1572 Race St., Denver, CO 80206. ☎ **303/331-0621** or 800/92-MARNE for reservations. Fax 303/331-0623. www.castlemarne.com. 11 units. A/C TEL. $95–$165 double; $200–$245 suite. Rates include breakfast and afternoon tea. AE, CB, DC, DISC, MC, V. Ample street parking. Not suitable for children under 10.

A National Historic Landmark, Castle Marne is a massive stone fortress, designed and built in 1869 by the renowned architect William Lang for a contemporary silver baron. It was so named because a previous owner's son had fought in the Battle of the Marne during World War I.

The inn is furnished with antiques, fine reproductions, and family heirlooms. Two suites have whirlpool tubs for two, three rooms with private balconies are equipped with outdoor hot tubs for two, and 1999 will see the addition of a third suite with an outdoor hot tub for two. The old-fashioned bathrooms in three rooms contain pedestal sinks and cast-iron clawfoot tubs. A gourmet breakfast is served in the original formal dining room (two seatings), and a proper afternoon tea is served daily in the parlor. The inn also provides a game room, library, gift shop, and an office for business travelers' use. Smoking is not permitted.

Haus Berlin. 1651 Emerson St., Denver, CO 80218. ☎ **800/659-0253** or 303/837-9527. Fax 303/837-9527. www.hausberlinbandb.com. E-mail: haus.berlin@worldnet.att.net. 4 units. A/C TV TEL. $95–$115 room; $130 suite. Rates include full breakfast. AE, CB, DC, DISC, MC, V. Free off-street parking. Not suitable for children.

A Victorian town house built in 1892, Haus Berlin is decorated with original art and collectibles gathered from around the world by owners Christiana and Dennis Brown. Rooms are furnished with queen- or king-size beds, fine linens, and down comforters. The suite, which encompasses the entire third floor, offers beautiful views of downtown Denver. Although located on a quiet tree-lined street, the Haus Berlin is just a 10-minute walk from the 16th Street Mall, State Capitol, several museums, and Denver's central business district. Smoking is not permitted.

Holtze. 818 17th St., Denver, CO 80202. ☎ **800/422-2092** or 303/607-9000. Fax 303/607-0101. www.holtze.com. E-mail: stay@holtze.com. 244 units. A/C TV TEL. Mon–Thurs $139–$149 double, $169–$179 suite; Fri–Sun $109–$119 double, $119–$129 suite; monthly rates available. Rates include continental breakfast. AE, CB, DC, DISC, MC, V. Valet parking $16, self-parking $10; 6 ft. 10 in. height limit.

This upscale lodging aims to please the discerning business traveler, but it's a good choice for the sophisticated vacationer as well. The lobby has a cozy, almost library-like feel, with comfortable leather couches and wing chairs grouped around a marble fireplace. Included in the rates are an evening reception (Monday through Saturday) with cocktails and appetizers, and expanded continental breakfast.

The rooms are decorated in contemporary European style. All have coffeemakers, and many have minifridges. The suites boast full kitchens, oversize tubs with showers, hair dryers, and ironing boards and irons, and some have gas fireplaces. All phones have modem hookups and voice mail; room service is available from noon to 10pm.

The Warwick. 1776 Grant St. (at E. 18th Ave.), Denver, CO 80203. ☎ **800/525-2888** or 303/861-2000. Fax 303/839-8504. 191 units. A/C TV TEL. $159 double; $150–$800 suite. Weekend rates $79–$85 single or double. Rates include European-style buffet breakfast. Children under 18 stay free in parents' room. AE, CB, DC, DISC, JCB, MC, V. Valet or self-parking $10 per day, underground.

One of six Warwicks in the U.S., this handsome midsize choice is reminiscent of hotels in Paris, where the corporate office is located. The small marbled lobby is accented by richly upholstered antique chairs and couches. A $2-million structural renovation was recently completed, with another $6 million to be invested in soft renovations by early 1999.

Even the standard rooms provide a full private balcony, and all but a few are equipped with fridge, wet bar, and dining table. Units are outfitted with simple brass and mahogany furniture, antique hunting prints on the walls, and a phone with a second line for modem connection.

The Liaison Restaurant serves continental cuisine for breakfast and dinner daily, plus lunch weekdays; lighter fare is offered in the lounge from 11am daily. Amenities include 24-hour room service and concierge, valet laundry, courtesy limousine service within a 5-mile radius, complimentary newspaper, secretarial services (available at an extra cost), rooftop pool (open seasonally), access to a nearby health club, and meeting space for 300.

MODERATE

✪ **Queen Anne Bed & Breakfast Inn.** 2147–51 Tremont Place, Denver, CO 80205. ☎ **800/432-4667** in North America, or 303/296-6666. Fax 303/296-2151. www.bedand-breakfastinns.org/queenanne. E-mail: queenanne@worldnet.att.net. 14 units. A/C TEL. $75–$145 double; $135–$175 suite. Rates include hot breakfast and Colorado wine each evening. AE, DC, DISC, MC, V. Free off-street parking.

A favorite of both business travelers and couples seeking a romantic getaway, the Queen Anne might be considered the perfect B&B in the perfect home. Actually, there are two Victorian homes: one built by well-known architect Frank Edbrooke in 1879 and the other constructed in 1886. Each unit is equipped with a phone and a writing desk; innkeeper Tom King also provides piped-in chamber music, fresh

---

ⓕ Family-Friendly Hotels

Loews Giorgio Hotel *(see p. 69)*   Kids get a coloring book, crayons, and animal crackers when they arrive; there's also a special children's menu in the Tuscany Restaurant.

Quality Inn Denver South *(see p. 63)*   This hotel has a great courtyard and provides free volleyball equipment.

---

flowers, and fax services. Each of the 10 double rooms in the 1879 Pierce House is unique, decorated with period antiques. Three of the rooms boast original murals: The Aspen Room's walls are filled with aspen trees (what else?); the third floor Park Room shows visitors the view from its windows in 1879; and the Tabor Room honors Augusta Pierce Tabor with a mural of an 1894 garden party she hosted at her mansion. Each of the four two-room suites in the adjacent 1886 Roberts house is dedicated to a famous artist (Norman Rockwell, Frederic Remington, John Audubon, and Alexander Calder). The suites have deep soaking tubs, and the Remington suite has its own hot tub. The Rooftop Room has a two-person jetted spa on its outdoor deck, and the Skyline Room has a two-person jetted tub/shower.

Located in the Clements Historic District, the Queen Anne borders downtown Denver and is within easy walking distance of just about everything. Continental breakfast includes coffee, juice, fresh fruit, hot scones, granola, muffins, and a hot entree. Smoking is not permitted.

Victoria Oaks Inn. 1575 Race St., Denver, CO 80206. ☎ **800/662-6257** or 303/355-1818. Fax 303/331-1095. E-Mail: vicoaksinn@aol.com. 9 units (7 with bathroom). A/C TEL. $64–$89 double. Rates include continental breakfast. AE, CB, DC, DISC, MC, V.

A European-style B&B, this circa-1896 Victorian home with handsome oak floors and leaded-glass windows is in fact a favorite of European travelers. The centrally located inn provides a continental breakfast of fruit, Danish, muffins, cereals, coffee, tea, and juice. A veranda has been added, and guests have kitchen and laundry privileges.

INEXPENSIVE

Hostel of the Rocky Mountains. 1530 Downing St., Denver, CO 80218. ☎ **303/861-7777**. 78 beds. $12 per person. Free pickup and delivery at bus and train stations, and from the Denver International Airport Park-n-Ride lots.

This centrally located hostel is within walking distance of more than 50 restaurants as well as all the major downtown attractions. As with most hostels, facilities are shared; they include a community room with TV, coin laundry, game room, and snack and soda machines. Each dorm room has no more than four beds. The front door is always locked, and someone is on the premises all night. The office is open from 8 to 10am and 5 to 10pm, and they're always reachable by phone. Pay phones are located on the second and third floors.

OUTSIDE DOWNTOWN
VERY EXPENSIVE

Loews Giorgio Hotel. 4150 E. Mississippi Ave., Denver, CO 80246. ☎ **800/345-9172** or 303/782-9300. Fax 303/758-6542. www.loewshotels.com. 202 units. A/C TV TEL. $199–$229 double; $259–$1,000 suite; weekend rates from $89, including continental breakfast. Children under 18 stay free in parents' room. AE, CB, DC, DISC, MC, V. Free valet and self-parking. Pets accepted on one floor.

Staying at Loews Giorgio is a little like taking a trip to Rome. Although the exterior is black steel with a reflecting-glass tower, inside it's bella Italia. Columns are finished in imitation marble, and the Renaissance-style murals and paintings look five centuries old. Throughout the hotel, much use has been made of floral patterns, Italian silk wall coverings, and marble-top furnishings. Each spacious room contains at least three phones, a coffeemaker, and hair dryer. The west-facing rooms offer superb views of the Rocky Mountains.

Dining: The top-rated Tuscany Restaurant serves fine Italian-style cuisine (three meals daily) in its elegant yet comfortable dining room.

Amenities: 24-hour room service, concierge, dry cleaning and laundry service, newspapers in lobby, twice-daily maid service, baby-sitting, secretarial services, courtesy van. Game rooms, boutiques, a fitness center, jogging track, access to nearby health club, business center, and meeting facilities for 100. Each room on the two floors for business travelers is equipped with two phone lines (including modem hookups) and in-room fax, and there is complimentary newspaper delivery.

MODERATE & INEXPENSIVE

Cameron Motel. 4500 E. Evans Ave. (I-25 exit 203), Denver, CO 80222. ☎ **303/757-2100**. Fax 303/757-0974. 35 units. A/C TV TEL. $52 double; $72 suite. AE, DISC, ER, MC, V. Pets accepted with $5 fee each.

A small mom-and-pop motel located about 10 minutes from downtown, the Cameron provides a clean, quiet alternative to some of the more expensive chains. Built in the 1940s, the property has been completely renovated. The walls of the rooms are of glazed brick; remote-control cable TVs offer 60 channels. Three units have kitchenettes. Fourteen rooms provide showers only, while 21 have tub/shower combinations. The owners live on-site, and their pride of ownership shows.

CAMPING

Chatfield State Park. 11500 N. Roxborough Park Rd., Littleton, CO 80125. ☎ **800/678-2267** for state park reservation service, or 303/791-7275. 193 sites. $9–$12, plus $4 day-use fee. MC, V only for advance reservations.

On the south side of Denver, 1 mile south of the intersection of Colo. 121 (Wadsworth) and Colo. 470, Chatfield offers a 1,550-acre reservoir with ample opportunities for boating, waterskiing, fishing, and swimming, plus 24 miles of trails for horseback riding, mountain biking, and hiking. Facilities include hot showers, picnic areas, a dump station, boat ramps and rentals, and electric hookups.

Delux R.V. Park. 5520 N. Federal Blvd., Denver, CO 80221. ☎ **303/433-0452**. 29 sites. $23 and up. MC, V.

This campground, with shaded sites, hot showers, laundry, and full hookups, provides the best Denver location for travelers who take their homes with them. It's convenient to buses (no. 31 RTD), shopping, and recreational facilities. Open year-round, the campground is located five blocks north of I-70 exit 272, and two blocks south of I-76 exit 3, on the east side of Federal Boulevard.

Denver North Campground. 16700 N. Washington St., Broomfield, CO 80020. ☎ **800/851-6521** (reservations only) or 303/452-4120. 150 sites. $18.50–$24.50. DISC, MC, V. Just off I-25 exit 229, 5 miles north of Denver.

The sites at this well-laid-out campground offer a variety of sizes and shapes, and about half are pull-through. Most sites have at least water and electric, and about half have full hookups. There's lots of grass and trees, with tent sites scattered about. All of the amenities—phone, showers, playground, pool, laundry, store, game room—are near the entrance. There are also two cabins ($30) and periodic entertainment such as cookouts and ice cream socials.

4 Dining

Denver has been inundated with chain and franchise eateries, mostly family restaurants, where the food is reliably good, but seldom great. The restaurants we've listed here are mostly independent, unique to this area, and a cut above others in their price ranges.

DOWNTOWN

VERY EXPENSIVE

The Broker Restaurant. 821 17th St. (near Champa St.). ☎ **303/292-5065.** Reservations recommended. Main courses $9–$16 lunch, $18–$35 dinner. AE, CB, DC, DISC, MC, V. Mon–Fri 11am–2:30pm; daily 5–11pm. STEAK/SEAFOOD.

The historic Denver National Bank building is the site of the Broker, with its circular 23-ton door still in place. Patrons sit in cherry-wood booths once used by bank customers to inspect safe-deposit boxes, and historic photos of Denver line the walls. Famous for its generous portions, the Broker's house favorites include New York and porterhouse steaks, Rocky Mountain trout, rack of lamb, and blackened catfish. Vegetarians can try the vegetarian pasta medley. The Broker's trademark is a complimentary large bowl of steamed gulf shrimp with a tasty and tangy sauce.

Two additional locations of Broker restaurants in Denver are the **Airport Broker** (near DIA), 12100 E. 39th Ave., at Peoria just south of I-70 (☎ **303/371-6420**), and **DTC Broker,** 5111 DTC Parkway, east of I-25 in Greenwood Village (☎ **303/70-5111**). In Boulder, there's the **Broker Inn Restaurant,** 555 30th St., between the turnpike and Baseline Road (☎ **303/444-3330**).

Buckhorn Exchange. 1000 Osage St. (at W. 10th Ave.). ☎ **303/534-9505.** Reservations recommended. Main courses $6.75–$14 lunch, $17–$39 dinner. AE, CB, DC, DISC, MC, V. Mon–Fri 11:30am–2pm; Sun–Thurs 5:30–10:30pm; Fri–Sat 5:30–11pm. ROCKY MOUNTAIN.

Thanks to Denver's new light-rail system, this restaurant is just minutes from the 16th Street Mall, the Convention Center, and all downtown hotels. Still occupying the same premises since it was founded in 1893, the restaurant displays its Colorado Liquor License No. 1 over the 140-year-old hand-carved oak bar in the upstairs Victorian parlor and saloon. Start with the Rocky Mountain oysters or smoked buffalo sausage, then choose from among slow-roasted buffalo prime rib or elk or beef steaks. There are even large-portion steaks to serve two to five persons. And for those who just can't make up their minds, several combination plates are offered. For dessert, try the chocolate "moose."

EXPENSIVE

✪ **Bravo! Ristorante.** Plaza Building of Adam's Mark Denver, 1550 Court Place. ☎ **303/626-2581,** or ext. 3164 from within the hotel. Reservations recommended. Main courses $4.50–$12.50 lunch, $12.50–$26 dinner. AE, CB, DC, DISC, MC, V. Mon–Fri 11:30am–2pm; Sun–Thurs 5:30–10:30pm; Fri–Sat 5:30–11pm. NORTHERN ITALIAN.

You'll think you're dining on an Italian piazza here: The room is open and airy, with a high ceiling, windows overlooking the 16th Street Mall, potted trees, and quartet groupings of booths with etched-glass dividers. Glass chandeliers increase the sparkle, and the mood is enhanced by the music served with your meal: The wait staff are also fine singers of both Broadway tunes and opera.

The sauces are lighter than you might expect, with sometimes-unusual flavors enhancing the generous portions of al dente pasta. Also on the menu are several unique pizzas, such as prawn, shrimp, and prosciutto. Several delightful pasta dishes are offered at both lunch and dinner, including lasagna with fennel sausage, eggplant, and sweet peppers, and fettuccine with diced tomatoes, roasted garlic, and

Downtown Denver Dining

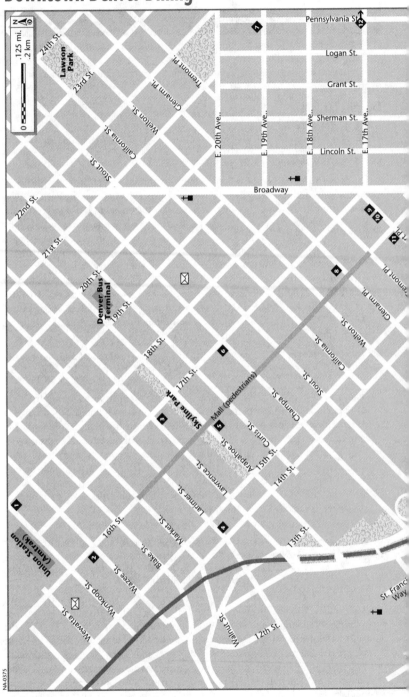

LEGEND
✝ Church
✉ Post Office

Bravo! Ristorante 🔟
The Broker Restaurant 6️⃣
Buckhorn Exchange 1️⃣4️⃣
The Delectable Egg 🔟
Denver Buffalo Company 1️⃣3️⃣
Duffy's Shamrock 9️⃣
Imperial Chinese Restaurant 1️⃣5️⃣
Las Delicias 🔟
The Little Russian Cafe 4️⃣
Marlowe's 8️⃣
The Palm 3️⃣
Palomino Euro Bistro 5️⃣
Vino Vino Ristorante Italiano 1️⃣2️⃣
The Wazee Supper Club 2️⃣
Wynkoop Brewing Company 1️⃣

73

red chiles. Other dinner selections include the specialty, filet Bravo!: tenderloin of beef with roasted cipollini onions, Gorgonzola cheese, balsamic dressed arugula, and chianti. Smoking is not permitted.

Denver Buffalo Company. 1109 Lincoln St. ☎ **303/832-0880.** Reservations recommended for dinner. Main courses $6–$12.50 lunch, $16–$38 dinner. DISC, MC, V. Mon–Sat 11am–2:30pm; Mon–Thurs 5–9pm; Fri–Sat 5–10pm.

You can't miss this busy restaurant, bar, deli, art gallery, and trading post, with the big bronze statue of a buffalo out front. The buffalo steaks, burgers, sausage, and even hot dogs come from the company's own Colorado ranch and are also available to take out or ship from the deli. For those not interested in buffalo, the restaurant also offers seafood, beef, poultry, and pasta dishes.

The bar is open all afternoon, serving a limited lunch menu, and there's live entertainment (country western, folk, or jazz) on Friday and Saturday nights.

Imperial Chinese Restaurant. 431 S. Broadway. ☎ **303/698-2800.** Reservations recommended. Individual dishes $8–$28. Complete multicourse dinners $15–$25. AE, CB, DC, MC, V. Mon–Thurs 11am–10pm; Fri 11am–10:30pm; Sat noon–10:30pm; Sun 4–10pm. CHINESE.

Considered by many locals to be the best Chinese restaurant in Denver, the Imperial offers classic and innovative Szechuan, Hunan, Mandarin, and Cantonese dishes. A laughing Buddha greets diners at the entrance, while two rather large tropical fish tanks, an exquisite hand-carved panel, and Chinese ceramics provide the right atmosphere for a family-style Chinese meal. Specialties include Nanking pork loin, seafood bird's nest, and sesame chicken.

The Palm. In The Westin Tabor Center, 1672 Lawrence St. ☎ **303/572-9100.** Reservations recommended. Main courses $8.50–$15 lunch, $12.50–$30 dinner. AE, CB, DC, DISC, ER, JCB, MC, V. Daily 11am–11pm. ITALIAN/STEAK/SEAFOOD.

Pio Bozzi and John Ganzi opened the first Palm restaurant in New York City in 1926, specializing in cuisine from their hometown of Parma, Italy. But whenever a customer requested steak, Ganzi ran to a nearby butcher shop, bought a steak, and cooked it to order! This eventually led to the Palm having its own meat wholesale company to ensure the quality of its steaks. Seafood was added by the current third-generation owners, who also opened a dozen more restaurants across the country. Most famous for its prime cuts of beef and huge lobsters, tradition holds firm at the Palm, with some of Ganzi's original Italian dishes still popular menu items. The dining room is decorated with fun on-the-wall drawings of celebrities; customers are seated at either booths or tables.

MODERATE

The Little Russian Cafe. 1424H Larimer St. ☎ **303/595-8600.** Lunch approximately $6.50, dinner $10–$15. AE, CB, DC, DISC, MC, V. Mon–Thurs 11:30am–2:30pm and 5:30–9:30pm; Fri 11:30am–10:30pm; Sat–Sun 5–10:30pm. RUSSIAN.

This quiet, charming cafe combines old-world atmosphere with authentic Russian cuisine. Russian scenes grace the walls of the dimly lit dining room; there's also an outdoor patio. In the Russian tradition, you can, if you wish, begin your meal with a shot of ice-cold vodka and a bowl of borscht. Main dishes include beef Stroganoff, goulash, stuffed cabbage, lamb stew, and a variety of traditional Russian selections.

There's another **Russian Cafe** in Englewood, at 2500 E. Orchard Rd. (☎ **303/347-0300**), plus the **Little Russian Cafe** in Boulder, 1430 Pearl St., at 15th Street (☎ **303/449-7696**).

Marlowe's. 511 16th St. (at Glenarm St.). ☎ **303/595-3700.** Reservations recommended. Main courses $7–$11 lunch, $9–$25 dinner. AE, DC, MC, V. Mon–Thurs 11am–11pm; Fri 11am–midnight; Sat 5pm–midnight. STEAK/SEAFOOD.

ⓘ Family-Friendly Restaurants

Casa Bonita *(see p. 77)* If the kids' attention isn't on the tacos, they'll be enthralled by puppet shows, high divers, a fun house, and a video arcade.

White Fence Farm *(see p. 77)* Meals are served family style, with Mom or Dad doling out the vegetables, but the best part is outside with the live farm animals and playground.

This popular eatery and saloon occupies a corner of the 1891 Kittredge Building (on the National Register of Historic Places), with an antique cherry-wood bar, granite pillars, and brass rails. It's a great spot for cocktails and appetizers, especially in warm weather, when tables are set up outside. House specialties include a pan-seared beef tenderloin, almond-crusted salmon, and live Maine lobster.

Palomino Euro Bistro. 1515 Arapahoe, on the 16th St. Mall. ☎ **303/534-7800.** Main courses $6–$14 lunch, $11–$15 dinner. AE, CB, DC, DISC, MC, V. Mon–Sat 11:15am– 2:30pm; Sun–Thurs 5–10pm; Fri–Sat 5–11pm. Closed Christmas and Thanksgiving. MEDITERRANEAN.

A lively, busy, and upbeat restaurant, with bright colors, rich wood, and hand-blown art-glass chandeliers, the Palomino also has a beautiful curving 48-foot bar of mahogany and marble. The menu changes monthly, with emphasis on wood-fired cooking. Specialties include spit-roasted garlic chicken, oven-roasted prawns and fresh fish, and Roman-style pizza baked crisp in a 600° oven. Lunch also includes sandwiches such as iron grill turkey with prosciutto, red onion, tomato, and provolone; and Moroccan lamb burger with sweet tomato chutney. Dinner might offer spit roasted lamb shanks from the wood oven, applewood-grilled chicken, or Atlantic salmon.

The Palomino also serves a wide selection of draft beers and wines by the glass, plus their signature drinks: "Palomino Cuvee," a sparkling wine created for them by Iron Horse Vineyards of Sonoma, California, and "Palomino Palini," a frozen blend of champagne, peach nectar, lemon, and cassis.

Vino Vino Ristorante Italiano. 708 E. 17th Ave. (at Washington). ☎ **303/837-9900.** Entrees $10–$17, pizza $8–$10. AE, DISC, MC, V. Mon–Fri 11am–2pm; Mon–Sat from 5:30pm. ITALIAN.

Chef Roberto C. Ravara trained in Basil and Milan, and his joy in creating tasty Italian dishes from choice ingredients is obvious. Vino Vino features walls finished to resemble a crumbling villa, with an inviting and intimate atmosphere complete with strolling Neapolitan singers. The house specialty is Osso Buco Alla Milanese: braised veal shank baked with carrots, onions, celery, pelati tomatoes, extra-virgin olive oil, white wine, lemon peel, bay leaves, and rosemary, and served over saffron rice. Among the two dozen other entrees are numerous pasta dishes, fish, beef, chicken, fresh seafood, and more veal. The extensive wine list of more than 300 domestic and imported selections can be confusing, but each menu item lists a wine recommendation.

Wynkoop Brewing Company. 1634 18th St. (at Wynkoop St.). ☎ **303/297-2700.** Reservations required for large parties. $5–$16. AE, CB, DC, DISC, MC, V. Mon–Sat 11am–2am, Sun 10am–midnight. REGIONAL AMERICAN/PUB.

When the Wynkoop opened its doors in 1988 as Denver's first new brewery in over 50 years, it started a mini-revolution: Since then, about 50 microbreweries have opened in Colorado. Wynkoop is located in a renovated warehouse across from

Union Station and near Coors Field. The menu offers pub fare, sandwiches, and soups and salads, plus dinners of steak, Denver cut elk medallions, and pan-fried Rocky Mountain trout. See also "Denver After Dark," in chapter 7.

INEXPENSIVE

The Delectable Egg. 1642 Market St. ☎ **303/572-8146.** Menu items $3.50–$6.25. AE, DC, DISC, MC, V. Daily 7am–2pm. AMERICAN.

Every city should have a cafe like this: There are more than two dozen egg dishes, pancakes, waffles, and French toast. Lunch includes a variety of salads and sandwiches. You can order eggs skillet-fried, baked in a frittata, scrambled into pita pockets, or smothered with chile or hollandaise. Accompany your meal with a plain coffee, latte, or espresso.

Another **Delectable Egg** can be found at 1625 Court Place (☎ **303/892-5720**).

✪ **Duffy's Shamrock.** 1635 Court Place. ☎ **303/534-4935.** Breakfast $1.75–$4.50; lunch $4–$7; dinner $5–$12. AE, CB, DC, MC, V. Mon–Fri 7am–2am; Sat 8am–2am; Sun 11am–2am. AMERICAN.

This traditional Irish bar and restaurant with fast, cheerful service has been thriving since the late 1950s. It specializes in Irish coffees and imported Irish beers. Daily specials may include prime rib, broiled mahimahi, or grilled liver and onions. Sandwiches, on practically every kind of bread imaginable, include corned beef, braunschweiger, and even a Dagwood.

Las Delicias. 439 E. 19th Ave. (at Pennsylvania St.). ☎ **303/839-5675.** Main courses $3–$10. AE, DISC, MC, V. Mon–Sat 8am–9pm, Sun 9am–9pm. MEXICAN.

Las Delicias, comprised of half a dozen red-brick-walled rooms, is known for its extensive menu of traditional Mexican dishes. Tamales, burritos, tacos, and fajitas are offered, along with generous portions of carne asada and carne de puerco adovado. Lots of fresh hot tortillas, chips, and salsa accompany each meal.

Other **Las Delicias** locations in Denver are at 50 E. Del Norte St., at Conifer (☎ **303/430-0422**), and 1530 Blake St. (☎ **303/629-5051**).

The Wazee Supper Club. 1600 15th St. (at Wazee St.). ☎ **303/623-9518.** Menu items $3.50–$8 (large pizzas cost more). AE, MC, V. Mon–Sat 11am–2am. PIZZA/SANDWICHES.

A former plumbing-supply store in lower downtown, the Wazee is a Depression-era relic with a black-and-white tile floor and a bleached mahogany burl bar, a magnificent example of 1930s art deco. It's been popular for more than 20 years with artists, architects, entertainers, businessmen, and others of good character. Pizza lovers throng the place (some believe the pizza here is the best in town, if not the world), but you'll also find an array of sandwiches from kielbasa to corned beef, plus buffalo burgers; about a dozen draft beers will quench your thirst. Don't miss the dumbwaiter used to shuttle food and drinks to the mezzanine floor—it's a converted 1937 garage-door opener.

OUTSIDE DOWNTOWN
EXPENSIVE

✪ **The Fort.** 19192 Colo. 8 (off W. Hampden Ave./U.S. 285), Morrison. ☎ **303/697-4771.** Reservations recommended. Main courses $15–$40. AE, CB, DC, DISC, MC, V. Mon–Fri 5–10pm; Sat 5–11pm; Sun 5–8pm. Special holiday hours. ROCKY MOUNTAIN.

There are several reasons to drive the 18 miles southwest from downtown Denver to visit the Fort. First is the atmosphere: The building is a full-scale reproduction of Bent's Fort, Colorado's first fur-trading post, and the staff is dressed as 19th-century Cheyenne. A second reason is the owner, Sam Arnold, a broadcast personality and master chef who opens champagne bottles with a tomahawk. He's had the menu translated into French, German, Spanish, Japanese, and Braille.

The third (and best) reason to go is the food. The Fort built its reputation on high-quality, low-cholesterol buffalo, of which it claims to serve the largest variety and greatest quantity of any restaurant in the world. There's buffalo steak, buffalo tongue, broiled buffalo marrow bones, and even "buffalo eggs"—hard-boiled quail eggs wrapped in buffalo sausage. Other house specialties include Taos trout, broiled with fresh mint and orange marmalade; a spicy-hot chicken stew; and elk medallions with wild huckleberry sauce. Diehards can get beefsteak.

MODERATE

Bull & Bush Pub & Brewery. 4700 Cherry Creek Dr. S., Glendale. ☎ **303/759-0333.** Main courses $5–$15. AE, DC, MC, V. Mon–Fri 11am–closing, Sat–Sun 10am–closing. BREWPUB.

This re-creation of a famous London pub always has eight of their own brewed beers on tap. Sunday evenings bring Dixieland jazz by regional groups, and Thursdays offer acoustic music. The menu includes English fish-and-chips and a Henry VIII platter: a combination of St. Louis–style ribs, smoked chicken leg thigh, bacon-wrapped water chestnuts, smoked cheddar and gouda, and assorted fruit. Several burgers and other sandwiches are available, plus salads and Mexican dishes. A weekend brunch menu from 10am to 2:30pm features several egg plates, such as the popular eggs Taos: eggs scrambled with avocados, scallions, and green chile, wrapped in a tortilla and smothered with green chile and melted cheddar. There are two happy hours most evenings. See also "Denver After Dark," in chapter 7.

White Fence Farm. 6263 W. Jewell Ave., Lakewood. ☎ **303/935-5945.** Reservations accepted for parties of 15 or more. Meals $10–$18. DISC, MC, V. Tues–Sat 5–9pm, Sun noon–8pm. Closed Jan. AMERICAN.

Locals come here for the family-style fried-chicken dinners: a delicately fried half chicken per person plus heaping bowls of potatoes, corn fritters, homemade gravy, coleslaw, cottage cheese, pickled beets, and bean salad. Also available are T-bone steaks, deep-fried shrimp, and broiled whitefish filet. For dessert, try the freshly baked pies. A children's menu is available, plus a playground, farm animals, carriage rides, and country store, all in a beautiful country setting 20 minutes from downtown Denver.

INEXPENSIVE

Casa Bonita. In the JCRS Shopping Center, 6715 W. Colfax Ave., Lakewood. ☎ **303/232-5115.** Reservations accepted for parties of 25 or more. Lunch or dinner $6.50–$9. AE, CB, DC, DISC, MC, V. Daily 11am–9:30pm. MEXICAN/AMERICAN.

A west Denver landmark, Casa Bonita is more of a theme park than a restaurant. A pink Spanish cathedral-type bell tower greets visitors, and inside are divers plummeting into a pool beside a 30-foot waterfall, puppet shows, fun house, and strolling mariachi bands. Food is served cafeteria style: enchiladas, tacos, fajitas, country-fried steak, and fried chicken. Hot sopaipillas (deep-fried sweet dough), served with honey, are included with each meal.

Healthy Habits. 865 S. Colorado Blvd. ☎ **303/733-2105.** All you can eat $8. AE, DC, DISC, MC, V. Daily 11am–9pm. AMERICAN.

This award-winning cafeteria-style restaurant offers what may be Denver's best deal for salad and pasta. The 70-item salad bar displays all the usuals, plus fresh fruit and a variety of pasta salads. A separate hot pasta bar offers pastas, fresh sauces, and pizza. The all-you-can-eat price includes fresh-baked desserts. Beverages, including beer and wine, are extra.

Additional **Healthy Habits** restaurants can be found at 7418 S. University Blvd., Littleton (☎ **303/740-7044**); 14195 W. Colfax Ave., Golden (☎ **303/277-9293**); and 4760 Baseline Rd., Boulder (☎ **303/494-9177**).

T-Wa Inn. 555 S. Federal Blvd. (near W. Virginia Ave.). ☎ **303/922-4584.** Lunch $4.50–$7.50, dinner $5–$15. AE, CB, DC, DISC, MC, V. Daily 11am–10pm. VIETNAMESE.

Denver's first Vietnamese restaurant still dishes up the authentic flavorful cuisine of Vietnam. The decor is simple but pleasant, with Viet folk songs providing atmospheric background. Try the egg rolls, with shrimp and crabmeat wrapped in rice paper; hearty meat-and-noodle soups; chicken salad; or soft-shell crab.

What to See & Do in Denver   7

An intriguing combination of modern American city and sprawling Old West town, Denver offers a wide variety of attractions, activities, and events. You'll discover art, history, sports, recreation, shopping, and, of course, dining, and it would be easy to spend a week in the city and never be bored. It's also a convenient base for easy day trips to Boulder, Colorado Springs, or up into the mountains.

1 Attractions

THE TOP ATTRACTIONS

✪ **Denver Art Museum.** 100 W. 14th Ave. (at Civic Center Park). ☎ **303/ 640-4433.** Admission $4.50 adults, $2.50 students and seniors, free for children under 6; free for everyone Sat. Tues–Sat 10am–5pm (until 9pm Wed), Sun noon–5pm. Bus: 7, 8, 50.

Founded in 1893 and recently renovated, this seven-story museum is wrapped by a thin 28-sided wall faced with one million sparkling tiles designed by Gio Ponti of Italy and James Sudler Associates of Denver. The new main entrance on Acoma Plaza boasts a dramatic steel canopy and is more convenient to the parking lots at Acoma and 13th Avenue. The original Ponti entrance door on 14th Avenue will also be accessible.

The museum's expanding collection of Western and regional works is housed on the seventh floor. Included are Frederic Remington's bronze *The Cheyenne,* Charles Russell's painting *In the Enemy's Country,* plus 19th-century photography and historical pieces.

The American Indian collection consists of more than 17,000 pieces from 150 tribes of North America, spanning nearly 2,000 years. The collection is growing not only through the acquisition of historic pieces, but also through the commissioning of works by contemporary artists. Other collections include architecture, design and graphics, Asian, modern and contemporary, Pre-Columbian, and Spanish Colonial.

The Bernadette Berger Discovery Library tantalizes visitors with cozy reading nooks, display drawers of art objects and prints, and a costume closet where you can try on old-style clothing, hats, and wigs. Also scattered about are computer stations offering CD-ROM activities and access to the Denver Public Library's online catalog.

Downtown Denver Attractions

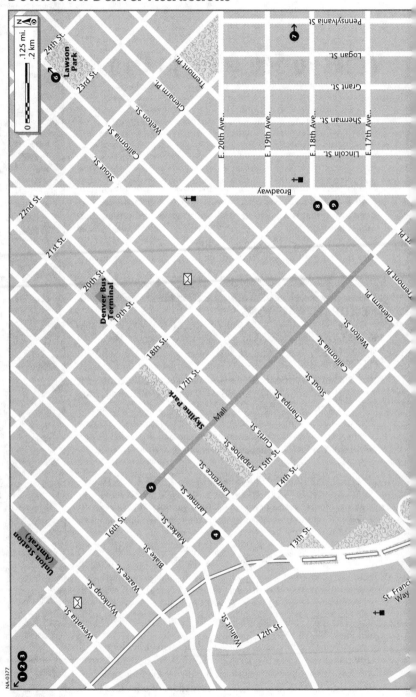

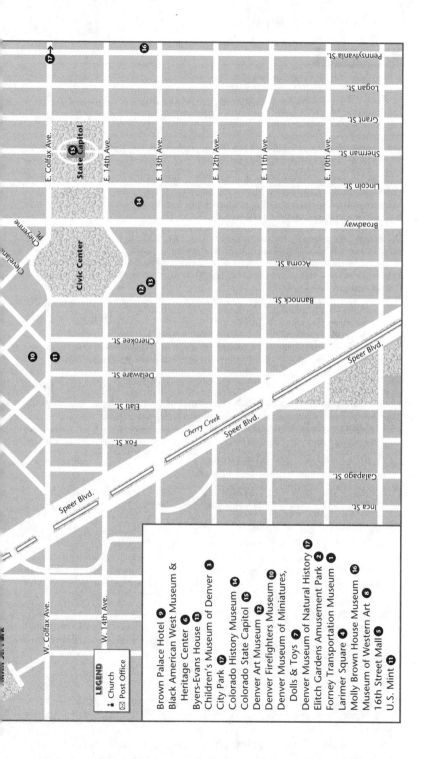

LEGEND
✝ Church
⊠ Post Office

Brown Palace Hotel **9**
Black American West Museum &
Heritage Center **6**
Byers-Evans House **13**
Children's Museum of Denver **3**
City Park **17**
Colorado History Museum **14**
Colorado State Capitol **15**
Denver Art Museum **12**
Denver Firefighters Museum **10**
Denver Museum of Miniatures,
Dolls & Toys **7**
Denver Museum of Natural History **17**
Elitch Gardens Amusement Park **2**
Forney Transportation Museum **1**
Larimer Square **4**
Molly Brown House Museum **16**
Museum of Western Art **8**
16th Street Mall **5**
U.S. Mint **11**

81

Impressions

. . . Cash! Why they create it here.

—Walt Whitman, on Denver in *Specimen Days*, 1879

Overview tours are available (Tuesday through Sunday at 1:30pm, plus 11am on Saturday), an in-depth tour of a different area of the museum is offered each Wednesday and Friday at noon, and a variety of child-oriented and family programs are scheduled regularly. The Museum Shop sells replicas of art treasures and books on art and southwestern lore. A restaurant and cafe are open Monday through Saturday from 11am and Sunday from noon.

✪ **Denver Museum of Natural History.** City Park, 2001 Colorado Blvd. ☎ **800/ 925-2250** or 303/322-7009; 303/370-8257 for the hearing impaired. Admission to museum, $6 adults, $4 children 3–12 and seniors 65 and older; IMAX, $6 adults, $4 children and seniors; planetarium, free with museum admission; group rates available. Daily 10am–5pm. Closed Christmas. Bus: 24, 32, 40.

This rambling three-story museum is the fifth-largest natural history museum in the United States. Exquisitely fashioned figures in more than 90 dioramas depict the history of life on earth on four continents. Displays explore ancient cultures, prehistoric American peoples, Colorado wildlife, and Australian ecology. Also on view are artifacts of early Native American tribes from Alaska to Florida, plus exhibits of South American wildlife and the habitats of Botswana.

The "Prehistoric Journey" traces the history of life on earth through 3.5 billion years. Fossils, interactive exhibits, and dioramas of ancient ecologies make this the museum's most popular attraction, especially enticing for children.

The **IMAX Theater** (☎ **303/370-6300**) presents science, nature, or technology-oriented films with sense-surround sound on a screen that measures 4½ by 6½ stories; the **Charles C. Gates Planetarium** (☎ **303/370-6487**) schedules frequent multimedia star programs and laser light shows.

✪ **United States Mint.** 320 W. Colfax Ave. (between Cherokee and Delaware sts.). ☎ **303/844-3582** or 303/844-3331. Free admission. Tickets available at the booth next to the visitor entrance on Cherokee St. Mon–Fri, 8am–2:45pm; tours every 20–30 minutes depending on visitor volume. Reservations not accepted; June–Labor Day expect a 40–45 min. wait. Closed 2 weeks in summer for audit, call for exact date. Cultural Connection Trolley. Bus: 7.

Opened in 1863, the Mint originally melted gold dust and nuggets into bars. In 1904 the office moved to this site, and 2 years later began making gold and silver coins. Copper pennies were added a few years later. The last silver dollars (containing 90% silver) were coined in 1935. In 1970 all silver was eliminated from dollars and half dollars (today they're made of a copper-nickel alloy). The Denver Mint stamps ten billion coins a year, and each has a small *D* on it. This is one of only four mints in the United States.

Video monitors along the visitors' gallery through the mint provide a close view of the actual coin-minting process, and new displays are frequently being added.

✪ **Colorado State Capitol.** Broadway and E. Colfax Ave. ☎ **303/866-2604.** Free admission. 30-minute tours offered year-round (more frequently in summer), Mon–Fri 9:30am–2:30pm (the dome is locked at 3:30pm). Bus: 2, 7, 8, 12, 15.

Built to last a thousand years, the Capitol was constructed in 1886 of granite from a Colorado quarry. The dome, which rises 272 feet above the ground, was first

Robbery at the Mint

A daring armed robbery took place at the Denver Mint in 1922, just a week before Christmas, and although police were certain they knew who the culprits were, no one ever served a day in jail for the crime. The most secure and theft-proof building in Denver, the mint seemed an unlikely target for a robbery. In fact, the thieves did not rob the mint itself—they simply waited for guards to carry the money out the front door.

A Federal Reserve Bank truck was parked outside the mint on West Colfax Avenue, around 10:30am on December 18. It was being loaded with $200,000 worth of brand-new five-dollar bills, to be taken to a bank about 12 blocks away, when a black Buick touring car pulled up. Two men jumped out and began firing sawed-off shotguns, killing one guard and spraying the mint and nearby buildings, while a third robber grabbed the bags of money. Guards inside the mint quickly pulled their guns and returned fire, but within a minute and a half the robbers were gone—$200,000 richer.

Mint guards were certain they had hit one of the thieves, and four weeks later in a dusty Denver garage they found the Buick. Lying in the front seat was the frozen and bloody body of one Nick Trainor, a convicted criminal who had recently been released on parole from the Nebraska State Penitentiary. Trainor had been shot several times.

Secret Service agents recovered $80,000 of the missing loot the following year in St. Paul, Minnesota, but no arrests were made, and little more was mentioned until 1934, when Denver police announced that they knew the identities of the other men involved. Still, no charges were filed. Two of the suspects were already serving life sentences for other crimes.

At the time, police said the robbery had been pulled off by a Midwest gang, who had immediately fled to the Minneapolis–St. Paul area, where they gave the money to a prominent Minneapolis attorney, who also was never charged.

sheathed in copper, but it was replaced with 200 ounces of gold after a public outcry: Copper was not a Colorado product.

Murals depicting the history of water in the state adorn the walls of the first-floor rotunda, which offers a splendid view upward to the underside of the dome. South of the rotunda is the governor's office, paneled in walnut and lit by a massive chandelier.

On the first floor, the west lobby has a display case of dolls in ball gowns—miniature versions of those worn by various governors' wives. To the right of the main lobby is the governor's reception room. The second floor has main entrances to the House, Senate, and old Supreme Court chambers, and entrances to the public and visitor galleries for the House and Senate are on the third floor. The Colorado Hall of Fame is located near the top of the dome, with stained-glass portraits of Colorado pioneers; on clear days, the views from the dome are spectacular. Capitol memorabilia is available for purchase at the tour guide desk.

MORE ATTRACTIONS
HISTORIC BUILDINGS

Byers-Evans House. 1310 Bannock St. (in front of the Denver Art Museum). ☎ **303/ 620-4933.** Admission $3 adults, $2.50 seniors, $1.50 children 6–16, free for children under 6. Tues–Sun 11am–3pm. Closed state holidays. Bus: 8.

Mile High City

Denver is exactly 1 mile high—the 15th step of the State Capitol Building is 5,280 feet above sea level

This elaborate 1883 Victorian home has been restored to its 1912–24 period, when it was owned by William Gray Evans, son of Colorado's second territorial governor. Guided tours describe the architecture and explain the fascinating lives of these prominent Denver families. Admission to the Byers-Evans House includes the renovated service wing and carriage house, which now houses the Denver History Museum. Here you will find changing displays and thousands of photos describing Denver's history, from the gold rush to World War II. In addition, interactive video displays depict historical events and issues, facts and figures, biographies of early Denverites, and historic photos.

Larimer Square. 1400 block of Larimer St. ☎ **303/534-2367,** or 303/607-1276 for the events line. Bus: 2, 7, 12, 15, 16, 28, 31, 32, 38, 44. The free Larimer Shuttle offers round-trip service from downtown hotels, the Denver Convention Center, and the Denver Performing Arts Complex (☎ 303/626-2326).

This is where Denver began. Larimer Street between 14th and 15th streets comprised the entire community of Denver City in 1858, with false-fronted stores, hotels, and saloons to serve gold-seekers and other pioneers. In the mid-1870s, it was the main street of the city and the site of Denver's first post office, bank, theater, and streetcar line. By the 1930s, however, it had deteriorated so much that it had become a "skid row" of pawnshops, gin mills, and flophouses. Plans had been made to level these structures with a wrecking ball when the entire block was purchased by a group of investors in 1965.

The Larimer Square project became Denver's first major historic preservation effort. All 16 of the block's commercial buildings, constructed in the 1870s and 1880s, were renovated, providing space for street-level retail shops, restaurants, nightclubs, and upper-story offices. A series of inner courtyards and open spaces was created, and in 1973 it was added to the National Register of Historic Places.

Larimer Square hosts numerous special events. A series of free concerts takes place on Thursday evenings in summer; Oktoberfest (September and October) features beers from all around the globe, particularly Germany; and December's Winterfest includes a huge tree-lighting, an outdoor ice-skating arena, carolers, and more.

✪ Molly Brown House Museum. 1340 Pennsylvania St. ☎ **303/832-4092.** Admission $5 adults, $3.50 seniors over 65, $1.50 children 6–12, free for children under 6. Year-round Tues–Sat 10am–4pm, Sun noon–4pm; June–Aug, also Mon 10am–4pm. Last tour of the day begins at 3:30pm. Closed major holidays. Bus: 2 on Logan St. to E. 13th, then 1 block east to Pennsylvania.

Built in 1889 of Colorado lava stone with sandstone trim, from 1894 to 1932 this was the residence of James and Margaret (Molly) Brown. The "unsinkable" Molly Brown became a national heroine in 1912 when the *Titanic* sank: She took charge of a group of immigrant women in a lifeboat and later raised money for their benefit.

Restored to its 1910 appearance, the Molly Brown House has a large collection of turn-of-the-century furnishings and art objects, many of which had belonged to the Brown family. A carriage house at the rear is also open to visitors.

MUSEUMS & GALLERIES

Black American West Museum & Heritage Center. 3091 California St. (at 31st St.). ☎ **303/292-2566.** Admission $3 adults, $2 seniors, $1 children 12–17, 50¢ children under 12, free for children under 3. May–Sept Mon–Fri 10am–5pm, Sat–Sun noon–5pm; Oct–Apr Wed–Fri 10am–2pm, Sat–Sun noon–5pm. Light Rail stop no. 1.

Nearly a third of the cowboys in the Old West were blacks, and this museum chronicles their little-known history, along with that of black doctors, teachers, miners, farmers, reporters, and state legislators. The 35,000-item collection is housed in the Victorian home of Dr. Justina Ford, the first black woman licensed to practice medicine in Denver. Known locally as the "Lady Doctor," Ford delivered more than 7,000 babies, most of them at home since she was denied hospital privileges, and consistently served the disadvantaged and underprivileged of Denver.

Paul Stewart, a black who loved to play cowboys and Indians as a boy but was always cast as an Indian because "There was no such thing as a black cowboy," began researching the history of blacks in the West after meeting a black cowboy who had actually led cattle drives in the early 20th century. Stewart explored almost every corner of the American West, gathering artifacts, memorabilia, photographs, oral histories—anything to document the fact of black cowboys—and his collection served as the nucleus for this museum when it opened in 1971.

Colorado History Museum. 1300 Broadway. ☎ **303/866-3682.** Admission $3 adults, $2.50 seniors, $1.50 students and children. Mon–Sat 10am–4:30pm, Sun noon–4:30pm. Bus: 8.

The Colorado Historical Society's permanent exhibits include "The Colorado Chronicle," an 1800 to 1949 time line that uses biographical plaques and a remarkable collection of photographs, news clippings, and various paraphernalia to explain Colorado's past. Dozens of dioramas portray various episodes in state history, including an intricate re-creation of 19th-century Denver; there's also a life-size display of early transportation and industry.

The museum recently opened a new exhibit titled "Invisible Hero: The Untold Story of the Black Cowboy," which will remain open through February 2000. Historic photos, artifacts, and biographical sketches tell the story of the estimated 9,000 black cowboys in the American West, while vignettes detail the rigorous trail life as well as the racism and prejudice they faced. You'll clearly see the differences between reality and the cowboy's life as portrayed by Hollywood.

The museum hosts traveling exhibits and offers a series of lectures and statewide historical and archaeological tours. Its gift shop is also worth a visit.

Denver Firefighters Museum. 1326 Tremont Place. ☎ **303/892-1436.** Admission $3 adults, $2 children 12 and under. Mon–Sat 10am–2pm.

The history of the Denver Fire Department is preserved and displayed here in historic Fire Station No. 1. Built in 1909 for Engine Company No. 1, it was one of the largest firehouses in Denver, occupying 1,100 square feet on two floors. In its early years, it lodged men, fire engines, and horses. Motorized equipment replaced the horse-drawn engines by 1924, and in 1932 this firehouse was "modernized." Concrete replaced the wooden floor, the stables and hayloft were removed, and the plumbing was improved. Visitors can see fire-fighting equipment dating back to 1866, plus historic photos and newspaper clippings.

Denver Museum of Miniatures, Dolls & Toys. 1880 Gaylord St. (just west of City Park). ☎ **303/322-3704.** Admission $3 adults, $2 seniors and children 2–16, free for children under 2. Tues–Sat 10am–4pm, Sun 1–4pm.

This early-20th-century property is home to an intriguing collection of antique and collectible dolls, from rag and wooden to exquisite German bisque. Also on display are dollhouses—from a Santa Fe adobe with hand-carved furniture to a replica of a 16-room home in Newport, Rhode Island—plus wonderful old toys, including teddy bears and a full circus, complete with tent and animals. The gift shop is equally delightful.

Forney Transportation Museum. 1416 Platte St. ☎ **303/433-3643.** Admission $4 adults, $3.50 seniors over 61, $2 youths 12–18, $1 children under 12. Mon–Sat 9am–5pm (10am–5pm in winter), Sun 11am–5pm. Take I-25 exit 211 (23rd Ave.) and go east on Water St. ¾ of a mile to Platte St.

More than 100 antique and classic cars and trucks are the centerpiece of this collection, which also includes some 350 other exhibits. You'll see a number of one-of-a-kind vehicles, including Amelia Earhart's "Gold Bug" roadster, a Rolls-Royce that once belonged to Prince Aly Khan, and a 1909 French taxicab that transported World War I soldiers from Paris to the Battle of the Marne. Other displays include locomotives, wagons, music boxes, historic fashions, farm equipment, and a model train. The museum's current home is the former Denver Tramway power building and surrounding grounds, but plans include a possible move to new quarters in late 1998; call or check with the visitor center before going.

✪ Four Mile Historic Park. 715 S. Forest St. ☎ **303/399-1859.** Admission $3.50 adults, $2 seniors and children 6–15, free for children under 6. Apr–Sept, Wed–Sun 10am–4pm; Oct–Mar, Fri–Sun 11am–3pm. Located 4 miles southeast of downtown Denver, at S. Forest St. and Exposition Ave.

The oldest log home (1859) still standing in Denver serves as the centerpiece for this 14-acre living-history facility. Everything is authentic for the period from 1859 to 1883, including the house (a former stagecoach stop), its furnishings, outbuildings, and farm equipment. There are draft horses and chickens in the barn and crops in the garden. Weekend visitors can enjoy stagecoach rides, weather permitting, and observe costumed volunteers engaged in various chores or crafts, from plowing and blacksmithing to quilting and cooking. Call for details on upcoming special events.

Lakewood's Heritage Center at Belmar Park. 797 S. Wadsworth Blvd., Lakewood. ☎ **303/987-7850.** Admission $2 adults, $1 children 4–18, free ages 3 and under. Tues–Fri 10am–4pm, Sat–Sun noon–4pm. Bus: 76.

In Denver's early days, many of its wealthy residents maintained summer estates in the rural Lakewood area, and this historic village tells their story as well as that of others who lived and worked here. Stop first at the visitor center for an introduction to the museum; this is also where you can begin a personalized guided or self-guided tour. The village includes an 1880s farmhouse, 1920s one-room school, and the Barn Gallery. There's an exhibit on "Lakewood People and Places," antique and vintage farm machinery, guided nature walks through the surrounding 127-acre park, changing art exhibits, and a picnic area. The center presents year-round lecture-luncheon programs, plus children's programs on most summer Saturdays. There's also an excellent gift shop with unique handmade items.

Mizel Museum of Judaica. 560 S. Monaco Parkway. ☎ **303/333-4156.** Free admission. Mon–Fri 10am–4pm, Sun noon–4pm. From downtown head east on Colfax Ave. for about 3½ miles, then south (right) on S. Monaco Parkway for about 2¼ miles to the museum; turn left onto Center Ave. and park in the east side lot.

The museum's permanent collection describes Jewish customs, ceremonies, and traditions in three groupings: *Torah, Hiddur Mitzvah,* and the Israel Arts and Crafts

Movement. Part of this collection is on display at all times in the corridor cases. Changing exhibits discuss the history, culture, and art of Judaism around the world. Recent exhibitions included a multicultural fiber show centered around the Wimpel Project from Pittsburgh; personal mementos, photographs, clothing, and letters describing the life of Colorado Jewish women between 1860 and 1960; and a remembrance of the horrors of the Holocaust that includes sculpture by Joe Nicrastri, paintings by Francia Tobacman offered as a *Kaddish* (memorial prayer) for the 6 million Jewish lives lost, and photographs by Judy Ellis Glickman that tell the story of Denmark's incredible feat in protecting 99% of its Jewish population.

Museum of Western Art. 1727 Tremont Place. ☎ 303/296-1880. Admission $3 adults, $2 seniors and students, free for children under 7. Tues–Sat 10am–4:30pm. Bus: 20.

This museum occupies a three-story Victorian brick house that was originally Denver's most notorious brothel and gambling casino. Among the more than 125 paintings and sculptures are classic western scenes by Frederic Remington and Charles Russell, as well as landscapes by Albert Bierstadt and Thomas Moran. The gift shop sells hard-to-find art books and prints.

Wings Over the Rockies Air & Space Museum. 7711 E. Academy Parkway, Hangar #1 in Lowry Air Force Base (gates at 6th Ave. and Dayton St., Quebec St. and 1st Ave., and Alameda Ave. between Havana and Monaco sts.). ☎ 303/360-5360. Admission $4 adults, $2 children 6–17 and seniors, free for children under 6. Group rates available. Mon–Sat 10am–4pm, Sun noon–4pm. Bus: 6.

More than 20 planes and spacecraft are housed in the cavernous Hangar No. 1, which became a museum when Lowry Air Force Base closed in 1995. On display are antique biplanes, a search-and-rescue helicopter, a massive B-1A bomber—one of only five ever built—and most of the F1 fighter series. You can also see World War I uniforms, a Norden bomb sight, U3A Blue Canoe, and the "Freedom" space module, plus traveling exhibits and changing private collections. Once a month, the museum hosts "Open Cockpit Day," when children get to climb into the planes' cockpits. The store is filled with aviation and space-oriented clothing, souvenirs, and toys for kids of all ages.

NEIGHBORHOODS WORTH EXPLORING

FAR EAST CENTER   Denver's Asian community is concentrated along this strip of Federal Boulevard, between West Alameda and West Mississippi avenues, which burgeoned in the aftermath of the Vietnam War to accommodate throngs of Southeast Asian refugees, especially Thai and Vietnamese. Look for authentic restaurants, bakeries, groceries, gift shops, and clothing stores. The Far East Center building at Federal and Alameda is built in Japanese pagoda style.

FIVE POINTS   The "five points" actually meet at 23rd Street and Broadway, but the cultural and commercial hub of Denver's black community, **from 20th to 38th Streets, northeast of downtown,** covers a much larger area and incorporates four historic districts. Restaurants offer soul food, barbecued ribs, and Caribbean cuisine, while jazz and blues musicians and contemporary dance troupes perform in theaters and nightclubs. The Black American West Museum and Heritage Center is also in this area.

LA ALMA LINCOLN PARK/AURARIA   Hispanic culture, art, food, and entertainment predominate along this strip of Santa Fe Drive, between West Colfax and West Sixth Avenues, notable for its southwestern character and architecture. You'll find numerous restaurants, art galleries, and crafts shops. Denver's annual Cinco de Mayo celebration takes place here each May.

LOWER DOWNTOWN (LODO)   A 25-block area surrounding Union Station, and encompassing **Wynkoop Street southeast to Market Street** and **20th Street southwest to Speer Boulevard,** this delightful and busy historic district was until recent years a somewhat seedy neighborhood of deteriorating Victorian houses and warehouses. But a major restoration effort has brought it back to life, so today it's home to chic shops, art galleries, nightclubs, and restaurants that are kept hopping by Denver's movers and shakers. Listed as both a city and county historic district, it boasts numerous National Historic Landmarks. In addition, the 50,000-seat stadium, Coors Field, home of the Rockies baseball team, opened here in the spring of 1995.

UPTOWN   Denver's oldest residential neighborhood, from **Broadway east to York Street (City Park)** and **23rd Avenue south to Colfax Avenue,** is best known today for two things: It's bisected by 17th Avenue's "Restaurant Row" (see "Dining," in chapter 6), and several of its classic Victorian and Queen Anne–style homes have been converted into captivating B&Bs (see "Accommodations," in chapter 6).

PARKS & GARDENS

✪ **Butterfly Pavilion & Insect Center.** 6252 W. 104th Ave., Westminster. ☎ **303/ 469-5441.** Admission $6.50 adults, $4.50 seniors, $3.50 children. Tues–Sun 9am–5pm. Take the Denver–Boulder Turnpike (U.S. 36) to West 104th Ave. and go east for about a block. The Pavilion is on your right.

A walk through the butterfly conservatory introduces the visitor to a world of grace and beauty. The constant mist creates a hazy habitat to support the lush green plants that are both food and home to the inhabitants. If you stand still for a few minutes, resident butterflies might land on you, but don't try to pick them up—the oils on your hands contaminate their senses, interfering with their ability to find food. One display describes the differences among butterflies, moths, and skippers, and color charts are available to help with identification (a butterfly guide costs 25¢).

In the insect room you'll discover that honeybees beat their wings some 200 times per second, and beetles comprise one-fifth of all living things on earth. Meet arthropods (the scientific name for insects) that are native to Colorado, and see exotic species from around the world. A fascinating "touch cart" allows you to get up close to a cockroach or tarantula—that is, if this is something you really want to do.

The walls of the entryway are lined with magnificent close-up photographs of insects by Fran Hall, many taken before macro lenses made such close-ups relatively easy. Hall started traveling and photographing in the mid-1930s, and many of the photos on display were taken with a special camera he designed with a toolmaker friend.

Also on the premises are a large gift shop and snack bar. Outside, a half-mile nature trail meanders among cactus and other desert-friendly plants.

City Park. E. 17th to E. 26th aves., between York St. and Colorado Blvd. Free admission to park, although the zoo, museum, golf course, and other sites charge independently. Daily 24 hours. Bus: 24, 32.

Denver's largest urban park covers 314 acres (96 square blocks) on the east side of Uptown. Established in 1881, and with its Victorian touches still evident, it includes two lakes (with boat rentals), athletic fields, jogging and walking trails, playgrounds, tennis courts, picnic areas, and an 18-hole municipal golf course.

In summer, band concerts are performed in the park, which is also the site of both the Denver Zoo and the Denver Museum of Natural History (including its planetarium and IMAX Theater).

✪ **Denver Botanic Gardens.** 1005 York St. ☎ **303/331-4000** or 303/331-4010 (24-hour recording). Admission May–Sept, $5.50 adults, $3.50 seniors and children 6–15; Oct–Apr, $4.50 adults, $2.50 seniors, $2 children 6–15; free for children under 6. Daily 9am–5pm. Closed Dec. 25, Jan. 1, and May 7. Cultural Connection Trolley. Bus: 2, 6, 10.

Twenty acres of outstanding indoor and outdoor gardens display plants native to the desert, plains, mountain foothills, and alpine zones; there's also a traditional Japanese garden, scripture garden (relating plants to biblical history), herb garden, home-demonstration garden, water garden, "wingsong" garden to attract songbirds, and new "Romantic Gardens" with a waterway, fragrance garden, and courtyard garden.

Even in the cold of winter, the dome-shaped, concrete-and-Plexiglas Boettcher Memorial Conservatory houses more than 1,000 species of tropical and subtropical plants. Huge, colorful orchids and bromeliads share space with a collection of plants used for food, fibers, dyes, building materials, and medicines. The Botanic Gardens also include a gift shop, library, and auditorium. Special events scheduled throughout the year range from garden concerts in summer to sunset strolls in mid-June to several holiday events.

✪ **Denver Mountain Parks.** Dept. of Parks and Recreation. ☎ **303/697-4545.** Free admission.

Formally established in August 1913, the city's Mountain Parks system immediately began acquiring land in the mountains near Denver to be set aside for recreational use. Today it includes more than 13,000 acres, with 31 developed mountain parks and 16 wilderness areas—wonderful places for hiking, picnicking, bird watching, golfing, or lazing in the grass and sun.

The first and largest, **Genesee Park,** is 20 miles west of Denver off I-70 exit 254; its 2,400 acres contain the Chief Hosa Lodge and Campground (the only overnight camping in the system), picnic areas with fireplaces, a softball field, scenic overlook, and an elk and buffalo enclosure.

Among the system's other parks is **Echo Lake,** located about 45 minutes from downtown Denver on Colo. 103. At 10,600 feet elevation on Mt. Evans, the park has good fishing, hiking, and picnicking, plus a restaurant and curio shop. Other parks include 1,000-acre **Daniels Park** (23 miles south of Denver via I-25 to Castle Pines Parkway, then west to the park), which offers picnic areas, a softball field, and a scenic overlook; and **Dedisse Park** (2 miles west of Evergreen on Colo. 74), which provides picnic facilities, a golf course, restaurant and clubhouse, and opportunities for ice-skating, fishing, and volleyball.

Denver Zoo. City Park, 23rd Ave. and Steele St. (main entrance is between Colorado Blvd. and York St.). ☎ **303/331-4110.** Admission $6 adults, $3 seniors 62 and over and children 4–12 (accompanied by an adult), free for children under 4. Apr–Sept, daily 9am–6pm; Oct–Mar, daily 10am–5pm. Cultural Connection Trolley. Bus: 24, 32.

More than 600 species of animals (over 3,000 individuals) live in this spacious zoological park. Feeding times are posted near the zoo entrance, so you can time your visit to see the animals at their most active. Bear Mountain, when it was built in 1918, was the first animal exhibit in the U.S. to be constructed of simulated concrete rock-work. At the other end of the time line, Northern Shores (1987) allows underwater viewing of polar bears and sea lions, while Tropical Discovery (1994) re-creates an entire tropical ecosystem under glass, complete with crocodiles, piranhas and king cobras, as well as an exhibit of the rare Komodo dragon. Exotic waterfowl inhabit several ponds, and 300 avians live in Bird World, which includes a hummingbird forest and a tropical aviary. The Primate Panorama is a 7-acre world-class primate exhibit with 29 species, ranging from a 6-ounce marmoset to a 581-pound gorilla.

The zoo is home to the nation's first natural-gas–powered train. The rubber-tired Zooliner tours all zoo paths, spring through fall. Full meals are served at the Hungry Elephant, a zoo cafeteria with an outdoor eating area, and snack bars are scattered about. Many visitors bring picnic lunches to eat on the expansive lawns.

Rocky Mountain Arsenal National Wildlife Refuge. Quebec St. and 72nd Ave. ☎ **303/289-0232** (most activities require reservations). Free admission. Daylight hours. Bus: 48.

Once a site where the U.S. Army manufactured chemical weapons such as mustard gas and GB nerve agent, and later leased to a private enterprise to produce pesticides, the Rocky Mountain Arsenal has become an environmental success story. The 27-square-mile Superfund cleanup site, comprised of open grasslands and wetlands just west of Denver International Airport, is home to more than 330 species, including deer, coyotes, prairie dogs, and birds of prey. An estimated 100 bald eagles make this one of the country's largest eagle roosting locales during the winter months.

The Rocky Mountain Arsenal Wildlife Society Bookstore is located at the visitor center. The U.S. Fish and Wildlife Service offers a drop-in visitor program on Saturdays, as well as many other programs; for reservations, call ☎ **303/289-0232**. For a guided tour, it's best to call a week in advance. The U.S. Army (☎ **303/289-0467**) offers a program of environment cleanup information and tours.

ESPECIALLY FOR KIDS

Denver abounds in child-oriented activities, and the listings below should appeal to young travelers of any age. Some sights listed in the sections above may appeal to families as well (the Butterfly Pavilion and Insect Center; Colorado History Museum; Denver Art Museum; Denver Museum of Miniatures, Dolls, and Toys; Denver Museum of Natural History; Denver Zoo; Four Mile Historic Park; and the U.S. Mint).

Adventure Golf. 9650 N. Sheridan Blvd. (at 96th Ave.). ☎ **303/650-7587.** Admission $5.95 adults, $5.45 seniors over 65 and children 4–12. Easter to Halloween, daily 10am–11pm, weather permitting. Hours may be shorter in spring and fall. Closed in winter. Bus: 51.

Each of the 54 holes at this miniature golf course has a theme to challenge you, such as a haunted house, pirate battle, fairy castle, fire-breathing dragon, and fiery volcano. Or perhaps you'd prefer to visit "The Lost Continent," with "deadly" piranha pools and quicksand pits.

✪ Children's Museum of Denver. 2121 Children's Museum Dr. ☎ **303/433-7444.** Admission $5 ages 3–59, $3 seniors 60 and over, $2 ages 1–2. Memorial Day–Labor Day, daily 10am–5pm plus first Mon of every month Twilight Theatre open 6:30–8pm; Labor Day–Memorial Day, Tues–Sun 10am–5pm plus Mon school holidays. Take exit 211 (23rd Ave.) east off I-25; turn right on 7th St., and again on Children's Museum Dr.

Denver's best hands-on experience for children, this intriguing museum is both educational and just plain fun. Kids will enjoy the "Inventions" exhibit, comprised of four areas: an updated and expanded wood shop, where creative carpenters use wood and real tools, then take home whatever they make; an assembly line, where kids build a car and then test-drive it, fill the gas tank, check the air in the tires and water in the radiator, and even vacuum the interior; the "How's it Done?" house, which starts out with videos of how some things are made and ends with a house building site; and an interactive car—a 7½-foot replica that demonstrates how an automobile works.

The "Wild Oats Community Market" is a grocery/deli/bakery where children learn to plan meals, create a shopping list, get a cart and choose items, and go through the checkout (as items are "scanned" they go into a bin to be returned to the shelves).

There's also a computer lab where kids can log on to the Internet; Discovery Labs for exploring light, sound, electronics, and biology; a TV weather-forecasting studio; an exhibit where participants learn what it feels like to have various disabilities; and a gigantic mountain with year-round ski lessons. In yet another area, kids can examine size relationships by looking at the Denver Nuggets basketball team. Special events such as live theater take place periodically; call for schedules.

Elitch Gardens Amusement Park. Speer Blvd., at I-25 exit 212A. ☎ **303/595-4386.** Gate admission with unlimited rides, $24 those taller than 4 feet; $14 those 4 feet and under, and seniors 55–69; free for ages 3 and under and 70 and over. Memorial Day–Labor Day, daily 10am–10pm. Call for off-season hours.

A Denver tradition established in 1889, this amusement park moved to its present site in 1995. The 30-plus rides include Twister II, an unbelievable 10-story roller coaster with a 90-foot drop and dark, black tunnel; Disaster Canyon, a raging river-rapids ride—yes, you will get wet; the 250-foot Total Tower; and a fully restored 1925 carousel with 67 hand-carved horses and chariots. Kiddieland is just for children under 54 inches tall, with rides sized to fit. The amusement park also has musical revues and other entertainment, games and arcades, food, shopping, and beautiful flower gardens.

Funplex. 9670 W. Coal Mine Ave. (at Kipling St.), Littleton. ☎ **303/972-4344.** Admission varies by activity, $4–$6.50 (multi-activity tickets available). Memorial Day–Labor Day, daily 11am–10pm; Labor Day–Memorial Day, daily 4–10pm, call for activity availability. Bus: 67, 76.

This large indoor entertainment mall, with activities for adults as well as kids, offers 40 lanes of bowling, two 18-hole mini-golf courses, LaserTag, roller skating, a large (160 games) video arcade, Kids Korner and rides, billiards, two restaurants, and a sports bar with big-screen TV.

Lakeside Amusement Park. I-70 exit 271 and Sheridan Blvd. ☎ **303/477-1621.** Gate admission, $1.50. Ride coupons 25¢ (rides require 2 to 6 coupons each); unlimited rides, $10.75 Mon–Fri, $12.75 Sat–Sun and holidays. May, Sat–Sun and holidays noon–11pm; June to Labor Day, Mon–Fri 6–11pm, Sat–Sun and holidays noon–11pm. Kiddie Playland, Mon–Fri 1–10pm, Sat–Sun and holidays noon–10pm. Closed Labor Day–Apr.

Among the largest amusement parks in the Rocky Mountains, Lakeside has about 40 rides, including a Cyclone roller coaster, a midway with carnival and arcade games, and a miniature train that circles the lake. There are also food stands and picnic facilities, plus a separate Kiddies Playland with 15 rides.

Water World. 88th Ave. and Pecos St., Federal Heights. ☎ **303/427-SURF.** Admission $19.95 adults, $18.95 children 4–12, free for seniors and children under 4. Memorial Day to Labor Day, daily 10am–6pm. Closed in winter. Take the Thornton exit (exit 219, 84th Ave.) off I-25 north.

This 60-acre complex, billed as America's largest family water park, has two ocean-like wave pools, river rapids for inner-tubing, twisting water slides, a small children's play area, plus other attractions—32 in all.

WALKING TOUR
Downtown Denver

Start: Civic Center Park.
Finish: State Capitol.
Time: 2 to 8 hours, depending on how much time you spend shopping, eating, and sightseeing.
Best Times: Any Tuesday through Friday in late spring.
Worst Times: Monday and holidays, when the museums are closed.

Start your tour of the downtown area at:

1. **Civic Center Park,** a 2-square-block oasis featuring a Greek amphitheater, fountains, statues, flower gardens, and 30 different species of trees, two of which (it is said) were originally planted by Abraham Lincoln at his Illinois home.

    Overlooking the park on its east side is the State Capitol. On its south side are the:

2. **Colorado History Museum,** a staircaselike building with exhibits that make the state's colorful history come to life; the Denver Public Library; and the:

3. **Denver Art Museum.** Designed by Gio Ponti of Milan, Italy, the museum is a 28-sided, ten-story structure that resembles a medieval fortress with a skin of more than a million tiny glass tiles. Inside are 35,000 works of art, including a renowned American Indian collection.

    On the west side of Civic Center Park is the:

4. **City and County Building,** decorated in spectacular fashion with a rainbow of colored lights during the Christmas season.

    A block farther west is the:

5. **U.S. Mint.** Modeled in the Italian Renaissance style, the building resembles the Palazzo Riccardi in Florence. More than 60,000 cubic feet of granite and 1,000 tons of steel went into its construction in 1904.

    Cross over Colfax and go diagonally northwest up 14th Street. Four blocks ahead, on the left, is the:

6. **Colorado Convention Center,** with its impressive five-story, steplike white facade. Opened in June 1990, the million-square-foot building contains a 7-acre exhibit room and the largest ballroom between Chicago and Los Angeles.

    It's another 2 blocks up 14th to the:

7. **Denver Center for the Performing Arts,** covering 4 square blocks between 14th Street and Cherry Creek, Champa Street and Arapahoe Street. The complex is entered under a block-long, 80-foot-high glass archway. The center includes seven theaters, a symphony hall in the round, a voice-research laboratory, and a smoking solar fountain. Free tours are offered.

    Two more blocks up 14th past the arts center is:

8. **Larimer Square,** Denver's oldest commercial district. Restored turn-of-the-century Victorian buildings accommodate more than 30 shops and a dozen restaurants and clubs. Colorful awnings, hanging flower baskets, and quiet open courtyards accent the square, once home to such notables as Buffalo Bill Cody and Bat Masterson. Horse-drawn carriage rides originate here for trips up the 16th Street Mall or through lower downtown.

    A walkway at the east corner of Larimer and 15th leads through:

9. **Writer Square,** another shopping-and-dining complex with quaint gas lamps, brick walkways, and outdoor cafes.

Walking Tour—Downtown Denver

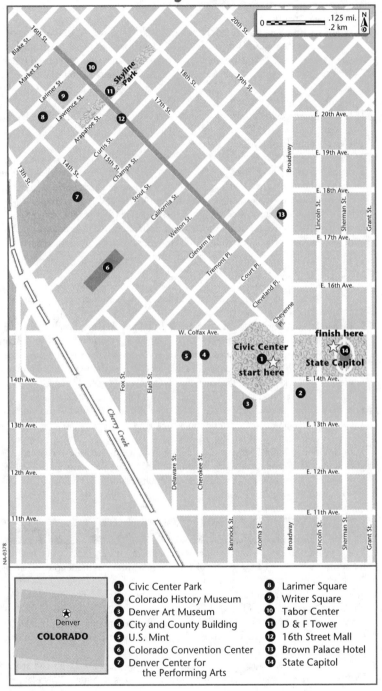

1 Civic Center Park
2 Colorado History Museum
3 Denver Art Museum
4 City and County Building
5 U.S. Mint
6 Colorado Convention Center
7 Denver Center for
   the Performing Arts
8 Larimer Square
9 Writer Square
10 Tabor Center
11 D & F Tower
12 16th Street Mall
13 Brown Palace Hotel
14 State Capitol

NA-0378

COLORADO
Denver

At 16th Street, cross to the:

10. Tabor Center, a glass-enclosed shopping complex on three levels. In effect a two-block-long greenhouse (with the Westin Hotel rising from within), the Tabor Center was developed by the Rouse Company, the same firm that created Faneuil Hall in Boston, South Street Seaport in New York, and Harborplace in Baltimore.

To the east, the Tabor Center is anchored by the:

11. D&F Tower, a city landmark patterned after the campanile of St. Mark's Basilica in Venice, Italy, in 1910.

Here, begin a leisurely stroll down the:

12. 16th Street Mall, with the State Capitol building to the southeast as your directional beacon. The $76-million pedestrian path is the finest people-watching spot in the city, where you'll see everyone from street entertainers to lunching office workers to travelers like yourself. Built of red and gray granite, it's lined with 200 red oak trees, a dozen fountains, and a lighting system straight out of *Star Wars*—not to mention the outdoor cafes, restored Victorian buildings, modern skyscrapers, and hundreds of shops, restaurants, and department stores. Through it run sleek European-built shuttle buses, offering free transportation up and down the mall as often as every 90 seconds.

You'll walk 7 blocks down 16th Street from the Tabor Center before reaching Tremont Place. Turn left, go a block farther, and across the street, on your right, you'll see the:

13. Brown Palace Hotel. One of the most beautiful grande dame hotels in the U.S., it was built in 1892 and features a nine-story atrium lobby topped by a Tiffany stained-glass ceiling. Step into the lobby for a look before continuing across Broadway on East 17th Avenue. Go 2 blocks to Sherman Street, turn right, and proceed 2 blocks south on Sherman to East Colfax Avenue.

You're back overlooking Civic Center Park, but this time, you're at the:

14. State Capitol. If you stand on the 15th step on the west side of the building, you're exactly 5,280 feet (1 mile) above sea level. Architects modeled the Colorado capitol after the U.S. Capitol building in Washington, D.C., and used the world's entire known supply of rare rose onyx in its interior wainscoting. A winding, 93-step staircase leads to an open-air viewing deck beneath the capitol dome; on a clear sunny day, your view can extend from Pikes Peak near Colorado Springs to the Wyoming border.

2 Organized Tours

Visitors who want in-the-know guides to show them the attractions of Denver and the surrounding areas have a variety of choices. In addition to the following, see the "Package Tours" section in chapter 3.

Half- and full-day bus tours of Denver and the nearby Rockies are offered by the ubiquitous **Gray Line,** P.O. Box 17646, Denver, CO 80217 (☎ **303/289-2841** for reservations and information, 800/348-6877 for information only). Included in fares are entry fees but no food. Tours depart the Denver Bus Center at 19th and Curtis streets.

Among other companies offering half- and full-day guided tours in and around Denver is **The Colorado Sightseer,** 6780 W. 84th Circle, Suite 60, Arvada, CO 80003 (☎ **303/423-8200**).

FOUR-WHEEL-DRIVE TOURS   For those who want to get off the well-traveled path, a back-roads mountain tour is just the ticket. Excursions to remote areas with spectacular scenery include trips to ghost towns, old mining camps, and historic wagon trails. Half- and full-day trips, plus nighttime star treks on mountaintops, are available.

One firm that offers these trips year-round is **Best Mountain Tours by the Mountain Men**, 3003 S. Macon Circle, Aurora, CO 80014 (☎ **303/750-5200** from 7am to 10pm). Destinations and daily availability vary. Typical rates are $35 per person for half-day tours, $60 to $65 for all-day tours. The Mountain Men also provide private group transportation to gambling casinos and ski resorts.

BICYCLING TOURS　A variety of bicycle tours are available in and around Denver. **WorldTrek Expeditions, Inc.** (☎ **800/795-1142** or 303/202-1142; www.worldtrekexpeditions.com) offers half-day bike tours of the Denver metropolitan area year-round, weather permitting, and half- and full-day tours in the mountains from May through September or October. Tours include round-trip transportation from Denver (hotel pickup and drop-off can be arranged), snack or lunch, front suspension bikes, protective gear, free water bottle, and professional guides. Reservations are required. Half-day trips cost $49 for adults, $39 children under 12; full-day, $75 and $55, respectively.

3　Outdoor Activities

Denver's proximity to the Rocky Mountains makes it possible to spend a day pursuing your favorite outdoor sport and return to the city by nightfall. Within the city limits and nearby, visitors will find more than 200 miles of jogging and bicycle paths, 100 or more free tennis courts, and several dozen public golf courses.

The city has an excellent system of **Mountain Parks** (☎ **303/697-4545**), covering some 13,488 acres (see "Parks & Gardens," earlier in this chapter).

Visitors tempted by the Denver area's outdoor recreation opportunities but who neglected to bring the necessary equipment are in luck, with several rental sources available. **Sports Rent,** 1402 S. Parker Rd., Unit A-108, Denver, CO 80231 (☎ **303/671-6700;** fax 303/671-9452), has just about everything imaginable. **Grand West Outfitters,** 801 Broadway, Denver, CO 80203 (☎ **303/825-0300**), rents camping gear and sells climbing gear, other equipment, and outdoor clothing; there's a rock-climbing wall in the store.

BALLOONING　You can't beat a hot-air balloon ride for viewing the magnificent Rocky Mountain scenery. **Life Cycle Balloon Adventures, Ltd.** (☎ **303/759-3907**) offers sunrise champagne flights daily, and has over 25 years of experience. **Colorado Balloon Rides** (☎ **800/873-8927**) generally schedules daily flights from Chatfield State Park southwest of the city, but will happily customize your flight. **Looney Balloons** (☎ **303/979-9476**) offers daily 1-hour flights year-round.

BICYCLING　Denver is crisscrossed everywhere by paved bicycle paths, including a 12-mile scenic stretch along the bank of the South Platte River and along Cherry Creek beside Speer Boulevard. All told, the city has 85 miles of off-road trails for bikers and runners. Bike paths link the city's 205 parks, and many city streets are marked with bike lanes. In all, the city has more than 130 miles of designated bike paths and lanes. For more information, contact the Denver visitor center or **Bicycle Colorado** (☎ **303/798-1429**). Contact WorldTrek Expeditions, Inc. (see "Organized Tours," above) for tours.

BOATING　A quiet way to view some of downtown Denver is from a punt on scenic Cherry Creek. **Punt the Creek** (☎ **303/893-0750**) operates Tuesday through Sunday from 4 to 9pm, Memorial Day to Labor Day. Guides describe the history of the city while pointing out famous landmarks. Tickets are available at the kiosk at Creekfront Plaza, Speer Boulevard and Larimer Street ($7 for adults, $3.50 for children, $6 for seniors).

Boaters enjoy the powerboat marinas at **Cherry Creek State Park,** 4201 S. Parker Rd., Aurora, CO 80014 (☎ **303/699-3860**), 11 miles from downtown off I-225; and **Chatfield State Park,** 11500 N. Roxborough Park Rd., Littleton, CO 80125 (☎ **303/791-7275**), 16 miles south of downtown Denver off Colo. 470. Both also permit jet skiing and sailboarding. Wakeless boating is popular at **Barr Lake State Park,** 13401 Picadilly Rd., Brighton, CO 80601 (☎ **303/659-6005**), 21 miles northeast of downtown via I-76.

BOWLING   One of Denver's biggest bowling centers is the 40-lane **Funplex,** 9670 W. Coal Mine Ave., Littleton (☎ **303/972-4344**), open Memorial Day to Labor Day, daily from 11am to 10pm; and in winter, daily from 4 to 10pm.

FISHING   A couple of good bets in the metropolitan area are Chatfield State Park, with trout, bass, and panfish, and Cherry Creek State Park, which boasts trout, walleye pike, bass, and crappie (see "Boating," above).

Sporting-goods stores can provide detailed information. The skilled and experienced staff at **The Flyfisher Ltd.,** 120 Madison St. (☎ **303/322-5014**), can help with equipment choices and recommendations for where to go on any given day. They also offers lessons, seminars, clinics, and guided trips.

GOLF   Throughout the Front Range, it's often said that you can play golf at least 320 days a year—that the sun always seems to be shining, and even when it snows, the little snow that sticks melts quickly. There are more than 50 courses in the Denver area, including seven municipal golf courses, with non-resident greens fees for 18 holes of $19 to $22. Among the city courses is **City Park Golf Course,** East 25th Avenue and York Street (☎ **303/295-4420**). For information and other locations, call the **Denver Department of Parks and Recreation** (☎ **303/964-2563**).

HIKING & BACKPACKING   For hikes specific to the Denver area, contact the city **Department of Parks and Recreation** (☎ **303/964-2500**) for information on Denver's park system. A good source for maps and hiking guides is **Maps Unlimited by Pierson Graphics,** 899 Broadway, Denver, CO 80203 (☎ **800/456-8703** or 303/623-4299). The Colorado Trail is a hiking, horse, and mountain-biking route stretching 500 miles from Denver to Durango (see "Hiking, Backpacking & Mountaineering," in chapter 5).

Mount Falcon Park offers excellent trails that are easy to moderate in difficulty, making this a good place for families with children. There are also picnic areas, shelters, and ruins of an old castlelike home. From Denver, go west on U.S. 285 and then south on Colo. 8; the park is open daily from dawn to dusk, and admission is free. Mountain bikes and horses are permitted, as are leashed dogs.

HORSEBACK RIDING   Equestrians can find a mount year-round at **Stockton's Plum Creek Stables,** 7479 W. Titan Rd., Littleton (☎ **303/791-1966**), near Chatfield State Park, 15 miles south of downtown. Guided rides, by appointment only, are about $20 per hour; children must be at least 8 years old. Stockton's also offers hayrides and barbecue picnics. **Paint Horse Stables,** 4201 S. Parker Rd., Aurora (☎ **303/690-8235**), at Cherry Creek State Park, also rents horses boards horses and provides riding lessons, hay rides, and pony rides for kids.

SKIING   Several ski resorts are close to Denver. See chapter 9 for details on **Eldora Mountain Resort,** 45 miles west via Boulder. See chapter 11 for information on **Loveland Basin,** 56 miles west via I-70; **Winter Park Resort,** 73 miles west of Denver via I-70 and U.S. 40; and **Berthoud Pass Ski Area,** near Winter Park. Eldora and Winter Park offer Nordic as well as alpine terrain.

Some useful Denver telephone numbers for skiers: **ski-area information** ☎ 303/825-7669, **snowboarding report** ☎ 303/573-7433, **weather report** ☎ 303/337-2500, **road conditions** ☎ 303/639-1111.

TENNIS   The Denver Department of Parks and Recreation (☎ **303/964-2500**) manages or owns close to 150 tennis courts, more than a third of them lit for night play. In all, you'll find tennis courts at 26 city parks, with lighted courts at 11 parks. Among the most popular courts are those located in City Park (York St. and E. 17th Ave.), Berkeley Park (Tennyson St. and W. 17th Ave.), Green Valley East Ranch Park (Jebel St. and E. 45th Ave.), Washington Park (S. Downing St. and E. Louisiana Ave.), and Sloan Lake Park (Sheridan Blvd. and W. 17th Ave.). Many public courts are free, and some charge about $5 per hour. It's generally easier to find space at an outlying court than one in downtown Denver. For more information on tennis possibilities, contact the **Colorado Tennis Association,** 1191 S. Parker Rd., Suite 101, Denver, CO 80231 (☎ **303/695-4116**).

GREAT NEARBY OUTDOOR AREAS

BARR LAKE STATE PARK   About 25 miles northeast of Denver via I-76 in Brighton, this wildlife sanctuary of 2,600 acres comprises a prairie reservoir and surrounding wetlands and uplands. Boats with motors exceeding 10 horsepower are not allowed, but you can sail, paddle, or row, as well as fish. On site are a 9-mile hiking and biking trail circling the lake, nature center, heron rookery, and three picnic areas. A commercial campground is opposite the park on the west side. The park entrance is at 13401 Picadilly Rd. Admission costs $4 per vehicle. Call ☎ 303/659-6005 for more information.

CASTLEWOOD CANYON STATE PARK   Steep canyons, a meandering stream, a waterfall, lush vegetation, and considerable wildlife distinguish this 1,000-acre park. You can see the remains of Castlewood Canyon Dam, which was built for irrigation in 1890; it collapsed in 1933, killing two people. The park, 30 miles south of Denver on Colo. 83, east of Castle Rock in Franktown, provides picnic facilities and hiking trails. The entrance is at 2989 S. State Highway 83; admission is $4 per vehicle. Call ☎ **303/688-5242** for more information.

CHATFIELD STATE PARK   Just 8 miles south of downtown Denver via U.S. 85 in Littleton, this park occupies 5,600 acres of prairie against a backdrop of the steeply rising Rocky Mountains. Chatfield Reservoir, with a 26-mile shoreline, invites swimming, boating, fishing, and other water sports. The area also has 18 miles of paved bicycle trails, plus hiking and horseback-riding paths. In winter, there's ice-fishing and cross-country skiing.

An observation area on the south side of the park permits viewing of a 27-acre nature-study grove, closed during nesting season. Facilities include 153 pull-through campsites, showers, laundry, and dump station. Admission is $4 per vehicle; camping, $9 to $12. The entrance is located a quarter-mile south of Deer Creek Canyon Road and Colo. 121 (☎ **303/791-7275**).

CHERRY CREEK STATE PARK   The 880-acre Cherry Creek Reservoir, created for flood control by the construction of a dam in 1950, offers swimming, water-skiing, boating, and fishing in summer; and skating, ice-fishing, and ice-boating in winter. The park comprises 3,900 acres about 12 miles southeast of downtown Denver (off Parker Road and I-225). There's a nature trail, dog-training area, model-airplane field with paved runways, rifle range, pistol range, and trap-shooting area. Six miles of paved bicycle paths and 10 miles of bridle trails circle the reservoir (horse rentals are available). Rangers offer evening programs and guided walks on a 1½-mile nature trail. Each of the park's 102 campsites (40 with electric hookups) has access to showers, laundry, and dump station.

Admission is $5 per vehicle; camping, $9 to $12. Campgrounds are closed November through March. The entrance is at 4201 S. Parker Rd. in Aurora. Call ☎ **303/690-1166** for general information or ☎ **800/678-2267** for camping reservations.

GOLDEN GATE STATE PARK   One hour west of Denver, this 14,000-acre park ranges in elevation from 7,600 to 10,400 feet, and offers camping, picnicking, hiking, biking, fishing, hunting, and horseback-riding opportunities. Admission costs $4; camping is $7 to $12 in developed campgrounds (168 developed sites, with a few electric hookups) and $3 to $5 for backcountry. Showers and laundry facilities are provided at Reverend's Ridge, the park's largest campground.

To get to Golden Gate, take Colo. 93 north from Golden 1 mile to Golden Gate Canyon Road. Turn left and continue 15 miles to the park. For more information, call ☎ **303/582-3707.**

4 Spectator Sports

Tickets to many sporting events can be obtained from **The Ticketman,** 6800 N. Broadway, #103, Denver, CO 80221 (☎ **800/200-TIXS** or 303/430-1111), with delivery to your hotel available; or **TicketMaster** (☎ **303/830-TIXS**), with several outlets in the Denver area.

AUTO RACING   For drag racing, head to **Bandimere Speedway,** 3051 S. Rooney Rd., Morrison (☎ **303/697-6001** or 303/697-4870 for a 24-hour recording), with races scheduled April through October. There are special events for high school students, motorcycles, pickup trucks, street cars, and sports cars, plus car shows, swap meets, and even volleyball tournaments.

Colorado National Speedway, at I-25 exit 232, 20 minutes north of Denver (☎ **303/665-4173**), has NASCAR Winston Racing, superstocks, and RMMRA midgets on a three-eighths-mile asphalt oval track, weekends from April through September.

BASEBALL   The **Colorado Rockies,** which began life as a National League expansion team in 1993, have taken over the Colorado sports scene with a vengeance. The team plays at Coors Field, in the historic lower downtown section of Denver. The 50,000-seat stadium, with its red-brick exterior, was designed in the style of baseball stadiums of old. For information and tickets, call **ROCKIES** (☎ **800/388-7625** or 303/762-5437; www.coloradorockies.com).

BASKETBALL   The **Denver Nuggets** (☎ **303/893-6700** for ticket information), of the National Basketball Association, play their home games at McNichols Sports Arena, 1635 Clay St. (☎ **303/640-7300**). There are 41 home games a year between November and April, with playoffs continuing into June. The **Colorado Xplosion** (☎ **303/832-2225**), a professional women's basketball team, play at the Denver Coliseum and McNichols Sports Arena.

The **University of Denver** (☎ **303/871-2336** for ticket office) plays a competitive college basketball schedule from late November through March, in addition to women's gymnastics, men's hockey, and other sports.

FOOTBALL   The **Denver Broncos** (☎ 303/433-7466 for tickets) of the National Football League make their home at Mile High Stadium, part of a sports complex reached at exit 210B of I-25. Home games are sold out months in advance, so call early. Your best bet may be to find someone hawking tickets outside the stadium entrance on game day.

You'll have better luck getting into a college game. The **University of Colorado Buffaloes** in Boulder play in the Big Eight Conference. For ticket information, call ☎ **303/492-8337.** Other top college football teams in the area can be found at Colorado State University in Fort Collins and at the Air Force Academy in Colorado Springs.

GREYHOUND RACING   The **Mile High Greyhound Park,** East 62nd Avenue and Colorado Boulevard, in Commerce City (☎ **303/288-1591**), has pari-mutuel dog races from June to February, with afternoon and evening events. Call for the current schedule.

HOCKEY   Denver's National Hockey League team, the **Colorado Avalanche** (☎ **303/893-6700** for ticket information), began playing in Denver during the 1995–1996 season, with games at McNichols Sports Arena, 1635 Clay St. The season runs from October through April.

Coloradans went wild in June 1996 when the Avalanche surprised everyone by winning the prestigious Stanley Cup, Colorado's first championship in any major league sport. The Avalanche had begun its season by beating the highly rated Detroit Red Wings, and then, led by Most Valuable Player Joe Sakic, demolished the Florida Panthers to bring the Stanley Cup home to Denver, where the team was met by a screaming throng of 450,000 fans and a ticker-tape parade.

HORSE RACING   Arapahoe Park, at 26000 E. Quincy Ave., Aurora (☎ **303/690-2400**), offers pari-mutuel horse racing each summer with simulcast racing the rest of the year.

RODEO   The **National Western Stock Show and Rodeo** (☎ **303/297-1166**) is held the second and third weeks of January, with the rodeo at the Denver Coliseum and other activities at the National Western Complex and the Event Center. With more than $400,000 available in prize money, this is one of the world's richest rodeos.

SOCCER   The **Colorado Rapids** (☎ **800/844-7777** or 303/299-1599) brought soccer fame to Denver in 1997 with major league soccer's Western Conference Championship. The team plays at Mile High Stadium.

5 Shopping

If you're in Denver on foot, you'll find that most visitors do their shopping along the **16th Street Mall** and adjacent areas, including **Larimer Square, The Shops at Tabor Center, Writer Square,** and (just slightly farther away) **Tivoli Denver.**

For those who don't mind leaving the downtown area, there are more options, primarily the huge **Cherry Creek Shopping Center**—a shopper's dream—located to the south of downtown. There are also numerous suburban shopping malls.

Business hours vary from store to store and from mall to mall. Generally, stores are open six days a week, with many open on Sunday, too; department stores usually stay open until 9pm at least one evening a week. Discount stores and supermarkets are often open later than other stores, and some supermarkets are open 24 hours a day.

SHOPPING A TO Z
ANTIQUES

Denver's main antiques area is along **South Broadway,** between Mississippi and Iowa Streets, with some 400 dealers selling all sorts of fine antiques, collectibles, and junk. It's great fun wandering through the gigantic rooms, where each dealer has his or her little space. Just remember that prices are often negotiable; unless you're quite knowledgeable about antiques, it wouldn't hurt to do some comparison shopping before making a major purchase.

A major part of Antique Row is taken up by the **Antique Guild** (☎ 303/ 722-3365), an antiques dealers' mall in the 1200 block of South Broadway and the adjacent **Antique Market** (☎ 303/744-0281). Together they have more than 250 dealers selling every type of antique and collectible imaginable, as well as an historic soda fountain.

Serious antiques hunters will also want to explore the **Antique Mall of Lakewood,** 9635 W. Colfax Ave. (☎ 303/238-6940), which has a 34,000-square-foot showroom where some 200 antiques dealers display a wide variety of items from the 18th and 19th centuries, as well as more recent collectibles.

ART & FINE CRAFTS

The renaissance of Denver's Lower Downtown (LoDo) has resulted in the creation of the **Lower Downtown Arts District,** where you can explore more than two dozen galleries. The district runs from Larimer to Wazee streets between 14th and 25th streets. Art walks take place from 5 to 9pm on the first Friday of each month. Call ☎ **303/820-3139** for additional information.

Camera Obscura. 1309 Bannock St. ☎ **303/623-4059.** Closed Mon.

This highly respected photographic gallery exhibits vintage and contemporary photographs, including works by such renowned photographers as Henri Cartier-Bresson and Annie Liebowitz.

Core New Art Space. 1412 Wazee St. ☎ **303/571-4831.**

This lower downtown cooperative gallery features experimental art. A move is planned in 1999; call for new location.

Merrill Gallery of Fine Art, Ltd. 1401 17th St. (at Market St.). ☎ **303/292-1401.**

Established national and emerging regional artists are represented at this beautiful gallery in LoDo, which is known for its traditional and contemporary works of realism.

Mudhead Gallery. 321 17th St. ☎ **303/293-9977.**

This gallery, located in the Brown Palace Hotel, has contemporary and historic American Indian pottery, baskets, weavings, and jewelry, plus western and southwestern art. There's another location at the Hyatt Regency Hotel, 555 17th St. (☎ **303/293-0007**).

Native American Trading Company. 1301 Bannock St. ☎ **303/534-0771.**

Older weavings, ceramics, baskets, jewelry, and other American Indian works are sold at this fine gallery. Appropriately, it's across the street from the Denver Art Museum.

Pismo Contemporary Art Glass. 235 Fillmore St. ☎ **303/333-2879.**

Nationally renowned glass artists as well as emerging artists are represented in this gallery, located in Cherry Creek North.

Turner Gallery. 301 University Blvd. ☎ **303/355-1828.**

Colorado's oldest gallery specializes in traditional art forms, including oils and landscapes (many of Colorado scenes) by American and European painters. Its collection also includes etchings, engravings, and antique botanicals by early Colorado artists.

BOOKS

Barnes & Noble Booksellers. 9370 Sheridan Blvd. (north of U.S. 36 Sheridan Blvd. exit), Westminster. ☎ **303/426-7733.**

It's hard to imagine any popular book or music item that you won't be able to find at Barnes & Noble, and often at a discounted price. There's a particularly good travel section, where you'll also find local and regional maps. The store has a well-stocked music department plus multimedia software, and of course there's a Starbucks Coffee attached.

Other Denver-area Barnes & Noble Booksellers are at 14015 E. Exposition Ave., Aurora (☎ **303/366-8928**); 8555 E. Arapahoe Rd., Englewood (☎ **303/796-8851**); 960 S. Colorado Blvd., Glendale (☎ **303/691-2998**); and 8136 W. Bowles Ave., Littleton (☎ **303/948-9565**).

Borders. 9515 E. County Line Rd. (at I-25 and E. County Line Rd., across from Park Meadows Shopping Center), Englewood ☎ **303/708-1735**.

You'll find a large selection of books of all types plus recorded music at Borders. There's a well-stocked travel section, local and regional maps, and all the latest fiction and nonfiction. You can also stop at the in-store Cafe Espresso for a cup of your favorite coffee and a fresh-baked pastry.

✪ **Tattered Cover Book Store.** 2955 E. First Ave. (opposite Cherry Creek Shopping Center). ☎ **800/833-9327** or 303/322-7727. www.tatteredcover.com.

This bookstore is so big, it supplies maps to help you find your way through its maze of shelves, which contain just about any book anyone could possibly want. Comfortable chairs are placed strategically throughout the building for those who want to check out the first chapter before buying, or to rest up after a hike to the fourth floor. The store also provides a wide selection of newspapers and magazines, a bargain book section, free gift wrapping, disabled access to all four floors via elevator, mail order, and out-of-print search services. In addition, there's a full-service coffee bar, an enclosed rooftop restaurant specializing in new American cuisine, and storytelling in the children's section every Tuesday at 11am and Saturday at 10:30am. Hours are Monday through Saturday from 9am to 11pm, Sunday from 10am to 6pm.

The **Tattered Cover** has a second location in Denver's LoDo at 16th and Wynkoop streets, on the 16th Street Mall (☎ **303/436-1070**).

The Hue-Man Experience. 911 Park Ave. West (between Curtis and Champa sts.). ☎ **303/293-2665.**

This bookstore specializes in African and African-American subjects, including children's books, fine art prints, and magazines.

FASHION

Eddie Bauer Outlet. 3000 E. Cherry Creek Ave. (in the Cherry Creek Mall). ☎ **303/377-2100.**

This is the place to come for good deals on the famous Eddie Bauer line of upscale outdoor clothing. You'll find discontinued and overstocked items at reduced prices.

Lawrence Covell. 225 Steele St. (in Cherry Creek North). ☎ **303/320-1023.**

This upscale shop, established in 1967 by Lawrence and Cathy Covell, offers the finest quality men's and women's fashions, including designer clothing by Ermenegildo Zegna, Vestimenta, Luciano Barbera, and Ralph Lauren Purple Label.

Sheplers. 8500 E. Orchard Rd., Englewood. ☎ **303/773-3311.** www.sheplers.com. At I-25 exit 198.

Billing itself as the world's largest western clothing store, Sheplers sells boots, cowboy hats, western shirts, fancy skirts, belt buckles, scarves, jackets, plenty of jeans, and just about everything else western.

Another **Sheplers** is at 10300 Bannock St., Northglenn, at 104th Avenue (☎ **303/450-9999**).

Timbuktu Station. 1512 Larimer St. ☎ **303/820-3739.**

A good selection of upscale casual clothing and unique accessories is available here.

The Woolrich Store. 6900 W. 117th Ave., Broomfield. ☎ **303/469-5257.**

This outlet store, located at the factory off U.S. 36 between Denver and Boulder, sells top-quality woolens and other outdoor clothing, plus accessories and wool blankets.

FOOD & DRINK

Safeway, King Soopers, and **Albertson's** are the main grocery-store chains.

Applejack Liquors. 3320 Youngfield St. (in the Applewood Shopping Center), Wheat Ridge (I-70 exit 264). ☎ **800/879-5225** or 303/233-3331.

This huge store, which covers some 40,000 square feet and claims to be Colorado's largest beer, wine, and liquor supermarket, offers some of the best prices in the area as well as delivery. The store has a wide choice of single malt Scotches; an extensive wine section, which includes a number of Colorado wines; and a good selection of cigars. It's open Monday through Thursday until 10pm, and Friday and Saturday until 11pm.

Argonaut Wine & Liquor Supermarket. 700 East Colfax Ave. (at Washington St.). ☎ **303/831-7788.** www.argonautliquor.com.

You'll find an excellent selection of wines, as well as beer and liquor, at good prices at this large store, which is located just 4 blocks east of the State Capitol. It's open Monday through Thursday until 10pm, Friday and Saturday until 11:45pm.

Stephany's Chocolates. 6770 W. 52nd St., Arvada (north of I-70 via Wadsworth Blvd.). ☎ **800/888-1522** or 303/421-7229. www.stephanys-chocolates.com.

Denver's largest manufacturer and wholesaler of gourmet confections is best known for its Denver Mint and Colorado Almond Toffee. In business for more than three decades, it offers tours twice daily on weekdays, by advance reservation only. Retail outlets are located in malls throughout the city.

Wild Oats. 201 University Blvd. ☎ **800/494-9453** or 303/320-9071. www.wildoats.com.

Already an institution in the Denver area, this huge natural-foods store—50,000 square feet in area—helps perpetuate Coloradans' healthy lifestyles. No food sold here contains artificial flavoring or preservatives, nor was any grown using pesticides, chemicals, or other additives. There's a juice and health-food bar as well. This Cherry Creek–area store opened in 1990; others are scattered throughout the metropolitan area.

Gifts & Souvenirs

Colorado History Museum Store. 1300 Broadway. ☎ **303/866-4993.**

This museum shop carries unique made-in-Colorado gifts and souvenirs, including American Indian jewelry and sand paintings, plus an excellent selection of books on Colorado.

Earth Works, Ltd. 1421-B Larimer Square. ☎ **303/825-3390.**

Here you'll find handcrafted work by Colorado artisans, including pottery, jewelry, photos, candles, and posters. Of special note are the Colorado-made hot sauces and salsas, plus other gourmet foods.

Lokstok 'N Barel. 1421 Larimer Square. ☎ **303/825-3436.**

This Larimer Square shop sells a variety of western and wildlife bronze sculptures, aspen vases, jewelry, antique toy reproductions, and a wide variety of Colorado-made souvenirs.

Made in Colorado. 4840 W. 29th Ave. (☎ **800/272-1046** or 303/480-9050. www.madeincolorado.com.

You can take home a piece of Colorado with a stop at this shop, which also has a mail-order department. The wide variety of gift and souvenir items ranges from Mesa Verde pottery and hand-blown glass to hand-dipped decorated candles, aspen wood vases, art, jewelry, and foods of many descriptions, all made in Colorado.

Jewelry

Atlantis Gems, Inc. 718 16th St. Mall. ☎ **800/659-6404** or 303/825-3366.

This store features unique custom jewelry plus a large selection of loose gemstones and exotic minerals. It also stocks fossils, estate jewelry, and vintage watches; a gemologist and goldsmith are on-site.

Jeweler's Center at the University Building. 910 16th St. ☎ **303/534-6270.**

Here you'll find 12 floors of retail and wholesale outlets, in what is billed as Denver's largest concentration of jewelers.

John Atencio. 1440 Larimer St. (on Larimer Square). ☎ **303/534-4277** or 800/466-6944, PIN 4277.

A highly regarded Colorado artist, John Atencio has received several awards for his unique jewelry designs. Located on historic Larimer Square in downtown Denver, his store offers 14- and 18-karat gold jewelry accented with high quality stones, plus special collections such as "Elements," unusual combinations of gold, sterling silver, and stones.

Malls & Shopping Centers

Castle Rock Factory Shops. I-25 exit 184, about 20 minutes south of Denver. ☎ **303/688-4494.**

This outlet mall between Denver and Colorado Springs has well over 100 outlet stores, including Corning Revere, Levi's, Van Heusen, Calvin Klein, Eddie Bauer, Black & Decker, Sony, Bass, Nike, Big Dog, Guess?, Athlete's Foot, Farberware, GAP, and Toy Liquidators, plus a food court. Although many prices are the same as you'd find during a sale at your local mall or discount store, there's a nice selection and a few real bargains, especially on end-of-season items, reconditioned Sony electronics and Black & Decker tools, and irregulars. An information booth in the food court has maps of the outlet center; wheelchair rentals are available. Open Monday through Saturday from 10am to 9pm, Sunday from 11am to 6pm.

Cherry Creek Shopping Center. 3000 E. First Ave. (between University Blvd. and Steele St.). ☎ **800/424-6360** or 303/388-3900.

Saks Fifth Avenue, Neiman Marcus, Foley's, and Lord and Taylor anchor this deluxe million-square-foot mall, with more than 160 shops, restaurants, and services, including an eight-screen movie theater. Across the street is Cherry Creek North, an upscale neighborhood retail area. Open Monday through Friday from 10am to 9pm, Saturday from 10am to 7pm, and Sunday from 11am to 6pm.

Larimer Square. 1400 block of Larimer St. ☎ **303/534-2367.**

This restored quarter of old Denver (see "Attractions," above) includes numerous art galleries, boutiques, restaurants, and nightclubs. Most shops are open Monday through Thursday from 10am to 8pm, Friday and Saturday from 10am to 9pm, and Sunday from noon to 5pm. Restaurant and nightclub hours vary, and hours are slightly shorter in winter.

Mile High Flea Market. 7007 E. 88th Ave. (at I-76), Henderson. ☎ **303/289-4656.**

Just 10 minutes northeast of downtown Denver, this huge market attracts more than 1.5 million shoppers a year to its 80 paved acres. Besides close-outs, garage sales, and seasonal merchandise, it has more than a dozen places to eat and snack, plus family rides. It's open year-round on Wednesday, Saturday, and Sunday from 7am to 5pm. Admission is $2 Saturday and Sunday, $1 Wednesday, and free for children under 12.

The Shops at Tabor Center. 16th Street Mall (at Lawrence St.). ☎ **303/572-6865.**

About 60 specialty shops, services, and eateries are in this 2-block, glass-enclosed galleria. You'll find upscale clothing, toys, books, gifts and collectibles, as well as more than a dozen dining spots. Open Monday through Friday from 10am to 9pm, Saturday from 10am to 6pm, and Sunday from noon to 5pm.

Tivoli Student Union. 900 Auraria Pkwy. ☎ **303/556-6329** or 303/556-6330.

Transformed from a 19th-century brewery, this building has been home to Auraria's Student Union since 1994. It contains shops, cafes, restaurants, and movie theaters, plus a TicketMaster outlet for both campus and city events and even ski-lift tickets. Shops are open Monday through Saturday from 10am to 9pm, Sunday from noon to 5pm.

SPORTING GOODS

Active travelers who want to pick up a few supplies will be pleased to discover that Denver has the world's largest sporting-goods store: **Gart Sports Castle,** on Broadway at 10th Avenue (☎ **303/861-1122;** www.gartsports.com). There are also a number of Gart outlets in the Denver area.

REI also has several stores in the metro area, including an outlet at 5375 S. Wadsworth Blvd. (☎ **303/932-0600;** www.rei.com); those in need of a new bike may want to stop at **Bicycle Village,** 6300 E. Colfax Ave. (☎ **303/355-5339;** www.bicyclevillage.com), which claims the distinction of being the world's largest Schwinn dealer.

Sports fans looking for that Rockies cap or Broncos shirt will have no trouble finding exactly what they seek at the appropriately named **Sportsfan,** 1720 Federal Blvd. (☎ **303/455-6303**). There are several other locations in the Denver area, and mail orders are accepted.

For information on where to rent sporting-goods equipment, see the "Outdoor Activities" section earlier in this chapter.

TOYS & HOBBIES

✪ **Caboose Hobbies.** 500 S. Broadway. ☎ **303/777-6766.**

Model-train buffs should plan to spend at least half a day here. Billed as the world's largest train store, there are electric trains, accessories, books, and so much train-related stuff that it's hard to know where to start. Knowledgeable employees will help you choose whatever you need, and they seem just as happy to talk about trains as to sell them. Naturally, there are model trains of every scale winding through the store, as well as test tracks so you can check out a locomotive before purchasing it. There are also mugs, patches, and decals from just about every railroad line that ever existed in North America.

The Wizard's Chest. 230 Fillmore St. ☎ **303/321-4304.**

The magical store design—a castle with drawbridge and moat—and legendary wizard out front are worth the trip alone, but be sure to go inside. The Wizard's Chest, located in Cherry Creek, is paradise for kids of all ages, specializing in games, toys, and puzzles. The costume department is fully stocked, from costumes, wigs, and masks to professional makeup.

6 Denver After Dark

Denver's performing-arts and nightlife scene, an important part of this increasingly sophisticated western city, is anchored by the 4-square-block, $80-million **Denver Performing Arts Complex,** located downtown just a few blocks from major hotels. The complex houses nine theaters, a concert hall, and what may be the nation's first symphony hall in the round. It is home to the Colorado Symphony, Colorado Ballet, Opera Colorado, and the Denver Center for the Performing Arts (an umbrella organization for resident and touring theater companies).

In all, Denver has some 30 theaters, more than 100 cinemas, and dozens of concert halls, nightclubs, discos, and bars. Clubs offer country-and-western music, jazz, rock, and comedy acts.

Current entertainment listings are presented in special Friday-morning sections of the two daily newspapers—the *Denver Post* and *Rocky Mountain News. Westword,* a weekly newspaper distributed free throughout the city every Wednesday, has perhaps the best listings of all. The *Denver Post* provides information on movie show times and theaters; call ☎ **303/777-FILM** or check out **www.777film.com**.

Tickets for nearly all major entertainment and sporting events can be obtained from **The Ticketman,** 6800 N. Broadway, #103, Denver, CO 80221 (☎ **800/ 200-TIXS** or 303/430-1111), with delivery to your hotel available. Also try **Ticket-Master** (☎ **303/830-TIXS**), with several outlets in the Denver area.

THE CLUB & MUSIC SCENE
ROCK, JAZZ & BLUES

Bluebird Theater. 3317 E. Colfax Ave. (at Adams St.). ☎ **303/322-2308**. www.thebluebird.com/bluebird.

This historic theater, built in 1913 to show silent movies, has been restored and now offers a diverse selection of jazz, rock, alternative, and other live music, as well as films.

El Chapultepec. 1962 Market St. ☎ **303/295-9126.**

Denver's oldest jazz club, the "Pec" offers live jazz nightly in a noisy, friendly atmosphere, where you'll often find standing room only.

Herman's Hideaway. 1578 S. Broadway (near Iowa Ave.). ☎ **303/777-5840.**

Considered one of the best spots in Denver to hear original rock music by bands on their way up, there's usually live music Wednesday through Saturday nights.

Jimmy's Grille. 320 S. Birch St., Glendale. ☎ **303/322-5334.**

If you're looking for live reggae, this is the place to go, at least on Thursday, Friday, and Saturday nights. Other nights you might catch blues, jazz, or whoever happens to be in town, but it's always live. Jimmy's also has drinks, burgers, sandwiches, and Tex-Mex specials galore, plus events such as the annual pig roast each May.

The Mercury Cafe. 2199 California St. (at 22nd St.). ☎ **303/294-9281**. www.mercurycafe.com.

It's hard to classify the Mercury as specializing in any one genre of music, but there's always something exciting happening, even on poetry night. Offerings range from avant-garde jazz to classical violin and harp to big band to progressive rock.

Synergy. 3240 Larimer St. ☎ **303/296-9515.**

The high energy here will keep you dancing all night, and it may take several days before you can hear again after a night at Synergy.

Supreme Court Cafe & Nightclub. 1550 Court Place. ☎ **303/892-6878.**

Pouring out onto the 16th Street Mall, the Supreme Court is the spot for live and loud dance music, food-laden happy hours, and beach parties complete with Hawaiian drinks and imported beach sand.

COUNTRY MUSIC

The Grizzly Rose. 5450 N. Valley Hwy. ☎ **303/295-1330.** At I-25 exit 215.

Known to locals as "the Griz" or "the Rose," its 5,000-square-foot dance floor beneath a one-acre roof draws such national acts as George Thorogood, Garth Brooks, Willie Nelson, Don Williams, Creedence Clearwater Revival, Tanya Tucker, and Johnny Paycheck. There's live music every night of the week; Sunday is family night. The cafe serves a full-service menu, and dance lessons are available.

Stampede Mesquite Grill & Dance Emporium. 2430 S. Havana St. (at Parker Rd.), Aurora. ☎ **303/337-6909.**

At this nightclub you'll find free country-western dance lessons nightly, a huge solid-oak dance floor, pool tables, a restaurant, and seven bars. It's located off I-225 exit 4 (north on Parker Road about 2 miles to Havana Street). Closed Mondays.

THE BAR SCENE

The first permanent structure built on the site of modern Denver was supposedly a saloon, and the city has been adding to that tradition ever since. Today there are sports bars, dance bars, lots of brew pubs, outdoor cafe bars, English pubs, Old West saloons, city-overlook bars, art-deco bars, gay bars, and a few bars we don't want to discuss here.

Appropriately, the newest Denver "in" spot for barhopping is also the oldest part of the city—LoDo—which has been renovated and upgraded, and now attracts all the smart generation Xers and other young professionals. Its trendy nightspots are often noisy and crowded, but if you're looking for action, this is where it's at.

Glendale, an enclave completely surrounded by southeastern Denver where Colorado Boulevard crosses Cherry Creek, is another popular hangout for Denver's smart set. An unusual zoning situation has led to more than a dozen drinking establishments built into a small, concentrated area.

Brewery Tours

Whether or not you drink beer, it can be fun to look behind the scenes and see how beer is made. Denver's first modern microbrewery—the **Wynkoop Brewing Co.,** 1634 18th St., at Wynkoop Street (☎ 303/297-2700)—offers tours every Saturday from 1 to 5pm. Housed in the renovated 1898 J. S. Brown Mercantile Building across from Union Station, the Wynkoop is also a popular restaurant (see "Dining," in chapter 6). Six beers are always on tap; the "taster set" provides a nice sampling: six 4-ounce glasses of different brews. For nonbeer drinkers, the Wynkoop offers some of the best root beer in town. On the second floor is a top-notch pool hall with billiards, snooker, and darts.

Since it opened in November 1991, **Rock Bottom Brewery,** 1001 16th St. (☎ 303/534-7616), has been one of the leading brew pubs in the area. Tours, given on request, offer great views of the brewing process, plus a sampling of the product. The Rock Bottom also has eight billiard tables and a good brew pub menu, starting at $6.

Another Denver brewery that lets you see the brewing process is **Brecken-ridge Brewery,** 2220 Blake St. (☎ 303/297-3644), located across from Coors Field. In addition to its award-winning ales, you can get traditional pub fare.

Over in Cherry Creek, **Bull & Bush Pub & Brewery,** 4700 Cherry Creek Dr. S. (☎ 303/759-0333), produces about eight handcrafted ales and will give tours of its facilities on request (see "Dining," in chapter 6).

Those who are really serious about visiting Colorado's microbreweries should consider an organized tour with **"Actually Quite Nice Brew Tours"** (☎ 800/951-7827 or 303/431-1440). Traveling in a 23-passenger bus, participants sample the beers at Denver- and Boulder-area microbreweries on 4- to 5-hour lunch or dinner tours, or strike out on full-day excursions for breweries in Breckenridge and other mountain towns, or the Front Range cities of Colorado Springs and Fort Collins. Prices range from $50 to $75, and include beer samples, a sampling glass, and lunch or dinner. Custom tours are also available.

For a look at the other side of the coin, take a trip to nearby Golden for a look at Coors, the world's largest single-site brewery (see below).

Other "strips" can be found along North and South Broadway, and along East and West Colfax Avenue.

The following are among the popular bars and pubs, but there are plenty more, so be sure to check out the publications mentioned above.

Bull & Bush Pub & Brewery. 4700 Cherry Creek Dr. S., Glendale. ☎ **303/759-0333.**

This re-creation of a famous London pub always has eight of their own brewed beers on tap, as well as Sunday evening Dixieland jazz by regional groups and acoustic music on Thursdays. A full brew house menu is available.

Charlie Brown's Bar & Grill. 980 Grant St. (at 10th Ave.). ☎ **303/860-1655.**

Just south of downtown, Charlie Brown's is a popular piano bar, some version of which has been in existence since 1927. The atmosphere is casual, with Elvis decanters, a baby grand piano, and a large central bar that attracts a diverse array of Denverites. The pianist plays a wide range of tunes, from Henry Mancini to Billy Joel, and the bartenders are not stingy. The grill serves breakfast, lunch, and dinner.

Churchill Bar. 321 17th St. (in the Brown Palace Hotel). ☎ **303/297-3111.**

You'll find an excellent selection of fine cigars, single malt Scotch, and after dinner drinks at this refined cigar bar, which caters to older, well-to-do Establishment types.

Club Proteus. 1669 Clarkson St. ☎ **303/869-4637.**

A large gay club near downtown, Club Proteus features lots of drink specials, happy-hour buffets, and dancing.

Cruise Room Bar. In the Oxford Hotel, 1600 17th St. (at Wazee St.). ☎ **303/825-1107.**

Modeled after a bar aboard the *Queen Mary* in the 1930s, the Cruise Room opened in 1934 on the day Prohibition ended. Recently restored to its art-deco best, it has a sophisticated atmosphere, a free jukebox, and the best martini in town.

Falling Rock Tap House. 1919 Blake St. ☎ **303/293-8338.**

This LoDo pub has 69 beers on tap—one of the best selections in Denver. You'll also find darts and pool, cigars, happy hours, and occasional live music.

Larry Walker's Sports Grill. 1701 Wynkoop St., #140. ☎ **303/534-1881.**

This sports grill, which serves a full lunch and dinner menu, claims to have Denver's largest big-screen TVs, plus numerous smaller screens, so you never have to miss a minute of play.

SandLot Brewery. 2145 Blake St. ☎ **303/298-1587.**

Located at Coors Field, home of the Colorado Rockies, this is considered America's first microbrewery located in a ballpark. Owned by the Coors Brewery in nearby Golden, you might get a sample of new products being tested by Coors. There's a restaurant nearby. Unless you're attending a ball game, stay away on game days, when SandLot is packed.

Sing Sing. 1735 19th St. ☎ **303/291-0880.**

Noisy college students dominate the scene at this LoDo hot spot, located beneath the Denver ChopHouse Restaurant. You'll often find low-priced beer specials, which encourage the partying college types to sing along (loudly and badly) with the dueling pianos. A fun place, but hang on tight.

Wynkoop Brewing Company. 1634 18th St. (at Wynkoop St.). ☎ **303/297-2700.**

Denver's first modern brew pub, many real beer fans say this is still the city's best. Among its most interesting offerings are the India pale ale and Scotch ale, but you can't go wrong here. An added attraction is a large pool hall.

THE PERFORMING ARTS
CLASSICAL MUSIC & OPERA

Colorado Symphony Orchestra. 821 17th St., #700. ☎ **303/98-MUSIC.**

This international-caliber orchestra performs more than 100 classical, pops, and family concerts each year at various locations throughout the metropolitan area.

Opera Colorado. 695 S. Colorado Blvd., # 20. ☎ **303/98-MUSIC** or 303/778-1500.

Each season three operas (12 performances) are staged, with English supertitles, at the Denver Performing Arts Complex. Internationally renowned singers and local favorites sing the lead roles. The typical schedule is three evening performances and one matinee each week from February through May.

THEATER

Denver Center for the Performing Arts. 14th and Curtis sts. ☎ **800/641-1222** or 303/893-4100, or 303/893-DCPA for recorded information. www.artstozoo.org/denvercenter.

An umbrella organization for resident and touring theater, youth outreach, and conservatory training, the DCPA includes the **Denver Center Theatre Company,** the largest professional resident theater company in the Rockies. With 40 artists on its payroll, the troupe performs about a dozen plays in repertory from October through June, including classical and contemporary dramas, musicals, and premieres of new plays.

Avenue Theater. 2119 E. 17th Ave. ☎ **303/321-5925.**

Original and off-Broadway plays are presented in an intimate 99-seat theater.

Chicken Lips Comedy Theater. 1624 Market St., #301. ☎ **303/534-4440.**

Productions include improvisational comedy, plays, and musicals, often with audience participation.

Comedy Works, Inc. 1226 15th St. ☎ **303/595-3637.**

Considered one of the region's top comedy clubs, this is your best bet for seeing America's hot comics at work.

El Centro Su Teatro. 4725 High St. ☎ **303/296-0219.** www.suteatro.org.

A Hispanic theater and cultural center, El Centro presents bilingual productions on a regular basis.

Germinal Stage Denver. 44th and Alcott Sts. ☎ **303/455-7108.**

In this 100-seat theater, plays by modern playwrights, such as Brecht, Albee, and Pinter, are presented.

Hunger Artists Ensemble Theatre. ☎ **303/893-5438.**

This award-winning theater group presents contemporary works at various locations throughout the city. Call for details.

DANCE

Colorado Ballet. 1278 Lincoln St. ☎ **303/837-8888.**

The state's premier professional resident ballet company performs in the Auditorium Theatre and Temple Hoyne Buell Theatre at the Denver Performing Arts Complex. The company presents four productions during its fall-through-spring season—a balance of classical and contemporary works that always includes *The Nutcracker* at Christmastime.

Cleo Parker Robinson Dance. 119 Park Ave. W. ☎ **303/295-1759.**

A highly acclaimed multicultural modern-dance ensemble and school, the Cleo Parker Robinson group performs a varied selection of programs each year, both on tour around the world and at several Denver locations.

MAJOR CONCERT HALLS & ALL-PURPOSE AUDITORIUMS

Arvada Center for the Arts & Humanities. 6901 Wadsworth Blvd., Arvada (2½ miles north of I-70). ☎ **303/431-3939.** Fax 303/431-3083. www.arvadacenter.org.

This multidisciplinary arts center is in use almost every day of the year for performances by internationally known artists and its own theater companies, its historical museum and art-gallery exhibitions, and hands-on education programs for all ages. The indoor theater seats 500, and the outdoor amphitheater seats 1,200. A fully handicapped-accessible playground has recently been added, and features a 343-foot sea creature by the name of Squiggles. The 1998/1999 theater season includes *Singin' in the Rain, Arsenic and Old Lace,* and the Pulitzer Prize–winning drama *The Young Man from Atlanta.* Scheduled musical events include the Nelson Riddle Orchestra, Asleep at the Wheel, and Blood, Sweat, and Tears.

Denver Performing Arts Complex. 14th and Curtis Sts. ☎ **800/641-1222** or 303/893-4100, or 303/893-DCPA for recorded information. www.artstozoo.org/denvercenter.

Covering four square blocks in downtown Denver from Speer Boulevard to 14th Street and Champa to Arapahoe streets, the Center for the Performing Arts (called the "PLEX" by locals) is impressive even to those not attending a performance. Its numerous theaters seat from 157 to 2,800, and there's also a restaurant and shopping promenade.

Fiddler's Green Amphitheatre. 6350 Greenwood Plaza Blvd., Englewood. ☎ **303/220-7000.**

Alfresco summer concerts at the Museum of Outdoor Arts feature national and international stars in rock, jazz, classical, and country music. The amphitheater has 7,500 reserved seats and room for plenty more on its spacious lawn. Located in the southwestern section of the metropolitan area, just west of I-25 between Arapahoe and Orchard roads, it's open from May to September.

Paramount Theatre. 1631 Glenarm Place. ☎ **303/825-4904.**

A performing-arts center since 1929, this restored 2,000-seat downtown theater is a wonderful place to enjoy jazz, pop, and folk performances, as well as comedy and films. Recent entertainers have included Pat Metheny and Roger Whittaker.

Red Rocks Amphitheatre. I-70 exit 259 S., 16351 County Rd. 93, Morrison. ☎ **303/640-7300.**

Denver's favorite venue for top-name outdoor summer concerts is set in the foothills of the Rocky Mountains, 15 miles west of the city. The 9,000-seat amphitheater is flanked by 400-foot-high, red sandstone rocks, and at night, with the lights of Denver spread across the horizon, the atmosphere is magical.

The Beatles performed here, as have U2, Paul Simon, Sting, Bonnie Raitt, Lyle Lovett, Merle Haggard, and top symphony orchestras from around the world. Visit the Red Rocks Trading Post/Visitor Center (☎ **303/697-8935**) to learn about the varied performances that have taken place here since it opened in 1941. The trading post also has a good selection of American Indian jewelry and pottery plus a variety of other curios and souvenirs.

7 A Side Trip to Colorado's Gold Circle Towns

Golden, Georgetown, and **Idaho Springs** comprise most of the fabled Gold Circle—those towns that boomed with the first strikes of the gold rush in 1859. The circle would be complete with the inclusion of Central City, once the richest of the four towns, but now the least attractive for today's visitor. Central City is trying to relive its glory days with a return to gambling, largely supported by locals from Denver, and although the exteriors of its historic buildings remain appealing, the rows of electronic slot machines and other gambling devices inside are a turn-off. Visitors to the area might like to make a brief stop, and then move on to Idaho Springs, where they can actively experience the area's past by panning for gold, riding a replica of a turn-of-the-century locomotive (the **Argo Express**), or donning a hard hat and following a working miner through the narrow tunnels of the **Phoenix Mine** (see below).

GOLDEN

Golden, 15 miles west of downtown Denver via U.S. 6 or Colo. 58 off I-70, is better known for the Coors Brewery (founded in 1873) and the Colorado School of Mines (established in 1874) than for its years as territorial capital.

For tourist information, contact the **Greater Golden Area Chamber of Commerce,** 1010 Washington Ave., Golden, CO 80401 (☎ **800/509-3113** or 303/279-3113; www.goldencochamber.com).

WHAT TO SEE & DO

Historic downtown Golden centers on the **Territorial Capitol** in the **Loveland Building** at 12th Street and Washington Avenue. Built in 1861, it housed the first state legislature from 1862 to 1867, when the capital was moved to Denver. Today it houses offices and a restaurant. The **Armory,** 13th and Arapahoe streets, is probably the largest cobblestone structure in the U.S.; 3,300 wagon loads of stone and quartz were used in its construction. The **Rock Flour Mill Warehouse,** Eighth and Cheyenne streets, dates from 1863; it was built with red granite from nearby Golden Gate Canyon and still has its original cedar beams and wooden floors.

Under development at press time was **Clear Creek Ranch Park,** a 3-acre creek-side park that illustrates the history of the area's ranching, with two log cabins and an 1870s one-room schoolhouse. The buildings were moved to this site to save them from development in nearby Golden Gate Canyon, their original location. Managed by the nonprofit Golden Landmarks Association, the park is located at 1022 11th Street in Golden. Call ☎ 303/278-3557 for current information.

In addition to the attractions listed below, see the section on Golden Gate State Park in "Outdoor Activities," above.

Astor House Museum. 822 12th St. ☎ **303/278-3557**. Admission $3 adults, $1 children 12 and younger. Daily 11am–4pm (museum officials hope to expand hours).

This handsome native stone structure, believed to be the first stone hotel built west of the Mississippi River, was constructed in 1867 to house legislators when Golden was the Territorial Capital. Scheduled for demolition to make space for a parking lot, the Astor House was instead restored in the 1970s and is now listed on the National Register of Historic Places. Today this western-style Victorian hotel offers glimpses into life during Golden's heyday in the late 19th century.

While there, you can obtain a walking-tour guide for the 12th Street Historic District, or visit the Victorian Gift Shop, whose proceeds benefit the museum.

Boettcher Mansion. 900 Colorow Rd. (on Lookout Mountain). ☎ **303/526-0855.** Free admission. Mon–Sat 8am–5pm, or by appointment.

This historic Jefferson County estate was built by Charles Boettcher in 1917 as a summer home and hunting lodge, and contains displays of furnishings and other items from the American Arts and Crafts period in the late 1800s and early 1900s. Other exhibits explore the history of Golden and the Boettcher family.

Buffalo Bill Museum & Grave. 987½ Lookout Mountain Rd. ☎ **303/526-0747.** Admission $3 adults, $2 seniors, $1 children 6–15, free for children under 6. May–Oct, daily 9am–5pm; Nov–Apr, Tues–Sun 9am–4pm. Closed Christmas. I-70 exit 260.

William Frederick Cody, the famous western scout, is buried atop Lookout Mountain, south of Golden. The adjacent museum contains memorabilia from the life and legend of "Buffalo Bill," who rode for the Pony Express, organized buffalo hunts for foreign royalty, and toured the world with his Wild West Show. There are also displays of American Indian artifacts, guns, and western art; an observation deck provides a great view of Denver. The museum is in 66-acre **Lookout Mountain Park,** a Denver municipal park popular for picnicking.

✪ **Colorado Railroad Museum.** 17155 W. 44th Ave. ☎ **800/365-6263** or 303/279-4591. www.colrailroad.com. Admission $4 adults, $3.50 seniors over 60, $2 children under 16, $9.50 families. June–Aug, daily 9am–6pm; Sept–May, daily 9am–5pm. Closed New Year's morning, Thanksgiving, and Christmas. Located 2 miles east of Golden. Follow the signs from I-70 exit 265 westbound, or exit 266 eastbound.

Housed in a replica of an 1880 railroad depot, this museum is a must-stop for railroad buffs. On display are more than 4 dozen narrow- and standard-gauge locomotives and cars, plus other historic equipment and artifacts, photos and documents, and model trains. The exhibits cover 12 acres, including the two-story depot. You can climb up into many of the old locomotives and wander through the parlor cars. The excellent gift shop sells hundreds of railroad-related items, from coffee mugs to posters to T-shirts.

✪ **Colorado School of Mines Geology Museum.** 16th and Maple Sts. ☎ **303/273-3815.** Free admission. School year, Mon–Sat 9am–4pm, Sun 1–4pm (closed for school holidays); summer, Mon–Sat 9am–4pm.

Explore the history of mining in Colorado with a replica of a gold mine and other displays. There are some 50,000 minerals, gems, fossils, and artifacts from around the world on exhibit, plus displays of geology, earth history, and paleontology. There's also a kids' corner. The Colorado School of Mines, founded in 1874, has an enrollment of about 3,000.

Coors Brewing Company. 13th and Ford sts. ☎ **303/277-2337.** Free admission. Tours Mon–Sat 10am–4pm; shop Mon–Sat 10am–5pm. Closed holidays.

The world's largest single-site brewery, producing 1½ million gallons of beer each day, Coors conducts free public tours of its brewery, followed by free samples of Coors' various beers. Tours leave a central parking lot at 13th and Ford streets, where visitors board a bus for a short drive through historic Golden before arriving at the brewery. There, a 30-minute walking tour covers the history of the Coors family and company, the barley-malting process, the 13,640-gallon gleaming copper kettles, and the entire process all the way to packaging. Children are welcome, and arrangements can be made for disabled or non-English-speaking visitors. There's also a gift shop and an interactive time line in the reception area.

Foothills Art Center. 809 15th St. ☎ **303/279-3922.** Free admission. Mon–Sat 9am–4pm, Sun 1–4pm.

Housed in an 1872 Gothic-style Presbyterian church (which is on the National Historic Register), this exhibition center evolved from the annual Golden Sidewalk Art Show and features changing national and regional exhibits. A gift shop next door, Foothills Two, sells crafts by local artisans.

Golden Pioneer Museum. 923 10th St. ☎ **303/278-7151.** Free admission. Summer, Mon–Sat 11am–4pm; winter, Mon–Sat noon–4pm. Closed major holidays.

This museum exhibits an impressive collection of furniture, household articles, photographs, and other items, including a re-created 19th-century parlor and boudoir.

✪ **Hakushika Sake USA.** 4414 Table Mountain Dr. ☎ **800/303-7253** or 303/279-7253. Free admission. Mon–Fri 10am–noon and 1–4pm by reservation. The Hakushika Sake brewery is located in the Coors Technology Center. From Denver, take I-70 exit 265, follow Colo. 58 toward Golden to the McIntyre St. exit. Go 2 miles north on McIntyre, turn left onto Service Dr., and then left onto Table Mountain Dr., where Hakushika is located.

The Hakushika company, founded in 1662 and today one of Japan's foremost sake-makers, has opened a brewery in Golden that produces sake for distribution throughout the United States and Europe. Sake, considered the Japanese national drink, is made from fermented steamed rice, has an alcohol content of 16%, and is traditionally, but not exclusively, consumed with meals.

Guided tours, by reservation only, follow a glass-enclosed mezzanine that permits an excellent view of the entire brewing and bottling process. Visitors can also see displays of traditional sake-brewing techniques, and an exhibit of fine Japanese art from the 19th and early 20th centuries. Also on the premises are a tasting room and gift shop. Children are welcome.

Heritage Square. U.S. 40. ☎ **303/279-2789.** Free admission, but individual activities impose their own charges. Memorial Day–Labor Day, daily 10am–9pm; rest of year, daily 10am–6pm. Located three-quarters of a mile south of the U.S. 6 and U.S. 40 interchange.

A shopping, dining, and entertainment village with a Wild West theme, Heritage Square features 30 Victorian specialty shops, a small museum, several fine restaurants, and a dinner theater. Warm-weather activities include go-carts, bumper boats, a water slide, a bungee tower, mountain-bike rentals, white-water rafting, and a 2,350-foot alpine slide with bobsled-style carts. The Lazy H Chuckwagon serves dinner with a western-style show. Heritage Square Music Hall offers shows for both adults and children, plus there's an ice-cream parlor and beer garden.

Lookout Mountain Nature Center. 910 Colorow Rd. (on Lookout Mountain). ☎ **303/526-0594.** Free admission. Trail, daily 8am–dusk; Nature Center, Tues–Sun 10am–4pm.

A 1¼-mile self-guided nature trail winds through this 110-acre preserve, among ponderosa pines and pretty mountain meadows. A free trail guide is available at the Nature Center (when it's open), and a map is on display at a kiosk for those walking the trail at other times. The nonprofit Nature Center has displays on the pine beetle, noxious weeds, and Colorado wildlife, plus a model of what the entire facility is expected to look like when all the exhibits are in place (scheduled for late 1999). The building, which opened in 1997, is also worth a look—it's constructed of used and recycled materials such as ground-up plastic soda containers and the pulp of aspen trees. A variety of free naturalist-guided environmental-education activities are offered year-round, mostly on weekends. Topics vary, but could include the flowers, butterflies, or wildlife of the area, or a look at the night sky. Advance registration is required, and some age restrictions may apply for certain programs. Call for details.

Mother Cabrini Shrine. 20189 Cabrini Blvd. (I-70 exit 259), Lookout Mountain. ☎ **303/526-0758.** Free admission, donations welcome. Summer, daily 7am–7pm; winter, daily 7am–5pm; masses Mon–Sat 7:30am, Sun 7:30am and 11am.

A 22-foot statue of Christ stands at the top of a 373-step stairway, adorned by carvings representing the stations of the cross and mysteries of the rosary. Terra-cotta benches provide rest stops along the way. The shrine is dedicated to the country's first citizen saint, St. Frances Xavier Cabrini, who founded the Order of the Missionary Sisters of the Sacred Heart. The order has a convent here with a gift shop, open daily from 9am to 5pm.

National Earthquake Information Center. 1711 Illinois St. ☎ **303/273-8500.** Free admission. Tues–Thurs, by appointment only.

The U.S. Geological Survey operates this facility to collect rapid earthquake information, transmit warnings via the Earthquake Early Alerting Service, and publish and disseminate earthquake data. Tours of 30 to 45 minutes can be scheduled.

Rocky Mountain Quilt Museum. 1111 Washington Ave. ☎ **303/277-0377**. Admission $2; free for children under 6. Tues–Sat 10am–4pm.

This museum presents changing exhibits, including works from its permanent collection of more than 140 quilts. Local crafters' work can be purchased in the gift shop.

WHERE TO STAY & DINE

La Quinta Inn–Golden, just off I-70 exit 264, at 3301 Youngfield Service Rd. (☎ **800/531-5900** or 303/279-5565), is a dependable choice for the night, with 129 units and rates of $69 to $79 single or double. **Table Mountain Inn,** 1310 Washington Ave. (☎ **800/762-9898** or 303/277-9898), is a slightly more expensive, if smaller, alternative, with 29 rooms and 3 suites; rates are $90 to $110 single or double, $140 suite. Open since 1992, it features southwest charm, beautiful views of the surrounding mesas, and a restaurant serving three meals daily.

For a good meal in an historic setting, try the **Old Capitol Grill** in downtown Golden, 1122 Washington Ave. at 12th Street (☎ **303/279-6390**), offering steak and seafood plus a good selection of sandwiches. Located in the Territorial Capitol Building constructed in 1862, the restaurant is open daily for lunch and dinner, with dinner prices in the $12 to $16 range.

✪ IDAHO SPRINGS

For visitor information, contact the **Idaho Springs Chamber of Commerce,** P.O. Box 97, Idaho Springs, CO 80452 (☎ **800/685-7785** or 303/567-4382). Information on Idaho Springs and the nearby towns of Empire, Georgetown, and Silver Plume can be obtained from the **Clear Creek County Tourism Board,** Box 100, Idaho Springs, CO 80452 (☎ **800/88-BLAST** or 303/567-4660).

WHAT TO SEE & DO

The scenic "Oh My God" dirt road winds from Central City through Virginia Canyon to Idaho Springs, although most visitors prefer to take I-70 directly to this community, 35 miles west of Denver. Site of a major gold strike in 1859, Idaho Springs today beckons visitors to try their luck at panning for any gold that may still remain.

The **Argo Gold Mine, Mill, and Museum,** 2350 Riverside Dr. (☎ **303/567-2421**), is listed on the National Register of Historic Places, and offers tours daily, from 10am to 7pm in summer, with shorter hours in winter. Visitors can see the Double Eagle Gold Mine, relatively unchanged since the early miners first worked it more than 100 years ago, and the mill, where ore was processed into gold. You can also ride the **Argo Express,** a one-half-scale replica of a turn-of-the-century steam locomotive, which operates in summer only. Allow at least 45 minutes. It costs $10 for adults, $8 for children 7 to 12, and $5 for kids 6 and under.

Still being worked is **Phoenix Gold Mine** on Trail Creek Road (☎ **303/567-0422**), where you can don a hard hat and follow a working miner through narrow tunnels to see what mining 100 years ago was really all about. You can also pan for gold on the property and relax in the picnic area. Open daily from 10am to 6pm year-round, the tours are informal and entertaining. Cost is $9 for adults, $8 for seniors, $5 for children 5 to 11, and free for children 4 and younger.

The Colorado School of Mines in Golden uses the **Edgar Experimental Mine,** less than a mile north of Idaho Springs on Eighth Avenue (☎ **303/567-2911**), as a research area and teaching facility for high-tech mining practices. Underground walking tours of 1 to 1½ hours are offered from mid-June to mid-August, Tuesday through Saturday at 9am, 11am, 1pm, and 3pm; group tours are available year-round by appointment, subject to guide availability. Tours are $6 for adults, $4.50 for seniors, $3 for ages 6 to 16, and free for kids under 6; there's a $15 maximum per family.

Just outside of Idaho Springs is **Indian Springs Resort**, 302 Soda Creek Rd. (☎ **303/567-2191**), a fine spot for a relaxing soak in the hot springs after a long day of skiing or hiking. There's a covered swimming pool, indoor and outdoor private baths, and a vapor cave with soaking pools. Rates are $10 per person per hour for the private baths, $10 for all-day use of the vapor cave, and $7 for all-day use of the pool. Lodging ($49 to $71 for two), meals, and weekend entertainment are also offered. The resort is open daily from 7:30am to 10:30pm, year-round.

Idaho Springs is the starting point for a 28-mile drive to the summit of 14,260-foot **Mount Evans**. From I-70 exit 240, follow Colo. 103—also called Mt. Evans Highway—as it winds along Chicago Creek through Arapahoe National Forest to **Echo Lake Park,** another Denver mountain park with fireplaces, hiking trails, and fishing. From here, Colo. 5—the highest paved auto road in North America—climbs to Mount Evans's summit. It's generally open from Memorial Day to Labor Day.

Another way to see this area's great scenery is by horseback. **A&A Historical Trails Stables,** 2380 Riverside Dr. (☎ **303/567-4808**), offers a variety of trail rides, including breakfast and moonlight rides, plus pony rides for children. Rides are usually offered from May through November, weather permitting. A 1-hour ride costs $15 per person, and a 2-hour ride costs $25.

WHERE TO STAY & DINE

H&H Motor Lodge, 2445 Colorado Blvd. (P.O. Box 1359), Idaho Springs, CO 80452 (☎ **800/445-2893** or 303/567-2838), is a mom-and-pop motel on the east side of town. It offers bright and cheery rooms, TVs with HBO, a hot tub, and sauna. The 34 rooms and suites here include several larger family units. Rates are about $54 double for a standard room, kitchenettes $10 extra; two-bedroom suites start at $69. Pets are welcome.

Beau Jo's Colorado Style Pizza, 1517 Miner St. (☎ **303/567-4376**), offers a wide variety of so-called "mountain pizzas," including standard pepperoni, a Thai Pie with sweet-and-sour sauce, and a roasted garlic and veggie combo. Sandwiches are also available, plus a soup and salad bar set up in a pair of old claw-foot bathtubs. Prices are $6 to $12. Smoking is not permitted.

GEORGETOWN

A pretty village of Victorian-era houses and stores, Georgetown, 45 miles west of Denver on I-70, at an elevation of 8,500 feet, is named for an 1860 gold camp. Among the best preserved of the foothills mining towns, Georgetown is one of the few that didn't suffer a major fire during its formative years. Perhaps to acknowledge their blessings, townspeople built eye-catching steeples on top of their firehouses, not their churches.

For information on attractions and travel services, drop by or contact the **Georgetown Chamber of Commerce,** P.O. Box 444, Georgetown, CO 80444

(☎ **800/472-8230** or 303/569-2888), which runs a visitor information center at Sixth Street across from the Georgetown post office; or **Historic Georgetown, Inc.,** at 15th and Argentine streets, P.O. Box 667, Georgetown, CO 80444-0667 (☎ **303/569-2840**).

WHAT TO SEE & DO

The Georgetown–Silver Plume Mining Area was declared a National Historic Landmark District in 1966, and more than 200 of its buildings have been restored.

A convenient place to begin a **walking tour** is the Old County Courthouse at Sixth and Argentine Streets. Now the Community Center and tourist information office, it was built in 1867. Across Argentine Street is the Old Stone Jail (1868); 3 blocks south, at Third and Argentine, is the Hamill House (see below).

Sixth Street is Georgetown's main commercial strip. Walk east from the Old Courthouse to, on your left, the Masonic Hall (1891), the Fish Block (1886), the Monti and Guanella Building (1868), and the Cushman Block (1874); and on your right, the Hamill Block (1881) and the Kneisel & Anderson Building (1893). The Hotel de Paris (see below) is at the corner of Sixth and Taos. Nearly opposite, at Sixth and Griffith, is the Star Hook and Ladder Building (1886), along with the town hall and marshal's office.

If you turn south on Taos Street, you'll find Grace Episcopal Church (1869) at Fifth Street, and the Maxwell House (1890) a couple of steps east on Fourth. Glance west on Fifth to see Alpine Hose Company No. 2 (1874) and the Courier Building (1875). North on Taos Street from the Hotel de Paris are the Old Georgetown School (1874) at Eighth Street, First Presbyterian Church (1874) at Ninth, Our Lady of Lourdes Catholic Church (1918) at Ninth, and the Old Missouri Firehouse (1870) at 10th and Taos.

If you turn west on Ninth at the Catholic church, you'll find two more historic structures: the Bowman-White House (1892) at Rose and Ninth, and the Tucker-Rutherford House (ca. 1860), a miner's log cabin with four small rooms and a trapper's cabin in back, located on Ninth Street at Clear Creek.

Georgetown Loop Railroad. 1106 Rose St., Georgetown. ☎ **800/691-4FUN,** 303/ 569-2403, or 303/670-1686 in Denver. Fax 303/569-2894. www.gtownloop.com. Admission for train ride $12.95 adults, $8.50 children 4–15, and free for children under 3 not occupying a seat; mine tour (only accessible by train) $5 adults, $3 children 3–15. There's no mine tour on the final run. Memorial Day–Labor Day, daily 9:20am–4pm; Labor Day–early Oct, full schedule on weekends, limited during the week. Departures from Georgetown and from Silver Plume.

An 1884 railroad bridge serves this restored narrow-gauge line, which runs daily trips in summer between Georgetown and Silver Plume. The steel bridge, 300 feet long and 95 feet high, was considered an engineering miracle a century ago. Although the direct distance between the terminals is 2.1 miles, the track covers 4.5 miles, climbing 638 feet in 14 sharp curves and switchbacks, crossing Clear Creek four times, and culminating with a 360° spiraling knot. Passengers may make a round-trip from either end: The whole trip takes about 2½ hours, including an optional walking tour of the Lebanon Mine and Mill, which can be reached only by train.

Mountain bikers might like to try a combination bike/train tour, priced from $65 to $95. This includes bicycling gear, uphill transportation, guided downhill tour, round-trip train ride, and lunch.

Hamill House. Third and Argentine Sts. ☎ **303/569-2840,** or 303/674-2625 in Denver. Admission $5 adults, $4 seniors 60 and older, $4 students of all ages, free for kids under 6. Memorial Day–Sept 30, daily 10am–4pm; Oct–Dec, Sat–Sun noon–4pm; closed Jan— Memorial Day.

Built in Country Gothic Revival style, this house dates from 1867, when it was owned by silver speculator William Hamill. When acquired by Historic Georgetown, Inc. (in 1971), the house had its original woodwork, fireplaces, and wallpaper. A delicately carved outhouse had two sections: one with walnut seats for the family the other with pine seats for servants.

Hotel de Paris. 409 Sixth St. (at Taos St.). ☎ **303/569-2311.** Admission $3.50 adults, $2.50 seniors 60 and older, $1.50 children 6–16, free for kids under 6. Memorial Day– Sept 30, daily 10am–5pm; rest of year, Sat–Sun noon–4pm. Closed major holidays.

The builder of the hotel, Louis Dupuy, once explained his desire to build a French inn so far away from his homeland: "I love these mountains and I love America, but you will pardon me if I bring into this community a remembrance of my youth and my country." The hotel opened in 1875 and soon became famous for its French provincial luxury.

Today it's a historic museum run by the National Society of Colonial Dames of America, embellished with many of its original furnishings, including Haviland china, a big pendulum clock, paintings and etchings of the past century, photographs by William Henry Jackson, and carved walnut furniture. The kitchen contains an antique stove and other cooking equipment, and the wine cellar houses early wine barrels, with their labels still in place.

WHERE TO STAY & DINE

Colorado's oldest continually operating hotel, about 5 minutes from Georgetown, is the **Peck House Hotel and Restaurant,** on U.S. 40 off I-70 exit 232, at 83 Sunny Ave., P.O. Box 428, Empire, CO 80438 (☎ **303/569-9870;** fax 303/569-2743). Established in 1862 as a stagecoach stop for travelers and immigrants from the East Coast, the hotel has an antique-filled parlor lined with photos of the Peck family and their late-19th- and early-20th-century guests. The rooms are comfortable and quaint (claw-foot tubs grace many bathrooms), and one of the best parts of a stay here is the fine panoramic view of the Empire Valley afforded by the wide veranda. There are 11 rooms (9 with private bathroom), with rates for two in the $50 to $110 range. The hotel's excellent **restaurant** serves fish and steak entrees and seriously delicious hot-fudge cake and raspberries Romanoff. The restaurant serves dinner and Sunday brunch only; prices for dinner entrees are $16 to $25, and the brunch costs $15.

Back in Georgetown, **The Happy Cooker,** 412 Sixth St. (☎ 303/569-3166), serves unusual soups, sandwiches on homemade breads, crepes, quiches, and more substantial fare such as lasagna and barbecued beef, in a converted home in Georgetown's historic business district. It's open Monday through Friday from 8am to 4pm, Saturday and Sunday from 8am to 6pm. Prices are in the $4 to $8 range.

8 Colorado Springs

Magnificent scenic beauty, a favorable climate, and dreams of gold have lured visitors to Colorado Springs and neighboring Pikes Peak Country for well over 100 years.

Nearly two centuries ago, in 1806, army lieutenant Zebulon Pike led a company of soldiers on a trek around the base of an enormous mountain. He called it "Grand Peak," declared it unconquerable, and moved on. Today, the 14,110-foot mountain we now know as Pikes Peak has been conquered so often that an auto highway and a cog railway have been built to take visitors to the top.

Unlike many Colorado towns, neither mineral wealth nor ranching was the cornerstone of Colorado Springs' economy during the 19th century: Tourism was. In fact, when founded in 1871, Colorado Springs was the first genuine resort community west of Chicago. General William J. Palmer, builder of the Denver & Rio Grande Railroad, established the resort on his rail line, at an elevation of 6,035 feet. The state's growing reputation as a health center, with its high mountains and mineral springs, convinced him to build at the foot of Pikes Peak. In an attempt to lure affluent easterners, he named the resort Colorado Springs, because most fashionable eastern resorts were called "springs." The mineral waters at Manitou were only 5 miles away, and soon Palmer exploited them by installing a resident physician, Dr. Samuel Solly, who exuberantly trumpeted the benefits of Manitou's springs both in print and in person.

The 1890s gold strikes at Cripple Creek, on the southwestern slope of Pikes Peak, added a new dimension to life in Colorado Springs. Among those who cashed in on the boom was Spencer Penrose, a middle-aged Philadelphian and Harvard graduate who arrived in the Springs in 1892, made some astute investments, and became quite rich. Penrose, who believed that the automobile would revolutionize life in the United States, promoted the creation of new highways. To show the effectiveness of motor cars in the mountains, he built (from 1913 to 1915) the Pikes Peak highway, using more than $250,000 of his own money. Then, during World War I, at a cost of more than $2 million, he built the luxurious Broadmoor hotel at the foot of Cheyenne Mountain. World War II brought the military and defense industry to this area, and in 1958 the $200-million U.S. Air Force Academy opened.

Modern Colorado Springs is a growing city of 323,000, with close to half a million people in the metropolitan area. The majority of its residents are conservative (one-third of its residents are active or retired military personnel), and in recent years, it has developed a reputation for right-wing political activism. The city is also home to some of the country's largest nondenominational churches and conservative groups, such as Focus on the Family.

To many visitors, the city retains the feel and mood of a small western town. Most tourists come to see the Air Force Academy, marvel at the scenery at Garden of the Gods and Pikes Peak, and explore the history of America's West.

1 Orientation

ARRIVING

BY PLANE   Major airlines offer some 100 flights a day to **Colorado Springs Airport,** located north of Drennan Road and east of Powers Boulevard in the southeastern part of the city (☎ **719/550-1900**).

Airlines serving Colorado Springs include **American** (☎ 800/433-7300), **America West** (☎ 800/235-9292), **Mesa** (☎ 800/637-2247), **Northwest** (☎ 800/225-2525), **Reno Air** (☎ 800/736-6247), **TWA** (☎ 800/221-2000 or 719/599-4400), and **United** (☎ 800/241-6522).

GETTING TO & FROM THE AIRPORT   The **Colorado Springs Airport Shuttle** (☎ **719/578-5232**) operates direct ground service from Colorado Springs Airport to local hotels and the Denver airport.

BY CAR   The principal artery to and from the north (Denver: 70 miles) and south (Pueblo: 42 miles), I-25 bisects Colorado Springs. U.S. 24 is the principal east–west route through the city.

Visitors arriving via I-70 from the east can take exit 359 at Limon and follow U.S. 24 into the Springs. Arriving on I-70 from the west, the most direct route is exit 201 at Frisco, then Colo. 9 through Breckenridge 53 miles to U.S. 24 (at Hartsel), and then east 66 miles to the Springs. This route is mountainous, so check road conditions before setting out in winter.

BY BUS   **Greyhound** and **TNM&O Coaches,** 120 S. Weber St. (☎ **719/635-1505**), provide regular service to communities throughout the state.

VISITOR INFORMATION

The **Colorado Springs Convention and Visitors Bureau** is located at 104 S. Cascade Ave., Colorado Springs, CO 80903 (☎ **800/DO-VISIT** or 719/635-7506; fax 719/635-4968; www.coloradosprings-travel.com). Ask for the free *Official Visitor Guide to Colorado Springs and the Pikes Peak Region,* a colorful booklet with a comprehensive listing of accommodations, restaurants, and other visitor services in the area, as well as a basic but efficient map. Inquire at the Visitor Information Center or local bookstores for more detailed maps (an excellent one is the Pierson Graphics Corporation's *Colorado Springs and Monument Valley Street Map*).

The **Visitor Information Center,** located in the same Sun Plaza Building at the corner of Cascade and Colorado Avenues, is open in summer, daily from 8:30am to 6pm; in winter, Monday through Friday from 8:30am to 5pm. From I-25, take the Bijou Street exit, head east, and turn right at the second stoplight onto Cascade. Just past the Antlers Doubletree Hotel, turn right onto Colorado Avenue, and almost immediately left into the parking lot for the Visitor Center. The center also operates a weekly events line with a 24-hour recording (☎ **719/635-1723**).

Additional information on regional attractions plus accommodations, restaurants, and special events in the Manitou Springs area can be obtained from the **Manitou Springs Chamber of Commerce,** 354 Manitou Ave., Manitou Springs, CO 80829 (☎ 800/642-2567 or 719/685-5089; fax 719/685-0355; www.manitousprings.org; e-mail: manitou@pikespeak.com). You can also contact the **Pikes Peak Country Attractions Association** at the same address (☎ 800/525-2250 or 719/685-5894; fax 719/685-5873; www.pikes-peak.com; e-mail: ppcaa@ pikes-peak.com).

CITY LAYOUT

It's easy to get around central Colorado Springs because it is laid out on a classic grid pattern.

If you focus on the intersection of I-25 and U.S. 24, downtown Colorado Springs lies in the northeast quadrant—bounded on the west by I-25 and on the south by U.S. 24 (Cimarron Street). Boulder Street to the north and Wahsatch Avenue to the east complete the downtown frame. Nevada Avenue (U.S. 85) parallels the freeway for 15 miles through the city, intersecting it twice; Tejon Street and Cascade Avenue also run north-south through downtown between Nevada Avenue and the freeway. **Colorado Avenue** and **Platte Avenue** are the busiest east-west downtown cross streets.

West of downtown, Colorado Avenue extends through the historic Old Colorado City district and the quaint foothill community of **Manitou Springs,** rejoining U.S. 24—itself a busy but less interesting artery—as it enters Pike National Forest.

South of downtown, **Nevada Avenue** intersects **Lake Avenue,** the principal boulevard into the Broadmoor, and proceeds south as Colo. 115 past Fort Carson.

North and east of downtown, **Academy Boulevard** (Colo. 83) is the street name to remember. From the south gate of the Air Force Academy north of the Springs, it winds through residential hills, crosses Austin Bluff Parkway, then runs without a curve 8 miles due south, finally bending west to intersect I-25 and Colo. 115 at Fort Carson. U.S. 24, which exits downtown east as Platte Avenue, and Fountain Boulevard, which leads to the airport, are among its cross streets. Austin Bluffs Parkway extends west of I-25 as **Garden of the Gods Road,** leading to that natural wonder.

City street addresses are divided by Pikes Peak Avenue into "north" and "south"; by Nevada Avenue into "east" and "west."

2 Getting Around

Although Colorado Springs has public transportation, most visitors prefer to drive. Parking and roads are good, and some of the best attractions, such as the Garden of the Gods, are accessible only by car (or foot or bike for the truly ambitious).

BY CAR

For regulations and advice on driving in Colorado, see "Getting Around," in chapter 3. The **American Automobile Association (AAA)** maintains an office in Colorado Springs at 3525 N. Carefree Circle (☎ 800/283-5222 or 719/ 591-2222), open Monday through Friday from 8:30am to 5:30pm and Saturday from 9am to 1pm.

CAR RENTALS Car-rental agencies in Colorado Springs, some of which have offices in or near downtown as well as at the airport, include **Avis** (☎ 800/ 831-2847 or 719/596-2751); **Budget** (☎ 800/527-0700 or 719/574-7400);

Dollar (☎ 800/800-4000 or 719/637-2620); **Enterprise** (☎ 800/325-8007 or 719/636-3900); **Hertz** (☎ 800/654-3131 or 719/596-1863); **National** (☎ 800/227-7368 or 719/596-1519); **Rent A Wreck** (☎ 800/535-1391 or 719/471-2100); and **Thrifty** (☎ 800/367-2277 or 719/390-9800).

PARKING   Most downtown streets have parking meters; the rate is 25¢ for a half hour. Look for city-run parking lots, which charge 25¢ per half hour and also offer day rates. Outside of downtown, free parking is generally available on side streets.

BY BUS

City bus service is provided by **Colorado Springs Transit** (☎ **719/475-9733**). Buses operate Monday through Friday from 6am to 10pm, and Saturday from 7am to 6pm, except holidays. Fares on in-city routes are 75¢ for adults; 35¢ for children 6 to 11, seniors, and the disabled; and free for kids under 6. Fares for routes outside the city limits are 25¢ higher. Bus schedules can be obtained at terminals, city libraries, and the Colorado Springs Convention and Visitors Bureau.

In Manitou Springs, the **Town Trolley** operates Memorial Day to Labor Day, daily from 10am to 8pm, and on weekends during September and October, weather permitting. The open-sided trolleys provide one-hour guided tours through Manitou Springs and a portion of Garden of the Gods. A one-day pass ($2 for adults, $1 for children) allows riders to stop to see the sights and then resume the tour later. The trolleys (named Morris and Charlie) depart from Seven Minute Springs Park every 30 minutes.

BY TAXI

Call **Yellow Cab** (☎ **719/634-5000**) or **American Cab** (☎ **719/637-1111**) for taxi service and tours.

ON FOOT

Each of the main sections of town can easily be explored without a vehicle. It's fun, for instance, to wander the winding streets of Manitou Springs or explore the Old Colorado City "strip." Between neighborhoods, however, distances are considerable. Unless you're particularly fit, it's wise to drive or take a bus or taxi.

FAST FACTS: COLORADO SPRINGS

American Express   To report a lost card, call ☎ **800/528-4800**; to report lost traveler's checks, call ☎ **800/221-7282.**

Area Code   The telephone area code is **719.**

Baby-sitters   Front desks at major hotels often can make arrangements on your behalf.

Business Hours   Most banks are open Monday through Friday from 9am to 5pm, and some have Saturday hours as well. Major stores are open Monday through Saturday from 9 or 10am until 5 or 6pm, and often Sunday from noon until 5pm. Stores that cater to tourists are usually open longer in the summer with shorter hours in winter. Some may close completely between October and April.

Car Rentals   See "Getting Around," earlier in this chapter.

Dentists   For 24-hour referrals, contact Colorado Springs Dental Society Emergency and Referral Service (☎ **719/598-5161**).

Doctors   For referrals, call Healthlink Physician Referral (☎ **719/444-2273**).

Drugstores   Walgreens Drug Stores has a 24-hour prescription service at 920 N. Circle Dr. (☎ **719/473-9090**).

Emergencies   To reach **Poison Control,** dial ☎ 800/332-3073.

Eyeglasses   You can get one-hour replacement of lost or broken glasses at **Pearle Vision Express** in Citadel Mall (☎ 719/550-0300). Another good choice is **LensCrafters,** in Erindale Centre (☎ 719/548-8650).

Hospitals   Full medical services, including 24-hour emergency treatment, are offered by **Memorial Hospital,** 1400 E. Boulder St. (☎ 719/475-5000). The **Penrose–St. Francis Health System** (☎ **719/776-5000**) operates health-care facilities throughout the city.

Newspapers/Magazines   The *Gazette Telegraph*, published daily in Colorado Springs, is the city's most widely read newspaper. Both Denver dailies—the *Denver Post* and *Rocky Mountain News*—are available at newsstands throughout the city. *Springs* magazine and the *Independent* are free arts-and-entertainment tabloids. *USA Today* and the *Wall Street Journal* can be purchased on the streets and at major hotels.

Photographic Needs   There are dozens of photo finishing outlets throughout the city, including **Walgreens Drug Stores** and **50-Minute Photo**, in the Woodmen Valley Shopping Center at 6902 N. Academy Blvd. (☎ 719/598-6412). For camera and video supplies and repairs, as well as photo finishing, go to **Robert Waxman Camera and Video,** 1850 N. Academy Blvd. (☎ 719/597-1575), or **Shewmaker's Camera Shop,** downtown at 30 N. Tejon St. (☎ 719/636-1696).

Post Office   The main post office is downtown at 201 E. Pikes Peak Ave. Call the U.S. Postal Service (☎ **800/275-8777**) for hours and locations of other post offices.

Radio/TV   More than a dozen AM and FM radio stations in the Colorado Springs area cater to all tastes in music, news, sports, and entertainment, including KCME (88.7 FM) for classical, KILO (94.3 FM) for album-oriented rock, KKFM (98.1 FM) for classic rock, KGFT (100.7 FM) and KCBR (1040 AM) for contemporary Christian, KCMN (1530 AM) for big band and hit parade, KKCS (101.9 FM) for country, KRDO (1240 AM) for sports talk, KKLI (106.3 FM) for adult contemporary, and KVOR (1300 AM) for all news.

Major television stations include Channels 5 (NBC), 8 (PBS), 11 (CBS), 13 (ABC), and 21 (FOX). Cable or satellite service is available at most hotels.

Safety   Although Colorado Springs is generally a safe city, it is not crime free. Try to be aware of your surroundings at all times, and ask at your hotel or the visitor center about the safety of neighborhoods you plan to explore, especially after dark.

Taxes   The Colorado state sales tax is 3%. In Colorado Springs the sales tax is about 7% and the lodging tax is about 9%. Rates in Manitou Springs are about 7.5% for general sales tax and almost 10% for lodging.

Useful Telephone Numbers   For **road conditions** and **time** call ☎ 719/630-1111. For **ski conditions** statewide, call ☎ 303/831-SNOW. For **weather information**, phone ☎ 719/475-7599.

3 Accommodations

You'll find a wide range of lodging possibilities here, from Colorado's fanciest resort—the Broadmoor—to clean basic budget motels. There are also several particularly nice B&Bs. The rates listed here are the officially quoted prices ("rack rates") and don't take into account any individual or group discounts. Generally, rates are highest from Memorial Day to Labor Day and lowest in the spring. During graduation and other special events at the Air Force Academy, rates will be at their absolute highest, and you may have trouble finding a room at any price.

In addition to the accommodations described below, a number of chain and franchise motels in Colorado Springs offer reliable moderately priced lodging. These include the **Best Western Palmer House,** 3010 N. Chestnut St., Colorado Springs, CO 80907 (☎ 800/528-1234 or 719/636-5201), which charges $49 to $99 double; **Econo Lodge Downtown,** 714 N. Nevada Ave., Colorado Springs, CO 80903 (☎ 800/553-2666 or 719/636-3385), with rates for two ranging from $35 to $85; and **Super 8,** 4604 Rusina Rd., Colorado Springs, CO 80907 (☎ 800/ 800-8000 or 719/599-8616), which charges $47 to $66 double. The nearest full-service hotel to the Air Force Academy is the **Radisson Inn North**, 8110 N. Academy Blvd. (I-25 exit 150A), Colorado Springs, CO 80920 (☎ **800/333-3333** or 719/598-5770), which charges $80 to $120 for two.

A lodging tax (about 9% in Colorado Springs, almost 10% in Manitou Springs) will be added to all bills.

VERY EXPENSIVE

✪ **The Broadmoor.** Lake Circle, at Lake Ave. (P.O. Box 1439), Colorado Springs, CO 80901. ☎ **800/634-7711** or 719/634-7711. Fax 719/577-5779. www.broadmoor.com. E-mail: info@broadmoor.com. 700 units. A/C TV TEL. Summer, $280–$425 double; $450–$2,000 suite. Winter, $180–$325 double; $350–$1,575 suite. Winter packages may cost as little as $75 per person per night. AE, CB, DC, MC, V. Free parking.

A Colorado Springs institution and a tourist attraction in its own right, the Broadmoor is a sprawling resort complex of historic pink Mediterranean-style buildings, set at the foot of Cheyenne Mountain. Built in the Italian Renaissance style, the Broadmoor opened in 1918. Its marble staircase, chandeliers, della Robbia tile, hand-painted beams and ceilings, and carved-marble fountain remain spectacles today, along with a priceless art collection.

The spacious and luxurious guest rooms, located in four separate buildings on the 3,000-acre grounds, are decorated with early-20th-century antiques and original works of art. Most units contain desks and tables, plush seating, and excellent lighting. The service is impeccable: The hotel staffs two employees for every guest.

Dining/Diversions: The elegant Penrose Room is the hotel's finest restaurant, serving breakfast and dinner daily. Charles Court (see "Dining," below) serves breakfast, high tea, and American continental cuisine for dinner. The Tavern serves steak and seafood in an informal setting. The Lake Terrace Dining Room serves the hotel's award-winning Sunday Brunch. There are several more casual dining choices and six lounges.

Amenities: 24-hour room service, full concierge service, in-room massage, valet laundry, shuttle bus between buildings. Sports and recreational facilities include three 18-hole championship golf courses, three pools, 12 all-weather tennis courts, bicycle rentals, a state-of-the-art fitness center and full-service spa, aerobics classes, saunas, and whirlpool tub. Horseback riding, paddleboating on Cheyenne Lake, and hot-air ballooning are also available. Other facilities include nearly 30 shops, a theater, car-rental agency, service station, and meeting facilities for 1,600.

Colorado Springs Accommodations & Dining

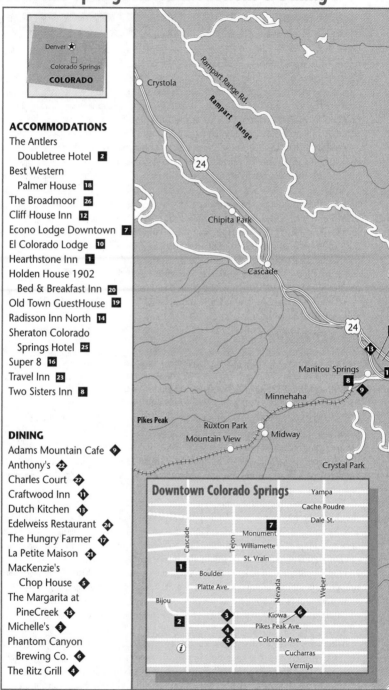

ACCOMMODATIONS
The Antlers
  Doubletree Hotel **2**
Best Western
  Palmer House **18**
The Broadmoor **26**
Cliff House Inn **12**
Econo Lodge Downtown **7**
El Colorado Lodge **10**
Hearthstone Inn **1**
Holden House 1902
  Bed & Breakfast Inn **20**
Old Town GuestHouse **19**
Radisson Inn North **14**
Sheraton Colorado
  Springs Hotel **25**
Super 8 **16**
Travel Inn **23**
Two Sisters Inn **8**

DINING
Adams Mountain Cafe **9**
Anthony's **22**
Charles Court **27**
Craftwood Inn **11**
Dutch Kitchen **13**
Edelweiss Restaurant **24**
The Hungry Farmer **17**
La Petite Maison **21**
MacKenzie's
  Chop House **5**
The Margarita at
  PineCreek **15**
Michelle's **3**
Phantom Canyon
  Brewing Co. **6**
The Ritz Grill **4**

Denver ★
Colorado Springs
COLORADO

Crystola

Rampart Range Rd
Rampart Range

24

Chipita Park

Cascade

24

Manitou Springs

Minnehaha

Pikes Peak

Ruxton Park
Mountain View
Midway

Crystal Park

Downtown Colorado Springs
Yampa
Cache Poudre
Dale St.
Monument
Williamette
St. Vrain
Boulder
Platte Ave.
Bijou
Kiowa
Pikes Peak Ave.
Colorado Ave.
Cucharras
Vermijo
Cascade
Tejon
Nevada
Weber

NA-0382

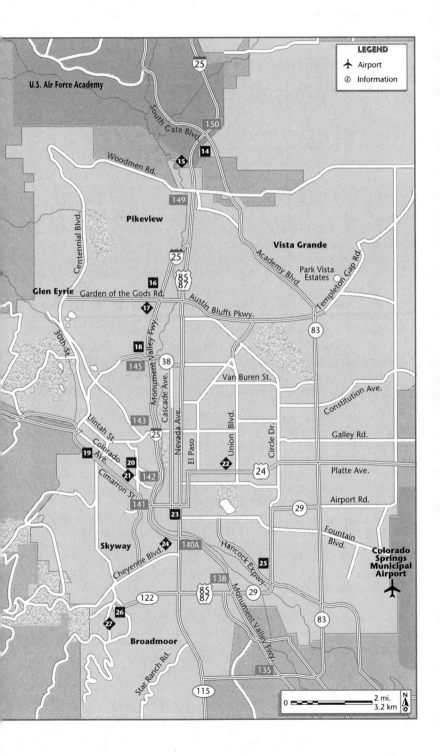

EXPENSIVE

The Antlers Doubletree Hotel. 4 S. Cascade Ave., Colorado Springs, CO 80903. ☎ **800/ 222-TREE** or 719/473-5600. Fax 719/444-0417. www.doubletreehotels.com. 290 units. A/C TV TEL. $120–$160 double; $300–$700 suite. AE, CB, DC, DISC, ER, JCB, MC, V. Parking $6 per day.

This hotel has been a Colorado Springs landmark for more than a century— although there have been three different Antlers on the same site. The first, a tur- reted Victorian showcase built in 1883, was destroyed by fire in 1898. The Italian Renaissance–style building that replaced it survived until 1964, when it was leveled to make room for the new Antlers Plaza. Doubletree Hotels purchased it, spent more than a year in renovation, and reopened it in October 1990.

Antique black-walnut nightstands from the preceding Antlers provide a touch of historic continuity in each guest room, which also have TVs, two phones, cof- feemakers, and ample closet space. The corner rooms are larger, and the west side rooms provide great views of the mountains.

The hotel offers a full range of services, including a beauty salon, fitness center, indoor pool, and whirlpool. It has two restaurants, including Colorado Springs' first microbrewery: Judge Baldwin's (see "Colorado Springs After Dark," below).

Cliff House Inn. 306 Cañon Ave., Manitou Springs, CO 80829. ☎ **888/212-7000** or 719/685-3000. Fax 719/685-3913. www.thecliffhouse.com. E-mail: canon306@aol.com. 56 units. A/C TV TEL. $99–$400 suite. Rates include breakfast buffet. AE, CB, DC, DISC, MC, V.

Scheduled to open in late 1998, the Cliff House has undergone a $5.5-million restoration and renovation to marry its Victorian charm to modern-day technology and amenities. Built in 1873, the Cliff House was designated a National Historic Landmark in 1980 and has hosted such eminent guests as Theodore Roosevelt, Clark Gable, and Thomas Edison.

Rooms vary in size and personality, offering a wide variety of choices from studio to celebrity suites. Some units have gas fireplaces, two-person spas, steam showers, and terrific views of the mountains. All have robes, heated toilet seats, Internet access and modem ports, coffeemakers, hair dryers, and irons and ironing boards.

Services include airport pick-up, valet parking, valet laundry service, room ser- vice from 7am to 11pm, and afternoon tea. The Cliff House Dining Room serves breakfast and dinner daily, plus Sunday brunch.

✪ **Old Town GuestHouse.** 115 S. 26th St., Colorado Springs, CO 80904. ☎ **888/ 375-4210** or 719/632-9194. Fax 719/632-9026. www.bbonline.com/co/oldtown. E-mail: oldtown@databahn.net. 8 units. A/C TEL TV. $95–$175. AE, DISC, MC, V. Off-road parking. Not recommended for children.

This three-story red-brick inn is just a half-block south of the main street of Col- orado Springs' historic Old Colorado City. It may appear to be from the 19th cen- tury, but innkeepers Kaye and David Caster designed and built it in 1997 to provide all the modern amenities in a warm and inviting atmosphere. An attractive library with fireplace, music, and overstuffed chairs entices you to relax and stay a while.

All eight guest rooms are individually decorated and named for flowers; each has individual climate control, VCR, CD player, coffeemaker, fridge, robes, ironing board and iron, and a queen or king bed. Several have gas-log fireplaces, seven have either a private porch or balcony, and some have either steam showers for two or private outdoor hot tubs. There's an elevator, and one room is ADA approved.

Wine and hors d'oeuvres are offered in the afternoon. Full homemade breakfasts are served, with lighter fare available, and special dietary needs can be accommo- dated with advance notice. Downstairs is a game room with pool table and exercise

---

⊕ Family-Friendly Hotels

Radisson Inn North *(see p. 123)*   Kids like the 24-hour pool and video games; for teens who want to hang out, Chapel Hills Mall is right across the street.

Sheraton Colorado Springs Hotel *(see p. 127)*   Two swimming pools, a separate children's pool, shuffleboard, and a putting green should keep most kids occupied.

---

equipment, plus a 20-person private conference room. On many weekends, Dave parks his 1936 Cadillac in front to add a festively historic touch.

Sheraton Colorado Springs Hotel. 2886 S. Circle Dr. (I-25 exit 138), Colorado Springs, CO 80906. ☎ **800/981-4012** or 719/576-5900, 800/325-3535 worldwide. Fax 719/576-7695. 516 units. A/C TV TEL. $99–$169 double; $310–$515 suite. AE, DC, DISC, MC, V. Free outdoor parking. Small pets accepted.

Eleven acres of landscaped grounds and a beautiful sky-lit indoor garden set this Sheraton apart from others. The indoor garden has a pool and whirlpool tub, while the outdoor garden features a second pool, sunbathing area, and children's play area. All guest rooms have coffeemakers and full-size mirrors, with refrigerators available on request. A half-dozen bi-level suites are furnished with a king-size bed in a loft and a sleeper sofa downstairs.

Amenities include a concierge, 24-hour room service, newspaper delivery, dry cleaning, secretarial services, and express checkout. On the premises are a restaurant and lounge, business center, car-rental desk, conference rooms, game rooms, health club, and two tennis courts. Executive Club Level rooms offer additional amenities.

MODERATE

○ **Hearthstone Inn.** 506 N. Cascade Ave., Colorado Springs, CO 80903. ☎ **800/521-1885** or 719/473-4413. Fax 719/473-1322. hearthstoneinn.com. E-mail: hearthstone@worldnet.att.net. 25 units (2 with shared bathroom). A/C. $90–$150 double with private bathroom, $70–$80 with shared bathroom; $150–$180 suite. Rates include full breakfast. AE, MC, V. Free off-street, lighted parking.

This comfortably elegant small downtown inn is actually two historic homes, built in 1885 and 1900, connected by a carriage house. Listed on the National Register of Historic Places and the winner of numerous preservation awards, the inn is decorated with old photographs, many antiques, and reproductions. Some of the comfortably furnished rooms can accommodate three or four people, and each unit has its own distinct personality. Breakfasts are wonderful: imaginative variations on the standard egg entrees, plus home-baked breads, fruit, and hot and cold cereals. A common parlor has games, a piano, and fresh coffee. No smoking is permitted inside the inn, but there is an outside porch designated for smokers.

○ **Holden House 1902 Bed & Breakfast Inn.** 1102 W. Pikes Peak Ave., Colorado Springs, CO 80904. ☎ **719/471-3980.** www.bbonline.com/co/holden. E-mail: holdenhouse@worldnet.att.net. 5 suites. A/C TEL. $115–$130 double. Rates include full breakfast. AE, CB, DC, DISC, MC, V. Not suitable for children.

Innkeepers Sallie and Welling Clark restored this storybook Colonial Revival–style Victorian house, and its adjacent 1906 carriage house, and filled the rooms with antiques and family heirlooms. Located near Old Colorado City, the inn has a living room with a tile fireplace, a front parlor with TV, and verandas. Guests enjoy a 24-hour coffee/tea service with bottomless cookie jar, plus a gourmet breakfast in the formal dining room. Smoking is not allowed.

Each guest room, which is named after a Colorado mining area, contains memorabilia of that district. All have queen-size beds, three have fireplaces, and several have tubs for two. The Independence Suite, in the adjacent building, is accessible to the disabled and is cat-free for those with allergies.

○ **Two Sisters Inn.** 10 Otoe Place, Manitou Springs, CO 80829. ☎ **719/685-9684.** 5 units (3 with private bathroom). $66 room with shared bathroom, $85 room with private bathroom; $105 cottage. Rates include full breakfast. DISC, MC, V. Suitable for well-supervised children over 10.

Built by two sisters in 1919 as a boardinghouse, this award-winning B&B is still owned and operated by two women—sisters in spirit if not actually in blood. Wendy Goldstein and Sharon Smith have furnished the four bedrooms and separate honeymoon cottage with family heirlooms and photographs, in a style best described as "informal elegance." The rooms in the main house feature Victorian frills and furnishings, while the cottage has a feather bed, gas-log fireplace, and fridge. Fresh flowers adorn each room, and homemade chocolates and baked goods are served in the evenings. Smoking is not permitted.

INEXPENSIVE

El Colorado Lodge. 23 Manitou Ave., Manitou Springs, CO 80829. ☎ **800/782-2246** or 719/685-5485. 26 cabins (8 with kitchen, 11 with shower only). A/C TV TEL. Summer $54–$125. Winter rates up to 30% off. AE, CB, DC, DISC, MC, V. Free parking by cabins.

Most of the cabins in this southwestern-style lodge have fireplaces and beamed ceilings. Each has from one to three clean, well-appointed rooms and can accommodate from two to six people. The lodge boasts the largest outdoor swimming pool in Manitou Springs and an outdoor pavilion for groups. Complimentary coffee is served.

Travel Inn. 512 S. Nevada Ave., Colorado Springs, CO 80903. ☎ **719/636-3986.** Fax 719/636-3980. 34 units. A/C TV TEL. Summer $45–$52 double, winter $32–$37 double. AE, DC, DISC, MC, V.

This two-story motel has turquoise trim that vies with the blue of the sky on a sunny day. It's conveniently located near downtown Colorado Springs, and the recently remodeled rooms are simple, clean, and comfortable, with white stucco walls and dark-wood furnishings. About a third of the units have tub/shower combinations, others showers only. A self-serve laundry is available.

CAMPING

Campsites are also available in Mueller State Park (see "Parks & Zoos," later in this chapter).

Garden of the Gods Campground. 3704 W. Colorado Ave., Colorado Springs, CO 80904. ☎ **800/345-8197** or 719/475-9450. www.coloradovacation.com/camp/gogc. $25–$30 for two people. Extra person $2. AE, DISC, MC, V. Closed mid-Oct–mid-Apr. Take I-25 exit 141, head west on U.S. 24, then north (right) on 31st St., then left on Colorado Ave. for 6 blocks (keep right), and turn right to gate.

Located near Garden of the Gods (see "Attractions," below), this large tree-shaded campground offers 250 full RV hookups (30 and 50 amp service), an adults-only section, and additional tent sites. Facilities include tables, a barbecue pit, grocery, bathhouses, laundry, heated pool, whirlpool tub, playground, and clubhouse with pool tables and game room.

4 Dining

Colorado Springs has an excellent variety of above-average restaurants, and surprisingly, almost all of them put a lot of effort into creating exciting desserts. See also the section on dinner theaters in "Colorado Springs After Dark," later in this chapter.

VERY EXPENSIVE

Charles Court. Broadmoor West, in the Broadmoor, Lake Circle. ☎ **719/634-7711.** Reservations recommended. Breakfast $7.75–$15.50, dinner main courses $18–$36. AE, CB, DC, DISC, MC, V. Daily 7–11am and 6–9:30pm. SEASONAL AMERICAN BOUNTY.

The English country-manor atmosphere of this outstanding restaurant, with picture windows looking across Cheyenne Lake to the renowned Broadmoor Hotel, lends itself to a fine dining experience complete with attentive service. The creative menu changes seasonally, but you'll usually find such delicacies as Colorado lamb chops, beef tenderloin, salmon fillet, and a wild-game selection. The wine list includes over 600 selections, and the desserts are extraordinary.

EXPENSIVE

✪ **Craftwood Inn.** 404 El Paso Blvd., Manitou Springs. ☎ **719/685-9000.** Reservations recommended. Main courses $12–$29.50. DISC, MC, V. Daily 5–10pm. Turn north off Manitou Ave. onto Mayfair Ave., go uphill 1 block, and turn left onto El Paso Blvd.; the Craftwood is on your right. COLORADO CUISINE.

Ensconced in an English Tudor building with beamed ceilings, stained-glass windows, and a copper-hooded fireplace, the Craftwood Inn, built in 1912, was originally a coppersmith's shop. Today this excellent restaurant specializes in regional game, plus seafood, chicken, and vegetarian dishes. You might try the grilled buffalo tenderloin served with a wild-mushroom cabernet-sauvignon glace, or Colorado mountain bass sautéed with crushed hazelnuts and deglazed with white wine and lemon. But be sure to save room for one of the superb desserts, such as jalapeño white-chocolate mousse with raspberry sauce, or prickly-pear sorbet.

✪ **La Petite Maison.** 1015 W. Colorado Ave. ☎ **719/632-4887.** Reservations recommended. Main courses $16–$26. AE. CB, DC, DISC, MC, V. Tues–Sat 5–10pm. CONTEMPORARY.

This delightful 1894 Victorian cottage houses a gem of a restaurant, providing a blend of classic French and eclectic modern cuisine, served in a friendly, intimate setting to the strains of chamber music. The food is top rate and the service impeccable; this is where locals go to celebrate special occasions. Our recommendations include grilled lamb loin with artichoke bottoms and mushroom essence, and grilled duck breast with a warm Marsala vinaigrette. Other choices include the evening's pasta selection and fresh fish, and several lighter dishes are offered between 5 and 6:30pm. Desserts might include white-chocolate mousse with fresh berries or a fresh fruit tart with almond paste.

✪ **MacKenzie's Chop House.** 128 S. Tejon St. ☎ **719/635-3536.** Reservations highly recommended. Lunch $6–$13, dinner $13–$35; Sun brunch $20 adults, $7 ages 6 to 12. AE, MC, V. Mon–Fri 11am–3pm, Sun brunch 10am–2pm; Sun–Thurs 5–10pm, Fri–Sat 5–11pm. STEAK HOUSE.

Located in a handsome brick building in downtown Colorado Springs, MacKenzie's large dining room is divided into numerous intimate sections, with

ⓘ　Family-Friendly Restaurants

Edelweiss Restaurant *(see p. 130)*　Kids will enjoy the strolling musicians who play German folk music on weekends, and they'll love the apple and cherry strudels.

The Hungry Farmer *(see p. 131)*　Lots of good basic food served in a fun semi-barn-like atmosphere should please the entire family.

dark woods and antique-like upholstery on the booths. The open-air patio gives the feeling of dining in a grotto, with a lovely waterfall cascading over rocks.

The food is both tasty and casually elegant. The crusty breads are made in-house, fresh seafood is flown in regularly, and the chops are special-ordered and cooked to perfection. Good choices include the fresh Atlantic salmon, oven-roasted on a cedar plank and coined with a compound butter; and the signature charbroiled chops, such as the southwestern fillet (two fillet medallions charbroiled to order and served with avocado salsa, cojita cheese, and chipotle puree). Lunch brings sandwiches and burgers, pasta, and pizza, and the Sunday champagne brunch is sumptuous.

MacKenzie's Martini Menu lists some three dozen martinis, from the traditional to the exotic, and even so-called "dessert" martinis. The bar lounge offers a full menu and seating at high tables. See also "Colorado Springs After Dark," below.

The Margarita at PineCreek. 7350 Pine Creek Rd. ☎ 719/598-8667. Reservations recommended. Fixed-price dinner $21–$25. AE, DISC, MC, V. Tues–Fri 11:30am–2pm; Tues–Sun 6–9pm. INTERNATIONAL.

A delightful spot to sit and watch the sun setting over Pikes Peak, the Margarita is tucked away above two creeks on the north side of the city. Decor is attractively simple, with tile floors and stucco walls; a tree-shaded outdoor patio is open in summer. Saturday evenings bring live harpsichord music in the dining room, and Friday nights often feature a Celtic band.

The emphasis here is on fresh ingredients and everything made "from scratch." Lunches feature a choice of soup, salad, and freshly baked bread, plus a southwestern special. Six-course dinners offer three choices of entrees.

MODERATE

Anthony's. 1919 E. Boulder St. ☎ 719/471-3654. Reservations recommended for groups of five or more. Main courses $5–$10 lunch, $8–$17.50 dinner. AE, DISC, MC, V. Mon–Fri 11am–2pm; Tues–Thurs 5–9pm, Fri–Sat 5–10pm. ITALIAN.

Situated in a quiet east-side neighborhood, Anthony's offers a tranquil escape from a hectic day. In summer, dine on the outdoor patio; in winter, stay warm by the blazing fire. All pastas are homemade. Regulars often choose chicken or veal parmigiana, or *saltimbocca alla Romana*. Dinners include soup, salad, garlic bread, sorbet, and Dorro (an Italian dessert liqueur); a plate of linguine accompanies meat dishes.

Edelweiss Restaurant. 34 E. Ramona Ave. ☎ 719/633-2220. Reservations recommended. Main courses $4.50–$7.25 lunch, $8.25–$17.25 dinner. AE, DC, DISC, MC, V. Mon–Fri 11:30am–2pm; Sun–Thurs 5–9pm, Fri–Sat 5–9:30pm. Located southwest of I-25, just west of Nevada Ave. GERMAN.

The Edelweiss has a big indoor fireplace and an outdoor patio, and underscores its Bavarian atmosphere with strolling folk musicians on weekends. It offers a hearty menu of Jägerschnitzel, Wiener schnitzel, sauerbraten, bratwurst, and other old-country specials, as well as New York strip steak, fresh fish, and chicken. The fruit strudels are excellent.

The Hungry Farmer. 575 Garden of the Gods Rd. ☎ **719/598-7622.** Lunch $4.75–$11, dinner $11–$19. AE, CB, DISC, DC, MC, V. Mon–Fri 11:30am–2pm and 5–9pm, Sat 11:30am–10pm, Sun 11:30am–9pm. AMERICAN.

Locally famous for its generous portions and slow-cooked prime rib, this restaurant has a somewhat unusual kind of farm atmosphere, with bales of hay, stained-glass windows, and chandeliers. There's a large selection of steak, chicken, seafood, ribs, and veal, and all dinners include a bottomless bucket of soup, corn on the cob, salad, potato, and hot homemade oatmeal muffins and cinnamon rolls. Children get their own menu.

Phantom Canyon Brewing Co. 2 E. Pikes Peak Ave. ☎ **719/635-2800.** Reservations required for groups of eight or more. Lunch $5.25–$7.50, dinner $9–$17. AE, CB, DC, DISC, MC, V. Mon–Thurs 11am–11pm, Fri–Sat 11am–2am, Sun 9am–10pm. URBAN COMFORT CUISINE.

This popular brewpub is located in the Cheyenne Building, home to the Chicago Rock Island & Pacific Railroad from 1902 to 1909. On any given day, five to eight of Phantom Canyon's specialty beers are on tap, including their homemade root beer.

The dining room is large and open, with hardwood floors, booths and tables, walls of windows facing two streets, and the large brewing vats in one corner. The lunch menu features several wood-fired pizzas, hearty salads, half-pound beef or buffalo burgers, fish-and-chips, shepherd's pie, and several pasta dishes. Dinner is varied, with unusual choices such as charbroiled garlic chicken breast with three-grain rice and honey-beer mustard, and charbroiled salmon fillet with smoked strawberry BBQ sauce, horseradish whipped potatoes, and skinny onion rings. The menu changes periodically. On the second floor is a billiard hall with its own menu of pizza, calzones, salad, and appetizers.

The Ritz Grill. 15 S. Tejon St. ☎ **719/635-8484.** Brunch and lunch $6–$10, dinner $8–$18. AE, MC, V. Mon–Sat 11am–2am, Sun 9:30am–2am. NEW AMERICAN.

This lively restaurant-lounge, with a large central bar, is where it's at for many of Colorado Springs' young professionals. The decor is art deco, and the service fast and friendly. The varied, trendy menu offers such specialties as the Ritz veggie pizza, with fresh spinach, sun-dried tomatoes, bell peppers, onions, mushrooms, pesto, and three cheeses; and southwest pasta—rock shrimp and chicken in a roasted red-pepper sauce, angel-hair pasta, and jack cheese. There's also a mesquite-grilled filet mignon, fish and chicken dishes, salads, and sandwiches. See also "Colorado Springs After Dark," below.

INEXPENSIVE

Adams Mountain Cafe. 110 Cañon Ave., Manitou Springs. ☎ **719/685-1430.** Breakfast and lunch $2.50–$7, dinner $6–$12. MC, V. Daily 7:30am–3pm, Tues–Sat 5–9pm. INTERNATIONAL/NATURAL FOODS.

This cafe has a country French–Victorian setting, with exposed brick and stone, antique tables and chairs, fresh flowers, and original watercolors. The menu includes grilled items and fresh fish, although the restaurant focuses on vegetarian offerings made with the freshest ingredients. Dinner options include shrimp margarita—sweet peppers, avocado, and fresh melon sautéed with Tiger shrimp, with tequila and lime, and served over spinach linguine or polenta. Breakfast specialties include the "P. W. Busboy Special"—two whole-grain pancakes, two scrambled eggs, and slices of fresh fruit. Lunch offerings include sandwiches, soups, salads, fresh pasta, and southwestern plates.

Fit for the Gods

In 1859 large numbers of pioneers were arriving in Colorado hoping to find gold (their motto: "Pikes Peak or Bust"); many of these pioneers established communities along what is now called the Front Range, including Colorado City (later incorporated within Colorado Springs).

Legend has it that certain pioneers who explored the remarkable sandstone formations in the area wanted to establish a beer garden there. However, one Rufus Cable objected: "Beer Garden! Why this is a fit place for a Garden of the Gods!"

Fortunately for posterity, the area was bought some 20 years later by Charles Elliott Perkins (head of the Burlington Railroad) and kept in its natural state. Upon Perkins' death in 1907, his heirs gave the remarkable area to Colorado Springs on condition that it be preserved as a park and open to the public. Now a Registered National Landmark, the park was dedicated in 1909.

Dutch Kitchen. 1025 Manitou Ave., Manitou Springs. ☎ **719/685-9962.** Lunch $3–$5, dinner $5.50–$7.25. Sat–Thurs 11:30am–3:30pm and 4:30–8pm. Closed Dec–Feb. AMERICAN.

Good, homemade food served in a casual, friendly atmosphere is what you'll find at this relatively small restaurant, which has been owned and operated by the Flynn family since 1959. The corned beef, pastrami, and ham sandwiches have been popular since the restaurant opened, and if you're there in summer be sure to try the fresh rhubarb pie. Other house specialties include buttermilk pie and homemade soups.

Michelle's. 122 N. Tejon St. ☎ **719/633-5089.** Reservations not accepted. Breakfast $2.50–$5, lunch and dinner $4–$7. AE, CB, DC, DISC, MC, V. Mon–Thurs 9am–11pm, Fri–Sat 9am–midnight, Sun 10am–11pm. AMERICAN/GREEK/SOUTHWEST.

The menu is eclectic, but it's amazing how many different dishes Michelle's prepares well—and at such reasonable prices. Since it opened in 1952, this restaurant has been known for its excellent handmade chocolates, fresh-churned ice cream, and Greek specialties such as gyros and spanakopita. But it also has good burgers, croissant sandwiches, salads, omelets, and a delicious breakfast burrito.

There's also a **Michelle's** in the Citadel Shopping Center, at East Platte Avenue and North Academy Boulevard (☎ **719/597-9932**).

5 Attractions

The attractions of the Pikes Peak region can be placed in two general categories: natural, such as Pikes Peak, Garden of the Gods, and Cave of the Winds, and historic and educational, including the Air Force Academy, Olympic Training Center, museums, historic homes, and art galleries. And there are also the gambling houses of Cripple Creek.

If you have just arrived in Colorado from a sea-level area, you might want to schedule any mountain excursions, such as the cog railway to the top of Pikes Peak, for the end of your stay; this will give your body time to adapt to the lower oxygen level at these higher elevations. See also "Health, Safety & Insurance," in chapter 3.

THE TOP ATTRACTIONS

United States Air Force Academy. Off I-25 exit 156B. ☎ **719/333-8723.** Free admission. Summer, daily 9am–6pm; winter, daily 9am–5pm; additional hours for special events.

Colorado Springs' pride and joy got its start in 1954, when Congress authorized the establishment of a U.S. Air Force Academy and chose this 18,000-acre site from among 400 prospective locations.

The academy is situated 12 miles north of downtown (I-25 exit 156B). Soon after entering the grounds, you'll see an impressive outdoor B-52 bomber display. In another mile or so, look to your left to see the Cadet Field House, where basketball and ice hockey games are played, and the Parade Ground, where cadets can sometimes be spotted marching.

Six miles from the entrance, signs mark the turnoff to the Barry Goldwater Air Force Academy Visitor Center. Open daily, it offers a variety of exhibits and films on the academy's history and cadet life, extensive literature and self-guided tour maps, and the latest information and schedules on academy activities, plus a large gift shop, coffee shop, public phones, and rest rooms.

A short trail from the visitor center leads to the Cadet Chapel, whose 17 gleaming aluminum spires soar 150 feet skyward. Hours are Monday through Saturday from 9am to 5pm, Sunday from 2 to 5pm; Sunday services at 9 and 11am are also open to the public. The chapel is closed for five days around graduation and during special events.

Also within easy walking distance of the visitor center are the Academy Planetarium, with periodic free public programs; Arnold Hall, offering historical exhibits, a cafeteria, and theater featuring a variety of public shows and lectures; and Harmon Hall, the administration building, where prospective cadets can obtain admission information.

After leaving the visitor center, you will pass Falcon Stadium, and then Thunderbird Airmanship Overlook, where you might be lucky enough to see cadets parachuting, soaring, and practicing takeoffs and landings in U.S. Air Force Thunderbirds.

For specific information about the academy, write Visitor Services Division, Directorate of Public Affairs, 2304 Cadet Dr., Ste. 318, U.S. Air Force Academy, CO 80840.

✪ **Garden of the Gods.** Ridge Rd., I-25 exit 146. ☎ **719/634-6666.** www.gardenofgods. com. Free admission. Park, May–Oct, daily 5am–11pm; Nov–Apr, daily 5am–9pm. Visitor Center, Jan–Feb 9am–5pm; Mar–Memorial Day and Labor Day–Dec 8:30am–5:30pm; Memorial Day–Labor Day 8am–9pm. Take Garden of the Gods Rd. west from I-25 exit 146 and turn south on 30th St.

One of the West's unique geological sites, the Garden of the Gods is a beautiful giant rock garden, composed of spectacular red sandstone formations sculpted by rain and wind over millions of years. Located where several life zones and ecosystems converge, the city-run park harbors a variety of plant and animal communities.

Hiking maps for the 1,300-acre park are available at the **Visitor Center,** which also offers an 8-minute geology show; displays on the history, geology, plants, and wildlife of the park; and a cafeteria. A 12-minute multimedia theater presentation—*How Did Those Red Rocks Get There?*—is a fast-paced exploration of the geologic history of the area ($2 for adults, $1 for children 12 and under). In summer, park naturalists lead 45-minute walks through the park and conduct afternoon interpretive programs. You may spot technical rock climbers on some of the park spires (they are required to register at the Visitor Center).

Also in the park is the **Rock Ledge Ranch Historic Site** (see "More Attractions," below).

Focus on the Family. 8685 Explorer Dr. ☎ **719/531-3328**. Free admission. Summer, Mon–Sat 9am–5pm; winter, Mon–Fri 9am–5pm, Sat 9am–4pm. Take I-25 exit 151 east to Explorer Dr.

Colorado Springs Attractions

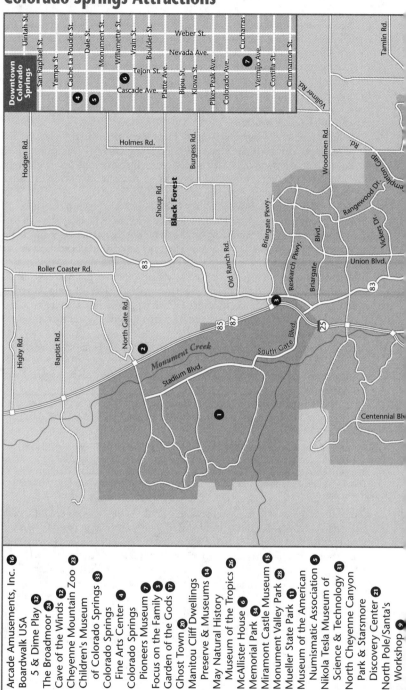

Downtown Colorado Springs

Uintah St.
San Raphael St.
Yampa St.
Cache La Poudre St.
Dale St.
Monument St.
Willamette St.
Vrain St.
Boulder St.
Weber St.
Nevada Ave.
Cucharras
Vermijo Ave.
Costilla St.
Cimmarron St.
Tejon St.
Pikes Peak Ave.
Platte Ave.
Bijou St.
Kiowa St.
Colorado Ave.
Cascade Ave.

Tamlin Rd.

Holmes Rd.
Hodgen Rd.
Burgess Rd.
Woodmen Rd.
Vollmer Rd.
Templeton Gap Rd

Black Forest
Shoup Rd.
Old Ranch Rd.
Briargate Pkwy.
Rangewood Dr.
Vickers Dr.

Roller Coaster Rd.
83
Research Pkwy.
Briargate Blvd.
Union Blvd.
83

Higby Rd.
Baptist Rd.
North Gate Rd.
85 87
South Gate Blvd.
25

Monument Creek
Stadium Blvd.

Centennial Blv

1-0509

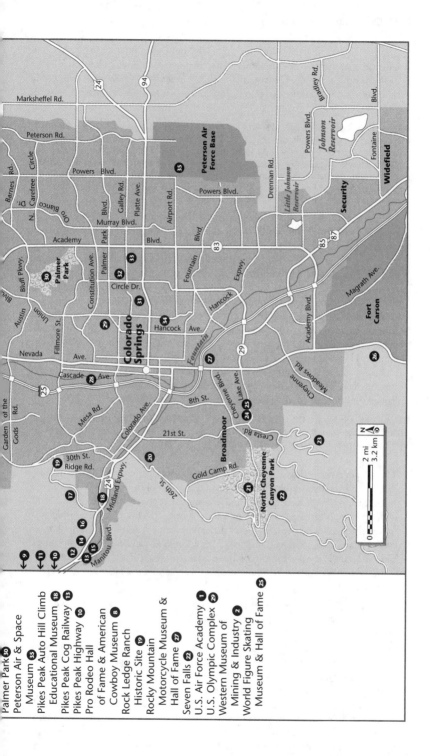

Palmer Park **30**
Peterson Air & Space
   Museum **35**
Pikes Peak Auto Hill Climb
   Educational Museum **18**
Pikes Peak Cog Railway **13**
Pikes Peak Highway **10**
Pro Rodeo Hall
   of Fame & American
   Cowboy Museum **8**
Rock Ledge Ranch
   Historic Site **19**
Rocky Mountain
   Motorcycle Museum &
   Hall of Fame **27**
Seven Falls **22**
U.S. Air Force Academy **1**
U.S. Olympic Complex **29**
Western Museum of
   Mining & Industry **2**
World Figure Skating
   Museum & Hall of Fame **25**

The attractive Welcome Center contains a large bookstore, interactive displays, and a theater that shows a 20-minute video narrated by Dr. James C. Dobson, founder of Focus on the Family. Downstairs is a Kids Korner with a play area, plus a soda fountain the entire family can enjoy. A cafeteria upstairs serves breakfast and lunch. There's also a free 45-minute guided tour of the campus.

Pikes Peak Cog Railway. 515 Ruxton Ave., Manitou Springs. ☎ **719/685-5401.** www.cograilway.com. Admission $25 adults, $12 children under 12 (but those under 5 held on an adult's lap ride free). June–Aug, eight departures daily; in late April and Sept–Oct, two to six departures daily. Late Apr–Oct departures from Manitou Springs at 9:20am and 1:20pm. Reservations recommended (and can be made online). Take I-25 exit 141 west on U.S. 24 for 4 miles, turn onto to Manitou Ave. west 1½ miles to Ruxton Ave., turn left and continue for about half a mile.

For those who enjoy rail travel, spectacular scenery, and the thrill of mountain climbing without all the work, this is the trip to take. The first passenger train climbed Pikes Peak on June 30, 1891, and diesel slowly replaced steam power between 1939 and 1955. Four custom-built Swiss twin-unit rail cars, each seating 216 passengers, were put into service in 1989. The 9-mile route, with grades up to 25%, takes 75 minutes to reach the top of 14,110-foot Pikes Peak, and the round-trip requires 3 hours and 10 minutes (including a 40-minute stopover at the top).

The view from the summit takes in Denver, 75 miles north; New Mexico's Sangre de Cristo range, 100 miles south; wave after wave of Rocky Mountain sub-ranges to the west; and the seemingly endless sea of Great Plains to the east. The Summit House at the top of Pikes Peak has a restaurant and gift shop.

Take a jacket or sweater—it can be cold and windy on top, even on warm summer days. This trip is not recommended if you have cardiac or respiratory problems. Even those in good health may feel faint or light-headed.

Pikes Peak Highway. Off U.S. 24 at Cascade. ☎ **719/684-9383.** Admission $10 per person over age 16 or $35 per car. Memorial Day–Labor Day, daily 7am–7pm; the rest of the year, daily 9am–3pm, except closed Tues–Wed, Jan–Feb. Take I-25 exit 141 west on U.S. 24 about 10 miles.

There is perhaps no view in Colorado to equal the 360° panorama from the 14,110-foot summit of Pikes Peak. Whether you go by cog railway (see above) or private vehicle, the ascent is a spectacular and exciting experience, although not for those with heart or breathing problems or a fear of heights. This 19-mile toll highway (paved for 7 miles, all-weather gravel thereafter) starts at 7,400 feet, some 4 miles west of Manitou Springs, with numerous photo stops as you head up the mountain. This 156-curve road is the site of the annual July Fourth Pikes Peak Auto Hill Climb, the Pikes Peak Marathon footrace in August, and the New Year's Eve climb and fireworks show.

✪ **Colorado Springs Pioneers Museum.** 215 S. Tejon St. ☎ **719/578-6650.** Free admission. Tues–Sat 10am–5pm; plus May–Oct Sun 1–5pm. Take I-25 exit 141 east to Tejon St., turn left for 2 blocks.

Housed in the former El Paso County Courthouse, built in 1903 and listed on the National Register of Historic Places, this museum is an excellent place to begin your visit to Colorado Springs. Exhibits depict the community's rich history, including its beginning as a fashionable resort, the railroad and mining eras, and its growth and development into the 20th century.

You can ride an 80-plus-year-old Otis birdcage elevator to the restored original courtroom, where several *Perry Mason* television episodes were filmed. The renovation uncovered murals of gold and silver images of goddesses, painted as a protest when the country was changing from a gold to silver monetary standard, and others depicting the history of the region.

Changing exhibit areas house traveling shows, and the museum hosts a wide range of events, including lectures, antique auto shows, and concerts. There's also an historic reference library and archives for public use.

United States Olympic Complex. 1 Olympic Plaza, corner of Boulder St. (entrance) and Union Blvd. ☎ **719/578-4618** for visitor center, 719/578-4644 for tour and events hotline. Tour reservations required for groups of 10 or more. Free admission. Complex open daily 9am–5pm. Take I-25 exit 143.

This 36-acre site houses a sophisticated training center for more than half of the 41 U.S. Olympic sports, providing a training ground for some 20,000 athletes of all ages each year. Free guided tours, available daily, begin with a film depicting the U.S. Olympic effort. A gift shop next to the visitor center sells Olympic-logo merchandise; the proceeds help support athlete training programs.

MORE ATTRACTIONS
ARCHITECTURAL HIGHLIGHTS

The Broadmoor. Lake Circle, at Lake Ave. ☎ **719/634-7711.** Free admission. Daily year-round.

This famous Italian Renaissance–style resort hotel has been a Colorado Springs landmark since it was built by Spencer Penrose in 1918. (See "Accommodations," above.)

Miramont Castle Museum. 9 Capitol Hill Ave., Manitou Springs. ☎ **719/685-1011.** Admission $3 adults, $1 children 6–11, free for children under 6. Memorial Day–Labor Day, daily 10am–5pm; Apr–Memorial Day and Labor Day–mid-December, Tues–Sun 11am–4pm; rest of year, Tues–Sun noon–3pm. Located just off Ruxton Ave., en route from Manitou Ave. to the Pikes Peak Cog Railway.

Built into a hillside by a wealthy French priest as a private home in 1895, and converted by the Sisters of Mercy into a sanatorium in 1907, this unique Victorian mansion has always aroused curiosity. At least nine identifiable architectural styles are incorporated into the four-story structure. It has 28 rooms and two-foot-thick stone walls. A separate building houses a model-railroad museum. In summer, light meals and tea are served from 11am to 4pm in the Queen's Parlour.

HISTORIC BUILDINGS

McAllister House. 423 N. Cascade Ave. (at St. Vrain St.). ☎ **719/635-7925.** oldcolo.com/hist/mcallister. Admission $3 adults, $2 seniors and students, $1 children 6–16, free for children under 6. Summer, Wed–Sat 10am–4pm, Sun noon–4pm; winter, Thurs–Sat 10am–4pm. Take I-25 exit 141 east to Cascade Ave., then left for about 6 blocks.

This 1873 Gothic cottage, on the National Register of Historic Places, was constructed of brick when the builder, Henry McAllister, learned that the local wind was so strong it had blown a train off the tracks nearby. The house has many original furnishings, including three marble fireplaces. Tea is served on certain holidays, and croquet is available on summer Sundays.

Rock Ledge Ranch Historic Site. Gateway Rd., Garden of the Gods. ☎ **719/578-6777.** Admission $3 adults, $2 seniors, $1 children 6–12, free for children under 6. June–Labor Day, Wed–Sun 10am–5pm; Labor Day–Christmas, Sat 10am–4pm, Sun noon–4pm. Closed Jan–May. Take I-25 exit 146, then follow signs west to Garden of the Gods.

Listed on the National Register of Historic Places, the Ranch presents the rigors of the homestead era at the 1860s Galloway Homestead, the agricultural difficulties of the working-ranch era at the 1880s Chambers Farm and Blacksmith Shop, and the more sophisticated estate period at the 1907 Orchard House. Special events include an old-fashioned Fourth of July celebration, an 1860s-vintage baseball game in late summer, and holiday celebrations from Thanksgiving through Christmas. The General Store offers historic reproductions, books, and gift items; proceeds help with preservation and restoration.

HISTORIC NEIGHBORHOODS

Manitou Springs, which is centered around Manitou Avenue off U.S. 24 West, is actually a separate town with its own government and is one of the country's largest National Historic Districts. Legend has it that Utes named the springs Manitou, or "Great Spirit," because they believed the Great Spirit breathed into the waters to create the natural effervescence of the springs.

Today, the elegant Victorian buildings house delightful shops, galleries, restaurants, and lodgings, and Manitou Springs is home to many fine artists and artisans. A small group of sculptors began the Manitou Art Project in 1992, whereby more than 20 sculptures were installed in various locations around town, creating a large sculpture garden for all to enjoy. The works are for sale, with 25% of the proceeds used to purchase permanent sculptures for the city. Five have been purchased to date.

Visitors are encouraged to take the self-guided tour of the nine mineral springs of Manitou that have been restored. Pick up the *Manitou Springs Complete Visitor's Guide,* which contains a map and descriptions to help you find each spring. It's available at the Chamber of Commerce, 354 Manitou Ave., open daily.

Old Colorado City, Colorado Avenue between 21st and 31st Streets, was founded in 1859, before Colorado Springs itself. The town boomed in the 1880s after General Palmer's railroad came through: Tunnels led from the respectable side of town to this saloon and red-light district so that the city fathers could carouse without being seen coming or going, or so the legend goes. Today this historic district has an interesting assortment of shops, galleries, and restaurants.

MUSEUMS & GALLERIES

Colorado Springs Fine Arts Center. 30 W. Dale St. (west of N. Cascade Ave.). ☎ **719/ 634-5581.** Admission to galleries and museum, $3 adults, $1.50 seniors and students, $1 children 6–12, free for children under 6. Free for everyone Sat 10am–noon. Separate admission for performing-arts events. Galleries and museum, Tues–Fri 9am–5pm, Sat 10am–5pm, Sun 1–5pm. Closed federal holidays. Take I-25 exit 143 east to Cascade St., turn right to Dale St., then turn right again.

Georgia O'Keeffe, Charles Russell, Albert Bierstadt, and other famed painters and sculptors are represented in the center's permanent collection, which also includes a world-class collection of American Indian and Hispanic works. Opened in 1936, the center also houses a performing-arts theater, art research library, the Bemis Art School, a tactile gallery for those who are visually impaired, and a delightful sculpture garden. Changing exhibits in two galleries showcase local collections as well as touring international exhibits.

Ghost Town. 400 S. 21st St. ☎ **719/634-0696.** www.pikes-peak.com/ghosttown. Admission $4.50 adults, $2.50 children 6–16, free for children under 6. Memorial Day–Labor Day, Mon–Sat 9am–6pm, Sun noon–6pm; Labor Day–Memorial Day, Mon–Sat 10am–5pm, Sun noon–5pm. Just west of I-25 exit 141, on U.S. 24 at 21st St.

Comprised of authentic 19th-century buildings relocated from other parts of Colorado, this "town" is sheltered from the elements in Old Colorado City. There's a sheriff's office, saloon, general store, blacksmith shop, and assay office. Animated frontier characters tell stories of the Old West, while a shooting gallery, antique arcade machines, and nickelodeons provide additional entertainment.

☼ Manitou Cliff Dwellings Preserve & Museums. U.S. 24, Manitou Springs. ☎ **800/ 354-9971** or 719/685-5242. Admission $6 adults, $5 seniors, $4 children 7–11, free for children under 7. June–Aug, daily 9am–8pm; May and Sept, daily 9am–6pm; Oct–Apr, daily 9am–5pm. Closed Christmas and Thanksgiving. Take I-25 exit 141, go west on U.S. 24 about 5 miles.

The cliff dwelling ruins here are real, although relocated from elsewhere. In the early 1900s, archaeologists, seeing such dwellings being plundered, dismantled some of the ancient buildings, gathered together artifacts, and hauled them away. Some may now be seen in this 12th-century village, placed here by archaeologists around 1900. American Indian dancers perform in summer.

May Natural History Museum of the Tropics. 710 Rock Creek Canyon Rd. ☎ **719/ 576-0450.** Admission $4.50 adults, $2.50 children. May–Sept, daily 9am–6pm. Take Colo. 115 and drive southwest out of Colorado Springs for 9 miles; watch for signs and the Hercules Beetle of the West Indies that marks the turnoff to the museum.

James F. W. May (1884–1956) spent more than half a century exploring the world's jungles and compiling his collection, now grown to over 100,000 invertebrates—about 8,000 of which are on display at any given time. The specimens are irreplaceable, since many came from areas so politically unstable now that no one can explore the backcountry to collect them again. Exhibits change periodically.

The **Museum of Space Exploration** offers a pictorial historical overview, beginning with man's first attempts to fly and continuing up to the most recent photos of Venus from the Mariner Space Craft.

Museum of the American Numismatic Association. 818 N. Cascade Ave. ☎ **719/ 632-2646.** Free admission, but donations are welcome. Mon–Fri 8:30am–4pm. Take I-25 exit 143 east to Cascade Ave., then turn right for about 6 blocks.

The largest collection of its kind west of the Smithsonian Institute, this museum consists of eight galleries of coins, tokens, and paper money from around the world. There's also a collectors' library, a gallery for the visually impaired, and an authentication department.

Nikola Tesla Museum of Science & Technology. 2220 E. Bijou St. ☎ **719/475-0918.** Free admission to gallery and bookstore; tours $5 adults, $3 children 12 and under. Mon–Fri 11am–4pm, Sat noon–4pm. Take I-25 exit 142 east to Cascade, turn left 1 block, then right onto Platte Ave. After about 2 miles, turn right onto Union Blvd. and left at the first block onto Bijou St. It's about 3 blocks down.

Science buffs will love this small but fascinating collection of early electronics and related gadgets. The museum's primary purpose is to display and demonstrate some of the many inventions of Nikola Tesla (1856–1943), who was awarded more than 100 U.S. patents. A contemporary of Thomas Edison's, Tesla perfected the alternating current and invented the Tesla coil, a transformer used to produce high-frequency power. Guided hands-on tours are usually given Saturdays at 2pm or by special arrangement. The museum also has an extensive science and technology bookstore.

Peterson Air & Space Museum. Peterson Air Force Base main gate, off U.S. 24. ☎ **719/ 556-4915.** Free admission. Tues–Sat 8:30am–4:30pm. Closed holidays and occasionally during military exercises. Take I-25 exit 141, then follow U.S. 24 east about 7½ miles.

This museum's exhibits trace the history of Peterson Air Force Base, NORAD, the Air Defense Command, and Air Force Space Command. Of special interest are 17

Impressions

The air is so refined that you can live without much lungs.

—Shane Leslie, *American Wonderland*, 1936

historic aircraft, including fighters from World War II, plus four missiles and jets from the Korean War to the present.

Pikes Peak Auto Hill Climb Educational Museum. 135 Manitou Ave., Manitou Springs. ☎ 719/685-4400. Admission $5 adults, $3 seniors, $2 children 6–12. May–Oct 1, daily 9am–7pm; rest of year, daily 9am–5pm. Take I-25 exit 141 west 4 miles on U.S. 24 to Manitou Ave., then east 1 block.

Commemorating the nation's second-oldest auto race (the oldest is the Indianapolis 500), this museum displays nearly a century of memorabilia and historic photos, plus almost two dozen complete race cars from the 1920s to today. The annual July Fourth race comprises 156 turns on a gravel highway to the summit of Pikes Peak, 14,110 feet above sea level.

Pro Rodeo Hall of Fame & American Cowboy Museum. 101 Pro Rodeo Dr. (off Rockrimmon Blvd.). ☎ 719/528-4764. Admission $6 adults, $3 children 5–12, free for children under 5. Daily 9am–5pm. Closed New Year's Eve and Day, Easter, Thanksgiving, and Christmas. Just off I-25 exit 147.

The development of rodeo, from its origins in early ranch work to major professional sport, is featured in two multimedia presentations. Heritage Hall showcases both historic and modern cowboy and rodeo gear and clothing, and rodeo greats are honored in the Hall of Champions. Changing exhibits of western art are featured throughout, and outside are a replica rodeo arena, live rodeo animals, and sculpture garden.

Rocky Mountain Motorcycle Museum & Hall of Fame. 308 E. Arvada St. ☎ 719/633-6329. Free admission, donations welcome. Mon–Sat 10am–7pm. From I-25 south, take exit 140B onto Arvada east about 3 blocks; the museum is on the left. From I-25 north, take exit 140B onto Tejon south and go 1 block to Arvada; turn left and go about 2 blocks to the museum. From downtown, take Nevada Ave. south; turn left onto Arvada just after you pass under I-25, and go about 2 blocks.

Adjoining southern Colorado's oldest and largest custom motorcycle shop, this museum has more than 75 classic motorcycles on display. Many are in superb condition—either original or restored—and others are in various states of disrepair awaiting their turn. Motorcycle memorabilia, photos, art, and sculpture fill the space between the machines.

✪ **Western Museum of Mining & Industry.** Gleneagle Drive, at I-25 exit 156A. ☎ 719/488-0880. Admission $6 adults, $5 seniors 60 and older and students 13–17, $3 children 5–12, and free for children under 5. Mon–Sat 9am–4pm; plus June–Sept Sun noon–4pm. The 27-acre site is located just east of the north gate of the U.S. Air Force Academy.

Historic hard-rock mining machinery and other equipment from turn-of-the-century Colorado gold camps form the basis of this museum's 3,000-plus-item collection. Visitors can see an operating Corliss steam engine with a 17-ton flywheel, a life-size underground mine reconstruction, and an exhibit on mining-town life. You can also pan for gold—there's a wheelchair-accessible trough—and view an 18-minute slide presentation on life in the early mining camps. Guided tours are available, with times varying seasonally; call for details.

World Figure Skating Museum & Hall of Fame. 20 First St. ☎ **719/635-5200.** Admission $3 adults, $2 seniors and children. June–Aug, Mon–Sat 10am–4pm; Sept–May, Mon–Fri and first Sat of each month 10am–4pm. Take I-25 exit 138 west on Lake Ave.; just before the Broadmoor, turn right onto First St.

This is the only museum of its kind in the world, exhibiting 1,200 years of ice skates—from early skates of carved bone to highly decorated cast-iron examples and finally the steel blades of today. There are also skating costumes, medals, and other memorabilia, changing exhibits, films, a library, and gift shop. The museum is the repository for the history and official records of figure skating, including the United States' national, regional, sectional, and international trophies.

NATURAL ATTRACTIONS

Cave of the Winds. U.S. 24, Manitou Springs. ☎ **719/685-5444.** Admission $12 adults, $6 children 6–15, free for children under 6. May–Labor Day, daily 9am–9pm; Labor Day–Apr, daily 10am–5pm. Adventure Tours depart every 15 minutes; in summer, Lantern Tours ($16 adult, $7 children 6–15, not recommended for those under 6) are conducted four times daily and Explorer Tours ($60 per person, children 13 to 17 must be accompanied by parent or guardian, under 13 not permitted) three times daily, other times by reservation. Visitors with heart conditions, visual impairment, or other physical limitations are advised not to take the Lantern Tour, and may not take the Explorer Tour. Take I-25 exit 141, go 6 miles west on U.S. 24.

Discovered by two boys on a church outing in 1880, this impressive underground cavern has offered public tours for well over a century. The 40-minute Discovery Tour follows a well-lit three-quarter-mile passageway through 20 beautiful subterranean chambers. The 1¼-hour Lantern Tour is a rather strenuous path along unpaved and unlighted corridors through some areas with low ceilings. The physically demanding, 4-hour Explorer Tour is guaranteed to get participants dirty: Armed only with flashlights and helmets, adventurers slither and scramble through remote tunnels.

Seven Falls. At the end of S. Cheyenne Canyon Rd. ☎ **719/632-0765.** Admission $7 adults, $4 children 6–15, free for children under 6. Memorial Day–Labor Day, daily 8am–11pm; reduced hours in other months. Take I-25 exit 141, head west on U.S. 24, turn south on 21st St. for about 3 miles, turn west on Cheyenne Blvd., and then left onto S. Cheyenne Canyon Rd.

A spectacular one-mile drive through a box canyon takes you between the Pillars of Hercules, where the canyon narrows to just 42 feet, ending at these cascading falls. Seven separate waterfalls dance down a granite cliff, illuminated each summer evening by colored lights; an elevator takes visitors to the Eagle Nest viewing platform. A mile-long trail atop the plateau ends at a panoramic view of Colorado Springs.

PARKS & ZOOS

✪ **Cheyenne Mountain Zoo.** Cheyenne Mountain Zoo Rd., above the Broadmoor. ☎ **719/633-9925.** Admission $7.50 adults, $6.50 seniors 65 and over, $4.50 children 3–11, free for children under 3. Summer, daily 9am–6pm and until 8pm Tues; rest of year, daily 9am–5pm. Take I-25 exit 140A, then head south on Colo. 115 to Lake Ave., which you follow west to Cheyenne Mountain Zoo Rd.; watch for a sign.

Located on the lower slopes of Cheyenne Mountain at 6,800 feet above sea level, this medium-sized zoo claims to be the country's only mountain zoo. Animals, many in "natural" environments, include lions, black leopards, elephants, otters, monkeys, giraffes, reptiles, and lots of birds. Rocky cliffs have been created for the mountain goats; there's a pebbled beach for penguins and an animal-contact area for children. The zoo is home to more than 50 endangered species, including the Siberian tiger, Amur leopard, and black rhinoceros.

In summer a tram makes a full loop of the zoo in about 15 minutes; you can ride all day for $1. It's stroller and handicapped accessible. Strollers, double strollers, wheelchairs, and wagons are available for rent at Thundergod Gift and Snack Shop.

Admission to the zoo includes road access to the Will Rogers Shrine of the Sun, a tall wooden tower built in 1937, with photos and information on the American humorist. It also provides a great view of the city and surrounding countryside.

Memorial Park. 1605 E. Pikes Peak Ave. (between Hancock Ave. and Union Blvd.). ☎ **719/ 385-5940.** Free admission. Daily year-round.

One of the largest parks in the city, Memorial is home to the Mark "Pa" Sertich Ice Center and the Aquatics and Fitness Center, as well as the famed 7-Eleven Velodrome, which is used for world-class bicycling events. Other facilities include baseball/softball fields, volleyball and tennis courts, a bicycle criterium, and jogging trails. At Prospect Lake on the south side of the park, you can fish, swim, and rent paddleboats (about $8 an hour). The park hosts a terrific fireworks display on Independence Day. See the sections on ice skating, swimming, and tennis under "Outdoor Activities," below.

Monument Valley Park. 170 W. Cache La Poudre Blvd. ☎ **719/385-5941.** Free admission. Daily year-round.

This long, slender park follows Monument Creek through downtown Colorado Springs. At its south end are formal gardens; in the middle are demonstration gardens of the Horticultural Art Society. Facilities include softball/baseball fields, a pool (open daily in summer; $4 adults, $2.50 children), volleyball and tennis courts, children's playgrounds, picnic shelters, and two trails—the 4¼-mile Monument Creek Trail for walkers, runners, and cyclists, and the 1-mile Monument Valley Fitness Trail at the north end of the park.

✪ Mueller State Park. P.O. Box 49, Divide, CO 80814. ☎ **719/687-2366.** Admission $4 per vehicle. Take U.S. 24 west from Colorado Springs to Divide (25 miles), then go 3½ miles south on Colo. 67.

Somewhat like a junior version of Rocky Mountain National Park, Mueller has 12,000 acres of prime scenic beauty along the west slope of Pikes Peak. There are 90 miles of trails for hikers, horseback riders, and mountain bikers, with opportunities to observe wildlife. The best times are spring and fall, just after sunrise and just before sunset. Trails north of the campground are closed for elk calving from May 15 to June 15. Rangers lead hikes and offer campfire programs in an 80-seat amphitheater.

The park has 134 campsites (☎ **800/678-2267** for reservations), with fees ranging from $9 for walk-in sites to $12 for drive-in sites with electricity; showers are available (bathhouse open from May 15 to October 15 only).

North Cheyenne Canyon Park and Starsmore Discovery Center. 2120 S. Cheyenne Cañon Rd. (west of 21st St.). ☎ **719/578-6146.** Free admission. Park, May–Oct, daily 5am–11pm; Nov–Apr, daily 5am–9pm. Starsmore Discovery Center, early June–Labor Day, daily 9am–10pm; Labor Day–early June, Wed–Sun 10am–4pm. Helen Hunt Falls Visitor Center, May–Aug, daily 9am–5pm; Sept–Oct, Sat–Sun 10am–4pm, closed Nov–Apr.

This city park includes North Cheyenne Creek, which drops 1,800 feet over the course of 5 miles in a series of cascades and waterfalls. There are picnic areas, hiking trails, and a seasonal tram; the visitor center at the foot of Helen Hunt Falls has exhibits on history, geology, flora, and fauna. The Starsmore Discovery Center, at the entrance to the park, offers maps, information, tram tickets ($5.75 adults, $3.25 children), and interactive exhibits for both kids and adults, including audio-visual programs and a climbing wall.

Palmer Park. Maizeland Rd. off Academy Blvd. ☎ **719/385-5941.** Free admission. Daily year-round.

Deeded to the city in 1899 by Colorado Springs' founder Gen. William Jackson Palmer, this 722-acre preserve permits hiking, biking, and horseback riding across a mesa overlooking the city. It boasts a variety of minerals, rich vegetation, considerable wildlife, picnic areas, softball/baseball fields, volleyball courts, and the self-guided Edna Mae Bennet Nature Trail. Other trails include those shared with riders from the adjoining Mark Reyner Stables.

ESPECIALLY FOR KIDS

In addition to the listings below, children will probably enjoy the **Cheyenne Mountain Zoo, May Natural History Museum,** and **Ghost Town,** described above.

Arcade Amusements, Inc. 930 Block Manitou Ave., Manitou Springs. ☎ **719/685-9815.** Free admission; arcade games range from 1¢ to 75¢. First weekend in May–Labor Day, daily 10am–midnight. In winter, open on nice weekends 11am–6pm; call first.

Among the West's oldest and largest amusement arcades, this games complex just might be considered a hands-on arcade museum as well as a fun place for kids of all ages. Some 250 machines range from original working penny pinball machines to modern video games, skee-ball, and 12-player horse racing.

Boardwalk USA 5 & Dime Play. 3275 E. Platt Ave. ☎ **719/227-3866.** Admission $3 for 1 hour, $5 for 2 hours, $10 for all day. Summer, Mon–Thurs 10am–11pm, Fri–Sat 10am–midnight, Sun 10am–9pm. Winter, Mon–Thurs noon–10pm, Fri–Sat 10am–midnight, Sun 10am–9pm.

This indoor family entertainment center provides lots of activities for kids of all ages, including ski ball and other games, plus over 80 video games.

Children's Museum of Colorado Springs. Upper level of Citadel Mall next to J.C. Penney, 750 Citadel Dr. ☎ **719/574-0077.** Admission $3.50. Summer, Mon–Sat 10am–5pm, Sun noon–5pm; school year, Wed–Thurs 11:30am–5pm, Sun noon–5pm, Mon–Tues and Fri–Sat 10am–5pm. Closed major holidays.

Come to this museum to "discover the art & science of being a kid." Children can crawl through a model of the human heart, explore the far corners of the globe on the computer-assisted geography display, and learn how technology helps disabled persons live independently. The nonprofit art and science museum offers many more hands-on activities, special programs on Sundays, a gift shop, and birthday parties by arrangement.

North Pole/Santa's Workshop. At the foot of Pikes Peak Hwy. off U.S. 24, 5 miles west of Manitou Springs. ☎ **719/684-9432.** Admission $9.50 ages 2–59, $3.95 seniors 60 and over, free for children under 2. Mid-May–May 31, Fri–Wed 9:30am–6pm; June–Aug, daily 9:30am–6pm; Sept–Dec 24 (weather permitting), Fri–Tues 10am–5pm. Closed Christmas to mid-May. Take I-25 exit 141, go west on U.S. 24 about 10 miles.

Santa's workshop is busy from mid-May right up until Christmas Eve. Not only can kids visit shops where elves have some early Christmas gifts for sale, but they can also see Santa himself and whisper their requests in his ear. This 26-acre village features numerous rides, including a miniature train, Ferris wheel, and a replica of the *Enterprise* space shuttle, as well as magic shows and musical entertainment, snack shops, and an ice-cream parlor.

Impressions

Could one live in constant view of these grand mountains without being elevated by them into a lofty plane of thought and purpose?

—General William J. Palmer, founder of Colorado Springs, 1871

ORGANIZED TOURS

Half- and full-day bus tours of Colorado Springs, Pikes Peak, the Air Force Academy, and other nearby attractions are offered by **Pikes Peak Tours/Gray Line,** 3704 W. Colorado Ave. (☎ **800/345-8197** or 719/633-1181). From May through October, a variety of other tours are offered, including an excursion to Royal Gorge and white-water-rafting trips. Prices range from $20 to $60 per person.

Historic walking tours, as well as customized individual and group tours, are available from **Talk of the Town,** 1313 Sunset Rd. (☎ **719/633-2724**); they also publish a book of walking tours, *Trips on Twos,* and a book of driving tours, *Trips on Wheels,* both of which are available at local bookstores.

A free downtown **Walking Tour** brochure, with a map and descriptions of more than 30 historic buildings, is available at the Colorado Springs Convention and Visitors Bureau, as well as at local businesses.

Another free brochure, titled *Old Colorado City,* not only shows the location of more than a dozen historic buildings, but also lists shops, galleries, and other businesses.

During the summer months, the **Town Trolley** provides tours and transportation through Manitou Springs and into part of Garden of the Gods (see "Getting Around," above).

Visitors to Manitou Springs should stop at the **Manitou Springs Chamber of Commerce,** 354 Manitou Avenue (☎ **800/642-2567** or 719/685-5089), to pick up a copy of the free *Manitou Springs Complete Visitor's Guide,* which includes a self-guided walking-tour map to Mineral Springs, plus the locations of outdoor sculptures. See "Historic Neighborhoods," above.

6 Outdoor Activities

For information on the city's parks and programs, contact the **Colorado Springs Parks and Recreation Department** (☎ 719/385-5940). Most of the state and federal agencies concerned with outdoor recreation are headquartered in Denver. There are branch offices in Colorado Springs for **Colorado State Parks,** 2128 N. Weber St. (☎ 719/471-0900); the **Colorado Division of Wildlife,** 2126 N. Weber St. (☎ 719/473-2945, or 719/227-5201 for a 24-hour recorded information line); and the **U.S. Forest Service,** Pikes Peak Ranger District of the Pike National Forest, 601 S. Weber St. (☎ 719/636-1602).

You can get hunting and fishing licenses at many sporting-goods stores, as well as at the Colorado Division of Wildlife office listed above.

AERIAL SPORTS　The **Black Forest Soaring Society,** 24566 David Johnson Loop, Elbert, CO 80106 (☎ **303/648-3623**), some 30 miles northeast of the Springs, offers glider rides, rentals, and instruction. Rides cost about $65, with rentals at $15 to $25 per hour (to those with gliding licenses). Advance reservations are required.

Those preferring a hot-air balloon ride can contact several commercial ballooning companies for tours, champagne flights, and weddings. **High But Dry Balloons,** P.O. Box 49006, Colorado Springs, CO 80949 (☎ **719/260-0011**), schedules sunrise and sunset flights daily year-round, weather permitting. Cost depends on the number of passengers, locations, and type of flight. Generally, flights last 2 or 3 hours, with a minimum of 1 hour. On Labor Day weekend, the **Colorado Springs Balloon Classic** sees more than 100 hot-air balloons launched from the city's Memorial Park. Admission is free. (☎ **719/471-4833**).

BICYCLING   Aside from the 4¼-mile loop trail around Monument Valley Park (see "Parks & Zoos" in "More Attractions," above), there are numerous other urban trails for bikers. You can get information at the city's Visitor Information Center, 104 S. Cascade Ave. (☎ **719/635-1632**).

For guided tours and rentals contact **Challenge Unlimited** (see "Mountain Biking," below).

FISHING   Most serious Colorado Springs anglers drive south 40 miles to the Arkansas River, or west to the Rocky Mountain streams and lakes, such as Eleven Mile State Park and Spinney Mountain State Park on the South Platte River west of Florissant. Bass, catfish, walleye pike, and panfish are found in the streams of eastern Colorado; trout is the preferred sport fish of the mountain regions.

Angler's Covey, 917 W. Colorado Ave. (☎ **800/753-4746** or 719/471-2984), is a specialty fly-fishing shop and a good source of general fishing information for southern Colorado. It offers guided half- and full-day trips ($125 to $175 for one person; discounts for two or more), as well as state fishing licenses, rentals, flies, tackle, and so forth. Another good source for licenses, advice, and equipment is **Blicks Sporting Goods,** 119 N. Tejon St. (☎ **719/636-3348**).

GOLF   Public courses include the **Patty Jewett Golf Course,** 900 E. Española St. (☎ 719/578-6827); **Pine Creek Golf Club,** 9850 Divot Trail (☎ 719/594-9999); and **Valley Hi Golf Course,** 610 S. Chelton Rd. (☎ 719/578-6351). Nonresident greens fees range from $24 to $28 for 18 holes.

The finest golf resorts in the Springs are private. Guests can enjoy the 54-hole **Broadmoor Golf Club** (☎ 719/577-5790) at the Broadmoor hotel.

HIKING   Opportunities abound in municipal parks (see "Parks & Zoos" in "More Attractions," above) and Pike National Forest, which borders Colorado Springs to the west. The U.S. Forest Service district office can provide maps and general information (see addresses and phone numbers, above).

Especially popular are the 7½-mile **Waldo Canyon Trail,** with its trailhead just east of Cascade Avenue off U.S. 24; the 10-mile **Mount Manitou Trail,** starting in Ruxton Canyon above the hydroelectric plant; and the 12-mile **Barr Trail** to the summit of Pikes Peak. **Mueller State Park** has 90 miles of hiking and backpacking paths (see "Parks & Zoos" in "More Attractions," above).

HORSEBACK RIDING   The **Academy Riding Stables,** 4 El Paso Blvd., near the Garden of the Gods (☎ **719/633-5667**), offers guided trail rides for children and adults by reservation ($18 to $30).

ICE SKATING   The **Mark "Pa" Sertich Ice Center** at Memorial Park (☎ **719/ 578-6883**) is open daily, offering prearranged instruction and rentals. In 1995, the United States Olympic Complex opened the **Colorado Springs World Arena Ice Hall,** located at 3205 Venetucci Blvd. (☎ **719/579-8014**), with public sessions daily (admission $1 to $4). To get there, take I-25 exit 138, go west on Circle Drive to Venetucci Boulevard, and south to the arena.

MOUNTAIN BIKING   There are abundant mountain-biking opportunities in the Colorado Springs area; contact the U.S. Forest Service for details (see address and phone number, above). From May through early October, **Challenge Unlimited,** 204 S. 24th St. (☎ **800/798-5954** or 719/633-6399), hosts fully equipped, guided rides for every level of experience. Your guide on the 19-mile ride down the Pikes Peak Highway, from the summit at 14,110 feet to the toll gate at 7,000 feet, presents an interpretation of the nature, history, and beauty of the mountain. Advance reservations are advised; minimum age 10 years. Rates are $60 to $80 for a 5-hour trip. Challenge Unlimited also rents bikes ($15 for 3 hours; $20 for full day), so you can explore the area on your own.

SWIMMING   Among the many attractions at the city-run Memorial Park (see "Parks & Zoos" above) is the pool at the **Aquatics and Fitness Center,** 270 Union Blvd. (☎ **719/ 578-6634**). Admission is $4 for adults, $2.50 for children. Call for seasonal hours. You can also swim at Memorial Park's **Prospect Lake** in summer, when it's open daily from 10am to 5pm ($2.50 adults, $1 children).

TENNIS   Many city parks have tennis courts, including **Memorial Park** (see "Parks & Zoos" above). Contact the Colorado Springs Parks and Recreation Department (☎ **719/ 385-5940**). Use of city courts is free.

7 Spectator Sports

The **Air Force Academy Falcons** (the football team) dominate the sports scene here, although there are also competitive baseball, basketball, hockey, and soccer teams. Call for schedules and ticket information (☎ **800/666-USAF** or 719/ 472-1895).

AUTO RACING   The annual **Pikes Peak Auto Hill Climb** (☎ **719/685-4400**), known as the "Race to the Clouds," is held on July 4. An international field of drivers negotiates the winding, hairpin turns of the final 12.4 miles of the Pikes Peak Highway, to the top of the 14,110-foot mountain. For information, contact the Pikes Peak Auto Hill Climb Educational Museum (see "Museums & Galleries" in "Attractions," above).

BASEBALL   The **Colorado Springs Sky Sox** of the Pacific Coast League, the Colorado Rockies AAA farm team, play a full 144-game season, with 72 home games at Sky Sox Stadium, 4385 Tutt Blvd., off Barnes Road east of Powers Boulevard (☎ **719/597-3000**). The season begins the second week of April and runs through Labor Day. Games are played afternoons and evenings. Tickets for reserved seating cost $7 for adults, $6 for children 2 to 12 and seniors 60 and over; for general admission, $4.50 and $3.50, respectively. Call the stadium or check the newspaper sports pages for schedule information.

GREYHOUND RACING   Dog racing takes place from April through September at **Rocky Mountain Greyhound Park,** 3701 N. Nevada Ave. (☎ **719/632-1391**), with both evening and weekend races.

RODEO   The **Pikes Peak or Bust Rodeo,** held annually (since 1941) in early August, is a major stop on the Professional Rodeo Cowboys Association circuit. Its purse of more than $150,000 makes it the second-largest rodeo in Colorado (after Denver's National Western Stock Show), 15th-largest in North America. Events are held at Penrose Stadium, 1045 W. Rio Grande Ave. off Fountain Creek Boulevard (☎ **719/635-3547**). Various events around the city, including a parade, mark rodeo week.

8 Shopping

Five principal areas attract shoppers in Colorado Springs. The Manitou Springs and Old Colorado City neighborhoods are excellent places to browse for art, jewelry, arts and crafts, books, and other specialty items. The Citadel and Chapel Hills malls combine major department stores with a variety of fashionable boutiques. Downtown Colorado Springs, of course, has numerous fine shops.

SHOPPING A TO Z

ANTIQUES

Nevada Avenue Antiques. 405 S. Nevada Ave. ☎ **719/473-3351**.

This is Colorado Springs' oldest multi-dealer mall, with 7,000 square feet filled with antiques.

The Villagers. 2426 W. Colorado Ave., Old Colorado City. ☎ **719/632-1400.**

Run by volunteers, proceeds from sales go to Cheyenne Village, a community of adults with developmental disabilities.

ART GALLERIES

Business of Art Center. 513 Manitou Ave., Manitou Springs. ☎ **719/685-1861.**

Primarily an educational facility to help artists learn the business end of their profession, there are numerous artists' studios (open for viewing by visitors), three exhibition galleries, a Cafe Gallery, and gift shop. Featured are renowned Colorado artists and juried exhibits of regional art. Theater, music, and dance performances are occasionally staged (donation requested).

Colorado Springs Art Guild/Gallery. 1700 E. Platte Ave. (in the lower suite of the First United bank). ☎ **719/630-1611.**

A showcase for local artists, with juried shows and classes, plus workshops and demonstrations by leading regional artists.

Michael Garman's Gallery. 2418 W. Colorado Ave., Old Colorado City. ☎ **800/731-3908** or 719/471-9391.

This gallery is a showcase for Garman's sculptures and casts depicting urban and western life, plus "Magic Town," a large model of an old-time inner city. Admission to "Magic Town" is $3 for adults, $2 for children 7 to 12, and free for children under 7.

BOOKS

Barnes & Noble Booksellers. 795 Citadel Dr. E. (on the edge of Citadel Mall). ☎ **719/637-8282.**

Pick up the latest best-seller at a discount, and just about any book you want. A Starbucks Coffee is here as well.

There's another Barnes & Noble near the Air Force Academy, at 1565 Briargate Blvd. (☎ **719/266-9960**).

The Book Sleuth. 2501 W. Colorado Ave. #105, Old Colorado City. ☎ **719/632-2727.**

For all your mysterious needs, visit this bookstore of mystery novels, puzzles, and games.

Borders. 110 Briargate Blvd. (in Chapel Hills Mall). ☎ **719/266-1600.**

Like others in this national chain, this Borders stocks a wide range of books, including regional titles and all the latest best-sellers, plus maps; it has an attached cafe.

The Chinook Bookshop. 210 N. Tejon St. ☎ **800/999-1195** or 719/635-1195.

This gem of a bookstore has 75,000 titles, including an extensive western Americana collection. One room is devoted to maps and globes, and the Children's Room offers a large, sunny area with a two-story playhouse and a carpeted and cushioned reading platform.

CRAFTS

Van Briggle Art Pottery. 600 S. 21st St., Old Colorado City. ☎ **719/633-7729.**

Founded in 1900 by Artus Van Briggle, who applied Chinese matte glaze to Rocky Mountain clays and imaginative art-nouveau shapes, this is one of the oldest active art potteries in the United States. Free tours are available.

GIFTS & SOUVENIRS

Horsetails Gourmet. 2530A W. Colorado Ave., Old Colorado City. ☎ **719/578-1386.**

Gourmet food made in Colorado, from salsas to chokecherry jelly, plus dishware, hand-painted glassware, and kitchen gift items are available here.

Penguin & Friends. 742 Manitou Ave., Manitou Springs. ☎ **719/685-0700.**

This unusual shop sells souvenirs of the Pikes Peak region, Christmas items, American Indian crafts, angels and other collectibles, and—of course—penguins.

Simpich Character Dolls. 2413 W. Colorado Ave., Old Colorado City. ☎ **719/636-3272.**

These exquisite handmade dolls are the creation of Bob and Jan Simpich, who made their first dolls in 1952 as Christmas gifts for their parents. Today there are dolls representing characters from literature and early American life, plus creations from the whimsical to the historical.

JEWELRY

Manitou Jack's Jewelry & Gifts. 814 Manitou Ave., Manitou Springs. ☎ **719/685-5004.**

Black Hills gold, 10- and 14-karat, is the specialty here, plus American Indian jewelry, pottery, sand paintings, and other art, as well as custom jewelry and repairs.

Megel & Graff Jewelers Ltd. 12 E. Pikes Peak Ave. ☎ **719/632-2552.**

A downtown institution since 1949, this well-respected shop offers full-service jewelry and watch repair, plus a large selection of diamonds and gems.

MALLS & SHOPPING CENTERS

Chapel Hills Mall. 1710 Briargate Blvd. (N. Academy Blvd., at I-25 exit 150A). ☎ **719/594-0111.**

Among the more than 135 stores here are Joslins, Sears, Mervyn's, J.C. Penney, Dillard's, and Kmart, plus an ice-skating arena, two movie theaters, and about two dozen food outlets.

The Citadel. 750 Citadel Dr. E. (N. Academy Blvd. at E. Platte Ave.). ☎ **719/591-2900.**

Southern Colorado's largest regional shopping mall has Dillard's, Foley's, J.C. Penney, Mervyn's, and more than 170 specialty shops and restaurants.

SPORTING GOODS

Leading sporting-goods dealers in the city include **Grand West Outfitters,** 3250 N. Academy Blvd. (☎ **719/596-3031**), which sells and rents camping gear, and also sells outdoor clothing, bikes, hiking and climbing gear, and winter-sports equipment. A good source for fishing, as well as camping and winter-sports equipment, is **Blicks Sporting Goods,** 119 N. Tejon St. (☎ **719/636-3348**).

WINE & LIQUOR

Coal Train Wine & Liquors. 330 W. Uintah St. ☎ **719/475-9700**.

Located on the north edge of downtown, this liquor store offers a good selection, personal service, and reasonable prices.

Pikes Peak Vineyards. 3901 Janitell Rd. (I-25 exit 138). ☎ **719/576-0075**.

This small award-winning winery produces 8 to 10 moderately priced red, white, and blush wines. Tours and tastings are offered by appointment. **The Winery** (☎ 719/538-8848), a restaurant featuring fresh seafood, steaks, lamb, veal, and duck, opened at the site in summer 1998. Call for additional information.

9 Colorado Springs After Dark

The Colorado Springs entertainment scene is spread throughout the metropolitan area. Pikes Peak Center, the Colorado Springs Fine Arts Center, City Auditorium, Colorado College, and the various facilities at the U.S. Air Force Academy are all outstanding venues for the performing arts. The city also supports dozens of cinemas, nightclubs, bars, and other after-dark attractions.

Current weekly entertainment schedules can be found in the Friday *Gazette Telegraph*. Also look at the listings in *Springs* magazine and *The Independent*, free entertainment tabloids. Or call the city's weekly events line at ☎ 719/635-1723.

Tickets for nearly all major entertainment and sporting events can be obtained from **TicketMaster** (☎ 719/520-9090).

THE CLUB & MUSIC SCENE

Cowboys. 3910 Palmer Park Blvd. ☎ **719/596-2152**.

Two-steppers and country-and-western music lovers flock to this east-side club, which boasts the largest dance floor in the area. It's open nightly, with dance lessons available.

Poor Richard's Restaurant. 324½ N. Tejon St. ☎ **719/632-7721**.

An eclectic variety of performers appears here one or two nights a week, presenting everything from acoustic folk to Celtic melodies, jazz to bluegrass.

The Underground. 130 E. Kiowa St. (at Nevada Ave.). ☎ **719/633-0590**.

This popular hangout attracts a diverse crowd, from college students and other young people to baby boomers and retirees. The music ranges from rock to jazz to reggae, with occasional folk.

THE BAR SCENE

The Golden Bee. Lower level entrance of the Broadmoor International Center, Lake Circle. ☎ **719/634-7111**.

An opulent English pub was disassembled, shipped from Great Britain, and reassembled piece by piece to create this delightful drinking establishment. Enjoy imported Bass Ale with a beef-and-kidney pie or other English specialties. Evenings bring a ragtime pianist to enliven the atmosphere.

Hide 'n' Seek. 512 W. Colorado Ave. ☎ **719/634-9303**.

The Hide 'n' Seek is one of the oldest—since 1972—and largest gay bars in the West. It has five bars, dance areas with DJ music most nights, and a restaurant.

Judge Baldwin's Brewing Company. In the Antlers Doubletree Hotel, 4 S. Cascade Ave. ☎ **719/473-5600**.

This popular and busy restaurant is also a good spot to stop and sample the local brews. Generally four to six of their brews are on tap, so order a sampler tray and try several. Beer is also available to go.

MacKenzie's Chop House. 128 S. Tejon St. ☎ **719/635-3536**.

MacKenzie's specializes in martinis—shaken not stirred—with some three dozen on the menu. The luxurious cigar lounge in back has a fragrant walk-in humidor (cigars priced from $4 to $30). The extensive wine list includes American, French, Italian, and South African choices. See also "Dining," above.

The Ritz Grill. 15 S. Tejon St. ☎ **719/635-8484.**

Especially popular with young professionals after work and the chic clique later in the evening, this noisy restaurant-lounge, with a large central bar, has live rock and blues weekends. See also "Dining," above.

THE PERFORMING ARTS

Among the major venues for performing arts in Colorado Springs is the 8,000-seat **Colorado Springs World Arena,** 3185 Venetucci Blvd., at I-25 exit 138 (☎ **719/477-2100**). The area's newest entertainment center, it presents big-name country and rock concerts and a wide variety of sporting events. Other major facilities include the handsome **Pikes Peak Center,** 190 S. Cascade Ave. (☎ **719/520-7453** for general information, or 719/520-7469 for the ticket office), a 2,000-seat concert hall in the heart of downtown with outstanding acoustics. It hosts the city's symphony orchestra, plus top-flight touring entertainers, Broadway musicals, and symphony orchestras. The **Colorado Springs Fine Arts Center,** 30 W. Dale St. (☎ **719/634-5581** for general information, or 719/634-5583 for the box office), is an historic facility (see "Museums & Galleries" in "Attractions," above) that includes a children's theater program, a repertory theater company, dance programs and concerts, and classic films. At the historic **City Auditorium,** 221 E. Kiowa St. (☎ **719/578-6652**), you can often attend a trade show or concert, or drop in at the Lon Chaney Theatre, with its resident Star Bar Players (see below).

CLASSICAL MUSIC & OPERA

Colorado Opera Festival. 219 W. Colorado Ave. ☎ **719/473-0073.**

Each summer, a variety of classical operas are staged at the Pikes Peak Center. Original-language productions with English supertitles feature nationally known opera singers. Call for schedule and prices.

Colorado Springs Symphony Orchestra. 619 N. Cascade Ave. ☎ **719/633-6698,** or 719/520-7469 for ticket information. Tickets $8–$40.

This fine professional orchestra annually performs about a dozen classical concerts, as well as youth, pops, chamber, holiday, and free summer concerts. Most performances are held at the Pikes Peak Center. Tchaikovsky's *The Nutcracker* kicks off the holidays on Thanksgiving weekend, and New Year's Eve is celebrated with Viennese waltzes.

THEATER & DANCE

Colorado Springs Dance Theatre. 7 E. Bijou St., Suite 209. ☎ **719/630-7434.** Tickets $13–$30, with discounts for students and seniors.

This nonprofit organization presents dance companies from around the world from September to May at various venues. Each year three to five performances of traditional, modern, ethnic, or jazz dance programs are scheduled, and frequently master classes, lectures, and other programs are offered.

Rocky Mountain Cloggers. 806 Cardinal St. ☎ **719/392-4791.**

The eight members of this national exhibition clog-dance team perform some three dozen shows in the Colorado Springs area each year. Call for a current schedule.

Star Bar Players. Lon Chaney Theatre, City Auditorium, 221 E. Kiowa St. ☎ **719/573-7411.**

Each year, this resident theater company presents several full-length plays, ranging from Greek comedies to modern murder mysteries, plus children's and other productions.

DINNER THEATERS

Flying W Ranch. 3330 Chuckwagon Rd. ☎ **800/232-FLYW** or 719/598-4000. Reservations strongly recommended. Admission: chuck-wagon dinners, $14 adults, $7 children 8 and under; winter steak house, $19 adults, $8 children 8 and under.

This working cattle and horse ranch just north of the Garden of the Gods treats visitors to a western village of more than a dozen restored buildings and a mine train. A western stage show features bunkhouse comedy, cowboy balladry, and foot-stompin' fiddle, mandolin, and guitar music. From mid-May through September the town opens daily at 4:30pm; a chuck-wagon dinner is served at 7:15pm and the show begins at 8:30pm. The winter steak house is open October to December and March to May on Friday and Saturday evenings, with seatings and a western stage show at 5 and 8pm.

Iron Springs Chateau Melodrama. 444 Ruxton Ave., Manitou Springs. ☎ **719/685-5104** or 719/685-5572. Reservations required. Tickets, dinner and show, $21 adults, $20 seniors, $12 children; show only, $11 adults, $10.50 seniors, $7 children.

Located near the foot of the Pikes Peak Cog Railway, this popular comedy/drama dinner theater urges patrons to boo the villain and cheer the hero. A family-style dinner offers oven-baked chicken and barbecued ribs with all the trimmings, plus free seconds. The show is followed by a sing-along intermission and a vaudeville-style olio show. It's open Tuesday through Saturday in summer, Friday and Saturday in winter, with dinner served between 6 and 7pm (arrive before 7pm); the show starts at 8:30pm.

10 A Side Trip to Florissant Fossil Beds National Monument

Approximately 35 miles west of Colorado Springs on U.S. 24 is the small village of Florissant, which means "flowering" in French. It couldn't be more aptly named—every spring its hillsides are virtually ablaze with wildflowers. And just 2 miles south is one of the most spectacular, yet relatively unknown, fossil deposits in the world, Florissant Fossil Beds National Monument (from Florissant, follow the signs along Teller County Road 1).

The fossils in this 6,000-acre National Park Service property are preserved in the rocks of ancient Lake Florissant, which existed 34 million years ago. Volcanic eruptions spanning half a million years trapped plants and animals under layers of ash and dust; the creatures were fossilized as the sediment settled and became shale.

The detailed impressions, first discovered in 1871, offer the most extensive record of its kind in the world today. Thousands of specimens have been removed by scientists, including 1,100 separate species of insects. Leaves and needles, many from extinct trees, have also been fossilized, and are very different from those living in the area today, demonstrating how the climate has changed over the centuries.

Mud flows also buried forests, petrifying the trees where they stood. Nature trails pass petrified tree stumps; one sequoia stump is 10 feet in diameter and 11 feet high. The visitor center offers interpretive programs, and there are some 14 miles of hiking trails.

Admission to the monument is $2 per person, up to a maximum of $4 per family, making a visit here an incredibly affordable outing. It's open June to September, daily from 8am to 7pm; the rest of the year, daily from 8am to 4:30pm. It's closed New Year's Day, Thanksgiving, and Christmas. Contact Florissant **Fossil Beds National Monument,** P.O. Box 185, Florissant, CO 80816 (☎ **719/ 748-3253**), for further information.

Boulder 9

Although Boulder is known primarily as a college town (the University of Colorado is here), it would be inaccurate to describe the town as just that. Sophisticated and artsy, Boulder is home to numerous high-tech companies and research concerns; it has also attracted countless outdoor sports enthusiasts who have been drawn by Boulder's delightful climate, vast open spaces, and close proximity to Rocky Mountain National Park.

Set at the foot of the Flatirons of the Rocky Mountains, just 30 miles northwest of downtown Denver and only 74 feet higher than the "Mile High City," Boulder was settled by hopeful miners in 1858 and named for the large rocks in the area. Welcomed by Chief Niwot and the resident southern Arapaho, the miners struck gold in the nearby hills the following year. By the 1870s, Boulder had become a regional rail and trade center for mining and farming. The university, founded in 1877, became the economic mainstay of the community after mining collapsed around the beginning of the 20th century.

Since the 1950s, Boulder has grown as a center for scientific and environmental research. The National Center for Atmospheric Research and the National Institute of Standards and Technology are located here, as are IBM, Storage Tek, and Ball Aerospace, among other companies.

Today's residents are a mix of students attending the University of Colorado (called C.U. by locals); employees of the many computer, biotech, and research firms in the area; and others who were attracted by the casual, environmentally aware, and hip lifestyle that prevails here. Whatever differences exist among the residents, they are joined by a common love of the outdoors. Boulder has 25,000 acres of open space within its city limits, 56 parks, and 150 miles of trails; on any given day, seemingly three-quarters of the population is outside making great use of this land, generally from the vantage point of a bicycle seat. With an estimated 93,000 bicycles—more than one per resident—it's the preferred mode of transport in Boulder.

1 Orientation

ARRIVING

BY PLANE   Boulder doesn't have its own commercial airport. Air travelers must fly into Denver International Airport, then make ground connections to Boulder. See chapter 6, "Arriving," for more information.

Getting to & from the Airport   The **Boulder Airporter** (☎ 303/444-0808) leaves Denver hourly from 8am to 11pm, and Boulder hourly from 4am to 9pm, with fewer departures on holidays. Scheduled pickups in Boulder are made from the University of Colorado campus and area hotels; pickups from other locations are made on call. The one-way fare from a scheduled pickup point to the airport is $19 per person, or $25 for residential pickup service from other points. Boulder Airporter also provides statewide charter services.

Boulder Yellow Cab (☎ 303/777-7777) charges $60 one-way to the airport for up to five passengers.

Buses operated by the **Regional Transportation District,** known locally as **RTD** (☎ 800/366-7433 or 303/299-6000, TDD 303/299-6089; www.rtd-denver. com), charge $8 for a one-way trip to the airport (exact change required). Buses leave from, and return to, the main terminal at 14th and Walnut Streets daily every hour from 6am to 11pm.

Boulder Limousine Service (☎ 800/910-7433 or 303/449-5466; www. whitedovelimo.com) charges $95 to take up to three people from Boulder to Denver Airport in a sedan limousine, $125 for a six-passenger stretch limo, $161 for an eight-passenger stretch limo, and $185 for a 10-passenger stretch limo. Charter services are also available.

BY CAR   The Boulder Turnpike (U.S. 36) branches off I-25 north of Denver and passes through the suburbs of Westminster, Broomfield, and Louisville before reaching Boulder some 25 minutes later.

If you're arriving from the north, take the Longmont exit from I-25 and follow Colo. 119 all the way. Longmont is 7 miles due west of the freeway; Boulder is another 15 miles southwest via the Longmont Diagonal Highway.

VISITOR INFORMATION

The **Boulder Convention and Visitors Bureau,** 2440 Pearl St. (at Folsom Street), Boulder, CO 80302 (☎ 800/444-0447 or 303/442-2911; visitor.boulder.co.us), is open Monday through Friday from 9am to 5pm, and can provide excellent maps, brochures, and general information on the city.

From Memorial Day to Labor Day, there are staffed visitor information centers on **Pearl Street Mall** and at the **Davidson Mesa overlook,** several miles southeast of Boulder on U.S. 36. Brochures are available at those sites year-round.

CITY LAYOUT

The north–south streets increase in number going from west to east, beginning with Third Street. (The eastern city limit is at 61st Street, although the numbers continue to the Boulder County line at 124th Street in Broomfield.) Where U.S. 36 enters Boulder (and does a 45-degree turn to the north), it becomes 28th Street, a major commercial artery. The Longmont Diagonal Highway (Colo. 119), entering Boulder from the northeast, intersects 28th Street at the north end of the city.

To reach downtown Boulder from U.S. 36, turn west on Canyon Boulevard (Colo. 119 west) and north on Broadway, which would be 12th Street if it had a number. It's 2 blocks to the Pearl Street Mall, a 4-block pedestrians-only strip from 11th to 15th Streets that constitutes the historic downtown district. Boulder's few one-way streets circle the mall: 13th and 15th Streets are one-way north, 11th and 14th one-way south, Walnut Street (a block south of the Mall) one-way east, and Spruce Street (a block north) one-way west.

Broadway continues across the Mall, eventually joining U.S. 36 north of the city. South of Arapahoe Avenue, Broadway turns to the southeast, skirting the University of Colorado campus and becoming Colo. 93 (the Foothills Highway to Golden) after crossing Baseline Road. Baseline follows a straight line from east Boulder, across U.S. 36 and Broadway, past Chautauqua Park and up the mountain slopes. To the south, Table Mesa Drive takes a similar course.

The Foothills Parkway (not to be confused with the Foothills Highway) is the principal north–south route on the east side of Boulder, extending from U.S. 36 at Table Mesa Drive to the Longmont Diagonal; Arapahoe Avenue, a block south of Canyon Boulevard, continues east across 28th Street as Arapahoe Road.

2 Getting Around

BY PUBLIC TRANSPORTATION

The **Regional Transportation District,** better known locally as the **RTD** (☎ **800/ 366-7433** or 303/299-6000, TDD 303/299-6089; www.rtd-denver.com), provides bus service throughout Boulder as well as the Denver greater metropolitan area. The Boulder Transit Center, 14th and Walnut Streets, is open Monday through Friday from 5am to midnight, Saturday and Sunday from 6am to midnight. Fares within the city are 75¢ for adults and children (25¢ for seniors and disabled persons during off-peak hours); schedules are available at the Transit Center, the Chamber of Commerce, and other locations. Buses are wheelchair accessible.

The City of Boulder runs a shuttle bus service, called **HOP** (☎ **303/447-8282**), connecting downtown, University Hill, the University of Colorado, and Crossroads Mall. It operates Monday through Wednesday from 7am to 7pm, Thursday and Friday from 7am to 10pm, and Saturday from 9am to 10pm. While the University of Colorado is in session, the night HOP runs Thursday through Saturday from 10pm to 2:30am to every destination except Crossroads Mall. Buses run about every 10 minutes during the day, every 15 to 20 minutes at night; fares are 75¢ (25¢ for seniors).

BY TAXI

You can get 24-hour taxi service from **Boulder Yellow Cab** (☎ **303/442-2277**), but you'll need to call for service because there are no taxi stands, and taxis won't stop for you on the street.

BY CAR

The **American Automobile Association (AAA)** has an office at 1933 28th St. #200 (☎ **303/753-8800,** ext. 8600). It's open Monday through Friday from 8:30am to 5:30pm, Saturday from 9am to 1pm.

CAR RENTALS   Although most people who fly to Colorado will land at Denver International Airport and rent a car there before proceeding to Boulder, those who find themselves in need of a car in Boulder can contact Avis (☎ **800/331-1212**),

Budget (☎ **800/527-0700**), Hertz (☎ **800/654-3131**), or National (☎ **800/ 227-7368**).

PARKING   Most downtown streets have parking meters, with rates of about 25¢ per half hour. Downtown parking lots cost about 35¢ for 3 hours before 5pm. Parking is hard to find around the Pearl Street Mall. Outside downtown, free parking is generally available on side streets.

BY BICYCLE

Boulder is a wonderful place for bicycling; there are bike paths throughout the city and an extensive trail system leading for miles beyond Boulder's borders (see "Outdoor Activities," below).

Among shops where you can rent and repair mountain bikes and buy copies of the handy *Boulder Bicycling Map* ($7) are **Doc's Ski and Sports,** 627 S. Broadway (☎ 303/499-0963), and **Full Cycle,** 1211 13th St., near the campus (☎ 303/ 440-7771). Bike rentals cost $16 to $30 daily. Maps and other information are also available at the **Boulder Chamber of Commerce,** 2440 Pearl St. (☎ 303/ 442-1044).

ON FOOT

Most of what's worth seeing in downtown Boulder can be reached by simple foot power, especially around the Pearl Street Mall and University of Colorado campus.

FAST FACTS: BOULDER

Area Code   Area codes are **303** and **720,** and local calls require 10-digit dialing. See the "Telephone, Fax & Telegraph" section under "Fast Facts: For the Foreign Traveler" in chapter 4.

Baby-sitters   The front desk at a major hotel often can make arrangements on your behalf. Boulder's **Child Care Referral Service** (☎ 303/441-3180), open Monday through Friday from 8am to 5pm, can also help.

Business Hours   Most banks are open Monday through Friday from 9am to 5pm, and some have Saturday hours, too. Major stores are open Monday through Saturday from 9 or 10am until 5 or 6pm, and often Sunday from noon until 5pm. Department and discount stores often have later closing times.

Car Rentals   See "Getting Around," earlier in this chapter.

Drugstores   Reliable prescription services are available at the Medical Center Pharmacy in the **Boulder Medical Center,** 2750 N. Broadway (☎ 303/ 440-3111), and **Jones Drug and Camera Center,** 1370 College Ave. (☎ 303/ 443-4420). The pharmacy at **King Soopers Supermarket,** 1650 30th St. (in Sunrise Plaza), is open from 6am to midnight (☎ 303/444-0164).

Emergencies   For the **Poison Control Center,** call ☎ 800/332-3073 or 303/739-1123. For the **Rape Crisis Hotline,** call ☎ 303/443-7300.

Eyeglasses   You can get fast repair or replacement of your glasses at **Boulder Optical,** 1928 14th St. (☎ **303/442-4521**), just off the Pearl Street Mall.

Hospitals   Full medical services, including 24-hour emergency treatment, are available at **Boulder Community Hospital,** 1100 Balsam Ave., at North Broadway (☎ **303/440-2273**).

Newspapers/Magazines   *Boulder's Daily Camera* is an award-winning daily newspaper, and the new *Boulder Planet* is a weekly local paper. Many townspeople also read the campus paper, the *Colorado Daily,* available all over town.

Both Denver dailies—the *Denver Post* and *Rocky Mountain News*—are available at newsstands throughout the city. You can also find the *New York Times, Wall Street Journal,* and *Christian Science Monitor* at many newsstands. The free *Boulder* magazine, published three times a year, lists seasonal events and other information on restaurants and the arts.

Photographic Needs   For standard processing requirements (including 2-hour slide processing) as well as custom lab work, contact **Photo Craft,** 3550 Arapahoe Ave. (☎ 303/442-6410). For equipment, supplies, and repairs, visit **Mike's Camera,** 2500 Pearl St. (☎ 303/443-1715).

Post Office   The main downtown post office is at 15th and Walnut Streets; call the U.S. Postal Service (☎ **800/275-8777**) for hours and other locations.

Radio/TV   Boulder radio stations include KBCO (97.3 FM) for alternative rock; KBVI (1490 AM) for local news, sports, and contemporary rock; and KGNU (88.5 FM) for Boulder and national public radio. Boulder is also within reception range of most Denver stations.

The following Denver television stations can be received in Boulder: Channels 2 (KWGN/WB), 4 (KCNC/CBS), 6 (KRMA/PBS), 7 (KMGH/ABC), 9 (KUSA/NBC), and 31 (KDVR/FOX). Boulder has two independent stations: Channel 20 (KTVD) and 59 (KUBD). Cable or satellite service is available at most motels.

Safety   Although Boulder is generally a safe city—safer than Denver, for instance—it is not crime free. Many locals say they avoid walking alone late at night along the Boulder Creek Path because of the transients who tend to hang out there.

Taxes   State and city sales tax total almost 7%.

Useful Telephone Numbers   Call ☎ 303/639-1111 for **road conditions**; ☎ 303/825-7669 for **ski reports**; and ☎ 303/398-3964 for **weather reports**.

3 Accommodations

You'll find a good selection of comfortable lodgings in Boulder, with a wide range of rates to suit almost every budget. Be aware, though, that the town literally fills up during the popular summer season, making advance reservations essential. It's also almost impossible to find a place to sleep during any major event at the University of Colorado, particularly graduation. Those who do find themselves in Boulder without lodging can check with the Boulder Convention and Visitors Bureau (see "Visitor Information," above), which keeps track of availability. Of course, you can usually find a room in Denver, a half hour away.

Major chains and franchises that provide reasonably priced lodging in Boulder include **Holiday Inn Boulder,** 800 28th St., Boulder, CO 80303 (☎ 800/465-4329 or 303/443-3322), with 165 units and rates of $82 to $99 double; **Best Western Golden Buff Lodge,** 1725 28th St., Boulder, CO 80301 (☎ 800/999-2833 or 303/442-7450), with 112 units, charging $66 to $101 double; **Best Western Boulder Inn,** 770 28th St., Boulder, CO 80303 (☎ 800/528-1234 or 303/449-3800), with 96 units and rates for two of $66 to $103; **Econo Lodge,** 2020 Arapahoe Ave., Boulder, CO 80302 (☎ 800/55-ECONO or 303/449-7550), with 46 units and rates for two of $75 to $110; and **Super 8,** 970 28th St., Boulder, CO 80303 (☎ 800/525-2149 or 800/800-8000), with 69 units and rates of $73 to $82 double.

Boulder Accommodations & Dining

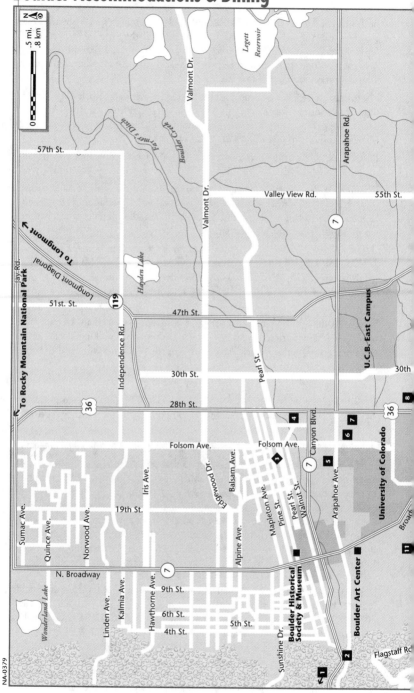

NA-0379

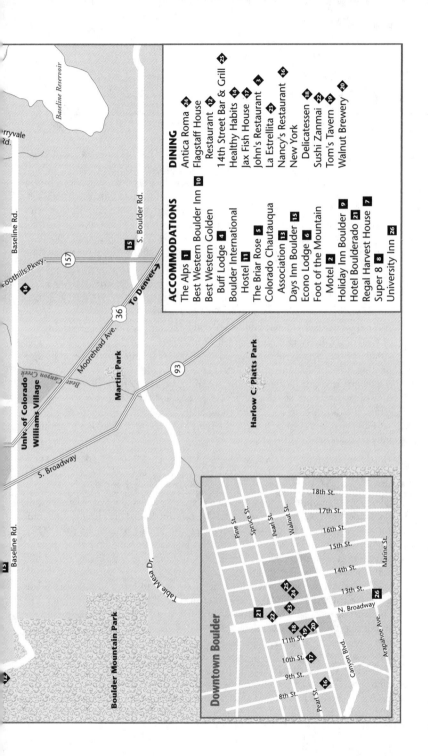

ACCOMMODATIONS

The Alps **1**
Best Western Boulder Inn **10**
Best Western Golden
Buff Lodge **4**
Boulder International
Hostel **11**
The Briar Rose **5**
Colorado Chautauqua
Association **13**
Days Inn Boulder **15**
Econo Lodge **6**
Foot of the Mountain
Motel **2**
Holiday Inn Boulder **9**
Hotel Boulderado **21**
Regal Harvest House **7**
Super 8 **8**
University Inn **26**

DINING

Antica Roma **24**
Flagstaff House
Restaurant **12**
14th Street Bar & Grill **25**
Healthy Habits **14**
Jax Fish House **17**
John's Restaurant **3**
La Estrellita **23**
Nancy's Restaurant **16**
New York
Delicatessen **18**
Sushi Zanmai **22**
Tom's Tavern **19**
Walnut Brewery **20**

Rates given below do not include the 9.5% sales tax that is added to all accommodation bills.

EXPENSIVE

✪ **The Alps.** 38619 Boulder Canyon Dr., Boulder, CO 80302. ☎ **800/414-2577** or 303/444-5445. Fax 303/444-5522. E-mail: alpsinn@aol.com. 12 units. TEL. $115–$250 double. Rates include full breakfast. AE, CB, DC, DISC, MC, V. Free parking.

A stage stop in the late 1800s, this historic log lodge has been turned into a beautiful B&B by its owners, Jeannine and John Vanderhart. Perched on a mountainside about 7 minutes west of downtown Boulder, the Alps is decorated with British antiques. Each room is different, although all have functional fireplaces with Victorian mantels and queen beds with down comforters. Most are spacious, with either a claw-foot or double whirlpool tub plus shower; many have private porches. Shared spaces include a beautiful lounge with a huge rock fireplace and TV/VCR, plus delightful gardens and patio areas. The entryway to the Alps is the original log cabin built in the 1870s. Smoking is not permitted.

The Briar Rose. 2151 Arapahoe Ave., Boulder, CO 80302. ☎ **303/442-3007**. Fax 303/786-8440. 9 units (4 with shower only). A/C TEL. May–Dec, $114–$159 double; Dec–Apr, $104–$149 double. Rates include continental breakfast. AE, DC, MC, V.

A country-style brick home built in the 1890s, this midcity B&B might remind you of Grandma's. Every room is furnished with antiques, and the lovely gardens offer a quiet escape. Several units have modem hook-ups, a large work table, and super lighting. Fax and copy machines are available.

Five rooms are in the main house, four in a separate cottage. Two in the main house have fireplaces, all have feather comforters, and the cottage rooms come with either a patio or a balcony. The continental breakfast is gourmet quality, and refreshments are available in the lobby from 8am to 10pm. Smoking is permitted only in the outside garden areas.

✪ **Hotel Boulderado.** 2115 13th St. (at Spruce St.), Boulder, CO 80302. ☎ **800/433-4344** or 303/442-4344. Fax 303/442-4378. www.boulderado.com. 160 units. A/C TV TEL. $151–$221 double; $229–$295 suite. Extra person $12. AE, CB, DC, DISC, MC, V. Free parking.

This elegant and historic hotel still has the same Otis elevator that wowed visiting dignitaries on opening day in 1909. The colorful leaded-glass ceiling and cantilevered cherry-wood staircase are other reminders of days past, along with the rich woodwork of the balusters around the mezzanine and the handsome armchairs and settees in the main-floor lobby. The hotel's Christmas tree, a 35-footer with 1,000 white lights, is a Boulder tradition.

The original five-story hotel, just a block off the Pearl Street Mall, has 42 bright and cozy guest rooms, each slightly different, but all with a Victorian flavor. The construction of a spacious North Wing a few years ago almost quadrupled the number of rooms, while continuing the turn-of-the-century feel in the wallpaper and reproduction antiques. All units have hair dryers and two-line phones (or dataports) and voice mail; some rooms have refrigerators.

Dining: Q's Restaurant (☎ **303/442-4880**) is run by chef/owner John Platt, who prefers locally grown organic vegetables and claims seafood as his specialty after years on Cape Cod. Rotisseried meats are also offered, plus pasta, roasted chicken and quail, venison, and beef. The Corner Bar (☎ **303/442-4560**) offers sandwiches, burgers, pasta, and light fare from 11am to midnight.

Amenities: Limited room service, dry cleaning and laundry service, business center, access to a nearby health club, bike rentals in summer.

ⓘ Family-Friendly Hotels

Foot of the Mountain Motel *(see p. 161)*   There's lots of space here where the kids can expend their energy. Across the street is a lovely park with a playground, as well as the Boulder Creek Path.

Holiday Inn *(see p. 157)*   At the "Holidome," kids can use the pool and play inside even when the weather is bad.

Regal Harvest House *(see p. 161)*   A good place to stay with the kids, especially in the summer. The Harvest House has a nice swimming pool and lots of nearby green space; it's also next to the Boulder Creek Path and within walking distance of the Crossroads Mall.

Regal Harvest House. 1345 28th St., Boulder, CO 80302. ☎ **800/222-8888** or 303/443-3850. Fax 303/443-1480. 269 units. A/C TV TEL. $129–$145 double; $175–$395 suite. AE, CB, DC, DISC, MC, V. Free parking.

The Harvest House looks like almost any other four-story hotel from the front, but its backyard melts into a park on the 10-mile Boulder Creek Path (see "Attractions," below). All rooms are furnished with one king or two double beds, a lounge chair and ottoman, and cable TV. Spacious VIP Tower accommodations provide upgraded amenities such as an extra phone jack for a modem, a continental breakfast, and cocktail hour in the Regal Club Room.

Dining/Diversions: The Fancy Moose has the look and feel of a mountain lodge, with large windows looking out on a waterfall on Boulder Creek Path. It puts an emphasis on Colorado fish and game, such as baked Colorado trout, buffalo rib-eye steak, and elk sausage. Lunch offers variations on the dinner menu, sandwiches, and lighter items; breakfasts feature standard American fare. The hotel also has a locally popular sports bar with a big fireplace.

Amenities: Room service, valet and self-service laundry, masseur, airport shuttle, 15 tennis courts (five indoors), indoor lap pool and hot tub, outdoor pool and hot tub, baby pool, fitness center, bicycle rentals at Boulder Creek Path, playground, volleyball, business center, facilities for the disabled, and meeting space for 200.

MODERATE

✪ **Days Inn Boulder.** 5397 S. Boulder Rd., Boulder, CO 80303. ☎ **800/329-7466** or 303/499-4422. Fax 303/494-0269. 74 units. A/C TV TEL. $74–$99 double; suite $20 extra. Rates include continental breakfast. AE, CB, DC, DISC, MC, V. Free parking. Small pets accepted.

One of the best values around, this four-story hotel offers great views of the mountains. The rooms are large, with night tables on each side of the beds. All units have cable TV, desks, and phones with modem hookups; fax and photocopy services are available. The continental breakfast is excellent, and there's a seasonal outdoor heated pool.

Foot of the Mountain Motel. 200 Arapahoe Ave., Boulder, CO 80302. ☎ **303/442-5688**. 18 units (2 with shower only). TV TEL. $75 double. AE, DISC, MC, V. Pets accepted.

A series of log cabins near the east gate of Boulder Canyon, this motel dates from 1930 but has been fully modernized. Across the street is Eben Fine Park, which accesses the Boulder Creek Path. There's free coffee in the lobby, and bicycle rentals are available. The pleasant pine-walled cabins are furnished with queen or double beds, refrigerators, and individual water heaters.

University Inn. 1632 Broadway (near Arapahoe Ave.), Boulder, CO 80302. ☎ **800/ 258-7917** or 303/442-3830. Fax 303/442-1205. www.u-inn.com. E-mail: info@u-inn.com. 39 units. A/C TV TEL. $62–$105 double. Rates include continental breakfast. AE, DC, DISC, MC, V. Free parking.

Conveniently located within walking distance of both the University of Colorado and the Pearl Street Mall, this two-story motel has simple, cozy, and well-maintained rooms outfitted with light-wood furnishings and refrigerators. Most have showers only; if you prefer a bathtub, ask. Family rooms are available, and facilities include a guest laundry and outdoor heated pool. Free refreshments and newspapers are available in the lobby.

INEXPENSIVE

Boulder International Hostel. 1107 12th St., Boulder, CO 80302-7029. ☎ **888/ 442-0522** or 303/442-0522. Fax 303/442-0523. E-mail: boulder.hostel@mail.com. 50 units. $15 for dorm bed; private room $25–$50. AE, DISC, MC, V.

As at most hostels, the toilets, showers, kitchen, laundry, and TV room are communal. Individual phones can be arranged for private rooms (with a deposit), but others share a phone. Two blocks from the University of Colorado campus, the hostel is open for registration daily from 7am to midnight.

Colorado Chautauqua Association. 900 Baseline Rd. (at 9th St.), Boulder, CO 80302. ☎ 303/442-3282 ext. 10 for lodging, 303/440-3776 for restaurant, 303/545-6924 for general information. Fax 303/449-0790. www.chautauqua.com. E-mail: chau@usa.net. 87 units. Summer, $52–$67 rm, $56–$68 apartment, $58–$110 cottage (minimum 4-night stay). Winter, renters must sign a lease for the entire season. MC. V. Bus: 203. Pets accepted in cottages for $100 fee; pets not permitted in lodges.

During the late 19th and early 20th centuries, more than 400 Chautauquas—adult education and cultural entertainment centers—sprang up around the U.S. This 26-acre park, on a hillside west of downtown, is one of the few left. In summer, there's a wide-ranging program of performing arts, including the Colorado Music Festival (see "Boulder After Dark," below).

Lodging is available in attractive but basic cottages and in rooms and apartments in two historic lodges. All units are completely furnished and have either private or shared kitchens. Cottages range from efficiencies to three-bedroom, two-bathroom units. Guests have access to a self-service laundry, the park's playgrounds, picnic grounds, tennis courts, and hiking trailheads. The historic Chautauqua Dining Hall, which first opened on July 4, 1898, serves three meals daily at moderate prices, Memorial Day to Labor Day.

4 Dining

Partly because Boulder is a young, hip community, it has attracted a variety of small, with-it restaurants—chef-owned and -operated—where innovative and often-changing cuisine is the rule. You'll find a lot of California influences here, but also a number of top-notch chefs doing their own thing.

A Boulder city ordinance prohibits smoking inside restaurants.

VERY EXPENSIVE

✪ **Flagstaff House Restaurant.** 1138 Flagstaff Rd. (west up Baseline Rd.). ☎ 303/442-4640. Reservations recommended. Main courses $25–$45. AE, DC, MC, V. Sun–Fri 6–10pm, Sat 5–10pm. NEW AMERICAN/REGIONAL.

People come to the Flagstaff House from across the state and nation to partake of its excellent cuisine and enjoy its spectacular nighttime view of the lights of

---

ⓕ Family-Friendly Restaurants

New York Deli *(see p. 165)*   Fifteen varieties of burgers are offered here, plus pizza, Coney Island hot dogs, and Dagwood-style sandwiches. Take-out and delivery service are available.

Sushi Zanmai *(see p. 163)*   Flashing knives and tableside cooking keep kids fully entertained.

Boulder, spread out 1,000 feet below. A local institution since 1951, this family-owned and -operated restaurant has an elegant, candlelit dining room with glass walls to maximize the view.

The menu, which changes daily, offers an excellent selection of seafood and Rocky Mountain game, prepared with a creative flair. Typical appetizers are smoked rabbit or duck, oysters, and cheeses. Entrees might include Colorado buffalo, Australian lobster tail, or soft-shell crabs. The restaurant also boasts dessert soufflés and a genuinely world-renowned wine cellar (undoubtedly the best in Colorado).

EXPENSIVE

John's Restaurant. 2328 Pearl St. ☎ **303/444-5232.** Reservations recommended. Main courses $15.50–$25. AE, DISC, MC, V. Tues–Sat from 5:30pm. CONTINENTAL/AMERICAN.

This small, charming restaurant has been winning awards and raves since it opened in 1974. Chef-owned, the restaurant serves the classic dishes of France, Italy, and Spain, along with contemporary American cuisine. House specialties include filet mignon with Stilton ale sauce, topped with grilled Bermuda onions, and shrimp Nancy—pan-grilled shrimp dusted with southwestern spices and flamed in brandy with cream and cayenne. John's also offers vegetarian items, homemade desserts (such as John's Chocolate Intensity), a well-chosen wine list, microbrewery and other beers, and cocktails.

Sushi Zanmai. 1221 Spruce St. (at Broadway). ☎ **303/440-0733.** Reservations requested for groups of four or more. Lunch $6–$10, dinner $12–$20. AE, MC, V. Mon–Fri 11:30am–2pm; Sun–Fri 5–10pm; Sat 5pm–midnight. JAPANESE.

For years locals have rated this Boulder's best Japanese restaurant. All the food is traditionally prepared while you watch—at the hibachi steak table, the sushi bar, or tableside. There are lunch specials and sushi happy-hour specials. Karaoke sing-along takes place Saturdays from 10pm to midnight.

MODERATE

Antica Roma. 1308 Pearl St. (on the Mall). ☎ **303/442-0378.** Reservations accepted. Main courses $8–$20, pizza $8–$10. DISC, MC, V. Mon–Sat 11:30am–2:30pm; Mon–Thurs 5–9pm; Fri–Sat 5–10pm. ROMAN ITALIAN.

Walking into Antica Roma is like entering a piazza in Rome: There's a lovely fountain, brick walls—even laundry hanging on the balcony. The food is equally authentic, with all the pasta made on the premises and hand-thrown pizza baked in the wood-burning oven. Particularly popular are the seafood dishes, such as salmon Mediterranean (a fresh salmon fillet marinated in white wine and fresh herbs, broiled with tomatoes, fresh mint, and thyme), and the award-winning lasagna. There's a full bar and more than 250 Italian wines.

14th Street Bar & Grill. 1400 Pearl St. ☎ **303/444-5854.** Main courses $5–$18. AE, CB, DC, DISC, MC, V. Mon–Sat 11:30am–10pm, Sun 5–10pm. AMERICAN.

Windows facing the corner of 14th and Pearl Streets make this a great spot for people watching as well as dining. The open wood grill and pizza oven and the long and crowded bar tell you this is a fun place. The constantly evolving menu centers around what chef/owner Kathy Andrade calls "American grill" cuisine, which includes grilled sandwiches, southwestern chicken salads, and unusual homemade pizzas, such as a pie topped with chorizo sausage, garlic, and roasted green chiles. A variety of pasta dishes are also offered, plus changing dinner specials.

Jax Fish House. 928 Pearl St. (1 block west of the Mall). ☎ **303/444-1811.** Reservations accepted for large parties only. Main courses $8–$18. MC, V. Mon–Thurs 4–10pm; Fri–Sat 4–11pm; Sun 4–9pm. SEAFOOD.

This small, usually crowded and noisy restaurant has clean lines, open space, brick walls, and both counter and table seating. The menu features the best seafood available, and usually includes shrimp, Atlantic salmon, Rocky Mountain trout, and Hawaiian tuna. Those who prefer beef can choose New York strip steak or a hamburger.

✪ **Nancy's Restaurant.** 825 Walnut St. ☎ **303/449-8402.** Breakfast $4–$8, lunch $6–$8, tea $10, dinner $8–$14. AE, MC, V. Daily 7:30am–2pm; Fri–Sat 5:30–9pm; afternoon tea Wed–Sat 2:30–4pm. CONTINENTAL.

A local favorite in a handsome Victorian home, Nancy's offers excellent food and a varied, imaginative menu. Breakfast is busy, offering omelets and other egg dishes, waffles, blintzes, and espresso drinks. For lunch, you might opt for breakfast again, or choose the grilled Cajun chicken sandwich or pan-braised salmon with raspberry-champagne sauce. A bit of Britain can be found at afternoon tea, comprised of properly brewed English tea (a rarity in American restaurants), sandwiches, currant scones with Devonshire-style cream, and pastries. Champagne, brandy, port, and sherry are also available. Dinner brings steaks, fresh seafood, several pasta and vegetarian dishes, and a number of chicken dishes. Desserts, such as the chocolate raspberry cake, are extra special.

Walnut Brewery. 1123 Walnut St. (near Broadway). ☎ **303/447-1345.** Lunch $4.50–$9.25, dinner $6.50–$17.50. AE, DC, DISC, MC, V. Food service available Sun 11am–10pm, Mon–Thurs 11am–11pm, Fri–Sat 11am–midnight. Bar open until midnight Sun–Wed, until 2am Thurs–Sat. AMERICAN.

Walnut Brewery boasts prominent brew tanks and big beer-label signs on brick walls. Order an appetizing taster of the brewery's eight handcrafted beers (including root beer), but don't ignore the food. Lunches feature a Caesar salad, the brew burger, and the brewer's club, as well as excellent beer-batter fish-and-chips made with cold-smoked salmon. The dinner menu includes the same brewery favorites, plus pasta and such entrees as brown ale chicken and St. Louis–style ribs.

INEXPENSIVE

In addition to the choices below, see chapter 6, "Dining," for a complete review of **Healthy Habits,** 4760 Baseline Rd. (☎ 303/494-9177), a cafeteria-style restaurant that offers all-you-can-eat salad, pasta, and more.

La Estrellita. 1718 Broadway (at Arapahoe Ave.). ☎ **303/939-8822.** Meals $4–$14. AE, DISC, MC, V. Sun–Thurs 11am–10pm, Fri–Sat 11am–11pm. MEXICAN.

Using recipes developed by his parents at the original La Estrellita in Fort Lupton in the 1950s and 1960s, John Montoya established this restaurant in 1986. You'll find all the standard tacos, tostadas, enchiladas, tamales, fajitas, and chile rellenos, in generous portions, plus Indian tacos and stuffed sopaipillas. In recent years

Hispanic Magazine chose La Estrellita as one of the 50 Best Mexican Restaurants in the United States. There's also a delightful outdoor patio.

New York Delicatessen. 1117 Pearl St. ☎ **303/447-DELI (3354)**. $2–$9. AE, CB, DC, DISC, MC, V. Daily 8am–10pm. DELI.

Remember television's *Mork and Mindy?* Back in the 1970s, Robin Williams and Pam Dawber made their home-away-from-home at this authentic New York–style deli on the Pearl Street Mall. You can join the local crowd munching Dagwood-style sandwiches, Coney Island hot dogs, or Reuben sandwiches. Soups, salads, and pastries are prepared fresh daily. The extensive menu also includes pizza and 15 different burgers. There's booth seating and a sunny outside deck, take-out service, and delivery.

✪ **Tom's Tavern.** 1047 Pearl St. ☎ **303/443-3893**. $5–$10. AE, CB, DC, DISC, MC, V. Mon–Sat 11am–midnight, Sun 1–9:30pm. AMERICAN.

Boulder's most popular place for a good hamburger, Tom's has been a neighborhood institution for almost 40 years. Located in a turn-of-the-century building that once housed an undertaker, the tavern has vinyl booths indoors and patio seating outdoors. Besides the one-third-pound burgers and other sandwiches, Tom's serves dinner anytime: a 10-ounce steak, fried chicken, or a vegetarian casserole.

ESPRESSO BARS

Espresso fans will have no problem finding a decent espresso, cappuccino, or latte, since there are outlets of **Starbucks** and **Brio,** as well as more interesting independent coffeehouses, throughout Boulder. Many of those, located in the vicinity of the Pearl Street Mall, provide outdoor seating in nice weather. **Bookend Cafe,** 1115 Pearl Street Mall (☎ **303/440-6699**), offers a variety of coffee drinks; baked goods and egg dishes for breakfast; and soups, salads, and sandwiches for lunch and supper. At the east end of the mall (at 18th Street) is the somewhat bohemian **Penny Lane** (☎ **303/443-9516**), a gathering place for talking, playing chess, or reading while you sip your favorite coffee drink and munch on a bagel or muffin. There's a wide variety of newspapers and nightly live entertainment, including poetry, an open stage, and a diverse range of music by local and regional performers. See also "Boulder After Dark," below.

5 Attractions

THE TOP ATTRACTIONS

✪ **Boulder Creek Path.** 55th St. and Pearl Pkwy. to the mouth of Boulder Canyon. ☎ **303/441-3400**. Free admission. Daily 24 hours. Bus: HOP.

Following Boulder Creek, this nature corridor provides about a 10-mile-long oasis and recreation area through the city and west into the mountains. With no street crossings (there are bridges and underpasses instead), the path is popular with Boulder residents, especially on weekends, when you'll see numerous walkers, runners, bicyclists, and in-line skaters. (Walkers should stay to the right since the left lane is for faster traffic.) The C.U. campus and several city parks are linked by the path, as are local office buildings. Near the east end, watch for deer, prairie dog colonies, and wetlands, where some 150 species of birds have been spotted. You may see Canada geese, mallard ducks, spotted sandpipers, owls, and woodpeckers.

At 30th Street, south of Arapahoe Road, the path cuts through Scott Carpenter Park (named for Colorado's native-son astronaut), with swimming in summer and sledding in winter. Just west of here you'll find Boulder Creek Stream Observatory,

Boulder Attractions

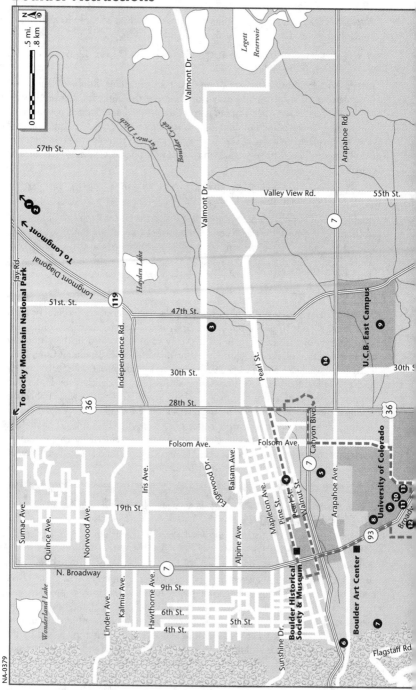

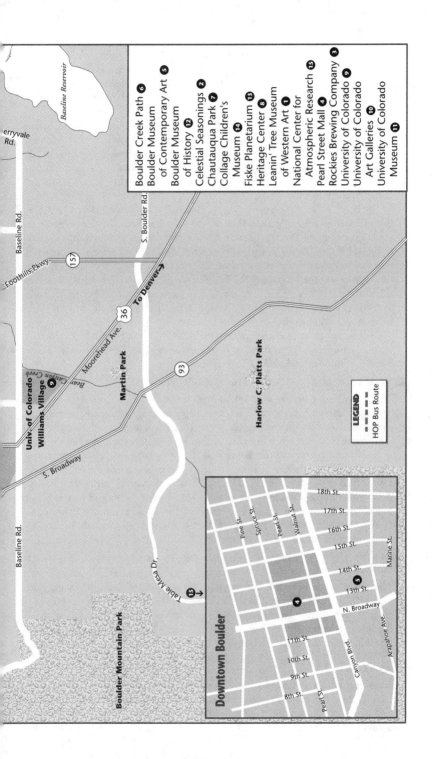

Boulder Creek Path **6**
Boulder Museum
  of Contemporary Art **5**
Boulder Museum
  of History **12**
Celestial Seasonings **2**
Chautauqua Park **7**
Collage Children's
  Museum **14**
Fiske Planetarium **13**
Heritage Center **8**
Leanin' Tree Museum
  of Western Art **1**
National Center for
  Atmospheric Research **15**
Pearl Street Mall **4**
Rockies Brewing Company **3**
University of Colorado **9**
University of Colorado
  Art Galleries **10**
University of Colorado
  Museum **11**

Baseline Reservoir

erryvale
Rd.

Baseline Rd.

S. Boulder Rd.

Foothills Pkwy

157

36

To Denver

Moorehead Ave.

Martin Park

93

Harlow C. Platts Park

Bear Canyon Creek

Univ. of Colorado
Williams Village **9**

S. Broadway

Baseline Rd.

Table Mesa Dr.

15

LEGEND

HOP Bus Route

Boulder Mountain Park

Downtown Boulder

18th St.
17th St.
16th St.
15th St.
14th St.
13th St.

Pine St.
Spruce St.
Pearl St.
Walnut St.

Marine St.

4

5

N. Broadway

Canyon Blvd.

Arapahoe Ave.

11th St.
10th St.
9th St.
8th St.

Pearl St.

adjacent to and maintained by the Regal Harvest House. In addition to observing aquatic wildlife, you're invited to feed the fish with food purchased from a vending machine (25¢). Central Park, at Broadway and Canyon Boulevard, preserves some of Boulder's history with a restored steam locomotive. The Boulder Public Library is also in this area.

Traveling west, watch for the Charles A. Heartling Sculpture Garden (with the stone image of local Indian Chief Niwot) and the Kids' Fishing Ponds, which are stocked by the Boulder Fish and Game Club and open only to children under 12, who can fish for free and keep what they catch. Near Third Street and Canyon Boulevard you'll find the Xeriscape Garden, where drought-tolerant plants are tested for reduced water intake.

The Eben G. Fine Park is named for the Boulder pharmacist who discovered Arapaho Glacier on nearby Arapaho Peak. To the west, Red Rocks Settlers' Park marks the beginning of the Boulder Canyon Pioneer Trail, which leads to a continuation of Boulder Creek Path. The park is named for Missouri gold-seekers who camped here in 1858 and later found gold about 12 miles farther west. Watch for explanatory signs along the 1.2-mile path. The Whitewater Kayak Course has 20 slalom gates for kayakers and canoeists to use free; to the west, Elephant Buttresses is one of Boulder's more popular rock-climbing areas. The path ends at Four Mile Canyon, the old town site of Orodell.

Note: Although the path is generally well populated and quite safe, Boulderites warn against using it late at night if you are alone; one of the problems is the number of transients who take refuge there.

✪ Pearl Street Mall. Pearl St. from 11th to 15th Sts. Bus: HOP.

This 4-block-long tree-lined pedestrian mall marks Boulder's downtown core and center for dining, shopping, strolling, and people watching. Musicians, mimes, jugglers, and other street entertainers hold court on the landscaped mall day and night, year-round. Buy your lunch from one of the many vendors and sprawl on the grass in front of the courthouse to relax and eat. Locally owned businesses and galleries share the mall with trendy boutiques, sidewalk cafes, and major chains (including Esprit, Banana Republic, and Pendleton). There's a wonderful play area for youngsters, with climbable boulders set in gravel. Don't miss the bronze bust of Chief Niwot (of the southern Arapaho) in front of the Boulder County Courthouse. Niwot, who welcomed the first Boulder settlers, was killed in southeastern Colorado during the Sand Creek Massacre of 1864.

University of Colorado. East side of Broadway, between Arapahoe Ave. and Baseline Rd. ☎ 303/492-1411. Bus: HOP.

The largest university in the state, with 25,000 students (including 4,600 graduate students), the University of Colorado dominates the city. Its student population, cultural and sports events, and intellectual atmosphere have helped to shape Boulder into the city it is today. The school boasts 15 alumni-astronauts who have flown in space, plus one in training.

Old Main, on the Norlin Quadrangle, was the first building erected after the university was established in 1876; at that time, it housed the entire school. Later, pink-sandstone Italian Renaissance–style buildings came to dominate the campus. Visitors may want to take in the university's Heritage Center, on the third floor of Old Main; the University of Colorado Museum (see "More Attractions," below), a natural-history museum in the Henderson Building on Broadway; the Mary Rippon Outdoor Theatre, behind the Henderson Museum, site of the annual Colorado Shakespeare Festival; Fiske Planetarium and Science Center, between

Kittredge Loop Drive and Regent Drive on the south side of campus; and the Norlin Library, on the Norlin Quadrangle, the largest research library in the state, with extensive holdings of American and English literature. Other attractions include the Fine Arts Galleries, University Memorial (the student center), and the new Integrated Teaching and Learning Laboratory in the College of Engineering. Prospective students and their parents can arrange campus tours by contacting the admissions office (☎ 303/492-6301).

Tours are available weekdays at the Laboratory for Atmospheric and Space Physics (☎ 303/492-6412), on the east campus, with at least one week's advance notice. The Sommers-Bausch Observatory (☎ 303/492-5002) offers tours and Friday evening open houses. Among the telescopes there are 16-, 18-, and 24-inch Cassegrain reflectors and a 10-inch aperture heliostat.

National Center for Atmospheric Research. 1850 Table Mesa Dr. ☎ **303/497-1174**. Free admission. Self-guided tours, Mon–Fri 8am–5pm, Sat–Sun and holidays 9am–3pm. Guided tours, June–Sept, Mon–Sat at noon; rest of year, Mon and Wed at noon. Take Broadway heading southwest out of town to Table Mesa Dr., and follow it west to the center.

I. M. Pei designed this striking pink-sandstone building, which overlooks Boulder from high atop Table Mesa in the southwestern foothills. Here, scientists study the greenhouse effect, wind shear, and ozone depletion to gain a better understanding of the earth's atmosphere. Among the technological tools on display are satellites, weather balloons, robots, and supercomputers that can simulate the world's climate. There are also hands-on, weather-oriented exhibits from the San Francisco Exploratorium Museum, now on permanent display. The Weather Trail outside the building's west doors is a 0.4-mile loop with interpretative signs describing aspects of weather and climate plus the plants and animals of the area. The center also hosts a changing art exhibit.

MORE ATTRACTIONS
INDUSTRIAL TOURS

✪ **Celestial Seasonings.** 4600 Sleepytime Dr. (off Spine Rd. at Colo. 119, Longmont Diagonal). ☎ **303/581-1202**. Free admission. Mon–Sat 9am–5pm, Sun 11am–5pm; tours on the hour. Reservations required for groups of 8 or more. Bus: J.

The nation's leading producer of herbal teas, housed in a modern building in northeastern Boulder, offers tours that are an experience for the senses. The company, which began in a Boulder garage in the 1970s, now produces more than 50 varieties of tea from more than 100 different herbs and spices, imported from 35 foreign countries. You'll understand why they invite you to "see, taste, and smell the world of Celestial Seasonings" as you move from a consumer taste test in the lobby, to marketing displays, and finally into the production plant where milling, packaging, and shipping can be seen. The overpowering "mint room" is a highlight. The tour lasts about an hour.

Rockies Brewing Company. 2880 Wilderness Place. ☎ **303/444-8448**. Free admission. Pub, Mon–Sat 11am–10pm; tours, Mon–Sat 2pm. Take U.S. 36 north to Valmont Rd. and then head east to Wilderness Place.

From the grinding of the grain to the bottling of the beer, the 25-minute tour of this microbrewery passes by glistening copper vats that turn out 300 to 400 kegs of Boulder Beer a day, and ends as all brewery tours should: in the pub. It's actually a restaurant overlooking the bottling area, so even if you visit without taking a tour, you still get a good view of the brewing process. The menu includes munchies, soup, fresh salads, and sandwiches; lunches run $5 to $8.

MUSEUMS & GALLERIES

There are three art galleries on the University of Colorado campus. The **C.U. Art Gallery,** in the Sibell Wolle Fine Arts building (☎ **303/492-8300**), is home to the Colorado Collection of about 3,000 works by international artists including Durer, Rembrandt, Tiepolo, Hogarth, Hiroshige, Matisse, and Picasso. There are also changing exhibits. Admission is free; hours are Monday through Friday from 8am to 5pm, and Saturday from noon to 4pm. Tuesday the gallery is open until 8pm. Bus: HOP.

At the University Memorial Center, **UMC Art Gallery** (☎ **303/492-7465**) organizes and hosts a variety of exhibitions featuring regional and national artists. In the music-listening rooms, visitors can peruse current periodicals while listening to modern and classical music. The gallery is on the second floor of the Center, just left of the information desk; it's open Monday through Thursday from 9am to 10pm, Friday from 9am to 5pm. Bus: HOP.

The **Andrew J. Macky Gallery** (☎ **303/492-8423**), at the main entrance of Macky Auditorium, shows touring exhibits and works by local artists. It's open Wednesday from 10am to 5pm. Bus: HOP.

Boulder Museum of Contemporary Art. 1750 13th St. ☎ **303/443-2122.** www.bmoca.org. Admission $2 adults, $1.50 students and seniors. Tues–Fri 11am–5pm, Sat 9am–5pm, Sun noon–5pm. Closed major holidays. Bus: HOP.

This multidisciplinary art center, originally created to exhibit the work of local artists, has gradually evolved into an exciting venue where one can expect to see almost anything art-related, from the light-hearted to the elegant, by local, regional, and international contemporary artists. There are special programs for young children, plus arts events throughout the year. Performing arts are presented in the museum's Public Theater, and an outdoor cinema takes place Saturday evenings in summer ($5 per person), where classic movies and cult classics are shown. Take a lawn chair or blanket.

Boulder Museum of History. 1206 Euclid Ave. ☎ **303/449-3464.** Admission $2 adults; $1 children, students, and seniors. Tues–Fri 10am–4pm, Sat–Sun noon–4pm. Closed major holidays. Bus: HOP.

Ensconced on University Hill in the 1899–1900 Harbeck-Bergheim House, a French château–style sandstone mansion with a Dutch-style front door and Italian tile fireplaces, this museum has an impressive collection of more than 20,000 artifacts, plus hundreds of thousands of photographs and historical documents from Colorado's early days up to the present. Built by a New York financier, it features a Tiffany window on the stairway landing, a built-in buffet with leaded-glass doors, and hand-carved mantels. Mannequins are used to depict cooking in the authentic old-fashioned kitchen. The wardrobes in the upstairs bedrooms contain an extensive collection of Victorian and Edwardian clothing, and there are exquisite quilts on the beds.

Owned by the Boulder Historical Society, the museum presents lecture programs, classes, and events such as a Victorian Fair, with barbershop quartets, carriage rides, and quilting.

Collage Children's Museum. 2065 30th St. ☎ **303/440-9894.** Admission $3.50, $1.75 seniors, free for kids under 2, $12 maximum per family. Mon and Wed–Sat 10am–5pm, Sun 1–5pm. Across from Crossroads Mall on the east side.

With 4,700 square feet of custom-designed interactive exhibits created to stimulate the imagination, children from preschool through elementary grades are encouraged to touch, dress up, and get involved. There's a 5-foot-tall magnetic poetry board, plenty of art supplies, and changing hands-on exhibits dealing with science, technology, literature, and more. Call for times of the museum's numerous planned activities. Children under 12 must be accompanied by an adult, but adults can play, too.

Heritage Center. Third floor of Old Main, University of Colorado. ☎ **303/492-6329.** Free admission. Tues–Fri 10am–4pm; and preceding most home football games. Bus: HOP.

Located in the oldest building on campus, this museum reflects the history of the university. Within seven galleries are exhibits on early student life (together with a complete set of yearbooks), C.U.'s contributions to space exploration, campus architecture, distinguished C.U. alumni, and an overview of the university's history.

Leanin' Tree Museum of Western Art. 6055 Longbow Dr. (off Spine Rd. and Longmont Diagonal). ☎ **800/777-8716** or 303/530-1442. www.leanintree.com. Free admission. Mon–Fri 8am–4:30pm, Sat–Sun 10am–4pm. Bus: 205.

You may know Leanin' Tree as the world's largest publisher of western-art greeting cards. What's not so well known is that here in the company's headquarters is an outstanding collection of original paintings and bronze sculptures by contemporary artists—all depicting scenes from the Old or New West, including a collection of humorous cowboy art. Some of the works have been reproduced on the company's greeting cards that are offered for sale in the gift shop. Free guided tours are available.

University of Colorado Museum. University of Colorado, Henderson Bldg., Broadway at 15th St. ☎ **303/492-6892.** Free admission, but donations accepted. Mon–Fri 9am–5pm, Sat 9am–4pm, Sun 10am–4pm. Bus: HOP.

The natural history and anthropology of the Rocky Mountains and Southwest are the focus of this campus museum, founded in 1902. Featured exhibits include ancestral Puebloan (also called Anasazi) pottery and collections pertaining to dinosaurs, geology, paleontology, botany, entomology, and zoology. A children's area has interactive exhibits, and the main gallery is devoted to special displays that change throughout the year.

ESPECIALLY FOR KIDS

City parks (see "Outdoor Activities," below), **Collage Children's Museum** (see above), and the University of Colorado's **Fiske Planetarium** offer the best diversions for children.

On the **Boulder Creek Path** (see "The Top Attractions," above), youngsters are fascinated by the underwater fish observatory behind the Regal Harvest House, and can feed the huge trout (machines cough up handfuls of fish food for 25¢). Farther up the path, on the south bank around Sixth Street, Kids' Fishing Ponds, stocked by the Boulder Fish and Game Club, are open to children under 12. There's no charge for either activity.

The **Fiske Planetarium** (☎ 303/492-5002) offers visitors a walk through the Solar System. Dedicated to the memory of C.U. alumnus Ellison Onizuka and the six other astronauts who died in the space shuttle *Challenger* explosion, the outdoor scale model of the system begins at the entrance to the planetarium with the sun and inner planets, and continues across Regent Drive to the outer planets, located along the walkway to the Engineering Center. Admission is free. Allow at least a half hour. The planetarium also offers after-school and summer discovery programs for kids, as well as star shows and other programs where you get a chance to look at the sky through the planetarium's telescopes. Admission for these events is usually $2 to $4 per person; call for the latest schedule. Bus: HOP.

6 Outdoor Activities

Boulder manages over 8,000 acres of park lands, including more than 100 miles of hiking trails and long stretches of bicycle paths. Several canyons lead down from the Rockies directly into Boulder, attracting mountaineers and rock climbers. Families enjoy picnicking and camping in the beautiful surroundings. It seems that everywhere you look, people of all ages are running, walking, biking, skiing, or engaged in other active sports.

The **Boulder Parks and Recreation Department** (☎ 303/441-3400) schedules many year-round activities for children as well as adults. Seasonal booklets on activities and city parks are available free from the Chamber of Commerce office. Although many of the programs last for several weeks or months, some are half- or full-day activities that visiting children can join, although usually at a slightly higher price than that charged for city residents. The department sponsors hikes, horseback rides, fitness programs, ski trips, water sports, special holiday events, and performances in local parks.

One destination where you can enjoy several kinds of outdoor activities is **Eldorado Canyon State Park**. This mountain park, just 8 miles southwest of Boulder in Eldorado Springs, is a favorite of technical rock climbers, but the 850-foot-high canyon's beauty makes it just as popular among hikers, picnickers, and others who want to get away from it all. The 1,165-acre park includes 12 miles of hiking and horseback-riding trails, plus 9 miles of trails suitable for mountain bikes; fishing is permitted, but not camping. Exhibits at the visitor center describe the canyon's geologic formations, bats, and the history of the park. There's also a climbing wall. Admission is $4 per vehicle; the park is open daily from dawn to dusk. For further information, contact Eldorado Canyon State Park, Box B, Eldorado Springs, CO 80025 (☎ 303/494-3943).

BALLOONING   Float above the majestic Rocky Mountains in a hot-air balloon, watching as the early morning light gradually brightens to full day. **Fair Winds Hot Air Balloon Flights** (☎ 303/939-9323; www.fairwindsinc.com) flies daily year-round, weather permitting. Prices are about $150 per person.

BICYCLING   On some days, you can see more bikes than cars in Boulder. Paths run along many of the city's major arteries, and racing and touring events are scheduled year-round. Night bicyclists are required to have lights; perhaps because of the large number of cyclists in Boulder, the local police actively enforce traffic regulations that apply to them—generally the same laws that apply to motor vehicles.

For current information on biking events, tips on the best places to ride, and equipment sales and repairs, check with **University Bicycles,** 839 Pearl St., about 2 blocks west of the Pearl Street Mall (☎ 303/444-4196; www.ubikes.com). The shop also provides bike rentals for about $20 per day, and has maps of the city's 80 miles of bike lanes, paths, and routes.

CLIMBING   If you'd like to tackle the nearby mountains and cliffs with ropes and pitons, contact **Boulder Mountaineer,** 1335 Broadway (☎ 303/442-8355), which sells clothing and technical equipment, and can also provide maps and advice on climbing and trail running. Another good information source is **Colorado Athletic Training School,** 2800 30th St. (☎ 303/939-9699).

The Flatiron Range (easily visible from downtown Boulder) and nearby Eldorado Canyon are two favorite destinations among expert rock scalers.

FISHING   A favored nearby fishing area is **Boulder Reservoir,** run by the Boulder Parks and Recreation Department (☎ 303/441-3456), North 51st Street, northeast of the city off the Longmont Diagonal. Other favorite fishing holes include Lagerman Reservoir, west of North 73rd Street off Pike Road, about 15 miles northeast of the city, where only nonmotorized boats can be used; Barker Reservoir, just east of Nederland on the Boulder Canyon Drive (Colo. 119), for bank fishing; and Walden Ponds Wildlife Habitat, about 6 miles east of downtown on North 75th Street.

GLIDER FLYING & SOARING   The atmospheric conditions generated by the peaks of the Front Range are ideal for year-round soaring and gliding. **Mile High Gliding,** 5534 Independence Rd. (☎ 303/527-1122), offers rides and lessons from Boulder Municipal Airport, 2 miles northeast of downtown. Rides for one person range from $60 to $160, and last from 15 minutes to an hour or more; a half-hour ride for two costs $130.

GOLF   Local courses include **Flatirons Golf Course** (run by Boulder Parks and Recreation Dept.), 5706 E. Arapahoe Ave. (☎ 303/442-7851), and **Lake Valley Golf Course**, 4400 Lake Valley Dr., several miles north of Boulder off Neva Road (☎ 303/444-2114). Non-resident greens fees for 18 holes range from $18 to $29.

HIKING & BACKPACKING   There are plenty of opportunities for hiking and backpacking in the Boulder area—the Boulder Mountain Parks system includes 4,625 acres bordering the Boulder city limits, including the Flatirons and Flagstaff Mountain. You can obtain a map with descriptions of more than 60 trails from the Boulder Convention and Visitors Bureau.

Numerous Roosevelt National Forest trailheads leave the Peak to Peak Scenic Byway (Colo. 72) west of Boulder. Check with the U.S. Forest Service, Boulder Ranger District, 2995 Baseline Rd., Room 110 (☎ 303/444-6600) for hiking and backpacking information, and during dry weather, check on possible fire and smoking restrictions before heading out into the forest.

West of Boulder, on the Continental Divide, is the Indian Peaks Wilderness Area (☎ 303/444-6003). More than half of the area is fragile alpine tundra; permits are required from June 1 to September 15.

RUNNING   The best place to get information about running or walking is the **Runners Roost,** 1129 Pearl St., on the Mall (☎ 303/443-9868). In addition to selling shoes and apparel, this shop can supply maps and information on area trails and outdoor fitness in general, plus it serves as headquarters for numerous scheduled races. Most of these are "fun runs," varying in distance from 5K (3.1 miles) to a half marathon (13 miles). The **Bolder Boulder** (☎ 303/444-RACE), held every Memorial Day, attracts 40,000 runners who circle its 10-kilometer (6.2-mile) course.

SKIING   Friendly **Eldora Mountain Resort,** P.O. Box 1697, Nederland, CO 80466 (☎ **888/235-3672** or 303/440-8700; fax 303/440/8797; www.eldora. com), is just 21 miles (about a 40-minute drive) west of downtown Boulder via Colo. 119 through Nederland. RTD buses leave Boulder for Eldora four times daily during ski season. For downhill skiers and snowboarders, Eldora has 47 trails, rated 20% novice, 50% intermediate, and 30% expert terrain among its 495 acres. It has snowmaking on 320 acres. The area has a new quad lift, one triple- and five double-chairlifts, three surface lifts, and a vertical rise of 1,400 feet. Lift tickets (1998–99 rates) are $35 for adults, $16 for children 6 to 12 and seniors 65 to 69, and free for kids 6 and under and seniors 70 and older. Skier and snowboarder packages that include lessons and rental equipment are available. The season runs from mid-November to mid-April, snow permitting.

For cross-country skiers, Eldora has 45 kilometers of groomed and backcountry trails, and an overnight hut available by reservation. Snowmaking equipment serves two 5-kilometer loops. About 15% of the trails are rated easy, 50% intermediate, and 35% difficult. The trail fee is $10, or $7 for seniors 65 to 69.

You can rent all your ski and snowboard equipment at the ski-rental center, and Nordic equipment at the Eldora Nordic Center. A free base-area shuttle runs throughout the day from the Lodge to the Little Hawk area and the Nordic Center. In Boulder, you can rent or buy telemark and alpine touring equipment from **Boulder Mountaineer,** 1335 Broadway (☎ **303/442-8355**).

SWIMMING   Five public pools are located within the city. Indoor pools, all open daily year-round, are at the **North Boulder Recreation Center,** 3170 N. Broadway (☎ 303 441-3444), the **East Boulder Community Center,** 5660 Sioux Dr. (☎ 303/ 441-4400), and the **South Boulder Recreation Center,** 1360 Gillaspie Dr. (☎ 303/441-3448). The two outdoor pools (both open daily from Memorial Day to Labor Day) are **Scott Carpenter Pool,** 30th Street and Arapahoe Avenue (☎ 303/441-3427), and **Spruce Pool,** 2102 Spruce St. (☎ 303/441-3426). Swimming fees are $4.25 for adults, $1.50 for children, and $2.25 for seniors.

TENNIS   There are more than 30 public courts in the city. The North and South Boulder Recreation Centers (see "Swimming," above) each have four lighted courts, and accept reservations ($8 for 1½ hours). The North Boulder Recreation Center also has two platform tennis courts. Play is free if you arrive and there's no one using the courts or with a reservation. For locations of other public tennis courts, contact the Boulder Parks and Recreation Department (☎ 303/441-3400).

WATER SPORTS   For both power and non-power boating, sailboard instruction, or swimming at a sandy beach, head for the 1,400-acre **Boulder Reservoir** (☎ 303/441-3456), on North 51st Street off the Longmont Diagonal northeast of the city. Non-powered boats and canoes can be rented starting at $5 an hour, with sailboards at $10 an hour. There's also a boat ramp and other facilities.

7 Spectator Sports

The major attractions are **University of Colorado football, women's volleyball,** and **men's and women's basketball**. For tickets, contact the Ticket Office, Campus Box 372, Boulder, CO 80309 (☎ **303/49-BUFFS**). Football tickets sell out early, particularly for homecoming and games with Nebraska, Texas A&M, and Oklahoma, so it would be wise to make reservations far in advance.

8 Shopping

For the best shopping in Boulder, head to the **Pearl Street Mall** (see "The Top Attractions," above), where you'll find shops and galleries galore.

If you're more interested in a typical shopping center, head to **Crossroads Mall** (☎ 303/444-0722), between 28th and 30th Streets off Arapahoe Road, with over 150 stores, including Sears, JC Penney, and Foley's. On rainy days, locals get their exercise at the mall's "Walker's Track," which begins next to the C.P.I. One-Hour Photo store.

SHOPPING A TO Z
ARTS & CRAFTS

Art Source International. 1237 Pearl St. ☎ **303/444-4080.**

You'll find natural-history prints, maps, and rare books on western Americana, all from the 18th and 19th centuries, plus a collection of late-19th-century Colorado photographs.

Boulder Arts & Crafts Cooperative. 1421 Pearl St. ☎ **303/443-3683.**

This shop, owned and operated by its artist members since 1971, features a wide variety of original handcrafted works, ranging from watercolors, serigraphs, and other fine art to top-quality crafts including blown or stained glass, jewelry, and pottery.

Maclaren Markowitz Gallery. 1011 Pearl St. ☎ **303/449-6807.**

Presented here are works by local and national artists in a variety of media and styles, including fine paintings, sculpture, ceramics, and wearable art jewelry.

BOOKS

Barnes & Noble Booksellers. 2915 Pearl St. ☎ **303/442-1665.**

You'll find all the usual best-sellers and other titles at this large bookstore, a good selection of local and regional titles, and numerous maps—from downtown Boulder to world atlases. They also sell tapes and CDs, and the cafe carries fresh-baked pastries and a variety of coffees.

FOOD & DRINK

Alfalfa's. 1651 Broadway. ☎ **303/442-0909.**

The original Alfalfa's still sells excellent produce (much of it certified organic) and chemical-free groceries; there's also a deli, soup-and-salad bar, juice-and-espresso bar, and a hot-food case.

Boulder Wine Merchant. 2690 Broadway. ☎ **303/443-6761.**

This store has a solid wine selection with more than 2,000 international varieties, plus a knowledgeable staff who can help you make the right choice.

Liquor Mart. 1750 15th St. (at Canyon Blvd.). ☎ **800/597-4440** or 303/449-3374.

Here you'll find a huge choice of discounted wine and liquor, including a wide selection of imported and microbrewed beers.

GIFTS & SOUVENIRS

Nature's Own Imagination. 1133 Pearl St. Mall. ☎ **303/443-4430.**

Stop by this store for a unique collection of candles, aromatherapy oils, and wind chimes, plus birdhouses, jewelry, fossils, geodes, and more.

Traders of the Lost Art. 1454 Pearl St. ☎ **303/440-9664.**

Here you'll find incense, candles, cards, jewelry, and colorful 100%-natural-dyed cotton clothing and accessories from around the world.

HARDWARE

✪ **McGuckin Hardware.** 2525 Arapahoe Ave. ☎ **303/443-1822.**

McGuckin's claims to have the world's largest hardware selection, with more than 200,000 items in stock. In addition to the usual hardware and assorted whatchamacallits that most hardware stores carry, you'll also find sporting goods, kitchen gizmos, automotive supplies, electronics, outdoor furniture, and a whole lot of other stuff.

JEWELRY

Antiquariat. 2014 Broadway. ☎ **303/443-6311.**

This shop focuses on American Indian jewelry, including many hard-to-find pieces. You'll also find estate and fine jewelry, figurines, and other collectibles.

MUSIC

⭐ **Boulder Early Music Shop.** 3200 Valmont Rd. #7. ☎ **800/499-1301** or 303/449-9231. www.bems.com.

Musicians and music lovers from across North America rely on this shop for sheet music, recordings, books, musical gifts, and instruments. Browsing is loads of fun, and the musician-shopkeepers are friendly, highly knowledgeable folks who obviously love their work.

SPORTING GOODS

There are a number of well-established sporting-goods stores in the city. **Mountain Sports,** 821 Pearl St. (☎ **800/558-6770** or 303/443-6770), which boasts it's Boulder's oldest mountaineering shop (it opened in 1958), specializes in equipment, clothing, and accessories for backpacking, camping, rock and ice climbing, mountaineering, backcountry and telemark skiing, skate skiing, and snowshoeing. Equipment rentals include sleeping bags, tents, backpacks, and snowshoes; backcountry and telemark ski packages are available as well, as are maps and guidebooks. The knowledgeable staff can help you plan your trip.

Outdoor enthusiasts are also on hand at **Doc's Ski and Sport,** 627 S. Broadway (☎ **303/499-0963**), which sells, rents, and repairs skis, snowboards, snowshoes, mountain bikes, and in-line skates. **Boulder Army Store,** 1545 Pearl St. (☎ **303/442-7616**), has the best stock of camping gear in the city, along with a limited amount of fishing equipment, plus a good supply of outdoor clothing and military surplus items, such as fatigues, helmets, and that disarmed hand grenade you've always wanted. **Gart Brothers,** 2525 Arapahoe Ave. (☎ **303/449-6180**), is a good all-purpose sporting-goods source.

9 Boulder After Dark

As a cultured and well-educated community (59% of Boulder's adult residents have at least one college degree), Boulder is noted for its summer music, dance, and Shakespeare festivals. Of course, major entertainment events take place year-round, both downtown and on the University of Colorado campus. There's also a wide choice of nightclubs and bars, but it hasn't always been so: Boulder was dry for 60 years, from 1907 (13 years before national Prohibition) to 1967. The first new bar in the city opened in 1969, in the Hotel Boulderado.

Entertainment schedules can be found in the *Daily Camera's* weekly *Friday Magazine;* in either of the Denver dailies, the *Denver Post* or the *Rocky Mountain News;* in *Westword,* the Denver weekly; or the free *Boulder Weekly.*

THE CLUB & MUSIC SCENE

Boulder Broker Inn. 555 30th St. (at Baseline Rd.). ☎ **303/444-3330.**

The dance music at this flashy singles bar tends to attract young professionals rather than college students. Tuesday is comedy night.

Boulder Theater. 14th and Pearl sts. ☎ **303/786-7030.**

Country, rock, jazz, and who knows what else is performed here.

The Catacombs. In the basement of the Hotel Boulderado, 13th and Spruce sts. ☎ **303/443-0486.**

This popular bar attracts a crowd to listen to live blues and jazz by local and regional performers. C.U. students like the loud, somewhat raucous atmosphere.

Fox Theatre and Cafe. 1135 13th St. ☎ **303/443-3399.**

A variety of live music (mainly alternative) is presented here every night, featuring a mix of local, regional, and national talent. This converted movie theater boasts three bars.

Penny Lane Coffee House. Pearl and 18th Sts. ☎ **303/443-9516.**

Quiet by day, this Greenwich Village–style coffeehouse comes alive at night. There's usually a poetry reading on Mondays, live jazz one night, several open-stage evenings, and a variety of live music by local and regional performers Friday and Saturday. See also "Espresso Bars," above.

Tulagi. 1129 13th St. ☎ **303/442-1369.**

An informal college bar on the Hill off campus, Tulagi features live rock music most nights, has frequent beer specials, and offers occasional no-alcohol nights when youths 16 and older are welcome.

West End Tavern. 926 Pearl St. (between 9th and 10th Sts.). ☎ **303/444-3535.**

The West End is consistently voted the "best neighborhood bar" by *Daily Camera* readers. Boulderites seem to love the wide-ranging selection of jazz, blues, and other live music in the trendy bar. Fare includes hot chili, pizza, and charbroiled sandwiches.

THE BAR SCENE

The Barrel House. 2860 Arapahoe Rd. ☎ **303/442-4594.**

Consistently voted the number-one sports bar in Boulder by local newspaper readers, the Barrel House offers a choice of 28 beers on tap, most of which are Colorado microbrews. There are close to three dozen TVs, including four big-screen sets, and food ranging from buffalo burgers to jambalaya to Maine lobster. There's also a roof-top patio and Boulder's longest happy hour: from 3 to 7pm and 10pm to closing, daily.

Mountain Sun Pub & Brewery. 1535 Pearl St. (east of the Mall). ☎ **303/546-0886.**

An English-style neighborhood pub and microbrewery, Mountain Sun produces 35 barrels of beer each week and provides tours on request. The menu features soups, salads, burgers, sandwiches, and a few Mexican dishes, and there's live folk, acoustic, and bluegrass music on Sunday nights (no cover).

Oasis II Brewery. 1095 Canyon Blvd. ☎ **303/449-0363.**

Probably the only brewpub with an Egyptian motif, Oasis II brews great beer. Try the award-winning Tut Brown Ale.

The Sink. 1165 13th St. ☎ **303/444-SINK (7465).**

Open since 1949, the new spacey wall murals make this one of Boulder's funniest nightspots. There's a full bar with over a dozen regional microbrews, live music, and fare such as Sinkburgers and "ugly crust" pizza.

Walnut Brewery. 1123 Walnut St. (near Broadway). ☎ **303/447-1345.**

This large microbrewery—popular with the after-work crowd, both young and old—has its restaurant/bar/brewery in a historic brick warehouse a block from the Pearl Street Mall. At least six beers, from a pale ale to a stout, are always available. The brewery produces its own root beer, plus several seasonal specials. See also "Dining," above.

The Yard. 2690 28th St., Unit C. ☎ **303/443-1987.**

A gay bar that attracts a diverse crowd, the Yard features dancing (no cover) on Fridays and Saturdays, as well as pool and a daily happy hour.

THE PERFORMING ARTS

Music, dance, and theater are important aspects of life for Boulder residents, and visitors are welcome to take full advantage of the numerous events scheduled. Many of these activities take place at **Macky Auditorium** at the University of Colorado (☎ 303/492-8008; www.colorado.edu/music), and other campus venues, as well as the **Chautauqua Auditorium,** 900 Baseline Rd. (☎ 303/442-3282; www. chautauqua.com), and the **Dairy Center for the Arts,** 2590 Walnut St. ☎ 303/440-7826; www.thedairy.com).

CLASSICAL MUSIC & OPERA

✪ **Boulder Bach Festival.** P.O. Box 1896, Boulder, CO 80306. ☎ **303/494-3159.**

First presented in 1981, this celebration of the music of Johann Sebastian Bach includes not only a late-January festival, but also concerts and other events year-round. Individual adult tickets cost $15 to $30, students pay $11, and series tickets are also available.

Boulder Philharmonic Orchestra. Dairy Center for the Arts, 2590 Walnut St. ☎ **303/449-1343.**

This acclaimed community orchestra performs from fall to spring, with world-class artists that have included singer Marilyn Horne, guitarist Carlos Montoya, and violinist Itzhak Perlman. Tickets are $8 to $90.

Colorado MahlerFest. P.O. Box 1314, Boulder, CO 80306. ☎ **303/494-1632** for information, ☎ 303/449-1343 for box office.

Begun in 1986, this international festival celebrates the work of Gustav Mahler for a week each January. There's a performance of one of his symphonies, plus films, discussions, seminars, and other musical programs. Some events are free; admission to others ranges from $8 to $30.

Colorado Music Festival. 1525 Spruce St., Suite 101, Boulder, CO 80302. ☎ **303/449-1397** for general information, or 303/449-2413 ext. 11 for tickets.www.coloradomusicfest.com.

Begun in 1976, this series is the single biggest annual arts event in Boulder, with world-class musicians performing in the acoustically revered Chautauqua Auditorium. The festival presents works by classical through modern composers, such as Bach, Beethoven, Mozart, Dvorak, and Gershwin, plus living composers. It usually runs from late June to mid-August, with symphony orchestra concerts Thursdays and Fridays at 8pm, chamber orchestra concerts Sundays at 7pm, and a chamber music series Tuesdays at 8pm. There's also a children's concert in late June and a 4th of July concert. Adult ticket prices range from $12 to $35.

C.U. Concerts. University of Colorado. ☎ **303/492-8008.** www.colorado.edu/music.

The university's College of Music presents the Artist Series, Lyric Theatre, Takács String Quartet Series, and Holiday Festival at Macky Auditorium and Grusin Music Hall. General admission tickets usually range from $10 to $30. The Artist Series features an outstanding lineup of classical soloists, jazz artists, dance companies, and multidisciplinary events.

THEATER & DANCE

Boulder Ballet Ensemble. Dairy Center for the Arts, 2590 Walnut St. ☎ **303/442-6944.**

This community group, established in 1984, presents classical ballet with professional, semi-professional, and amateur dancers. It is best known for its production of *The Nutcracker* with the Boulder Philharmonic on Thanksgiving weekend.

Colorado Dance Festival. P.O. Box 356, Boulder, CO 80306. ☎ **303/442-7666.**

Dancers from around the world flock to Boulder for this 4-week event each July. Varied performances (tickets range from $18 to $28) are interspersed with classes, workshops, lectures, film and video screenings, and panel discussions.

✪ **Colorado Shakespeare Festival.** Campus Box 460, University of Colorado, Boulder, CO 80309. ☎ **303/492-1527,** or 303/492-0554 for the box office.

Considered one of the top three Shakespearean festivals in the United States, this 2-month annual event attracts over 40,000 theatergoers between late June and late August. Held since 1958 in the University of Colorado's Mary Rippon Outdoor Theatre, and indoors at University Theatre, it offers more than a dozen performances of each of four Shakespearean plays. Actors, directors, designers, and everyone associated with the productions are fully schooled Shakespearean professionals. Tickets run $14 to $38 for single performances, with series packages available. During the festival, company members conduct 45-minute backstage tours before each show; special events include an opening night party and the Barbecue for the Bard.

The Guild Theatre. Dairy Center for the Arts, 2590 Walnut St. ☎ **303/442-1415.**

The Guild Theatre is actually the umbrella for five resident theater companies—the Upstart Crow, Actors Ensemble, Boulder Conservatory Theater, Director's Theatre, and Trouble Clef—which perform in a 99-seat theater where no seat is more than three rows from the stage.

10 Northeastern Colorado

Here are the spacious skies, stretching without obstacle or interruption hundreds of miles eastward from the foot of the Rocky Mountains. Here are the golden, rolling, irrigated fields of wheat and corn, spreading along the valleys of the South Platte and Republican Rivers and their tributaries.

A different Colorado exists on the sparsely populated plains, one that inspired James Michener's novel *Centennial*. Alive are memories of the Folsom buffalo hunters who first inhabited the region; trailblazers and railroad crews who opened up the area to Anglo settlement; hardy pioneer farmers who endured drought, economic ruin, and so many other hardships; and ranchers like John W. Iliff, who carved a feudal empire built on longhorn cattle. Pioneer museums, frontier forts, old battlefields, and preserved downtown districts won't let history die. Vast open stretches—wetlands swollen with migrating waterfowl, the starkly beautiful Pawnee National Grassland—remain to remind us that the Rockies are not the sole domain of Colorado wilderness.

1 Fort Collins

65 miles N of Denver, 34 miles S of Cheyenne, Wyoming

A bustling college town, Fort Collins began in 1864 as a military post on the Cache la Poudre (pronounced *Poo*-der) River, named for a powder cache left by French fur traders. The fort, named for Lieutenant Colonel William O. Collins, was abandoned in 1867, but the settlement prospered, first as a center for quarrying and farming, and by 1910 with sugar-beet processing and lamb feeding.

Today Fort Collins is regarded as one of the fastest-growing cities in the United States, with an average annual growth rate of 3½ %. Population leaped from 43,000 in 1970 to 65,000 in 1980 to more than 100,000 today, not including the many Colorado State University students. CSU was established in 1870; today it is nationally known for its forestry and veterinary medicine schools, as well as its research advances in space engineering and bone cancer.

Fort Collins, at just under 5,000 feet elevation, makes a good base for fishing, boating, and rafting, or exploring Rocky Mountain National Park (see chapter 11).

Northeastern Colorado

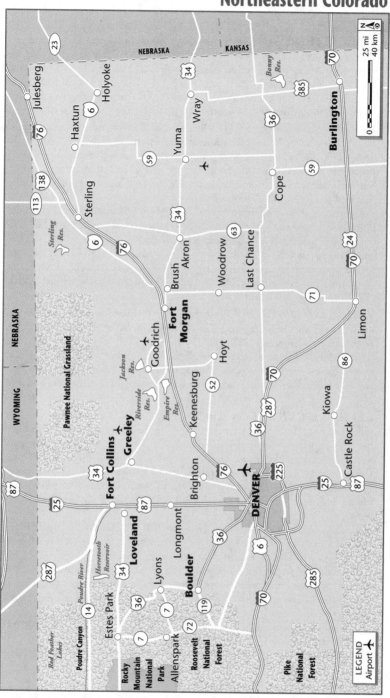

ESSENTIALS

GETTING THERE   By Car   Coming from south or north, take I-25 exit 269 (Mulberry Street, for downtown Fort Collins), exit 268 (Prospect Road, for Colorado State University), or exit 265 (Harmony Road, for south Fort Collins). From Rocky Mountain National Park, follow U.S. 34 to Loveland, then turn north on U.S. 287. The drive takes about 1¼ hours from Denver or Estes Park, about 40 minutes from Cheyenne, Wyoming.

By Plane   Many visitors to Fort Collins fly into **Denver International Airport** (see chapter 6). The **Fort Collins Municipal Airport** (☎ 970/962-2850), off I-25 exit 259, 7 miles northeast of downtown Loveland, serves charter, corporate, and private planes, but does not currently offer regularly scheduled commercial service. Fuel and other services are provided by the airport's fixed base operator, Fort Collins Loveland Jet Center (☎ **970/667-2574**).

Car rentals at the airport are provided by **Hertz** (☎ 800/654-3131 or 970/962-9323). Rental companies that will deliver cars to the airport are **Avis** (☎ 800/331-1212 or 970/229-9115) and **Enterprise** (☎ 800/325-8007 or 970/669-7119). **Airport Express** (☎ 970/482-0505) provides daily shuttle services between Denver and Fort Collins ($15 one-way), but does not serve Fort Collins Municipal Airport. Shuttle service from DIA is also available from **Shamrock Airport Shuttle** (☎ 970/686-9999) at similar rates.

VISITOR INFORMATION   The **Fort Collins Convention & Visitors Bureau** has a visitor information center at 420 S. Howes St., Suite 101 (P.O. Box 1998), Fort Collins, CO 80522 (☎ **800/274-FORT** [3678] or 970/482-5821; fax 970/493-8061; www.ftcollins.com; e-mail: ftcollin@ftcollins.com). That's 2 blocks west of the intersection of College Avenue and Mulberry Street. A new state **Welcome Center** was scheduled to open in early 1999 along I-25 at Prospect Road (exit 268).

GETTING AROUND   Fort Collins is located on the Cache la Poudre River, four miles west of I-25. College Avenue (U.S. 287) is the main north-south artery and the city's primary commercial strip; Mulberry Street (Colo. 14) is the main east-west thoroughfare. Downtown Fort Collins extends north of Mulberry Street on College Avenue to Jefferson Street; Old Town is a triangle east of and bounded by College Avenue, 4 blocks north of Mulberry. The main Colorado State University campus is a square mile on the west side of College Avenue 2 blocks south of Mulberry.

The city bus system, known as **Transfort** (☎ 970/221-6620), operates ten routes throughout Fort Collins Monday through Saturday from 6:30am to 6:30pm, except major holidays. Limited evening service (until 11pm) is provided while CSU is in session; call for details. All buses are accessible to those with disabilities, and all have bike racks. Fares are 90¢ for adults, 45¢ for seniors and those with disabilities; youths 17 and under ride free. Exact change is required. A 10-ride ticket costs $6.40.

Taxi service is provided 24 hours a day by **Fort Collins Taxi** ☎ 970/690-8294) and **Shamrock Yellow Cab** (☎ 970/224-2222).

Bicycling is a popular and viable means of transportation in Fort Collins. Just about the only place you can't ride is College Avenue. See "Sports & Outdoor Activities," below, for information about bike rentals.

FAST FACTS   The **Poudre Valley Hospital** is at 1024 S. Lemay Ave. (☎ 970/495-7000), between Prospect Road and Riverside Avenue just east of downtown.

The main **post office** is located at 301 E. Boardwalk Dr. Contact the U.S. Postal Service (☎ **800/275-8777**) for hours and other post office locations.

SPECIAL EVENTS   Cinco de Mayo in Old Town and Lee Martinez Park, first weekend in May; Colorado Brewers' Festival on Old Town Square, last full weekend in June; New West Fest in Old Town and Library Park, third weekend in August; and Oktoberfest in Old Town, mid-October.

WHAT TO SEE & DO

✪ **Anheuser-Busch Brewery.** 2351 Busch Dr. (I-25 exit 271). ☎ **970/490-4691.** Free admission. June–Aug, daily 9:30am–5pm; Sept, daily 10am–4pm; Oct–May, Thur–Mon 10am–4pm. Closed some major holidays.

One of Fort Collins's leading employers—and its top tourist attraction—this Anheuser-Busch brewery produces some six million barrels of beer each year, distributed to 10 western states. The 1¼-hour tours leave from the visitor center and gift shop, and include exhibits on the history of the Anheuser-Busch company, nostalgic displays of ads from the 1950s and other periods, and a complete look at the brewing process, from the huge brew kettles to the high-speed packaging plant that fills 2,000 cans per minute. The tours end at the tasting room for a free sample. You can also visit the barn and see the giant Clydesdale draft horses used to promote Budweiser and other Anheuser-Busch beers since 1933, and the first Saturday of each month (year-round) from 1 to 3pm is Clydesdale Camera Day, when the horses are brought out to pose with visitors.

Avery House. 328 W. Mountain Ave. ☎ **970/221-0533.** Admission by donation. Wed and Sun 1–3pm except Easter, Christmas, and New Year's Day.

Custom-built in 1879 for banker-surveyor Franklin Avery and his wife, Sara, this Victorian home at the corner of Mountain Avenue and Meldrum Street was constructed of red-and-buff sandstone from the quarries west of Fort Collins. The Poudre Landmarks Foundation and the city of Fort Collins purchased the house in 1974, restoring it to its original Victorian splendor—from furniture to wallpaper to wallpapered ceilings. The Foundation holds an Annual Historic Homes Tour in September and celebrates a Victorian Christmas in December to help raise funds for the restoration, which is nearing completion. The grounds, with a gazebo, carriage house, and fountain, are popular for weddings and receptions.

Colorado State University. University and College aves. ☎ **970/491-1101.**

Fort Collins revolves around the university, with its 22,000 students and 4,500 faculty and staff. Founded in 1870 as the Agricultural College of Colorado, it was renamed Colorado A&M in 1935, and it became Colorado State University in 1957. The "A" constructed on the hillside behind Hughes Stadium by students and faculty in 1923 stands for "Aggies" and remains a cherished tradition, even though athletic teams have been called the Rams for decades.

   Those wanting to see the campus should stop first at the **visitor center,** at the southwest corner of College avenue and Pitkin Street (☎ 970/491-6222), for information, maps, and parking passes. Among suggested stops are the **Administration Building**, on the Oval where the school began, and **Lory Student Center,** University and Center avenues (☎ 970/491-6444), which houses a food court, bookstore, art gallery, floral shop, activities center, ballroom, and other facilities. Appointments can be made to visit the renowned **Veterinary Teaching Hospital,** 300 W. Drake Rd. (☎ 970/221-4535), and the **Equine Teaching Center** at the Foothills Campus, Overland Trail (☎ 970/491-8373). The **Art Department,** on

Horsing Around

Firecracker, the world's first test-tube horse, was born July 2, 1996, at Colorado State University's very own Animal Reproduction and Biotechnology Laboratory.

Pitkin Street (☎ 970/491-6774), has five different galleries with revolving exhibits; and the **University Theatre** in Johnson Hall, on East Drive (☎ 970/491-5562, or 970/491-5116 for tickets), presents student productions year-round. The university's **Environmental Learning Center,** located on East Drake Road 1 mile east of the Drake and Timberline intersection, covers some 200 acres, and has 2½ miles of trails, with opportunities to see wildlife such as golden eagles, muskrats, and white-tail deer, and a variety of plants. Dogs, horses, and bikes are not permitted on the trails.

The Farm at Lee Martinez Park. 600 N. Sherwood St. ☎ **970/221-6665.** Free admission. Summer, Tues–Sat 10am–5:30pm; Sun noon–5:30pm. Winter, Wed–Sat 10am–5:30pm; Sun noon–5:30pm.

Early-20th-century farm machinery is on display, crafts are sold in the Silo Store, and oats are available to feed the animals. The Farm Museum has exhibits depicting farming techniques from the late 19th and early 20th centuries. Special programs are scheduled year-round, and kids can take advantage of the weekend pony rides ($2) from mid-March through October. One-hour trail rides ($10) along the Poudre River are offered to adults and children ages 8 and older from May through September. A gift shop is open from mid-March through October.

Fort Collins Municipal Railway. Oak & Roosevelt, at City Park. ☎ **970/224-5372.** Admission $1 adults, 75¢ seniors, 50¢ children 12 and under. May–Sept, weekends and holidays only, noon–5pm.

One of the few remaining original trolley systems in the nation, this restored 1919 Birney streetcar runs on its original route, along Mountain Avenue for 1½ miles from City Park to Howes Street. It's certainly more for fun than practical urban transport.

Fort Collins Museum. 200 Mathews St. ☎ **970/221-6738.** Fax 970/416-2236. www.fort-collins.co.us/arts_culture/museum. Free admission, donations accepted. Tues–Sat 10am–5pm, Sun noon–5pm.

Located in the 1903 Carnegie Library Building just a block south of Old Town, this museum boasts the largest collection of Folsom points of any western museum, plus military artifacts from Fort Collins as well as pioneer and Victorian objects. You can see an 1850s cabin that is among the oldest surviving pioneer buildings in Colorado, the 1864 log officers' mess hall known locally as "Auntie Stone's cabin," and a log one-room schoolhouse built in 1905. Annual events include Rendezvous and Skookum Day in July, a living-history day with blacksmithing, quilting, weaving, branding, and milking demonstrations.

Old Town. Between College and Mountain aves. and Jefferson St.

A redbrick pedestrian walkway, flanked by street lamps and surrounding a bubbling fountain, is the focus of this restored historic district. The main plaza extends diagonally to the northeast from the intersection of College and Mountain avenues; on either side are shops and galleries, restaurants, and nightspots. Outdoor concerts and a string of special events keep the plaza lively, especially from mid-spring to mid-fall. Walking-tour maps are available from the Convention and Visitors

Brewery Tours

One might say that Fort Collins is a beer town. Not only is it home to the giant ✪ **Anheuser-Busch Brewery,** with its famous Clydesdale horses (see above), but the city has also become a center for microbreweries and brew pubs.

Coopersmith's Pub & Brewing Co. (see "Where to Dine," below) provides patrons a view of the brewing process from inside the restaurant, and also offers guided tours on Saturdays from 1 to 4pm. Using English malted barley and hops from the Pacific Northwest, Coopersmith's brews from 6 to 10 ales. For those who don't like beer, the brewery also makes its own root beer, ginger ale, and cream soda.

Just northeast of Old Town, across the railroad tracks, **New Belgium Brewing Company,** 500 Linden St. (☎ 970/221-0524), concentrates on beer-making only, producing top-quality Belgian-style ales. The brewery is open Monday through Saturday from 10am to 6pm. Tours are offered weekdays at 2pm, and Saturdays on the hour from 11am to 2pm, with self-guided tours any-time. Beer can be purchased, along with glasses, caps, T-shirts, and other sou-venirs.

You'll find **Odell's Brewing Company** at 800 E. Lincoln Ave. (☎ 970/498-9070; www.odells.com). Specializing in English-style ales, Odell's produces draft and bottled beers, which are available in restaurants and bars throughout the Rocky Mountains and the Southwest. Tours are given Monday through Friday at 3pm, on the hour between 11am and 2pm on Saturdays, and by appointment. The tasting room is open Monday through Friday from 9am to 6pm, Saturday from 10am to 6pm. Beer, which you can sample before making your choice, plus beer glasses, shirts, mouse pads, and other souvenirs, are all available.

H.C. Berger Brewing Company, 1900 E. Lincoln Ave. (☎ 970/493-9044), produces handcrafted German-style ales using a cold-maturation process. Up-close personalized brewery tours are offered Saturdays from 1 to 5pm and by appointment, and the tasting room is open Monday through Thursday from 8am to 5pm, Friday from 8am to 6pm, and Saturday from 1 to 5pm. Ales can be purchased at the brewery in brewery jugs and kegs, and in smaller bottles at local stores.

Bureau, individual merchants, and city offices. You'll find public rest rooms just east of the intersection of South College Avenue and Oak Street, open daily from 8am to 9pm.

✪ **Swetsville Zoo.** 4801 E. Harmony Rd. ☎ **970/484-9509.** Free admission, donations appreciated. Daily, dawn to dusk. The zoo is one-quarter mile east of I-25 exit 265.

Don't come to Bill Swets's zoo expecting to find animals—not live ones, that is. The Sculpture Park is a constantly growing menagerie of about 150 dinosaurs and other real and imaginary animals, flowers, and windmills—all constructed from car parts, farm machinery, and other scrap metal. The humorous creatures in the Bungled Jungle are the only pieces for sale, and are located at the southeast end of the parking lot. There's also an outdoor museum of oddities displaying relics from the past, including old farm equipment and a 10-seat bicycle.

SPORTS & OUTDOOR ACTIVITIES

With its prime location, nestled in the foothills of the Rockies, Fort Collins is ideally situated for those who want to get out under Colorado's clear blue sky and experience the delights of nature. There are several convenient multi-use trails. The **Poudre River Trail** is an 8.35-mile paved trail that follows the Poudre River from North Taft Hill Road to East Drake Road and the CSU Environmental Learning Center, passing Lee Martinez Park along the way. The **Spring Creek Trail,** which is also paved, runs 6.6 miles along Spring Creek, passing through several city parks, from West Drake Road to East Prospect Road at the Poudre River, where you can pick up the Poudre River Trail. Both are popular with hikers, cyclers, and skaters during warm weather and cross-country skiers when the snow flies. Contact the Fort Collins Convention & Visitors Bureau (see "Visitor Information," above) for additional information.

Major Fort Collins city parks include: **City Park,** 1500 W. Mulberry St. (☎ **970/221-6640**), with a lake, picnic shelters, playgrounds, playing fields, tennis courts, a fitness course, miniature train rides, a nine-hole golf course, and an outdoor swimming pool; **Edora Park,** 1420 E. Stuart St. (☎ **970/221-6640**), with the excellent Edora Pool Ice Center (combination indoor swimming pools and ice rink), plus playgrounds, ball fields, tennis courts, a disc golf course, a fitness course, and horseshoe pits; and **Rolland Moore Park,** 2201 S. Shields St. (☎ **970/ 221-6667**), which features an outdoor complex for racquetball and handball players, plus tennis courts, picnic grounds, softball fields, and basketball courts. **Fort Collins Senior Center,** 1200 Raintree Dr. (☎ **970/ 221-6644** or TDD 970/224-6006), is open to anyone 18 and older, and offers a four-lane indoor lap pool, a spa, a walk-jog track, billiards, a limited amount of exercise equipment, and a library with computers. Admission costs $2.50 for those 18 to 59 and $2 for those 60 and older. For additional information on the city's park system, call the administration office at ☎ **970/221-6640**.

Among the most popular areas for outdoor recreation is **Horsetooth Reservoir,** about 15 minutes west of downtown, just over the first ridge of the Rocky Mountain foothills. The 6½-mile-long, man-made lake is named for a distinctive tooth-shaped rock that has long been an area landmark. It's reached via County Road 44E or 42C, both off Overland Trail, or County Road 38E off Taft Hill Road (☎ **970/ 226-4517**). At the reservoir and nearby **Horsetooth Mountain Park,** located several miles west via County Road 38E (same phone as above), you'll find a wide array of outdoor activities from fly-fishing to rock climbing to swimming and water-skiing.

Lory State Park, just west of Fort Collins along the northwest edge of Horsetooth Reservoir (☎ **970/493-1623**), is known for its scenic beauty and extensive trail system. To get to the park, take U.S. 287 north out of Fort Collins, leaving it to take 54G Rd. through Laporte, then head west on County Road 52E for 1 mile, turn left (south) onto County Road 23N for about 1½ miles to County Road 25G, where you turn right and drive about 1½ miles to the park entrance. ✪ **Colorado State Forest Park,** about 75 miles west of Fort Collins via Colo. 14 (☎ **970/ 723-8366**), covers 70,000 acres with spectacular mountain scenery, alpine lakes, an abundance of wildlife, camping, and numerous trails. See below for details on activities at these areas.

BICYCLING   There are more than 75 miles of designated bikeways in Fort Collins, including the Spring Creek and Poudre River Trails, both paved (see above). There's also a dirt trail, the 5.8-mile Foothills Trail, parallel to Horsetooth Reservoir from Dixon Reservoir north to Campeau Open Space and Michaud

Lane. For bike rentals ($18 to $25 per day), repairs, accessories, maps, and tips on where to ride, stop at **Lee's Cyclery,** 202 W. Laurel St. (☎ **800/748-2453** or 970/482-6006), or its second location at 931 E. Harmony St. (☎ **970/226-6006**). Also see "Mountain Biking," below.

FLY-FISHING   Guided fly-fishing trips and clinics are available from **Rocky Mountain Adventures,** 1117 N. U.S. 287 (P.O. Box 1989), Fort Collins, CO 80522 (☎ **800/858-6808** or 970/493-4005; www.omnibus.com/rma.html). They access the Big Thompson, Cache la Poudre, and North Platte Rivers, plus waters on two private ranches. Guided trips start at $80 for a half day. Those who'd like to strike out on their own might try nearby Roosevelt National Forest. For further information, contact the U.S. Forest Service Information Center, 1311 S. College Ave. (☎ **970/498-2770**), and the Colorado Division of Wildlife, 317 W. Prospect Rd. (☎ **970/484-2836**). Anglers heading out to Colorado State Forest Park have a good chance of catching a variety of trout species; only artificial flies and lures are permitted in some lakes there.

GOLF   Fort Collins has three municipal courses: **Collindale Golf Course,** 1441 E. Horsetooth Rd. (☎ **970/221-6651**), **City Park Nine,** 411 S. Bryan Ave. (☎ **970/221-6650**), and **Southridge Golf Club,** 5750 S. Lemay Ave. (☎ **970/ 226-2828**). Greens fees are in the $16 to $19 range for 18 holes, and tee times should be reserved 3 days in advance. Two privately owned courses that are open to the public are **Link-N-Greens Golf Course**, 777 E. Lincoln Ave. (☎ **970/ 221-4818**), with fees of $14 to $15 for 18 holes, and **Mountain Vista Greens Golf Course,** 2808 NE Frontage Rd. (☎ **970/482-4847**), which charges $5 to $16 for 18 holes. Courses are open year-round, weather permitting.

HIKING   The **Comanche Peak Wilderness area,** 67,500 acres of pine and spruce-fir forests below expanses of alpine tundra, offers scenic hiking trails along the north and east sides of Rocky Mountain National Park. Contact the U.S. Forest Service Information Center, 1311 S. College Ave. (☎ **970/498-2770**).

   Colorado State Forest Park has miles of hiking trails and even gives overnight visitors the opportunity to stay in a yurt (see "Skiing," below), and there are 26 miles of trails at Horsetooth Mountain Park that are shared by hikers, mountain bikers, and horseback riders. Finally, **Lory State Park** has about 25 miles of hiking trails, where the top of Arthur's Rock—a hike of 2 miles—offers a marvelous view across Fort Collins and the northeastern Colorado plains.

HORSEBACK RIDING   For the most part, riding is permitted anywhere in the Estes-Poudre District of the Roosevelt National Forest without special permit or license. Horsetooth Mountain Park, Colorado State Forest Park, and Lory State Park have horse trails as well. Lory State Park has the added advantage of the **Double Diamond Stable** (☎ **970/224-4200**), which offers guided trail rides, hayrides, and chuck-wagon dinners. Prices for trail rides start at about $15 per hour, and hay rides are about $5 per person.

KAYAKING   **Rocky Mountain Adventures,** P.O. Box 1989, Fort Collins, CO 80522 (☎ **800/858-6808** or 970/493-4005; www.omnibus.com/rma.html), offers kayaking classes covering the Eskimo roll, paddling techniques, and white-water skills. Prices are about $50 for the roll, $35 for paddling, and $165 to $179 for white water. Private instruction starts at $95.

   Classes for all levels are also available from **Poudre River Kayaks, Inc.,** 1524 W. Oak St., Fort Collins, CO 80521 (☎ **970/484-8480**). The introductory lesson begins with a classroom session, followed by three 3-hour flatwater classes and an optional half-day river class. The full session cost is $150, or without the river class,

$100. The river class alone is $60, 2-hour roll clinics cost $20, and an ACA instructor certification 4-day class costs $350. In addition, they rent and service equipment, and sell used items. Rental rates are $15 to $40 per day for a boat or kayak (plus a deposit), and $5 to $8 for helmet, life vest, wetsuit, and so on. Multi-day rates are available.

LLAMA PACKING   Using llamas as pack animals is relatively new in the United States, but they are rapidly becoming the pack animal of choice in the Rocky Mountains. The **Buckhorn Llama Company,** Box 64, Masonville, CO 80541 (☎ 800/318-9454 or 970/667-7411; www.llamapack.com), offers a wide range of services, including guided llama hikes. You'll still travel on your own two feet, but instead of carrying a heavy pack, the llamas—natives of altitudes of 9,000 to 18,000 feet—do the heavy work. Prices for fully guided overnight pack trips start at $150 daily per person, or you can do it yourself and rent a llama. Visitors are welcome to view the llamas at the ranch, and guided tours are available for groups of 25 or more. Increasingly popular are instructional trips, so that next time the client can do it on his own. Other services offered include llama boarding, transportation, and training.

MOUNTAIN BIKING   The Foothills Trail for mountain bikers runs along the east side of Horsetooth Reservoir from Dixon Dam north to Michaud Lane. Horsetooth Mountain Park, Lory State Park, and Colorado State Forest Park have excellent trails appropriate for mountain biking as well. In addition, there are yurts for overnighting at Colorado State Forest Park (see "Skiing," below). Also see "Bicycling," above.

RIVER RAFTING   River-rafting enthusiasts have ample opportunities for boating the Cache la Poudre, a nationally designated wild and scenic river. **Rocky Mountain Adventures,** P.O. Box 1989, Fort Collins, CO 80522 (☎ 800/858-6808 or 970/493-4005; www.omnibus.com/rma.html), offers half-day, full-day, and overnight trips on the Cache la Poudre. Costs range from $34 to $56 for a half day, $74 for a full day, and to $169 for overnight. For 1- or 2-day trips on the pristine, high altitude (8,000 feet) North Platte River, expect to pay $83 to $189. **A Wanderlust Adventure,** 3500 Bingham Hill Rd., Fort Collins, CO 80521 (☎ 800/745-7238 or 970/484-1219), offers half-day trips on the Cache la Poudre River for $35 to $55, and full-day trips for about $80.

ROCK CLIMBING   There are plenty of opportunities for rock climbing on the northwestern shore of Horsetooth Reservoir in Lory State Park.

SKIING & OTHER WINTER SPORTS   Cross-country skiers will find plenty of trails and rolling hills at Lory State Park, surrounding national forests (☎ 970/498-2770), and in Colorado State Forest Park, where they can stay overnight in a backcountry yurt system owned by **Never Summer Nordic, Inc.,** P.O. Box 1983, Fort Collins, CO 80522 (☎ 970/482-9411). The yurts, which are circular, tent-like canvas-and-wood structures on a high wood deck, have wood-burning stoves, padded bunks, and complete kitchens. Most sleep up to six, and one sleeps at least 10. Winter rates for the entire yurt are $75 to $99. In summer, rates are $45 to $59. Seven yurts (one near Lake Agnes and the other six at North Michigan Reservoir) can be rented by reservation (☎ 800/678-2267). Colorado State Forest Park also has an extensive system of snowmobile trails, either groomed or packed, that is separate from its cross-country ski trail system.

There's year-round **ice-skating** at Edora Pool Ice Center (EPIC) at Edora Park, 1801 Riverside Dr. (☎ 970/221-6683). Call for rates and hours.

SWIMMING   Edora Pool Ice Center (EPIC), at 1801 Riverside Dr. in Edora Park, (☎ **970/221-6683**), has swimming and water exercise programs and diving. The indoor **Mulberry pool,** 424 W. Mulberry St. (☎ **970/221-6659**), has lap lanes, a diving area, and "Elrog the Frog," a poolside slide. Both have recreational swimming most afternoons and evenings, and lap swimming at other times; call for the current schedule. The **City Park Outdoor Pool,** 1599 City Park Ave. (☎ **970/ 484-7665**), is open afternoons during warm weather (closed in inclement weather). Admission at the three above pools costs $2.50 for adults, $1.75 for youths 17 and younger, and $2 for seniors 60 and older. There's also swimming at the Fort Collins Senior Center and at Horsetooth Reservoir (see the "Sports & Outdoor Activities" introduction, above).

WATER SPORTS   Inlet Bay Marina, 4314 Shoreline Dr. (☎ **970/223-0140**), at Horsetooth Reservoir, is a full-service marina open from April through mid-October. There's a boat launching ramp; convenience store with snacks, fishing supplies, and live bait; a full service gas dock; and boat rentals. Fishing boats, with 10-horsepower motors, cost $10 per hour or $50 per day; personal watercraft cost $50 per hour or $150 per half day Friday through Sunday and $35 per hour or $105 per half day Monday through Thursday; and ski boats (with skis) rent for $35 to $50 per hour or $150 to $200 per day, depending on size. Gas and oil are extra. There's also a swimming beach and nearby restaurant, and banana boat rides were planned for the 1999 season.

WILDLIFE WATCHING   Although you'll see some wildlife and water birds at Lory State Park and Horsetooth Reservoir, go to Colorado State Forest Park to try to catch a glimpse of the state's largest moose population, along with elk, mule deer, mountain lions, big horn sheep, and black bears. State Forest Park's Moose Visitor Center has wonderful displays and wildlife-viewing information.

SHOPPING

Visitors enjoy shopping in **Old Town Square,** at Mountain and College avenues, with numerous shops, galleries, and restaurants. Also downtown is **OneWest Art Center,** 201 S. College Ave. (☎ **970/482-2787**), housed in a 1911 Italian Renaissance–style building that for six decades was the Fort Collins post office. The visual-arts complex now has three galleries that offer changing shows with a wide variety of contemporary art. It's open Tuesday through Saturday from 10am to 5pm, year-round. Suggested donation is $2 for adults, $1 for students and seniors, free for children under 6, and free for everybody on Saturdays.

Northern Colorado's largest enclosed shopping mall is the **Foothills Fashion Mall,** at South College Avenue and Horsetooth Road (☎ **970/226-2441; www.ffmall.com**). Anchored by four department stores—Foley's, JC Penney, Sears, and Mervyn's—it has more than 120 specialty stores and a food court, and is open Monday through Saturday from 10am to 9pm and on Sunday from 11am to 6pm.

WHERE TO STAY

Lodging rates in Fort Collins are usually higher in summer, and rooms can be especially expensive and hard to find during college graduation and other college events. The city has numerous major chain motels, including **Best Western Kiva Inn,** 1638 E. Mulberry St. (☎ **888/299-5482** or **970/484-2444**), with rates for two of $59 to $138; **Best Western University Inn,** 914 S. College Ave. (☎ **800/ 528-1234** or **970/484-1984**), with rates for two of $48 to $67; **Hampton Inn,** 1620 Oakridge Dr. (☎ **800/526-7866** or **970/229-5927**; fax **970/229-0854**), with rates for two of $85 to $115; the all-suite **Ramada Limited**, 4001 S. Mason St. (☎ 800/272-6232 or 970/282-9047), with rates for two of $88 to $92; and **Super 8 Motel**, 409 Centro Way (☎ 800/800-8000 or 970/493-7701), with rates for two of $46 to $100. Room taxes add about 9% to hotel bills.

MODERATE

Edwards House Bed & Breakfast. 402 W. Mountain Ave., Fort Collins, CO 80521. ☎ **970/493-9191**. Fax 970/484-0706. 9 units. A/C TV TEL. $85–$105 double; $135–$145 suites. Rates include full breakfast. AE, DISC, MC, V.

Every room in this beautiful 1904 Denver Foursquare is individually and comfortably furnished with lovely antiques from the late 1800s and early 1900s, yet all the modern amenities are here, too. Each spacious room has a gas fireplace, TV and VCR hidden in an armoire (the inn has a vast collection of videos available for guest use), and either whirlpool tub/shower or claw-foot tub with separate shower. The electrical and plumbing have been completely redone, a modern smoke detection system and central air-conditioning have been installed, and telephones have modem hookups. For breakfast you will enjoy a selection of fresh fruit and juice, gourmet coffee, homemade baked goods and granola, plus an entree such as orange cinnamon French toast, blueberry pecan pancakes, or southwestern quiche.

Elizabeth Street Guest House. 202 E. Elizabeth St., Fort Collins, CO 80524. ☎ **970/493-BEDS**. Fax 970/493-6662. 3 units (1 with bathroom). $67 double without bathroom, $87 double with bathroom. Rates include breakfast. AE, DISC, MC, V.

This 1905 American Foursquare brick home, just a block from CSU at Elizabeth and Remington streets, is furnished with antiques, handmade crafts, and old quilts, setting off the handsome leaded windows and oak woodwork. All three guest rooms have been recently redecorated. Guests have access to a TV, phone, and refrigerator. Full breakfasts include home-baked pastries and granola and entrees such as Scotch eggs. Smoking is not permitted inside.

Helmshire Inn. 1204 S. College Ave., Fort Collins, CO 80524. ☎ **970/493-4683**. Fax 970/495-0794. 25 units. A/C TV TEL. May–Sept $95–$99 double; Oct–Apr $79–$85 double. Discounts for stays over 5 days. Rates include breakfast. AE, DC, MC, V. Infant or one child welcome.

A three-story custom-built inn across from the CSU campus, the Helmshire has a lobby like a living room and a lovely adjoining dining room. Each spacious guest room is unique, but all are furnished with antiques and reproductions. Each unit has a kitchenette with microwave, refrigerator, and wet bar. There's also an elevator and wide covered porches. Guests have privileges at a health club in town. Smoking is not permitted inside.

Holiday Inn University Park. 425 W. Prospect Rd., Fort Collins, CO 80526. ☎ **800/HOLIDAY** or 970/482-2626. Fax 970/493-6265. 259 units, including 50 minisuites. A/C TV TEL. $99 double; $99–$109 minisuite. AE, CB, DC, DISC, MC, V.

Conveniently located across the street from the main campus of CSU and adjacent to the Spring Creek trail for bikers and runners, this is the city's largest hotel. All rooms overlook the beautiful lush garden atrium and the hotel restaurant.

Standard rooms have one king or two oversize double beds and all standard hotel furnishings, including a TV, direct-dial phone, and attractive serigraphs on the walls. King executive minisuites have kitchenettes. The hotel offers a full range of concierge services, room service (from 6am to 10pm), fitness center, indoor pool, a big-screen TV in the lounge, piano bar, and restaurant featuring daily specials and international cuisine (open daily from 6am to 10pm).

INEXPENSIVE

Budget Host Inn. 1513 N. College Ave., Fort Collins, CO 80524. ☎ **800/825-4678** or 970/484-0870. Fax 970/224-2998. E-mail: budget@webaccess.net. 30 units. A/C TV TEL. Mid-May to Sept, $36–$62 double; Oct to mid-May, $32–$48 double. Rates include continental breakfast. AE, DISC, MC, V.

At the north end of town on U.S. 287 near Willox Lane, this motel has been owned and operated by Tom and Karen Weitkunat since 1975. Kids enjoy the playground, while adults like the outdoor hot tub. Eight units have kitchenettes; all have coffeemakers and firm queen or double beds. Some of the rooms have a shower only, so if you need a tub, request it. The queen rooms have been recently renovated.

Mulberry Inn. 4333 E. Mulberry St., Fort Collins, CO 80524. ☎ **800/234-5548** or 970/493-9000. Fax 970/224-9636. www.mulberry-inn.com. E-mail: mulberry@verinet.com. 120 units. A/C TV TEL. $48–$95 double; $85–$125 suite; $59–$105 Jacuzzi unit. Rates include morning coffee and muffins. AE, DC, DISC, MC, V. Pets accepted.

Each room in this pleasant motel has a quality queen or king bed (some have king-size waterbeds), a desk, and other standard furnishings. VCRs and movies are available for rent. There are hot tubs in 35 rooms; some suites have wet bars and large private decks. Facilities include a heated, seasonal outdoor swimming pool and a restaurant serving Italian cuisine each evening.

CAMPING

There are few full-service campgrounds in the Fort Collins area. The **Fort Collins KOA** is about 10 miles northwest of downtown on Colo. 14 (☎ **970/493-9758**), open spring through autumn, with rates of $17 for tent sites and $23 for RV sites. A second **KOA,** open year-round, is just off I-25 exit 281, north of Fort Collins at Wellington (☎ **970/568-7486**), with rates of $15 for tent sites and RV hookups costing $21.

Nearby Arapahoe and Roosevelt national forests have a number of established campgrounds, most with rest rooms, water, and picnic tables. Cost is $9 per site per night. Call ☎ **970/498-2770** for more information. There's also camping at Colorado State Forest Park (☎ **303/723-8366**), 75 miles west of Fort Collins via Colo. 14.

WHERE TO DINE
EXPENSIVE

Nico's Catacombs. 115 S. College Ave. ☎ **970/482-6426.** Reservations recommended. Main courses $17.50–$32.50. AE, CB, DC, DISC, MC, V. Mon–Sat 5–10pm. CONTINENTAL.

A classic, dimly lit cellar restaurant, with a richly decorated lounge separated from the main dining room by a stained-glass partition, Nico's features tableside service and daily specials (including fresh seafood) announced on blackboards. You might start with a shellfish dish such as mussels Marseilles, or perhaps the Galantine de foie gras, then move on to steak Diane flambé, shrimp parmesan, or one of the house specialties, such as rack of lamb paloise or chateaubriand bouquetière for two. The lounge offers a bar menu including baked brie and oysters Rockefeller, plus desserts and cappuccinos.

MODERATE

✪ **Bisetti's.** 120 S. College Ave. ☎ **970/493-0086.** Reservations accepted for parties of 6 or more only. Main courses $4.25–$7 lunch, $6.50–$16 dinner. AE, DISC, MC, V. Mon–Fri 11am–2pm; Sun–Thurs 5–9pm, Fri–Sat 5–10pm. ITALIAN.

The first thing you notice upon entering this long-standing family business is the ceiling: From one end to the other dangle empty Chianti bottles signed by over a decade of patrons. This is a dark, candlelit room; two adjoining rooms are brighter and more modern. The menu features a variety of homemade pastas, from spaghetti and lasagna to rigatoni and manicotti. Full main courses include veal saltimbocca, basil fettucine with chicken, and smoked salmon Alfredo. Arrive before 6pm for early-bird dinner specials.

Coopersmith's Pub & Brewing Co. 5 Old Town Sq. ☎ **970/498-0483.** www. coopersmithspub.com. $6–$13. AE, MC, V. Fri–Sat 11am–2am, Sun–Thurs 11am–midnight. BRITISH PUB.

This modern brew pub isn't just a place for knocking back a few. Within its brick walls is an open kitchen that prepares such traditional pub specialties as fish-and-chips, bangers and mash, and Highland cottage pie. You can also get hamburgers, sandwiches, salads, and soups, plus pizzas baked in a wood-fired oven. Breads, rolls, and desserts are prepared in Coopersmith's in-house bakery. Portions are generous, and the outdoor patio is a favorite in good weather. There's also a children's menu and a "poolside" area with 13 pool tables.

Jay's American Bistro. 151 S. College Ave. ☎ **970/482-1876.** Main courses $4–$8 lunch, $10–$25 dinner. AE, DC, DISC, MC, V. Mon–Fri 11am–10pm; Sat 5–10pm; Sun 5–9pm. CREATIVE AMERICAN.

An eclectic menu and a friendly, casual atmosphere are what you'll find at Jay's. Appetizers include crab cakes, and there's a decidedly southwestern influence in many of the main entrees, such as seafood enchiladas or the chipotle pasta (a smoked jalapeño pasta with tequila lime sauce). Other choices include Northern Italian–style pastas, wild game, a variety of fresh seafood, steak, veal, and California-style pizza.

INEXPENSIVE

Cozzola's Pizza North. 241 Linden St. ☎ **970/482-3557.** Reservations not accepted. Pizza $5.40–$14; lunch $4–$4.50. AE, MC, V. Tue–Fri 11am–10pm, Sat 11:30am–10pm, Sun 4–9pm. PIZZA.

This is the place to come for the best pizza in Fort Collins, or so the vote in the local newspaper has shown for the last 15 years. You serve yourself during the day, as waiters don't appear until evening. The wooden booths and tables, rough wood walls, and hanging plants give the small dining room a homey feel. In addition to the traditional chewy white crust, they offer whole-wheat poppy-seed or herb crust, in three sizes—10, 12, and 14 inch. Next choose your sauce: sweet basil, fresh garlic, *salsa del drago* (sauce of the dragon), pesto, or Spanish ricotta. As if that's not enough, there are more than two dozen toppings, from the expected pepperoni, black olives, green peppers, and extra cheese, to more unusual items like pineapple, almonds, black beans, and yellow squash! If you're not in the mood for pizza, you might try the spinach calzone or stromboli. Takeout and delivery are available.

Cozzola's Pizza South is located at 1112 Oakridge Dr. (☎ **970/229-5771**).

The Egg & I. 2809 S. College Ave. ☎ **970/223-5271.** Reservations not accepted on weekends. $3.35–$6.50. AE, DISC, MC, V. Mon–Sat 6am–2pm; Sun 7am–2pm. AMERICAN.

Consistently voted by locals as offering the best breakfast in town, The Egg and I creates a number of imaginative egg dishes such as scrambled eggs with shrimp, a Wisconsin scramble with four types of cheese, and several variations on eggs Benedict. There are also omelets, fritattas, skillet breakfasts, huevos rancheros, and other Mexican dishes. Pancakes, French toast, sandwiches, and salads round out the menu.

El Burrito. 404 Linden St. ☎ **970/484-1102.** $3.50–$10.00. AE, MC, V. Daily, 11am–2pm and 5–10pm. MEXICAN.

The Godinez family has been concocting authentic Mexican specialties at this tiny north-of-downtown restaurant since 1960, and year-in, year-out, Fort Collins residents have been filling up on the restaurant's popular burritos. It also serves good tacos, enchiladas, and chile rellenos, and you can eat in or order your food to go.

✪ **Silver Grill Cafe.** 218 Walnut St., Old Town. ☎ **970/484-4656.** $3–$7. DISC, MC, V. Mon–Sat 6am–2pm, Sun 7am–2pm. AMERICAN.

Continually operated since 1933, this working-man's cafe attracts blue- and white-collar types, as well as seniors, students, and families. When there's a line outside, as there often is on weekends, coffee is served to those waiting. Come for the giant cinnamon rolls or standard American fare: eggs, pancakes, and biscuits 'n' gravy for breakfast; burgers, other sandwiches, or the excellent homemade soups for lunch; and "noontime dinners" like chicken-fried steak and beef pot roast. Everything's prepared fresh daily. Grilling and frying are done in salt-free and cholesterol-free vegetable oil.

PERFORMING ARTS & NIGHTLIFE

The college crowd does much of its drinking and partying at **Trunks Bar and Grill,** a large dance club near the railroad tracks at 450 N. Linden St. (☎ **970/ 407-7389**), with a variety of recorded music and drink specials. There's live music a few blocks away in Old Town at **Linden's Brewing Company,** 214 Linden St. (☎ **970/482-9291**), the spot for jazz, blues, zydeco, occasional comedy, and hand-crafted beers. You might also try **Avogadro's Number,** 605 S. Mason St. (☎ **970/ 493-5555**), for live bluegrass and acoustic music. Also popular is **Suite 152,** 23 Old Town Square (☎ **970/224-0888**), a nightclub that has a variety of recorded dance music. Country-and-western fans head to the big dance floor at the **Sundance Steak House and Country Club,** 2716 E. Mulberry St. (☎ **970/484-1600**), for live country music and swing dance lessons. Sports freaks like the **SportsCaster Bar & Grill,** 165 E. Boardwalk (☎ **970/223-3553**), which has 50 TV screens and 20 beers on tap; smoking is not permitted.

When you just want to have cool beer at the end of the day, **Coopersmith's Pub & Brewing Co.,** 5 Old Town Sq. (☎ **970/498-0483**), may be the best place in town. It attracts everyone from students to business executives with its pub menu and custom beers. Nearby, **Old Chicago,** 147 S. College Ave. (☎ **970/482-8599**), is another good bet, with its international list of 125 beers.

Many Fort Collins folk drive 24 miles up the Poudre River to the **Mishawaka Amphitheatre & Restaurant,** 13714 Poudre Canyon, (☎ **970/482-4420**; www. mishawakaconcerts.com), where top regional bands—and occasional national acts—perform during the summer in an outdoor amphitheater on the banks of the Poudre River. Concert tickets range from $9 to $18, and you can also dine on an outside deck over the river or inside with a view of the water.

Fort Collins's principal venue for the performing arts is **Lincoln Center,** 417 W. Magnolia St., at Meldrum Street (☎ **970/221-6730** box office, 970/221-6735 administration; www.ci.fort-collins.co.us/arts_culture). Built in 1978, the center includes the 1,180-seat Performance Hall and the 220-seat Mini-Theatre, as well as three art galleries and an outdoor sculpture and performance garden. It is home to the Fort Collins Symphony, Opera Fort Collins, Canyon Concert Ballet, Larimer Chorale, OpenStage Theatre, and the Children's Theater. Annual concert, dance, children's, and travel film series are presented. The center is wheelchair accessible and has an infrared sound system for the hearing impaired. The box office is open Monday through Saturday from noon to 6pm, with tickets ranging from $5 to $28.

Fort Collins Symphony (☎ 970/482-4823), established in 1948, performs both classical and pops music plus special events with guest performers. For those who enjoy a casual atmosphere with their classical music, there's the popular *Beethoven in Blue Jeans* concert each January, which concludes with a party.

The **OpenStage Theatre Company** (☎ 970/484-5237) is the area's leading professional stage group. It offers six contemporary productions annually, as well as various popular, classical, and operatic performances. Recent productions have included *Becket* and *Dial M for Murder.*

Those who enjoy an intimate theater experience head to the 49-seat **Bas Bleu Theatre Company,** 216 Pine St., in Old Town (☎ 970/498-8949), which presents a variety of plays, musicals, readings, and other events.

Notable **summer concert programs** include the "Concert Under the Stars Series," with concerts in Old Town Square each Thursday evening, featuring rock, bluegrass, country, jazz, and swing; the "Lagoon Summer Concert Series," with a variety of music, Wednesday evenings on the west lawn of the Lory Student Center at CSU; the "Noontime Notes Concert Series," which offers symphony, classical, and jazz performances at lunchtime each Tuesday on Oak Street Plaza; and the "Out to Lunch Concert Series," offering an assortment of live music, theater, and other events each Friday at noon at Lincoln Center. The series take place from early June through early August. Admission to all four of these programs is free; for information contact the Fort Collins Convention & Visitors Bureau (see "Visitor Information," above).

Broadway musicals are presented year-round at **Carousel Dinner Theatre,** 3509 S. Mason St. (☎ 970/225-2555; fax 970/225-2389; www.carouseltheatre. com), Thursday through Saturday at 6pm and Sunday at noon. A choice of three entrees is offered, and prices are $29 to $33, which include dinner, show, and tax, but not beverages or dessert. Recent productions have included *Hello Dolly, Phantom of the Opera, Father of the Bride,* and *Forever Plaid.* The company also has a summer conservatory program for children ages 6 to 18; call for details.

The **Colorado State University Department of Music, Theater, and Dance** (☎ 970/491-5529) presents a variety of dramas and musicals, plus concerts by music faculty ranging from jazz to classical during the school year at Johnson Hall on the CSU campus. Live performances and movies are also presented at Lory Student Center (☎ 970/491-5402).

2 Loveland

13 miles S of Fort Collins, 52 miles N of Denver

Named for Colorado Central Railroad President W. A. H. Loveland in the 1870s, this former trading post now calls itself the "Sweetheart City" because every February some 300,000 Valentine's Day cards are remailed from here with a Loveland postmark. Established as a trading post in the late 1850s, this community at the foot of the Rockies grew around a flour mill in the late 1860s, before being platted on a wheat field near the railroad tracks in 1877. Today the city is a shipping and agriculture center with a population of just over 37,000. It also has a growing arts community and several foundries.

ESSENTIALS

GETTING THERE By Car Loveland is at the junction of U.S. 287 and U.S. 34. Coming from south or north, take I-25 exit 257. From the west (Rocky

Valentines from Loveland

To get your Valentine's Day cards remailed with a four-line Valentine cachet from Loveland, address and stamp each one individually, making sure to leave room in the lower-left-hand corner of the envelopes for the special Loveland stamp, and mail them in a large envelope to the Postmaster, Attn.: Valentines, Loveland, CO 80538-9998. To ensure delivery by February 14, mail for the United States must be received in Loveland by February 9, and foreign mail should be received by February 4.

Mountain National Park) or east (Greeley), follow U.S. 34 directly to Loveland. The drive takes about 1 hour from Denver.

By Plane   Visitors to Loveland can fly into **Denver International Airport** (see chapter 6). The **Fort Collins Municipal Airport** (☎ 970/962-2850), off I-25 exit 259, 7 miles northeast of downtown Loveland, serves charter, corporate, and private planes, but does not currently offer regularly scheduled commercial service. (See "Getting There" in the Fort Collins section, above.) **Airport Express** (☎ 970/482-0505) provides daily shuttle services between Denver and Loveland ($13 one-way), but does not serve Fort Collins Municipal Airport. Shuttle service from DIA is also available from **Shamrock Airport Shuttle** (☎ 970/226-6886) at similar rates.

VISITOR INFORMATION   The **Loveland Chamber of Commerce** operates a visitor center at 5400 Stone Creek Circle, Suite 100, Loveland CO 80538, near the junction of I-25 and U.S. 34 (☎ 800/258-1278 or 970/667-5728; fax 970/667-5211; www.loveland.org).

GETTING AROUND   U.S. 34, Eisenhower Boulevard, is the main east-west thoroughfare and does a slight jog around Lake Loveland, just west of city center. Lincoln Avenue (one-way northbound) and Cleveland Avenue (one-way southbound) comprise U.S. 287 through the city. The downtown district is along Lincoln and Cleveland south of Seventh Street, 7 blocks south of Eisenhower. For a taxi, call **Shamrock Yellow Cab** (☎ 970/667-6767).

FAST FACTS   The hospital, with a 24-hour emergency room, is **McKee Medical Center,** 2000 Boise Ave. (☎ 970/669-4640), in the northeastern part of the city. The **post office** is at 446 E. 29th St., just off Lincoln Avenue. Contact the U.S. Postal Service (☎ 800/275-8777) for hours and locations of other nearby post offices.

SPECIAL EVENTS   Annual Rotary Sweetheart Sculpture Show and Sale, February; Corn Roast Festival and Larimer County Fair and Rodeo, August; Pumpkin Festival, October.

FOUNDRY TOURS

Several foundries will provide tours by appointment. **Art Castings of Colorado** (☎ 970/667-1114) gives foundry tours several weekday mornings, at a charge of $4 per person. **Loveland Sculpture Works** (☎ 970/667-0991) offers tours several times each week to groups of at least five people. Cost is $5 per person.

SPORTS & OUTDOOR ACTIVITIES

Loveland has more than two dozen city parks, a mountain park, three golf courses, and hiking trails, many of which are discussed below. The city's **Hatfield-Chilson**

Recreation Center, 700 E. Fourth St. (☎ **970/962-2458**), has a swimming pool with slide, two gyms, two weight rooms, cardiovascular exercise equipment, racquetball courts, and other facilities. Entrance fee, which allows use of all facilities, is $3 for those 18 to 61, $2 for youths 6 to 17 and seniors 62 and older, and free for children 5 and under. Full information on all city-run recreation sites is available from **Loveland Parks and Recreation Department,** 500 E. Third St. (☎ **970/962-2727**).

○ **Boyd Lake State Park** (☎ **970/669-1739**) is located a mile east of downtown Loveland via Madison Avenue and County Road 24E. One of the largest lakes in the northern Front Range, with 1,800 surface acres when full, Boyd Lake is geared to water sports, including waterskiing (on the south end of the lake only), sailing, and windsurfing. There are sandy beaches for swimming, 148 campsites ($9), showers, a dump station, picnic areas, a children's playground, a paved walking/biking trail that connects to the city's path system, two paved boat ramps, and excellent fishing (especially for walleyes). Visitors often see foxes, beavers, coyotes, great-horned owls, hawks, eagles, and other wildlife. The daily park entrance fee is $4 per vehicle. A commercially run **marina** (☎ **970/663-2662**) is open in summer, with boat slips and moorings, a full-service gas dock, boat rentals from May to September, bait, groceries, and other supplies. Rentals are $10 per hour or $50 per day for fishing boats, including gas; $45 per hour or $175 per day for ski boats, including skis but not fuel; and $50 per hour for personal watercraft, plus gas. A **restaurant** (☎ **970/663-3314**) is open from 10am to 6pm in summer, with hot food, snacks, and rentals of beach toys, chairs, and umbrellas.

BICYCLING/JOGGING   A combination biking/jogging/walking path that will eventually circle the city, joining with a 3-mile path at Boyd Lake State Park, is gradually being constructed. For a map showing completed sections, stop at the Loveland Chamber of Commerce (see above).

GOLF   Golfers can enjoy two 18-hole municipal golf courses: **Olde Course at Loveland**, 2115 W. 29th St., which charges $14 for nine holes and $22 for 18 holes; and **Marianna Butte,** 701 Clubhouse Dr., with greens fees of $18 for nine holes and $29 for 18 holes. The nine-hole **Cattail Creek Golf Course,** 2116 W. 29th St. (across the street from Olde Course), charges $8 for nine holes. For tee times and other information for all three courses, call ☎ **970/669-5800.**

HIKING   The city-run **Viestenz-Smith Mountain Park,** in Big Thompson Canyon 8 miles west of Loveland along U.S. 34 (☎ **970/962-2727**), is one of your best bets for hiking, with two trails. The **Summit Adventure Trail,** a moderately difficult 4¾-mile (one-way) hike, climbs 2,750 feet to offer scenic views of the mountains to the west and plains to the east. Those not interested in that much exercise will enjoy the easy 1-mile (one-way) **Foothills Nature Trail.** The park, which is open year-round, also has picnic tables, a playground, and a fishing stream.

LLAMA PACKING   Loveland's proximity to Rocky Mountain National Park offers many hardier challenges. One outfit that makes roughing it a bit easier and certainly more interesting is the **Buckhorn Llama Co.** (☎ **800/318-9454** or 970/667-7411; www.llamapack.com), based in Masonville, a small community about 10 miles northwest of Loveland via County Road 27. You'll still do your mountain travel by foot power, but instead of carrying a heavy pack, the llamas do the work. Prices for fully guided overnight pack trips start at $150 daily per person; or you can do it yourself and rent a llama.

SWIMMING   **North Lake Park,** at 29th Street and Taft Avenue, has a free swimming beach, fishing, tennis and racquetball courts, a playground, and a miniature narrow-gauge train. The **Winona Outdoor Swimming Pool** (☎ 970/669-6907), in Osborn Park on S.E. First Street, is open in summer and has a pool, water slide, diving area, bathhouse, and children's wading pool and water play area. Admission is $2 for adults 18 to 61, $1.50 for youths 6 to 17 and seniors 62 and older, 75¢ for children 3 to 5, and free for children under 3. There's also swimming at Hatfield-Chilson Recreation Center and Boyd Lake State Park (see above).

IN-TOWN ATTRACTIONS

Benson Park Sculpture Garden. 29th St. between Aspen and Beech streets. ☎ 970/663-2940.

Several dozen sculptures are permanently displayed among the trees, plants, and ponds at this city park, and three or four more are added each year. This is also the site of "Sculpture in the Park," one of the largest outdoor sculpture shows in the United States, which takes place each year in mid-August. The juried show, with all submissions available for purchase, features from 175 to 200 works by sculptors from across the United States and Canada.

Loveland Museum/Gallery. 503 N. Lincoln Ave., at E. Fifth St. ☎ 970/962-2410. Free admission. Tues–Wed and Fri 10am–5pm, Thurs 10am–9pm, Sat 10am–4pm, Sun noon–4pm.

Changing exhibits of local historical subjects and the work of regional, national, and international artists fill this fine, small museum. A "Life on Main Street" exhibit area depicts Loveland at the turn of the 20th century. The New Great Western Sugar Factory exhibit opened in fall 1998. The museum also sponsors programs on art and history, workshops, concerts, and poetry readings.

WHERE TO STAY

Note that state and county taxes add about 9% to hotel bills.

Best Western Coach House Resort. 5542 E. U.S. 34 (I-25 exit 257B), Loveland, CO 80537. ☎ 888/818-6223 or 970/667-7810. Fax 970/667-1047. E-mail: andrzej@colorado.net. 88 units. A/C TV TEL. $59–$79 double. Rates include continental breakfast. AE, CB, DC, DISC, MC, V. Small pets accepted with a fee.

Located along U.S. 34 as it enters Loveland from the east, this expansive, modern motel features rooms with coffeemakers, 25-inch TVs with VCRs, and direct-dial phones with data ports and voice mail. Refrigerators and microwave ovens are also available. Facilities include indoor and outdoor pools, a tennis court, two indoor hot tubs, barbecue area, and a sports lounge with big-screen TV, pool tables, and shuffleboard. Directly across the street is a factory-outlet mall with 85 stores.

Budget Host Exit 254 Inn. 2716 S. E. Frontage Rd. (I-25 exit 254), Loveland, CO 80537. ☎ 800/283-4678 or 970/667-5202. 30 units. A/C TV TEL. Summer $52–$68 double, $65–$70 hot-tub room. Lower rates at other times. AE, CB, DC, DISC, MC, V.

A basic modern motel beside the freeway, this Budget Host has individually heated rooms with good quality king or queen beds, tub/shower combinations, 25-inch TVs, and direct-dial phones. One room has a hot tub. There's a coin-operated laundry, a playground for the kids, free coffee in the lobby, and a restaurant next door.

Lovelander Bed-and-Breakfast Inn. 217 W. Fourth St., Loveland, CO 80537. ☎ 800/459-6694 or 970/669-0798 reservations. Fax 970/669-0797. www.bbonline.com/co/lovelander. E-mail: love@ezlink.com. 11 units. A/C TV TEL. $100–$150 double. Rates include full breakfast. AE, DISC, MC, V. Children over 10 welcome.

Lauren and Gary Smith's rambling 1902 Victorian, just west of downtown, is Loveland's most charming accommodation. Every room has period antiques, including vintage iron or hardwood beds and writing tables. All units have private bathrooms, one has a steam shower for two, two have whirlpools, and many have claw-foot tubs. One room also has a fireplace, and several have balconies. Breakfast is served in the dining room, porch, or garden; complimentary homemade cookies and beverages are available at all times; and complimentary dessert is served nightly. Outside, guests can enjoy the rose and herb gardens. Laundry and fax services are available, and picnic lunches can be prepared with advance notice from May through September. Smoking is not permitted indoors.

✪ **Sylvan Dale Guest Ranch.** 2939 N. County Rd. 31D, Loveland, CO 80538. ☎ **970/ 667-3915.** Fax 970/635-9336. www.sylvandale.com. E-mail: ranch@sylvandale.com. 25 units, including 11 cabins. Mid-June to Aug, 6-night packages only, $838 per adult, $669 per youth (ages 5–12), $481 per child (ages 1–4). Packages include all meals. Sept to mid-June, including full breakfast, $75–$105 double; $85–$105 cabin; $12.50 extra person. Two-bedroom units and guest houses available (call for details). No credit cards. 7 miles west of Loveland via U.S. 34.

A working cattle-and-horse ranch on the banks of the Big Thompson River, the Jessup family invites guests to join in with daily ranch chores and roundups, or just kick back and relax and enjoy the many activities available. Accommodations here are delightful, quiet, and comfortable; the homey rooms and cabins have a touch of western charm, and are carpeted and furnished with antiques. Some cabins have fireplaces. A new lodge, the Heritage, opened in 1998, and provides a gathering room with a large stone fireplace, game room, library, gift shop, and exhibits on the 50-plus-year history of the ranch.

Ranch facilities and activities include an outdoor heated pool, two tennis courts, horseshoe pits, basketball and volleyball courts, lakes stocked with rainbow trout, trophy fly-fishing, hayrides, guided nature walks, an indoor recreation room, live western music, country-western dancing, and a children's program. There are extra fees for horseback riding (including overnight pack trips and weekly gymkhanas), white-water rafting, and trips to Rocky Mountain National Park. Summer guests must schedule 6-day full-board stays; the rest of the year, overnight guests are welcome, and the ranch is also open for retreat packages (including all meals) for groups from 6 to 60. The ranch offers complimentary van service from Loveland for packages. Smoking is not permitted inside any buildings.

WHERE TO DINE

The Peaks Cafe. 425 E. Fourth St. ☎ **970/669-6158.** Reservations not accepted. Breakfast $1.75–$5.50; lunch $3–$5.50. No credit cards. Mon–Fri 7am–3pm. INTERNATIONAL.

Come to this cheery little cafe in the morning for breakfast burritos, porridge, yogurt parfait, and homemade scones or other fresh-baked items. Lunch offers salads, soups, a healthy spinach lasagna, build-your-own deli sandwiches, barbecued beef and chicken, chicken green-chile burritos, meatloaf, and eggplant Parmesan. In addition, each day a different Persian dish is featured. The cafe also serves excellent home-baked goods, ice cream, and espresso.

The Summit. 3208 W. Eisenhower Blvd. (U.S. 34). ☎ **970/669-6648.** Reservations recommended. Main courses $5–$8 lunch, $8–$25 dinner. AE, DC, DISC, MC, V. Sun 10am–2pm, Mon–Fri 11:30am–2pm; Sun–Thurs 4:30–9:30pm, Fri–Sat 4:30–10pm. STEAK/SEAFOOD.

The Summit offers magnificent views of the Rockies through south-facing windows and from the back deck, where alfresco dining is popular in warm weather. The interior is a bit dark, but the large wood beams and different dining levels add interest. The menu includes three cuts of prime rib, New York and sirloin steaks, tenderloin of elk, chicken piccata or chipeta, fresh fish, and Alaskan snow crab. There are daily specials, wines by the glass, homemade pies, and a children's menu. Thursday through Saturday evenings you can dine to live music, ranging from easy listening to light rock to jazz.

PERFORMING ARTS & NIGHTLIFE

Outdoor concerts and presentations are staged all summer long at **Foote Lagoon,** in **Civic Center Park,** and at **Peters Park,** next to the Loveland Museum/Gallery. Call the museum (☎ **970/962-2410**) or the Chamber of Commerce (☎ **800/ 258-1278** or 970/667-6311) for information on performances by the community's chamber orchestra, choral society, concert band, theater orchestra, and community theater group.

3 Greeley

30 miles SE of Fort Collins, 54 miles N of Denver

Greeley is one of the few cities in the world that owes its existence to a newspaper. It was founded in 1870 as a sort of prairie Utopia by Nathan C. Meeker, farm columnist for the *New York Tribune.* Meeker named the settlement—first known as Union Colony—in honor of his patron, *Tribune* publisher Horace Greeley. Through his widely read column, Meeker recruited more than 100 pioneers from all walks of life and purchased a tract on the Cache la Poudre from the Denver Pacific Railroad. Within a year, the colony's population was 1,000, and it's been growing steadily ever since, to around 70,000 today.

Greeley's economy is supported in large part by agriculture, with more than 96% of Weld County's 2.5 million acres devoted to either farming or raising livestock. A combination of irrigated and dry-land farms produce grains, including oats, corn, and wheat, and root vegetables such as sugar beets, onions, potatoes, and carrots. In recent years the community has been attracting major corporations, and its list of top employers includes Kodak, Hewlett Packard, Amoco, ConAgra, and State Farm. The University of Northern Colorado (UNC), with about 10,000 students, offers undergraduate and graduate degree programs.

ESSENTIALS

GETTING THERE   By Car   Greeley is located at the crossroads of U.S. 34 (east-west) and U.S. 85 (north-south), midway between Denver and Cheyenne, Wyoming—both of which are more directly reached by U.S. 85 than by I-25. U.S. 34 heads west 17 miles to I-25, beyond which are Loveland and Rocky Mountain National Park. To the east, U.S. 34 connects Greeley to Fort Morgan via I-76, 37 miles away.

By Airport Shuttle   Visitors who fly into Denver International Airport can travel on to Greeley with **Rocky Mountain Shuttle** (☎ 970/356-3366).

VISITOR INFORMATION   Contact the **Greeley Convention & Visitors Bureau,** 902 Seventh Ave., Greeley, CO 80631 (☎ **800/449-3866** or 970/ 352-3566; www.greeleycvb.com; e-mail: greeleycvb@ctos.com).

GETTING AROUND   Greeley is laid out on a standard grid, and is an easy city to navigate—provided you don't get confused by the numbered streets (which run east-west) and numbered avenues (which run north-south). It helps to know which is which when you're standing at the corner of 10th Street and 10th Avenue. Eighth Avenue (U.S. 85 north) and 11th Avenue (U.S. 85 south) are the main north-south streets through downtown. Ninth Street is U.S. 34 Business, jogging into 10th Street west of 23rd Avenue. The U.S. 34 Bypass joins U.S. 85 in a cloverleaf just south of town.

The city bus system, called simply **The Bus,** provides in-town transportation. For route information, call ☎ **970/350-9287.** All buses are lift-equipped, but those who cannot use them because of mobility impairments can call for information on paratransit service (☎ **970/350-9290**). For a taxi call **Shamrock Yellow Cab** (☎ **970/352-3000**).

FAST FACTS The hospital, **North Colorado Medical Center,** is at 1801 16th St. (☎ **970/352-4121**), just west of downtown. The **post office** is at 925 11th Ave. Contact the U.S. Postal Service (☎ **800/275-8777**) for hours and locations of other area post offices.

SPECIAL EVENTS Colorado Farm Show, late January; the UNC Jazz Festival, April; Semana Latina and Cinco de Mayo, early May; Independence Stampede, late June and early July; Weld County Fair, second largest in the state, early August; Potato Day celebrates Greeley's heritage, early September; Festival of Trees, early December; Homesteaders Holiday, mid-December; Northern Lights, throughout December.

SPORTS & OUTDOOR ACTIVITIES

Beginning about 25 miles northeast of Greeley and extending 60 miles east, the **Pawnee National Grassland** is a popular destination for hiking, mountain biking, birding, wildlife viewing, and horseback riding. Nomadic tribes lived in this desert-like area until the late 19th century, and farmers subsequently had little success in cultivating the grasslands. Although primarily grassland, the dramatic ✪ **Pawnee Buttes,** in the eastern section, are a pair of sandstone formations that rise some 250 feet. The most popular springtime activity is bird watching, when you're apt to see white-crowned sparrows, lark buntings, meadowlarks, thrushes, orioles, and burrowing owls among the 200-plus species known to frequent the area. Antelope, coyotes, mule deer, prairie dogs, and short-horned lizards are among the prolific wildlife.

There are many routes to the grasslands; one is to follow U.S. 85 north 11 miles to Ault, then east on Colo. 14 toward Briggsdale, 23 miles away. Those planning to explore the grasslands are advised to pick up a map and other free information before setting out by stopping at the U.S. Forest Service office, 660 O St., Greeley (☎ **970/353-5004**).

Spectator Sports

FOOTBALL The **Denver Broncos** of the National Football League hold pre-season training at UNC each summer. For practice and scrimmage information, call ☎ **970/351-1099** or 970/351-2007.

RODEO The **Greeley Independence Stampede** comes to town for 2 weeks, starting in late June, and boasts the world's largest Fourth of July Rodeo. Hundreds of professional cowboys compete for over $300,000 in prize money at Greeley's Island Grove Park, with bareback bronc riding, calf roping, saddle bronc riding, team roping, steer racing, barrel racing, and bull riding. Festivities include concerts by top country-western stars, art shows, a carnival, a children's rodeo, fun-runs, a demolition derby, barbecues, and a parade and fireworks display. For information, call ☎ **800/982-2855** or 970/356-2855.

IN-TOWN ATTRACTIONS

Centennial Village Museum. 1475 A St. at N. 14th Ave., adjacent to Island Grove Park. ☎ **970/350-9224.** Admission $3.50 adults, $3 seniors 60 and older, $2 children 6–12, free for children under 6. MC, V. Memorial Day–Labor Day, Tues–Sat 10am–5pm; mid-Apr to Memorial Day and Labor Day to mid-Oct, Tues–Sat 10am–3pm.

This collection of more than 30 structures—more are added each year—on 5½ acres depicts life on the High Plains of Colorado from the 1860s to the 1940s. Visit the blacksmith shop, print shop, and fire station of the commercial district, and stroll through Hannah Square, surrounded by elegant Victorian homes, a school, depot, and church. Living-history demonstrations and special events bring the past alive.

Meeker Home Museum. 1324 Ninth Ave. ☎ **970/350-9221.** Admission $3.50 adults, $3 seniors 60 and older, $2 children 6–12, free for children under 6. Memorial Day–Labor Day, Tues–Sat 10am–5pm; Labor Day to mid-Oct and mid-April to Memorial Day, Tues–Sat 10am–3pm.

This two-story adobe residence, built in 1870 for Greeley founder Nathan Cook Meeker and now on the National Register of Historic Places, is furnished with original Meeker family belongings and 19th-century antiques. Interpretive panels discuss the history of Greeley and northeastern Colorado, with emphasis on the Meeker family and their struggle for survival after Nathan's death in the 1897 Meeker Massacre.

WHAT TO SEE & DO SOUTH OF GREELEY

South from Greeley, U.S. 85 heads to Denver, but there are interesting stops en route in **Platteville,** 16 miles from Greeley; **Fort Lupton,** 25 miles; and **Brighton,** 32 miles.

One mile south of Platteville on U.S. 85 is **Fort Vasquez** (☎ 970/785-2832), an adobe reconstruction of a fur trader's fort from the 1830s, with exhibits on Colorado's fur trading days, including a display of bead work and other artifacts from local American Indian tribes of the period. There's a museum store, visitor center, and picnic area. In summer it's open Monday through Saturday from 9:30am to 4:30pm, Sunday from 1 to 4:30pm; limited hours and days at other times. Admission is free.

The **Fort Lupton Museum,** at 453 First St. (Colo. 52), Fort Lupton (☎ 303/857-1634), is a small museum packed to the rafters with artifacts and displays from the beginnings of the community as a fort and fur trading post in the 1830s through modern times. Many exhibits come from local families, and include historic photos, wedding gowns and even football uniforms from the 1800s, handmade quilts, American Indian blankets, a cannonball from the original fort, and memorabilia from the various ethnic groups that found their way to Fort Lupton over the years. You'll also see exhibits on the local industry—dairies and tomato canning—plus dinosaur bones, minerals, an arrowhead collection, and military uniforms from the 1830s to the present. The fort is long gone, but there's a diorama of what it would have looked like, and plans are underway to build a reconstruction. The museum is open Monday through Friday from 9am to 4pm, year-round. Admission is free, but donations are welcome.

The five buildings that comprise the **Adams County Museum Complex,** 9601 Henderson Rd., Brighton (☎ 303/659-7103), house displays on a wide variety of subjects, including area art and culture, restored agricultural equipment, and archeology and anthropology. There's a 1940s-era barber shop, a 1902 electric car, and an Earth Science Section with a fully operational blacksmith shop from the 1930s and 1940s. The museum also has a fully equipped 1930s-style Conoco gas station and a 1930s-style one-room schoolhouse. The complex is open Tuesday through Saturday from 10am to 4:30pm. Admission for individuals and families is free, but donations are appreciated; call for group rates.

WHERE TO STAY

A building boom of chain and franchise motels in the past few years has greatly increased lodging choices. Highest rates are during the summer. Among your options are the **Best Western Ramkota Inn**, 701 Eighth St. (☎ 800/528-1234 or 970/353-8444), with double rates of $80 to $88; the handsome **Country Inn & Suites by Carlson,** 201 W. 29th St. (☎ 800/456-4000 or 970/330-3404), with rates for two of $60 to $102; **Fairfield Inn**, 2401 W. 29th St. (☎ 800/228-2800 or 970/339-5030), with rates for two of $69 to $79; the brand-new (in 1998) **Microtel Inn & Suites,** 5630 W. 10th St. (☎ 888/771-7171 or 970/392-1530), with double rates of $45 to $65 Sunday through Thursday, and $55 to $75 Friday and Saturday; and the **Super 8,** 2423 W. 29th St. (☎ 800/800-8000 or 970/330-8880), with rates for two of $52 to $62. Rates for the last four facilities include a continental breakfast. State and city taxes add about 9% to hotel bills.

Sod Buster Inn Bed & Breakfast. 1221 Ninth Ave., Greeley, CO 80631. ☎ **888/300-1221** or 970/392-1221. Fax 970/392-1222. www.colorado-bnb.com/sodbuster. E-mail: sodbuster@ctos.com. 10 units. AC TEL. $89–$119 double. Rates include full breakfast. AE, DC, MC, V. Well-behaved children accepted with advance notification.

The octagonal shape and wraparound veranda of this attractive three-story inn grab your attention immediately. Although situated in an historic district and surrounded by 100-year old structures, the Sod Buster was actually built in 1997, designed to blend in with its older neighbors. Innkeepers LeeAnn and Bill Sterling have created what may be the best of both worlds—an exceedingly comfortable and attractive modern inn with the look and feel of an historic property, but without the steep staircases, noisy pipes, creaks, groans, and other "charms" you often find in old buildings.

Each guest room is individually decorated with a blend of antiques and country-style furnishings, and all include a king or queen bed, desk, phone with data port, a direct cable to the inn's main computer printer, good reading lamps, CD player (CDs available), comfortable seating, and individual climate control. Several rooms have jetted tubs, while others offer soaker tubs or old-fashioned claw-foot tubs, and all have separate showers. An ADA handicapped-accessible room is available. The inn's common area has comfortable overstuffed furniture, a fireplace, big-screen TV with VCR and a variety of videotapes, CD player, chess and other games, and a selection of reading materials. Refreshment bars on the first and second floors, open each morning and evening, are stocked with a variety of home-baked items, coffee, tea, and soft drinks. Full country-style breakfasts might include an egg entree, pancakes, a meat dish, fruit, fresh-baked breads, juices, and hot beverages. Smoking is permitted on the veranda only.

WHERE TO DINE

The Armadillo. 111 S. First St., La Salle. ☎ **970/284-5565.** $3–$9. AE, DC, MC, V. Mon–Thurs 11:30am–8:30pm, Fri–Sat 11:30am–9:30pm, Sun 11am–8:30pm. MEXICAN.

Occupying a large brick building beside the Union Pacific tracks in La Salle, 5 miles south of Greeley, this popular Mexican restaurant, with a decor reminiscent of a Mexican cantina, offers an extensive menu. Many of the recipes come from the family that has run this restaurant since 1970. Specialties include the Mexican Turnover (a deep-fried meat pie) and the Burrito Supreme. Fajitas are also popular.

Another **Armadillo** is located in Greeley at 819 Ninth St. (☎ **970/304-9024**).

Cable's End Italian Grille. 3780 W. 10th St. ☎ **970/356-4847.** $6–$14. AE, CB, DC, DISC, MC, V. Mon–Sat 11am–1am, Sun 11am–11pm. ITALIAN.

Locally popular for its homemade pastas with a choice of toppings, Cable's End also offers several chicken dishes, New York steak, and thin- or thick-crust pizza. Also on the menu are several calzones and strombolis, including the Cables Stromboli: salami, pepperoni, mushrooms, onion, mozzarella, and provolone. Sandwiches, which are served with pasta salad, French fries, or onion rings, include the Power House, consisting of roast beef, salami, green chile, onion, and melted provolone, with tomato sauce on the side.

Potato Brumbaugh's Restaurant & Saloon. 2400 17th St., in Cottonwood Square shopping center. ☎ **970/356-6340.** Reservations recommended. Lunch $5–$8; dinner $9–$30. AE, DC, DISC, MC, V. Mon–Fri 11:15am–2pm; Mon–Sat 5–10pm, Sun 4–9pm. AMERICAN.

Named for a character in James Michener's *Centennial,* this casually elegant restaurant follows the novel's theme in its western decor. The prime rib is especially popular, as is the daily fresh fish selection. The menu also features filet mignon, chicken, and pastas, such as pasta primavera, which is available with chicken or shrimp and in a marinara or Alfredo sauce.

PERFORMING ARTS & NIGHTLIFE

Greeley's cultural focus is the **Union Colony Civic Center,** 701 10th Ave., at Seventh Street (☎ **800/315-2787** or 970/356-5000; www.ci.greeley.co.us/uccc), which hosts several hundred performances during its September through May season, featuring national performers and touring groups as well as local and regional productions. Recent productions and those scheduled for the 1998–99 season have included *The King and I,* A Conversation with Gregory Peck, singer Roger Whittaker, the Vienna Choir Boys, *Smokey Joe's Cafe,* and comedians Elaine Boosler, Paula Poundstone, Gallagher, Paul Rodriguez, and George Carlin. The center is also the performance home for local theater and music groups, including a children's chorale and the Greeley Philharmonic Orchestra, the oldest continually performing orchestra west of the Mississippi River.

Each summer, the **Little Theater of the Rockies (☎ 970/351-2200)** presents five productions: usually a comedy, a drama or two, and several musicals. A summer series of free films and concerts, called **Neighborhood Nights (☎ 970/350-9454)**, is presented outdoors at various city parks. The **University Garden Theater** is the scene of Concerts Under the Stars in July and August. For information or tickets, call the University of Northern Colorado box office at ☎ **970/351-2200.** Other cultural programs scheduled by the university are also open to the public (for information call ☎ **970/351-2265**).

Among Greeley's more popular nightspots are the **Smiling Moose Brew Pub & Grill,** 2501 11th Ave. (☎ 970/356-7010), and **Potato Brumbaugh's Restaurant & Saloon,** 2400 17th St. (☎ 970/356-6340). The college crowd particularly enjoys the **Union Colony Brewery,** 1412 Eighth Ave. (☎ 970/356-4116), offering locally brewed beer, billiards, and darts. There's dancing Thursday through Saturday nights to live country music at **The Gambler,** 618 25th St. (☎ 970/351-7575).

4 Fort Morgan

51 miles E of Greeley, 81 miles NE of Denver

A laid-back city of nearly 11,000 people, Fort Morgan may be best known as the childhood home of famed big-band leader Glenn Miller, who graduated from Fort Morgan High School in 1921 and formed his first band, the Mick-Miller Five, in the city. Established as a military outpost in 1864, the original Fort Morgan housed about 200 troops who protected stagecoaches and pioneers traveling the Overland Trail from marauding Cheyenne and Arapahoe warriors. The threat had passed by 1870, and the fort was dismantled, but the name stuck when the city was founded in 1884. A monument on Riverview Avenue marks the fort's site. The town grew in the 20th century with the establishment of the Great Western Sugar Company for sugar-beet processing, and with a pair of oil discoveries in the 1920s and 1950s. Cattle and sheep ranching remain important today, as well as dairy farming. In addition to sugar beets, the area grows alfalfa, onions, beans, corn, potatoes, sorghum, and wheat.

About 10 miles east of Fort Morgan is the community of **Brush,** with a population of about 5,000. Also a farming and ranching center, Brush offers food and lodging, easy access to a popular pheasant-hunting area, and a variety of special events.

ESSENTIALS

GETTING THERE   By Car   Fort Morgan is located on U.S. 34 at I-76, the main east-west route between Denver and Omaha, Nebraska. U.S. 34 proceeds west to Greeley and Estes Park, east to Wray and southern Nebraska. Colo. 52 is the principal north-south route through Fort Morgan.

By Plane   Denver International Airport is less than 90 minutes away (see chapter 6).

By Train   Amtrak trains make daily stops on the Denver-to-Chicago route at the Fort Morgan depot, located on Ensign Street south of Railroad Avenue (☎ **800/ 872-7245**).

VISITOR INFORMATION   Contact the **Fort Morgan Area Chamber of Commerce,** 300 Main St. (P.O. Box 971), Fort Morgan, CO 80701 (☎ **800/354-8660** or 970/867-6702; www.fmchamber.org; e-mail: fmchamber@twol.com). The chamber is located in a handsome old stone bank building that's listed on the National Register of Historic Places. For information on events and activities in the nearby community of Brush, contact the **Brush Chamber of Commerce,** 1215 Edison St., Brush, CO 80723 (☎ **800/354-8659** or 970/842-2666; fax 970/ 842-3828; www.brushchamber.org; e-mail: brush@brushchamber.org).

GETTING AROUND   Platte Avenue (U.S. 34) is Fort Morgan's principal east-west thoroughfare. The north-south artery, Main Street, divides it and other streets into east and west designations. I-76 exits onto Main Street north of downtown.

FAST FACTS   The **Colorado Plains Medical Center,** with a 24-hour emergency room, is located at 1000 Lincoln St. (☎ **970/867-3391**). The **Fort Morgan Post Office** is at 300 State St. Contact the U.S. Postal Service (☎ **800/275-**8777) for hours and the addresses of other area post offices.

SPECIAL EVENTS   Brush Antique Show, February; Huck Finn & Becky Thatcher Days in Fort Morgan, June; the Glenn Miller Festival in Fort Morgan, third weekend in June; the Brush Rodeo, early July; Festival in the Park in Fort Morgan, mid-July; Morgan County Fair in Brush, August.

WHAT TO SEE & DO

✪ **Fort Morgan Museum.** City Park, 414 Main St. ☎ **970/867-6331.** www. ftmorganmus.org. Free admission. Mon–Fri 10am–5pm, plus Tues–Thurs 6–8pm; Sat 11am–5pm.

An impressive collection of northeastern Colorado American Indian artifacts, beginning with 13,000-year-old Clovis points, is the highlight of this museum— the smallest one in Colorado to be accredited by the American Association of

Museums. Other permanent exhibits focus on farming, ranching, and the military and railroad history of Morgan County, plus a display on the life of native son Glenn Miller and a fully restored 1920s soda fountain. The museum also hosts traveling exhibits and stages temporary shows from its collection, and is a good source for genealogical information in the area. There's a gift shop, and you'll find picnic areas and a playground in the surrounding City Park.

Oasis on the Plains Museum. 6877 County Rd. 14. ☎ **970/432-5200.** Free admission, donations appreciated. Sun noon–4pm, or by appointment.

This working-ranch museum about 15 miles southwest of Fort Morgan displays artifacts, antiques, collectibles, and other items from the northeastern Colorado plains pioneer days.

Rainbow Bridge. At the northwest corner of Riverside Park (I-76 and Colo. 50).

Also called the James Marsh Arch Bridge, this 11-arch concrete bridge was built over the South Platte River in 1923, at a construction cost of $69,290. Listed on the National Register of Historic Landmarks and the National Register of Engineering Landmarks, the 1,110-foot bridge is the only rainbow-arch design in Colorado. For information, contact the Fort Morgan Museum (see above).

Sherman Street National Historic District. 400 and 500 blocks of Sherman St. ☎ **970/867-6331.**

The Fort Morgan Museum (see above) publishes a walking-tour brochure both for Sherman Street and for the 9-block downtown district, the latter noting 44 buildings that comprised the early town. These are available at the Chamber of Commerce and the museum.

Four Victorian mansions in the Sherman Street District are of special interest. Located around the intersection of Sherman Street and East Platte Avenue, they include the Warner House, an 1886 Queen Anne home; the Curry House, an 1898 Queen Anne with decorative spindlework porches, a barn, carriage house, and water tower; the Graham House, a 1914 American Foursquare home; and the Bloedorn House, a 1926 brick Georgian revival–style building. Each is associated with a prominent city pioneer. They are private homes, not open to the public.

SPORTS & OUTDOOR ACTIVITIES

The main outdoor recreational facility in town is **Riverside Park** (☎ 970/867-3808), off Main Street between I-76 and the South Platte River. Admission is free, and it has a large children's playground, walking paths, tennis courts, an archery range, playing fields, a picnic area, a duck pond (open to fishing by children 16 and younger, and adults accompanied by a child 16 or younger), ice-skating in winter, and a swimming pool open in summer ($1). The park also has free overnight RV camping.

Outside of town is **Jackson Lake State Park** (☎ 970/645-2551), with swimming, boating, fishing, and picnicking in summer; and ice-fishing, ice-skating, and cross-country skiing in winter ($4 day-use fee). There's also a half-mile nature trail, plus 250 campsites with electric hookups, showers, and a dump station ($9 to $12). To get to Jackson Lake, follow Colo. 144 northwest for about 22 miles; the park is about 2½ miles north of the community of Goodrich via County Road 3.

FISHING   In addition to Riverside Park (see above), anglers fish year-round (ice-fishing in winter) at Jackson Lake State Park for trout, walleye, bass, catfish, and perch, except when fishing is prohibited during the migratory waterfowl season. **Jackson Lake Marina** (☎ 970/768-6011) has supplies and services. See "Water Sports," below.

HUNTING   Pheasant and duck hunting is popular in the Brush Prairie Ponds State Wildlife Area near Brush. Information is available from the Brush Chamber of Commerce (see above).

WATER SPORTS   Waterskiing, sailboarding, and boating are the most popular activities on the 2,700-acre reservoir at Jackson Lake State Park, which has sandy beaches and boat ramps. A **marina** (☎ **970/768-6011**) has fuel, fishing and boating supplies, a snack bar, and boat rentals from May through September. Fishing boats cost $18 per hour, personal watercraft and 18-foot pontoon boats are $45 per hour, and ski boats cost $65 per hour (skis are extra). Those who prefer traveling under their own power can rent paddleboats for $15 per hour. The lake is closed to motorized boats from November until all the ice is gone in spring.

Spectator Sports

RODEO   The **Brush Rodeo,** billed as the world's largest open rodeo (both amateurs and professionals compete), is held in the town of Brush, 10 miles east of Fort Morgan, over the Fourth of July weekend, with all the usual rodeo events, plus a parade, kids' games, a dance, and fireworks. Contact the Brush Chamber of Commerce (see above).

STOCK-CAR RACING   Fans head to Fort Morgan's I-76 Speedway (☎ **970/867-2101**), where they can see late-model, street stocks, minisprints, microsprints, dwarf cars, and IMCA modifieds race on a quarter-mile, high-banked dirt oval track from April through October.

WHERE TO STAY

Note that state and county taxes add just under 7% to hotel bills.

Best Western Park Terrace Inn. 725 Main St., Fort Morgan, CO 80701. ☎ **800/528-1234** or 970/867-8256. Fax 970/867-8257. 24 units. A/C TV TEL. $55–$78 double. AE, CB, DC, DISC, MC, V. The inn is 4 blocks south of I-76. Pre-approved pets accepted with a $25 deposit.

Family-owned since 1980, rooms in this attractive two-story Best Western have queen-size beds, individual heating, modem hookups, and coffeemakers. Amenities include a swimming pool, hot tub, and fax and copier services. The restaurant, decorated with antiques and collectibles, serves three meals daily from an extensive menu that includes steaks, seafood, and Mexican, Italian, and American dishes.

Budget Host Empire Motel. 1408 Edison St., Brush, CO 80723. ☎ **800/283-4678** or 970/842-2876. 18 units. A/C TV TEL. $34–$45 double. AE, DISC, MC, V. Pets accepted for a fee.

A comfortable roadside motel, this mom-and-pop operation provides small but clean and completely adequate rooms with good-quality beds, showers only, cable TV, and at-your-door parking.

WHERE TO DINE

Country Steak Out. 19592 E. Eighth Ave., Fort Morgan. ☎ **970/867-7887.** $5–$20. AE, MC, V. Tues–Sat 11am–9pm, Sun 11am–2pm. STEAK/SEAFOOD.

This open and airy restaurant, with high ceilings and lots of wood and brick, is a favorite of locals. In addition to the popular steaks and prime rib, there's salmon, halibut, and trout, plus homemade soups, daily luncheon specials, and an extensive salad bar at both lunch and dinner.

Stroh's Inn. 901 W. Platte Ave., Fort Morgan. ☎ **970/867-6654.** Breakfast $2.25–$5.25; lunch and dinner $3.25–$12. AE, MC, V. Mon–Sat 6am–9pm, Sun 6am–2pm. AMERICAN.

This family-owned and -operated restaurant is known for its generous portions of homemade food, with an extensive menu that includes eight different burgers, 18 sandwiches, a half dozen Mexican dishes, plenty of salads, and a variety of steaks, pork, roasted chicken, and seafood. Pies are baked fresh daily. The breakfast menu offers all the American standards, and there's a children's menu.

5 Burlington

163 miles E of Denver, 385 miles W of Topeka, Kansas

As the first major Colorado community to greet motorists traveling I-70 from the east, Burlington is an excellent place to overnight and spend some time at the beginning of a Colorado vacation. It's the largest town in east-central Colorado, with a population of about 3,000, and has preserved its turn-of-the-century heritage with an impressive Old Town and famous carousel. Dry-land farmers established Burlington and other "Outback" communities along the Kansas City–Denver rail line in the 1880s, and while wheat is very much the dominant crop today, you'll also find corn and dry beans.

ESSENTIALS

GETTING THERE   By Car   Burlington is located on east-west I-70, 13 miles from the Kansas border. U.S. 385, which runs the length of Colorado's eastern frontier, makes a north-to-south pass through the town.

VISITOR INFORMATION   The **Colorado Welcome Center** is on I-70 beside Burlington Old Town (☎ **719/346-5554**). For information specifically on Burlington, contact the **Burlington Chamber of Commerce,** 415 15th St., Burlington, CO 80807 (☎ **719/346-8070**).

GETTING AROUND   The town lies on the north side of I-70. Rose Avenue (U.S. 24) runs east-west through the center of Burlington. Main north-south streets are Eighth Street (U.S. 385 north) on the east side of town, 14th Street (which locals call Main Street), and Lincoln Street (U.S. 385 south) on the west side of town.

FAST FACTS   The **Kit Carson County Memorial Hospital** is at 186 16th St. (☎ **719/346-5311**). The **post office** is at 259 14th St. Contact the U.S. Postal Service (☎ **800/275-8777**) for hours and other information. During inclement weather (but not at other times), you can get a **road condition report** by calling ☎ **719/346-8778**.

SPECIAL EVENTS   Kit Carson County Fair, August; Old Town's Outback Hoedown, September; Old Town Ghost Town, late October; Old Town Christmas and Parade of Lights, December.

SPORTS & OUTDOOR ACTIVITIES

As soon as the winter snows are gone, the folks in Burlington and other eastern Colorado communities head to the beach, and that means **Bonny State Park,** 23 miles north of Burlington on U.S. 385, then east on County Roads 2 or 3 for about 1½ miles (☎ **970/354-7306**). Built as a flood control project in 1951, the reservoir contains 1,900 surface acres of relatively warm water, perfect for swimming, water-skiing, windsurfing, and fishing. Daily entrance fee is $4 per vehicle.

The lake has two swimming areas (no lifeguards) and four campgrounds with a total of 190 campsites ($7 to $12 per night). Some sites have electric hookups, and several are handicapped-accessible. Facilities include rest rooms, showers, picnic areas, a self-guided nature trail (not handicapped-accessible), and a fish cleaning station. Fishing is good for walleye, northern pike, and a variety of bass.

Boat launching ramps are available, and the **Bonny Dam Marina** (☎ 970/354-7339) sells fuel, groceries, and boating and fishing supplies. The marina also rents fishing boats, 20- to 24-foot pontoon boats, and personal watercraft between mid-May and mid-September. Call for current rates. The 5,000-acre park provides opportunities to see wildlife, with some 250 species of birds, mule and whitetail deer, coyotes, badgers, muskrats, bobcats, beavers, and rabbits.

If you're traveling this way in winter, stop by for an afternoon of cross-country skiing, ice-skating, or ice-fishing, but don't forget your long underwear—winter winds are bone-chilling out here on the plains. During winter, electric and water are available in the campgrounds, and there are vault toilets, but the showers and flush toilets are shut down.

WHAT TO SEE & DO

✪ **Kit Carson County Carousel.** County Fairgrounds, 15th St. at Colorado Ave. ☎ **719/346-8070.** Admission 25¢ per ride. Memorial Day–Labor Day, daily 1–8pm. Private tours given at other times; write P.O. Box 28, Stratton, CO 80836, with 2 weeks' advance notice.

This is the town's pride and joy, the only National Historic Landmark in eastern Colorado. Carved in 1905 by the Philadelphia Toboggan Company, it is fully restored and operational, and is one of the few wooden carousels left in America that still wears its original coat of paint. The 46 stationary animals—mostly horses, but also including giraffes, zebras, camels, a hippocampus (sea horse), lion, tiger, and others—march counterclockwise around three tiers of oil paintings, representing the lifestyles and interests of the American Victorian middle class. A Wurlitzer Monster Military Band Organ, one of only two of its size and vintage in operation today, provides the music.

✪ **Old Town.** 420 S. 14th St. ☎ **800/288-1334** or 719/346-7382. Admission $6 adults 19–59, $4 youths 12–18, $2 children 3–11, $5 seniors 60 and older. Memorial Day–Labor Day, daily 8:30am–7pm; rest of the year, Mon–Sat 9am–6pm, Sun noon–6pm.

Close to 2 dozen turn-of-the-century-style Old West buildings make up this living-history museum, where you're likely to see a gunfight, or, in the summer months, a cancan show in the Longhorn Saloon. Ten of the buildings are original historic structures, moved to Old Town, and the rest are reproductions, all furnished with genuine Old West artifacts to show what it was like here 100 years ago.

Visit the blacksmith shop, bank, law office, newspaper office and operating print shop, general store, schoolhouse, and barn. The railroad depot, built in 1889 in Bethune, Colorado, is the oldest structure in Old Town. Of course there's the saloon, where you're likely to find the local madam during the summer, or perhaps you'd prefer to stop at the church, built in 1921 and still used for weddings.

The dollhouse is home to a number of unique dolls, and in the wood shop you'll see tools more than 100 years old. The original Burlington town jail cells are also here; and the two-story, six-bedroom Manor house, built in the early 1900s, is magnificent, furnished with splendid antiques of the period. Heritage Hall contains a large collection of 45 wagons, guns, and other exhibits. There's also a 2,000-square-foot gift shop, with handcrafted items and other souvenirs. On summer weekends the horse-drawn "Old Town Express" gives rides from Old Town to the Kit Carson County Carousel (see above).

WHERE TO STAY

Because for many travelers Burlington is simply an overnight stop along the inter-state highway, you won't have any trouble finding a room here, with all the motels easily accessible from I-70 exits 437 and 438. In addition to the motels discussed below, there's a **Comfort Inn,** 282 S. Lincoln St. (☎ **800/228-5150** or 719/346-7676), with rates for two of $74 to $79; and **Super 8,** 2100 Fay St. (☎ **800/800-8000** or 719/346-5627), with double rates of $40 to $47. Tax adds about 7% to lodging bills.

Sloan's Motel. 1901 Rose Ave., Burlington, CO 80807. ☎ **800/362-0464** or 719/346-5333. Fax 719/346-9536. 29 units. A/C TV TEL. Memorial Day–Labor Day $42 double. Labor Day–Memorial Day $34 double. Family units $42–$48. AE, CB, DC, DISC, MC, V. Small pets accepted.

A well-kept, comfortable establishment, this motel has a children's playground and enclosed heated swimming pool. All rooms have firm queen or double beds and 27-channel cable TV. One family unit has two rooms, and the ADA room has a roll-in shower. Fifteen rooms have shower/tub combos, and the remaining 14 have shower only. Free coffee is available in the lobby, and a fax machine is available.

Travelodge. 450 S. Lincoln St., Burlington, CO 80807. ☎ **719/346-5555.** Fax 719/346-5555. 112 units. A/C TV TEL. $36–$46 double; from $51 suite. A child under 16 stays free with parent. AE, CB, DC, DISC, MC, V. Pets accepted at $5 per day.

This conveniently located motel offers recently remodeled spacious rooms, with cable TV and coffeemakers. There's an outdoor heated swimming pool, lounge, and dining room serving three meals daily.

WHERE TO DINE

Mitten's Interstate House Restaurant. 415 S. Lincoln St., at I-70 exit 437. ☎ **719/346-7041.** Breakfast $1.50–$6.25; lunch and dinner $3–$15. DISC, MC, V. Daily 6am–9pm. AMERICAN.

Called the "Yellow Top" by locals because of its distinctive bright yellow roof, this family restaurant is a favorite because of its good home-cooked food, quick service, and low prices. House specialties include the aged, charbroiled steaks that are cut in-house, plus the waffles, which, like many of the other breakfast entrees, are served all day. There are also burgers, sandwiches, seafood selections, pork chops, tacos, burritos, chile, and a steak-and-eggs special.

Western Motor Inn Restaurant. 123 Lincoln St. ☎ **719/346-8115.** Main courses $4–$14. CB, DC, MC, V. Mon–Sat 6am–9pm (until 9:30pm Fri–Sat in summer). AMERICAN.

This cheery family-style restaurant, with tables or window booths, specializes in steak, roasted chicken, and homemade pies. There's an all-you-can-eat lunch buffet weekdays ($5.35); a salad, soup, and dessert bar; and a full bar. Known for its gen-erous portions, the restaurant also serves a variety of sandwiches and burgers, plus gulf shrimp and halibut steak. Everything is available to go, and there's children's and senior citizens' menus as well.

The Northern Rockies

Literally and figuratively, this is the mother lode. It's where scrappy silver and gold miners struck it rich time and time again in the late 19th century (and you might still find an ore deposit while hiking or fishing here today), yet it's also where Colorado's rugged beauty is shown off to fullest effect.

The northern Rockies begin just outside of Denver and extend on either side of the meandering Continental Divide down saw-tooth ridgelines, through precipitous river canyons, and across broad alpine plains. Here, snowfall is measured in feet, not inches; it's where you'll find Colorado's hottest ski resorts—Aspen, Vail, and Steamboat—as well as a few smaller areas that are making head-lines, such as Winter Park. And then there's Summit County, with possibly more major ski areas within a half-hour's drive than any-where else in the country. If you're easily bored, rent a condo or take a room in Breckenridge and spend your days skiing a different mountain every day. With Copper, Keystone, Arapahoe Basin, and even tiny Loveland Basin all within a few miles' drive, you've got plenty of choices.

When spring's sun finally melts away the walls of white, a whole new world opens up amid the brilliantly colored alpine wildflowers. You can head to any of the area's ski resorts and shop their stores, and hike or cycle their trails. Perhaps best of all, though, is a trip to the West's premier mountain vacation land, and our very favorite mountain destination in Colorado: Rocky Mountain National Park, where you'll discover what many of us feel is the American West's most spectacular scenery, with a broad range of outdoor activities, from hiking to wildlife viewing to cross-country skiing.

1 Estes Park & Grand Lake: Gateways to Rocky Mountain National Park

71 miles NW of Denver, 42 miles SW of Fort Collins, 44 miles NW of Boulder

Estes Park is the eastern gateway to Rocky Mountain National Park, and Grand Lake is the closest town to the park's western entrance. Of the two, Estes Park is more developed. It has more lodging and dining choices, as well as a few noteworthy sights that are worth a visit. If you're driving to Rocky Mountain National Park via Boulder or Denver, you'll want to make Estes Park your base camp.

Grand Lake is a more rustic spot, with plenty of spots to camp,

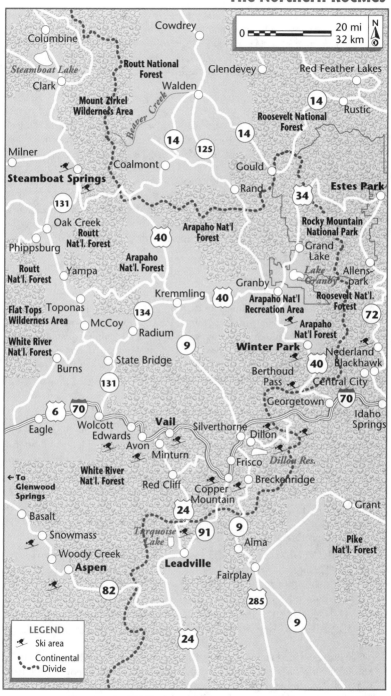

The Northern Rockies

0 — 20 mi
32 km

N

Columbine
Steamboat Lake
Clark
Cowdrey
Glendevey
Red Feather Lakes

Routt National Forest
Walden
14
Rustic
Mount Zirkel Wilderness Area
Roosevelt National Forest

Milner
Coalmont
14
125
Gould
Rand

Steamboat Springs
131
34
Estes Park

Oak Creek
Routt Nat'l. Forest
40
Arapaho Nat'l Forest
Rocky Mountain National Park
Grand Lake

Phippsburg
Yampa
Arapaho Nat'l. Forest
Granby
Lake Granby
Allenspark

Routt Nat'l. Forest
Kremmling
40
Arapaho Nat'l Recreation Area
Roosevelt Nat'l. Forest
72

Flat Tops Wilderness Area
Toponas
134
Radium
Arapaho Nat'l. Forest

McCoy
9
Winter Park
40
Nederland
Blackhawk

White River Nat'l. Forest
State Bridge
Berthoud Pass
Central City

Burns
131
Georgetown
70
Idaho Springs

6
70
Vail
Silverthorne
Dillon

Eagle
Wolcott
Edwards
Avon
Minturn
Frisco
Dillon Res.

To Glenwood Springs
White River Nat'l. Forest
Red Cliff
Copper Mountain
Breckenridge
Grant

Basalt
24
91
9
Alma
Pike Nat'l. Forest

Snowmass
Turquoise Lake

Woody Creek
Leadville
Fairplay

Aspen
82
285
9

24

LEGEND

- Ski area
- Continental Divide

a number of motels, and a few guest ranches. If you're coming from Steamboat Springs or Glenwood Springs, Grand Lake is a more convenient base. At any time of year, you can get there via U.S. 34. In summer, you can also get to Grand Lake by taking the Trail Ridge Road through Rocky Mountain National Park from Estes Park. Both routes are scenic, although the national park route (closed in winter) is definitely prettier.

ESTES PARK

Unlike most Colorado mountain communities, which got their starts in mining, Estes Park (elevation 7,522 feet) has always been a resort town. Long known by Utes and Arapahoes, it was "discovered" in 1859 by rancher Joel Estes. He soon sold his homestead to Griff Evans, who built it into a dude ranch. One of Evans's guests, the British Earl of Dunraven, was so taken by the region that he purchased most of the valley and operated it as his private game reserve, until thwarted by such settlers as W. E. James, who built Elkhorn Lodge as a "fish ranch" to supply Denver restaurants.

But the growth of Estes Park is inextricably linked with two individuals: Freelan Stanley and Enos Mills. Stanley, a Bostonian, who, together with his brother Francis, invented the kerosene-powered Stanley Steamer automobile in 1899, settled in Estes Park in 1907, launched a Stanley Steamer shuttle service from Denver, and in 1909 built the landmark Stanley Hotel. Mills, an innkeeper-turned-conservationist, was one of the prime advocates for the establishment of Rocky Mountain National Park. Although much less well known than John Muir, Mills is an equally important figure in the history of the U.S. conservation movement. His tireless efforts as an author and stump speaker increased sentiment nationwide for preserving our wild lands, and resulted in President Woodrow Wilson signing a bill to set aside 400 square miles for Rocky Mountain National Park in 1915. Today the park attracts some three million visitors annually.

ESSENTIALS

GETTING THERE   By Car   The most direct route is U.S. 36 from Denver and Boulder. At Estes Park, U.S. 36 joins U.S. 34, which runs up the Big Thompson Canyon from I-25 and Loveland, and continues through Rocky Mountain National Park to Grand Lake and Granby. An alternative scenic route to Estes Park is Colo. 7, the "Peak-to-Peak Scenic Byway" that goes through Central City (Colo. 119), Nederland (Colo. 72), and Allenspark (Colo. 7) under different designations.

By Plane   The closest airport is Denver International Airport, 80 miles away.

By Bus   Charles Tour and Travel Services (☎ **800/586-5009** or 970/586-5151) connects Estes Park with Boulder and Denver.

VISITOR INFORMATION   The **Estes Park Chamber Resort Association,** 500 Big Thompson Ave., Estes Park, CO 80517 (☎ **800/44-ESTES** or 970/586-4431; www.rockymtntrav.com/estes), has a visitor center on U.S. 34, just east of its junction with U.S. 36.

GETTING AROUND   In summer, a free national-park **shuttle bus** runs from the Glacier Basin parking area to Bear Lake, with departures every 15 to 30 minutes.

There's year-round taxi service with **Charles Tour and Travel Service** (☎ **800/586-5009** or 970/586-5151), which also provides tours into Rocky Mountain National Park during the summer. Similar services are offered by **Emerald Taxi, Shuttle, Tour, and Travel Service** (☎ **970/586-1992**).

FAST FACTS The hospital, **Estes Park Medical Center,** with a 24-hour emergency room, is at 555 Prospect Ave. (☎ **970/586-2317**). The **post office** is at 215 W. Riverside Dr. Call the U.S. Postal Service (☎ **800/275-8777**) for hours and locations of other post offices. For statewide **road conditions,** call ☎ **303/639-1111.** For a **current weather report,** call ☎ **970/586-5555.**

SPECIAL EVENTS Stanley Steamer Tour, May; Scandinavian Mid-Summer Festival, on the weekend closest to the summer solstice; the Rooftop Rodeo and Western Heritage Days, third week in July; Estes Park Music Festival, July and August; and Scottish-Irish Highland Festival, second weekend in September.

WHAT TO SEE & DO

Enos Mills Cabin and Gallery. 6760 Colo. 7 (opposite Longs Peak Inn). ☎ **970/586-4706.** Memorial Day–Labor Day, Tues–Sun 11am–4pm. By appointment in other seasons.

The 1885 cabin and homestead of the late-19th- and early-20th-century conservationist is owned and operated by Mills's family. There's a 5-minute walk down a nature trail to the cabin, where members of the Mills family discuss his life and work. Memorabilia in the cabin includes copies of his 15 books and the cameras he used to take thousands of photos of the mountains he loved. Summer nature walks ($20 per hour) are available by appointment, and evening talks are scheduled during the winter (call for details). There's also a bookshop, photo gallery, and nature center.

Estes Park Aerial Tramway. 420 E. Riverside Dr. ☎ **970/586-3675.** Admission $8 adults, $4 children 6–11, free for children 5 and under. Summer, daily 9am–6:30pm.

This lift provides panoramic views of Longs Peak and the Continental Divide, plus Estes Park village itself. Its lower terminal is a block south of the post office. Its upper terminal has a gift shop, snack bar, and observation deck with binoculars (25¢). Numerous trails converge atop the mountain.

Estes Park Area Historical Museum. 200 Fourth St. at U.S. 36. ☎ **970/586-6256.** estes.on-line.com\epmuseum. E-mail: epmuseum@juno.com. Admission $2.50 adults, $1 children 12 and under; $10 maximum for families. May–Oct, Mon–Sat 10am–5pm, Sun 1–5pm; Nov–Apr, Fri–Sat 10am–5pm, Sun 1–5pm; extended Dec holiday hours.

The lives of early homesteaders in Estes Park are depicted in this excellent small museum, which includes a completely furnished turn-of-the-century log cabin, an original Stanley Steam Car, and a changing exhibit gallery, all housed in the original headquarters building of Rocky Mountain National Park, which has been moved here. The museum also features a permanent "Tracks in Time" exhibit that helps visitors see the impact that ordinary people, from the region's American Indians and women pioneers to today's area residents and travelers, have had on Estes Park. In addition, the museum sponsors a variety of programs and distributes a historical walking-tour brochure of downtown Estes Park.

Michael Ricker Pewter Casting Studio and Museum. 2050 Big Thompson Ave. ☎ **800/373-9837** or 970/586-2030. Free admission. Summer, Mon–Thurs 9am–9pm, Fri–Sat 9am–6pm, Sun 10am–6pm; winter, Mon–Sat 9am–5pm, Sun 11am–5pm.

Ricker is an internationally recognized artist and sculptor, whose works have been displayed in the Great Hall of Commerce in Washington, D.C., and at both Disneyland and Disney World. There are more than 1,000 pewter sculptures in the museum and gallery, including Ricker's masterpiece, "Park City," claimed to be the world's largest miniature pewter sculpture. Free guided tours are available daily.

SHOPPING

The **Art Center of Estes Park** in the Stanley Village Shopping Center (up the stairs behind the fountain), 517 Big Thompson Ave. (☎ **970/586-5882**), is a community visual-arts center featuring changing exhibits of a wide variety of local and regional art, workshops, and classes. Cost is usually in the $40 to $75 range, including materials. It's open daily from 11am to 5pm in summer; call for winter hours.

Among the notable galleries and gift shops are those in the **Old Church Shops,** 157 W. Elkhorn Ave., and **Sundance Center for the Arts,** 150 E. Riverside Dr. Also of note are **The Glassworks,** 323 W. Elkhorn Ave. (☎ **800/490-6695** or 970/586-8619), a gallery and studio with hand-glass-blowing demonstrations; and **Serendipity Trading Company,** 117 E. Elkhorn Ave. (☎ **970/586-8410**), traders in American Indian arts and crafts.

Ten miles south of Estes Park is **Eagle Plume's** store and museum, 9853 Colo. 7, Allenspark (☎ **303/747-2861**). A University of Colorado graduate (now deceased), Charles Eagle Plume was one-quarter Blackfeet (a Montana tribe, not the better-known Blackfoots of Canada) and an entertainer and entrepreneur. His fascinating collection of museum-quality artifacts is not for sale, but in this museum (free admission) you'll get to see antique Indian beadwork and quill work, historic and prehistoric pottery, Navajo and Pueblo textiles dating from the 1870s, plus old pawn jewelry. In the trading post, you can purchase contemporary works by American and Canadian Indians, including crafts, pottery, jewelry, baskets, beadwork, and rugs. Eagle Plume's is open April through December, daily from 9am to 5pm; weekends only from January through March.

WHERE TO STAY

Highest rates here are in summer. For help finding accommodations, call the **Estes Park Area Chamber of Commerce Lodging Referral Service** (☎ **800/443-7837** or 970/586-4431). National chains here include **Best Western Lake Estes Resort,** 1650 Big Thompson Ave. (U.S. 34), (☎ **800/292-8439** or 970/586-3386), with rates of $98 to $210 per double from mid-June to mid-September, and $50 to $132 per double the rest of the year; and **Comfort Inn,** 1459 Big Thompson Ave. (☎ **800/228-5150** or 970/586-2358), charging $74 to $159 per double in summer, and $51 to $129 per double the rest of the year. Taxes add about 8% to hotel bills. See also the National Park Resort, Cabins, and Campground in the "Camping" section, below.

Expensive

✪ **Aspen Lodge at Estes Park.** 6120 Colo. 7, Longs Peak Route, Estes Park, CO 80517. ☎ **800/332-6867** from outside Colorado (reservations only) or 970/586-8133. Direct from Denver 303/440-3371. Fax 970/586-8133. 36 rms, 23 cabins. TEL. June–Aug: 3-day minimum, packages include three meals, children's program, entertainment, and recreation (horseback riding extra). 3 days, shared room $450 each adult, $270 each child ages 3–12, free for children under 3; single adult $580. 4 days, shared room $580 each adult, $365 each child ages 3–12, free for children under 3; single adult $780. 7 days, shared room $930 each adult, $610 each child ages 3–12, free for children under 3; single adult $1245. For horseback riding, add $245 to the weekly rate. Sept–May: $79–$169 double per night, including full breakfast. Holiday rates higher. AE, DISC, DC, MC, V.

Among Colorado's top dude ranches, Aspen Lodge is a full-service western-style resort, offering horseback riding, tennis, hiking, mountain biking, fishing, cross-country skiing, ice-skating, snowshoeing, and a myriad other activities. Guests stay in the handsome log lodge, which has a commanding stone fireplace in the lobby, or in cozy one-, two-, or three-room cabins nestled among the aspens. All lodge rooms have balconies, and most rooms and cabins have splendid views of Longs Peak, the tallest mountain in Rocky Mountain National Park. Trails on the lodge's 82 acres of grounds lead directly into the national park. Guests can also enjoy an outdoor heated swimming pool and hot tub, as well as the sports center, which has racquetball, a weight room, and a sauna. Meals are varied and delicious. The lodge also schedules numerous activities to entertain both children and teens.

✪ **Boulder Brook.** 1900 Fall River Rd., Estes Park, CO 80517. ☎ **800/238-0910** or 970/586-0910. Fax 970/586-8067. www.estes-park.com/boulderbrook. 16 suites. TV TEL. $89–$169 double; $129–$199 spa suite. AE, DISC, MC, V.

It would be hard to find a more beautiful setting for a lodging than this. Surrounded by tall pines, all suites face the Fall River, and feature private riverfront decks and either full or partial kitchens. The spa suites are equipped with two-person spas, and one-bedroom suites offer whirlpool tub and shower combinations. Both have king beds. There's also a year-round outdoor hot tub. VCRs, in-room movies, and fax service are available, and packages for special occasions can be arranged year-round.

Romantic RiverSong Inn. P.O. Box 1910, Estes Park, CO 80517. ☎ **970/586-4666**. Fax 970/577-0699. www.romanticriversong.com. E-mail: riversng@frii.com. 9 units. $135–$250 double. Rates include full breakfast. MC, V. Not suitable for small children.

A 1920 Craftsman mansion on the Big Thompson River, this elegant bed-and-breakfast has 27 forested acres with hiking trails and a trout pond, as well as prolific wildlife and beautiful wildflowers. Very quiet, the inn is at the end of a country lane, the first right off Mary's Lake Road after it branches off U.S. 36 south. The cozy bedrooms are decorated with a blend of antique and modern country furniture, and all have fireplaces and firewood. Some feature ornate brass beds and claw-foot tubs; several boast jetted tubs for two. Smoking is not permitted. Gourmet candlelight dinners are available by advance arrangement ($69 per couple), but you must supply your own alcoholic beverages.

Stanley Hotel. 333 Wonderview Ave. (P.O. Box 1767), Estes Park, CO 80517. ☎ **800/ 976-1377** or 970/586-3371. Fax 970/586-3673. www.grandheritage.com. 133 units. TV TEL. Late May to mid-Oct, $169–$209 double, $269–$299 suite; mid-Oct to late May, $139–$179 double, $219–$249 suite. AE, DISC, MC, V.

F. O. Stanley, inventor of the Stanley Steam Car, built this elegant, white-pillared hotel in 1909. The equal of European resorts of the time, it was constructed into solid rock. Today the hotel and grounds are listed on the National Register of Historic Places. The entire building, both guest rooms and public areas, was remodeled in 1997. As often happens in historic hotels, each room differs in size and shape, offering a variety of views of Longs Peak, Lake Estes, and surrounding hillsides. Amenities include a heated outdoor pool, tennis and volleyball courts, sundeck, access to a nearby health club, two restaurants, shops, and a business center.

Streamside Cabins. 1260 Fall River Rd., Moraine Rte. (P.O. Box 2930), Estes Park, CO 80517. ☎ **800/321-3303** or 970/586-6464. Fax 970/586-6272. www.streamsidecabins. com. E-mail: resv@streamsidecabins.com. 19 units. TV. Late Oct to early May, $70–$145 single or double; early May to late Oct, $95–$215; extra person $15. AE, DISC, MC, V.

These cabin suites, on 17 acres along the Fall River, about a mile west of Estes Park on U.S. 34, are surrounded by woods and meadows of wildflowers. Deer, elk, and occasional bighorn sheep are such regular visitors that many have been given names.

Everything is top drawer in these cabins. All have king- or queen-size beds, fireplaces, cable TV, VCRs, and decks or patios with gas grills. Most also have full kitchens, and many have beamed cathedral ceilings, skylights, and whirlpool tubs or steam showers. Extras include an indoor hot tub/swim spa and nature trails. A variety of special-occasion packages are offered.

Moderate

Allenspark Lodge Bed & Breakfast. Colo. 7 Business Loop (P.O. Box 247), Allenspark, CO 80510. ☎ **303/747-2552.** 13 units (5 with bathroom). $60–$105 double. Rates include breakfast. AE, DISC, MC, V.

This three-story lodge, built in 1933 of hand-hewn ponderosa pine logs, boasts a large native stone fireplace. Located 16 miles south of Estes Park, in a tiny village at the southeast corner of the national park, all rooms offer mountain views and original handmade 1930s pine furniture. Guests share the large sunroom, the stone fireplace in the Great Room, Ping-Pong and videos in the recreation room, and books in the library. Complimentary afternoon and evening coffee, tea, and cookies are served. There's also a hot tub, self-service laundry, conference rooms, an espresso coffeeshop, and a wine and beer bar.

✪ **Baldpate Inn.** 4900 S. Colo. 7 (P.O. Box 4445), Estes Park, CO 80517. ☎ **970/ 586-6151.** E-mail: baldpatein@aol.com. 16 units. $80 double with shared bathroom, $95 double with private bathroom; $140 cabin. Rates include full breakfast. DISC, MC, V. Closed Oct–Apr.

Built in 1917, the Baldpate was named for the novel *Seven Keys to Baldpate,* a murder mystery in which seven visitors believe each possesses the only key to the hotel. In 1996 the Baldpate was added to the National Register of Historic Places. Guests today can watch several movie versions of the story, read the book, and add their keys to the hotel's collection of more than 20,000 keys.

Baldpate is located 7 miles south of Estes Park, adjacent to Rocky Mountain National Park at an elevation of 9,000 feet. Guests can enjoy complimentary refreshments by the handsome stone fireplace in the lobby, relax on the large sundeck, view free videos on the library VCR, or walk the nature trails. Each of the early-20th-century–style rooms is unique, with handmade quilts on the beds. In summer, an excellent soup-and-salad buffet is served for lunch and dinner daily (see "Where to Dine," below). Smoking is not permitted.

✪ **Estes Park Center/YMCA of the Rockies.** 2515 Tunnel Rd., Estes Park, CO 80511-2550. ☎ **970/586-3341,** or 303/448-1616 direct from Denver. 530 rms (450 with bathroom), 205 cabins. Lodge rooms, summer $48–$89, winter $34–$62; cabins, year-round $53–$223. YMCA membership required (available at a nominal charge). No credit cards. Pets are permitted in the cabins but not the lodge rooms.

This extremely popular family lodge is an ideal place to get away from it all and serves as a great home base while exploring the Estes Park area. Lodge units are basic but perfectly adequate, and many were completely renovated in 1998. The spacious mountain cabins are equipped with two to four bedrooms (accommodating up to 10), complete kitchens, and phones; some have fireplaces. The center, which occupies 860 wooded acres, offers hiking, horseback riding, miniature golf, an indoor heated swimming pool and children's pool, fishing, biking (rentals available), three tennis courts, and cross-country skiing. Other facilities include conference rooms and a self-service laundry.

Glacier Lodge. Colo. 66 (P.O. Box 2656), Estes Park, CO 80517. ☎ **800/523-3920** or 970/586-4401. 28 units. TV. Early June to late Aug, $95–$160; late May to early June and late Aug to late Sept, $85–$130. Early to late May and late Sept through Oct, $80–$98. Closed Nov–Apr. MC, V.

Deer and elk frequently visit these lovely cottages, spread across 15 wooded acres along the Big Thompson River. Poolside chalets sleep up to six; cozy, homey river duplexes with decks overlook the stream; and river triplexes range from earthy to country quaint in decor. All have a porch or patio, and almost all feature kitchens and fireplaces, with firewood provided. Facilities include a swimming pool, sport court, playground, fishing, gift shop, ice-cream shop, lending library, and stables. Breakfast cookouts, barbecues, and special kids' activities are held in summer (extra charge).

Inexpensive

H-Bar-G Ranch Hostel. 3500 H-Bar-G Rd., off Dry Gulch Rd. (P.O. Box 1260), Estes Park, CO 80517. ☎ **970/586-3688.** Fax 970/5869-5004. E-mail: h-bar-g@indra.com. 100 beds (20 with bathroom). Memorial Day–Labor Day, $9 per bed. Hostelling International membership required. Closed Labor Day to Memorial Day. MC, V.

Bring a sleeping bag to throw on your dorm bunk, and be prepared to pitch in with daily chores—that's the hostelling tradition. There are separate accommodations for men and women, and family cabins with private bathrooms are available by advance reservation. Everyone shares the kitchen and game room. Other facilities include tennis and volleyball courts, barbecues, and a fireplace. Hiking trails lead into the national forest. The hostel is located 5½ miles northeast of Lake Estes in the national forest (elevation 8,200 feet), with easy access to Rocky Mountain National Park. Check-in is between 5:15 and 9pm. Pickup is available at 5pm daily at the Estes Park Tourist Information Center.

CAMPING

In addition to the following commercial campgrounds in the Estes Park area, see "Camping" in Rocky Mountain National Park, later in this chapter.

Mary's Lake Campground. 2120 Mary's Lake Rd. (P.O. Box 2514), Estes Park, CO 80517. ☎ **800/445-6279** or 970/586-4411. Fax 970/586-4493. E-mail: maryslake@aol.com. 150 sites. $19–$25 per campsite for two people. Extra person (over age 5) $2. Rates include cable TV hookups; $2 extra for A/C or electric heater use. Open May 15 through Sept. AE, DISC, MC, V.

Here you'll find campsites for everything from tents to 40-foot RVs, with full hookups. Facilities include bathhouses, laundry, dump station, playground, basketball court, small store, heated swimming pool, and game room. Fishing licenses, bait, and tackle for shore fishing at the lake and stream fishing in the national park are available.

National Park Resort, Cabins, and Campground. 3501 Fall River Rd., Estes Park, CO 80517. ☎ **970/586-4563.** 100 sites. $19–$22 per campsite for two people; extra person $2. Lodging units $50–$130; extra person $10. DISC, MC, V. Campground and motel units open May–Sept; cabins open year-round.

This wooded campground can accommodate both tents and RVs. Full hookups include electric, water, sewer, and cable TV. Facilities include bathhouses, laundry, grocery store, and a livery stable. There are also four cabins and five motel units.

Spruce Lake R.V. Park. U.S. 36 and Mary's Lake Rd. (P.O. Box 2497), Estes Park, CO 80517. ☎ **970/586-2889.** 110 sites. $15–$28 with hookups. Extra fees for cable TV and A/C or electric heater use. MC, V. Open Apr–Oct 15.

This meticulously well-maintained campground offers a heated pool, free miniature golf, large playground, stocked private fishing lake, large sites, and spotless bathhouses. There are Sunday pancake breakfasts and weekly ice-cream socials. Ground tents are not permitted. Reservations are strongly recommended, especially in summer.

WHERE TO DINE

In addition to the restaurants described here, see the Lazy B Ranch under "Arts & Entertainment," below.

Expensive

The Dunraven Inn. 2470 Colo. 66. ☎ **970/586-6409.** Reservations highly recommended. Main courses $8–$28. AE, DISC, MC, V. Sun–Thurs 5–10pm; Fri–Sat 5–11pm; closes slightly earlier in winter. ITALIAN.

Images of the *Mona Lisa*—ranging from a mustachioed lady to opera posters—litter the walls, and autographed dollar bills are posted in the lounge area. House specialties include shrimp scampi, linguine with white clam sauce, and Dunraven Italiano (an 11-ounce charbroiled sirloin steak in a sauce of peppers, onions, and tomatoes). There's a wide choice of pastas, seafood, vegetarian plates, and desserts, plus a children's menu. Smoking is permitted in only one room.

Moderate

La Casa of Estes Park. 222 E. Elkhorn Ave. ☎ **970/586-2807.** Reservations recommended. Main courses $5–$15. AE, CB, DC, DISC, MC, V. Daily 11am–9:30pm. MEXICAN/CAJUN/AMERICAN.

This downtown restaurant, which looks out at the park across the street, is a good choice when you're in the mood for Kansas City–style barbecue. Or you might try blackened fish, mesquite chicken, or a spicy beef burrito. Burgers and sandwiches are also on the menu.

Molly B's. 200 Moraine Ave. ☎ **970/586-2766.** Reservations recommended for dinner. Breakfast $2.50–$7, lunch $4–$7, dinner $6–$17. AE, MC, V. Apr–Sept, Thurs–Tues 6:30am–3pm and 4–9pm; closed Oct–Mar. AMERICAN.

The friendly staff makes you feel right at home in this casual, popular restaurant. Menu choices include vegetarian entrees, fresh seafood, pasta, prime rib, and steak. Desserts are homemade, and beer and wine are served. A children's menu is available, plus patio dining in good weather.

Inexpensive

✪ **Baldpate Inn.** 4900 S. Colo. 7. ☎ **970/586-6151.** Reservations recommended. Buffet $9.75 adults, $7.75 children under 10. DISC, MC, V. Memorial Day–Oct 1, daily 11:30am–7pm. SOUP/SALAD.

Don't be misled by the simple cuisine—the buffet is deliciously filling and plentiful. Everything is freshly prepared on the premises, with the cooks barely staying one muffin ahead of the guests. Soups—a choice of two is offered each day—include hearty stews, chili, a marvelous chicken rice, garden vegetable, and classic French onion. The salad bar provides fresh greens and an array of toppings, chunks of cheese, and fruit and vegetable salads. Honey-wheat bread is a staple, plus wonderful rolls, muffins, and cornbread. Topping off the meal are fresh homemade pies and cappuccino. Smoking is not permitted.

Estes Park Brewery. 470 Prospect Village Dr. ☎ **970/586-5421.** $5–$7. AE, CB, DC, DISC, MC, V. Summer daily 11am–midnight; closes earlier in winter. AMERICAN.

Pizzas, burgers, sandwiches—including meatball and grilled turkey—and bratwurst made with the brewery's own beer are the fare here. There's also a veggie burger and a variety of salads, plus a children's menu. The brewery specializes in Belgian-style ales, such as Longs Peak Raspberry Wheat, and also produces an excellent India pale ale.

ARTS & ENTERTAINMENT

There's plenty to do in Estes Park, especially in summer, ranging from chamber music concerts to Broadway musicals to knee-slapping western music. For details on what's going on when you plan to be in town, contact the **Cultural Arts Council of Estes Park,** P.O. Box 4135, Estes Park, CO 80517 (☎ **970/586-9203;** www.estes.on-line.cacep or www.longspeak.com/highway/arts-council), an umbrella organization for about 30 area arts groups.

Among individual organizations presenting live productions is the **Fine Arts Guild of the Rockies,** which sponsors a musical and two plays each year; past offerings have included *South Pacific, Crimes of the Heart, Mame,* and *Harvey.* The Guild also produces arts-and-crafts shows and festivals. **Estes Park Music Festival** presents a series of classical music concerts each summer, and the **Chamber Music Society of Estes Park** offers three concerts in early October.

The **Lazy B Ranch,** 1915 Dry Gulch Rd. (☎ **800/228-2116** or 970/586-5371), serves a chuck-wagon supper with a western show. There's also a program on the history of western music. Cost is $14 for everyone 13 and older, $11 for those 10 to 12 years old, and $7 for children 3 to 9. To get there, take U.S. 34 east from Estes Park about 1½ miles, turn left at Sombrero Stables, and follow the signs. The ranch is open from early June to Labor Day.

For live rock music and dancing, check out **Lonigan's Saloon,** 110 W. Elkhorn Ave. (☎ **970/586-4346**).

GRAND LAKE

The western entrance to Rocky Mountain National Park is at the picturesque little town of Grand Lake, in the shade of Shadow Mountain at the park's southwestern corner.

Here, in the crisp mountain air at 8,370 feet above sea level, you can stroll down an old-fashioned boardwalk on Grand Avenue alongside a local resident on horseback. Located within the Arapahoe National Recreation Area, Grand Lake is surrounded by three lakes—Grand Lake, Shadow Mountain Reservoir, and Lake Granby—each with a marina that offers boating (with rentals), fishing, and other water sports. Throughout the recreation area you'll also find miles of trails for hiking, horseback riding, four-wheeling, and mountain biking that become cross-country skiing and snowmobiling trails in winter.

The Grand Lake Yacht Club hosts the **Grand Lake Regatta** and **Lipton Cup Races** every August. The club was organized in 1902, and the regatta began 10 years later. Sailboats from around the world compete to win the prestigious Lipton Cup, given to the club by Thomas Lipton in 1912. Other summer events include an enormous Fourth of July fireworks display; Western Week, with a buffalo barbecue and mountain man rendezvous, in mid-July; and the Arts and Crafts Festival in late August.

Open daily in summer is the **Kaufman House,** 407 Pitkin Ave. (☎ **970/627-3351**), an early log structure that serves as the museum of the Grand Lake Historical Society. Golfers may want to test their skills at the 18-hole championship **Grand Lake Golf Course** (☎ **970/627-8008**), altitude 8,420 feet.

For further information on these and other activities, stop at the Visitor Information Center on U.S. 34 at the turnoff into town; or contact the **Grand Lake Area Chamber of Commerce,** P.O. Box 57, Grand Lake, CO 80447 (☎ **800/531-1019** or 970/627-3372; 970/627-3402 visitor center; fax 970/627-8007;

www.grandlakecolorado.com). Information is also available from the forest service's **Sulphur Ranger District office,** (P.O. Box 10), 9 Ten Rd., off U.S. 40 about a half-mile south of Granby, CO 80446 (☎ 970/887-4100).

There are plenty of places to stay and eat in Grand Lake. Lodging possibilities include the **Bighorn Lodge,** 613 Grand Ave. (☎ 800/341-8000 or 970/627-8101), a well-maintained motel with rates of $60 to $85 for two persons in summer, $5 to $10 less in winter; and the **Daven Haven Lodge,** 604 Marina Dr. (☎ 970/627-8144; fax 970/627-5098), with a variety of cabins that cost $68 to $140 for two. Among our choices for a bite to eat are **Chuck Hole Cafe,** 1131 Grand Ave. (☎ 970/627-3509), open daily for breakfast and lunch ($2 to $6); and **EG's Garden Grill,** 1000 Grand Ave. (☎ 970/627-8404), also open daily, serving light, healthy lunches and dinners ($7 to $20).

2 Rocky Mountain National Park

Snow-covered peaks—17 mountains above 13,000 feet—stand over lush valleys and shimmering alpine lakes in the 415 square miles (265,727 acres) that comprise Rocky Mountain National Park. The highest, at 14,255 feet, is Longs Peak.

But what really sets the park apart (after all, this sort of eye-popping beauty is not unusual in the Rockies) is its variety of distinct ecological zones. As you rise and descend in altitude, the landscape of the park changes dramatically. In relatively low areas, from about 7,500 to 9,000 feet, a lush forest of ponderosa pine and juniper cloaks the sunny southern slopes, with Douglas fir on the cooler northern slopes. Thirstier blue spruce and lodgepole pine cling to streamsides, with occasional groves of aspen. Elk and mule deer thrive. On higher slopes, a subalpine ecosystem exists, dominated by forests of Engelmann spruce and subalpine fir, but interspersed with wide meadows alive with wildflowers during spring and summer. This is also home to bighorn sheep, which have become unofficial mascots of the park. Above 11,500 feet, the trees become increasingly gnarled and stunted, until they disappear altogether and alpine tundra predominates. Fully one-third of the park is at this altitude, and in this bleak, rocky world, many of the plants are identical to those found in the Arctic.

Trail Ridge Road, the park's primary east–west roadway, is one of America's great alpine highways. It cuts west through the middle of the park from Estes Park, then south down its western boundary to Grand Lake. Climbing to 12,183 feet near Fall River Pass, it's the highest continuous paved highway in the United States. The road is usually open from Memorial Day into October, depending on the snowfall. The 48-mile scenic drive from Estes Park to Grand Lake takes about three hours, allowing for stops at numerous scenic outlooks. Exhibits at the **Alpine Visitor Center** (open in summer, daily from 9am to 5pm) at Fall River Pass, 11,796 feet above sea level, explain life on the alpine tundra.

Fall River Road, the original park road, leads to Fall River Pass from Estes Park via Horseshoe Park Junction. West of the Endovalley picnic area, the road is one-way uphill, and closed to trailers and motor homes. As you negotiate its gravelly switchbacks, you get a clear idea of what early auto travel was like in the West. This road, too, is closed in winter.

One of the few paved roads in the Rockies that leads into a high mountain basin is **Bear Lake Road**; it is kept open year-round, with occasional half-day closings to clear snow. Numerous trails converge at Bear Lake, southwest of the Park Headquarters/Visitor Center, via Moraine Park.

Rocky Mountain National Park

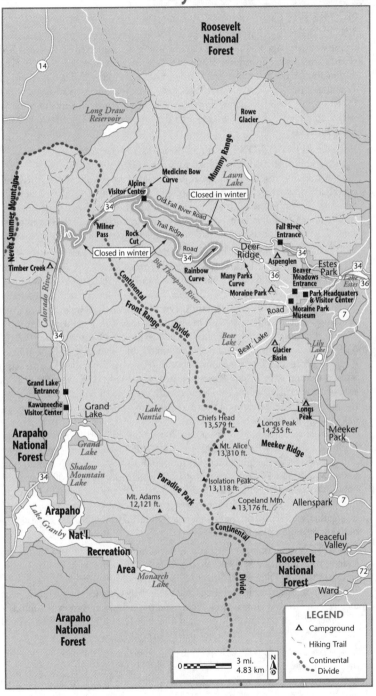

Roosevelt National Forest

14

Long Draw Reservoir

Rowe Glacier

Mummy Range

Lawn Lake

Medicine Bow Curve

Alpine Visitor Center

Old Fall River Road

Closed in winter

Milner Pass

34

Rock Cut

Trail Ridge

Fall River Entrance

Road

34

Timber Creek △

Closed in winter

Road

34

Rainbow Curve

Deer Ridge

Aspenglen △

Estes Park

34

Many Parks Curve

Beaver Meadows Entrance

36

36

Big Thompson River

Continental

Moraine Park

Park Headquaters & Visitor Center

Lake Estes

Colorado River

Front Range

Divide

Road

Moraine Park Museum

7

Bear Lake

Bear Lake

Glacier Basin △

Lily Lake

34

Grand Lake Entrance

Kawuneeche Visitor Center

Grand Lake

Lake Nantia

Chiefs Head 13,579 ft. ▲

Longs Peak △

Longs Peak 14,255 ft. ▲

Meeker Park

Arapaho National Forest

Grand Lake

Shadow Mountain Lake

Mt. Alice 13,310 ft. ▲

Meeker Ridge

34

Paradise Park

Isolation Peak 13,118 ft. ▲

Lake Granby

Arapaho Nat'l.

Mt. Adams 12,121 ft. ▲

Copeland Mtn. 13,176 ft. ▲

Allenspark

7

Recreation

Continental

Peaceful Valley

Area

Monarch Lake

Roosevelt National Forest

72

Ward

Arapaho National Forest

Divide

LEGEND

△ Campground

Hiking Trail

Continental Divide

0   3 mi.
4.83 km

N

JUST THE FACTS

ENTRY POINTS   Entry into the park is from either the east (through Estes Park) or the west (through Grand Lake). The two sides are connected by the **Trail Ridge Road**. The **Beaver Meadows Entrance,** west of Estes Park via U.S. 36, is the national park's main entrance and the best way to get to the visitor center and Park Headquarters. U.S. 34 west from Estes Park takes you to the **Fall River Entrance** (north of the Beaver Meadows Entrance). Those entering the park from the west side should take U.S. 40 to Granby and then follow U.S. 34 north to the **Grand Lake Entrance**.

FEES & REGULATIONS   Park admission is $10 per week per vehicle, $5 for bicyclists and pedestrians. An annual park pass costs $20.

As is true for most of the national parks, wilderness permits are required for all overnight backpacking trips, and camping is allowed only in specified campsites. Pets must be leashed at all times, and are not permitted on trails or into the backcountry. Both motor vehicles and bicycles must remain on the roads or in parking areas. Do not feed or touch any park animals, and do not pick any wildflowers.

VISITOR CENTERS & INFORMATION   Entering the park from Estes Park, it's wise to stop first at **Park Headquarters/Visitor Center,** U.S. 36, west of Colo. 66 (☎ **970/586-1206**). Here you will find knowledgeable people to answer questions and give advice, a wide choice of books and maps for sale, and an interpretive exhibit, including a relief model of the park and an audiovisual program. In summer, this center is open daily from 8am to 9pm; in winter, daily from 8am to 5pm.

Near the park's west side entrance is the **Kawuneeche Visitor Center** (☎ **970/627-3471**), open in summer daily from 7am to 7pm, in winter daily from 8am to 4:30pm. Located high in the mountains (11,796 feet above sea level) is the **Alpine Visitor Center,** at Fall River Pass, open in summer only, daily from 9am to 5pm; exhibits here explain life on the alpine tundra. Visitor facilities are also available at the **Moraine Park Museum** on Bear Lake Road, open mid-June to mid-September, daily from 9am to 5pm.

For more specifics on planning a trip, contact Superintendent, Rocky Mountain National Park, Estes Park, CO 80517 (☎ **970/586-1206**; www.nps.gov/romo). You can also get detailed information from the **Rocky Mountain Nature Association** (☎ **800/816-7662** or 970/586-0108), which sells a variety of maps, guides, books, and videos (including some in PAL format). Those who would like to help this nonprofit association, and receive a 15% discount on purchases at this and most other national parks and monuments, can join. Memberships cost $15 for individuals and $25 for families.

SEASONS   Even though the park is technically open daily year-round, Trail Ridge Road, the main east-west thoroughfare through the park, is almost always closed in winter. The road is usually open by late May (after the snow has been cleared) and closes again between mid- and late October. However, it is not uncommon for snow storms to close the road for several hours or even a full day at any time, but especially in early June and October. The high country is open during the summer and as snow conditions permit in winter.

AVOIDING THE CROWDS   Because large portions of the park are closed half the year, practically everyone visits during the other half of the year: spring and summer. The busiest period, though, is from mid-June to mid-August—essentially during school vacations. In order to avoid the largest crowds, try to visit just before or just after that period. For those who don't mind chilly evenings, late September and early October are less crowded and can be beautiful, although there's always the chance of an early winter storm. Regardless of when you visit, the absolute best way to avoid crowds is by putting on a backpack or climbing onto a horse. Rocky Mountain has 355 miles of trails leading into all corners of the park (see "Sports & Outdoor Activities In & Around the Park," below).

RANGER PROGRAMS   Campfire talks and other programs are offered at each visitor center between June and September. Consult the park's free *High Country Headlines* newspaper for scheduled activities, which vary from photo walks to fly-fishing and orienteering.

SEEING THE HIGHLIGHTS

Although Rocky Mountain National Park is generally considered the domain of hikers and climbers, it's surprisingly easy to thoroughly enjoy this park without working up a sweat. For that we can thank **Trail Ridge Road**.

Built in 1932 and undoubtedly one of America's most scenic highways, it provides expansive and sometimes dizzying views in all directions. The drive from Estes Park to Grand Lake covers some 48 miles through the park, rising above 12,000 feet in elevation and crossing the Continental Divide. It offers spectacular vistas of snow-capped peaks, deep forests, and meadows of wildflowers, where bighorn sheep, elk, and deer browse. Allow at least 3 hours for the drive, and possibly more if you'd like to take a short hike from one of the many vista points.

To get a close look at the tundra, pull off Trail Ridge Road into the **Rock Cut** parking area (elevation 12,110 feet), about halfway along the scenic drive. The views of glacially carved peaks along the Continental Divide are spectacular, and signs on the half-mile Tundra Nature Trail identify the hardy plants and animals that inhabit the region and explain how they have adapted to the harsh environment.

SPORTS & OUTDOOR ACTIVITIES IN & AROUND THE PARK

Estes Park is a major center for outdoor recreation. In addition to Rocky Mountain National Park, many activities take place in the 1,240-square-mile Roosevelt National Forest. Obtain information on hiking, horseback riding, fishing, and other activities in advance from the **Canyon Lakes Ranger District Office,** 1311 S. College Ave., Fort Collins, CO 80524 (☎ **970/498-2770**). In Estes Park, a **Forest Service Information Center** is located at 161 Second St. (☎ **970/ 586-3440**); it's open daily from 9am to 5pm in summer, and from 9am to 2pm several days a week in winter.

BICYCLING   Bicyclists must pay a $5 weekly fee to enter Rocky Mountain National Park, and in most cases will have to share the roadways with motor vehicles along narrow roads with 5% to 7% grades. Like most national parks, bikes are not permitted off established roads. However, bicyclists still enjoy the challenge and scenery. One popular 16-mile ride is the **Horseshoe Park/Estes Park Loop,** which goes from Estes Park west on U.S. 34 past Aspenglen Campground and the park's Fall River entrance, and then heads east again at the Deer Ridge Junction, following U.S. 36 through the Beaver Meadows park entrance. There are plenty of beautiful mountain views; allow from 1 to 3 hours. A free park brochure provides information on safety, regulations, and other suggested routes. Tours, rentals, and repairs are available at **Colorado Bicycling,** 184 E. Elkhorn Ave., Estes Park (☎ **800/607-8765** or 970/586-4241). Bike rentals start at about $6 per hour, and the company also offers guided road trips in the park ranging in price from $50 to $70 per person.

BOATING   The small Lake Estes, with a marina a half-mile east of Estes Park along U.S. 34, covers 185 acres. It's popular with boaters and fishermen, although a bit cool for swimming. The marina (☎ **970/586-2011**), open from Memorial Day to mid-September, sells fishing licenses and supplies (plus a few groceries) and rents boats and bikes. Canoes rent for $10 an hour, paddleboats for $13 an hour, fishing boats with a small outboard motor for $15 an hour, small sportboats for $18 an hour, and seven-person pontoon boats for $29 an hour. Rental mountain bikes cost $5 per hour, tandem bikes cost $6 an hour, and surrey bikes cost $12 per hour.

CLIMBING & MOUNTAINEERING   **Colorado Mountain School,** P.O. Box 2062, Estes Park, CO 80517 (☎ **970/586-5758**), is a year-round guide service and a national-park–sanctioned technical climbing school that caters to all ages. The most popular climb is Longs Peak (the highest mountain in the park). It can be ascended by those without experience via the "Keyhole," but its north and east faces are for experts only. Rates vary, and the larger the group the less per person, but the base rate for one person for half- and full-day excursions ranges from $75 to $300. The school also operates a small store, and offers lodging in a hostel-type setting, at about $20 per night per person. (See also "Hiking & Backpacking," below.) Be sure to stop at the ranger station at the Longs Peak trailhead for current trail and weather information before attempting to ascend Longs Peak.

EDUCATIONAL PROGRAMS   The **Rocky Mountain Nature Association,** Rocky Mountain National Park, Estes Park, CO 80517 (☎ **970/586-0108**), offers a wide variety of seminars and workshops, ranging from half- and full-day to several days. Subjects include songbirds, flower identification, edible and medicinal herbs, painting, wildlife photography, tracking park animals, and edible mushrooms. Rates range from $25 to $50 for half- and full-day programs, and $65 to $175 for multi-day programs. Nature Association members receive 10% discounts. (See "Visitor Centers & Information," above.)

FISHING   Four species of trout are fished in national park and national forest streams and lakes: brown, rainbow, brook, and cutthroat. A state fishing license is required, and only artificial lures or flies are permitted in the park. A number of lakes and streams in the national park are closed to fishing, including Bear Lake; a list of open and closed bodies of water plus regulations and other information are available in a free park brochure that's available at visitor centers. Trout fishermen also head to Lake Estes (see "Boating," above).

GOLF   There are two nearby courses: **Estes Park Golf Course** (18 holes), 1080 S. St. Vrain St. (☎ **970/586-8146**), just off Colo. 7, charges $30 for 18 holes; and **Lake Estes Executive Golf Course**, 690 Big Thompson Hwy. (☎ **970/ 586-8176**), along U.S. 34 east of downtown Estes Park, charges $11 for nine holes and $16 for 18 holes.

HIKING & BACKPACKING   The Park Headquarters/Visitor Center offers U.S. Geological Survey topographic maps and guidebooks for sale, and rangers can direct you to lesser-used trails.

One particularly easy park hike is the **Alberta Falls Trail** from the Glacier Gorge Parking Area (0.6 mile one-way), which rises in elevation only 160 feet as it follows Glacier Creek to pretty Alberta Falls.

A slightly more difficult option is the **Bierstadt Lake Trail,** accessible from the north side of Bear Lake Road about 6.4 miles from Beaver Meadows. This 1.4-mile (one-way) trail climbs 566 feet through an aspen forest to Bierstadt Lake, where you'll find excellent views of Longs Peak.

Starting at Bear Lake, the trail up to **Emerald Lake** offers spectacular scenery en route, past Nymph and Dream Lakes. The half-mile hike to Nymph Lake is easy, climbing 225 feet; from there the trail is rated moderate to Dream Lake (another 0.6 miles) and then on to Emerald Lake (another 0.7 miles), which is 605 feet higher than the starting point at Bear Lake. Another moderate hike is the relatively uncrowded **Ouzel Falls Trail,** which leaves from Wild Basin Ranger Station and climbs about 950 feet to a picture-perfect waterfall. The distance one-way is 2.7 miles.

Among our favorite moderate hikes here is the ✪ **Mills Lake Trail,** a 2½-mile (one-way) hike, with a rise in elevation of about 700 feet. Starting from Glacier Gorge Junction, the trail goes up to a picturesque mountain lake, nestled in a valley among towering mountain peaks. This lake is an excellent spot for photographing dramatic Longs Peak, especially in late afternoon or early evening, and it's the perfect place for a picnic.

If you prefer a more strenuous adventure, you'll work hard but be amply rewarded with views of timberline lakes and alpine tundra on the **Timber Lake Trail,** in the western part of the park. It's 4.8 miles one-way, with an elevation gain of 2,060 feet. Another strenuous trail, only for experienced mountain hikers and climbers in top physical condition, is the 8-mile (one-way) **East Longs Peak Trail,** which climbs some 4,855 feet along steep ledges and through narrows to the top of Longs Peak.

Backcountry permits (required for all overnight hikes) can be obtained ($15 from May through October, free from November through April) at Park Headquarters and ranger stations (in summer); for information call ☎ **970/586-1242.** There is a seven-night backcountry camping limit from June to September, with no more than three nights at any one spot. Tents are not permitted in the backcountry in summer.

HORSEBACK RIDING   Many of the national park's trails are open to horseback riders, and a number of outfitters provide guided rides, both within and outside the park, ranging from one hour (about $20) to all day (about $75), plus breakfast and dinner rides and multi-day pack trips. Recommended companies include **Sombrero Ranch Stables,** opposite the Lake Estes dam at 1895 Big Thompson Hwy. (U.S. 34) (☎ 970/586-4577); the **National Park Village Stables** at the Fall River Entrance of the national park on U.S. 34 (☎ 970/586-5269); and the **Cowpoke Corner Corral,** at Glacier Lodge 3 miles west of town, 2166 Colo. 66 (☎ 970/ 586-5890). **Hi Country Stables** operates two stables inside the park—**Glacier Creek Stables** (☎ 970/586-3244) and **Moraine Park Stables** (☎ 970/586-2327).

RIVER RAFTING   For trips down the Colorado or Poudre Rivers, contact **Rapid Transit Rafting,** P.O. Box 4095, Estes Park, CO 80517 (☎ **800/367-8523** or 970/586-8852); they provide half-day and full-day river trips with transportation from Estes Park, starting at about $40 per person.

SKIING & SNOWSHOEING   A popular spot for cross-country skiing and snowshoeing in the park is Bear Lake, south of the Beaver Meadows entrance. A lesser known area of the park is Wild Basin, south of the park's east entrances off Colo. 7, about a mile north of the community of Allenspark. A 2-mile road, closed to motor vehicles for the last mile in winter, winds through a subalpine forest to the Wild Basin Trailhead, which follows a creek to a waterfall, a rustic bridge, and eventually to another waterfall. Total distance to the second falls is 2.7 miles. Along the trail, your chances are good for spotting birds such as Clark's nutcrackers, Steller's jays, and the American dipper. On winter weekends, the Colorado Mountain Club often opens a warming hut at the Wild Basin Ranger Station.

Before you set forth, stop by Park Headquarters for maps, information on where the snow is best, and a permit if you plan to stay out overnight. Ski rentals, instruction, and guide service are available from **Colorado Mountain School,** P.O. Box 2062, Estes Park, CO 80517 (☎ **970/586-5758**). Rangers also often lead guided snowshoe walks on winter weekends.

SNOWMOBILING   Snowmobiling is permitted on the west side of the park only, accessible in winter only from Grand Lake. Register at the **Kawuneeche Visitor Center** (☎ **970/627-3471**). The park speed limit for snowmobiles is 25 mph.

WILDLIFE VIEWING & BIRD WATCHING   Rocky Mountain National Park is a premier wildlife-viewing area; fall, winter, and spring are the best times. Large herds of elk and bighorn sheep can often be seen in the meadows and on mountainsides. In addition, you may spot mule deer, beavers, coyotes, and river otters. Watch for moose among the willows on the west side of the park. In the forests are lots of songbirds and small mammals; particularly plentiful are gray and Steller's jays, Clark's nutcrackers, chipmunks, and golden-mantled ground squirrels. There's a good chance of seeing bighorn sheep, marmots, pikas, and ptarmigan along Trail Ridge Road. For detailed and current wildlife viewing information, stop by one of the park's visitor centers, and check on the many interpretive programs, including bird walks.

CAMPING

The park has five campgrounds with a total of 589 sites. Nearly half (247 sites) are at **Moraine Park;** another 150 are at **Glacier Basin.** Moraine Park, **Timber Creek** (100 sites), and **Longs Peak** (26 tent sites) are open year round; Glacier Basin and **Aspenglen** (54 sites) are seasonal. Camping is limited to three days at Longs Peak and seven days at other campgrounds. Arrive early in summer if you hope to snare one of these first-come, first-served campsites. Moraine Park and Glacier Basin require reservations from Memorial Day through early September. Contact **Biospherics** (☎ **800/365-2267**). Campsites cost $12 to $14 per night during the summer, $10 in the off-season. No showers or RV hookups are available.

3 Steamboat Springs

158 miles NW of Denver, 194 miles E of Grand Junction, 335 miles E of Salt Lake City, Utah

A resort town that effectively fuses two very different worlds—a state-of-the-art ski village with a genuine western ranching center—Steamboat is where ranchers still go about their business in cowboy boots and Stetsons, seemingly unaware of the fashion statement they are making to city-slicker visitors.

At an elevation of 6,695 feet, Steamboat Springs' numerous mineral springs and abundant wild game made this a summer retreat for Utes centuries before the arrival of white settlers. Mid-19th-century trappers swore they heard the chugging sound of "a steamboat comin' round the bend" until investigation revealed a bubbling mineral spring. Prospectors never thrived here as they did elsewhere in the Rockies, though coal mining has proven profitable. Ranching and farming—cattle and sheep, hay, wheat, oats, and barley—were the economic mainstays until tourism arrived, yet agriculture remains of key importance today.

But this area is perhaps best known as the birthplace of organized skiing in Colorado. Although miners, ranchers, and mail carriers used primitive skis as a means of transportation as early as the late 1880s, it wasn't until a Norwegian ski-jumping and cross-country champion, Carl Howelsen, built a ski jump here in 1914 (Howelsen Hill) that skiing began to be considered a recreational sport in Colorado. In

Steamboat Springs

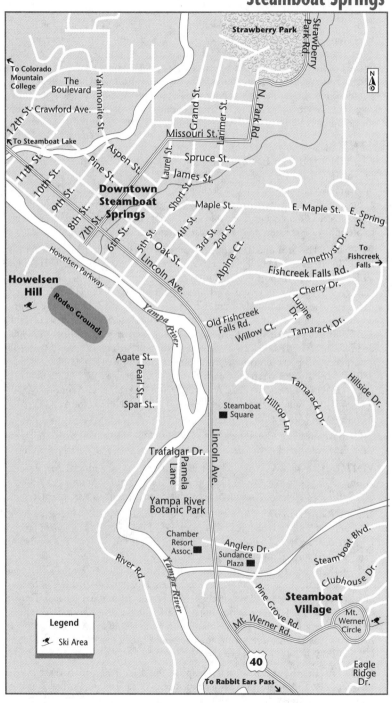

Strawberry Park

Strawberry Park Rd.

To Colorado Mountain College

The Boulevard

Crawford Ave.

Yahmonite St.

Grand St.

Larimer St.

N. Park Rd.

12th St.

Missouri St.

To Steamboat Lake

Aspen St.

Pine St.

Laurel St.

Spruce St.

James St.

11th St.

10th St.

9th St.

8th St.

7th St.

Downtown Steamboat Springs

Short St.

Maple St.

E. Maple St.

E. Spring St.

6th St.

5th St.

4th St.

3rd St.

2nd St.

Oak St.

Lincoln Ave.

Alpine Ct.

Amethyst Dr.

To Fishcreek Falls

Fishcreek Falls Rd.

Howelsen Parkway

Howelsen Hill

Rodeo Grounds

Old Fishcreek Falls Rd.

Cherry Dr.

Lupine Dr.

Willow Ct.

Tamarack Dr.

Yampa River

Agate St.

Pearl St.

Spar St.

Tamarack Dr.

Hillside Dr.

Steamboat Square

Hilltop Ln.

Trafalgar Dr.

Pamela Lane

Lincoln Ave.

Yampa River Botanic Park

Chamber Resort Assoc.

Anglers Dr.

Sundance Plaza

Steamboat Blvd.

River Rd.

Yampa River

Pine Grove Rd.

Clubhouse Dr.

Steamboat Village

Mt. Werner Circle

Legend

Ski Area

Mt. Werner Rd.

40

To Rabbit Ears Pass

Eagle Ridge Dr.

1963, a nearby mountain, Storm Mountain, was developed for skiing, and Steamboat's future as a modern ski resort was ensured. Renamed Mount Werner after the 1964 avalanche death in Europe of Olympic skier Buddy Werner, a Steamboat Springs native and staunch supporter of developing Storm Mountain into a full-fledged resort, today the mountain is managed by the Steamboat Ski & Resort Corporation and, more often than not, is called simply Steamboat. Howelsen Hill, owned by the city of Steamboat Springs, continues to operate primarily as a facility for ski jumpers.

ESSENTIALS

GETTING THERE   By Car   The most direct route to Steamboat Springs from Denver is via I-70 west 68 miles to Silverthorne, Colo. 9 north 38 miles to Kremmling, and U.S. 40 west 52 miles to Steamboat. (*Note:* Rabbit Ears Pass, 25 miles east of Steamboat, can be treacherous in winter.) If you're traveling east on I-70, exit at Rifle, proceed 88 miles north on Colo. 13 to Craig, then take U.S. 40 east 42 miles to Steamboat. For statewide **road-condition reports,** call ☎ **303/639-1234**.

By Plane   The **Steamboat Springs Airport,** 3 miles northwest of town on Elk River Road (☎ 970/879-9042), serves charter and private flights. The **Yampa Valley Regional Airport,** 22 miles west of Steamboat Springs near Hayden (☎ 970/276-3669), is served by **United Express** (☎ 800/241-6522 or 970/276-4116), with year-round commuter service from Denver. During the winter, direct flights to major U.S. cities are available from **American Airlines** (☎ 800/433-7300), **United Airlines** (☎ 800/241-6522), **Continental Airlines** (☎ 800/523-3273), **TWA** (☎ 800/221-2000), and **Northwest Airlines** (☎ 800/225-2525).

Ground transportation is provided by **Alpine Taxi-Limo** (☎ 800/343-7433 or 970/879-2800) and **Western Coach Limousine Service** (☎ 970/870-0771). Local car-rental agencies include **Avis** (☎ 970/879-3785) and **Alamo** (☎ 800/327-9633). At Yampa Valley Regional Airport (see above), look for **Avis** (☎ 970/276-4377) and **Dollar** (☎ 970/276-3702).

By Airport Shuttle   **Alpine Taxi-Limo** (☎ **800/343-7433** or 970/879-2800), provides daily year-round service between Denver International and Steamboat Springs.

VISITOR INFORMATION   The **Steamboat Springs Chamber Resort Association,** 1255 S. Lincoln Ave. (P.O. Box 774408), Steamboat Springs, CO 80477 (☎ **970/879-0880**; www.steamboat-chamber.com), operates a visitor center.

GETTING AROUND   There are really two Steamboats. The ski resort, known as Steamboat Village, is about 2 miles southeast of the historic Steamboat Springs. If you're coming from Denver, U.S. 40 approaches Steamboat from the south and parallels the Yampa River through town. Mount Werner Road, which turns east off U.S. 40, leads directly to the ski resort, centered around Mount Werner Circle and Ski Time Square. U.S. 40 is known as Lincoln Avenue through the town of Steamboat, where it is crossed by 3rd through 13th Streets. **Steamboat Springs Transit** (☎ **970/879-5585**) provides free rides throughout the area. During ski season, buses run every 15 minutes in peak hours; during the rest of the year, buses run less frequently, about once every half hour at peak travel times. **Alpine Taxi-Limo** (☎ **970/879-8294**) provides taxi service.

FAST FACTS   Routt Memorial Hospital, 80 Park Ave., off Seventh Street (☎ **970/879-1322**), provides 24-hour medical service. The **post office** is at 200 Lincoln Ave. For hours and other information contact the U.S. Postal Service (☎ **800/275-8777**). For **road information,** call ☎ 970/879-1260.

SPECIAL EVENTS   Cowboy Downhill, second week in January; Winter Carnival, early February; Yampa River Festival and Steamboat Marathon, early June; Cowboy Roundup Days, Fourth of July weekend; Vintage Auto Race, Labor Day weekend; Fall Foliage Festival, late September; Torchlight Parade, New Year's Eve.

SKIING & OTHER WINTER ACTIVITIES

STEAMBOAT   When devoted skiers describe Steamboat, they practically invent adjectives to describe its incredibly light powder.

Five peaks comprise the ski area: Mount Werner, Christie, Storm, Sunshine, and Thunderhead. Christie Peak, the lower mountain area, is ideal for beginners. Thunderhead Peak, served by a high-speed detachable quad chairlift called the Thunderhead Express and the Silver Bullet gondola, is great for intermediate and advanced skiers and riders. Arrowhead Glade provides an advanced playground for everybody.

The Morningside Park lift accesses the extreme double black diamond terrain—chutes, advanced mogul runs, powder bowls, and one-of-a-kind tree skiing, all from the top of Mt. Werner. "Buddy's Run," one of the Rockies' great intermediate cruisers, is located on Storm Peak. The most famous tree runs—"Shadows," "Closet," and "Twilight"—are on Sunshine Peak, along with more bump runs and cruising slopes. Morningside Park includes 179 acres on the back of Storm Peak, with intermediate to advanced terrain served by a triple chair.

Three separate restaurants, not including the ski-school cafeteria, are located at the top of the gondola terminal. In Rendezvous Saddle, midmountain in the saddle of "High Noon," are two more restaurants.

The 1997–98 season saw the opening of 260 acres on Pioneer Ridge, with eight trails for intermediate and advanced skiers and riders. The 1998–99 season will see the addition of seven trails and four glades in that area plus a new high-speed detachable quad lift, the Pony Express. Top to bottom snowmaking coverage goes into effect this season also, assuring quality snow throughout the ski area.

The vertical drop here is among the highest in Colorado: 3,668 feet from the 10,568-foot summit. Skiable terrain of 2,939 acres (61% groomable) includes 139 named runs, served by 22 lifts—an eight-passenger high-speed gondola, four high-speed express quad chairs, six triple chairs, six double chairs, and four surface lifts.

Lift tickets (1998–99 rates) are $48 per day for adults, $28 per day for children 12 and under, and $29 per day for ages 65 to 69; seniors 70 and over ski free with photo ID. Lessons and rentals are available, and the resort also has 30km of cross-country skiing at the **Steamboat Ski Touring Center** (☎ 907/879-8180).

Steamboat is a great mountain for snowboarders, with several terrain parks: The Dude Ranch is a competition halfpipe; Sunshine Reef has various jumps, slides, and obstacles; and Beehive, just for kids, is on the Giggle Gulch Trail on Christie Peak.

Snowshoe tours provide an alternative way to see Mt. Werner. They're offered for all levels of snowshoers, departing from the top of the Silver Bullet Gondola. Rentals are available from **Steamboat Ski Rentals** (☎ 970/879-6111, ext. 345).

The Mountain Hosts, Steamboat's information and mountain tour specialists, provide information about skiing, snowboarding, and snowshoeing, plus daily grooming sheets, mountain tours, lost and found, and general information. Hosts can be found in the Information Center (across from the lift ticket windows, open daily from 8am to 5pm) and on the mountain.

Steamboat is usually open from the third week in November through mid-April, daily from 8:30am to 4pm. For further information, contact **Steamboat Ski & Resort Corporation,** 2305 Mt. Werner Circle, Steamboat Springs, CO 80487

(☎ 800/922-2722 or 970/879-6111; fax 970/879-4757; www.steamboat-ski. com; e-mail: steamboat-info@steamboat-ski.com). For daily **ski reports,** dial ☎ 970/879-7300.

HOWELSEN HILL   In addition to Steamboat, there's Howelsen Hill (☎ 970/ 879-8499; www.ci.steamboat.co.us), which has remained open every winter since its first day in 1915. The first accredited public-school ski classes in North America were taught on this slope. It offers both day and night skiing on its 30 acres of terrain served by a double chair, a poma lift, and a pony tow. It rises 440 feet to a 7,136-foot summit elevation. Tickets (1998–99 rates) are $10 for adults and $5 for children 12 and under, with lower rates for night skiing.

Howelsen Hill has bred more North American skiers for international competition than any other—primarily because of its ski-jumping complex. The U.S. ski-jumping team trains each year on the 20-, 30-, 50-, 70-, and 90-meter jumps.

CROSS-COUNTRY SKIING   Seasoned cross-country skiers swear by the **Steamboat Ski Touring Center** at the Sheraton Steamboat Resort and Conference Center, Clubhouse Road (☎ 970/879-8180). Some 30 kilometers (about 18½ miles) of groomed cross-country trails are set across the fairways beside Fish Creek, near the foot of the mountain. Fees are about $10 a day; equipment rentals and lessons are available. There are also cross-country trails at Howelsen Hill.

Popular cross-country skiing trails in nearby national forest land include **Rabbit Ears Pass,** 25 miles east of Steamboat on U.S. 40, and **Dunkley Pass,** 25 miles south on Colo. 131. For trail maps and information, contact **Medicine Bow-Routt National Forest,** Hahns Peak/Bears Ears Ranger Station, 57 10th St. (P.O. Box 771212), Steamboat Springs, CO 80477 (☎ 970/879-1870).

ICE CLIMBING   For equipment and tips on the best spots for ice climbing, contact **Backdoor Sports of Steamboat,** 811 Yampa St. (☎ 970/879-6249).

ICE DRIVING   America's first school of ice driving is based in Steamboat Springs at the foot of Mount Werner. Bridgestone Winter Driving School teaches safe winter driving the smartest way possible—hands-on, on a 1-mile circuit packed with frozen water and snow, and guarded by high snow banks. Classes combine instruction with on-track practice, and are available for average drivers as well as professionals. Classes include a half-day introductory course ($115) and the most popular—a full-day course for $225. There's also a two-day performance course for $975. The school is open daily from mid-December to early March, and reservations are recommended. Contact **Bridgestone Winter Driving School,** 1850 Ski Time Square Dr. (P.O. Box 774167), Steamboat Springs, CO 80477 (☎ 800/ 949-7543 WHYSKID or 970/879-6104; www.winterdrive.com).

ICE-SKATING   The **Howelsen Ice Arena,** 243 Howelsen Parkway (☎ 970/ 879-0341), rents skates; offers lessons in hockey and figure skating; organizes figure-skating, ice-hockey and broomball competitions; and hosts birthday parties. The season generally runs from early October through late May. Admission is $3.50, free for children 5 and under; skate rentals are $2. Call for the rink schedule.

SNOWMOBILING   Snowmobilers consider the **Continental Divide Trail,** running over 50 miles from Buffalo Pass north of Steamboat to Gore Pass, west of Kremmling, to be one of the finest maintained trails in the Rockies, with some of the most spectacular scenery you'll see anywhere. For information, check with Medicine Bow-Routt National Forest (see "Cross-Country Skiing," above). Among those offering snowmobile tours are **High Mountain Snowmobile Tours** (☎ 970/ 879-9073), **Steamboat Snowmobile Tours** (☎ 970/879-6500), and **Steamboat**

Lake Outfitters (☎ 970/879-4404). All offer half-day, day, and dinner tours, with rates starting at about $70 for a 2-hour ride.

WARM-WEATHER & YEAR-ROUND ACTIVITIES

Most outdoor recreation pursuits are enjoyed in 1.1-million-acre **Routt National Forest,** which virtually surrounds Steamboat Springs. With elevations ranging from 6,750 to 13,553 feet, the national forest offers opportunities for camping, hiking, backpacking, mountain biking, horseback riding, fishing, and hunting. For trail maps and information, contact **Medicine Bow-Routt National Forest,** Hahns Peak/Bears Ears Ranger Station, 57 10th St. (P.O. Box 771212), Steamboat Springs, CO 80477 (☎ **970/879-1870**).

Howelsen Hill (☎ **970/879-8499**) offers several warm-weather activities. You'll find a BMX and skateboard park, tennis, softball, volleyball, horseback riding, and mountain biking, plus the rodeo grounds (see below).

Two wilderness areas in the forest are easily reached from Steamboat. Immediately north of town is the **Mount Zirkel Wilderness Area,** a region of rugged peaks approached through 10,800-foot Buffalo Pass, on Forest Road 60 off Strawberry Park Road via Seventh Street. Southwest of Stillwater Reservoir, some 40 miles south of Steamboat via Colo. 131 through Yampa, is the **Flat Tops Wilderness Area,** with picturesque alpine meadows and sheer volcanic cliffs. No motorized vehicles or mountain bikes are allowed in wilderness areas.

Some 28 miles north of Steamboat Springs on Routt County Road 129 is **Steamboat Lake State Park** (☎ **970/879-3922**), encompassing 1,053-acre Steamboat Lake. At an elevation of 8,000 feet, activities include summer camping (183 campsites with fees of $9 to $12), picnicking, fishing, hunting, boating, swimming, canoeing, horseback riding, and nature walks. There's an attractive sandy beach (the sand was trucked in) and three boat launching ramps. Scheduled to open by summer 1999 are a group of camper cabins, with rates for two people expected to be about $50. **Steamboat Lake Marina** (☎ **970/879-7019**), usually open from mid-May through September, has a small store, boat fuel, and boat rentals. Canoes rents for $15 per hour, paddleboats cost $12.50 an hour, small fishing boats are $32.50 for 2 hours; and 20-foot pontoon boats cost $82.50 for 2 hours. There are discounts for longer time periods, and rates for powerboats include fuel. Boat reservations are strongly recommended. In winter, the park offers ice-fishing, cross-country skiing, snowmobiling, and snowshoeing. Day-use fee is $4 per vehicle.

Stagecoach State Park (☎ **970/736-2436**), about 19 miles south of Steamboat Springs, offers camping, picnicking, fishing, boating, and other water sports. From Steamboat Springs, head 3 miles south on U.S. 40 to Colo. 131, turn southwest (right) and go about 6 miles to Routt County Rd. 14, turn south (left) about 5 miles to the park entrance. A recent addition to the state parks system, Stagecoach Reservoir is set among rolling hills, interspersed with forests and grasslands. The reservoir is fairly evenly divided for water-skiing and wakeless boating. There are 92 campsites in four campgrounds, two of which have pull-through sites; one has electric hook-ups. Camping fees are $5 to $12; day-use fee is $4. The elevation at the park is 7,250 feet.

The Steamboat Springs Chamber Resort Association produces a **Trails Map,** available at the information center on Lincoln Avenue, showing which trails are open to what sport: biking, horseback riding, hiking, 4WD, or ATVs. On the reverse side of the map are descriptions of several trails in the area.

A good source for camping, climbing, and kayaking equipment (both sales and rentals) is **Backdoor Sports of Steamboat,** 811 Yampa St. (☎ **970/879-6249;** www.cmn.net/~backdoor.com).

BICYCLING & MOUNTAIN BIKING   The 5-mile, dual-surface **Yampa River Trail** connects downtown Steamboat Springs with Steamboat Village, and links area parks and national forest trails. The **Mount Werner Trail** links the river to the ski area, which has numerous slopes open to mountain bikers in summer. **Spring Creek Trail** climbs from Yampa River Park into Routt National Forest. Touring enthusiasts can try their road bikes on the 110-mile loop over Rabbit Ears and Gore passes, rated one of the 10 most scenic rides in America by *Bicycling* magazine.

Stop at **Sore Saddle Cyclery,** 1136 Yampa St. (☎ **970/879-1675**), for information on the best local trails (maps are on display), accessories, repairs, and rentals. This full-service bike shop also has a manufacturing plant for Moots Cycles, handmade titanium road and mountain bikes that are sold worldwide (about $4,500). Ask for a free tour of the facility. Rentals are also available from **Steamboat Trading Company**, at the Mountain Village in Ski Time Square (☎ **970/879-0083**), and **SportStalker**, in Gondola Square at 2305 Mt. Werner Road (☎ **970/879-0371**). Rentals cost about $14 for a half day and $18 for a full day, with hourly rates and multi-day reductions generally available.

CATTLE DRIVES   ✪ **Broken Skull Cattle Company,** 47080 Elk River Rd. (☎ **970/879-0090**), is a working cattle ranch—not some Hollywood-style dude ranch—that offers a genuine Old West experience. Each July its herd of longhorns is taken some 50 miles over the Continental Divide to summer pasture, and in September the herd is brought back to the Steamboat Springs ranch. On each 9-day trip, up to 10 greenhorns ride and work alongside seasoned cowboys, sleep in tents, and eat chuck-wagon grub. Cost is $1,600 for the entire 9 days, $900 for 5 days, or $190 per day for those who want to join for only part of the drive. Those who bring their own horses get a discount.

FISHING   There are nearly 150 lakes and reservoirs and almost 600 miles of streams in Routt County. Trout—rainbow, brown, brook, and cutthroat—are prolific; and the Yampa River and Stagecoach Reservoir are known for northern Pike. Contact **Straightline Outdoor Sports,** 744 Lincoln Ave. (☎ **800/354-5463** or 970/879-7568), for information, licenses, and either rental or purchase of equipment. Straightline also offers guide services: a half-day wading trip on the Yampa costs $145 for one person, $50 for each additional person; a full-day wading trip is $195 for one and $50 for each additional person; and a full-day float trip costs $325 for two anglers. The company also schedules free casting classes several evenings each week.

GOLF   The new 18-hole municipal **Haymaker Golf Course** is a challenging links-style course designed by Keith Foster, with only 110 of its 233 acres used for fairways and greens. It conforms to the open-space philosophy of the Steamboat community, with native grasses, wetlands, and contours mimicking the surrounding valley and mountains. The course offers four sets of tees and a substantial practice range. Preferred tee times are available with lodging reservations at participating properties through Steamboat Central Reservations (☎ **800/922-9722**).

The course at **Sheraton Steamboat Resort and Conference Center,** 2000 Clubhouse Drive (☎ **970/879-2220**), designed by Robert Trent Jones, Jr., in 1972, is considered one of the Rockies' finest. The 18-hole, 6,906-yard course offers spectacular scenery and challenging fairways. Greens fees, including cart, are $80 for Sheraton guests, $110 for the public.

HIKING & BACKPACKING   There are numerous trails in the **Mount Zirkel Wilderness Area,** immediately north of Steamboat, and the **Flat Tops Wilderness Area,** 48 miles southwest. An especially scenic 4-hour hike in the Flat Tops area takes you from Stillwater Reservoir to the Devil's Causeway, with unforgettable views. Contact the U.S. Forest Service (see above) for information.

HORSEBACK RIDING   Trail rides by the hour, half day, full day, and overnight are offered by **Del's Triangle 3 Ranch,** 55675 County Rd. 62 (P.O. Box 333, Clark, CO 80428; ☎ **970/879-3495**). Adult rates in summer start at $25 for a 1-hour ride, $60 for a half day, and $125 for a full day, including lunch. Winter rates are higher.

Saddle Mountain Ranch, 23760 U.S. 40 West (☎ **970/879-0179**), offers 1½-hour rides four times daily for $25. Reservations are requested by 5pm the previous day. **Steamboat Stables**, behind the rodeo grounds in town, P.O. Box 770885, Steamboat Springs, CO 80477 (☎ **970/879-2306**), offers 1- and 2-hour rides from June through mid-September, plus (by reservation only) breakfast rides, evening steak rides, and pack trips for fishing and hunting. Prices range from $18 for an hour to $38 for the evening steak ride. Also see "Cattle Drives," above.

HOT SPRINGS   More than 150 mineral springs are located in and around the Steamboat Springs area. Black, Heart, Iron, Lithia, Soda, Sulphur, and Steamboat—the springs for which the town was named—are located in city parks. Their healing and restorative qualities were recognized for centuries by Utes, and James Crawford, the area's first white settler, regularly bathed in Heart Spring and helped build the first log bathhouse over it in 1884.

Today, Heart Spring is part of the **Steamboat Springs Health & Recreation complex,** 136 Lincoln Ave. (☎ **970/879-1828**), in downtown Steamboat Springs. In addition to the man-made pools into which the spring's waters flow, there's a lap pool, water slide, spa, whirlpool, weight room, and massage therapy. Pool admission is $6 for adults, $4 for youths 13 to 17, and $2.50 for children under 13 and seniors 62 and over. Suit and towel rentals are available. It's open year-round, Monday through Friday from 6:30am to 9:45pm, and Saturdays and Sundays from 8am to 9:45pm. The slide is open from noon to 6pm in summer and 4 to 8pm in winter. The complex also has tennis courts ($6 per hour).

The **Hot Springs at Strawberry Park,** 44200 County Rd. 36 (☎ **970/ 879-0342**), are 7 miles north of downtown (from Seventh Street, follow the signs). It's a wonderful experience to spend a moonlit evening in a sandy-bottomed, rock-lined soaking pool, kept between 102° and 104°, with snow piled high around you. It's open daily from 10am to midnight; daytime admission is $5, Sunday through Thursday nights $7; and Friday and Saturday $10. Massages are available, and cabins can be rented year-round ($35 weeknights, $40 weekends, with a 2-night minimum on weekends); tent sites at $25 and $30, respectively. Pets are not permitted on the property.

A free city parks department brochure, *The Springs of Steamboat: A Walking Tour,* will acquaint you with other local mineral springs.

KAYAKING   **Backdoor Sports of Steamboat** (see above) offers kayaking lessons ($85 for a 4- to 6-hour class) in spring and summer, and also sells and rents kayaking equipment.

MOUNTAINEERING   Your best source for equipment sales and rentals, plus maps and information, is **Backdoor Sports of Steamboat** (see above).

RODEO   The **Steamboat Springs PRCA Summer Prorodeo Series** (☎ **970/ 879-1818**) takes place each year from mid-June to Labor Day at Howelsen Park.

Professional rodeo cowboys and cowgirls compete in bull riding, bareback and saddle bronco riding, steer wrestling, calf roping, team roping, and barrel racing. In the Wrangler Calf Scramble, children are invited to try to pluck a ribbon from the tail of a calf. Admission costs $9 for anyone over age 12; free for those 12 and younger.

MORE TO SEE & DO

You can learn about Steamboat's history at the **Lodge at Howelsen Hill** (☎ 970/ 879-4300), where there's an informative exhibit on the building of the ski jump (open daily from 8am to 10pm, free admission); and the ✪ **Tread of Pioneers Museum,** 800 Oak St. (☎ 970/879-2214), a beautifully restored Victorian home that features exhibits on pioneer ranch life, the Utes, and 100 years of skiing history. Museum admission is $2.50 for adults, $2 for seniors, and $1 for children 6 to 12; it's open from 11am to 5pm, daily in summer, Monday through Saturday in winter, Tuesday through Saturday in spring and fall. While there, ask for a copy of the Steamboat Springs **self-guided historical walking tour**, which starts at the museum.

For a pleasant and relaxing stroll among lovely gardens, stop at the **Yampa River Botanic Park,** located along the river between the ski mountain and downtown. Several ponds are set among low rolling hills, surrounded by a wide variety of flowering and non-flowering plants and trees of the Yampa River Basin. A brochure describes the planted areas, with a map to help you navigate the many paths. There are wetlands on each side of the park, and the Yampa River Core trail connects to the park on its west side. The park is not wheelchair accessible.

To get to the park, turn west toward the river on Trafalger Drive (the traffic light north of the Chamber Resort office light), then left on Pamela Lane, and go to the parking lot at the far end. A graveled walk leads to the main gate for the park. Admission is free, but donations are welcome and can be made at the kiosk in the park. For more information, contact Steamboat Springs Park & Recreation, P.O. Box 776269, Steamboat Springs, CO 80477 (☎ 970/879-4300).

Just 4 miles from downtown in Routt National Forest is **Fish Creek Falls**. A footpath leads to a historic bridge at the base of this breathtaking 283-foot waterfall. There's also a special overlook with a short one-eighth-mile trail and ramp designed for the disabled, as well as a picnic area and hiking trails. Turn right off Lincoln Avenue onto Third Street, go one block, and turn right again onto Fish Creek Falls Road. For more information, call ☎ 970/879-1870.

Amaze'n Steamboat Maze, 1255 U.S. 40, behind the Chamber office (☎ 970/ 870-8682), lets you test your skills, or perhaps luck, in finding your way through a confusing maze. A free observation deck gives a bird's-eye view of the maze, allowing your quicker companions to point and laugh as you stumble into one dead-end after another. In addition to the human maze, there is an 18-hole miniature golf course that uses items from Colorado's history, from a mine shaft to a Conestoga wagon. Admission for the maze is $5 for adults, $4 for children 5 to 12; for golf, $6 for adults, $5 for children; for both the maze and golf, $8 for adults, $7 for children; free for children under 5. Additional maze runs cost $2, and additional rounds of golf cost $3. The maze and golf are open from Memorial Day weekend to mid-September daily, weekends only thereafter; call for hours.

SHOPPING

Lincoln Avenue, between Fifth and Ninth Streets, is where most of the more interesting shops and galleries are located. Art lovers will enjoy **Artisans' Market of**

Steamboat, 626 Lincoln Ave. (☎ **970/879-7512**), a nonprofit cooperative of local artists; and **Steamboat Art Company,** 903 Lincoln Ave. (☎ **970/879-3383**), which offers western art, jewelry, and crafts in wood, glass, and pottery. **The Homesteader,** 821 Lincoln Ave. (☎ **970/879-5880**), is a delightful kitchen shop with gourmet coffee, espresso, and cappuccino.

If you forgot to pack your cowboy hat, there's a tremendous selection of Stetsons, plus just about everything else a westerner wears, at **F. M. Light & Sons,** 830 Lincoln Ave. (☎ **970/879-1822**). And while hardware stores might not be on everyone's list of tourist sites, take a few minutes to stop at **Bogg's Hardware,** established in 1939, at 730 Lincoln Ave. (☎ **970/879-6250**), where you'll find snowshoes, art and antiques, and just about every nut, bolt, and tool imaginable.

Lyon's Corner Drug & Soda Fountain, at the corner of Ninth and Lincoln (☎ **970/879-1114**), isn't just a drugstore and card shop; it also has a great old Wurlitzer jukebox spinning golden oldies, and an old-time soda fountain where you can get real malts, ice-cream sodas, egg creams, phosphates, sundaes, and fresh-squeezed lemonade.

WHERE TO STAY

As at all Colorado ski resorts, rates get progressively higher the closer you get to the slopes. You'll pay the highest rates during the Christmas holiday season (mid-December to New Year's Day). Next highest are the rates charged during February and March. Value season is usually January, and the low season runs from Thanksgiving to mid-December and from April until the ski areas close. Rates are normally much lower during the summer, from Memorial Day to mid-October. Because vacancy rates are so high during shoulder seasons—April to May and October to November—many accommodations close at these times.

Steamboat Central Reservations (☎ **800/922-2722** or 970/879-0740; fax 970/879-4757) can book your lodging and make virtually all of your travel arrangements. Be sure to ask about special packages and programs.

Steamboat Premier Properties, 1855 Ski Time Square Dr., Steamboat Springs, CO 80487 (☎ **800/228-2458** or 970/879-8811; fax 970/879-8485; www.steamboat-premier.com; e-mail: spp@steamboat-premier.com), manages 168 rental units spread among nine properties. There are both condos and town homes, with accommodations for four to twelve persons; several of the properties are described below. A few larger homes are available, with lodging for 11 to 18 persons.

Steamboat Resorts, 1847 Ski Time Square Dr., P.O. Box 772995, Steamboat Springs, CO 80477 (☎ **800/525-5502** or 970/879-8000; fax 970/879-8060; www.steamboatresorts.com; e-mail: ski@steamboatresorts.com), manages 13 properties, offering a variety of possibilities, from small lodge rooms for two to condos that will accommodate up to eight.

Several of the properties are described below. Room tax adds about 9½ % to lodging bills.

VERY EXPENSIVE

Château Chamonix. 2340 Apres Ski Way, Steamboat Springs, CO 80487. ☎ **800/ 833-9877** or 970/879-7511. Fax 970/879-9321. www.chateau-chamonix.com. E-mail: lodging@chateau-chamonix.com. 27 units. TV TEL. Two-bedroom, $140–$160 summer, $395–$560 winter; three-bedroom, $170–$190 summer, $545–$710 winter. Holiday rates higher; discounts possible between seasons. AE, MC, V. Free parking in covered lot.

Located a few steps from the base of the Silver Bullet gondola, this is one of the most convenient accommodations at Steamboat Village. Two buildings have condominium units with private decks facing the slopes. All have fireplaces, fully equipped kitchens, wet bars, VCRs, and pine, walnut, or oak furnishings. Most units are two-bedroom suites, with twin beds in one room, a king bed in the master bedroom, and a whirlpool tub in the adjoining bathroom. Facilities include an outdoor heated swimming pool, whirlpool, sauna, ski lockers, business center, and conference facilities for 70.

✪ **Torian Plum at Steamboat.** 1855 Ski Time Square Dr. (Steamboat Premier Properties, see above). ☎ **800/228-2458** or 970/879-8811. Fax 970/879-8485. 47 units. TV TEL. One- to three-bedroom units, $115–$195 summer, $195–$375 early and late ski season, $410–$760 regular ski season, $515–$985 holiday season. AE, MC, V. Free parking in underground lot.

These slope-side ski-in/ski-out condominiums have handsome light-wood furnishings, a fully equipped tile kitchen (with microwave and dishwasher), washer/dryer, gas fireplace, private balcony, ski locker, and two phone lines with voice mail and data port. Services during ski season include concierge, shuttle service, and free coffee. Facilities include an outdoor heated swimming pool, two outdoor and two indoor hot tubs, sauna, four tennis courts, and video rentals. Fax and photocopy services are available.

EXPENSIVE

The Meadows at EagleRidge. Walton Creek Rd. (Steamboat Premier Properties, see above). ☎ **800/228-2458** or 970/879-8811. Fax 970/879-8485. 31 units. TV TEL. Two- to four-bedroom units, $135–$425 summer, $150–$825 early and late ski season, $245–$875 regular ski season, $375–$1,075 holiday season. AE, MC, V. Check-in at Trappeur's Crossing.

As with most condominiums, these are individually owned, so each is individually decorated. All have fully equipped kitchens, stereos with CD player, TV/VCR, and gas fireplace. Some units overlook the creek. There's an indoor pool and hot tub, concierge, and ski shuttle.

The Ranch at Steamboat. 1 Ranch Rd. (off Clubhouse Dr.), Steamboat Springs, CO 80487. ☎ **800/525-2002** or 970/879-3000. Fax 970/879-5409. www.ranch-steamboat.com. E-mail: info@ranch-steamboat.com. 88 units. TV TEL. Double, $75–$125, summer; $115–$250 regular ski season. Higher rates on winter holidays. AE, DISC, MC, V. Free parking in private garages.

Spread across a 36-acre hillside on Burgess Creek, not far from Ski Time Square, these impressive condominiums offer a peaceful, quiet location. The two-story units have full kitchens (including microwaves), large fireplaces, private barbecue decks, and washer/dryers. There's a direct entrance from the private garage into the kitchen. Facilities include a swimming pool, hot tub, sauna, recreation center, four tennis courts, fitness center, game room, and meeting facilities for 200, plus shuttle vans in ski season.

✪ **Sheraton Steamboat Resort.** 2200 Village Inn Court, Steamboat Springs, CO 80477. ☎ **800/848-8878** or 970/879-2220. Fax 970/879-7686. www.steamboat-sheraton. com. E-mail: traci_gillan@ittsheraton.com. 322 units. A/C TV TEL. Late May–mid-Oct, $89–$109; winter, low-season $99–$179, value season $179–$259, Christmas and regular season $209–$289. Children under 17 stay free in parents' room in summer. AE, CB, DC, MC, V. Free parking in underground lot. Closed 1 month in spring and fall. Pets accepted with $50 fee.

Steamboat Springs' premier hotel is located in the heart of Ski Time Square, at the foot of the Silver Bullet gondola. The Sheraton opens directly onto the ski slopes, and every room has a view of the mountain, valley, or slopes. In summer, sports lovers enjoy its golf club, one of the finest in the Rockies.

Most units have one king or two queen beds, a private balcony, and in-room movies. All have coffeemakers, humidifiers, and mini-refrigerators. Phase I of an $18-million renovation and expansion project was completed in early 1998, featuring an entirely remodeled entrance and lobby, outdoor hot tubs on a rooftop spa deck, a full service health club, and three new restaurants. By 1999, Phase II should be finished: an all-new exclusive 23-unit luxury suite tower plus additional retail shopping space.

Dining/Diversions: Sevens Fine Dining offers magnificent views of the mountain and the Headwall chairlift. Breakfast and dinner are served daily. The restaurant has rotisserie selections, steak, seafood, and poultry dishes ($12 to $19). Buddy's Run, open winters only (from 8am to 5pm), serves breakfast and lunch; in the early evening, it's an après-ski comedy club. The hotel also offers year-round deck dining at 3 Saddles Bar & Grill, featuring lunch, appetizers, and dinner in a casual western atmosphere.

Amenities: Room service (from 7am to 10pm), concierge (from 8am to 6pm), valet and guest laundry services, children's day programs; cross-country ski course (see "Skiing & Other Winter Activities," above), golf club (see "Warm-Weather & Year-Round Activities," above), year-round heated swimming pool, hot tubs, saunas, steam rooms, fitness center, masseuse, game room, ski storage and rental; meeting facilities for 600; retail shops.

MODERATE

The Cascades at EagleRidge. Walton Creek Rd. (Steamboat Premier Properties, see above). ☎ **800/228-2458** or 970/879-8811. Fax 970/879-8485. 28 units. TV TEL. Three- to five-bedroom units, $165–$265 summer, $235–$625 early and late ski season, $375–$675 regular ski season, $595–$995 holiday season. AE, MC, V. Check-in at Trappeur's Crossing.

Each of these town houses, situated about half a mile from the ski slopes, has a two-car garage. Many are decorated in southwestern style, and some have stone fireplaces. The four- and five-bedroom units have a family room in addition to the living room. A hot tub, concierge, and ski shuttle are available.

The Harbor Hotel. 703 Lincoln Ave. (P.O. Box 774109), Steamboat Springs, CO 80477. ☎ **800/543-8888** out of state, 800/334-1012 in Colorado, or 970/879-1522. Fax 970/879-1737. 65 units. TV TEL. Double, $50–$75 summer and low ski season, $75–$160 value and regular seasons, $150–$205 holiday season; Condo, $95–$105 summer and low-season, $145–$175 value and regular seasons, $240–$290 holiday season. Rates include continental breakfast in winter only. AE, CB, DC, DISC, MC, V. Free off-street parking. Pets are accepted in summer, with some restrictions.

A European-style hotel built in 1939, the Harbor has expanded in recent years with an adjoining motel and condominium complex. Guests enter the hotel through polished bronze doors from a turn-of-the-century London bank, and register in a small, antique-filled lobby.

Each of the 15 hotel guest rooms has a different decor, with period furnishings; motel units are basic and economical; and the condos have well-equipped kitchens, including microwaves. Services and facilities include free winter shuttle pass, ski and bicycle storage, two whirlpools, sauna, steam room, coin-operated laundry, gift shop, and boutique.

The Lodge at Steamboat. 2700 Village Dr. (Steamboat Resorts, see above). ☎ **800/525-5502** or 970/879-8000. Fax 970/870-8061. 120 units. TV, TEL. One- to three-bedrooms, winter $110–$675; summer $130–$175. AE, MC, V.

These condominiums are just 200 yards from the Silver Bullet Gondola, and there's a free shuttle to take you to the mountain village, downtown, or shopping. The individually-owned and -decorated units have fully-equipped kitchens, VCRs (video rentals available), and balconies; upper-floor units have a cathedral ceiling with clerestory windows. Facilities include an outdoor heated pool, one indoor and two outdoor hot tubs, a sauna, two tennis courts, and a guest laundry. A typical average-sized unit is simply but pleasantly decorated in what might be termed mountain western style, and includes an attractive brick fireplace, a sunny dining area, a counter island with high stool seating between the kitchen and living area, a queen bed in the master bedroom, and twin beds in the second bedroom. In-room massage and baby-sitting are available.

Sky Valley Lodge. 31490 E. U.S. 40 (P.O. Box 3132), Steamboat Springs, CO 80477. ☎ 800/499-4759 or 970/879-7749. Fax 970/879-7752. www.steamboat-lodging.com. E-mail: sjmyler@amigo.net. 31 units. TV TEL. Late May to Thanksgiving, $78–$109 double. Winter, $108–$168 double. Extra person $10. Rates include breakfast—full in ski season, continental the rest of the year. AE, CB, DC, DISC, MC, V. Free parking. Pets accepted, with restrictions. Closed mid-Apr–late May.

Located below Rabbit Ears Pass with a spectacular view of the upper Yampa River Valley, this lodge—actually two rustic lodges, 8½ miles east of Steamboat Springs—offers country-manor charm in a woodsy setting, where guests can relax around a big fireplace in the lobby. Each room is a bit different, but all have an old-fashioned ski-lodge atmosphere. Only four units have full bathrooms; others have showers only, and sinks are in the bedroom. Features include king and queen brass and feather beds, fine views from every window, an outdoor hot tub, sauna, sundeck, and game room. No smoking is permitted in the lodge.

Vistas Restaurant serves dinner Wednesday through Saturday from late December to mid-March and mid-June to mid-September, with entrees such as ruby red trout in a light garlic-and-dill butter, and slow-baked prime rib rubbed with spices and then grilled.

Thunderhead Lodge & Condominiums. 1965 Ski Time Square (Steamboat Resorts, see above). ☎ 800/525-5502 or 970/879-8000. Fax 970/870-8061. 125 units. TV, TEL. Winter $89–$279 double, $139–$699 condo; summer $75–$95 double, $95–$175 condo. AE, MC, V.

This ski-in/ski-out property offers a variety of accommodations, from lodge and hotel rooms to one- and two-bedroom condos. Condo units have either full kitchens or kitchenettes, and most have gas fireplaces, but lodge and hotel rooms have neither. Some units have a sleeping loft, all except lodge rooms have balconies, and most boast great views of the ski mountain or valley. Hotel rooms have louvered doors separating the bedroom from the sitting area. The lodge rooms are somewhat small, with a queen bed, a loveseat, and no desk. The condos are generally spacious, even the studios, which have a queen bed and queen sofa sleeper. Facilities include three indoor hot tubs, an outdoor heated pool, sauna, sundeck, and self-service laundry, plus concierge and free coffee in the lobby. The Thunderhead is located in the heart of the mountain village, close to shopping and dining, and there's a complimentary shuttle to grocery stores and downtown. In-room massage and baby-sitting are available.

Trappeur's Crossing. Village Dr. and Medicine Springs Rd. (Steamboat Premier Properties, see above). ☎ 800/228-2458 or 970/879-8811. Fax 970/879-8485. 34 units. TV TEL. One- to four-bedroom units, $125–$215 summer, $140–$495 early and late ski season, $225–$545 regular ski season, $295–$765 holiday season. AE, MC, V.

The least expensive of the Steamboat Premier Properties, Trappeur's Crossing offers indoor and outdoor hot tubs, an indoor-outdoor swimming pool, private balconies, tennis courts (summer only), concierge, and ski shuttle. As with the others, these are individually owned and decorated, with completely equipped kitchens.

INEXPENSIVE

The Inn at Steamboat. 3070 Columbine Dr. (P.O. Box 775084), Steamboat Springs, CO 80477. ☎ **800/872-2601** or 970/879-2600. Fax 970/879-9270. 33 units. TV TEL. Double, $39–$85 summer, $45–$139 winter; extra person $10, children under 13 stay free (some restrictions apply). Rates include continental breakfast. AE, DISC, MC, V. Free parking.

A large ranch-style bed-and-breakfast, this is one of the least expensive accommodations in the Steamboat Village area. Etched-pine decor and a large stone fireplace add flair. Rooms are spacious, with two queen beds and sliding glass doors that lead to private decks or terraces. A condo has five bedrooms, two bathrooms, and a kitchenette.

Amenities at the Inn include an outdoor swimming pool, sauna, sundeck, service bar, self-serve laundry, VCR and video rental, game room, nature trail, mountain-bike rentals, 20 tennis courts, access to nearby health club, ski-tuning, and a private ski shuttle. Smoking is not permitted.

✪ **Rabbit Ears Motel.** 201 Lincoln Ave. (P.O. Box 770573), Steamboat Springs, CO 80477. ☎ **800/828-7702** or 970/879-1150. Fax 970/870-0483. www.rabbitearsmotel.com. E-mail: ski-rabbit-ears@toski.com. 65 units. A/C TV TEL. Christmas holiday $125–$165, early Jan–late Mar $95–$135, late Mar–mid-Dec $75–$115. Children under 12 stay free. Rates include continental breakfast. DC, DISC, MC, V. Free parking. Pets accepted.

The original ten rooms of this property were built in 1952, with additional units added through 1991, some of which overlook the Yampa River. Completely remodeled in 1996, all rooms are clean and comfortable. The decor is southwestern, with simple but attractive furnishings and prints or photos adorning the mostly white walls; even the smallest rooms (which are definitely tiny) have a desk and two upholstered chairs. The motel is conveniently located on the east end of the downtown shopping district, with the river behind and the hot springs pool across the street (discount passes are available), and on the local free shuttle bus route. All rooms have coffeemakers and hair dryers; some have microwaves, refrigerators, and private balconies. The continental breakfast is above average, and a coin-operated laundry and fax and copy service are available.

Steamboat Bed & Breakfast. 442 Pine St. (P.O. Box 775888), Steamboat Springs, CO 80477. ☎ **970/879-5724**. Fax 970/870-8787. 7 units. Mid-Apr–mid-Nov, $75–$125 double. Mid-Nov–mid-Apr $105–$155 double. Rates include full breakfast. AE, DISC, MC, V. Off-street parking.

Steamboat Springs' first house of worship, an 1891 Congregational Church that lost its steeple and top floor to lightning, is now a fine bed-and-breakfast with many stained-glass windows. There are beautiful European and American Victorian antiques in every room, reproduction antique beds, hardwood floors in the common areas and bathrooms, and carpeting in the bedrooms. Guests share a huge living/dining room with stone fireplace, where they can enjoy complimentary fresh fruit and baked goods. Other facilities include an upstairs library, hot tub, sundeck, and a music conservatory with piano, TV, and VCR (videos are available). In summer guests can enjoy an attractive deck, set in a lovely flower garden and lush lawn, or nap in a hammock under shady trees. Smoking is not allowed.

Steamboat Valley Guest House. 1245 Crawford Ave. (P.O. Box 773815), Steamboat Springs, CO 80477. ☎ **800/530-3866** or 970/870-9017. Fax 970/879-0361. www. steamboatvalley.com. E-mail: george@steamboatvalley.com. 4 units. Queen $80–$126, king $108–$148. Rates include full breakfast. AE, DC, DISC, MC, V. Free covered parking.

This western-style log house has spectacular views of the ski area and town. The four guest rooms are individually decorated with antiques and family heirlooms; the honeymoon suite, for instance, has a king bed and ceramic fireplace. Homemade breakfasts are different each day and might include Swedish pancakes or a green-chile cheese soufflé. A common room has a fireplace, baby grand piano, and TV, and guests have access to a cordless phone (some rooms have phones as well). There's also a sundeck and seasonal hot tub. Smoking is not permitted.

WHERE TO DINE

Those on a budget can save quite a bit by stopping at local supermarkets. **City Market,** 1825 City Park Plaza (☎ **970/879-3290**), is not only a good grocery store, but has a great salad bar (salads-to-go by the pound), bakery, deli, and pharmacy. **Safeway,** 37500 E. U.S. 40 (☎ **970/879-3766**), also has a bakery, deli, and pharmacy, but no salad bar.

EXPENSIVE

✪ **Hazie's.** 2305 Mt. Werner Circle, Thunderbird Terminal, Silver Bullet Gondola. ☎ **970/879-6111,** ext. 465. Reservations recommended for lunch, required for dinner. Lunch main courses $7–$16; four-course fixed-price dinner $60, including round-trip gondola ride; summer dinner main courses $17–$25. AE, CB, DC, DISC, MC, V. Early Dec–mid-Apr daily 11:30am–2:30pm; Tues–Sat 6:30–9:30pm. Mid-June–Labor Day, Sun brunch 10am–1:30pm; Fri–Sat 6:30–9:30pm. AMERICAN CREATIVE & CLASSIC CONTINENTAL.

Steamboat Springs' most exciting dining experience can be found at the top of the gondola, midway up Mount Werner. The views of the upper Yampa River valley are spectacular by day and romantic by night, as the lights of Steamboat Springs spread out at the foot of the mountain. Lunch features a variety of salads and sandwiches, plus a daily chef's special. But it's at dinner that Hazie's really struts its stuff. In winter a fixed-price four-course meal is offered: Start with an appetizer such as hot oak-smoked salmon or grilled Jamaican shrimp, then try the soup du jour or the delicious gourmet salad of mixed greens, bell peppers, tomatoes, black olives, cucumbers, and artichoke hearts. Finally, the entree might be châteaubriand béarnaise—a beef tenderloin seasoned with a blend of four crushed peppercorns, oven roasted and served with béarnaise sauce; rack of lamb Madagascar—sliced lamb rack served with a green peppercorn and tomato-cognac demi glaze; or tender duck breast marinated in walnut and olive oils with honey and spices, charbroiled and served with red currant sauce. The summer à la carte menu includes sea scallops and rock shrimp tossed with basil, rosemary, and thyme, with a light dry-wine/cream sauce and served on a bed of angel hair. Smoking is not permitted. Evening child-care is available in winter (☎ 970/879-6111, ext. 218).

L'Apogée. 911 Lincoln Ave. ☎ **970/879-1919.** Reservations recommended. Main courses $21–$34. AE, MC, V. Daily 5:30–10:30pm. CLASSIC & CONTEMPORARY FRENCH.

Located in a circa 1886 building in downtown Steamboat, L'Apogée has been serving fine French cuisine with an Asian flair to appreciative patrons since 1979. The candlelit atmosphere is enhanced by live piano music, contemporary artwork, white-linen tablecloths, and graceful cane-backed chairs. The service is excellent and the award-winning wine list is extensive. The menu changes often to take advantage of the freshest ingredients. Appetizers might include fruits de la mer au gratin—fresh bay scallops and Gulf rock shrimp simmered in cream with a hint of nutmeg, then finished under the broiler with gruyere and Parmesan cheeses. For the main course, you might choose from canard rôti à l'orange—a half duckling, twice baked and glazed with Cointreau orange syrup; or filet de boeuf à l'Oscar—center cut filet of aged beef tenderloin, skillet seared and finished in the oven, garnished with crabmeat and asparagus, then ladled with sauce bearnaise.

La Montaña. Village Center Shopping Plaza, 2500 Village Dr. at Apres Ski Way. ☎ **970/879-5800.** Reservations recommended. Main courses $10–$24. AE, DISC, MC, V. Daily 5–10pm (bar daily 4:30pm–closing). Hours vary in spring, summer, and fall. MEXICAN/SOUTHWESTERN.

This isn't your everyday Mexican restaurant; it's a gourmet experience. The festive decor sets the mood, with greenhouse dining and handsome photos by owner Tom Garrett on the stuccoed walls. Southwestern dishes include unusual combinations such as grilled elk loin with a pecan-nut crust and bourbon-cream sauce; the chef's award-winning dish of braided sausage: a mesquite-grilled combination of elk, lamb, and chorizo sausage; and enchiladas (which have been featured in *Gourmet* magazine) composed of blue corn tortillas, goat and Monterey Jack cheeses, roasted peppers, and onions.

MODERATE

Riggio's Fine Italian Food. 1106 Lincoln Ave. in the Old West Building. ☎ **970/879-9010.** Main courses $9–$19. AE, DISC, MC, V. Daily from 5:30pm, lounge from 5pm. Closed Tues in summer. ITALIAN. Located at the western edge of the downtown business district.

The large, open dining room has light-colored walls and an attractive solid wood bar. The decor is simple, with white tablecloths and bentwood chairs, a row of plates along one wall, and classic and contemporary art. The menu, however, is anything but simple. There's pizza choices such as pomodori (roasted garlic, fresh basil, and tomatoes) and Italiano (sausage, mushrooms, peppers, and onions). Pasta selections include fresh steamed mussels in white wine, garlic, and herbs, served with linguini and red or cream sauce. Riggio's house salad is served with a gorgonzola vinaigrette and bread. Entrees might include fresh salmon fillet seared with herbs and spices, topped with roasted red peppers and finished with a sweet red pepper white wine sauce; or scallopine of veal sautéed in olive oil with mushrooms, onions, and red and green peppers in demiglaze. Espresso and cappuccino are available.

✪ **Slopeside Grill.** Ski Time Square in Torian Plum Plaza. ☎ **970/879-2916.** Pizza $7.50–$10; main courses $6–$17. AE, DISC, MC, V. Daily 11am–10pm; pizza oven open until midnight; bar open until 2am. AMERICAN/ITALIAN.

A large U-shaped light-colored wooden bar dominates the dining room, where diners look at the ski slopes through large windows, and the walls are decorated with old western and early skiing memorabilia. In fine weather, alfresco dining is popular on the patio under large umbrellas.

Steamboat's only brick-oven pizza offers choices such as "Mother Nature" (fresh tomatoes, basil, and garlic) and "The Chutes" (sweet and hot Italian sausage, fresh tomatoes, red onions, and mushrooms). Grill options include a 12-ounce New York strip grilled with wood-smoked flavor, slow-roasted baby-back barbecue ribs, and chicken Parmesan. Burger lovers can choose from among the basic half-pound ground beef burger with lettuce, tomato, onion, and pickle; a red chili pesto burger topped with a zesty red chili pesto and jack cheese; and the boat burger, topped with mushrooms, cheese, bacon, and caramelized onions. Our top choices include the sausage calzone—hot and sweet Italian sausage, mushrooms, onions, and hot peppers with ricotta, mozzarella, and provolone cheese wrapped in pizza dough and served with a side of marinara sauce; and the pesto primavera—fresh garden vegetables in a white wine pesto sauce over linguine. Beware: The portions are rather large, so take a big appetite.

Steamboat Brewery & Tavern. 435 Lincoln Ave. (at 5th St.). ☎ **970/879-2233.** Reservations not accepted. Main courses $6–$8 lunch, $9–$13 dinner. AE, DISC, MC, V. Daily 11:30am–10pm, pizza available until 11pm, bar open until 2am. BREWPUB.

This modern brewpub has a long bar, polished wood trim, and white stucco walls decorated with early-20th-century–style prints and metal advertising signs. It offers a full bar, with about a dozen wines available by the glass, and five or six micro-brewed beers on tap. There's a wide selection of soups, sandwiches, burgers, and salads, plus hand-twirled pizza and their own bread, baked fresh daily. Dinner entrees might include garlic basil fettuccine with fresh vegetables, broiled salmon with raspberry mustard sauce, or brisket of beef with mashed potatoes and gravy. Tours of the brewery are available by request.

INEXPENSIVE

✪ **Cugino's Pizzeria.** 825 Oak St. ☎ **970/879-5805.** Reservations not accepted. Pizzas $6.50–$16; entrees $4.50–$15. No credit cards. Daily 11am–10pm. Delivery available 5–9:30pm. ITALIAN.

Local families pack this restaurant in downtown Steamboat Springs, and for good reason—good food, generous portions, and low prices. The simple decor consists of posters of Italian operas. The extensive menu includes pizza, of course, plus hoagies and steak sandwiches, pasta, seafood, and calzones. Those with healthy appetites might want to try a stromboli—fresh-baked pizza dough stuffed with mushrooms, onions, peppers, mozzarella and provolone cheeses, ham, Genoa salami, and capa-cola. A vegetarian version is also served. Beer and wine are available any time, and liquor is served after 5pm. Fedora's, a bar and waiting area upstairs, serves meals in summer and appetizers only in winter.

Full Moon Bakery and Cafe. Central Park Plaza (next to Blockbuster). ☎ **970/870-1888.** Breakfast $2.50–$4.75; lunch and dinner $3.50–$7. AE, MC, V. Mon–Sat 7am–7pm; Sun 8am–3pm. CREATIVE AMERICAN.

This comfortable casual cafe and bar offers fast friendly service and great food. Original art and plants contribute to the cheerful atmosphere. You can get a break-fast burrito, quiche, or Belgian waffle for breakfast, plus fresh-baked pastries, muffins, and scones. Lunch and dinner selections include oversized sandwiches served with chips or fruit, a special wrap every day (such as Greek veggie, chicken Caesar, or Thai veggie), pasta dishes, and entrees such as curried Bangkok chicken with rice or roasted potatoes, and curried Moroccan lamb stew with root vegetables.

The Tugboat Saloon & Eatery. Ski Time Square. ☎ **970/879-7070.** Reservations not accepted. Entrees $4.25–$14.25. AE, DC, MC, V. Winter, daily 7:30am–10pm; summer, daily 11am–10pm; bar Mon–Sat until 1:30am, Sun until midnight. Closed April 15–May 1. AMERICAN.

Oak floors and rough barn-wood walls cloaked with game and fishing trophies, sports memorabilia, and celebrity photographs are the trademark of this foot-of-the-slopes establishment. The hand-carved cherry-wood bar, circa 1850, came from the Log Cabin Saloon in Baggs, Wyoming, a Butch Cassidy hangout; look for the bullet hole in one of the columns. The fare includes omelets, huevos rancheros, and pancakes for breakfast; a variety of burgers, burritos, deli sandwiches, fish, soups, and salads for lunch and dinner. Many folks sup on nachos, teriyaki wings, and other generous appetizer plates. Live music starts nightly at 9:30pm.

PERFORMING ARTS & NIGHTLIFE

Summer is a musical time in Steamboat Springs. **Strings in the Mountains Festival of Music,** P.O. Box 774627, Steamboat Springs, CO 80477 (☎ **970/879-5056**), offers events Monday through Saturday from early July to mid-August, in the Performing Arts Tent at Torian Plum Plaza. A variety of performances and free "Musical Talks" feature award-winning classical and jazz musicians. Youth and family concerts cost $5 for adults, $1 for children; Tuesday and Thursday night chamber music concerts cost $12 to $18 for adults, $5 for juniors; Friday night programs of jazz, country, bluegrass, or other genres cost $20; and Saturday night classical concerts cost $14 to $18.

The bar scene in Steamboat, while never dull, comes especially alive in winter. **Heavenly Daze Brewery,** Ski Time Square (☎ 970/879-8080), has 20 beers on tap, five pool tables, video games, foosball, sandwiches, burgers, steak, and seafood; it claims to be Steamboat's biggest nightclub. Among other popular venues are the **Inferno,** Gondola Square (☎ 970/879-5111), a hot dance club with live music; and the rustic **Tugboat Saloon & Eatery,** Ski Time Square (☎ 970/879-7070), which attracts a local crowd for rock music and dancing. In downtown Steamboat, **Tap House Sports Grill,** 729 Lincoln Ave. (☎ 970/879-2431), has 23 TVs showing just about any sporting event you'd want to see.

4 Winter Park

67 miles NW of Denver

Originally an Arapahoe and Ute hunting ground, today most of the hunting is for the best ski runs. First settled by whites in the 1850s, the laying of a rail track over Rollins Pass in 1905 and the completion of the 6.2-mile Moffat Tunnel in 1928 opened forests here to logging, which long supported the economy while providing Denver with raw materials for its growth.

The birth of the Winter Park ski area in January 1940, at the west portal of the Moffat Tunnel, helped give impetus to the Colorado ski boom. Although it hasn't yet achieved the notoriety of Vail or Aspen, Winter Park still manages to attract more than a million skier visits per season. One of its draws is the Winter Park Ski Train, the last of its kind in the West. While skiers should find enough lodgings and restaurants to meet their needs, shoppers accustomed to the bounty in Aspen may be disappointed—at least for now. The development of a base village has begun. In the summer of 1998, construction started on Phase I, which will include an underground parking garage, a lodge with more than 200 units, plus restaurants, pubs, shops, and a health club. The lodge should be ready for occupancy for the 1999–2000 ski season.

ESSENTIALS

GETTING THERE   By Car   From Denver or other points east or west, take I-70 exit 232, at Empire, and climb 24 miles north on U.S. 40 over Berthoud Pass to Winter Park. U.S. 40 links Winter Park directly to Steamboat Springs, 101 miles northwest, and, via U.S. 34 (at Granby) through Rocky Mountain National Park, to Estes Park, 84 miles north.

By Plane   Visitors fly into Denver International Airport and can continue to Winter Park with **Home James Transportation Service** (☎ 800/451-4844 or 970/726-5060).

By Train   Winter Park Resort is the only ski area in the western United States to have rail service directly to the slopes. The dramatically scenic **Winter Park Ski Train** (☎ 303/296-4754) has been making regular runs between Denver and Winter Park since 1940, stopping just 50 yards from the foot of the lifts. On its 2-hour run, the train climbs almost 4,000 feet and passes through 29 tunnels (including the 6.2-mile Moffat Tunnel). The train operates weekends from late December to early April.

The **Amtrak California Zephyr** (☎ **800/USA-RAIL**) stops twice daily (once in each direction) in Fraser, 2 miles north of Winter Park, on its Chicago–West Coast run.

VISITOR INFORMATION   Main sources of visitor information are the **Winter Park/Fraser Valley Chamber of Commerce,** P.O. Box 3236, Winter Park, CO 80482 (☎ **800/903-7275** or 970/726-4118 for general information, 800/722-4118 for lodging; www.winterpark-info.com), and the **Winter Park Resort,** P.O. Box 36, Winter Park, CO 80482 (☎ **970/726-5514**). The chamber of commerce's visitor center, on the east side of U.S. 40 in the center of town, is open year-round, daily from 8am to 5pm.

GETTING AROUND   U.S. 40 (Winter Park Drive) runs almost directly north–south through the community. Vasquez Road, one of the few side roads with accommodations, is the first major left turn as you arrive from the south. Two miles north on U.S. 40 is Fraser, site of the Amtrak terminal and several condominium developments. **The Lift** (☎ **970/726-4163**), a free local shuttle service, runs between most accommodations and the ski area in winter. **Home James Transportation Service** (☎ **970/726-5060**) provides taxi service. **Car rentals** are available from **Hertz** (☎ **800/654-3131** or 970/726-8993).

FAST FACTS   The hospital, **Seven Mile Medical Clinic,** at the Winter Park Resort (☎ **970/726-8066**), can handle most medical emergencies (call for hours). The **post office** is in the heart of Winter Park on U.S. 40. For hours and other information contact the U.S. Postal Service (☎ **800/275-8777**). For **road information,** call ☎ **970/639-1111.**

SPECIAL EVENTS   National Women's Ski and Snowboard Week, late January; American Music and Winter Park Jazz Festivals, mid-July; High Country Stampede Rodeo, Saturday nights from early July through August; Rocky Mountain Wine and Food Festival, early August; King of the Rockies Mountain Bike Festival, late August; Flamethrowers High Altitude Chili Cookoff, late August; Torchlight Parade, Christmas Eve.

SKIING & OTHER WINTER ACTIVITIES

Winter Park is one of those rare resorts that seems to have something for everyone. Experts rave about the chutes and steep mogul runs on Mary Jane Mountain and the extreme skiing in the Vasquez Cirque, but intermediates and beginners are well served on other slopes. Moreover, Winter Park is noted for wide-ranging programs for children and those with disabilities.

The resort includes three interconnected mountain areas totaling 121 trails on 2,581 acres of skiable terrain. Twenty lifts include seven high-speed express quads, five triples, and eight double chairs.

Winter Park Mountain has 12 lifts and 46 trails, with mostly beginner and intermediate terrain. **Discovery Park** encompasses more than 20 acres of prime beginner terrain served by three lifts.

Mary Jane Mountain has seven chairlifts and 50 trails on intermediate and expert terrain. **Vasquez Ridge,** the resort's third mountain area, offers primarily intermediate terrain on 13 trails. All are served by one quad lift. Fans of tree-line skiing will like **Parsenn Bowl,** more than 200 acres of open-bowl and gladed-tree skiing that fan out from the summit at North Cone and merge with Mary Jane's Backside.

Vasquez Cirque, which opened in February 1998, contains 435 acres of steep chutes and gladed pockets for advanced and expert skiers and snowboarders. Accessed by a short hike from the top of the Timberline chair in Parsenn Bowl, skiers and snowboarders can choose from numerous entrances along a groomed "ski-way" that runs from the top of Parsenn Bowl along the perimeter of the Cirque. The most difficult areas are at the farthest end of the traverse. The upper area boasts above-tree-line skiing in steep chutes or wide open snow fields. Lower down, the glades gradually tighten, ending on a trail that brings skiers and snowboarders to the base of the pioneer Express chair.

Annual snowfall at Winter Park averages 370 inches (almost 40 feet). The vertical drop is 3,060 feet, from the 12,060-foot summit off North Cone. There are 11 restaurants and three bars, including the Lodge at Sunspot, a mountaintop restaurant.

Winter Park's 32,000-square-foot **Children's Center** includes a play area, rental shop, rest rooms, and a children's instruction hill. The **National Sports Center for the Disabled,** founded in 1970, is one of the largest programs of its kind in the world. Each year, more than 2,500 children and adults take over 23,000 lessons.

Lift tickets (1998–99 rates) are $46 per day for adults, $15 per day for children 6 to 13, $22 per day for seniors 62 to 69, and free for those under 5 and over 70. Full-rental packages are available, as are alpine, telemark, and snowboard lessons. On-mountain snowshoe tours are scheduled daily and cost about $25 per person, including equipment.

Winter Park is open from early November to late April, Monday through Friday from 9am to 4pm; Saturday, Sunday, and holidays from 8:30am to 4pm. Mary Jane mountain stays open through April, then Friday through Sunday until Memorial Day weekend. It is open for summer operations weekends only from Memorial Day weekend to mid-June, then daily through Labor Day weekend, and weekends again until the end of September. For more information, contact **Winter Park Resort,** P.O. Box 36, Winter Park, CO 80482 (☎ **970/726-5514,** or 303/892-0961 in Denver; www.skiwinterpark.com; e-mail: wp@mail.skiwinterpark.com). For daily ski reports, call ☎ **303/572-7669.**

OTHER SKIING NEARBY   Silver Creek Ski Area, U.S. 40, Granby (☎ **800/ 448-9458** or 970/887-3384; www.silvercreek-resort.com), is a compact, family-oriented area mainly known for its beginner's trails and intermediate slopes. Terrain is rated 30% beginner, 50% intermediate, and 20% advanced. With a 1,000-foot vertical drop to a base elevation of 8,202 feet, it is served by two triple chairs, one double, a poma, and a surface lift. Full-day lift tickets (1998–99 rates) are $34 for adults, $28 for youths 13 to 17, $15 for children 6 to 12, $18 for seniors 62 to 69, and free for those under 6 and over 69.

Berthoud Pass Ski Area, 93475 U.S. 40 (P.O. Box 3314, 80482), Winter Park (☎ **800/754-2378,** 970/726-0287, or 303/569-0100; fax 303/569-3472; www.berthoudpass.com), is a small but historically significant ski area 65 miles west of Denver and 5 miles south of Winter Park. In the early 1930s, ski enthusiasts drove to the top of the 11,307-foot Berthoud Pass to ski down either Seven-Mile Run on the west or Hoop Creek on the east, then piled into cars to ride back to the top to do it again. The first rope tow in Colorado was completed here in early February 1937, and in the 1940s was home to the world's first double chairlift. Berthoud pass was also the first Colorado ski area to welcome snowboarders, allowing them full access to lifts and terrain.

After being closed for 10 years, the resort reopened for the 1997–98 season. Its season runs from November until July 4th, conditions permitting. The 65 runs are

Totally Tubular

The **Fraser Valley Tubing Hill** (behind Safeway), Fraser (☎ 970/726-5954), offers a return to childhood for many adults, as well as a lot of fun for kids (who must be 7 or older to ride alone). A lift pulls you and your big inner tube to the top of a steep hill, and then you slide down, sometimes reaching speeds of 45 mph. Open 4 to 10pm Monday through Friday, and 10am to 10pm Saturday, Sunday, and during holiday periods. Call for current rates.

---

rated 70% expert, and 15% each intermediate and beginner, and are served by one quad and one triple lift. Vertical drop is 1,100 feet (top elevation of 12,407 feet to the base of 11,307 feet). Lift tickets (1998–99 season) are $28 for adults, $15 for ages 6 to 12, and free for those under 6 and over 69. Three shuttle buses help skiers get around. The lifts and shuttles operate November through mid-April, daily from 9am to 4pm; and mid-April until the area closes, daily from 10am to 5pm. The day lodge has a pub and restaurant, open year-round, plus seasonal cafeteria dining. Also available are ski lessons; rentals of skis, snowshoes, and snowboards; and a shop with discounted sports equipment. In summer, the area is popular for mountain biking and hiking, with chairlift rides available.

CROSS-COUNTRY SKIING The outstanding cross-country skiing in the Winter Park area is highlighted by what the *Denver Post* calls "the best touring center in Colorado." The **Devil's Thumb Cross-Country Center at Devil's Thumb Ranch Resort** (see "Where to Stay," below) has more than 100 kilometers (67 miles) of groomed trails. Full rentals and instruction are available.

Snow Mountain Ranch–YMCA Nordic Center, on U.S. 40 between Tabernash and Granby (☎ 970/887-2152), features 100 kilometers (60 miles) of groomed trails for all abilities, including 3 kilometers (2 miles) of lighted track for night skiing.

SLEIGH RIDES Winter Park Resort has evening horse-drawn sleigh rides Thursday through Sunday nights. Gondola cars are attached to the ✪ **Zephyr Express** to take guests to the Lodge at Sunspot on the 10,700-foot summit of Winter Park mountain. The 20-minute sleigh rides, available between 7 and 9pm, follow a loop from the Lodge to the summit of Mary Jane. Guests can visit the Lodge before or after their ride to sip hot cocoa, cider, or one of their specialty drinks, or splurge on a decadent dessert. Cost for the gondola and sleigh rides is $14 for adults, $7 for children 13 and under. For more information, contact Winter Park Resort (☎ 970/726-5514, or 303/892-0961 from Denver).

Another option is to have dinner at the Lodge at Sunspot. They offer a five-course prix fixe dinner on those nights, which may include rack of lamb, aged steaks, or grilled salmon. The cost for the dinner plus gondola and sleigh rides is $50 per person. Holidays and specialty dinners may be higher. Seating begins at 5:30pm and reservations are required (☎ 970/726-1466, or 303/316-1446 from Denver).

Sleigh rides and dinner sleigh rides are also provided at **Devil's Thumb Ranch** and its exceptional **Ranch House Restaurant** (☎ 970/726-5632). See "Where to Stay," below.

SNOWCAT, SNOWMOBILE & SNOWSHOE TOURS For the non-skier, or for a break from skiing, there is plenty to do at Winter Park. Stop at the Tour Center desk in Balcony House at the base of Winter Park mountain for information and reservations (☎ 970/726-5514, ext. 1732).

Scenic **snowcat tours** leave at 10am, noon, and 1pm daily through mid-April for a 2-hour ride. Guides discuss the history of the valley and the surrounding mountains, and there's plenty of opportunity for photos. Coach seats cost $22 per person, $17 for seniors, and lap-sitters ride free.

Moonlight **snowmobile tours** depart at 5pm Thursday through Sunday from mid-December to mid-April. Guests pilot their own snowmobile on a two-hour trip to the summits of Winter Park and Mary Jane, and then head to a cafe for hot drinks and snacks. Cost is $50 per single rider, $25 per passenger, and includes snowmobile, helmet, and goggles. If the first tour fills up, a second is offered at 7:30pm.

Snowshoe tours head out at 10:30am and 1pm daily through mid-April, and follow game paths and summer bike trails. Cost for the two-hour trek is $25 per person, and includes snowshoes, poles, and a one-time lift pass.

WARM-WEATHER & YEAR-ROUND ACTIVITIES

There are plenty of recreational opportunities in the **Arapahoe National Forest** and **Arapahoe National Recreation Area**. Maps and brochures on hiking, mountain biking, and other activities are available at the Sulphur Ranger District office, P.O. Box 10, 9 Ten Rd., off U.S. 40 about half a mile south of Granby, CO 80446 (☎ **970/887-4100**). The **Devil's Thumb Ranch Resort** (see "Where to Stay," below) is famous for its numerous recreation packages, including rafting, hiking, mountain biking, and fly-fishing.

ALPINE SLIDE   Colorado's longest alpine slide, at 1½ miles long, cools summer visitors. Rates are $6 for adults, $5 for children 13 and under and seniors 62 and over. Those under 6 and over 69 are admitted free. For information, contact Winter Park Resort (☎ **970/726-5514**).

FISHING   Fraser Valley and surrounding Grand County are renowned among anglers. Head to Williams Fork Reservoir and the Three Lakes District for kokanee salmon, lake trout, brookies, and browns. Fishing ponds stocked with various species are in Fraser, across from the Fraser Valley Center on U.S. 40. The upper pond is reserved for children and people in wheelchairs; the lower pond is open to everyone. Ponds are generally open and stocked by mid-May.

GOLF   **Pole Creek Golf Club,** 10 miles northwest of Winter Park on U.S. 40 (☎ **970/726-8847**), considered among the finest mountain courses in the state, continues to be highly rated by *Golf Digest* magazine. Mountain views on the Ron Kirby/Gary Player–designed course are terrific. The course usually opens by Memorial Day (or as soon as the snow melts) and remains open until the middle of October. Rates in midsummer are $40 for 9 holes and $62.50 for 18 holes Monday through Thursday; $42 for 9 holes and $72.50 for 18 holes Friday through Sunday. Rates are lower at the beginning and end of the season. After 5pm, for $45, you can play as many holes as you can manage before the light fails.

HIKING & BACKPACKING   Check with Arapahoe National Forest (see above) for trail maps and other information. Beautiful Rocky Mountain National Park is less than an hour's drive north (see section 1 of this chapter).

MOUNTAIN BIKING   Winter Park and the Fraser Valley have won national recognition for their expansive trail system and established race program. Many off-road bike trails connect to the 600 miles of backcountry roads and trails in the adjacent national forest. The King of the Rockies Off-Road Stage Race and Festival, held each year in August, is one of the top professional mountain-bike races in America; part of it is run on the 30-mile ✪ **Tipperary Creek Trail,** among Colorado's best mountain-bike trails.

For advice, information, and maps, talk to the knowledgeable folks at **Winter Park Sports Shop** in Kings Crossing Shopping Center, at the intersection of Winter Park Drive and Kings Crossing Road (☎ **800/222-7547** or 970/726-5554). In business since 1946, the shop is open daily year-round, providing mountain and road bike sales, repairs, and rentals (about $15 per day). For specific information on trails and races, and to pick up a free trail map, call the **Winter Park/Fraser Valley Chamber of Commerce** (☎ **800/903-7275**, ext. 1) or the **Winter Park Competition Center** (☎ **970/726-1590**).

RIVER RAFTING   Half-day, full-day, and multi-day trips on the Colorado, Arkansas, Eagle, North Platte, and other rivers are offered by numerous local outfitters, including Colorado River Runs (☎ 800/826-1081), Mad Adventures (☎ 800/359-7530 or 970/726-5290), and Raven Adventure Trips (☎ 800/332-3381 or 970/887-2141). Half-day trips cost $35 to $40; full-day trips are $55 to $60.

RODEOS   Every Saturday night for about 8 weeks beginning in July, the **High Country Stampede Rodeos** hold forth at John Work Arena in nearby Fraser (☎ **800/903-7275**). Professional and top amateur cowboys compete in bronco riding, calf roping, and other events. A barbecue precedes the rodeo.

MORE TO SEE & DO

Amaze'n Winter Park. At the base of Winter Park Resort. ☎ **970/726-0214.** Admission $4 adults, $3 children 5–12, free for children under 5. Additional maze runs $2. Memorial Day weekend–Sept. Call for hours.

A human maze by Amaze'n Colorado, this two-level labyrinth of twists and turns offers prizes to participants who can "beat the clock." The maze is constructed in such a way that it can be easily changed, which is done weekly to maintain interest for repeat customers. A free observation deck gives a bird's-eye view of the maze, as well as the surrounding scenery.

Cozens Ranch House Museum. U.S. 40 between Winter Park and Fraser. ☎ **970/726-5488.** www.rkymtnhi.com. Admission $4 adults, $3 seniors 62 and over, $2 students 6 to 18, free for children under 6. Memorial Day–Sept, Mon–Sat 10am–5pm, Sun noon–5pm; late Nov–Memorial Day, Wed–Sat 11am–4pm, Sun noon–4pm. Closed Oct–late Nov.

This 1870s homestead presents a glimpse into Colorado's pioneer past, with a restored and furnished family residence, small hotel, stage stop, and the original Fraser Valley post office. There's also a replica of a stagecoach that traveled roads near here between 1875 and 1910.

WHERE TO STAY

There are more than 100 accommodations in the Fraser Valley, including hotels, condominiums, family-style mountain inns (serving breakfast and dinner daily), bed-and-breakfasts, lodges, and motels. Bookings can be made by **Winter Park Central Reservations,** P.O. Box 36, Winter Park, CO 80482 (☎ **800/729-5813** or 970/726-5587; fax 970/726-5993; e-mail: cenres@rkymtnhi.com). The agency can also book air and rail tickets, rental cars, airport transfers, lift tickets, ski-school lessons, ski rentals, and other activities.

In addition to the properties listed below, Winter Park has a **Super 8,** downtown on U.S. 40 (☎ **800/541-6130** or 970/726-8088), with rates for two of $52 to $67. Taxes add about 9% to lodging bills.

✪ **Devil's Thumb Ranch Resort.** Grand County Rd. 83 (P.O. Box 750), Tabernash, CO 80478. ☎ **800/933-4339** or 970/726-5632. Fax 970/726-9038. www.rkymtnhi.com/devthumb. 14 units (about half with private bathroom), plus 6 cabins, 1 dormitory. $20–$63 per person. Weekly discounts available; minimum stay required for some accommodations. MC, V.

This is the sort of place that attracts outdoor sports freaks in droves. Established in 1937, the ranch—8 miles north of Winter Park—is as famous today for its cross-country skiing in winter (see "Skiing & Other Winter Activities," above) as for its horseback riding and fly-fishing in summer. Accommodations are available for all pocketbooks, from a honeymoon cabin with a fireplace to dormitory beds in the bunkhouse. Most guests stay in one of the cozy rooms in the log Elk Lodge, where they have access to a whirlpool, TV, and billiards room. The Ranch House Restaurant & Saloon (open June through September and November 15 to April 15, daily from 8am to 9pm; the rest of the year, Thursday through Sunday for dinner only) lures Winter Park residents for creative country cuisine and seasonal specialties.

Engelmann Pines. 1035 Cranmer Ave. (P.O. Box 1305), Winter Park, CO 80482. ☎ **800/992-9512** or 970/726-4632. Fax 970/726-5458. 7 units (5 with private bathroom). $59–$65 shared bathroom; $75–$95 private bathroom. Rates include full breakfast. AE, DISC, MC, V. Closed mid-Dec to mid-April.

In this contemporary home outside Winter Park, Heinz and Margaret Engel have created a homey and comfortable bed-and-breakfast inn, where American and European antiques, including some family heirlooms, add an elegant touch. Each room is unique—several have rocking chairs, a few have wood-burning fireplaces (wood provided), some have balconies, and all have whirlpool tubs. There's a mountain-biking and hiking trailhead across the street from the inn, and guests have access to enclosed mountain-bike storage. The hearty breakfasts include fresh fruit; a cold Swiss specialty of apples, bananas, oats, and milk; fresh-baked pastries; and a hot entree such as eggs Benedict, German pancakes, or berry crepes. Swiss confections and other treats are provided in the afternoon. There's also a guest kitchen. Smoking is not permitted.

Gästhaus Eichler. 78786 U.S. 40 at Vasquez Creek (P.O. Box 3303), Winter Park, CO 80482. ☎ **800/543-3899** or 970/726-5133. Fax 970/726-5175. 15 units. TV TEL. Summer, $30–$40 per person per unit, double occupancy. Winter, $55–$75 per person per unit, double occupancy. AE, DC, MC, V.

The charm of this small inn is exactly what you'd expect to find at a European resort. Lace curtains and down comforters grace the rooms, and each has its own whirlpool. The restaurant offers innovative specials, fresh fish, and lighter fare, three meals daily.

The Inn at Silver Creek. U.S. 40 (Silver Creek Lodging, P.O. Box 4222), Silver Creek, CO 80446. ☎ **800/926-4386** or 970/887-2131. Fax 970/887-2350. www.innatsilvercreek.com. E-mail: innkeeper@innatsilvercreek.com. 211 units. TV TEL. Summer, $69 double; $169 suite. Peak season, from $89 double; $199 suite. Christmas, from $159 double; $300 suite. Low season, $59 double; $129 suite. AE, DC, DISC, MC, V. Pets accepted in some units for $12.

This outstanding resort is located 15 miles north of Winter Park and 2 miles southeast of Granby. It's becoming a popular conference location with its meeting area, all-season athletic facilities, and a wide range of in-season activities.

Every room has a whirlpool and steam cabinet in the bathroom, and each has a deck or balcony. Third-floor rooms and suites have vaulted ceilings, skylights, and lofts. Suites and studios come with a fireplace, wet bar (with minifridge and microwave), and dining-and-living area.

Silver Creek Lodging also offers units in the nearby Mountainside at Silver Creek. Spacious one- and two-bedroom spa condos range from $129 to $189 in summer, $169 to $249 peak, $249 to $369 Christmas, and $109 to $159 low season.

Snowblaze. U.S. 40 (P.O. Box 66), Winter Park, CO 80482. ☎ **800/525-2466** or 970/726-5701. Fax 970/726-4208. E-mail: wpadventures@rkymtnhi.com. 73 units. Double: low-season $77–$180, value season $109–$290, pre-Christmas $124–$316, Christmas $196–$506, summer $70–$130 (additional summer discounts in certain months). AE, MC, V.

One of Winter Park's more prestigious condominiums, Snowblaze features the Fraser Valley's leading athletic club on site. The units are in downtown Winter Park, 1½ miles from the ski area by shuttle. All have full bathrooms (one per bedroom), fully equipped kitchens, electric stoves, and/or microwaves. Two- and three-bedroom units also have fireplaces (with wood provided) and private dry saunas. All have simple but handsome decor, with big picture windows and rich wood furnishings. Winter Park Adventures, the property management firm for Snowblaze, also manages 14 other area properties.

The Vintage. 100 Winter Park Dr. (P.O. Box 1369), Winter Park, CO 80482. ☎ **800/472-7017** or 970/726-8801. Fax 970/726-9230. E-mail: vintage@rkymtnhi.com. 138 units. A/C TV TEL. Summer (includes continental breakfast), $65–$95 double; $150–$200 suite. Winter, $85–$195 double; $235–$475 suite. AE, DC, DISC, MC, V.

The château-like Vintage rises five stories above the foot of Winter Park's ski slopes, not far from the Mary Jane base facilities. A full-service resort hotel, it offers convenient access, excellent dining and atmosphere, and luxury accommodations. Every room in the hotel has a view of either the ski slopes or the Continental Divide, and many have balconies. Some have fireplaces, kitchens, and whirlpool tubs. Amenities include an outdoor heated pool, sauna, self-serve laundry, and on-site ski rentals, plus access to a nearby health club.

WHERE TO DINE

Deno's Mountain Bistro. U.S. 40, downtown Winter Park. ☎ **970/726-5332.** Burgers and sandwiches $4–$8; main courses $8–$17. AE, CB, DC, DISC, MC, V. Daily 11:30am–11pm; bar open later. BISTRO.

A favorite of locals and visitors alike, this self-proclaimed mountain bistro on Winter Park's main street has a casual atmosphere and impressive bar, with 50 national and international beers and an award-winning wine list of more than 300 selections. The restaurant is on two levels—the upstairs pub features copper-topped tables, while downstairs is casually elegant fine dining. The gourmet cuisine includes such dishes as angel-hair pomadora, with fresh basil and rock shrimp; aged New York strip steak; and prime rib. There are fresh seafood specials nightly, plus burgers, sandwiches, salads, and pizzas. During busy times—ski season and summer—there's live entertainment on Friday and Saturday evenings.

The Last Waltz. King's Crossing Shopping Center, U.S. 40. ☎ **970/726-4877.** Lunch $3.50–$7.50; dinner $7–$17. AE, DC, DISC, MC, V. Daily 7am–9pm. Sun brunch available until 2pm. AMERICAN/MEXICAN.

A favorite of those who enjoy good home-style cooking, this cafe treads the line between cultures at every meal: flapjacks or *migas* (a south-of-the-border egg scramble) for breakfast; Bayou ham, Rocky Mountain Reuben, or quesadilla sandwiches for lunch. In the evening, choices include crabmeat enchiladas, pork chops, or a 12-ounce rib-eye steak. There are also a variety of pasta dishes, including pasta with shrimp and mussels, seasoned with saffron. Children's and senior's portions available.

Rome on the Range. Downtown on U.S. 40. ☎ **970/444-4444.** Main courses $5–$19.50. AE, DC, DISC, MC, V. Daily 11:30am–10pm; bar open until 2am. STEAKHOUSE.

Downtown Winter Park's largest restaurant, Rome on the Range is also a saloon and dance hall (see "Winter Park After Dark," below). Decor is strictly western, with high ceilings, original western art, a fireplace, old saddles, and lots of Old West memorabilia. The restaurant specializes in steak—try the choice, aged, 22-ounce, Colorado T-bone, prepared on a wood-fired grill—but also offers rotisserie chicken, seafood such as grilled prawns glazed with roasted garlic, and pizza and pasta. There's an outdoor patio for warm-weather dining.

WINTER PARK AFTER DARK

Winter Park and the Fraser Valley offer several options for a night on the town. The **Derailer Bar & Grill** (☎ 970/726-5514), at the base of Winter Park, is where everyone gathers to swap tall tales of the day's best run or biggest fall. They also offer live entertainment and sports TV. If you're looking for munchies and drink specials, stop at the **Club Car Restaurant** on Mary Jane (☎ 970/726-1442). Country-and-western lovers should head for **Rome on the Range**, downtown on U.S. 40 (☎ 970/444-4444), where you can also get dance lessons, shoot pool, or sample some of the 20 Colorado beers on tap. Those who feel like hearing a local band can head for the **Slope,** half a mile from the ski area on U.S. 40 (☎ 970/726-5727), or the **Crooked Creek Saloon** in downtown Fraser (☎ 970/726-9250). The **Winter Park Pub**, 78260 U.S. 40 (☎ 970/726-4929), offers something different every night, from disco to mystery beer night. They have 15 beers on tap and Chicago-style pizza, with the atmosphere of an Irish pub.

5 Breckenridge & Summit County

67 miles W of Denver, 114 miles NW of Colorado Springs, 23 miles E of Vail

By and large, Summit County is a relatively modern creation. The mountain towns that surround its excellent ski areas—Arapahoe Basin, Breckenridge, Copper, Keystone, and Loveland (just beyond the county line)—were barely on the map in the 1880s, when the rest of the state was laying claim to its stake of history. Breckenridge was a prosperous mining town in 1887 when the largest gold nugget ever found in Colorado, "Tom's Baby," was unearthed here. It weighed 13 pounds, 7 ounces, and is now in the Colorado History Museum in Denver. Copper Mountain gained a modest reputation for the copper ore it produced around the same time, but both towns had fallen on comparatively hard times before their respective ski areas opened in 1961 and 1972.

Today, Summit County is a major recreational sports center, with skiing in winter, and fishing, hiking, and mountain biking in summer. Though skiers began coming to Arapahoe Basin and Loveland in the immediate postwar period, Summit County wasn't known for its ski areas until Breckenridge opened, and its reputation was only enhanced with the openings of Keystone and Copper a few years later.

ESSENTIALS

GETTING THERE   By Car   I-70 runs through the middle of Summit County. For Keystone, exit on U.S. 6 at Dillon; the resort is 6 miles east of the interchange. For Breckenridge, exit on Colo. 9 at Frisco and head south 9 miles to the resort. Copper Mountain is right on I-70 at the Colo. 91 interchange.

By Airport Shuttle   Most visitors fly into Denver International or Colorado Springs and continue to Breckenridge, Frisco, Keystone, and/or Copper Mountain via shuttle. **Resort Express** (☎ 800/334-7433 or 970/468-7600) offers shuttles; **People's Choice Transportation** (☎ 800/777-2388 or 303/659-7780) offers luxury transport to Summit County resorts. (For listings of airlines servicing Denver and Colorado Springs, see chapters 6 and 8, respectively.)

VISITOR INFORMATION   For additional information on Breckenridge and other parts of Summit County, contact the Breckenridge Resort Chamber, with an information center at 309 N. Main St. and administrative offices at 311 S. Ridge St. (P.O. Box 1909), Breckenridge, CO 80424 (☎ 800/221-1091 or 970/453-6018; www.gobreck.com). For information about activities in Breckenridge, contact the Activity Center, 137 S. Main St., in Blue River Plaza (☎ 970/453-5579). For other communities, contact the following: the Copper Mountain Resort Chamber, P.O. Box 3003, Copper Mountain, CO 80443 (☎ 970/968-6477); and Keystone Resort, P.O. Box 38, Keystone, CO 80435 (☎ 970/496-2316 for general information; ☎ 800/404-3535 for reservations and snow conditions; www. snow. com).

A source of visitor information for the entire region is the **Summit County Chamber of Commerce,** P.O. Box 214, Frisco, CO 80443 (☎ **970/668-2051**). The chamber has an information center in Frisco (I-70 exit 203), and another in Dillon just off U.S. 6.

GETTING AROUND   Dillon Reservoir is at the heart of Summit County, and I-70 lies along its northwestern shore, with Frisco at its west end, and Dillon and Silverthorne toward the east. From Dillon take U.S. 6 about 5 miles east to Keystone and another 15 miles to Arapahoe. Breckenridge is about 10 miles south of Frisco on Colo. 9, and Copper Mountain is just south of I-70 exit 195 (Colo. 91). Loveland is just across the county line at exit 216 on the east side of the Eisenhower Tunnel.

Summit Stage (☎ **970/668-0999**) provides free year-round service between Frisco, Dillon, Silverthorne, Keystone, Breckenridge, and Copper Mountain, daily from 6am to midnight, late November to mid-April; shorter hours the rest of the year.

You can get around Breckenridge on the free **Town Trolley** (☎ **970/547-3127**), and there's also free shuttle service at Keystone Resort (☎ **970/453-5241**).

FAST FACTS   Hospitals include the **Centura Health Summit Medical Center,** Colo. 9 at School Road, Frisco (☎ **970/668-3300** for emergencies, 24 hours); the **Breckenridge Medical Center,** The Village at Breckenridge, 555 S. Park St., Plaza II, Breckenridge (☎ **970/453-9000**); and **Mountain Medical Center,** 130 Ski Hill Rd., Breckenridge (☎ **970/453-7600**). **Post offices** are at 300 S. Ridge St., Breckenridge; and 65 W. Main St., Frisco. For hours and other information contact the U.S. Postal Service (☎ **800/275-8777**). For **weather and road conditions,** call ☎ **970/668-1090.**

SPECIAL EVENTS   International Snow Sculpture Championships, second week in January; Ullr Fest, third week in January, in Breckenridge; Ski Fiesta, fourth Saturday in February, in Keystone; John Elway Celebrity Ski Race and Eenie Weenie Bikini Contest, first and second weekends in April, in Copper Mountain; Taste of Breckenridge and Beachin' at the Basin Spring Skiing Blowout, Memorial Day weekend, in Arapahoe Basin; the Breckenridge Music Festival, from late June to late August; Frisco Founders Day, third weekend in September; Monte Carlo Magic, second week in November.

SKIING & OTHER WINTER ACTIVITIES

Breckenridge and Keystone ski areas are now part of Vail Resorts, and any lift ticket purchased at Vail or Beaver Creek is valid without restriction at Breckenridge and Keystone. However, only multi-day lift tickets for three or more days purchased at Breckenridge or Keystone are also valid at Vail and Beaver Creek.

Breckenridge/Summit County

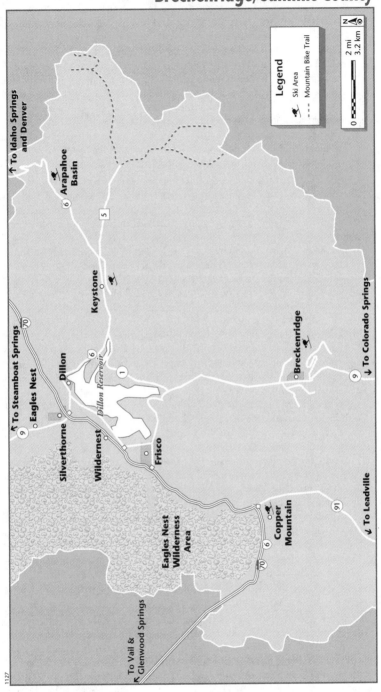

Legend

- Ski Area
- - - - Mountain Bike Trail

2 mi
3.2 km

N

↑ To Idaho Springs and Denver

Arapahoe Basin

6

5

Keystone

↖ To Steamboat Springs

70

Eagles Nest

9

Dillon

6

1

Dillon Reservoir

Silverthorne

Wildernest

Frisco

Eagles Nest Wilderness Area

Breckenridge

↓ To Colorado Springs

9

Copper Mountain

91

↓ To Leadville

6

70

↙ To Vail & Glenwood Springs

1127

ARAPAHOE BASIN   Arapahoe Basin, 28194 U.S. 6, between Keystone and Loveland Pass, is one of Colorado's oldest ski areas, having opened in 1945. It is now operated by **Dundee Realty,** P.O. Box 8787, Keystone, CO 80435 (☎ **888/ 272-7263** or 970/496-0718; www.arapahoebasin.com). Several features make Arapahoe exceptional. Most of its 490 acres are intermediate and expert terrain, much of it above timberline, and with an average of 360 inches of snow a year, it is often the last Colorado ski area to close for the season—usually not until early June. Arapahoe offers a 2,250-foot vertical drop from its summit at 13,050 feet. It is served by one triple and four double chairs.

Lift tickets (1998–99 season) are $39 for adults, $29 for seniors 60 to 69, $12 for children 6 to 12, and free for kids under 6 and seniors 70 and over.

✪ BRECKENRIDGE   Spread across four large mountains on the west side of the town of Breckenridge, this area ranks third in size among Colorado's ski resorts. Once known for its wealth of open, groomed beginner and intermediate slopes, Breckenridge in recent years has expanded its acreage for expert skiers as well.

Peak 8, the original ski mountain, is the highest of the three at 12,998 feet and has the greatest variety. Peak 9, heavily geared to novices and intermediates, rises above the principal base area. Peak 10, served by a single high-speed quad chair, is predominantly expert territory. The vast bowls of Peak 8 and the North Face of Peak 9 are likewise advanced terrain. There are restaurants high on Peaks 8, 9, and 10 and three cafeterias at the base of the slopes. Peak 7, opened in 1994, is a double black diamond challenge on over 1,200 feet of vertical.

All told, the resort has 2,031 skiable acres, with 136 trails served by 19 lifts—six high-speed quad superchairs, one triple chair, eight double chairs, and four surface lifts for beginners. Available vertical drop is 3,398 feet; average annual snowfall is 255 inches (more than 21 feet).

Lift tickets (1998–99 season) cost $47 for adults and $12 for children 5 to 12, with higher Christmas holiday rates. Children 4 and younger and seniors 70 and older ski free. Tickets purchased at Breckenridge are also valid at Keystone, and multi-day tickets for three or more days are also valid at Vail and Beaver Creek.

Among Breckenridge's programs are its women's ski seminars, taught exclusively by women for women skiers of all abilities. Three- and four-day seminars are offered in January, February, March, and April. Women-only ski-school classes are available throughout the ski season. For more information, call ☎ **888/576-2754.**

Breckenridge is open from late October to early May, daily from 8:30am to 4pm. From Memorial Day weekend to late September, the alpine slide is in operation, and the trails are open to mountain bikers; mini-golf is also available. Call ☎ **970/ 453-5000** for off-season hours and chairlift schedule. For further information, contact Breckenridge Ski Area, **Breckenridge Ski Resort,** P.O. Box 1058, Breckenridge, CO 80424 (☎ **970/453-5000,** or 970/453-6118 for 24-hour ski conditions; www.snow.com).

COPPER MOUNTAIN   From Copper Mountain village, the avalanche chutes on the west face of Ten Mile Mountain seem to spell out the word SKI. Though this is a natural coincidence, locals like to say the mountain has terrain created for skiing.

Terrain is about half beginner and intermediate, with the rest ranging from advanced to "you better be really good." The area has a vertical drop of 2,601 feet from a peak elevation of 12,313 feet. There are 2,433 skiable acres. The 119 trails are served by 19 lifts—three high-speed quads, six triple chairs, eight double chairs, and four surface lifts. Average annual snowfall is 280 inches.

There are three restaurants on the mountain and several more in the base village. Also at the base are 25 kilometers (15 miles) of cross-country track, an ice-skating pond, a tubing hill, and a full-service racquet and athletic club.

For the 1998–99 season, lift tickets cost $47 for adults, $17 for children 6 to 14, and $29 for seniors 60 to 69. Tickets are free for seniors over 70 and children 5 and under.

Copper Mountain is open from mid-November to early May, Monday through Friday from 9am to 4pm, Saturday and Sunday from 8:30am to 4pm. For information, contact **Copper Mountain Resort,** P.O. Box 3001, Copper Mountain, CO 80443 (☎ **970/968-2882;** www.ski-copper.com). For reservations, call ☎ **800/458-8386;** for a snow report, call ☎ **800/789-7609.**

KEYSTONE   Keystone is not only a superb mountain for intermediate skiers, but also one of the best spots for night skiing in America, with 14 trails and three lifts open daily until 9pm.

Spacious Keystone Mountain offers some 860 acres of intermediate terrain and ample beginner slopes. Over its back side are North Peak and the Outback region, both with advanced intermediate and expert runs.

From its peak elevation of 12,200 feet, Keystone's vertical drop is 2,900 feet. Keystone's three inter-connected mountains offer 1,755 acres of skiing, 92 trails, and 20 lifts—including two connecting high-speed gondolas, four high-speed quads, one quad chair, three triple chairs, five double chairs, and five surface lifts. Average annual snowfall is 230 inches (about 19 feet).

For the 1998–99 season, lift tickets cost $47 for adults and $12 for children 5 to 12, with higher rates during holidays. Children 4 and younger and seniors 70 and older ski free. Tickets purchased at Keystone are also valid at Breckenridge, and multi-day tickets for three or more days are also valid at Vail and Beaver Creek.

Excellent on-mountain dining is available at the Alpenglow Stube, located in The Outpost, a log-and-stone lodge atop North Peak (elevation 11,444 feet). Access is via two scenic gondola rides.

Keystone is open from mid-October to early May, daily from 8:30am to 9pm. For further information, contact **Keystone Resort,** P.O. Box 38, Keystone, CO 80435 (☎ **970/496-2316;** www.snow.com). For snow reports call ☎ **800/ 404-3535** or 970/496-4111.

LOVELAND   Just across the county line, on the east side of I-70's Eisenhower Memorial Tunnel, is **Loveland Ski Area,** P.O. Box 899, Georgetown, CO 80444 (☎ **800/736-3754** or 303/569-3203; www.skiloveland.com; e-mail: loveland@ pcisys.net). Comprised of Loveland Basin and Loveland Valley, it was created in the late 1930s by a Denver ski club wanting to take advantage of the area's heavy snowfall (400 inches, more than 33 feet, annually). You can still see the original ropetow cabins from 1942, when all-day tickets cost $2. Inflation (and the cost of many improvements) has taken a toll. Today, tickets (1998–99 season) are $37 for adults, $28 for seniors 60 to 69, and $18 for children 6 to 14; children under 6 and seniors 70 and older ski free.

There's good beginner–intermediate terrain on the 965 lift-served acres—22% and 55% respectively, leaving 23% expert, plus another 400 acres accessible by hiking to The Ridge, all of which is expert. The vertical drop is 2,410 feet from a top elevation of 13,010 feet. Lifts include two quad chairs, two triples, four doubles, one poma, and one Mitey Mite. The resort opens in mid-October and generally remains open until mid-May, with lifts operating from 9am to 4pm Monday through Friday, from 8:30am to 4pm weekends and some holidays.

CROSS-COUNTRY SKIING   The **Frisco Nordic Center,** on Colo. 9 south of Frisco (☎ **970/668-0866**), sits on the shores of Dillon Reservoir. Its trail network includes 37 kilometers (22 miles) of set tracks and groomed skating lanes, and access to backcountry trails. The lodge has a snack bar and a shop with rentals and retail sales; instruction and backcountry and snowshoe tours are also offered. From the Frisco Nordic Center you can ski to the **Breckenridge Nordic Ski Center,** on Willow Lane near the foot of Peak 8 (☎ **970/453-6855**), with its own series of 28 kilometers (17.4 miles) of groomed trails. Trail passes ($10 for adults, $6 for seniors and children) are interchangeable.

The **Copper Mountain Cross-Country Center** has 25 kilometers (15.5 miles) of track and skating lanes through the wooded valley and is adjacent to 1,200 acres of alpine skiing terrain (☎ **970/968-2882,** ext. 6342). An all-day pass costs $10. **Keystone Cross-Country Center** features 18 kilometers of groomed trails for both skiers and snowshoers, and another 57 kilometers of ungroomed trails in the back-country of the Arapaho National Forest.

For information on the numerous cross-country skiing possibilities in the area's national forests, contact the **Dillon Ranger District,** located in the town of Silverthorne at 680 Blue River Pkwy., half a mile north of I-70 exit 205 (P.O. Box 620, Silverthorne, CO 80498; ☎ **970/468-5400**).

SNOWBOARDING   Snowboarding is permitted at all local resorts. Enthusiasts can get equipment and lessons from the **Breckenridge Ski Resort** (☎ **800/ 789-7669** or 970/453-5000), where snowboarding has been popular since the early 1980s. They offer both class and private lessons.

Copper Mountain has a snowboard terrain park on the west side of the mountain near the American Flyer high-speed quad. Big floater jumps are spread out across an entire run, with proper take-off and landing ramps; there's a regulation half-pipe, and several drainage and gladed runs have been thinned to provide challenging tree riding for the more advance snowboarders.

In 1996, **Keystone** opened its mountains to snowboarders after investing $5 million in on-mountain improvements and skier/snowboarder services. Area 51 is a 20-acre terrain garden with two half-pipes, which is lit for night riding.

Loveland's snowboard park offers an 80-foot sidewinder quarter-pipe.

SNOWMOBILING   Snowmobilers can join guided tours from **Aspen Canyon Ranch** (☎ **800/321-1357** or 970/725-3600) or **Good Times, Inc.** (☎ **800/ 477-0144** or 970/453-7604). Tours vary considerably, but often include stops at ghost towns and old mining camps. Rates for a 2-hour trip, including lunch, are usually in the $60 to $90 range for one person on a snowmobile and $100 to $125 for two.

ICE-SKATING   All three major resort communities have groomed ponds for ice-skating, with rentals and lessons available. Five-acre **Keystone Lake** claims to be the largest maintained outdoor ice-skating lake in North America. The rink is generally open from late November to early March, with public skating sessions from 10am to 2pm, 2 to 6pm, and 6 to 10pm daily. Admission is $6 for adults, $5 for youths 13 to 17, $3.50 for children 5 to 12, and $1 for children 4 and under. Skate, sled, and hockey-stick rentals, as well as ice-skating lessons, are available.

WARM-WEATHER & YEAR-ROUND ACTIVITIES

Two national forests—**Arapahoe** and **White River**—overlap the boundaries of Summit County. These recreational playgrounds offer opportunities not only for downhill and cross-country skiing and snowmobiling in winter, but also for hiking and backpacking, horseback riding, boating, fishing, hunting, and bicycling in summer. White River National Forest encompasses the **Eagles Nest Wilderness Area** and Arapahoe National Forest includes **Green Mountain Reservoir,** both in the northern part of the county.

The **U.S. Forest Service's Dillon Ranger District,** located in the town of Silverthorne at 680 Blue River Pkwy., half a mile north of I-70 exit 205 (☎ **970/ 468-5400,** or write P.O. Box 620, Silverthorne, CO 80498), has an unusually good selection of information on outdoor recreation possibilities, including maps and guides to hiking and mountain-biking trails, jeep roads, cross-country skiing, snowmobiling, fishing, and camping. You can also get information on a wide variety of outdoor activities from the **Breckenridge Activity Center,** 137 S. Main St., in Blue River Plaza (☎ **970/453-5579**).

BICYCLING   There are more than 40 miles of paved bicycle paths in the county, including a path from Breckenridge (with a spur from Keystone) to Frisco and Copper Mountain, continuing across Vail Pass to Vail. This spectacularly beautiful two-lane path is off-limits to motorized vehicles of any kind. Also see "Mountain Biking," below.

BOATING   Dillon Reservoir, a beautiful mountain lake along I-70 between Dillon and Frisco, is the place to go. Also called Lake Dillon, the 3,300-acre reservoir, which provides drinking water to Denver, is more than 200 feet deep in spots. At 9,017-feet elevation, it claims to have America's highest altitude yacht club and holds colorful regattas most summer weekends. The popular Dillon Open, a huge sailboat race, occurs the first weekend in August. Swimming is not permitted.

The full-service **Dillon Marina,** 150 Marina Dr. (☎ **970/468-5100**), is open from the last weekend of May through the last weekend of October, offering boats for 2-hour, half-day, or full-day rental; sailing instruction; and charter cruises. Half-day boat-rental fees run $45 for small fishing boats, $105 for runabouts, and $160 for 24-foot pontoon boats. Fuel is extra. Half-day rates for sailboats are $95 to $150 for boats ranging from 18 to 23 feet. There's also a small store, repair shop, restaurant and bar.

FISHING   Major fishing rivers within an hour of Breckenridge include the South Platte, Arkansas, Eagle, Colorado, and Blue Rivers, and for lake fishing, try Dillon Reservoir and Spinney Mountain Reservoir. The Blue River, from Lake Dillon Dam to its confluence with the Colorado River at Kremmling, is rated a gold-medal fishing stream.

For tips on where they're biting, as well as supplies, fishing licenses, and all the rest, stop at **Mountain Angler,** 311 S. Main St. in the Main Street Mall (☎ **800/ 453-4669** or 970/453-4665), which also offers year-round guide service. Fly-fishing instruction is given weekends in July (4-hour lessons cost $110 to $180, 2-day lessons cost $279). Guided fly-fishing trips, on both public and private waters, are $135 to $205 for a half day; $185 to $285 for a full day, including lunch. A float-fishing guided trip, limited to two anglers, costs $275 for one and $325 for two, and includes transportation, lunch, and gear. The shop is open every day of the year, from 8am to 9pm in summer, 9am to 9pm in winter.

GOLF   Among area golf courses are **Breckenridge Golf Club,** 200 Clubhouse Dr., Breckenridge (☎ **970/453-9104**), designed by Jack Nicklaus, with fees ranging from $25 (9 holes in low season) to $78 (18 holes in high season, mid-June to mid-September); **Copper Creek Golf Club,** 122 Wheeler Place, Copper Mountain Resort (☎ **970/968-2882**), among the highest 18-hole courses in North America at 9,650 feet, with fees of $33 for 9 holes and $65 for 18 holes, including cart; and **Keystone Ranch Golf Course,** Keystone Ranch Road, Keystone (☎ **970/496-4250**), a highly-rated course, charging $101 for 18 holes.

HIKING & BACKPACKING   The ✪ **Colorado Trail** cuts a swath through Summit County. It enters from the east across Kenosha Pass, follows the Swan River to its confluence with the Blue River, then climbs over Ten Mile Mountain to Copper Mountain. The trail then turns south toward Tennessee Pass, north of Leadville.

There are myriad hiking opportunities in the national forests. Consult the U.S. Forest Service, the Breckenridge Activity Center, or a visitor information center for maps and details.

HORSEBACK RIDING   For some spectacular views of this area from atop a horse, take a ride with **Breckenridge Stables,** located just above the Alpine Super Slide parking area, 1700 Ski Hill Rd., Breckenridge (☎ **970/453-4438**). The company offers rides of 1 and 2 hours, plus breakfast and dinner rides, starting at about $20 per person.

MOUNTAIN BIKING   Numerous trails beckon mountain bikers as they wind through the mountains, often following 19th-century mining roads and burro trails and ending at ghost towns. Energetic fat-tire fans can try the Devil's Triangle, a difficult 80-mile loop that begins and ends in Frisco after climbing four mountain passes (including 11,318-foot Fremont Pass). Check with the U.S. Forest Service or Breckenridge Activity Center for directions and tips on other trails; for mountain bikers who prefer to not work so hard, check with the Breckenridge Activity Center on times and costs for taking your bike up the mountain on the Breckenridge chairlift.

Among companies providing bike rentals, repairs, accessories, and information is **Backcountry Bikes,** Bell Tower Mall, Breckenridge (☎ **800/525-9624** or 970/453-2194), which charges $12 for a basic bike and $21 for a full-suspension bike for a half day, and $15 and $30, respectively, for a full day.

RIVER RAFTING   Trips through the white water of the Blue River—which runs through Breckenridge to Frisco—as well as longer journeys on the Colorado and Arkansas Rivers, are offered by various companies, including **Kodi Rafting** (same phone as Backcountry Bikes, above), with rates per person of $30 for a half day and $60 for a full day. Similar trips are offered by **Performance Tours Rafting** in Breckenridge (☎ **800/328-7238** or 970/453-0661).

THE FESTIVAL SCENE

The **Breckenridge Music Festival** includes more than 50 classical and non-classical music performances, with concerts in the Riverwalk Center from late June through mid-August. Tickets cost from $10 to $22, with discounts for seniors; they're only $5 for students under 18. There is also a free Fourth of July concert. Contact the Breckenridge Music Institute, P.O. Box 1254, Breckenridge, CO 80424 (☎ **970/453-2120;** e-mail: bmi@csn.net).

Genuine Jazz in July, on the second weekend of the month, showcases Colorado jazz ensembles with styles ranging from Dixieland to bebop to New Age. Local bars and nightclubs host Friday- and Saturday-night performances. Free Saturday- and Sunday-afternoon concerts are outdoors at Maggie Pond, at the base of Peak 9. Call ☎ **970/453-6018** for schedules.

The **Breckenridge Festival of Film,** held the third full weekend of September, attracts Hollywood directors and actors to town to discuss some two dozen films in all genres. Contact the Breckenridge Festival of Film office for information (☎ **970/453-6200**).

Copper Fest, over Labor Day weekend, is a country-and-western music and art festival, featuring over 24 hours of entertainment with such performers as Clint Black, Don Edwards, Red Steagall, and Waddie Mitchell. Lumberjack exhibitions, children's activities, and art and artifacts are also on the bill. For more information call ☎ **970/968-2318,** ext. 6301.

MORE TO SEE & DO

Amaze'n Breckenridge. 710 S. Main St. at the base of Peak 8, Breckenridge. ☎ **970/453-7262.** Admission $4 adults, $3 children 5–12, free for children under 5. Additional maze runs $2. Mid-June to Labor Day. Call for hours.

Colorado's largest human maze, this is the original by Amaze'n Colorado. The two-level labyrinth of twists and turns offers prizes to participants who can "beat the clock." The maze is constructed in such a way that it can be easily changed, which is done weekly to maintain interest for repeat customers. A free observation deck provides a bird's-eye view of the maze, as well as the surrounding scenery.

Breckenridge National Historic District. Breckenridge. ☎ **970/453-9022.** Guided tours of historic district and gold mines, and slide shows, $5 adults, $3 children 12 and younger. Edwin Carter Museum tours, $3 all ages. Historic district and gold mine tours June–Aug; Edwin Carter Museum and historic district slide shows year-round (call for times).

The entire Victorian core of this 19th-century mining town has been carefully preserved. Colorfully painted shops and restaurants occupy the old buildings, most dating from the 1880s and 1890s. The Summit Historical Society conducts guided 2-hour walking tours in summer. Most of the historic district focuses on Main Street, and extends east on either side of Lincoln Avenue. Among the 254 buildings in the district are the **1875 Edwin Carter Museum,** 111 N. Ridge St., and the **1896 William Harrison Briggle House,** 104 N. Harris St., in Milne Park. The society also leads tours during the summer to the outskirts of town to visit the underground shaft of the hard-rock **Washington Gold Mine** and the gold-panning operation at **Lomax Placer Gulch.** In winter, the historical society offers tours of the Edwin Carter Museum once each week, and slide shows on the historic district, at the Edwin Carter Museum, twice a week (call for times).

Country Boy Mine. 0542 French Gulch Rd., P.O. Box 8569, Breckenridge. ☎ **970/453-4405.** Mine tour $11 adults, $6 children 4–12, free for kids under 4; hay ride $10 adults, $5 children 4–12, free for kids under 4; combination tickets available. Special rates and hours are available for families and groups. MC, V. Summer, daily 10am–5pm; winter, daily 11am–4pm.

The hundred-year-old Country Boy Mine is the place to take a guided tour 1,000 feet underground, pan for gold in Eureka Creek, explore the mining exhibit and the five-story 75-year-old mill, and listen to the legends. Or take a hay ride up the mountain on old mining trails and enjoy hot chocolate and roasted marshmallows around a campfire. The mine is a constant 55°F year-round, so take a jacket even in August. Future plans include the restoration of a blacksmith shop and an "ore chute" ride. Every summer sees the addition of a baby burro.

Frisco Historic Park. 120 Main St. (at Second St.), Frisco. ☎ **970/668-3428.** Free admission. Summer, Tues–Sun 11am–4pm; winter, Tues–Sat 11am–4pm.

Nine historic buildings, including the town's original 1881 jail, a one-room schoolhouse, log chapel, and homes dating to the 1880s, comprise this beautifully maintained historic park. The schoolhouse contains displays and artifacts from Frisco's early days, and a trapper's cabin has a hands-on exhibit of animal pelts. Artisans sell their wares in several buildings, and a variety of events are scheduled during the summer. A self-guided walking tour of historic Frisco can be obtained at the park.

Summit Historical Museum. 403 LaBonte St., Dillon. ☎ **970/453-9022**. Admission by donation. Museum, Memorial Day–Labor Day, tours Tues–Sat 1:30 and 3pm; or by appointment.

A one-room country school—filled with such artifacts of early Colorado education as desks with inkwells, McGuffey readers, and scientific teaching apparatus—is the highlight of Dillon's historic park. Also on the site are the 1885 Lula Myers ranch house and the depression-era Honeymoon Cabin. All buildings were moved from Old Dillon (now beneath the waters of the reservoir) or Keystone. Tours are also conducted (by appointment) of an 1884 Montezuma Schoolhouse, located at 10,200 feet elevation in the 1860s mining camp of Montezuma.

SHOPPING

Breckenridge is the place to shop in Summit County, with a variety of shops and galleries in the historic buildings along Main Street.

For contemporary art and sculpture, from realism to impressionism, check out **Breckenridge Gallery,** 124 S. Main St. (☎ 970/453-2592). Western art in a variety of media and techniques can be found at **Paint Horse Gallery,** 226 S. Main St. (☎ 970/453-6813). Art glass and jewelry, plus occasional glass-blowing demonstrations, are offered at **Fineline Studios Inc.,** 108 S. Main St. (☎ 970/453-2116). For beautiful photos of Colorado, stop at **Colorado Scenics,** 124 S. Main St. (☎ 970/453-4922); photographer Steve Tohari has been photographing his adopted state (he's originally from London) since 1983.

If you're in the market for a special hat, try the **Sundance Hat Co.,** Four Seasons Plaza, 411 S. Main St. (☎ 970/453-2737). Authentic traditional and contemporary American Indian jewelry, pottery, and other crafts can be found at **Southwest Designs,** 101 S. Main St. (☎ 970/453-6008). The **Silverthorne Factory Stores** (☎ 970/468-9440) has more than four dozen outlet shops—from fashion and athletic wear to home accessories; take I-70 exit 205.

WHERE TO STAY

Thousands of rooms are available here at any given time. Even so, during peak seasons, finding accommodations may be difficult. In many cases it will be best to simply call one of the reservation services, tell them when you plan to visit and how much you want to spend, and ask for their suggestions. As a general rule, avoid the Christmas holidays, when lodging is most expensive (especially the closer you are to the ski slopes). You'll usually get the best rates in late spring—after the ski season ends but before the summer rush begins.

Throughout the county, condominiums prevail. While they often offer the best value, they're sometimes short on charm. If you're planning to spend much time in one, it pays to ask about views and fireplaces before booking. Local reservation services include **Summit County Guest Services** (☎ 800/530-3099), **Breckenridge Central Reservations** (☎ 800/221-1091), **Keystone Central Reservations** (☎ 800/427-8308), and **Copper Mountain Resort** (☎ 800/458-8386).

In addition to the properties discussed below, there's a **Comfort Suites** in Dillon, 276 U.S. 6 (☎ **800/228-5150** or 970/513-0300), with rates of $119 to $229 double; and two motels at the I-70 Dillon Silverthorne exit (#205): **Days Inn** (☎ **800/329-7466** or 970/468-1421), with rates for two of $48 to $99; and **Super 8** (☎ **800/800-8000** or 970/468-8888), with rates for two of $50 to $60.

Room taxes add about 9.5% to hotel bills.

✪ **Allaire Timbers Inn Bed & Breakfast.** 9511 Colo. 9 (P.O. Box 4653), Breckenridge, CO 80424. ☎ **800/624-4904** or 970/453-7530. Fax 970/453-8699. www.allairetimbers. com. E-mail: allairetimbers@worldnet.att.net. 10 units. TV TEL. $130–$195 double; $200–$280 suite. Rates include full breakfast. AE, DISC, MC, V.

This is a lovely contemporary log lodge, with a stone wood-burning fireplace in the living room, an outside hot tub, and magnificent views of the mountains and town. All rooms are named for and decorated around the motif of a Colorado mountain pass. There are hand-painted tiled showers—no tubs—in standard rooms, but the two suites have hot tubs and river-rock gas-burning fireplaces. All units come with private decks, robes, and fuzzy fleece socks. Located just outside the town limits, there is an easy path that takes you right into town. The homemade gourmet breakfast includes a choice of a meat or vegetarian entree, plus fruit and muffins. In the afternoon guests can enjoy hot citrus cider (an old family recipe), beer, or wine; and the beverage bar is available 24 hours. Smoking is not allowed.

East West Resorts at Breckenridge. 295 S. Main Street. (P.O. Box 2009), Breckenridge, CO 80424. ☎ **800/525-2258** or 970/453-2222. Fax 970/453-0463. www.eastwestresorts. com. E-mail: breckres@eastwestresorts.com. 220 units. TV TEL. Summer, $59–$260; winter, $95–$815. Weekly and monthly rates in summer. AE, DISC, MC, V. Free parking in underground lot.

There are several condominium complexes to choose from here, offering everything from simple studios to luxurious and spacious five-bedroom units. Most have mountain views or are nestled among tall pines, provide ski lockers, and have a fireplace and access to a pool and hot tub; many are ski-in and -out.

East West Resorts also has properties at Keystone, 22869 U.S. 6, P.O. Box 8936, Keystone, CO 80435 (☎ **888/953-9737** or 970/468-2601; fax 970/262-0124; e-mail: keyres@eastwestresorts.com), and Copper Mountain, 760 Copper Rd, P.O. Box 3868, Copper Mountain, CO 80443 (☎ **800/525-3887** or 970/968-6840; fax 970/968-0317; e-mail: coppres@eastwestresorts.com), with similar properties and rates.

Holiday Inn–Summit County. I-70 exit 203 (P.O. Box 4310), Frisco, CO 80443. ☎ **800/ 782-7669** or 970/668-5000. Fax 970/668-0718. 217 units. A/C TV TEL. Dec–Apr, $89–$199 double; spring and fall, $69–$89 double; summer, $79–$119 double. Children 19 and under stay free in parents' room. AE, DC, DISC, MC, V.

Located beside the shoreline wetlands of Dillon Reservoir, this Holiday Inn maintains the feel of a ski lodge. Many second-floor rooms have balconies with views across the lake. A complete remodeling project—inside and out—was recently completed. There are four whirlpool suites, and all rooms have coffeemakers and hair dryers. The restaurant serves three meals daily and offers a prime rib and crableg buffet on Saturday nights. Amenities include limited room service, refreshments in the lobby, indoor heated swimming pool, two whirlpools, a sauna, game room, guest laundry, access to a nearby health club, squash and racquetball courts nearby, and meeting space for 250. Ski rentals and repairs are available.

Little Mountain Lodge Bed & Breakfast. 98 Sunbeam Dr. (P.O. Box 2479), Breckenridge, CO 80424. ☎ **800/468-7707** or 970/453-1969. Fax 970/453-1919. www.littlemountainlodge. com. E-mail: lml@colorado.net. 10 units. TV TEL. $130–$215 double; $160–$260 suite. Rates include full breakfast. AE, MC, V. Children over 12 welcome.

This handsome, whitewashed log lodge is nestled among the trees in Breckenridge, with breathtaking views of the mountains from the front rooms and the aspen forest from the back. All units are open and airy, and boast a balcony or deck, handmade log furnishings, ceiling fans, and TV/VCRs (a video library is available). Some rooms have jetted tubs, and back rooms feature vaulted ceilings. There's one handicapped-accessible room with a roll-in shower.

The living room has a huge fireplace made from river rock, with overstuffed sofa and chairs comfortably arranged around it. A game room contains a gas fireplace, pool table, and TV. There's also a ski storage room with a boot dryer. No smoking is permitted.

The Lodge & Spa at Breckenridge. 112 Overlook Dr. (P.O. Box 391), Breckenridge, CO 80424. ☎ **800/736-1607** or 970/453-9300. Fax 970/453-0625. 45 units. TV TEL. $150–$400 double. AE, DISC, MC, V.

You enter this European-style spa through the landscaped garden, and stone fireplaces and deer-antler chandeliers give it a Rocky Mountain atmosphere. Rooms, decorated in different themes, have American Indian decor and artwork, balconies (or views), and a king or two double beds. The Longs Peak Room has colorful floral prints in a rustic setting, pedestal sinks, and other antique touches. Suites contain sitting areas and kitchens.

The Top of the World Restaurant & Bar, named the community's best in recent "Taste of Breckenridge" competitions, serves American dinners with a regional flair ($18 to $50). Room service, a 24-hour front desk, ski and boot storage, and a complimentary shuttle for skiers and dinner guests are available. Facilities include a spa, free weights and nautilus equipment, indoor pool, four whirlpools, sauna, steam room, spa treatments, wellness programs, and meeting space for 110.

Ridge Street Inn Bed & Breakfast. 212 Ridge St. (P.O. Box 2854), Breckenridge, CO 80424. ☎ **800/452-4680** or 970/453-4680. www.colorado.net/ridge. E-mail: ridge@colorado.net. 6 units (4 with bathroom). Summer, $70–$85 with private bathroom, $65 with shared bathroom; winter, $100–$115 with private bathroom, $90 with shared bathroom; early and late season, $80–$90 with private bathroom, $70 with shared bathroom. Holidays, $115–$135 with private bathroom, $98 with shared bathroom. Rates are for double occupancy and include full breakfast. MC, V.

This 1890 Victorian-style inn, located in the heart of the Breckenridge Historic District, is close to restaurants, shops, the town trolley, and shuttle services. The star of the inn is the Parlor Suite, furnished with butter-print antiques. It has bay windows, a queen bed and queen sofa sleeper, large private bathroom, TV, and private entrance. Rooms with private bathrooms also have TVs; the two rooms that share a bathroom also share a sitting room. Home-cooked breakfasts might include waffles, fresh strawberry crêpes, or omelets. Children over 5 are welcome. Smoking is not permitted.

CAMPING

✪ **Tiger Run R.V. & Chalet Resort.** 85 Tiger Run Rd. (3 miles north of Breckenridge off Colo. 9), Breckenridge, CO 80424. ☎ **970/453-9690.** Fax 970/453-6782. E-mail: tiger@colorado.net. 200 sites. Apr to mid-Nov $30–$35; mid-Nov to Mar $33–$35. Rates include water, sewer, electric, and cable TV hookups. Weekly rates available. DISC, MC, V.

Named for a historic mine in the area, Tiger Run is both conveniently and beautifully located. There is a full-time activities director, with skiing and snowmobiling available in the winter, and live music Friday and Saturday nights in summer. The clubhouse lodge, in the middle of the park, is open year-round, with an indoor swimming pool, hot tubs, game room, TV room, laundry facilities, rest rooms with showers, and telephones. Amenities include a convenience store; tennis, volleyball, and basketball courts; a children's playground; and sports equipment available at the office, including bicycles for rent. Pets are welcome. There are also 50 chalet-style cabins on the property, with rates of $80 to $130 double.

WHERE TO DINE
EXPENSIVE

Briar Rose Restaurant. 109 E. Lincoln St. ☎ **970/453-9948.** Reservations recommended. Main courses $15–$30. AE, DISC, MC, V. Ski season, daily 5–10pm; rest of year, Mon–Sat 6–10pm. REGIONAL.

Located uphill from the Main Street traffic light, the Briar Rose is among the town's most elegant (but still casual) restaurants. Classical paintings, fine music, and white-linen service underscore Briar Rose's sophisticated atmosphere. The adjoining trophy lounge has big-game heads, a few paintings, and a hundred-year-old bar. You can start with escargot, crab-stuffed mushrooms, or homemade soup. Dinners feature game when available—usually elk, moose, buffalo, and caribou. Other popular choices include slow-cooked prime rib, veal, steaks, duck, and seafood. Vegetarian meals are also available, plus a children's menu and an extensive wine list.

Hearthstone Casual Dining. 130 S. Ridge St. ☎ **970/453-1148.** Reservations recommended. Main courses $5–$8 lunch, $13–$26 dinner. AE, MC, V. Daily 5:30–10pm; plus in summer 11:30am–3pm. REGIONAL.

A favorite of locals, the Hearthstone is in an historic home built in 1886. Blue on the outside, with white trim and wrought iron, it has a rustic yet elegant interior, with fine mountain views from the upstairs lounge. Lunch is served only in summer, when you can get great jalapeño-stuffed shrimp, turkey-and-avocado sandwiches, and half-pound burgers. But dinners, served all year, are what the Hearthstone is known for. Start with baked Brie or steamed mussels. Then choose from fresh seafood, such as Hearthstone shrimp (with garlic and ginger) or yellowfin tuna; chicken; slow-roasted prime rib; and a variety of steaks and wild game. Especially popular is Rocky Mountain trout topped with blue crab in a lemon-basil wine sauce. Vegetarian choices are also offered.

Keystone Ranch. Keystone Ranch Rd., Keystone. ☎ **970/496-4161.** Reservations highly recommended. Six-course dinner $67. AE, CB, DC, DISC, MC, V. Summer and winter, daily 5:30–9pm, two seatings; spring and fall, Wed–Sat, same hours. CREATIVE REGIONAL.

A working cattle ranch for more than three decades until 1972, the Keystone Ranch now boasts riding stables, a golf course, and this outstanding gourmet restaurant, located in a 1940s ranch house with a mountain-lodge decor. The six-course menu offers a choice of appetizer, followed by soup, salad, and fruit sorbet. Main dishes, which vary seasonally, might include rack of lamb, beef, fresh seafood, elk, or other regional game. An extensive array of desserts is served in the living room in front of a handsome stone fireplace. There's valet parking and a full bar.

MODERATE & INEXPENSIVE

Breckenridge Brewery and Pub. 600 S. Main St. ☎ **970/453-1550.** Reservations not accepted. Lunch $4.75–$8.25; dinner $7–$17. AE, DISC, MC, V. Daily 11am–midnight, bar open until 2am. AMERICAN/SOUTHWEST.

This brewpub was designed around its brewery, giving diners a first-hand view of the brewing process. Try the India Pale Ale or the Avalanche, a local favorite. Lunch choices include fish-and-chips, half-pound burgers, charbroiled chicken sandwiches, chicken or vegetable burritos, soups and salads, and gourmet wraps. The dinner menu adds baby-back ribs, New York sirloin, North Atlantic grilled salmon, and daily pasta, seafood, and vegetarian specials. Desserts are homemade, and this brewpub also caters to abstainers—they brew their own root beer.

Horseshoe II Restaurant. 115 S. Main St. ☎ **970/453-7463.** Breakfast $2.75–$6; lunch $4–$6.50; dinner $9.50–$17.50. AE, MC, V. Winter and summer, Mon–Thurs 11am–10pm; Fri–Sun 8am–10pm. Call for hours in spring and fall. AMERICAN.

A family-style restaurant in an historic 19th-century building, the Horseshoe II (yes, there was once a I) is set in the heart of downtown Breckenridge. It has a sunny split-level patio, ornate walls and ceilings, lace curtains, and, of course, mounted horseshoes. The popular bar has over 15 varieties of draft beer, including micro-brewed choices.

Lunch offers salads, burgers, and sandwiches. Dinners are more elaborate. We particularly recommend the chicken-fried steak (breaded beefsteak topped with country sausage cream gravy) and the fresh grilled Colorado trout. Other menu items include various types of pasta and a selection of light and vegetarian dishes. On weekends, start your day with the HAB (high-altitude breakfast), consisting of two eggs, two pancakes, breakfast meat, and juice. Smoking is not permitted anywhere in the establishment, including the bar.

Mi Casa. 600 Park Ave. ☎ **970/453-2071.** Reservations not accepted. Main courses $5–$15. AE, MC, V. Daily 11:30am–3pm and 5–9pm. MEXICAN.

A large room with stuccoed walls, a tile floor, wooden furniture, and baskets of silk flowers hanging from a beamed ceiling, Mi Casa is considered Breckenridge's best Mexican restaurant. Its popular adjoining cantina offers margaritas by the liter. In addition to the standard burritos, tostadas, fajitas, and enchiladas, the restaurant is known for its Yucatan shrimp—sautéed rock shrimp in a spicy mushroom-chipotle cream sauce. There is also a good selection of beef, seafood, chicken, southwestern, and vegetarian dishes.

O'Shea's Copper Bar. Copper Junction Bldg. opposite Mountain Plaza, Copper Mountain. ☎ **970/968-2882,** ext. 6504. Reservations not accepted. Main courses $7–$15. AE, CB, DC, MC, V. Late Nov–late Apr, daily 11am–midnight. AMERICAN/MEXICAN.

There are two floors to this restaurant—a casual, mountain-style cafe on the main level, and a sports bar in the basement. Try buffalo burgers, buffalo ribs, mesquite chicken, or their famous Gold Spike Nachos. There's also a full bar with a large selection of microbrews.

Poirrier's Cajun Café. 224 S. Main St. ☎ **970/453-1877.** Main courses $6–$11 lunch, $13–$20 dinner. AE, CB, DC, DISC, MC, V. Daily 11:30am–2:30pm and 5:30–10pm. CAJUN/CREOLE.

This brownstone is straight out of New Orleans, with sidewalk cafe seating behind a wrought-iron railing. Two rooms inside display harlequin masks and photos of Louisiana. Indeed, owners Bobby and Connie Poirrier are native Cajuns. For lunch, order a po-boy, New Orleans–style red beans and rice, or seafood gumbo. At dinnertime, there's poisson Hymel (a catfish fillet surrounded with crayfish étoufée, served with steamed rice and gumbo), blackened catch of the day, chicken à la Poirrier (with a mushroom sauce), and rib-eye steak. Finish your meal with Lafayette bread pudding. A children's menu is available.

SUMMIT COUNTY AFTER DARK

Breckenridge has the best nightlife in the area, but every community has its watering holes.

The **Backstage Theatre**, at the Pond Level at the Village at Breckenridge, 655 S. Park St. (☎ **970/453-0199**), has been presenting live theater since 1974. Recent productions have included Neil Simon's *Lost in Yonkers* and Beth Henley's *The Miss*

Firecracker Contest. Tickets cost $12.50 for adults and $5 for children under 12, and reservations are strongly recommended.

Popular bars in Breckenridge include **Breckenridge Brewery & Pub,** 600 S. Main St. (☎ 970/453-1550), where the microbrews include Avalanche, a full-bodied amber ale billed as "the one you can't get away from"; and **JohSha's,** 500 S. Park St. (☎ 970/453-4146), a popular live-music dance club where you'll hear practically everything but country. For live blues and jazz, try **Alligator Lounge,** 318 S. Main St. (☎ 970/453-7782); and for both live and recorded dance music, there's **Eric's Underground** at **Downstairs at Eric's,** a bar and restaurant at 111 S. Main St. (☎ 970/453-1401). For a smoker-friendly atmosphere and the area's best selection of single malt Scotches and other exotic alcoholic beverages, it's **Cecilia's Cigar Bar & Coffee House,** in La Cima Mall, 520 S. Main St. (☎ 970/453-2243).

6 Vail & Beaver Creek

109 miles W of Denver, 150 miles E of Grand Junction

Consistently ranked the country's most popular ski resort by skiers and ski magazines almost since its inception, Vail is the big one. In fact, it's hard to imagine a more celebrated spot to schuss. Off the slopes, Vail is an incredibly compact Tyrolean village, frequented by almost as many Europeans as Americans, a situation which lends its restaurants, lodgings, and trendy shops a more transatlantic feel than other Colorado resorts. But the size of the mountain and the difficulty and excitement of its trails are still what draw the faithful.

Historically speaking, there was very little in the town's past to indicate that Vail would become the mega-destination it has. No substantial amount of gold was found in the Gore Valley, as it was then known, and until U.S. 6 was built through Vail Pass in 1939, the only inhabitants were a handful of sheep ranchers. Dropping farther back into history, it's worth noting that the resort could never have been possible if it weren't for the Ute tribe's reaction to the first incursions into this valley by white gold-seekers in the 1850s and 1860s. In response to the disturbance these profiteers caused to their way of life, the Utes set the valley's forests alight in "spite fires"—burnings that created the wide-open ridges and back bowls that make skiers the world over quiver in their boots.

It was only when veterans of the Tenth Mountain Division, who trained during World War II at Camp Hale, 23 miles south of the valley, returned in the 1950s that the reality of skiing the Rockies was realized. One of them, Peter Siebert, urged development of this mountain land in the White River National Forest. His investment company began construction in 1962, and the entire ski resort—immediately among the three largest ski areas in the United States—was completed and ready to open in December 1963. Additional ski-lift capacity made Vail America's largest ski resort by 1964. Elevation is 8,150 feet.

Beaver Creek, built in 1980, has quickly garnered a reputation as an elegant, if expensive, place to vacation. Like Vail, it is a fully equipped four-season resort that offers golf (the course was designed by Robert Trent Jones, Jr.), hot-air ballooning, mountain biking, fishing, and horseback riding, in addition to skiing. Its atmosphere is a bit more formal than the surrounding area, and its nightlife tends more toward refined piano bars than rowdy saloons, but the exclusivity of its après-ski spots isn't reflected on the slopes. At Beaver Creek, there's a trail for everyone. Experts are challenged but beginners aren't left out—they too can head straight to the top and then ski all the way down on a trail that matches their skill level.

ESSENTIALS

GETTING THERE   By Car   Vail is right on the I-70 corridor, so it's exceedingly easy to find. Just take exit 176, whether you're coming from the east (Denver) or the west (Grand Junction). A more direct route from the south may be U.S. 24 through Leadville; this Tennessee Pass road joins I-70 5 miles west of Vail.

By Plane   From mid-December to early April visitors can fly directly into **Eagle County Airport,** 35 miles west of Vail between I-70 exits 140 and 147 (☎ 970/524-7700), with **American** (☎ 800/433-7300), **Continental** (☎ 800/523-3273), **Delta** (☎ 800/221-1212), **Northwest** (☎ 800/225-2525), and **United** (☎ 800/241-6522). Call for possible availability of flights at other times.

By Airport Shuttle   Many visitors fly into Denver International Airport and continue to Vail aboard a shuttle service: **Airlink Shuttle** (☎ 800/554-8245 or 970/845-7119), **Airport Luxury Express** (☎ 800/708-1160), **Colorado Mountain Express** (☎ 800/525-6363 or 970/949-4227), or **Vail Valley Transportation** (☎ 800/882-8872 or 970/476-8008). **Eagle Transportation Services** (☎ 970/524-1100) offers shuttles from the Eagle County Airport. For private charter service from DIA and the Eagle County Airport call **Peak Service** (☎ 970/949-4886).

VISITOR INFORMATION   For information or reservations in the Vail Valley, contact the **Vail Valley Tourism and Convention Bureau,** 100 E. Meadow Dr., Vail, CO 81657 (☎ **800/525-3875** or 970/476-1000; www.vail.net/vvtcb; e-mail: vvtcb@vail.net); or **Vail Associates, Inc.,** P.O. Box 7, Vail, CO 81658 (☎ **800/525-2257** or 970/476-5601; www.snow.com; e-mail: vailbcr@vail.net).

Information centers are located at the parking structures in Vail and Lionshead on South Frontage Road.

GETTING AROUND   Vail is one of only a few Colorado communities where you really don't need a car. The Town of Vail runs a **free shuttle-bus service** between 7am and 2am daily, although hours may be shorter in shoulder seasons. Shuttles in the Vail Village–Lionshead area run every 3 to 5 minutes, and there are regularly scheduled trips to West Vail and East Vail (☎ **970/328-8143**). Shuttles between Vail and Beaver Creek, an 11-mile trip, plus regional bus service to Avon, Edwards, and Leadville run daily for a nominal charge (☎ **970/949-6121**).

Vail Valley Taxi (☎ **970/476-8008**) operates throughout the area, around-the-clock.

For **car rentals,** including four-wheel-drive vehicles, try **Hertz** (☎ 800/654-3131 or 970/524-7177) or **Avis** (☎ 800/831-2847 or 970/524-7571) at the Eagle County Airport; **Thrifty** (☎ 800/367-2277, 970/476-8718 in Vail, or 970/949-7787 in Beaver Creek), or **Enterprise** (☎ 800/325-8007 or 970/845-8393).

FAST FACTS   The hospital, **Vail Valley Medical Center**, with 24-hour emergency care, is at 181 West Meadow Drive between Vail Road and East Lionshead Circle (☎ **970/476-2451,** or 970/479-7219 for TDD). The **post office** is on North Frontage Road West, opposite Donovan Park. For hours and other information contact the U.S. Postal Service (☎ **800/275-8777**). For **road conditions,** call ☎ **970/479-2226.**

SPECIAL EVENTS   Taste of Vail, first weekend in April; Vail America Days, July 4; Eagle County Fair and Rodeo, second weekend in August in Eagle; Beaver Creek Arts Festival, third weekend in August in Beaver Creek; Minturn Jazz and Blues Fest, October and November in Minturn; and Torchlight Parade, December 31. Also see "The Festival Scene," below.

Vail

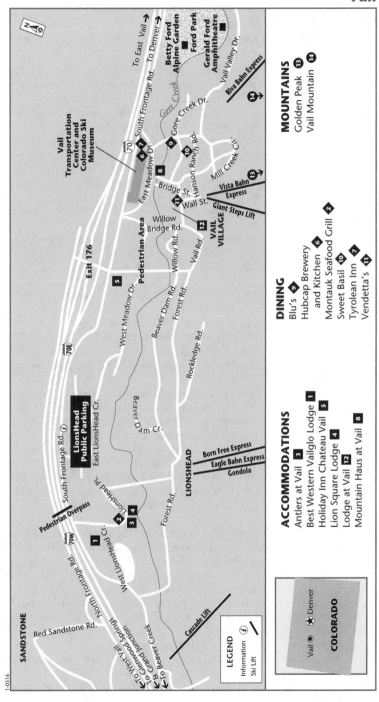

ACCOMMODATIONS

Antlers at Vail **3**
Best Western Vailglo Lodge **1**
Holiday Inn Chateau Vail **5**
Lion Square Lodge **4**
Lodge at Vail **12**
Mountain Haus at Vail **8**

DINING

Blu's **9**
Hubcap Brewery and Kitchen **6**
Montauk Seafood Grill **2**
Sweet Basil **10**
Tyrolean Inn **7**
Vendetta's **11**

MOUNTAINS

Golden Peak **13**
Vail Mountain **14**

LEGEND

ⓘ Information
╱ Ski Lift

COLORADO

Vail ◉
★ Denver

1-0516

Map labels:
SANDSTONE
Red Sandstone Rd.
North Frontage Rd.
South Frontage Rd. ⓘ
To Glenwood Springs
To West Vail
To Beaver Creek
Grand Junction
West LionsHead Cr.
Pedestrian Overpass
70W
LionsHead Public Parking
East LionsHead Cr.
LionsHead Pl.
LIONSHEAD
Forest Rd.
Beaver Dam Cr.
Born Free Express
Eagle Bahn Express Gondola
Cascade Lift
Rockledge Rd.
Beaver Dam Rd.
Willow Dam Rd.
West Meadow Dr.
Exit 176
Pedestrian Area
East Meadow Dr.
Forest Rd.
Willow Bridge Rd.
Vail Rd.
Bridge St.
Wall St.
VAIL VILLAGE
Giant Steps Lift
Vista Bahn Express
Hanson Ranch Rd.
Mill Creek Cir.
70E
70
Vail Transportation Center and Colorado Ski Museum
Gore Creek Dr.
Gore Creek
South Frontage Rd.
To East Vail
To Denver
Betty Ford Alpine Garden
Ford Park
Gerald Ford Amphitheatre
Vail Valley Dr.
Riva Bahn Express

267

SKIING & OTHER WINTER ACTIVITIES

You'll find many of the activities and companies discussed below on the Internet at **www.vail.net**.

✪ **VAIL**   In his *Skiing America* guide, author Charles Leocha writes, "Vail comes closest of any resort in America to epitomizing what many skiers would call perfection." You can arrive at the base village, unload and park your car, and not have to drive again until it's time to go. You'll find all the shops, restaurants, and nightlife you could want within a short walk of your hotel or condominium.

Ski area boundaries stretch 7 miles from east to west along the ridge top, from Outer Mongolia to Game Creek Bowl, and the skiable terrain is measured at 4,644 acres. Virtually every lift on the front (north-facing) side of the mountain has runs for every level of skier, with a predominance of novice and intermediate terrain. The world-famous Back Bowls are decidedly not for beginners, and there are few options for intermediates. The seven bowls—from west to east: Sun Down, Sun Up, Tea Cup, China, Siberia, Inner Mongolia, and Outer Mongolia—are strictly for advanced and expert skiers; snow and weather conditions determine just how expert you ought to be. They are served by four lifts, one of them a short surface lift to access the Mongolias. One trip down the Slot or Rasputin's Revenge will give you a fair idea of just how good you are.

From Mongolia Summit, at 11,450 feet, Vail has a vertical drop on the front side of 3,250 feet; on the back side, 1,850 feet. Average annual snowfall is 334 inches (nearly 28 feet). All told, there are 174 named trails served by 30 lifts—a gondola, 11 quad chairs, three triple chairs, five double chairs, and ten surface lifts. "Meet the Mountain" tours begin at Lionshead and Vail Village daily at 9am. Snowboarders are welcome, and there are two half-pipes at Golden Peak and one at Eagle's Nest.

Eighteen **mountain restaurants** include two that ask for reservations: the **Cook Shack** (☎ 970/479-2030), with creative American cuisine, at mid-Vail, and the **Wine Stube** (☎ 970/479-2034) at Eagle's Nest, with international cuisine atop the Eagle Bahn Gondola. **Two Elk Restaurant** on the Far East summit has southwestern cuisine and pasta, plus baked potato and salad bars. **Wok 'n' Roll,** in China Bowl, is a ski-by pagoda with Asian fast food; the **Dog Haus** offers ski-by hot dogs at the foot of the Northwoods Express; **Wildwood Shelter** specializes in smoked or barbecued foods; **Eagle's Nest** has salad, potato, and pasta bars. And Mid-Vail has two levels of cafeterias: **Golden Peak** and **Trail's End** serve breakfast, lunch, and après-ski drinks.

Vail has a highly respected children's program. The **Golden Peak Children's Skiing Center** and the **Lionshead Children's Skiing Center** (☎ 970/476-3239 for both) are under the aegis of the Ski School. Call ☎ 970/476-9090 for recorded information on a wide range of day and night family activities. There are daily NASTAR races at the Black Forest Race Arena.

Lift tickets (1998–99 season) are $54 per day for adults, $20 per day for children 5 to 12, $45 per day for seniors 65 to 69, and free for seniors 70 and older and children 4 and younger. Holiday rates are higher. Any lift ticket purchased at Vail is also valid at Beaver Creek, Keystone, and Breckenridge ski areas.

Vail is open from early November to early May, daily from 8:30am to 4pm. For further information, contact **Vail Mountain,** Vail Associates, Inc., P.O. Box 7, Vail, CO 81658 (☎ **800/404-3535** or 970/476-5601, 970/476-4888 for snow report; fax 970/845-5729; www.snow.com).

BEAVER CREEK   Vail Resort's other mountain is an outstanding resort in its own right, one with a more secluded atmosphere than its better-known neighbor. Located in a valley 1½ miles off the I-70 corridor, Beaver Creek combines European château–style elegance in its base village with expansive slopes for novice and intermediate skiers. The Grouse Mountain Express lift reaches expert terrain.

From the village, the Centennial Express lift to Spruce Saddle and Birds of Prey Express lift reach wide-open northwest-facing midmountain slopes and the Flattops beginners' area atop the mountain, offering a unique beginner's experience. Opposite, the Strawberry Park Express lift accesses Larkspur Bowl and the McCoy Park cross-country ski and snowshoe area at 9,840 feet. Three other lifts—Larkspur, Grouse Mountain, and Westfall (serving the expert Birds of Prey area)—leave from Red-Tail Camp at midmountain.

The Arrowhead Mountain is now part of Beaver Creek. The two are connected through Bachelor Gulch, offering village-to-village skiing.

Beaver Creek's vertical drop is 4,040 feet from the 11,440-foot summit. There are 1,625 developed acres, though Vail Associates are licensed to develop up to 5,600. Currently, 14 lifts (six quad chairs, three triples, four doubles, and one surface) serve 146 trails and the average annual snowfall is 330 inches. Snowboarding is permitted, and there is a snowboarding park with a half-pipe located off the Moonshine trail.

There are seven **mountain restaurants,** including the highly praised **Beano's Cabin** (see "Where to Dine," below). Others include **Rafters,** at Spruce Saddle (☎ **970/845-5528** for reservations); the **Spruce Saddle Cafeteria**; the **Red-Tail Camp** fast-food stop; **McCoy's,** offering breakfast, lunch, and après-ski entertainment at the base; and **Gundy's Barbecue** in Bachelor Gulch.

Lift tickets (1998–99 season) are $54 per day for adults, $20 per day for children 5 to 12, $45 per day for seniors 65 to 69, and free for seniors 70 and older and children 4 and younger. Holiday rates are higher. Any lift ticket purchased at Beaver Creek is also valid at Vail, Keystone, and Breckenridge ski areas.

Beaver Creek is open daily from 8:30am to 4pm. For more information, contact **Beaver Creek Resort,** Vail Associates, Inc., P.O. Box 7, Vail, CO 81658 (☎ **800/404-3535** or 970/949-5750, 970/476-4888 for snow reports; fax 970/845-5729; www.snow.com).

BACKCOUNTRY SKI TOURS   **Paragon Guides,** P.O. Box 130, Vail, CO 81658 (☎ **970/926-5299;** fax 970/926-5298; e-mail: paragonguides@vail.net), is one of the country's premier winter guide services, offering backcountry ski trips on the Tenth Mountain Trail and Hut System between Vail and Aspen. A variety of trips are available, lasting from 3 to 6 days and designed for all ability levels. Costs start at $580 per person for the 3-day trip, and $1,210 for the 6-day trip (for experienced backcountry skiers only).

CROSS-COUNTRY SKIING   Cross-country skiers won't feel left out here, with trails at both resorts as well as a system of trails through the surrounding mountains. **Vail's Nordic Center** (☎ **970/845-5313**) has 33 kilometers (20 miles) of trails, part of them on the Vail Golf Course, and offers guided tours, lessons, and snowshoeing. The **Beaver Creek Nordic Center** (☎ **970/949-5750**), on its golf course, has a 32-kilometer (21-mile) mountaintop track system with a skating lane in 9,840-foot McCoy Park. Most of the high-altitude terrain here is intermediate, though there's some for both beginner and advanced cross-country skiers; telemarking lessons are available.

For general information on the network of backcountry trails in the Vail area, contact the **Holy Cross Ranger District Office,** White River National Forest, P.O. Box 190, Minturn, CO 81645 (☎ 970/827-5715). Of particular note is the system of trails known as the **Tenth Mountain Division Hut System,** 1280 Ute Ave., Aspen, CO 81611 (☎ 970/925-5775). Generally following the World War II training network of the Camp Hale militia, the trails cover 300 miles and link Vail with Leadville and Aspen. There are 14 overnight cabins ($22 to $32 per person per night), and hikers and mountain bikers also use this trail.

SLEIGH RIDES   Horse-drawn sleigh rides, including dinner rides, are offered by several companies in the Vail area, including **4 Eagle Ranch** (☎ 970/926-3372). Rates for a sleigh ride with dinner are about $60 for adults and $30 for children, and a 30- to 40-minute afternoon sleigh ride costs $10.

SNOWMOBILING   You can see a lot of beautiful country in a short amount of time on a snowmobile. Among companies offering guided trips are **Nova Guides** (☎ 888/949-6682 or 970/949-4232) and **Timber Ridge Adventures** (☎ 800/ 282-9070 or 970/668-8349). Rates are about $105 for two people on a snowmobile for a 2-hour ride.

WARM-WEATHER & OTHER YEAR-ROUND ACTIVITIES

Vail doesn't shut down once the skiers go home. Instead, visitors and locals alike trade their skis for mountain bikes and hiking boots, and hit the trails again. The resort closes parts of the mountain to access from early May to late June to protect elk calving habitats, but other than that, warm-weather activities cover the mountains.

The **Piney River Ranch**, about 12 miles north of Vail on Piney Lake (☎ 970/ 76-9090), offers a variety of outdoor activities, including horseback rides, hay rides, a fishing lake, and a cattle roundup (see below). **Nova Guides,** P.O. Box 2018, Vail, CO 81658 (☎ 888/949-6682 or 970/949-4232; e-mail nova@vail.net), offers guided fishing, mountain-bike, and off-road tours, plus white-water rafting. The town of Avon's **Nottingham Lake** (☎ 970/949-4280) has fishing and paddleboats in summer. The **Tenth Mountain Division Hut System,** which runs for 300 miles, is open to hikers and mountain bikers (see "Cross-Country Skiing," above).

Contact **Vail Recreation District** (☎ 970/479-2294) for information on various activities, including the town's children's programs. You'll find many of the companies listed below on the Internet at **www.vail.net.** For maps and information on the numerous activities in the White River National Forest, consult the **Holy Cross Ranger District Office,** 24745 U.S. 24 (P.O. Box 190), Minturn, CO 81645 (☎ 970/827-5715). The office is on the south side of U.S. 24 just off I-70 exit 171.

BALLOONING   **Camelot Balloons** (☎ 800/785-4743 or 970/926-2435) and **Balloon America** (☎ 970/468-2473) fly year-round, with rides lasting from a half hour to well over an hour, and usually concluding with a champagne toast. Rates start at $125.

CATTLE DRIVES   For a taste of the Old West, climb onto a horse and join a half-day cattle round-up ($85, including a light breakfast) at **4 Eagle Ranch,** which can be reached via I-70. Take exit 157, and drive 4 miles north on Colo. 131 (☎ 970/926-3372).

FISHING   The streams and mountain lakes surrounding Vail are rich with rainbow, brook, brown, and cutthroat trout, plus mountain whitefish. Gore Creek through the town of Vail is a popular anglers' venue, especially toward evening from its banks along the Vail Golf Course. Also good are the Eagle River, joined by Gore Creek 5 miles downstream near Minturn; the Black Lakes near the summit of Vail Pass; and 60-acre Piney Lake (see directions under "Mountain Biking," below). The **Piney River Ranch** (see above) rents canoes ($13 per hour) and fishing gear ($7 per hour or $11 per day).

For a guided fishing trip call **Nova Guides** (see above); **Gorsuch Outfitters**, 263 E. Gore Creek Dr. (☎ 970/476-4700; www.gorsuch-outfitters.com); or **Fly Fishing Outfitters, Inc.,** P.O. (☎ 800/595-8090 or 970/476-3474; www.vail.net/flyfish; e-mail: fish@vail.net). For fishing supplies, stop at **Gore Creek Fly Fisherman,** Inc., 183 E. Gore Creek Dr., Vail (☎ 970/476-3296). Ask about the company's guided fishing trips, 3-day fishing school, boat trips, and horseback fishing trips.

FOUR-WHEEL-DRIVE TOURS[em]The mountains are accessible to virtually anyone in four-wheel-drive vehicles. Contact **Nova Guides** (see above) or **Timber-line Tours** (☎ **800/831-1414** or 970/476-1414) for guided trips ($60 and up).

GOLF   The season for golf varies in the Vail valley, depending on snow condi-tions, but courses are usually open from mid-May to mid-October. The **Vail Golf Course,** 1778 Vail Valley Dr., Vail (☎ **970/479-2260**), charges $45 for 9 holes and $70 for 18; and the **Eagle-Vail Golf Course,** 6 miles west of Vail at 431 Eagle Dr., Avon (☎ **970/949-5267**), is a challenging course that charges $85 for 18 holes.

HIKING & BACKPACKING   The surrounding White River National Forest has a plethora of trails leading to pristine lakes and spectacular panoramic views. The Holy Cross Wilderness Area, southwest of Vail, encompasses 14,005-foot Mount of the Holy Cross and is an awesome region with over 100 miles of trails. Eagle's Nest Wilderness Area lies to the north, in the impressive Gore Range. For information and maps for these and other hiking areas, consult the **Holy Cross Ranger District Office,** 24745 U.S. 24 (P.O. Box 190), Minturn, CO 81645 (☎ **970/827-5715**). Also see the information on the Tenth Mountain Division huts in "Cross-Country Skiing," above.

For supplies and more information, visit **Vail Mountaineering,** 500 E. Lion-shead Circle, Vail (☎ **970/476-4223**).

HORSEBACK RIDING   One of the best ways to explore this beautiful and rugged mountain country is on the back of a horse. The **Spraddle Creek Ranch,** 100 N. Frontage Rd. E. (☎ **970/476-6941**), is especially geared to families, with rides for beginners to experts. A one-hour ride costs $22. Also providing horseback rides are **4 Eagle Ranch** (see "Cattle Drives," above), charging $20 to $96 for trips ranging from 1 hour to a full day with lunch; and **Piney River Ranch** (see above), which offers guided horseback rides starting at $24 for one hour, pony rides for kids under 8 for $11, and hay rides for $5.

LLAMA TREKKING   **Paragon Guides,** P.O. Box 130, Vail, CO 81658 (☎ **970/926-5299;** fax 970/926-5298; www.vail.net/paragonguides; e-mail: paragonguides@vail.net), offers llama-trekking trips, lasting from 3 to 6 days, July through September. They are limited to eight persons for camping, slightly larger groups for hut trips, and start at $630 per person for 3 days. Custom treks are also available, from an overnight to one week.

MOUNTAIN BIKING   Summer visitors can take the Lionshead Gondola to Eagle's Nest on Vail Mountain, rent mountain bikes (and helmets) there, and cruise downhill to return their bikes at the base of the gondola.

There are many choices for avid bikers, both on backcountry trails and road tours. A popular trip is the 12½-mile Lost Lake Trail along Red Sandstone Road to Piney Lake. The 30-mile Vail Pass Bikeway goes to Frisco, with a climb from 8,460 feet up to 10,600 feet. Pick up a trail list (with map) at an information center.

Mountain bike rentals are available at a number of shops, including **Vail Bike Tech,** in the Lift House Lodge (☎ 970/476-5995); **Performance Sports,** at the east end of Lionshead Mall (☎ 970/476-1718); and **Wheel Base** in both Lionshead (☎ 970/476-5799) and Vail Village (☎ 970/476-0913). Rates are about $7 for the first hour and $2.50 for each additional hour.

Paragon Guides (see "Llama Trekking," above) offers a 5-day mountain-biking and hiking tour from late July into late September, along old logging and mining roads in the backcountry, starting at $1,200 per person. Rentals are available starting at $24 per day, and they will also custom design a trip for a group. Contact **Nova Guides** (see above) for half-day bike tours.

RIVER RAFTING   The Eagle River, just a few miles west of Vail, offers thrilling white water, especially during the May to June thaw. Families can enjoy the relatively gentle (Class II–IV) lower Eagle, west of Minturn; the upper Eagle, above Minturn, is significantly rougher (Class IV–V rapids). Area rafting companies also take trips on the Colorado River, which they access about 35 miles northwest via Colo. 131, at State Bridge.

One respected company that has been running area rivers for close to 25 years is **Colorado River Runs** (☎ 800/826-1081 or 970/653-4292). Although the company offers all types of trips, from calm to rough, it specializes in the easier trips, suitable for families. Rates for half-day trips are in the $26 to $36 range, while full-day trips, including lunch, are usually $55 to $65. Other companies offering raft trips include **Nova Guides** (see above), **Lakota River Guides** (☎ 970/476-7238), and **Timberline Tours** (☎ 800/831-1414 or 970/476-1414), with similar rates, although trips on rougher white water will be higher.

TENNIS   There are many public courts in the Vail valley, including nine hard and eight clay courts, run by the Vail Tennis Center, 700 S. Frontage Road E., open daily from 8am to 7pm in summer. For information call the Vail Recreation District (see above).

THE FESTIVAL SCENE

The summer season's big cultural event is the **Bravo! Colorado Vail Valley Music Festival,** from late June through early August. Established in 1988, the festival features everything from classical orchestra and chamber music to vocal and pops, baroque to modern jazz. In residence are the Detroit Symphony and Rochester Philharmonic Orchestras. Tickets, which go on sale May 1, range from $10 to $35; contact the festival office at P.O. Box 2270, Vail, CO 81658 (☎ **970/827-5700;** fax 970/827-5707; e-mail: bravo@vail.net).

The **Vail International Dance Festival** features both classes and performances. The Bolshoi Ballet Academy at Vail is the satellite school of the famous Bolshoi of Moscow and teaches the Russian style of artistic expression, and presents a series of performances each summer. For information, contact the Vail Valley Foundation, P.O. Box 309, Vail, CO 81658 (☎ **888/883-8245** or 970/949-1999; fax 970/949-9265).

Vail's Ford Amphitheatre hosts **Hot Summer Nights,** free concerts of contemporary rock, jazz, or blues on weeknight evenings in July and August.

NEARBY MUSEUMS & OTHER ATTRACTIONS

Betty Ford Alpine Gardens. Ford Park, east of Vail Village, Vail. ☎ **970/476-0103.** Free admission. Snowmelt to snowfall, daily dawn–dusk.

At 8,200 feet, these alpine gardens are the highest public botanical gardens in North America. The alpine display, perennial garden, and mountain meditation garden together represent about 2,000 varieties of plants, demonstrating the wide range of choices to be grown at high altitudes.

Colorado Ski Museum–Ski Hall of Fame. Vail Transportation Center, Level 3. ☎ **970/476-1876.** Free admission. Tues–Sun 10am–5pm. Closed May and Oct, except by appointment.

The history of more than a century of Colorado skiing—from the boards that mountain miners first strapped on their feet, to the post–World War II resort boom, to Coloradans' success in international racing—is depicted in this popular showcase. Also included is the evolution of ski equipment and fashions, plus the role of the U.S. Forest Service. There's one room devoted to the Tenth Mountain Division, the only division of the military trained in ski warfare. A theater presents historical and current ski videos. The museum incorporates the Colorado Ski Hall of Fame with plaques and photographs honoring Vail founder Peter Seibert, film-maker Lowell Thomas, Olympic skier Buddy Werner, and others.

Minturn Cellars. 107 Williams St., Minturn. ☎ **970/827-4065.** Summer, daily noon–6pm; winter, Wed–Sun noon–6pm. Minturn is located between Vail and Beaver Creek on U.S. 24, just a few miles south of I-70 exit 171.

A small winery, Minturn Cellars produces red, white, blush, and dessert wines, with up to a half dozen on hand at any given time for free tastings. Free tours of the winery are available on request. Prices start at $8, with most in the $12 to $18 range. Alfresco dining is available in summer.

SHOPPING

There are a wide variety of shops and galleries in Vail and Beaver Creek, but this is not a place for bargain-hunters.

Among art galleries of note are **Vail Vine Art,** Vail Village Crossroads Center, 141 E. Meadow Dr. (☎ **970/476-2900**), with beautiful sculptures and fine paintings; and **Gotthelf's Gallery,** 122 E. Meadow Dr. (☎ **970/476-1777**), featuring glass and innovative jewelry. You can get a complete listing of galleries and information on evening art walks from the **Vail Valley Arts Council,** P.O. Box 1153, Vail, CO 81658 (☎ **970/476-4255**).

Other interesting shops include **Noel the Christmas Shop,** in the Sitzmark Building, 183-2 Gore Creek Dr. (☎ **970/476-6544**), with unusual nutcrackers and exclusive ornaments; **Currents,** 285 Bridge St. (☎ **970/476-3322**), offering original designs in platinum, gold, and silver jewelry plus fine Swiss watches; **Colorado Style Furnishings & Decor,** 910 Nottingham Rd., Avon (☎ **970/949-0903**), featuring mountain classic, lodge, southwest, and traditional styles of everything for the home: furniture, rugs, window treatments, lighting, bedding, and accessories; and **Kitchen Collage,** at Riverwalk, the Crystal Building, Edwards (☎ **970/926-0400**), which carries fine cookware, gourmet foods, linens, and a multitude of handy gadgets.

WHERE TO STAY

Like most of Colorado's ski resorts, Vail has an abundance of condominiums, and it seems that more are built every day. Many are individually owned and available for rent when the owners aren't in town, so you'll find that they have more individuality and homey touches than you often find in a hotel. We discuss some of the better condominium developments below (along with other lodging choices), and there are scores more. Contact the **Vail Valley Tourism and Convention Bureau** (see "Visitor Information," above), which can provide additional lodging information or make your reservations for you, as well as provide information on skiing and other activities.

As in most ski areas, rates are highest during ski season, particularly Christmas, and can sometimes be half that after the lifts close. During ski season, you'll find the lowest rates at the very beginning, from opening to about December 20. Room taxes add about 8% to lodging bills in Vail, and about 9.5% in Beaver Creek.

IN VAIL

Reliable chain properties in Vail include **Best Western Vailglo Lodge,** 701 W. Lionshead Circle (P.O. Box 189), Vail, CO 81658-0189 (☎ **800/541-9423** or 970/476-5506), with rates for two of $235 to $260 from mid-November to late April, and $87 to $104 the rest of the year; and the **Holiday Inn Chateau Vail,** 13 Vail Rd., Vail, CO 81657 (☎ **800/HOLIDAY** or 970/476-5631), which charges $125 to $299 for two from late November to March, and much less at other times.

Expensive

The Lodge at Vail. 174 E. Gore Creek Dr., Vail, CO 81657. ☎ **800/331-LODG** or 970/476-5011. Fax 970/476-7425. www.vail.net/thelodge. E-mail: thelodge@vail.net. 150 units. TV TEL. Winter (includes full breakfast) $350–$750 double; $560–$1,300 suite. Summer (includes breakfast buffet), $220–$295 double; $285–$825 suite. 10-day minimum stay over Christmas holidays. AE, DC, DISC, JCB, MC, V. Free valet and self-parking. Directions: Follow Vail Rd. south from the main Vail interchange, through one stop sign and around a curve to the left, to the end of the road.

Vail's original deluxe hotel sits at the base of the Vista Bahn Express in the heart of Vail Village. As with most Vail properties, everything you need is within a few steps of your room: winter and summer recreation, restaurants, lounges, boutiques, galleries, and stunning views.

The lodge offers hotel rooms and one-, two-, and three-bedroom suites. Most have private balconies, mahogany furnishings and paneling, minifridges, and full-view mirrors. The bathrooms, finished with marble, have hair dryers and heated towel racks. Many deluxe rooms were recently refurbished and now include two-poster beds with duvets, antique armoires, and high-backed leather chairs. Suites, each with a fireplace and full kitchen, are individually owned and decorated.

Dining/Diversions: The Wildflower Inn serves creative American cuisine in a garden atmosphere, and is consistently rated the top restaurant in Vail. The Cucina Rustica, a Tuscan grill, offers smoked salmon, crab salad, pasta dishes, and grilled meats on winter evenings. Mickey's piano bar has featured the well-regarded Mickey Poage for almost 20 years.

Amenities: Concierge, 24-hour room service, valet laundry, international currency exchange, business center, baby-sitting, ski storage and rental, heated swimming pool, whirlpool, sauna, exercise room, and meeting space for 400.

Vail Cascade Hotel & Club. 1300 Westhaven Dr., Vail, CO 81657. ☎ **800/420-2424** or 970/476-7111. Fax 970/479-7020. www.vailcascade.com. E-mail: cascadehotel@vail.net. 316 units, including 27 suites. TV TEL MINIBAR. Winter $199–$400 double, $975 suite, higher at Christmas; summer $129–$249 double, $600 suite. AE, CB, DC, DISC, MC, V. Underground parking (7 ft. height limit), $12 winter, $5 summer. Take I-70 exit 173 for West Vail, head east on South Frontage Rd. to Westhaven Dr., and turn right.

The Vail Cascade might be described as having a "Ralph Lauren mountain eclectic" decor. Rooms contain cherry-wood armoires, other wood furnishings and trim, and beds with wicker headboards. Deluxe rooms (480 square feet) have the vanity outside the bathing area, and standard rooms (390 square feet) boast marble vanities. Suites have 600 to 1,000 square feet in two rooms, and most have a king bed plus a hide-a-bed. All units boast good mountain or courtyard views. The courtyard entrance is beautifully landscaped, with tall Colorado blue spruce, aspens, and vast amounts of flowers in summer. There are elevators accessing the four floors, and interior corridors everywhere so you never have to go outside until you're ready to ski—and the Cascade Village chairlift is just outside the door.

Also available are about 65 condos and several private homes.

Dining/Diversions: Alfredo's restaurant serves northern Italian cuisine for dinner in winter, and offers more regional fare in summer (all three meals). In summer you can dine outside on the patio. Relax around the fireplace in the welcoming Lobby Lounge/Bar in the evenings and enjoy the nightly entertainment provided by local pianists or guitarists. Downstairs, the Café serves all three meals in winter.

Amenities: Complimentary shuttle service, concierge, 24-hour room service, two movie theaters with first-run films. Outdoor pool (open year-round); sporting-goods stores offering rentals and apparel; the Cascade Club with three squash courts, raquetball, basketball, four indoor tennis courts plus three outdoor ones in summer, Cybex and free weights, cardiovascular equipment, indoor track, numerous classes, and child-care service; the Cascade Spa with a health and beauty salon, massage, hot tub, whirlpool, sauna, and steam room.

Moderate

Antlers at Vail. 680 W. Lionshead Place, Vail, CO 81657. ☎ **800/843-VAIL** or 970/476-2471. Fax 970/476-4146. E-mail: antlers@csn.net. 69 units. TV TEL. Winter, $260–$785; summer, $90–$245. AE, DC, DISC, MC, V.

This luxurious condominium property near the foot of the Lionshead Gondola has a reputation for friendly service and unobstructed views of Vail Mountain. Units range in size from studios to three-bedrooms, and each has a fully equipped kitchen, fireplace, and private balcony. Facilities include a heated outdoor pool, whirlpool, sundeck, two saunas, guest laundry, ski storage, and meeting space for 150.

Lion Square Lodge. 660 W. Lionshead Place, Vail, CO 81657. ☎ **800/525-5788** or 970/476-2281. Fax 970/476-7423. www.vail.net/lionsquare. E-mail: lionsquare@vail.net. 108 units. TV TEL. Winter, $110–$350 double; $150–$1,300 condo. Summer, $89–$135 double; $99–$159 condo. Children under 17 stay free in parents' room. AE, DC, DISC, MC, V. Free parking.

A ski-in/ski-out property on Gore Creek at the base of the Lionshead Gondola, the Lion Square offers deluxe lodge rooms and one-, two-, and three-bedroom condominiums. All condo units have mountain views, spacious living rooms with balconies and fireplaces, and fully equipped kitchens.

There are complimentary coffee, cookies, and newspapers in the lobby, and the restaurant offers steak, seafood, and an extensive salad bar. Amenities include a concierge, valet laundry and dry cleaning, baby-sitting arrangements, a heated outdoor pool, hot tubs, sauna, jogging track, ski and bicycle storage, guest laundry, and meeting space for 300.

Mountain Haus at Vail. 292 E. Meadow Dr., Vail, CO 81657. ☎ **800/237-0922** or 970/476-2434. Fax 970/476-3007. www.vail.net/mtnhaus. E-mail: mtnhaus@vail.net. 74 units. TV TEL. Winter, $120–$225 double lodge room; $205–$1,210 condo. Summer, $95 double lodge room; $125–$280 condo. Continental breakfast included in rates in winter. AE, DC, MC, V. Parking free in summer, $12 in winter.

Located in Vail Village on East Meadow Drive at the covered bridge across Gore Creek, the Mountain Haus offers guests the choice of handsome hotel rooms or spacious one- to four-bedroom condo units. All have gas fireplaces, VCRs, private balconies, and fully equipped kitchens. Two-bedroom units sleep six; there's a sleeper sofa in the living room, two bathrooms, and a ski room at the entrance.

Amenities include a heated outdoor pool, indoor and outdoor whirlpools, men's and women's steam rooms and saunas, massage, exercise room, guest laundry, valet laundry service, a concierge, express checkout, and complimentary coffee and refreshments.

Inexpensive

Park Meadows Lodge. 1472 Matterhorn Circle, Vail, CO 81657. ☎ **970/476-5598.** Fax 970/476-3056. 28 units. TV TEL. Winter, $74–$225; summer, $54–$89. Weekly rates available; children 12 and under stay free in parents' room. MC, V. Take I-70 exit 173 for West Vail, head east on South Frontage Rd. to Matterhorn Circle and turn right.

Located in West Vail, adjacent to the bicycle path, and an 8-minute walk from the Cascade Village Lift and terminus of the free Vail shuttle, the Park Meadows is one of the few family-style economy lodges left in the Vail valley. A condominium property, units range from efficiency studios to one- and two-bedrooms, and each has a full kitchen and a hide-a-bed. There's a common area with a large fireplace, board games, pool, and Ping-Pong tables; a hot tub in an outdoor courtyard; and a coin laundry.

The Roost Lodge. 1783 N. Frontage Rd. W., Vail, CO 81657. ☎ **800/873-3065** or 970/476-5451. Fax 970/476-9158. www.roostlodge.com. E-mail: roostldg@vail.net. 72 units. TV TEL. Ski season, $69–$205; rest of year, $69–$95. Rates include continental breakfast and afternoon refreshments. AE, DC, DISC, MC, V. Take I-70 exit 173 for West Vail, head east on North Frontage Rd. and go about a quarter-mile to the hotel. Pets accepted in smoking rooms at $10 each per night.

Personal attention in a country-inn atmosphere is the boast of the Roost, a family-run ski lodge on the north side of I-70 in West Vail. Rooms, which received new beds, carpeting, and other improvements in 1998, are cozy and homey. There are also some larger family rooms with additional beds, and deluxe units with refrigerators and microwaves. The lodge has an indoor heated pool, outdoor whirlpool, and sauna. There are nature trails nearby, and bicycle rentals are available. The free Vail shuttle bus runs to Vail Village every 15 minutes during the height of the ski season (less frequently at other times), and the lodge also provides a ski shuttle.

WEST OF VAIL & BEAVER CREEK

Very Expensive

✪ **Hyatt Regency Beaver Creek.** 50 W. Thomas Place (P.O. Box 1595), Avon, CO 81620. ☎ **800/233-1234** or 970/949-1234. Fax 970/949-4164. www.vail.nte/hyatt. 275 units. TV TEL. Winter, $370–$575 double; $975–$2,600 suite. Summer, $205–$320 double; $425–$1,050 suite. Spring and fall, $115–$260 double; $340–$940 suite. Rates are for double occupancy. Children 18 or under stay free in parents' room. AE, CB, DC, DISC, JCB, MC, V. Valet parking $13.

An architecturally unique hotel at the foot of the Beaver Creek lifts, this luxurious ski-in/ski-out Hyatt blends features of medieval European alpine monasteries with Rocky Mountain styles and materials. The exterior is native stone, offset with stucco and rough timbers. The interior is of rough-hewn pine and sandstone; wall-size fireplaces enhance numerous cozy alcoves furnished with overstuffed chairs and sofas. Elk-antler chandeliers and works by contemporary artisans lend a western ambiance.

Guest rooms have a European country elegance, with knotty-pine furnishings and TVs hidden in armoires. The raised beds have dust ruffles, pillow shams, and quilted comforters. Most rooms have private balconies. Bathrooms feature a marble-top vanity, hair dryer, heated towel rack, and coffeemaker.

Dining/Diversions: The Patina, open for three meals daily, has an open fireplace for cold days and an outdoor terrace for warm ones, and the cuisine is Pacific Rim with a southwestern influence. The Crooked Hearth Tavern specializes in lunches—outdoors in warm weather—and après-ski around another large fireplace, and offers live entertainment most nights. The Double Diamond Deli has all manner of snacks and sandwiches, and prepares picnic baskets for mountain hikes and rides.

Amenities: Room service, concierge, complimentary ski valet, and children's programs; indoor/outdoor swimming pool, six open-air whirlpools, saunas, weight-and-exercise room, aerobics and water aerobics classes, facials and massages, six tennis courts; retail boutiques, coin-operated laundry, and meeting space for 750.

Expensive

The Charter at Beaver Creek. 120 Offerson Rd. (P.O. Box 5310), Beaver Creek, CO 81620. ☎ **800/525-6660** or 970/949-6660. Fax 970/949-6709. www.vail.net/charter. E-mail: charter @vail.net. 156 units. TV TEL. Winter, $165–$375 double, $240–$1,800 condo; summer, $135 double, $175–$600 condo. AE, MC, V. Free underground parking, height limit 7 ft. 6 in.; valet parking available. Closed late April to late May.

This elegant European-style lodging offers the luxury of a world-class hotel and the convenience of condominiums, set in the magnificent Rocky Mountains. Lodge rooms, simply decorated with light-wood furnishings, can accommodate up to four persons; most have two queen beds, though some have a king. All units have a VCR, minifridge, coffeemaker, wall safe, iron and ironing board, and hair dryer; and some have a balcony with grand views of the valley or surrounding mountains. Condominiums have a full kitchen, fireplace—some of lovely river rock—and balcony or patio. All are decorated by the owners—some in western motif, some more traditional. The property is ski-in, ski-out, with ski valet service.

Dining: The traMonti Restaurant offers northern Tuscan and Italian cuisine in an elegant setting for dinner; the more casual Terrace Restaurant serves three meals daily.

Amenities: Concierge, limited room service, valet dry cleaning and laundry, self-service laundry, newspaper delivery, limited secretarial services, and baby-sitting. Full-service rental and retail sports shop; full-service spa and health club with a 20-meter lap pool, aerobic equipment, large hot tub, and sauna; outdoor heated pool in summer with separate children's pool; jogging trail; 18-hole golf course; game room; nature trails; and meeting facilities for up to 150.

The Lodge & Spa at Cordillera. 2205 Cordillera Way (P.O. Box 1110), Edwards, CO 81632. ☎ **800/877-3529** or 970/926-2200. Fax 970/926-2486. E-mail: ldgcord@vail.net. 48 units. A/C TV TEL. $255–$450 double; $480–$600 suite. Extra person $20; children under 12 stay free in parents' room. AE, DC, MC, V. Free valet parking.

Like a mountain château in the Pyrenees of southwestern France, this luxurious hideaway nestles in 3,200 acres of private forest 13 miles west of Vail, and about 3 miles from Beaver Creek.

Rocky Mountain timber and stone, along with elegant wrought iron, are prominent in the handsome, residential-style guest rooms. More than half the rooms feature wood-burning fireplaces; all have king or queen beds with down comforters, and most have private balconies or decks with views of the New York Range of the Rockies. All bathrooms have bidets. Smoking is not permitted.

Dining: The Restaurant Picasso is one of the Vail Valley's better dining options, serving light interpretations of continental cuisine. The Chapparal offers steaks, chops, and seafood at lunch and dinner, and the Timber Hearth Grille serves contemporary American dinners.

Amenities: Room service, concierge, valet laundry and dry cleaning; outdoor swimming pool, indoor lap pool, indoor and outdoor whirlpool, steam room, sauna, weight-and-exercise room, aerobics, massage, hydrotherapy; two 18-hole golf courses and a 10-hole short course; 15 miles of mountain biking/cross-country ski trails, Nordic ski center; bicycle rentals, two tennis courts, volleyball; and meeting facilities for 80.

Moderate

✪ **Black Bear Inn of Vail.** 2405 Elliott Rd. in West Vail, Vail, CO 81657. ☎ **970/ 476-1304.** Fax 970/476-0433. 12 units. TEL. $106–$245 double; Christmas $215. Rates include full breakfast. DISC, MC, V.

This overgrown log cabin, with huge Engelmann spruce ceiling timbers, has solid pine furniture made in Colorado. Rooms have down comforters on the good-quality beds, and quilts and watercolors by local artists on the walls. Breakfast and afternoon refreshments are served in the main room. Downstairs is a game room with pool table, pinball machine, books, TV, and VCR and movies; outside is a hot tub. There's a meeting room for 12. No smoking is permitted anywhere in the inn.

Eagle River Inn. 145 N. Main St. (P.O. Box 100), Minturn, CO 81645. ☎ **800/344-1750** or 970/827-5761. Fax 970/827-4020. E-mail: eri@vail.net. 12 units (all with three-quarter bathrooms). TV. Winter, $125–$180; summer, $98. Rates are for double occupancy and include breakfast. AE, DISC, MC, V. Closed mid-April to late May.

Built in 1894 when the Denver & Rio Grande Railroad made the village of Minturn a stop on its route, the picturesque Eagle River Inn has had many incarnations. Its latest makeover, in 1986, turned it into a fine bed-and-breakfast. It has a southwestern feel throughout, from the sala-style lobby (complete with kiva fireplace and bancos) to the bright and breezy second- and third-story guest rooms, with tiled bathrooms and down comforters. Wine and hors d'oeuvres are served each evening, and breakfast includes homemade granola, fresh fruit, and baked goods. The hot tub on a deck overlooking the Eagle River is always available. Smoking is not permitted.

Inexpensive

Comfort Inn. 161 W. Beaver Creek Blvd. (P.O. Box 5510), Avon, CO 81620. ☎ **800/ 423-4374** or 970/949-5511. Fax 970/949-7762. 146 units. A/C TV TEL. Winter, $97–$260 double. Summer, $87–$109 double. Rates include continental breakfast. Children under 18 stay free in parents' room. AE, DC, DISC, MC, V. Located just off I-70 exit 167.

This comfortable four-story lodging has a big stone fireplace in its lobby lounge and a southwestern decor. Most of the spacious rooms have two queen beds; a few have kings, plus comfortable chairs. There's indoor ski storage and a free shuttle to Beaver Creek Resort, a heated outdoor pool, whirlpool, and guest laundry.

CAMPING

Sylvan Lake State Park. ☎ **800/678-2267** for reservations, or 970/625-1607 for park information. 46 sites. $7 per site, plus $4 state parks pass. MC, V for reservations; cash only at the park. Take I-70 exit 147 to Eagle, drive south through town on Main St. to West Brush Creek Rd., turn right, and go 16 miles to the park entrance.

Two separate campgrounds at this beautiful 115-acre park put visitors close to trout fishing and boating on a 40-acre lake in the White River National Forest. The park has flush toilets, fire pits, and water, but no showers, RV hookups, or dump station. The elevation is 5,000 feet.

WHERE TO DINE
VERY EXPENSIVE

Beano's Cabin. Foot of Larkspur Lift, Beaver Creek Resort. ☎ **970/949-9090.** Reservations required. Fixed-price, $85 adults, $35 children under 12. AE, DC, DISC, MC, V. Departures from Rendezvous Cabin 5–9:30pm, winter daily, summer Tues–Sun. REGIONAL.

A splurge that many Beaver Creek visitors consider one of the highlights of their stay is the sleigh-ride dinner trip (or in summer, the horse-drawn wagon ride) to Beano's. This isn't the log homestead that Chicago lettuce farmer Frank "Beano" Bienkowski built on Beaver Creek Mountain in 1919—it's far more elegant. Diners board the 42-passenger, snowcat-driven sleighs at the base of the Centennial Lift, arriving 15 minutes later for a candlelit five-course dinner around a crackling fire with musical entertainment.

There's a choice of entrees, which generally include beef, seafood, chicken, and pasta. Vegetarian meals may be requested. A full bar, extensive wine list, and children's menu are also available.

EXPENSIVE

The Golden Eagle Inn. Village Hall, Beaver Creek Mall. ☎ **970/949-1940.** Main courses $8.50–$14 lunch, $15–$27 dinner. AE, MC, V. Daily 11:30am–10pm. CREATIVE AMERICAN.

Sidewalk tables on the Beaver Creek promenade are the outstanding feature of this restaurant, owned by Austrian Pepi Langegger of Vail's Tyrolean Inn. Appetizers might include chili-dusted soft-shell crab or black-bean soup. Main courses include roast duckling with sherried apple cider sauce, which is slow roasted and served with honey and walnuts; plus innovative variations of steak, seafood, pasta, lamb, and game. Among the game specialties is roast loin of elk, which is crusted with raspberry whole-grain mustard and served medium rare with a marsala-lingonberry pan jus.

Sweet Basil. 193 E. Gore Creek Dr. ☎ **970/476-0125.** Reservations recommended. Main courses $7–$9.50 lunch, $21–$29 dinner. AE, MC, V. Daily 11:30am–2:30pm and 5:30–10pm. CREATIVE AMERICAN.

Simple modern decor, with contemporary art, large windows, and the tasteful use of mirrors, is the earmark of this pleasant restaurant. A deck overlooks the Lodge Promenade in the center of Vail Village; diners sit at private tables or at the wine bar. Menus change seasonally but include items such as almond-crusted rack of lamb, honey-baked pork chop, and grilled New York steak; creative seafood dishes are the specialty, such as seared tuna with portabello mushroom Napoleon, crispy potatoes, and merlot sauce.

Tyrolean Inn. 400 E. Meadow Dr. ☎ **970/476-2204.** Reservations recommended. Main courses $16–$35. AE, MC, V. Daily 6–10pm. CREATIVE EUROPEAN & AMERICAN.

The Langegger family is proud of its Old World roots. Pepi established this Vail landmark in 1972, and the ambiance today remains decidedly alpine, with gracious, friendly service and authentic Tyrolean decor. In summer, there's dining on an outdoor patio beside Gore Creek.

Wild game is the house specialty, and choices might include Tyrolean game grill (herbed elk loin, marinated quail, and buffalo sausage) or chile-rubbed buffalo. Other items might range from Wiener schnitzel to roast rack of New Zealand lamb to Long Island pepper duck. Pasta and vegetarian dishes are also available. The wine list is extensive—more than 250 choices—and in addition to standard domestic beers, there are several Colorado microbrews plus a number of fine European beers.

Vendetta's. 291 Bridge St. ☎ **970/476-5070.** Reservations recommended. Main courses $6–$9 lunch, $15–$29 dinner. AE, MC, V. Daily 11am–3pm and 5:30–10pm. NORTHERN ITALIAN.

Located on busy Bridge Street in the heart of Vail Village, Vendetta's is a casual, friendly spot as famous for its après-ski (on a sunny deck) as for its fine Italian cuisine. Pasta lovers would enjoy the manicotti (baked with four cheeses), or lasagna (baked with beef and sausage). Osso bucco and muscovy duck chambord (grilled duck breast in a chambord cherry demi-glace with roasted potatoes) are favorites, and seafood specials range from Parmesan encrusted salmon to cioppino to fettuccine frutti di mare.

MODERATE

Blu's. 193 E. Gore Creek Dr. ☎ **970/476-3113.** Reservations not accepted. Breakfast/lunch $4.50–$9, main courses $9–$19. AE, CB, DC, MC, V. Daily 9am–11pm. CONTEMPORARY AMERICAN.

This eatery, located downstairs from the Children's Fountain by Gore Creek, is a local favorite—in no small part because it offers breakfasts daily until 5pm. There's a wide selection of breakfast/lunch items, including green eggs and ham, omelets, vegetarian specialties, pasta dishes, salads, sandwiches, and burgers. Dinner entrees include jambalaya, mushroom ravioli, mustard pepper steak, and "Kick Ass" California chicken relleno; there's also an extensive wine list.

Hubcap Brewery and Kitchen. 143 E. Meadow Dr., Crossroads Shopping Center. ☎ **970/ 476-5757.** Reservations not accepted. Main courses $4.75–$9 lunch, $7–$15 dinner. AE, MC, V. Daily 11:30am–1am. AMERICAN.

A state-of-the-art brewpub with a glass-enclosed brew house, the Hubcap serves unfiltered, unpasteurized beer. Sandwich offerings include grilled chicken, BLTs, steak, and tuna. There are also burgers, chicken pot pie, meat loaf, salads, and soups. Dinner selections, which come with homemade beer bread, include barbecued chicken, New York strip steak, a vegetarian platter, barbecued ribs, and fresh fish. Apple pie tops the decadent dessert selections.

Montauk Seafood Grill. 549 Lionshead Mall. ☎ **970/476-2601.** Reservations recommended. Main courses $16–$23. AE, MC, V. Daily 5–10pm. SEAFOOD.

Owner Gary Boris grew up around the harbors of Montauk Point, New York. Now that he's landlocked, he flies fresh fish in daily from both coasts, Hawaii, and the Gulf of Mexico; all are grilled, and creatively sauced if desired. Steak, chops, chicken, and pasta are also available.

The Red Lion. 304 Bridge St. ☎ **970/476-7676.** Main courses $8–$19. AE, DISC, MC, V. Daily 11am–11pm (bar open later). BARBECUE/BURGERS.

Established soon after the village of Vail was incorporated, this has been a popular spot for more than three decades. The traditional food is good and filling: The Red Lion's hallmark is hickory-smoked barbecue, but the burgers, specialty salads, and sandwiches are also popular, and there's a children's menu as well. Beer drinkers are drawn by the Around the World Beer Club (more than 40 varieties). There's live entertainment nightly in winter (Fridays and Saturdays in summer), plus 14 TVs for sporting events.

VAIL AFTER DARK

For up-to-date listings of what's going on where, pick up a free copy of *The Source,* Vail's weekly entertainment guide.

Vail's greatest concentration of late-night haunts can be found in a 1½-block stretch of Bridge Street from Hanson Ranch Road north to the covered bridge over Gore Creek. From mountainside to creek, they include the **Club** (☎ 970/479-0556), the **Red Lion** (☎ 970/476-7676), **Vendetta's** (☎ 970/476-5070), and **Nick's** (☎ 970/476-3433). Another popular place for hanging out is **Garton's Bar & Grill,** 143 E. Meadow Dr. (☎ 970/479-0607).

Pool enthusiasts should check out the **Sundance Saloon,** 675 Lionshead Place (☎ 970/476-3453); or the **Jackalope,** West Vail Mall (☎ 970/476-4314), which also has video games and 13 TVs. Piano bars draw quieter types to **Mickey's,** in the Lodge at Vail (☎ 970/476-5011); and the **Lobby Lounge/Bar** in the Vail Cascade (☎ 970/476-7111).

Vail's first brewpub, **Hubcap Brewery and Kitchen,** at the Crossroads Shopping Center (☎ 970/476-5757), invites beer connoisseurs to relax on its large deck and sip White River Wheat Ale and Vail Pale Ale.

7 Leadville

38 miles S of Vail, 59 miles E of Aspen, 113 miles W of Denver

There was a time, not much more than a century ago, when Leadville was the most important city between St. Louis and San Francisco. It was the stopping point for Easterners with nothing to lose and everything to gain from the promise of gold and silver. Today, Leadville is one of the best places to rediscover the West's mining heritage.

Founded in 1860 on the gold that glimmered in prospectors' pans, the Oro City site quickly attracted 10,000 miners who dug $5 million in gold out of a 3-mile stretch of the California Gulch by 1865. When the riches were gone, Leadville was deserted, although a smaller lode of gold-bearing quartz kept nearby Oro City alive for another decade. Then in 1875 two prospectors discovered that the lead ore in the valley's heavy black soil contained 15 ounces of silver to the ton, and located the California Gulch's first paying silver lode. Over the next two decades, Leadville grew to an estimated 30,000 residents—among them Horace Tabor, who parlayed his mercantile-and-mining investments into unimaginable wealth; and "the Unsinkable" Molly Brown, whose husband made his fortune here before moving to Denver, where the family lived at the time of Molly's Titanic heroism.

Many buildings of the silver boom (which produced $136 million between 1879 and 1889) have been preserved in one of Colorado's most complete National Historic Districts. So for those who want to take a break from playing outdoors to explore Colorado's frontier past, Leadville's just the place to do it.

ESSENTIALS

GETTING THERE   By Car   Coming from Denver, leave I-70 at exit 195 (Copper Mountain), and proceed south 24 miles on Colo. 91. From Grand Junction, depart I-70 at exit 171 (Minturn), and continue south 33 miles on U.S. 24. From Aspen, in the summer take Colo. 82 east 44 miles over Independence Pass (closed in winter), then turn north on U.S. 24 for 15 miles. There's also easy access from the south via U.S. 24.

It Doesn't Get Any Higher

Leadville has the highest elevation of any incorporated city in the United States: 10,430 feet, nearly 2 miles above sea level.

By Plane **Leadville Airport,** 915 County Rd. 23 (☎ **719/486-2627**), 2 miles south of downtown, at 9,927 feet elevation, is said to be America's highest airport. Air service is limited to air-taxi, charter, sightseeing, and private planes.

VISITOR INFORMATION   Contact the **Greater Leadville Area Chamber of Commerce,** 809 Harrison Ave. (P.O. Box 861), Leadville, CO 80461 (☎ **888/532-3845** or 719/486-3900; www.leadville.com; e-mail: leadville@leadville.com). The chamber's visitor center is open daily, from 9am to 5pm.

GETTING AROUND   U.S. 24 is Leadville's main street. Entering from the north, it's named Poplar Street; then it turns west on Ninth Street for a block and then left on Harrison Avenue. The next seven blocks south, to Second Street, are the heart of this historic town. Leadville's stoplight is at the intersection of Harrison Avenue and Sixth Street, which heads west to civic and recreational complexes. A block north, Seventh Street climbs east to the old train depot and 13,186-foot Mosquito Pass, among America's highest, open to four-wheel-drive vehicles in summer.

Car rentals are available through **Leadville Leasing** at the airport (☎ **719/486-2627**). **Dee Hive Tours,** 506 Harrison Ave. (☎ **719/486-2339**), offers **taxi** service plus year-round charter service.

FAST FACTS   There's a 24-hour emergency room at **St. Vincent's General Hospital,** 822 W. Fourth St. (☎ **719/486-0230**). The **post office** is at West Fifth and Pine Streets, a block west of Harrison Avenue. For hours and other information contact the U.S. Postal Service (☎ **800/275-8777**). The Lake County Sheriff's office (☎ **719/486-1249**) provides **road reports.**

EXPERIENCING LEADVILLE'S PAST

A great many residences of successful mining operators, engineers, and financiers are preserved within the **Leadville National Historic Landmark District,** which stretches along seven blocks of Harrison Avenue and part of Chestnut Street, where it intersects Harrison at the south end of downtown. A self-guided walking tour of this district, with map, is in the free *Leadville Magazine,* available at the chamber's visitor center.

An informative 30-minute film, *The Earth Runs Silver: Early Leadville,* is shown at the Fox Theater, 115 W. Sixth St. (☎ **719/486-3900**). It gives a good overview of Leadville's place in American mining history. Admission is $3 for adults, $2 for children 2 to 12. Call for times of daily showings or ask at the chamber's visitor center, which also sells tickets.

At the ✪ **National Mining Hall of Fame and Museum,** 120 W. Ninth St. (☎ **719/486-1229**), you'll find working models of mining machinery and dioramas depicting the history of Colorado mining from coal to gold. Admission is $3.50 for adults, $3 for seniors 62 and older, $2 for children 6 to 12, and free for children under 6. Open May through October, daily from 9am to 5pm; November through April, Monday through Friday from 10am to 2pm.

Peer into Horace Tabor's Matchless Mine, 1¼ miles east up Seventh Street, and tour the **Matchless Mine Cabin** where Tabor's widow, Baby Doe, spent the final 36 years of her life, hoping to strike it rich once more. Admission is $3 for adults,

$1 for children 6 to 12, and free for kids under 6. Open June to Labor Day, daily from 8am to 4:45pm.

To get an up-close look at where a few fortunate miners were able to escape the rough-and-tumble atmosphere of the mines, if only for an evening, visit **Healy House and Dexter Cabin,** 912 Harrison Ave. (☎ **719/486-0487**). Healy House was built by smelter owner August Meyer in 1878, and later converted into a lavish boardinghouse by Daniel Healy. The adjacent rough-hewn log cabin was built by John Dexter and furnished in an elegant style. Admission is $3.50 for adults, $3 for seniors 65 and older, $2 for children 6 to 16, and free for children under 6. Open Memorial Day weekend to Labor Day, daily from 10am to 4:30pm.

The **Tabor Opera House,** 308 Harrison Ave. (☎ **719/486-1147**), is where Leadville's mining magnates and their wives kept up with cultural happenings back East. Opened in 1879, over the years it has hosted everything from the Ziegfeld Follies and the Metropolitan Opera to prizefighter Jack Dempsey (a Colorado native) and magician Harry Houdini (whose vanishing square is still evident on the stage floor). Visitors are welcome to explore the 880-seat theater, backstage, and dressing rooms. Admission is $4 for adults, $2 for children 12 and under. Open summers, Sunday through Friday from 9am to 5:30pm.

Another historic site worth stopping at is **Western Hardware Antiques & Variety,** 431 Harrison Ave. (☎ **719/486-2213**), which operated as a hardware store from 1880 until 1985. Today, however, it's an antiques shop with a lot of other stuff, such as candy and novelties, that's open seven days a week. It's also a fascinating look at an old-fashioned store, with much original detail including a wall lined with 1,000 drawers, and a ladder on rollers that clerks used to retrieve items from them.

MORE TO SEE & DO

Leadville, Colorado & Southern Railroad. 326 E. Seventh St. at Hazel St. ☎ **719/486-3936.** www.leadville-train.com. Admission $22.50 adults, $12.50 children 4–12, free for children 3 and under. Daily, Memorial Day–early Oct, call for schedule.

This spectacularly scenic ride, in a modern diesel train, departs the 1893 C&S Depot, three blocks east of U.S. 24, and follows the old "high line" along the headwaters of the Arkansas River, to a splendid view of Fremont Pass. The return takes you to the French Gulch Water Tower for a dramatic look at Mount Elbert, Colorado's tallest mountain, at 14,431 feet. The ride lasts about 2½ hours, and because of the high elevations, jackets or sweaters are recommended even on the hottest summer days.

Leadville National Fish Hatchery. 2844 Colo. 300 (6 miles southwest of Leadville off U.S. 24). ☎ **719/486-0189.** Free admission. Summer, daily 7:30am–5pm; rest of the year, daily 7:30am–4pm.

Established in 1889, this is the second-oldest hatchery operated by the U.S. Fish and Wildlife Service. Rainbow, brook, brown, and cutthroat trout are raised here, at an elevation of 10,000 feet on the east side of Mount Massive. Visitors can also enjoy self-guided nature trails, with breathtaking views of the surrounding mountains and occasionally deer and elk. One trail passes by the remains of a late-1800s resort, the Evergreen Hotel, and several connect to the Colorado Trail. In winter, take cross-country skis or snowshoes.

SPORTS & OUTDOOR ACTIVITIES

FISHING   There's good trout and kokanee fishing at Turquoise Lake, Twin Lakes, and other small high-mountain lakes, as well as at beaver ponds located on side streams of the Arkansas River. There's also limited stream-fishing.

Licenses, supplies, and information can be obtained from **Buckthorn Sporting Goods,** 616 Harrison Ave. (☎ **719/486-3944**), and other local stores. Huck Finn Pond at City Park, West Fifth Street at Leiter Street, is open for free children's fishing in summer.

GOLF   The Mount Massive Golf Course, 3½ miles west of town at 259 County Rd. 5 (P.O. Box 312), Leadville, CO 80461 (☎ **719/486-2176**), claims to be North America's highest golf course, at 9,700 feet. Greens fees are $12 for 9 holes and $22 for 18, and views of surrounding mountain peaks are magnificent.

HIKING & MOUNTAINEERING   Adventurous hikers can attempt an ascent of Mount Elbert (14,433 feet) or Mount Massive (14,421 feet); either can be climbed in a day without technical equipment, though altitude and abruptly changing weather conditions are factors that should be weighed. The **San Isabel National Forest** office, 2015 Poplar St. (☎ **719/486-0749**), has detailed maps, as well as information on other hiking possibilities in the area.

SKIING   **Ski Cooper,** P.O. Box 896, Leadville, CO 80461 (☎ **719/486-3684,** or 719/486-2277 for snow reports), began as a training center for Tenth Mountain Division troops from Camp Hale during World War II. Located 10 miles north of Leadville on U.S. 24 near Tennessee Pass, it offers numerous intermediate and novice runs, and hosts backcountry Chicago Ridge Snowcat Tours for experts. The lifts—a triple chair, double chair, T-bar, and beginners' poma—serve 26 runs on a 1,200-foot vertical. Full-day tickets (1998–99 rates) are $25 for adults, $15 for children 6 to 12, $16 for seniors 60 to 69, and free for seniors 70 and over and kids under 6. The **Piney Creek Nordic Center** (☎ **719/486-1750**), at the foot of the mountain, has a 25-kilometer (15.5-mile) skate and classic cross-country track, plus rentals and lessons.

WHERE TO STAY

Taxes add just under 9% to lodging bills.

Apple Blossom Inn. 120 W. Fourth St., Leadville, CO 80461. ☎ **800/982-9279** or 719/486-2141. Fax 719/486-0994. E-mail: applebb@rmi.net. 8 units (3 with bathroom). $64–$99 double; from $128 suite. Rates include breakfast. AE, DC, DISC, MC, V.

An 1879 Victorian structure on Leadville's millionaires' row, this inn features the original handcrafted woodwork, detailed mantels, and crystal lights installed by its original owners. Rooms range from warm and cozy to large and sunny. Estelle's Room has a large fireplace, brass queen feather bed, and sitting area; while the Library features a 14-foot ceiling, five stained-glass windows, parquet floor, and a four-poster queen feather bed. Smoking is not permitted.

✪ **Delaware Hotel.** 700 Harrison Ave., Leadville, CO 80461. ☎ **800/748-2004** or 719/486-1418. Fax 719/486-2214. 36 units. TV TEL. $70–$80 double; $95–$100 family room; $115–$125 suite. Rates include breakfast. Inquire about special packages for skiing, golfing, and theme weekends. AE, CB, DC, DISC, MC, V.

Built in 1886, this hotel was restored in 1985 and is once again a Victorian gem. The lobby is beautiful in the style of grand old hotels, with a turn-of-the-century player piano, crystal chandeliers, and magnificent Victorian furnishings. Guest rooms have brass or iron beds, quilts, and lace curtains. Rooms have private bathrooms with showers but no tubs; the four suites have full bathrooms with tub/shower combos. The hotel also has a whirlpool and access to a nearby health club.

Pan Ark Lodge. 5827 U.S. 24, Leadville, CO 80461. ☎ **800/443-1063** or 719/486-1063. 48 units. $55–$61 double. DISC, MC, V.

Located 9 miles south of Leadville, this comfortable motel has spacious, well-maintained rooms, all with natural moss-rock fireplaces and beautiful mountain views. Some rooms have TVs, and some have kitchenettes. There's a coin-operated laundry.

CAMPING

Sugar Loafin' Campground. 303 Colo. 300, Leadville, CO 80461. ☎ **719/486-1031.** E-mail: sugarloafin@sni.net. $20–$25 for two. AE, MC, V. Pets accepted. Closed late Sept to mid-May.

Located 3½ miles northwest of downtown Leadville via West Sixth Street, this campground has spectacular mountain views and clean bathhouses with plenty of hot water. There are tent and full-hookup RV sites. Located at a 9,696-foot elevation, the campground provides a playground, rec room, planned activities, self-service laundry, phone, and a general store. A public golf course is nearby.

WHERE TO DINE

Columbine Cafe. 612 Harrison Ave. ☎ **719/486-3599.** Reservations not accepted. Main courses $4–$8. Daily 6:30am–3pm. Closed mid-Apr to early May. AMERICAN/VEGETARIAN.

This is a simple cafe with historic tools and some old wooden skis on the walls. Breakfasts range from traditional eggs and pancakes to more exotic dishes such as malted Belgian waffles and eggs Benedict, which can be prepared with avocados or tomatoes for vegetarians. Lunches include basics such as home-style roast beef, sandwiches, and burgers, plus more unique items like the spicy Cajun burger.

The Golden Burro Café. 710 Harrison Ave. ☎ **970/486-1239.** Main courses $3.50–$13. MC, V. Summer, daily 6am–10pm; winter, daily 7am–9pm. AMERICAN.

People have been enjoying good food in a comfortable western setting at the Golden Burro since it opened in 1938. Old photos and drawings hang on the white walls above wainscoting, glass-and-brass chandeliers cast a warm glow, and the large front windows provide views of the mountains. The emphasis at the Burro is on food like Grandma used to make, such as a hot meat-loaf sandwich (homemade meat loaf, served open-faced with brown gravy, mashed potatoes, and a vegetable), pork chops, chicken-fried steak, and liver and onions, plus burritos with your choice of red or green chile. Especially popular are the freshly-baked cinnamon rolls.

The Grill. 715 Elm St. ☎ **719/486-9930.** Main courses $4.75–$9.75. MC, V. Daily 11am–10pm. MEXICAN.

The Grill serves authentic south-of-the-border food and what many think are the best margaritas in Colorado's mountains. You can get one or two tacos, enchiladas, tamales, and burritos, or complete dinners such as the house specialty: sopaipillas stuffed with a variety of items. Vegetarian and children's plates are available.

The Leadville Prospector. 2798 Colo. 91. ☎ **800/844-2828** or 719/486-3955. Reservations recommended. Main courses $9–$20. MC, V. Tues–Sun 5–9pm. STEAK/SEAFOOD.

Lodged in a spacious log cabin with a stone entrance, 3 miles north of town in a picturesque mountain setting, the Prospector has long been considered one of Leadville's finest restaurants. Dinners include steaks, baby-back ribs, rack of lamb, chicken, pasta, seafood, and prime rib. There are daily specials, plus a salad bar, soup and bean kettles, and menus for children and light appetites. There's also a full bar, with a number of Colorado microbrews.

LEADVILLE AFTER DARK

Leadville is on the quiet side. If it's lively anywhere, it will be the **Silver Dollar Saloon,** 315 Harrison Ave. (☎ **719/486-9914**), an Irish-style bar decorated with pictures of "Baby Doe" Tabor. The **Delaware Hotel** (see above) has an oak lobby bar, with occasional piano entertainment.

8 Aspen

172 miles W of Denver, 130 miles E of Grand Junction

Like Vail, Aspen's reputation precedes it. Anyone with a pulse knows that, come winter, it's more than likely to wind up in the tabloids when two celebrities—who are married to other people—are captured on film sharing a chairlift together; and, yes, we guess it's possible that Hunter S. Thompson may serve you a drink downtown, if he happens to be tending bar somewhere as a favor to the owner, but that's not particularly likely.

If you take the time to dig beneath the media hype, you may be surprised by what you find. Aspen, at an elevation of 7,908 feet, is a real town with a fascinating history, some great old buildings, and spectacular mountain scenery. If you're a serious skier, you owe yourself at least a few days' worth of hitting the slopes (as if you need us to tell you that); but if you've never strapped on boards, and you're thinking of visiting in summer, you'll be doubly pleased: Prices are significantly lower, and the crowds thin out. Many of the fabulous restaurants are still open, the surrounding forests are teeming with great trails for hiking, biking, and horseback riding, and it becomes one of the best destinations in the country for summer music and dance festivals.

Aspen was "discovered" when silver miners from nearby Leadville wandered a bit further afield. When the Smuggler Mine produced the world's largest silver nugget (1,840 lb.), prospectors started heading to Aspen in droves. The city soon had 12,000 citizens—but just as quickly the population dwindled to one-tenth that number after the 1893 silver crash.

It took almost 50 years for Aspen to begin its comeback, which came as a result of another natural resource—snow. Shortly before World War II, a small ski area with a primitive boat tow was established on Aspen Mountain. During the war, Tenth Mountain Division ski-soldiers training near Leadville spent weekends in Aspen and were enthralled with its possibilities. An infusion of money in 1945 by Chicago industrialist Walter Paepcke, who moved to Aspen with his wife, Elizabeth, resulted in the construction of what was then the world's longest chairlift. The Aspen Skiing Corporation (now Company) was founded the following year, and in 1950 Aspen's status as an international resort was confirmed when it hosted the alpine world skiing championships. Then came the opening in 1958 of Buttermilk Mountain and Aspen Highlands, and in 1967, the birth of Snowmass.

The Paepckes' vision of the resort was not exclusively commercial, however. They saw Aspen as a year-round intellectual and artistic community that would nourish the minds and spirits as well as the bodies of those who visited. Chief among their accomplishments was the establishment of the Aspen Institute for Humanistic Studies and the Aspen Music Festival and School.

Their love of ideas and high-minded discourse attracted the likes of Thornton Wilder, Ortega y Gasset, and Albert Schweitzer to the Paepckes' resort, and the

Aspen

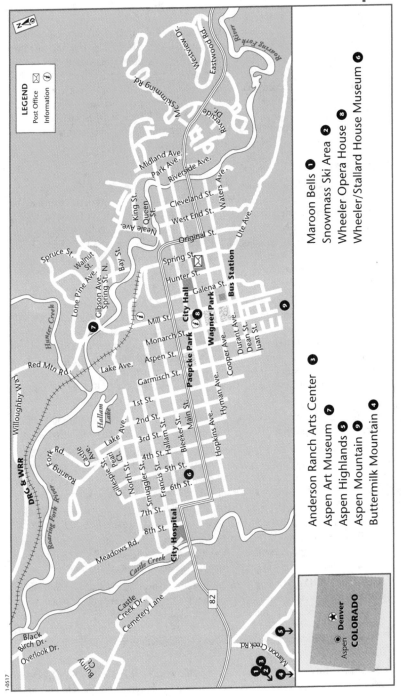

LEGEND
- ⊠ Post Office
- ⓘ Information

Anderson Ranch Arts Center ❸
Aspen Art Museum ❼
Aspen Highlands ❺
Aspen Mountain ❾
Buttermilk Mountain ❹

Maroon Bells ❶
Snowmass Ski Area ❷
Wheeler Opera House ❽
Wheeler/Stallard House Museum ❻

COLORADO
★ Denver
● Aspen

1-0517

couple became important promoters of Walter Gropius's Bauhaus design movement in America. The Paepckes believed in discipline, individual rights and responsibilities, and hard work. After Walter's death in 1960, Elizabeth strived to continue this tradition but found a less receptive audience among those who moved to Aspen in the 1960s and 1970s. By the 1980s, relatives reported that Elizabeth was disillusioned with the excesses that two decades of new, free-wheeling money had brought, but she remained—in many respects Aspen's conscience—living out her ideals with purpose, but also grace and élan, until her death in 1994. The continuing success—and critical praise—of the Institute's programs ensures that the Paepckes' vision for Aspen has not been forgotten.

ESSENTIALS

GETTING THERE   By Car   Aspen is located on Colo. 82, halfway between I-70 at Glenwood Springs (42 miles northwest) and U.S. 24 south of Leadville (44 miles east). In summer, it's a scenic 3½-hour drive from Denver: Leave I-70 West at exit 195 (Copper Mountain); follow Colo. 91 south to Leadville, where you pick up U.S. 24; turn west on Colo. 82 through Twin Lakes and over 12,095-foot Independence Pass. In winter, the Independence Pass road is closed, so you'll have to take I-70 to Glenwood Springs, and head east on Colo. 82. In optimal winter driving conditions, it'll take about 4 hours from Denver.

By Plane   Visitors who wish to fly directly into Aspen can arrange to land at **Pitkin County Airport/Sardy Field,** 3 miles northwest of Aspen on Colo. 82 (☎ 970/920-5380). Operating year-round flights are **United Express** (☎ 800/241-6522) and **America West** (☎ 800/930-3030). Other airlines sometimes operate during ski season. In summer, **Northwest** (☎ 800/225-2525) has a daily flight from Minneapolis/St. Paul.

Another option is the **Eagle County Airport** near Vail (☎ 970/524-7700); see section 6, above.

By Airport Shuttle   Colorado Mountain Express (☎ 800/525-6363) offers shuttle service from both Denver International Airport and Eagle County Airport.

By Train   En route from San Francisco or Chicago, **Amtrak** (☎ 800/872-7245) stops in Glenwood Springs (passenger station ☎ 970/945-9563), 42 miles northwest of Aspen. Taxis, as well as rental cars, are available at the depot, and the Aspen bus system also provides transportation (see "Getting Around," below).

VISITOR INFORMATION   For information, contact the **Aspen Chamber Resort Association,** 425 Rio Grande Place, Aspen, CO 81611 (☎ 970/925-1940; www.aspen.com), or drop by the **Aspen Visitor Centers** at the Wheeler Opera House, Hyman Avenue and Mill Street or Rio Grande Place. In summer, a **Kiosk** is set up on the Cooper Avenue Mall (next to Banana Republic).

GETTING AROUND   Entering town from the northwest on Colo. 82, the arterial jogs right (south) two blocks on Seventh Street, then left (east) at Main Street. "East" and "West" street numbers are separated by Garmisch Street, the next cross street after First Street. Mill Street is the town's main north–south street. There are several pedestrian malls downtown, which throw a curve into the downtown traffic flow.

By Shuttle Bus   Free bus service is available within the Aspen city limits, beyond which you can get connections west as far as Glenwood Springs. The fare from Aspen to Snowmass is $2 for adults, $1 for children 6 to 16, and free for children under 6 and seniors 65 and older. Exact fare is required. Normal hours are 6:15am to 2:15am daily. Further information can be obtained at the **Rubey Park Transit Center,** Durant Avenue between Mill and Galena Streets, Aspen (☎ 970/925-8484). Schedules, frequency, and routes vary with the seasons; services include free ski shuttles in winter between all four mountains, shuttles to the Aspen Music Festival, and tours to the Maroon Bells scenic area in summer.

Free shuttle transportation within Snowmass Village is offered daily during ski season and on a limited schedule in summer, by the **Snowmass Transportation Department** (☎ 970/923-2543).

By Taxi   For a cab, call High Mountain Taxi (☎ **970/925-8294**).

By Rental Car   Car-rental agencies include **Alamo** (☎ 800/327-9633 or 970/926-2603), **Avis** (☎ 800/831-2847 or 970/925-2355), **Budget** (☎ 800/527-0700 or 970/925-2151), **Eagle** (☎ 800/282-2128 or 970/925-2128), and **Thrifty** (☎ 800/367-2277 or 970/920-2305).

FAST FACTS   The **Aspen Valley Hospital**, 401 Castle Creek Rd., near Aspen Highlands (☎ **970/925-1120**), has a 24-hour emergency room. The **post office** is at 235 Puppy Smith St., off Mill Street north of Main; there's another in the Snowmass Center. For hours and other information contact the U.S. Postal Service (☎ **800/275-8777**). For **road reports,** call ☎ **970/920-5454.**

SPECIAL EVENTS   Wintersköl Carnival, third week in January, in Aspen/Snowmass; Gay Ski Week, last week in January; Snowmass Mardi Gras, late February or early March; Aspen Writers Conference, late June or July; Snowmass Children's Festival, first weekend in August; Aspen Filmfest, late September. Also see "The Festival Scene," below.

SKIING & OTHER WINTER ACTIVITIES

Skiing Aspen really means skiing the four Aspen area resorts—Aspen, Aspen Highlands, Buttermilk, and Snowmass. All are managed by Aspen Skiing Company, and one ticket gives access to all. Lift tickets (1998–99 season) cost $59 for adults 28 to 64, $39 for those 13 to 27, $35 for children 7 to 12, and $49 for seniors 65 to 69. Children 6 and under and seniors 70 and older ski free. For further information, contact **Aspen Skiing Company** (P.O. Box 1248), Aspen, CO 81612 (☎ **970/925-1220**; www.skiaspen.com). Call ☎ **970/925-1221** for snow reports.

ASPEN   Aspen Mountain—previously called Ajax for an old miner's claim—is not for the timid. It is the American West's original hard-core ski mountain, with no fewer than 23 of its named runs double diamond—for experts only. One-third of the mountain's runs are left forever ungroomed—sheer ecstasy for bump runners. There are mountain-long runs for intermediates as well as advanced skiers, but beginners should look to one of the other Aspen areas.

From the **Sundeck** restaurant at the mountain's 11,212-foot summit, numerous intermediate runs extend on either side of Bell Mountain—through Copper Bowl and down Spar Gulch. To the east of the Gulch, the knob of Bell offers a mecca for mogul mashers, with bump runs down its ridge and its east and west faces. To the west of the Gulch, the face of Ruthie's is wonderful for intermediate cruisers, while more mogul runs drop off International. Ruthie's Run extends for over 2 miles down the west ridge of the mountain, with an extension via Magnifico Cut Off and Little Nell to the base, and is accessed by the unique Ruthie's high-speed double chair.

Mid-mountain restaurants include **Bonnie's,** at Tourtelotte Park near the top of Ruthie's Lift, and **La Baita,** at the bottom.

Aspen Mountain has a 3,267-foot vertical drop, with 76 trails on 700 skiable acres. There are eight lifts—the high-speed Silver Queen gondola, three quad chairs, and four double chairs—and snowcats deliver advanced-and-expert skiers to an additional 1,500 acres of powder skiing in back bowls. Average annual snowfall at the 11,212-foot summit is 300 inches (25 feet).

Aspen is open from mid-November to mid-April, daily from 9am to 3:30pm.

ASPEN HIGHLANDS Highlands has the most balanced skiable terrain—novice to expert, with lots of intermediate slopes—in the Aspen area.

It takes two lifts to reach the 11,800-foot Loge Peak summit, where most of the advanced expert runs are found in the Steeplechase area and 199 acres of glades in the Olympic Bowl. Kandahar, Golden Horn, and Thunderbowl give the intermediate skier a long run from top to bottom, and novices are best served mid-mountain on trails like Red Onion and Apple Strudel. There are two restaurants: **Highland's Cafe** and **Merry-Go-Round** at Midway.

Freestyle Friday, a tradition at Aspen Highlands for 25 years, boasts some of the best freestyle bump and big air competitors in the state of Colorado every Friday from early January to mid-April. In this technical head-to-head competition, competitors bump their way down Scarlett's Run, and finish with a final jump that lands them within perfect view of lunchtime guests at the Merry-Go-Round Restaurant.

Highlands opened a terrain park in 1998, where all snowriders are welcome. Located on nine acres on the Grand Prix run, there are two moto jumps, a 16-by-35-foot tabletop fun box with a jib barrel, and a spine ramp with a log slide. The terrain is appropriate for intermediate to expert snowriders.

Highlands has 81 trails on 651 acres, served by nine lifts (two high speed quads, five double chairs, and two surface lifts).

Highlands is open from early December to early April, daily from 9am to 4pm.

BUTTERMILK MOUNTAIN Buttermilk is a premier beginners' mountain. In fact, *Ski* magazine has rated it the best place in North America to learn how to ski. But there's plenty of intermediate and ample advanced terrain as well.

The smallest of Aspen's four mountains has three segments: Main Buttermilk, rising from the Inn at Aspen, with a variety of intermediate trails and the long, easy, winding Homestead Road; Buttermilk West, a mountaintop (9,900 feet) novice area; and Tiehack, the intermediate-advanced section where Aspen town-league races are held. The **Cliffhouse** restaurant, which serves Mongolian barbecue, is atop Main Buttermilk, and there are cafes at the foot of the other two segments.

Seven lifts (one high-speed quad, five double chairs, and a platter-pull) serve 45 trails on 410 acres, with a 2,030-foot vertical drop. Average annual snowfall at the summit is 200 inches (16 ft., 8 in.).

Special features include the Kevin Delaney Snowboard Camp, which offers an intensive adult learn-to-snowboard program; the Powder Pandas for 3- to 6-year-olds; and a snowboard park with a 23% grade.

Buttermilk is open from early December to early April, daily from 9am to 4pm.

SNOWMASS A huge, intermediate mountain with something for everyone, Snowmass has 33% more skiable acreage than the other three Aspen areas combined! Actually four distinct self-contained areas, each with its own lift system and restaurant, its terrain varies from easy beginner runs to the pitches of the Cirque and the Hanging Valley Wall, the steepest in the Aspen area.

Big Burn, site of a forest fire set by 19th-century Utes to discourage settlers, boasts wide-open advanced and intermediate slopes and the expert drops of the

Cirque. Atop the intermediate Alpine Springs trails is the advanced High Alpine Lift, from which experts can traverse to the formidable Hanging Valley Wall. Elk Camp is ideal for early intermediates who prefer long cruising runs. Sam's Knob has advanced upper trails diving through trees, and a variety of intermediate and novice runs around its northeast face and base. All areas meet in the scattered condominium developments that surround Snowmass Village Mall.

Hungry skiers head for **Ullrhof** restaurant at Big Burn's base, **Up 4 Pizza** atop Big Burn, **High Alpine** atop Alpine Springs, **Café Suzanne** at the foot of Elk Camp, and **Sam's Knob** at that peak's summit.

All told, there are 2,655 skiable acres at Snowmass, with a 4,406-foot vertical drop. The mountain has 80 trails served by 22 lifts (7 quad chairs, 2 triple chairs, 6 double chairs, 3 platter-pulls, 2 handle tows, and 2 magic carpets). Average annual snowfall at the 12,510-foot summit is 300 inches (25 feet).

The renowned Snowmass ski school has hundreds of instructors, as well as Snow Cubs and Big Burn Bears programs for children 18 months and older. The area also caters to snowboarders with a half-pipe that is 545 feet long and 55 feet wide, with a 22% grade.

Snowmass is open from early December to early April, daily from 8:30am to 3:30pm.

CROSS-COUNTRY SKIING   The Aspen/Snowmass Nordic Council operates a free Nordic trail system with nearly 50 miles of groomed double track extending throughout the Aspen-Snowmass area, and incorporating summer bicycle paths. Instruction and rentals are offered along the trail at the **Aspen Cross-Country Center,** Colo. 82 between Aspen and Buttermilk (☎ 970/925-2145), and the **Snowmass Touring Center**, Snowmass Village (☎ 970/923-3148), both of which provide daily condition reports and information regarding the entire trail system.

Independent backcountry skiers should consult **White River National Forest,** 806 W. Hallam St. (☎ 970/925-3445). Two hut systems provide shelter on multi-day trips—the 14-hut **Tenth Mountain Trail Association** toward Vail, and the six-hut **Alfred A. Braun Hut System** (☎ 970/925-5775 for both) toward Crested Butte. Call for hut reservations. Guided backcountry ski trips on the hut system routes are offered by **Aspen Alpine Guides, Inc.** (☎ 800/643-8621 or 970/925-6618), with 4-day trips at $695 per person and 5-day trips at $870 per person.

DOGSLEDDING   For rides in winter or a kennel tour in summer, call **Krabloonik,** 4250 Divide Rd., Snowmass Village (☎ 970/923-3953). Every day in winter, teams of 13 Alaskan sled dogs pull guests into the Snowmass-Maroon Bells Wilderness Area. Half-day trips, departing at 8:30am and 12:30pm, include lunch at **Krabloonik's** restaurant (see "Where to Dine," below) and cost $195 per adult and $125 for children 3 to 8 years of age. Children under 3 are not permitted on the ride. One-hour kennel tours run from mid-June to Labor Day, Wednesday through Sunday. They depart at 11am and 2:30pm from the restaurant, at a cost of $4.50 for those over 12, $4 for 12 and under. Private and group tours can be arranged by calling the number above, or writing to P.O. Box 5517, Snowmass Village, CO 81615.

ICE-SKATING   There's year-round ice-skating at the indoor **City of Aspen Ice Garden,** 233 W. Hyman Ave. (☎ 970/920-5141); and outdoor skating in winter at the **Silver Circle** at the base of Aspen Mountain next to the Rubey Park Transit Center (☎ 970/925-6360).

SNOWMOBILING   There's snowmobiling on 26 miles of groomed trails from the **T Lazy 7 Ranch,** 3129 Maroon Creek Rd. (☎ 970/925-4614), all the way to

Natural Attractions

The two sheer, pyramidal peaks called **Maroon Bells,** on Maroon Creek Road 10 miles west of Aspen, are probably the most photographed mountains in the Rockies south of Wyoming's Grand Tetons. They're a beautiful scene any time, but especially in the fall, when their reflection in Maroon Lake is framed by the changing colors of the aspen leaves. For a nominal fee you can take a 30-minute narrated bus tour up the Maroon Creek Valley (☎ **970/925-8484**).

the base of the Maroon Bells. Guided 2-hour tours cost about $100 for one person and about $150 for two.

WARM-WEATHER & YEAR-ROUND ACTIVITIES

There's no lack of guides, outfitters, and sporting-goods shops in Aspen. Among the best one-stop outfitters is **Blazing Adventures,** Mill Street and Hyman Avenue (P.O. Box 2127), Aspen, CO 81612 (☎ **800/282-7238** or 970/925-5651; www.blazingadventures.com), which offers river-rafting, mountain-biking, hiking, four-wheeling, ballooning, and horseback-riding excursions. **Aspen Alpine Guides** ☎ **800/643-8621** or 970/925-6618; www.aspen.com/aspenalpine) gives guided mountain-biking, hiking, and backcountry ski trips.

Your best source for information on a wide variety of outdoor activities in the mountains around Aspen, including hiking, mountain biking, horseback riding, four-wheeling, fishing, and camping, is the **White River National Forest,** 806 W. Hallam St. (☎ **970/925-3445**). Another good source of information and maps is **Ute Mountaineer,** 308 S. Mill St. (☎ **970/925-2849**), which also sells and rents gear and clothing.

BALLOONING Unicorn Balloon Company (☎ **800/468-2478** or 970/ 925-5752) offers spectacular bird's-eye views from hot-air balloons. Prices start at $180 per person.

BICYCLING There are two bike paths of note. One connects Aspen with Snowmass Village; it begins at Seventh Street south of Hopkins Avenue, cuts through the forest to Colo. 82, then follows Owl Creek Road and Brush Creek Road to the Snowmass Mall. Extensions link it with Aspen High School and the Aspen Business Park. The Rio Grande Trail follows the Roaring Fork River from near the Aspen Post Office, on Puppy Smith Street, through Henry Stein Park to the community of Woody Creek, off Colo. 82 near Snowmass.

CATTLE DRIVES Those yearning for a taste of the real Old West can satisfy that urge by participating in a cattle drive. Contact **Rocky Mountain Cattle Moovers** (☎ **800/826-9666** or 970/963-9666) or **Blazing Adventures** (see above).

FISHING Perhaps the best of a great deal of good trout-fishing in the Aspen area is to be found in the Roaring Fork and Frying Pan Rivers, both considered gold medal streams. The Roaring Fork follows Colo. 82 through Aspen from Independence Pass; the Frying Pan starts near Tennessee Pass, northeast of Aspen, and joins the Roaring Fork at Basalt, 18 miles down valley.

Stop at **Oxbow Outfitting Co.,** at the Little Nell Hotel (☎ 970/925-1505); **Aspen Outfitting Co.,** 520 E. Cooper Ave. #5 (☎ **800/421-1505** or 970/ 925-1505); or **Aspen Sports,** with locations at 303 E. Durant Ave. (☎ 970/ 925-1505) and Snowmass Center (☎ 970/923-3566), for your fishing needs.

GOLF There are two public 18-hole championship courses in the Aspen valley. **Aspen Golf Course,** Colo. 82, 1 mile west of Aspen (☎ **970/925-2145**), is one of the longer courses in Colorado at 7,165 yards, and also has a restaurant and a marvelous view of the scenic Maroon Bells. Fees are $35 for 9 holes and $65 for 18 holes. **Snowmass Lodge & Golf Course,** Snowmass Club Circle (☎ **970/923-3148**), is an 18-hole championship golf course charging $95 for 18 holes ($55 in spring and summer), $85 for hotel guests.

HIKING & MOUNTAINEERING   Among the best ways to see the spectacular scenery here is on foot. You can get maps and tips on where to go from **White River National Forest** offices (see above). One popular trail is the route past the Maroon Bells to Crested Butte; the trek would take 175 miles by mountain road, but it's only about 30 miles by foot—14 from the end of Aspen's Maroon Creek Road.

Guided half- and full-day wilderness hikes are offered by **Blazing Adventures** (see above), with rates of $52 for a half day and starting at $70 for a full day.

Hikers can also make use of two hut systems for multi-day trips—the 14-hut **Tenth Mountain Trail Association** toward Vail, and the six-hut **Alfred A. Braun Hut System** (☎ **970/925-5775** for both) toward Crested Butte. Call for hut reservations. Guided backcountry hikes are offered by **Aspen Alpine Guides, Inc.** (see above), with a 5-day, 55-mile trip costing $890 per person.

HORSEBACK RIDING   Several stables in the Aspen valley offer a variety of rides, and some outfitters even package gourmet meals and country-western serenades with their expeditions. Rates start at $42. Inquire at **Blazing Adventures** (see above); **Capitol Peak Outfitters,** 0554 Valley Rd., Carbondale (☎ 970/963-0211); **H2J Riding School,** P.O. Box 8534, (☎ 970/923-9297), which offers riding lessons and an overnight camp for children; or **T Lazy 7 Ranch,** 3129 Maroon Creek Rd. (☎ 970/925-4614). The T Lazy 7 also offers lodging year-round (☎ 970/925-7254), plus hayrides, fishing, and hiking in summer; and snowmobiling, cross-country skiing, sleigh rides, and ice-skating in winter.

MOUNTAIN BIKING   There are hundreds of miles of trails through the White River National Forest that are perfect for mountain bikers, offering splendid views of the mountains, meadows, and valleys. Check with the forest service (see above) and local bike shops for tips on the best trails. Among full-service bicycle shops are **Hub of Aspen,** 315 E. Hyman Ave. (☎ 970/925-7970), and **Aspen Velo Bike Shop,** 465 N. Mill St. (☎ 970/925-1495). Typically, a full-day rental is $25 to $35, but fancier bikes can cost a lot more.

Among those leading guided mountain-biking tours are **Timberline Bicycle Tours** (☎ 800/842-2453 or 970/920-3217), **Rocky Mountain Bicycle Vacations,** 300 S. Spring St. (☎ 800/778-8586 or 970/925-1505), and **Blazing Adventures** (see above), with rates starting at $60 for a half-day trip. Guided multi-day trips on the Tenth Mountain Hut System are available from **Aspen Alpine Guides, Inc.** (see above), with a 4-day trip costing $640 per person.

RIVER RAFTING, KAYAKING & CANOEING   **Colorado Riff Raft,** 555 E. Durant (☎ **800/759-3939,** 970/925-5405, or 970/923-2220 in Snowmass), has been rafting the rapids since 1979. Trips are offered on the Roaring Fork, Arkansas, and Colorado Rivers, with refreshments on half-day trips and lunch on full-day trips. Prices start at $69 for a half day, and $89 for a full day. Also offering raft trips is **Blazing Adventures** (see above), charging $65 to $78 for half-day trips and $78 to $110 for full-day excursions.

Blazing Adventures also offers white-water canoeing trips for $65, and **Aspen Kayak School** (☎ 970/925-4433) offers weekend and week-long kayaking classes, starting at $185.

THE FESTIVAL SCENE

The **Aspen Music Festival and School** (☎ 970/925-8077 box office) originated in 1949. Lasting 9 weeks from mid-June to late August, it offers more than 150 events, including classical music, opera, jazz, choral, and children's programs. Most concerts take place in the 1,700-seat Bayer-Benedict Music Tent and 500-seat Joan and Irving Harris Concert Hall at Third and Gillespie Streets. Free events include the popular Saturday "Music on the Mountain" concerts atop Aspen Mountain. **Aspen Music Tours** (☎ 800/778-8576) offers a variety of packages to the festival every summer. For more information, contact the festival office at 2 Music School Rd., Aspen, CO 81611. Most individual event tickets are $12 to $30, with some events as high as $46.

Janus Jazz Aspen at Snowmass, 110 E. Hallam St., Suite 204, Aspen, CO 81611 (☎ 970/920-4996), takes place at Snowmass Village in late June, and again on Labor Day weekend. Legendary performers such as Lou Rawls, the Neville Brothers, the Zion Harmonizers, B. B. King, Patti LaBelle, and Ray Charles have appeared. The series includes two free outdoor concerts; call for ticket prices and schedule.

Aspen Theatre in the Park, P.O. Box 8677, Aspen, CO 81612 (☎ 970/925-9313), which began in 1983, is the only professional theater company in the Roaring Fork Valley. In recent years it has presented *I Do! I Do!*, *Wait Until Dark*, and *Greater Tuna*. Performances are held June through August, in the company's tent in the Art Park near the Rio Grande parking garage. Plays run in repertoire, and tickets start at $20.

MUSEUMS, ART CENTERS & HISTORIC SITES

The **Aspen Historical Society,** 620 W. Bleeker St. (☎ 970/925-3721; e-mail: ahistory@rof.net), offers two walking tours of Aspen from mid-June to mid-September. One begins at the visitor center and covers the downtown area; the other is a 1-mile walk beginning on the grounds of the Wheeler/Stallard House Museum (see below) that explores the West End residential area. Both tours end in the lobby of the historic Hotel Jerome (see "Where to Stay," below). Cost is $10 per person. Guided tours of Ashcroft and Independence ghost towns are offered June through August, from Tuesday to Sunday (no set admission price, but donations suggested). The Society has brochures with maps of the ghost towns for those who prefer to wander about on their own.

Tours to two historic area mines are also available, by reservation only. A year-round walking tour through the **Smuggler Mine** goes 1,200 feet into the mine, where the world's largest silver nugget—weighing 1,840 pounds—was found in 1894. Cost is $20 for adults and $15 for children 5 to 11. During the summer, tours are offered of the **Compromise Mine,** located high on Aspen Mountain. This tour is in an electric mine train, and goes 2,000 feet underground. Cost, including four-wheel-drive transportation to the mine, is $30 for adults and $20 for children 5 to 11. Children under 5 are not permitted on either tour. Call ☎ 970/925-2049 for schedules and reservations.

Anderson Ranch Arts Center. 5263 Owl Creek Rd. (P.O. Box 5598), Snowmass Village. ☎ 970/923-3181. E-mail: artranch@rof.net. Free admission to the gallery. Workshop tuition: $400–$850 per week; $85–$175 for children's programs. Housing and meals are extra. Gallery: Mon–Sat 9am–5pm, Sun noon–5pm.

What was once a sheep ranch in the Brush Creek Valley is now a highly respected visual-arts center with an art gallery and a nationally acclaimed program.

The summer workshop program caters to all levels, offering nearly 100 workshops in ceramics, painting, drawing, sculpture, photography, computer imaging, printmaking, woodworking, furniture design, and creative studies; there's also a children's program. Slide lectures by faculty are held Sunday and Tuesday evenings, and a free guided tour of the studios is offered at 4pm on Mondays. Self-guided tours of the ranch are welcome after 4pm weekdays and from 1 to 5pm weekends.

The winter studio residency program offers artists an opportunity to work outside professional or academic atmospheres, and receive critical feedback from their peers.

Aspen Art Museum. 590 N. Mill St., Aspen. ☎ **970/925-8050.** Admission $3 adults, $2 students and seniors, free for children under 12; free general admission Sat. Tues–Sat 10am–6pm, Sun noon–6pm, plus Thurs evening until 8pm.

The museum presents rotating exhibits highlighting the work of local and nationally known contemporary artists. Lectures and art education programs for adults and children are offered year-round, and there's a free reception every Thursday evening from 6 to 8pm.

Wheeler/Stallard House Museum. 620 W. Bleeker St., Aspen. ☎ **970/925-3721.** Admission $3 adults, 50¢ children. Walking tours $10 per person. Mid-June–mid-Sept, Tues–Fri 1–4pm.

Silver baron Jerome B. Wheeler had this three-story Victorian brick home built in 1888, and its steeply pitched roofs, dormers, and gables have made it a landmark in Aspen's West End neighborhood. A museum and archives of the Aspen Historical Society since 1969, the exterior of the house has been restored to its appearance in the heady days of silver mining. Exhibits describe Aspen's history from Ute culture through the mining rush, and from railroads and ranching to the founding of the skiing industry. The Museum Annex presents changing exhibits, and the gift shop offers a variety of souvenirs.

SHOPPING

To truly appreciate the Aspen experience, one must shop Aspen. Note that we say shop (meaning browse) rather than buy, because if you're not careful you just might blow next month's mortgage payment on some western fashion accessory that you probably won't wear much back home. No one ever brags about the great bargain they snagged last season in Aspen.

On the other hand, quality is usually tops, shop clerks are friendly, and there's a good chance your neighbor doesn't already have one. Having said all that, we suggest you lock up your credit cards, put on some good walking shoes, and spend a few hours exploring the galleries and shops of Aspen. Following are a few of our favorites.

For **original art,** check out: **Aspen Grove Fine Arts,** 525 E. Cooper Ave., upper level (☎ 970/925-5151), featuring paintings, graphics, and sculpture by acclaimed artists; **Susan Duval Gallery,** 525 E. Cooper Ave. (☎ 970/925-9044), for contemporary American paintings, graphics, and glass; **Heather Gallery,** 555 E. Durant St. (☎ 970/925-6170), which focuses on contemporary American crafts by regional and national artists; and **Hills of Aspen Gallery of Photography,** 312 E. Hyman Ave. (☎ 970/925-1836), for wildlife and landscape photography.

For **clothing,** the best places are: **Spurs,** 207 S. Galena St. (☎ 970/925-6029), for western wear; **Stefan Kaelin,** 447 E. Cooper St. (☎ 970/925-2989), for ski and casual wear; the **Freudian Slip,** 416 S. Hunter St. (☎ 970/925-4427), for lingerie; **Funky Mountain Threads,** 520 E. Durant St., suite 205 (☎ 970/925-4665), for unique clothing, gifts, jewelry, hats, candles, and beads; and **Crazy Shirts,** 316 S. Galena St. (☎ 970/920-3145), for good-quality souvenir T-shirts and sweatshirts.

When it's time to pick up a gift, we like **Aspen Mountain Christmas,** 616 E. Hyman Ave. (☎ 970/925-8142), for handcrafted and unique ornaments, nativities, and nutcrackers; **Chepita,** 525 E. Cooper Ave. (☎ 970/925-2871), a toy store for adults; **Stars Memorabilia,** 521 E. Cooper Ave. (☎ 970/920-9044), for historical documents and rock, Hollywood, and sports memorabilia; and **Curious George Collectibles,** 410 E. Hyman Ave. (☎ 970/925-3315), for western artifacts that used to belong to notorious cowboys.

WHERE TO STAY

Occupancy rates run 90% or higher during peak winter and summer seasons, so it's essential to make reservations as early as possible. The easiest way to do so is to call **Aspen Central Reservations** (☎ 888/290-1324 or 970/925-9000; fax 970/925-9008; skiaspen.com; e-mail: acrone@rof.net). Additional lodging is available in Snowmass, 12 miles west of Aspen; call **Snowmass Central Reservations** (☎ 800/598-2004; www.snowmassvillage.com). Those on especially tight budgets will find lower room rates in Glenwood Springs, 42 miles away over a sometimes icy and snowpacked road (see chapter 12).

Many accommodations close during the spring and fall; if they're open, rates during those months are typically the lowest of any time during the year. Tax of just over 8% is added to hotel bills, with an additional civic assessment of 4% added in Snowmass.

VERY EXPENSIVE

✪ **Hotel Jerome.** 330 E. Main St., Aspen, CO 81611. ☎ **800/331-7213** or 970/920-1000. Fax 970/925-2784. www.aspen.com/jerome. E-mail: hjerome@aol.com. 93 units. A/C MINIBAR TV TEL. Mid-Apr–early June and late Sept–mid-Nov, $160–$250 double; $395–$790 suite. Late Mar–mid-April and early June–late Sept, $295–$395 double; $595–$1,190 suite. Mid-Nov–mid-Dec and early Jan–late Mar, $325–$525 double; $625–$1,470 suite. Christmas season, $645–$805 double; $1,000–$2,000 suite. AE, CB, DC, MC, V. Underground valet parking. Pets permitted.

Jerome B. Wheeler built the Jerome during the peak of the silver boom. It opened in 1889 as Colorado's first hotel with electricity and indoor plumbing, and the first west of the Mississippi with an elevator. The silver crash of 1893 ended Aspen's prosperity and the glory years of the Hotel Jerome. Happily, in the mid-1980s, a multimillion-dollar renovation of the Jerome began, restoring it to its original splendor. With its Eastlake Victorian architecture lovingly preserved, and furnished with period antiques, the Jerome is now on the National Register of Historic Places.

Each guest room is spacious and unique, containing period antiques and furnishings, iron and brass double or king beds, down comforters, and crocheted bed dressings. Amenities include TVs, VCRs, multiline phones that are fax- and modem-ready, in-room safes, and iron and board. Bathrooms, finished with white Carrera marble and reproduction 19th-century octagonal tiles, contain showers, oversize tubs, hair dryers, and plush terrycloth robes.

Dining: The Century Room offers savory American fare served in Victorian elegance. Main courses vary, but there's generally a choice of beef, seafood, poultry, wild game, and pasta, with prices in the $20 to $30 range. One of the chef's specialties is lobster crab cakes. Jacob's Corner offers more casual surroundings for breakfast and lunch dining ($6 to $13). Guests with lighter appetites can get sandwiches and salads at the historic J-Bar.

Amenities: 24-hour room service, concierge, 24-hour front desk, valet laundry, complimentary shuttle van, ski concierge, business and secretarial services, heated pool with sundeck, two whirlpools, fitness room, retail ski shop, and meeting space for up to 200.

The Little Nell. 675 E. Durant Ave., Aspen, CO 81611. ☎ **888/843-6355** or 970/ 920-4600. Fax 970/920-4670. 92 units. A/C MINIBAR TV TEL. Early winter and early spring $320–$430 double; $625–$2,100 suite. Winter, $475–$625 double; $875–$3,800 suite. Summer, $295–$395 double; $575–$1,925 suite. Fall, $205–$290 double; $425–$1,500 suite. Call for holiday rates. AE, CB, DC, DISC, MC, V. Valet parking $15 per day. Pets accepted.

Located just 17 paces (yes, it's been measured) from the base terminal of the Silver Queen gondola, the Little Nell boasts the virtues of an intimate country inn as well as the personalized service and amenities of a grand hotel. All rooms have a view of either the town or the mountain.

No two guest rooms are alike, but each has a gas fireplace, Belgian-wool carpeting, down-filled lounge chairs or sofa, TV, VCR, oversized bed with down comforter, three two-line phones, and marble-finished bathroom with two vanities, hair dryer, and Crabtree & Evelyn toiletries. Suites have separate whirlpool tubs and steam showers. Five executive suites have all this and more, including fax machines.

Dining/Diversions: The Restaurant serves three meals daily in an arty atmosphere with large windows looking toward the hotel courtyard and Aspen Mountain. Featuring American alpine cooking by award-winning chef Keith Luce, the menu is constantly changing, offering fish and seafood, beef, chicken, and game with a regional flair. The Bar at the Little Nell is a plush living room with rich wood, a two-sided sandstone fireplace, historic photos of the Aspen ski scene, and outdoor terrace seating. The adjoining Ajax Tavern offers a more relaxed atmosphere.

Amenities: 24-hour room service, full-service concierge, winter ski concierge, ski technician on staff, same-day valet laundry, complimentary shuttle, express checkout, year-round outdoor heated swimming pool and whirlpool, fitness club (with Paramount equipment and free weights, steam room, and spa services, including massage), video rentals, arcade with eight shops, meeting space for 200.

✪ **The St. Regis Aspen.** 315 E. Dean St., Aspen, CO 81611. ☎ **888/454-9005** or 970/920-3300. Fax 970/925-8998. 257 units. A/C MINIBAR TV TEL. $125–$1,500 double. AE, CB, DC, DISC, MC, V. 24-hour valet parking.

Located at the base of Aspen Mountain, between the Gondola and Lift 1A, the St. Regis Aspen offers luxurious comfort in a casual but definitely upscale western atmosphere. The hotel is built of more than 800,000 Colorado red bricks, and guarded by a massive elk sculpture at the entrance. Inside, the lobby is decorated with rich wood, muted earth tones, and original paintings by 19th- and 20th-century artists. The lobby also offers cozy seating, a large granite fireplace, and magnificent views of Aspen Mountain.

Most rooms have views of either the mountains or town, and a few on the ground floor offer views of the hotel's flower-filled courtyard. Each unit is richly decorated in wildflower pastels of peach and green, with artwork reminiscent of Aspen's western heritage. Every room has either two double beds or a king, a personal safe, humidifier, three telephones with dual phone lines, and voice mail. Marble bathrooms feature double vanities, hair dryer, scale, and terry bathrobes.

The Club Floor offers keyed access to the floor for extra security, concierge for personalized service, and five complimentary food and beverage servings throughout the day. In winter, a ski concierge coordinates ski rentals, lift tickets, and lessons.

Dining/Diversions: The full-service Starwood Restaurant serves an eclectic combination of bistro and Mediterranean cuisine, and also offers several regional specialties such as roast venison and sautéed Colorado trout. In summer, the flower-filled courtyard is open to dining, with Aspen Mountain providing a magnificent backdrop. The Lobby Lounge is where guests gather around the granite fireplace to relax and sip cocktails. Burgers, sandwiches, and items from the Starwood's regular menu can be ordered. Later in the evening, live music draws guests to the lobby.

Amenities: Twice-daily housekeeping, turndown service, 24-hour room service, morning newspaper, free morning coffee in the lobby, 24-hour copy and fax services, secretarial service, baby-sitting, concierge, free ski shuttle. Fitness center with weight room, sauna and steam rooms, indoor and outdoor whirlpool spas, massage, and outdoor heated pool with sundeck; gift shop; sports shop; hair and body salon; conference space for 900; nature trails, jogging track nearby, bicycle rentals.

EXPENSIVE

The Sardy House. 128 E. Main St. (at Aspen St.), Aspen, CO 81611. ☎ **800/321-3457** or 970/920-2525. Fax 970/925-3840. www.aspen.com/sardylenado. E-mail: hotlsard@rof.net. 20 units. TV TEL. Early/late ski season, $150–$280 double; $275–$550 suite. Jan–Mar, $280–$380 double; $450–$650 suite. Holiday period, $380–$490 double; $550–$750 suite. Spring & fall, $90–$140 double; $150–$200 suite. Summer, $180–$300 double; $300–$480 suite. Rates include breakfast. AE, DC, MC, V.

A red-brick Victorian mansion built in 1892, the handsome Sardy House stands among majestic spruce trees. Inside, lace curtains and period antiques lend a delicate elegance. An enclosed gallery bridges a private brick walkway, joining the Sardy House to its Carriage House wing. Rooms combine antique Victorian and modern furnishings: cherry-wood beds and armoires, wicker chairs and sofas. There are whirlpool tubs in all but two units, which have antique claw-foot tubs. Other touches include down comforters, terrycloth robes, and heated towel racks. Suites have entertainment centers with VCRs and stereos, kitchenettes, and hideaway sofas. Three have private entrances; one has a private balcony and sitting room; and one has a fireplace. The Carriage House Suite features a winding, wrought-iron staircase to its second floor.

The Sardy House restaurant presents candlelit American dinners (5:30 to 9:30pm) with silver service in a plush fireplace room. Popular main courses include mushroom ragout, smoked trout, and roasted red pepper linguine. It's also open for breakfast (7:30 to 10:30am, until noon on Sunday). Room service morning and evening, a concierge, in-room massage, and valet laundry services are available. Facilities include a heated outdoor pool, hot tub, sauna, private ski storage, and heated boot lockers.

MODERATE

Hearthstone House. 134 E. Hyman Ave. (at Aspen St.), Aspen, CO 81611. ☎ **888/ 925-7632** or 970/925-7632. Fax 970/920-4450. www.hearthstonehouse.com. E-mail: hearthstone@aspeninfo.com. 17 units. TV TEL. Summer, $118–$158 double; $168–$188 with whirlpool bath. Winter, $188–$228 double; $248–$288 with whirlpool bath. Rates include breakfast and afternoon tea. AE, CB, DC, DISC, MC, V.

Small and sophisticated, the Hearthstone House is located just two blocks west of the Wheeler Opera House. Guests share a large, elegant living room with teak-and-leather furnishings and a wood-burning fireplace, dining room with bright flowers, and an extensive library. Rooms are bright and homey, with queen-size or twin beds, and one room has a king-size bed. Three units feature whirlpool tubs. The inn also offers access to a nearby health club, whirlpool, and sauna. Smoking is not permitted.

The Inn at Aspen. 38750 Colo. 82, Aspen, CO 81611. ☎ **800/952-1515** or 970/ 925-1500. Fax 970/925-9037. www.innataspen.com. E-mail: innataspen@aspeninfo.com. 124 units. A/C TV TEL. Winter, $150–$435 double; $225–$800 suite. Summer, $100–$190 double; $150–$325 suite. Higher rates during holiday period. AE, MC, V.

Nestled at the foot of Buttermilk Mountain, this ski-in/ski-out hotel offers views of either the slopes or the Roaring Fork valley. The recent $2-million renovation has given the inn a comfortable but rich mountain atmosphere. Rooms have balconies, coffeemakers, and refrigerators. Kitchenettes are stocked for four people and come with microwaves and toasters. The restaurant serves three meals daily (closed mid-April to early June and mid-September to Thanksgiving). The hotel also offers a heated outdoor pool, hot tub, whirlpool, sauna, health club, masseuse, meeting space for 220, limited room service, concierge, valet dry cleaning, and guest laundry.

Limelite Lodge. 228 E. Cooper Ave. (at Monarch St.), Aspen, CO 81611. ☎ **800/ 433-0832** or 970/925-3025. Fax 970/925-5120. www.aspen.com/limelite. E-mail: limelite@rof.net. 63 units. TV TEL. Early/late ski season, $68–$98 double, $130 suite. Holiday period, $168–$208 double, $275 suite. Jan, $108–$138 double, $185 suite. Feb–Mar, $160–$185 double, $230 suite. May–June, $58–$98 double, $130 suite. July–Aug, $88–$125 double, $170 suite. Sept–Oct, $68–$98 double, $130 suite. Rates include continental breakfast. AE, CB, DC, DISC, MC, V. Pets accepted.

Located within walking distance of practically everything in town, the lodge has two separate buildings facing each other across Cooper Avenue—one three stories, the other two—each with its own heated outdoor swimming pool and whirlpool. Rooms are well kept. Most have queen beds with comforters, a large dresser and other wood furnishings, floral wallpaper, and a small private bathroom on the other side of a walk-through closet/vanity. One whirlpool room is available. Hot beverages are available 24 hours a day. Services and facilities include a 24-hour desk, in-room massage, two heated outdoor swimming pools, whirlpool, sauna, sundeck, guest laundry, and ski lockers.

Snowflake Inn. 221 E. Hyman Ave., Aspen, CO 81611. ☎ **800/247-2069** or 970/ 925-3221. Fax 970/925-8740. 38 units. TV TEL. Early/late ski season, $99–$189; holiday period, $249–$369; Jan–mid-Feb, $165–$249; mid-Feb–late Mar, $205–$285; spring and fall, $49–$79; summer, $125–$179. Call for 2- and 3-bedroom suite rates. Rates include continental breakfast in winter. AE, DC, DISC, MC, V.

This is a comfortable ski-lodge–style inn with a variety of accommodations. Rooms have painted rough-wood walls, overstuffed chairs and sofas, good lighting, and in-room safes; some have gas fireplaces and some have skylights; all have kitchenettes. There's an outdoor heated pool, whirlpool, sauna, coin-operated laundry, 24-hour desk, and complimentary coffee in the lobby. Centrally located just one block from downtown Aspen, it's within easy walking distance of the Aspen lifts.

INEXPENSIVE

Innsbruck Inn. 233 W. Main St., Aspen, CO 81611-1796. ☎ **970/925-2980**. Fax 970/925-6960. E-mail: innsbruck@rof.net. 31 units. TV TEL. Jan–Mar, $129–$186 double; $200–$250 suite. Apr–Dec, $75–$105 double; $125–$153 suite; higher during holiday season. Rates include full breakfast in winter, continental breakfast in summer. AE, DC, DISC, MC, V.

This Tyrolean-style inn has a homey lobby, with a stone fireplace where you can relax and enjoy complimentary après-ski munchies. Each room is slightly different, though all have stucco walls, shower/tub combos, and ski racks. Upstairs rooms have hand-carved ceiling beams, and many have down comforters. There's a year-round outdoor heated pool, sauna, and hot tub (robes are available). There are also 2 one-bedroom apartments; call for rates.

The Mountain Chalet. 333 E. Durant Ave., Aspen, CO 81611. ☎ **800/321-7813** or 970/925-7797. Fax 970/925-7811. 51 units. TV TEL. Winter, $80–$225 double, $360 apt, rates higher during holidays; spring and fall, $45–$125 double, $180 apt. Rates include full breakfast in winter, continental breakfast in summer. CB, DC, DISC, MC, V. Free parking underground.

You'll find a friendly, ski-lodge atmosphere here, just 1½ blocks from the lifts. The lobby contains a TV and piano. Rooms are light-colored, with wood furnishings, and good-quality twin, double, queen, or king beds, plus a few trundle beds. There are even some bunk rooms with four beds, rented by the bed at greatly reduced rates in ski season. Facilities include a year-round heated outdoor pool, large indoor whirlpool, sauna and steam room, coin-operated laundry, exercise room, game room, and ski lockers.

WHERE TO DINE

Most restaurants in the Aspen-Snowmass area are open during the winter (Thanksgiving to early April) and summer (mid-June to mid-September) seasons. Between seasons, however, some close their doors or limit hours. Call ahead if you're visiting at these times.

EXPENSIVE

Krabloonik. 4250 Divide Rd., off Brush Creek Rd., Snowmass Village. ☎ **970/923-3953.** Reservations recommended at lunch, essential at dinner. Three-course prix fixe lunch $25, dinner main courses $23–$50. AE, MC, V. Winter, daily 11am–2pm and 5:30–9:30pm. Summer, Wed–Mon 6–9pm. INTERNATIONAL/GAME/SEAFOOD.

There's something very wild, something that hearkens back to Jack London, perhaps, about sitting in a log cabin watching teams of sled dogs come and go as you bite into a tender caribou loin or wild-boar chop. That's part of the pleasure of Krabloonik. A venture of the largest dog kennel in America's lower 48 states, this rustic restaurant has huge picture windows with mountain views and seating around a sunken fireplace. Skiers drop into the restaurant from the Campground lift for lunch, and visitors can dine before or after an excursion on a dogsled (see "Dogsledding," above). You might try a buffalo burger or roasted elk loin for lunch, or a grilled boneless breast of quail. For dinner there's Krabloonik smoked trout for starters and a wide variety of game, beef tenderloin, lamb, and fish for the main course. Those with hearty appetites can choose between two combination game entrees: caribou, elk, and deer; or caribou, quail, and boar. Smoking is not permitted.

Piñons. 105 S. Mill St. ☎ **970/920-2021.** Reservations recommended. Main courses $22–$34. AE, MC, V. Daily 6–10pm. Closed late spring and fall. CREATIVE REGIONAL.

Tremendous attention to detail went into creating the contemporary western ranch setting of Piñons, with its aged stucco walls and braided whip leather around the stairwell. The innovative menu includes sautéed Colorado pheasant, roasted Colorado striped bass, fresh fish, wild game, and grilled meats. In summer lighter fare is also offered.

Renaissance. 304 E. Hopkins St. ☎ **970/925-2402.** Reservations recommended. Entrees $24–$36; complete five-course wine-tasting dinners, $115 ($79 without wine). AE, DC, DISC, MC, V. Daily 6:30–10:30pm. Possible spring and fall closures. MODERN FRENCH.

Award-winning chef/owner Charles Dale has created a beautiful, intimate, and contemporary setting for his creative dishes, served à la carte or as part of an elaborate wine-tasting dinner. The menu changes frequently, but nightly specials might include a crispy fillet of Chilean sea bass with fresh artichoke hearts, served with sweet potato crisps; an exotically spiced grilled lamb loin; and honey-smoked duck breast. A choice from the award-winning wine list is a delightful addition.

MODERATE & INEXPENSIVE

Flying Dog Brew Pub. 424 E. Cooper Ave. ☎ **970/925-7464.** Most entrees $5.50–$16. AE, DISC, MC, V. Daily 11:30am–2am (may close 1 week in spring and fall). BREWPUB.

This is a cafe-style pub with red-brick walls, tables and booths, and a view into the brewery on the side. As the name suggests, the decor celebrates all things canine. The food is good, and there's a wide variety, with entrees such as fish-and-chips, sandwiches, chicken pub pie, and brewpub bratwurst. The dinner menu is heavy on beef, and also has great ribs and several pasta selections. The brewery keeps about 20 different ales in its inventory, with four to six available at any given time. A patio is open in summer, and there's a bluegrass band most Wednesday evenings.

✪ **La Cocina.** 308 E. Hopkins Ave. ☎ **970/925-9714.** Reservations not accepted. Main courses $7–$11. No credit cards. Daily 5–10pm. Closed mid-Apr–May and mid-Oct–Nov. SOUTHWESTERN.

Locals love this place, and we fully agree. The menu, although somewhat limited, reminds us of some of our favorite stops in Santa Fe and Taos, and no lard is used. A basket of chips and spicy-hot salsa have greeted diners here since La Cocina opened in 1972. You might start with the green-chile soup, then slide into a platter of blue-corn chicken enchiladas with a side of posole, an assertive burrito, or, for those prefer less spiciness, a seafood quesadilla. Top it off with a slice of chocolate velvet cake or bread pudding with whiskey sauce for dessert.

Little Annie's Eating House. 517 E. Hyman Ave. ☎ **970/925-1098.** Reservations not accepted. Most items $6–$20. AE, MC, V. Daily 11:30am–11pm (bar open until 2am). AMERICAN.

A casual, western-style place, Little Annie's is locally famous for its barbecued ribs, chicken, and outrageous burgers. It's becoming equally popular for its newer, lighter offerings, including healthy summer salads, fresh pastas, vegetarian lasagna, and fresh fish specials.

Red Onion. 420 E. Cooper St. ☎ **970/925-9043.** Reservations not accepted. Main courses $6–$13. AE, MC, V. Daily 11:30am–10pm (bar open until 2am). Check on possible spring closure. AMERICAN/MEXICAN.

Aspen's oldest surviving bar started out as a saloon and casino during the silver boom. Now it has an indoor ski corral for folks just off the slopes. Burgers and Philadelphia steak sandwiches are big favorites at lunch; Mexican cuisine holds forth at night, with the likes of burritos, fajitas, and taco salads. Daily specials feature traditional American fare.

Takah Sushi. 420 E. Hyman Ave. ☎ **970/925-8588.** Reservations recommended. Main courses $15–$25. AE, DC, DISC, MC, V. Winter, daily 5:30–11pm; summer, daily 6–11pm. JAPANESE/PACIFIC RIM.

This lively sushi bar and Japanese restaurant has been praised by the *New York Times,* which called its sushi "some of the best between Malibu and Manhattan." A wide variety of sushi is sliced and rolled here, from halibut to octopus. For those not desiring sushi or sashimi, the menu also includes crisp Chinese duck, several vegetarian dishes, Chilean sea bass, and a teriyaki-tempura combination with beef, chicken, or salmon.

Wienerstube. 633 E. Hyman Ave., at Spring St. ☎ **970/925-3357.** Reservations not accepted. Breakfast $4–$11; lunch $7–$16. AE, CB, DC, DISC, MC, V. Tues–Sun 7am–2:30pm. AUSTRIAN.

Gerhard Mayritsch, a native of the Austrian city of Villach, has been serving genuine Austrian food in this beautiful garden restaurant since 1965, with the Aspen powers-that-be often gathered around the Stammitsch, a large community dining table. There are also private tables and booths where you can enjoy a changing menu that might include eggs Benedict for breakfast, and Austrian sausages, Wiener schnitzel, and other specialties at lunch. Viennese pastries are available any time.

✪ **Woody Creek Tavern.** Upper River Rd., Woody Creek. ☎ **970/923-4585.** Reservations not accepted. $4–$16. No credit cards. Daily 11:30am–10:30pm. Drive west on Colo. 82, three-quarters of a mile past the Snowmass Village turnoff, turn right on Smith Rd. into Woody Creek Canyon, turn left at the first fork, and continue 1¼ miles. This road can be icy in winter. AMERICAN/MEXICAN.

Woody Creek is a true local hangout. They say that celebrities like to visit, too, but we didn't meet any on our last visit. Probably the only old-time, rustic tavern left in the Aspen area, its walls are covered with a variety of news clippings and other paraphernalia. You'll find a good selection of well-prepared tavern food, including barbecued pork ribs, thick steaks, burgers, and red snapper, as well as excellent Mexican food, which goes well with the house specialty drink—fresh lime-juice margaritas.

ASPEN AFTER DARK

The focus of the performing arts in Aspen is the 1889 **Wheeler Opera House,** 320 E. Hyman Ave., at Mill Street (☎ **970/920-5770** box office). Built at the peak of the mining boom by silver baron Jerome B. Wheeler, this stage—meticulously restored in 1984—hosts a year-round program of music, theater, dance, film, and lectures. The building itself is worth a visit, with brass wall sconces, crystal chandeliers, gold trim and stencils on the dark-blue walls, rich wood, red carpeting, and red velvet seats. The box office is open Monday through Saturday from 10am to 5pm.

For more information on the performing arts, see "The Festival Scene," above.

Among Aspen's clubs, **The Tippler,** 535 E. Dean St. (☎ 970/925-4977), near the gondola base, draws après-skiers, with enough energy remaining to get down on the dance floor. Country-music lovers appreciate **Shooters Saloon,** 220 S. Galena St. (☎ 970/925-4567), and **Cowboys,** at the Silvertree Hotel in Snowmass (☎ 970/923-5249).

In Aspen, it seems the fashion to do one's drinking at a historic bar. The Hotel Jerome's **J-Bar** (our favorite), Main and Mill Streets (☎ 970/920-1000), and the **R-Bar** in the Renaissance, 304 E. Hopkins St. (☎ 970/925-2402), have universal appeal, each with live music periodically. **Bentley's at the Wheeler,** 328 E. Hyman Ave. (☎ 970/920-2240), is an elegant English-style pub, good for the older crowd. Aspen's oldest bar is the **Red Onion,** 420 E. Cooper Ave. (☎ 970/925-9043), a noisy, popular hangout with occasional live music.

Also big in the Aspen music scene is **Howling Wolf,** 316 E. Hopkins Ave. (☎ 970/920-7771), and **Acme Bar & Grill,** 320 S. Mill St. (☎ 970/925-3775). Aspen's requisite **Hard Rock Café,** 210 S. Galena St. (☎ 970/920-1666), opened in 1991. The **Lobby Lounge** at the St. Regis, at the base of Aspen Mountain (☎ 970/920-3300), draws scores of après-skiers. **Flying Dog Brew Pub,** at 424 E. Cooper Ave. (☎ 970/925-7464), has a bluegrass band most Wednesday evenings.

The Western Slope **12**

Separated from Colorado's major cities by the mighty Rocky Mountains, the communities along the state's western edge are not only miles, but also years away from the hustle-and-bustle of Denver and the California-style sophistication of Boulder. Even Grand Junction, the region's largest city, remains a sprawling western town, and the rugged canyons and stark rocky terrain make you feel like you've stepped into a John Ford western. The lifeblood of this semi-desert land is its rivers—the Colorado, Gunnison, and Yampa—for not only have they brought life-giving water, but over tens of thousands of years their ceaseless energy has also gouged out stunning canyons that lure visitors from around the world. Colorado National Monument, west of Grand Junction, is remarkable for its land forms and prehistoric petroglyphs; Dinosaur National Monument, in the state's northwestern corner, preserves a wealth of dinosaur remains; and the Black Canyon of the Gunnison, a dark, narrow, and almost impenetrable chasm east of Montrose, challenges adventurous rock climbers and rafters.

But it's not all rocks and dinosaurs here. In the tiny community of Palisade, outside Grand Junction, some of the West's best wine is produced; and downtown Grand Junction boasts a continually changing and evolving outdoor art exhibit with its delightful Art on the Corner sculpture display.

1 Grand Junction and Colorado & Dinosaur National Monuments

251 miles W of Denver, 169 miles N of Durango

Among our favorite Colorado cities, Grand Junction is an excellent base camp for those who want to drive or hike through the awe-inspiring red-rock canyons and sandstone monoliths of Colorado National Monument, or explore the canyons at Dinosaur National Monument, about 2 hours north. Grand Junction is also the eastern entrance to one of the West's most scenic and challenging mountain-biking treks, Kokopelli's Trail, which ends in Moab, Utah. For the less athletically inclined, the Grand Junction area boasts half a dozen wineries.

Located at the confluence of the Gunnison and Colorado rivers, the city was founded in 1882 where the spike was driven to connect Denver and Salt Lake City by rail. It quickly became the primary

The Western Slope

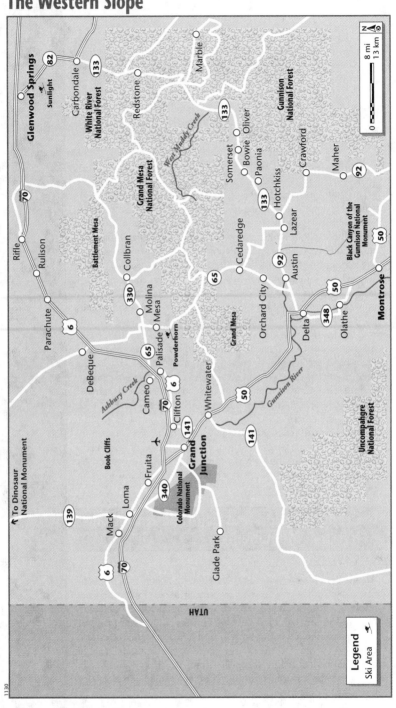

trade and distribution center between the two state capitals, and its mild climate, together with the fertile soil and irrigation potential of the river valleys, helped it grow into an important agricultural area. Soybeans, and later peaches and pears, were the most important crops. The city was also a center of the western Colorado uranium boom in the 1950s and the oil-shale boom in the late 1970s, and today is a fast-growing trade center serving practically all of western Colorado and eastern Utah.

ESSENTIALS

GETTING THERE   By Car   Grand Junction is located on I-70. U.S. 50 is the main artery from the south, connecting with Montrose and Durango.

By Plane   On the north side of Grand Junction, **Walker Field,** 2828 Walker Field Dr. (☎ **970/244-9100;** fax 970/241-9103; www.walkerfield.com; e-mail: gjt@ gj.net), is less than a mile off I-70's Horizon Drive exit. More than 25 commercial flights connect Grand Junction with Denver, Phoenix, Salt Lake City, and other cities.

Airlines serving Walker Field include **America West Express** (☎ 800/235-9292 or 970/728-4868), **SkyWest–The Delta Connection** (☎ 800/453-9417 or 970/242-5365), and **United Express** (☎ 800/241-6522).

By Train   Amtrak has a passenger station at 337 S. First Street (☎ **800/ USA-RAIL** or 970/241-2733). The *California Zephyr* stops twice daily, once in each direction, on its main route from San Francisco and Salt Lake City to Denver and Chicago.

VISITOR INFORMATION   Contact the **Grand Junction Visitor & Convention Bureau,** 740 Horizon Dr., Grand Junction, CO 81506 (☎ **800/962-2547** or 970/244-1480; fax 970/243-7393; www.grand-junction.net). There's a visitor center on Horizon Drive at I-70 exit 31, and a Colorado Welcome Center at I-70 exit 19 (Fruita and Colorado National Monument), 12 miles west of Grand Junction.

GETTING AROUND   Main Street and named avenues run east-west, and numbered streets and roads run north-south. Downtown Grand Junction lies south of I-70 and north of the Colorado River, encompassing one block on each side of Main Street between First and Seventh streets.

Sunshine Taxi (☎ 970/245-8294) offers 24-hour service. Car rentals are available in the airport area from **Avis** (☎ 970/244-9170), **Budget** (☎ 970/244-9155), **Enterprise** (☎ 970/242-8103), **Hertz** (☎ 970/243-0747), **National** (☎ 970/ 243-6626), **Sears** (☎ 970/244-9157), and **Thrifty** (☎ 970/243-7556).

FAST FACTS   There's a 24-hour emergency room at **St. Mary's Hospital**, Patterson Road and Seventh Street (☎ **970/244-2273**). The main post office is at 241 N. Fourth St.; contact the U.S. Postal Service (☎ **800/275-8777**) for hours and other information. For **weather conditions,** call ☎ **970/243-0914;** for **road conditions,** call ☎ **970/245-8800**.

SPECIAL EVENTS   Southwest Fest, late April; Cinco de Mayo, early May; Colorado Stampede Parade and Rodeo, late June; Dinosaur Days, late July; Junior College Baseball World Series, starting Memorial Day weekend; Mesa County Fair, early August; Peach Festival, mid-August in Palisade; Colorado Mountain Wine Fest, late September.

✪ COLORADO NATIONAL MONUMENT

Just minutes west of Grand Junction, this relatively undiscovered national monument is a delight, offering a colorful maze of steep-walled canyons filled with an array of naturally sculpted spires, pinnacles, and other impressive sandstone rock formations. Easy to get to and easy to see, in many ways it's a miniature Grand

Canyon, without the crowds. You can see much of the monument from your car on the 23-mile Rim Rock Drive, and there are ample opportunities for hiking, horseback riding, and cross-country skiing. Bighorn sheep, mountain lions, golden eagles, mule deer, and lizards are among the monument's residents.

Carved by water and wind over millions of years, Colorado National Monument encompasses 32 square miles of red-rock canyons and sandstone monoliths, more than 1,000 feet above the Colorado River. A combination of upward lifts and erosion caused the chaos of formations here. Each layer visible in the striations of the canyon walls marks a time in the land's history. Fossils permit scientists to date these rocks back through the Mesozoic era of 225 million to 65 million years ago, and the Precambrian formation dates back 1.67 billion years.

The east entrance is only 5 miles west of Grand Junction, off Monument Road, but the best way to explore the monument is to begin at the west entrance, following the signs off I-70 from Fruita, 15 miles west of Grand Junction. It's here that **Rim Rock Drive,** created during the Great Depression as a Civilian Conservation Corps project, begins. Snaking up dramatic Fruita Canyon, it offers panoramic views of fanciful and bizarre natural stone monuments, to the cliffs and mesas beyond. At 4 miles it reaches the national monument headquarters and **visitor center**. Exhibits on geology and history, plus a slide show, introduce the park, and rangers can help you plan your visit. Guided walks and campfire programs are offered during the summer.

Rim Rock Drive—open to bicycles as well as motor vehicles—offers access to hiking trails varying in length from 400 yards to 8½ miles. Many of the short, easy trails lead to spectacular canyon overlooks, while the longer backcountry trails head out across the mesas or down into the canyons. Strange formations such as Window Rock, the massive rounded Coke Ovens, the boulder-strewn Devils Kitchen, and the free-standing Independence Monument—all of which can be viewed from the road—are easily reached by foot.

If you're looking for an easy walk, try the 1-mile (round-trip) **Canyon Rim Trail,** which follows the edge of a cliff to spectacular views of the colorful rock formations in Wedding Canyon. Allow about an hour. An even shorter walk—the **Window Rock Trail**—also affords views of Wedding Canyon; a free brochure available at the visitor center helps you identify the plants you'll see along the way. Allow a half hour for the quarter-mile loop.

Those who want to get down into the monument, rather than viewing it from above, will want to tackle one of the backcountry trails. The relatively difficult 12-mile round-trip **Monument Canyon Trail** drops 600 feet from the plateau into the canyon, amongst many of the monument's more dramatic rock formations, such as the aptly named Kissing Couple. This is home to rattlesnakes and scorpions, so you'll want to watch where you put your feet and hands. Also, it's hot and dry down there, so be sure to carry plenty of water. If you'd like some panoramic views of the countryside, even to the canyonlands of Utah, try the **Black Ridge Trail.** The national monument's highest-elevation trail, it follows the rugged terrain of Black Ridge. Allow about 6 hours for the 11-mile round-trip hike, and, again, carry plenty of water.

Winter visitors may want to take their skis along. Among your best choices here is **Liberty Cap Trail,** which meanders across gently sloping Monument Mesa through a piñon-juniper forest and sagebrush flatlands. The trail is 14 miles round-trip, but cross-country skiers may want to turn back before the last 1½ miles, which drop sharply into the Grand Valley.

While the monument is worth visiting at any time of year, the best time is fall, when the air is crisp but not cold, the cottonwood trees turn a brilliant gold, and the summer crowds have departed. Those visiting in May and June will want to carry insect repellent to combat the clouds of gnats that invade at this time.

The monument's **Saddlehorn Campground,** located in a piñon-juniper forest near the visitor center, has 80 sites, some shady, with rest rooms but no showers or RV hookups. Cost is $10 per night. Like most areas administered by the National Park Service, pets must be leashed and are not allowed on trails or in the backcountry.

The national monument is open year-round. The day-use fee is $4 per vehicle or $2 per person for cyclists and pedestrians from late spring through summer, and is free at other times. From Memorial Day to Labor Day, the visitor center is open daily from 8am to 7pm; the rest of the year, daily from 9am to 5pm. To obtain a brochure and other information, contact **Colorado National Monument,** Fruita, CO 81521-9530 (☎ **970/858-3617;** www.nps.gov/colm). Those who want more in-depth information can order topographic maps, books, and other materials from the nonprofit Colorado National Monument Association at the monument's address and phone number above.

DINOSAUR NATIONAL MONUMENT

This national monument, about 2 hours north of Grand Junction, is really two separate parks, divided by the Utah–Colorado border. One side takes a close-up look at the world of dinosaurs, while the other opens into a scenic wonderland of colorful rock, deep river canyons, and a forest of Douglas firs.

About 150 million years ago this region had abundant vegetation, making it a suitable habitat for dinosaurs, both vegetarians and sharp-toothed carnivores. Most of their skeletons decayed and disappeared, but in at least one spot floodwaters washed their carcasses onto a sandbar, where they were preserved in sand and covered with sediment.

This **Dinosaur Quarry** is accessible only from the Utah side of the park. From Dinosaur, Colorado, head 20 miles west on U.S. 40 to Jensen, Utah, and then go 7 miles north. This is the only place in the monument to see dinosaur bones. The quarry contains the remains of many long-vanished species, including fossils of sea creatures much older than any land dinosaurs, in one of the world's most concentrated and accessible deposits of the petrified remains of dinosaurs, crocodiles, turtles, and clams. There's one section of bones you can touch, plus models that show what paleontologists believe these dinosaurs looked like when they had their skin. Sometimes visitors can see workers carefully chiseling away the hard rock to expose more bones, and park naturalists are on hand to explain the process.

But visitors who limit their Dinosaur National Monument trip to its namesake dinosaur quarry miss quite a bit. Encompassing 325 square miles of stark canyons at the confluence of the Yampa and Green Rivers in Colorado, there are hiking trails to explore, spectacular panoramic vistas, and the thrill of white-water rafting. Your first stop should be the small **visitor center** located about 2 miles east of the town of Dinosaur, Colorado, at the intersection of U.S. 40 and Harpers Corner Drive. (You have to return to U.S. 40 to get to the dinosaur quarry in the Utah section of the park.)

Allow about 2 hours for the scenic **Harpers Corner Drive.** This paved 62-mile round-trip drive has several overlooks offering panoramic views into the gorges carved by the Yampa and Green Rivers, a look at the derby-shaped Plug Hat Butte, and close-ups of a variety of other colorful rock formations. The drive also offers access to the easy half-mile round-trip **Plug Hat Nature Trail**, and the moderately difficult 2-mile round-trip **Harpers Corner Trail,** highly recommended for a magnificent view of the deep river canyons. In addition to several developed trails, experienced hikers with the appropriate maps can explore miles of unspoiled canyons and rock benches.

To many, the best way to see this rugged country is on the river, crashing through thrilling white water and gliding over the smooth, silent stretches. About a dozen outfitters are authorized to run the Yampa and Green rivers through the monument, offering trips ranging from 1 to 5 days, usually from mid-May through mid-September. Among companies providing river trips is **Hatch River Expeditions,** ☎ **800/342-8243** or 435/789-4316), with prices starting at $60 to $70 for a 1-day trip. A complete list of authorized river-running companies is available from monument headquarters.

Fishing in the Green and Yampa most often yields catfish, although there are also some trout. Several endangered species of fish—including the Colorado squawfish and humpback chub—must be returned unharmed to the water if caught. You'll need Utah and/or Colorado fishing licenses, depending on which side of the state line you're fishing.

There are **campgrounds** in both sections of the monument, although there are more sites in the Utah part. There are no showers or RV hookups, and fees range from $5 to $10 per night.

The national monument entrance near Dinosaur, Colorado, is about 110 miles north of Grand Junction. From Grand Junction, head west on I-70 about 12 miles to exit 15, turn right (north) onto Colo. 139 and go about 75 miles to Colo. 64, where you turn left, and follow it west for 20 miles to the town of Dinosaur. Then turn right onto U.S. 40 and go east about 2 miles to the monument entrance. The monument is open around-the-clock, and the visitor centers are open daily year-round, except Thanksgiving, Christmas, and New Year's Day. Admission fee, charged only at the Utah entrance as of this writing, is $10 per vehicle, and $5 per person for those on foot, motorcycles, bicycles, or in buses.

Rangers warn that rivers are not safe for swimming or wading; the water is cold, and the current is stronger than it may first appear. For information contact **Dinosaur National Monument,** 4545 U.S. 40, Dinosaur, CO 81610-9724 (☎ **970/374-3000**; www.nps.gov/dino). In addition, the nonprofit **Dinosaur Nature Association,** 1291 E. U.S. 40, Vernal, UT 84078 (☎ **800/845-3466;** fax 801/781-1304), offers numerous publications, maps, posters, and videos on the park, its geology, wildlife, history, and especially its dinosaurs.

SPORTS & OUTDOOR ACTIVITIES

In addition to activities in Colorado and Dinosaur National Monuments, there are numerous opportunities for hiking, camping, mountain biking, off-roading, horseback riding, cross-country skiing, snowmobiling, and snowshoeing on other public lands administered by the federal government. Contact the **Bureau of Land Management,** 2815 H Rd., Grand Junction, CO 81506 (☎ **970/244-3000**), and the **Grand Junction Ranger District of Grand Mesa National Forest,** 2777 Crossroads Blvd. (off Horizon Drive), Grand Junction, CO 81506 (☎ **970/242-8211**).

You'll also find plenty to do at the three units of **Colorado River State Park,** such as hiking, picnicking, fishing, and other activities. Two park units are day-use only, and one has camping (see "Camping," below). Check at the Grand Junction Visitor & Convention Bureau or call the state park office (☎ **970/434-3388**) for current information.

The city's **Parks and Recreation Department** (☎ 970/244-3866) manages more than 30 parks and other facilities, which offer picnicking, hiking, tennis, playgrounds, swimming pools, softball, playing fields, horseshoe pits, and golf courses.

GOLF   The 18-hole **Tiara Rado Golf Course,** 2063 S. Broadway (☎ 970/245-8085), is at the base of the Colorado National Monument canyons. The nine-hole **Lincoln Park Golf Course,** 14th Street and Gunnison Avenue (☎ 970/242-6394), is in the center of town. Fees at both courses are $8.50 for 9 holes and $15 for 18 holes Monday through Thursday, and $10.50 and $18, respectively, Friday through Sunday. The 18-hole **Adobe Creek Golf Course,** 876 18½ Rd., Fruita (☎ 970/858-0521), is 9 miles west of Grand Junction. On weekdays it charges $9 for 9 holes and $16 for 18 holes; weekend fees are $11 and $22, respectively.

HIKING   Hikers and walkers who want to stay close to town can explore the trails in the Colorado Riverfront Project. Collectively known as the **Colorado River Trails,** the system includes almost 20 miles of paved trails that meander along the Colorado and Gunnison rivers, offering the chance to see ducks, geese, blue heron, deer, and rabbits. They are open to walkers and hikers, runners, bikers, in-line skaters, and horseback riders, but closed to all motorized vehicles (except wheelchairs). Dogs are permitted if leashed, and owners are asked to clean up after their dogs. Most of the trails are between half a mile and 2 miles long, and they can be combined for longer hikes. An excellent brochure with maps of the various river trails and directions to their trailheads is available free at the Grand Junction Visitor & Convention Bureau (see "Visitor Information," above).

You'll also find hiking trails at **Colorado River State Park** (see the introduction to this section, above).

HORSEBACK RIDING   Trail rides near the west entrance of Colorado National Monument are available through **Rim Rock Adventures** (☎ 970/858-9555; fax 970/858-9465; www.rradventures.com; e-mail: info@rradventures.com), with stables about a mile south of Fruita on Colo. 340. Rates for a 1-hour ride are $16 for adults and $14 for children 5 to 12, and a half-day ride into the wilderness of Devil's Canyon costs $45 for adults and $40 for children. Kids' pony rides, lasting about 15 minutes, cost $5. Those who thought to bring their own horses will enjoy the 14-mile (round-trip) Liberty Cap Trail through Colorado National Monument, which winds through a scrub forest and over a sagebrush mesa before dropping steeply into a valley.

Based in the nearby community of Collbran, **Wallace Guide & Outfitters** (☎ 970/487-3235; fax 970/487-0118) offers a variety of horseback-riding trips, from 1-hour ($12) to full-day rides ($75 including lunch), plus overnight pack trips and dinner rides.

MOUNTAIN BIKING   Grand Junction has become important to mountain bikers as the eastern terminus of **Kokopelli's Trail** to Moab, Utah. Winding for 142 miles through sandstone and shale canyons, it has an elevation differential of about 4,200 feet. There are primitive campsites at intervals along the trail. The Colorado gateway is at the Loma Boat Launch, 15 miles west of Grand Junction off I-70.

For information on Kokopelli's Trail and several other area trails, send a self-addressed, stamped envelope to **Colorado Plateau Mountain-Bike Trail Association,** P.O. Box 4602, Grand Junction, CO 81502.

There's also a bike route through and around Colorado National Monument (see above). Covering 33 miles, it follows Rim Rock Drive through the park and 10 additional miles on rural South Camp Road and South Broadway at the base of

Wine Tasting & More Amid the Canyons

If you head east from Grand Junction, about 12 miles up the Grand Valley along U.S. 6 (or I-70 exit 42), you'll come to the farming community of **Palisade,** famous for its fruit orchards and vineyards. Most fruit is picked between late June and mid-September, when it's available at roadside fruit stands. For a fruit directory, harvest schedule, and map, contact the **Palisade Chamber of Commerce,** 309 S. Main (P.O. Box 729), Palisade, CO 81526 (☎ 970/464-7458; fax 970/464-4757).

Area wineries use the grapes and some of the fruits grown here, and they all welcome visitors for tastings and sometimes tours. The state's oldest existing winery, **Colorado Cellars,** 3553 E Rd., Palisade (☎ 800/848-2812), produces an excellent selection of award-winning wines, including a few chardonnays, a cabernet, rieslings, fruit wines, champagnes, and port. The winery grows its own grapes and produces some 15,000 cases of wine annually, plus more than 30 varieties of wine-based food products. Tastings are given year-round, Monday through Friday from 9am to 4pm, and Saturday from noon to 4pm.

Carlson Vineyards, 461 35 Rd., Palisade (☎ 970/464-5554), is a winery with a sense of humor, as well as a good product. Its wines have names such as Prairie Dog White and Tyrannosaurus Red, and are made with Colorado grapes. Visitors are welcome year-round, daily from 11am to 6pm.

Unique in Colorado is **Rocky Mountain Meadery,** 3701 G Rd., Palisade (☎ 800/720-2558 or 970/464-7899), which produces honey wine—also known as mead. Popular in medieval times, mead was known as "the drink of the gods," and is often served at Shakespearean festivals. It contains no grapes, but is made from orange-blossom honey from citrus groves in Arizona, and ranges from very sweet to quite dry—appropriate as a table wine. Rocky Mountain Meadery also produces blends of honey wine and fruit, using fruit from local orchards, as well as hard apple and pear cider. The tasting room, with large windows affording a view of the winery, is open daily from 10am to 5pm.

Other local wineries include **Grande River Vineyards,** 787 Elberta Ave., Palisade (☎ 800/264-7696 or 970/464-5867), which produces a variety of wines including a merlot and chardonnay. The tasting room is open in summer, daily from 9am to 7pm; in spring and fall, daily from 10am to 6pm; and in winter, daily from 10am to 5pm. **Plum Creek Cellars,** 3708 G Rd., Palisade (☎ 970/464-7586), is open daily from 10am to 5pm. The area's newest winery, **Canyon Wind Cellars,** 3907 U.S. 6, Palisade (☎ 970/464-0888), asks that visitors call for an appointment.

the canyons. Rim Rock Drive does not have a separate bike lane, nor shoulders, so be alert for motor traffic. The national monument publishes a free brochure.

Also see the "Hiking" section, above.

A variety of guided mountain-bike tours, including pampered excursions with gourmet meals, are available from **Adventure Quest Expeditions** (☎ 888/237-8378 or 970/245-9058; www.gj.net/~adquest; e-mail: adquest@gj.net). Costs run from $45 for a half-day ride near Grand Junction to $650 for a 5-day tour on Kokopelli's Trail from the Grand Junction area to Moab, Utah. Adventure Quest also offers a women-only mountain-biking camp trip on Kokopelli's Trail that includes instruction in mountain-biking techniques and bike repairs; custom tours can be arranged as well. Groups are small—usually six or fewer riders—and the company can arrange bike rentals at an additional cost.

RIVER RAFTING   Colorado river-rafting trips through beautiful red sandstone canyons are provided by **Rim Rock Adventures,** Box 608, Fruita, CO 81521 (☎ **970/858-9555;** fax 970/858-9465; www.rradventures.com; e-mail: info@ rradventures.com). Cost for a 1½-hour trip about 5 miles down the Colorado is $15 for adults and $13 for children 12 and under; a 30-mile full-day float trip costs $75 per adult and $55 per child. The company also rents rafts ($40 to $75 per day), canoes ($35 per day), and tubes ($8 per day) for those who want to explore the river on their own.

SKIING & SNOWBOARDING   **Powderhorn Resort,** Colo. 65, 7 miles south of Mesa (☎ **800/241-6997** for reservations only, or 970/268-5700; fax 970/ 268-5351; www.powderhorn.com; e-mail: ski@powderhorn.com), is located 35 miles east of Grand Junction on the north face of the Grand Mesa. A favorite among local skiers and snowboarders of all ability levels, it offers 500 acres of ski-able terrain with an average annual snowfall of more than 225 inches. The resort has one quad lift, two doubles, and a surface lift serving 27 trails, which are rated 20% beginner, 50% intermediate, 15% advanced, and 15% expert. Located at the resort are two condominium buildings, a cafeteria/restaurant and lounge, a rental shop, and repair center. Elevation at the top is 9,850 feet, and there's a vertical drop of 1,650 feet. Lift ticket prices (1998–99 season) are $31 for adults, $26 for college students, and $23 for students 7 to 18 and seniors 55 to 69. Those 6 and younger and 70 and older ski free, and use of the beginner lift is free for everyone. The resort is usually open from Thanksgiving until early April.

Cross-country skiers often head to Colorado National Monument (see above).

SNOWMOBILING   A trail connects Powderhorn Resort to Ski Sunlight, running 120 miles from Grand Junction's local ski area to Glenwood Springs, the longest multi-use winter recreational trail in Colorado, traversing White River and Grand Mesa National Forests. It is fully marked and continuously groomed. Other trails can be accessed from the parking areas along Colo. 65, between Mesa Lakes and Grand Mesa. Snowmobile rentals are available at Mesa Lakes Resort (☎ **970/ 268-5467**).

SWIMMING   Centrally located **Lincoln Park,** at 12th Street and North Avenue, has a 50-meter outdoor heated pool with a 351-foot water slide, open in summer, along with lighted tennis courts, playgrounds, picnic areas, and a nine-hole golf course. The **Orchard Mesa Community Center,** 2736 C Rd., has an indoor pool, open year-round, with a diving area and shallow-water section. For hours, fees, and other specifics, contact park offices (☎ **970/244-3866**).

THE MUSEUM OF WESTERN COLORADO

For a huge step through time—from 150 million years ago all the way up to the present—you'll want to visit the various facilities of the **Museum of Western Colorado** (☎ **888/488-3466** or 970/242-0971; www.mwc.mus.co.us). These include the **Regional History Museum, Dinosaur Valley Museum,** and **Cross Orchards Historic Farm** (each of which is discussed below). Combination passes for all three facilities are available ($6 for adults, $5 for seniors 60 and over, and $4 for children 11 and under).

In addition, the Museum of Western Colorado manages three **natural resource areas** (free admission, open 24 hours), where you can get a first-hand look at the geology and paleontology of western Colorado. **Rabbit Valley,** located at I-70 exit 2, 25 miles west of Grand Junction, encompasses a significant dinosaur quarry.

There's also a 1½-mile self-guided walking tour, the "Trail through Time," offering a close-up view of dinosaur fossils preserved in ancient stream channels. **Riggs Hill,** located on South Broadway in Grand Junction, is the site of the first official dinosaur excavation in western Colorado. It's named for paleontologist Elmer S. Riggs of Chicago's Field Museum of Natural History, who discovered huge fossilized bones of the previously unknown dinosaur Brachiosaurus altithorax here in 1900. The site has a three-quarter-mile self-guided interpretive trail. **Dinosaur Hill**, in Fruita, near the Fruita Welcome Center exit off I-70, is western Colorado's second excavated site, also made by Riggs. It contains a 1-mile self-guided interpretive trail.

Cross Orchards Historic Farm. 3073 F Rd. ☎ **970/434-9814.** Admission $4 adults, $3.50 seniors 60 and over, $2 children 11 and under. Memorial Day–Labor Day, Tues–Sat 9am–4pm, Sun noon–4pm; Labor Day–Oct and Apr–Memorial Day, Tues–Sat 10am–4pm. Closed Nov–Mar except for special events.

With over 22,000 apple trees covering 243 acres, Cross Orchards was one of the largest apple orchards in western Colorado during the first quarter of the 20th century. Today, the remaining 24.4 acres of the historic site preserve the feel of an old working farm and orchard, where blacksmiths and woodworkers continue to ply their trades, and visitors often smell ginger cookies baking in wood-burning stoves. Costumed guides lead tours through the original barn and packing house, workers' bunkhouse, and farm owner's gazebo. The site contains an extensive collection of vintage farm and road construction equipment, plus narrow gauge rail cars; there's also a gift shop.

Among annual events at the historic farm are the **Apple Jubilee,** a harvest festival in early October that includes a mountain man rendezvous, cowboy poetry, music, kids' games, blacksmithing demonstrations, an antique car and engine show, and, of course, plenty of fresh apple cider and other apple goodies. In early to mid-December it's **Country Christmas,** with candlelit walkways, live entertainment, ornament making, taffy pulls, hayrides, a visit from Santa, and homemade toys, gifts, and foods. Then in late April, the farm hosts **Western Colorado Heritage Days,** with numerous activities, including a ranch rodeo, a mountain man rendezvous, cowboy dance, Ute Indian dancers, weaving and gunsmithing demonstrations, and a Dutch-oven cookoff.

Dinosaur Valley Museum. 362 Main St., at Fourth St. ☎ **970/241-9210.** Admission $5 adults, $4.50 seniors 60 and over, $3 children 11 and under. Memorial Day–Labor Day Mon–Sat 9am–5pm, Sun 10am–4pm; Labor Day–Memorial Day Tues–Sat 10am–4pm.

Here you can visit a working paleontology lab, see living fossils and petrified bones, and compare yourself to gigantic dinosaur skeletons. You'll also find million-year-old bugs, plants, and feathers, plus animated dinosaurs that stomp and roar. Children can uncover dinosaur bones in the kids' excavation pit, and learn more about dinosaurs with their parents in the reading alcove. Visitors can join in a real dinosaur dig at one of the museum's quarries with advance registration (☎ **888/ 488-3466**).

Regional History Museum. 248 S. Fourth St., at Ute St. ☎ **888/488-3466** or 970/ 242-0971. Admission $3 adults, $2.50 seniors 60 and over, $2 children 11 and under. Memorial Day–Labor Day, Mon–Sat 9am–5pm, Sun noon–4pm; Labor Day–Memorial Day, Tues–Sat 10am–4pm.

At this worthwhile museum you can see ancient tools, baskets, pots, and weapons; peer at Spanish cannons and helmets; and learn about the mines, railroads, and orchards of the American West. There's an extensive collection of firearms—used by western Colorado's most famous and infamous citizens—and you can try to delve into the psyche of Alferd Packer, Colorado's notorious cannibal. In the one-room

schoolhouse exhibit, squeeze into old-time desks and practice Spencerian penman-
ship on slates. The museum also has a time line spanning a century of regional history beginning in the 1880s.

MORE TO SEE & DO

As we went to press, **Doo Zoo Children's Museum** (☎ 970/241-5225), which
specializes in educational hands-on activities for children and young teens, was in
search of a new location. Those traveling with kids may want to call to see if the
museum has finally found a home.

Art on the Corner. Main St., from First to Seventh sts. ☎ **970/245-2926.** Free admission.
Daily 24 hours, with shops and restaurants open usual business hours.

This outdoor sculpture exhibit, with more than 60 works, helps make Grand Junction's Downtown Shopping Park one of the most attractive and successful in the
country. About half of the sculptures are loaned by the artists for one year, during
which time they are for sale, while the rest are on permanent display. The sculptures
were created in a variety of styles in bronze, chrome, iron, and other materials. We
particularly like the large bronze pig named *Sir*, located on the east side of Sixth
Street at Main, and *Greg La Rex*, a sculpture in steel that depicts a dinosaur skeleton
atop a bicycle, at the corner of Third and Main. The shopping park has art galleries,
antiques shops, restaurants, and a variety of retail stores, with wide, tree-lined
pedestrian walkways.

Dinosaur Discovery Museum. 550 Jurassic Court, Fruita (just south of I-70 exit 19).
☎ **800/DIG-DINO** or 970/858-7282. Admission $5.50 adults, $3.50 children 3–12, $4.50
seniors 55 and over, free for children under 3. Mon–Sat 9am–5pm, Sun 10am–5pm.

Enter a virtual time machine to journey back to the Jurassic period, where you'll
encounter a mother stegosaurus defending her young from the fearsome allosaurus,
and visit the last ice age alongside a mighty mammoth. There are more than 125
cast specimens of dinosaurs and other prehistoric animals. The cleverly designed
and constructed full-size models move, bellow, and occasionally spit. Hands-on,
interactive exhibits allow kids of all ages to learn about and experience the forces
that created the lands around us. Feel the earth shake on an earthquake simulator,
make a sandstorm, or touch the icy face of a glacier.

Rim Rock Adventures. On Colo. 340 about half a mile south of I-70 exit 19, Fruita.
☎ **970/858-9555.** Free admission to museum and Indian village. Admission to deer park,
$2.50 adults, $1.50 children 3–13, free for children under 3. May–Labor Day, daily 8am–5pm.

Exotic deer from around the world are the highlight of this park/zoo, where you can
also see goats, sheep, and Roscoe the elk, who loves to be hand-fed by visiting children. Wild West rodeos are scheduled weekly in summer.

Western Colorado Botanical Gardens. 655 Struthers Ave. ☎ **970/245-3288.** Admission (1998 rates) $3 adults, $2 students and seniors, $1.50 children 5–12, free for kids 4 and
under. Wed–Sun 10am–4pm; call for possible change in days and times. Located at the south
end of 7th St.

This new botanical garden along the Colorado River was still being developed in
late 1998, but even though it's only partially completed, it offers plenty to see and
do. Located on 12.3 acres of land leased from the city of Grand Junction, the
facility includes a butterfly house, greenhouse, paved trails, and some outside
gardens—with extensive outdoor gardens and demonstration areas planned.

In the butterfly house visitors stroll through a lush forest of flowering plants,
ferns, and ponds. The adjacent greenhouse contains hundreds of plants, including
orchids and other colorful tropical varieties, plus a desert section of cactus. Also in

the greenhouse are fish ponds and several whimsical metal sculptures of animals, including one of the friendliest-looking snakes you've ever seen. The metal sculptures are for sale, along with numerous other botanically related items in the well-stocked gift shop. Walkways connect the botanical gardens with the Colorado River Trails system, which is discussed under "Hiking," above. By the way, when you're in the butterfly house, don't let butterflies land on the palms of your hands. Butterflies' taste buds are in pores on their feet, and natural oils on people's hands clog those pores, preventing the butterflies from locating food.

Western Colorado Center for the Arts. 1803 N. Seventh St. ☎ **970/243-7337.** Admission $2 adults, free for children under 13. Tues–Sat 9am–4pm.

This museum has hundreds of works of art, many with western themes, as well as traveling exhibits. The collection includes lithographs by Paul Pletka and more than 50 Navajo weavings dating from the early 1900s. There's also a gift shop featuring unique handcrafted items, as well as community theater performances (call for schedule).

SHOPPING

For Colorado's most artful shopping experience, head to Grand Junction's **Downtown Shopping Park**, where you'll find a variety of shops, art galleries, and restaurants set amid an outdoor sculpture garden that runs some 7 blocks along Main Street. (See "Art on the Corner," above.)

The Western Slope's largest indoor shopping mall, **Mesa Mall,** is located at 2424 U.S. 6 and 50 (☎ **970/242-0008**). It's anchored by Sears, Mervyn's, JC Penney, Target, and Herberger's, and contains about 100 specialty shops, services, and eateries.

WHERE TO STAY

Major chains offering reasonably priced lodging in Grand Junction, and all conveniently lined up along Horizon Drive, include **Best Western Sandman Motel,** 708 Horizon Dr. (☎ 800/528-1234 or 970/243-4150), with rates of $48 to $64; **Comfort Inn,** 750 Horizon Dr. (☎ 800/228-5150 or 970/245-3335), with rates of $55 to $77; **Days Inn,** 733 Horizon Dr. (☎ 800/329-7466 or 970/245-7200), with rates of $58 to $84; **Holiday Inn,** 755 Horizon Dr. (☎ 800/465-4329 or 970/243-6790), with rates of $74 to $79; **Ramada Inn,** 725 Horizon Dr. (☎ 800/ 272-6232 or 970/243-5150), charging $50 to $79; and **Super 8,** 728 Horizon Dr. (☎ 800/800-8000 or 970/248-8080), with rates of $49 to $55. All rates here are for two people, with the highest rates during the summer. Room tax adds almost 11% to lodging bills.

Country Inns of America. 718 Horizon Dr., Grand Junction, CO 81506. ☎ **800/ 990-1143** or 970/243-5080. Fax 970/242-0600. 141 units. A/C TV TEL. $48–$53 double. AE, CB, DC, MC, V. Pets accepted with charge of $5 per day.

This modern motel has spacious, quiet, comfortable rooms surrounding a courtyard with trees and a large lawn. Most units have two sinks, and either one or two queen beds or a king. Facilities include a heated pool and kiddie pool (open in summer), game room, self-serve laundry, cafe, and lounge. The motel also has meeting rooms and banquet facilities.

Grand Junction Hilton. 743 Horizon Dr., Grand Junction, CO 81506. ☎ **800/445-8667** or 970/241-8888. Fax 970/242-7266. 264 units. A/C TV TEL. $79–$129 double; $129–$225 suite. Children under 12 stay free in parents' room. AE, CB, DC, DISC, MC, V.

A modern eight-story hotel just off I-70 exit 31, the Hilton offers spacious guest rooms with southwestern decor, one king or two double beds, full-length curtains to separate the entry and bathroom from the sleeping area, and contemporary furnishings such as clear-glass lamps and mirrored closet doors. Rooms with refrigerators and coffeemakers are available. There are two restaurants and two lounges, one with entertainment, and a concierge. The Hilton also offers room service (limited hours), valet laundry, newspaper delivery, an outdoor heated pool, whirlpool, three lighted tennis courts, fitness center, sand volleyball court, basketball court, croquet, children's playground, game room, courtesy transportation, and meeting space for 600.

✪ **Grand Vista Hotel.** 2790 Crossroads Blvd., Grand Junction, CO 81506. ☎ **800/ 800-7796** or 970/241-8411. Fax 970/241-1077. E-mail: sales@grandvistahotel.com. 158 units. A/C TV TEL. Apr–Oct $79–$89 double, lower at other times. AE, CB, DC, DISC, MC, V. Small pets accepted for a $10 fee.

The aptly named Grand Vista does indeed have grand views, especially from the upper floors of its six stories. On the south side of the building you'll be looking out over Colorado National Monument, while guests on the building's north side see the Book Cliffs and Grand Mesa. Pleasantly outfitted in what might be described as modern American hotel decor, units here have good lighting, comfortable seating, and even the smallest rooms have a table and two upholstered chairs. The mini-suites are especially spacious, and come with a king bed, recliner, modem dataport, and whirlpool tub for one.

Oliver's Restaurant serves three meals daily—mostly American fare—and Bailey's Lounge is a handsome Old English–style pub with great deals on drinks and appetizers weekday evenings. Amenities include a heated indoor pool and whirlpool (open 24 hours), on-demand movies and video games, complimentary shuttle service to the airport or train and bus stations, meeting and banquet facilities for up to 300, and golf and rafting packages. Fax and copier services are available. Four floors are designated completely no-smoking.

The Orchard House. 3573 E. ½ Rd., Palisade, CO 81526. ☎ **970/464-0529.** Fax 970/464-0681. E-mail: oliver@iti2.net. 4 units (3 with private bathroom). A/C TEL. $60–$75 double. Rates include full breakfast. MC, V. Call for information on the inn's suitability for children.

Situated in the midst of the scenic Grand Valley orchard and wine country, this pleasant country farmhouse is more than just a bed-and-breakfast. Innkeeper Stephanie Schmid has created a true home environment, comfortable and laid-back, but elegant in a country sort of way. Rooms are named for the resident dog and three cats. The large upstairs honeymoon suite, named Conrad's Room for Conrad the cat, is furnished in brass and oak, with a king-sized bed, extra-large bathroom, separate sitting area, and wonderful views of the Grand Mesa and Book Cliffs. Next door, Zoe's Room (without its own bathroom) is available only in combination with Conrad's Room, good for two couples traveling together who don't mind sharing a bathroom. Cost for both is $125. Zoe's room has a large window seat and a four-poster queen bed. Downstairs, Cameo's Room (named for the resident dog) has cherry furnishings and woodland scenes, a wicker chair, and twin beds; and Oliver's Room has country-style cherry furnishings and a queen-sized bed. Rooms have ceiling fans, and TVs are available on request. Breakfasts, prepared fresh in-house, include fresh fruits (this is the Orchard House, after all), with a hot entree such as a vegetable fritatta or blueberry pancakes and sausage. Gourmet home-cooked candlelight dinners, complete with wine, are also available at additional cost. Smoking is not permitted.

Stonehaven Bed & Breakfast. 798 N. Mesa St., Fruita, CO 81521. ☎ **800/303-0898** or 970/858-0898. Fax 970/858-7765. www.innsofcolorado.org. E-mail: stonehvn@gj.net. 5 units (3 with bathroom). A/C TEL. $65–$135 double. Rates include full breakfast. AE, DISC, MC, V.

This elegant Victorian home, built in 1908, offers a relaxed country atmosphere within a few miles of both Grand Junction and Colorado National Monument. Listed on the National Register of Historic Places, the inn has a delightful wrap-around veranda. Inside it's decorated with antiques and reproductions—mostly Victorian, but some earlier. The Grey Room, especially popular with honeymooners and those celebrating anniversaries, contains an 1840s brass bed, gas fireplace, whirlpool tub, and large windows that provide spectacular views of Colorado National Monument. In the Cherry Suite you'll find an old-fashioned bathroom, queen bed in the sleeping room, a TV, and a day bed in the sitting room. Home-made breakfasts vary, but might include such items as baked potatoes stuffed with eggs or strawberry whole-wheat crêpes. At least once each month there is a murder-mystery night, complete with a full dinner, at a cost for two of $150 to $180. The Stonehaven is smoke-free.

CAMPING

In addition to campgrounds at **Colorado National Monument** (see above), the Island Acres unit of **Colorado River State Park**, 10 miles east of Grand Junction at I-70 exit 47 (☎ **970/434-3388**), has 80 campsites, ranging from tent-only ($9) to electric ($12) to full RV hookups ($16). The park also has showers and laundry facil-ities, a playground, naturalist programs, picnicking, fishing, swimming, and hiking.

There are also several commercial campgrounds in the Grand Junction area, com-plete with full RV hookups, hot showers, and all the usual niceties. We like **Junction West R.V. Park,** 793 22 Rd., Grand Junction (☎ **970/245-8531**), which not only has about the cleanest bathhouses we've seen anywhere, but is also quiet and conve-niently located. There are 61 large, somewhat-shaded sites, a store, coin-operated laundry, and game room. The park is open to RVs only (no tents), and no registra-tions are accepted after 9pm. Rates are in the $15 to $19 range. To get to Junction West, take U.S. 6 and 50 to 22 Road (or I-70 exit 26), and go north half a mile.

WHERE TO DINE
EXPENSIVE & MODERATE

G. B. Gladstone's. 2531 N. 12th St., at Patterson Rd. ☎ **970/241-6000.** Reservations rec-ommended. Main courses $4.75–$9 lunch, $8–$18 dinner. AE, DC, DISC, MC, V. Daily 11am–10pm. STEAK/SEAFOOD.

Nostalgia dominates the mood of this popular restaurant. The Croquet Room, for instance, is decorated with early-20th-century sports regalia, and the Library would delight any bibliophile. The sunken central bar is most nostalgic and most packed on Friday nights, when blues records blast. Local businesspeople enjoy the lunches: an innovative selection of hot and cold sandwiches, flame-broiled burgers, soups (including an excellent baked French onion soup), salads, quiche, and fish-and-chips. Dinners include exotic pastas, such as the Thai pesto linguine with broiled chicken strips, served with a spicy cream sauce of basil, garlic, and chile; plus steaks, fresh seafood, and chicken. Arrive early for the slow-roasted prime rib, a popular house specialty.

The Winery. 642 Main St. ☎ **970/242-4100.** Reservations recommended. Main courses $9.50–$30. AE, CB, DC, DISC, MC, V. Daily 5–10pm. STEAK/SEAFOOD.

Fine dining in an atmosphere of western elegance is what you'll experience at the Winery, considered by many as having the best food in Grand Junction. The dining room, of red brick and weathered barn wood, is decorated with lots of plants, stained glass, and wine barrels and bottles. It's hard to go wrong here, especially if you choose from the Winery Favorites section of the menu. We recommend the prime rib (get there early—it often sells out) and the salmon fillet. The salmon and a catch of the day are always fresh. You can also get a variety of steaks, steak and seafood combos, rack of lamb, or pork chops.

INEXPENSIVE

Crystal Cafe and Bake Shop. 314 Main St. ☎ **970/242-8843.** Breakfast $2–$5.75; lunch $4.50–$7.50. No credit cards. Mon–Fri 7am–1:30pm; Sat 8:30am–1:30pm. AMERICAN.

You may have to wait for a table at this popular breakfast and lunch spot, but it's worth it. The simple, modern decor includes hardwood tables and bentwood cafe-style chairs, with woven place mats and napkins. Selections are mostly innovative variations on standard American dishes, highlighted by the cafe's own fresh-baked breads, rolls, pastries, and desserts. For breakfast there is a variety of pancakes, as well as egg dishes that include a Greek omelet—a two-egg omelet with fresh tomatoes, black olives, red onions, oregano, and feta cheese. Lunches include plenty of salads, hot and cold sandwiches, and a quiche of the day. Sandwiches, of course, are prepared on the bakery's own bread and rolls, and often include uniquely seasoned mayonnaise. We particularly enjoyed the smoked turkey with red onion and basil mayonnaise.

✪ **Pomidori's Italian Deli.** 319 Main St. ☎ **970/242-5272.** Main courses $4–$10. MC, V. Mon–Sat 11am–8pm. ITALIAN.

For great homemade-style Italian food—the kind your grandmother might have made if she were Italian—at good prices, in a friendly, casual atmosphere, this is the place. Using many of his mother's recipes and a few of his own, Bronx-born Tony Checco creates all his own sauces, sausage, and meatballs, which he serves in a simple, storefront cafe-style deli, under the watchful eye of the *Mona Lisa*. Two pastas are featured each day, available with a choice of six different sauces. We loved the spicy sausage tomato sauce, but then we like food with an attitude. There are also salads, soups, meatball and sausage sandwiches (served hot), calzones, Italian subs, and a design-it-yourself cold sandwich menu. Sauces, meatballs, and sausage are available to go, and all the deli meats and cheeses are also sold by the pound. Those wanting complete meals delivered can call **Dinner Dashers** (☎ **970/255-9800**).

7th Street Café. 832 S. Seventh St. ☎ **970/242-7225.** Breakfast $1.75–$5.50; lunch $2.75–$5.75. DISC, MC, V. Mon–Sat 7am–3pm, Sun 7am–2pm. AMERICAN.

The fifties are back at 7th Street Café, with an old-fashioned soda fountain (there's also plenty of seating at tables), photos of Marilyn and Elvis, and 45-r.p.m. records. Breakfasts include bacon and eggs, pancakes, and for the more adventurous, several spicy combinations. For lunch, there are numerous sandwiches and salads, good burgers, and hot-plate specials including Italian-style meat loaf. Recently added to the menu are several vegetarian items. Leave room for a banana split or hot-fudge sundae.

2 Glenwood Springs

84 miles E of Grand Junction, 41 miles NW of Aspen, 169 miles W of Denver

Scenic beauty and hot mineral water are the lures here. Members of the Ute tribe visited the Yampah mineral springs on the banks of the Colorado River for centuries. Calling it "big medicine," they came from miles around to heal their wounds or use nearby vapor caves as a natural sauna. But it wasn't until the 1880s that the springs were commercially developed. The three Devereux brothers, who had made a small fortune in silver at Aspen, built what was at the time the largest hot-springs pool in the world, then added a red-sandstone bathhouse and built the Hotel Colorado. Soon everyone from European royalty to movie stars to President Theodore Roosevelt made their way to Glenwood Springs.

The springs supported the town until the Great Depression and World War II caused a decline in business. After the war, with the growth of the ski industry at nearby Aspen, Glenwood Springs began to reemerge as a resort town, but on a smaller scale. Today, this city of 7,700 is a popular recreational center. The hot-springs complex underwent a total renovation in the 1970s, and additional improvements were made in 1993, as it celebrated its centennial.

Also completed that year was a 12-year, $490-million project to build a four-lane interstate through the 18-mile Glenwood Canyon. One of the most expensive road-ways ever built—as well as one of the most beautiful interstate highway drives in America—the road offers a number of trailheads and raft-launching areas as well as viewpoints from which travelers can safely gaze at the Colorado River and its spectacular canyon.

ESSENTIALS

GETTING THERE   By Car   I-70 follows the Colorado River through Glenwood Springs. Colo. 82 (the Aspen Highway) links the city with Aspen, 42 miles southeast.

By Bus   Roaring Fork Transit Agency (☎ 970/920-8484) offers service between Glenwood Springs and Aspen, with numerous stops along the route, daily from 6am to midnight, at a cost of $6 each way.

By Shuttle Van   Transportation from Denver to Glenwood Springs and Aspen is provided by **Colorado Mountain Express** (☎ 800/525-6363); there's also daily commuter service to and from Aspen, and east on I-70 as far as Rifle, from **Aspen Limousine** (☎ 800/222-2112 or 970/945-9400). Call each for rates and times.

By Train   There's **Amtrak** (☎ 800/USA-RAIL) service to Glenwood Springs daily aboard the *California Zephyr,* direct from Denver and Salt Lake City. The depot is at Seventh Street and Cooper Avenue.

VISITOR INFORMATION   The **Glenwood Springs Chamber Resort Association,** 1102 Grand Ave., Glenwood Springs, CO 81601 (☎ **970/945-6589;** fax 970/945-1531; www.glenscape.com; e-mail: glenwood@rof.net), maintains a visitor center on the south side of downtown, on the southeast corner of 11th and Grand. Brochures are available 24 hours a day.

GETTING AROUND   The confluence of the Roaring Fork and the Colorado rivers forms a "T" in the heart of Glenwood Springs, and streets follow the valleys carved by the two streams. Downtown Glenwood is south of the Colorado and east of the Roaring Fork.

The city-run bus service, **Ride Glenwood Springs**, operates daily, providing rides to and from hotels, motels, restaurants, shopping areas, and the Hot Springs Pool. Passes cost $1 per person for unlimited rides (exact change required), and can be obtained from bus drivers. Schedules are available at the Chamber Resort Association office (see above). In-town transportation is also available, around the clock, from **Alpine Action Taxi** (☎ 970/947-1818).

FAST FACTS   Valley View Hospital, providing 24-hour emergency care, is at 1906 Blake Ave. (☎ **970/945-6535**), a block east of Colo. 82 at 19th Street. The **post office** is at 113 Ninth Street; contact the U.S. Postal Service (☎ **800/ 275-8777**) for hours and additional information.

SPECIAL EVENTS   Ski Spree Winter Carnival, from late January to early February; Summer of Jazz, June through August; the Strawberry Days Festival, second full week of June; Doc Hollidays, August; and the Fall Art Festival, late September.

Historic Fairy Caves to Reopen

Billed as the Eighth Wonder of the World, guided tours of Glenwood Springs' Fairy Caves were a major tourist attraction in the late 1890s and early 1900s. Located on Iron Mountain, a half-mile north and 1,300 feet above the town, the caves attracted visitors from around the world until the onset of World War I shut down the operation. They were a sight to see—numerous stalactites and stalagmites, needles, gypsum flowers, bacon, soda straws, and other delicate and colorful formations, illuminated by electric lights—all for the 1897 price of 50¢. Visitors would either walk to the caves' entrance or ride a burro.

Now, after being closed since 1917, efforts are underway to open the Fairy Caves—as well as a section of the caves that remained undiscovered until more recent times—to the public again. Caving fan Steve Beckley expects to open the caves to the public in 1999, and offer guided tours each year from mid-April through October. He's putting in trails, hand rails, and new lighting for a 1-hour tour, but leaving much of the caves in as natural a state as possible for guided 3- to 4-hour trips for small groups of physically fit individuals who don't mind crawling on their stomachs through dirty narrow passages wearing knee pads and helmet lights.

Formed in limestone that was deposited some 325 million years ago, the cave system is believed to be one of the largest in the state, with one room—the barn—over five stories tall. These caves are also significant because, unlike a number of other caves, they're live, meaning that they remain moist and continue to produce new formations. Beckley says he plans to manage the caves to protect them, and keep them alive. To do this he is building trails that allow visitors to see the caves' features but keep the delicate formations out of reach—natural oils from our fingers are death on growing cave formations—and he also is installing systems to maintain proper temperatures and humidity.

The caves are to be called Glenwood Caverns and Historic Fairy Caves, and plans call for a desk in the Hotel Colorado and a shuttle to take visitors to the caves. For the latest on the project's progress, as well as hours and prices when it opens, contact the Glenwood Springs Chamber Resort Association (see "Visitor Information," above).

SPORTS & OUTDOOR ACTIVITIES

A busy local shop where you can get information on the best spots for hiking, mountain climbing, rock climbing, kayaking, camping, and cross-country skiing is **Summit Canyon Mountaineering,** 732 Grand Ave. (☎ **800/360-6994** or 970/945-6994). In addition to selling a wide variety of outdoor-sports equipment, it rents cross-country ski gear, tents, sleeping bags, and backpacks.

BICYCLING   A paved bike trail runs from the Yampah Vapor Caves into Glenwood Canyon, and trails and four-wheel-drive roads in the adjacent White River National Forest are ideal for mountain bikers (see "Hiking," below). You'll find bike rentals (about $5 per hour or $15 to $18 per day), plus repairs and accessories, at **BSR Sports,** 210 Seventh St. (☎ 970/945-7317); **Canyon Bikes,** at the Hotel Colorado, 526 Pine St. (☎ 970/945-8904), which also offers a shuttle service; and **Sunlight Ski & Bike Shop,** 309 Ninth St. (☎ 970/945-9425). Also offering bike rentals is **Rock Gardens,** 1308 County Rd. 129, at I-70 exit 119 (☎ 800/958-6737 or 970/945 6737), which is located in Glenwood Canyon along the Glenwood Canyon Recreational Trail.

FISHING   Brown and rainbow trout are caught in the Roaring Fork and Colorado Rivers, and fishing for rainbow and brook trout is often good in the Crystal River above the community of Redstone. Get licenses, equipment, and advice from **Roaring Fork Anglers,** 2022 Grand Ave. (☎ **970/945-0180**), offering guided fly-fishing trips since 1975. Rates for one or two people on a full-day float trip are $295, including lunch; a full-day wading trip is $200 for one and $250 for two. Half-day trips are available as well, and Roaring Fork also has 4 miles of private waters, with a charge of $40 per rod for a full day.

GOLF   Glenwood Springs has two nine-hole courses: **Glenwood Springs Golf Club,** 193 Sunny Acres Rd. (☎ **970/945-7086**), and **Westbank Ranch Golf Club,** 1007 Westbank Rd. (☎ **970/945-7032**). Fees are $19 for 9 holes and $27 for 18 holes at Glenwood Springs, and $16 and $20, respectively, at Westbank. Some 27 miles west of Glenwood Springs, near Rifle, is the championship 18-hole **Rifle Creek Golf Course,** at 3004 Colo. 325, off I-70 exit 90 (☎ **888/247-0370** or 970/625-1093), which charges $16 for 9 holes and $26 for 18 holes.

Fans of miniature golf will discover two beautifully landscaped 18-hole water obstacle courses at **Johnson Park Miniature Golf,** 51579 U.S. 6 and 24, in West Glenwood Springs (☎ **970/945-9608**). Open from April through October, rates for 18 holes are $4.50 for adults and $3.50 for children under 12 and seniors over 60.

HIKING   There are plenty of hiking opportunities in the area. Stop at the **White River National Forest office**, Ninth Street and Grand Avenue (☎ **970/945-2521**), for free Recreational Opportunity Guide (ROG) sheets for many local trails. The forest service office also sells detailed forest maps and has other information.

One convenient walk is the **Doc Holliday Trail,** which climbs about half a mile from 13th Street and Bennett Street to an old cemetery that contains the grave of notorious gunslinger Doc Holliday (see "Exploring Glenwood Springs' Frontier Past," below).

Hikers will also find numerous trailheads along the **Glenwood Canyon Recreation Trail** in Glenwood Canyon, with some of the best scenery in the area. Among them, **Hanging Lake Trail,** 9 miles east of Glenwood Springs off I-70, is especially popular. The trailhead is accessible from eastbound I-70; westbound travelers must make a U-turn and backtrack a few miles to reach the parking area. The trail climbs 1,000 feet in 1 mile—allow several hours for the round-trip—and just beyond Hanging Lake is Spouting Rock, with an underground spring shooting out of a hole in the limestone cliff. The **Grizzly Creek Trailhead** is in the Grizzly Creek Rest Area, along I-70 in Glenwood Canyon, where there is also a launching area for rafts and kayaks. The trail climbs along the creek, past wildflowers and dogwood trees.

The **Glenwood Springs Chamber Resort Association** offers a free map of the recreation path with trailheads marked, and also sells a much more detailed map and trail guide for the Glenwood Springs area ($1).

RIVER RAFTING   Travel down the Colorado River through spectacular ✪ **Glenwood Canyon** in rafts or inflatable kayaks with **Rock Gardens,** 1308 County Rd. 129, at I-70 exit 119 (☎ **800/958-6737** or 970/945-6737); **Blue Sky Adventures,** 319 Sixth St. (☎ **970/945-6605**); or **Whitewater Rafting,** 2000 Devereux Rd., off I-70 exit 114 (☎ **970/945-8477**). Half-day trips cost about $35; full-day trips, which usually include lunch, cost about $60.

SKIING & SNOWBOARDING **Sunlight Mountain Resort,** 10901 County Rd. 117, Glenwood Springs, CO 81601 (☎ **800/445-7931** or 970/945-7491; www.sunlightmtn.com), is located 10 miles south of Glenwood Springs in the White River National Forest. Geared toward families, Sunlight has more than 460 skiable acres and a 2,010-foot vertical drop from its 9,895-foot summit; it's served by one triple and two double chairlifts and a ski-school surface lift. There are 57 runs, rated 20% beginner, 55% intermediate, 20% advanced, and 5% expert. There's also a special area for snowboarders, plus an ice-skating rink. The ski area is usually open from late November to mid-April. A full-day lift ticket (1998–99 rates) is $28 for adults, $18 for children 6 to 12 and seniors 60 to 69, and free for kids under 6 and seniors 70 and over. For equipment rentals and repairs, see the **Sunlight Ski Shop,** 309 Ninth St. (☎ **970/945-9425**). You can also rent, buy, or repair snowboards at **BSR Sports,** 210 Seventh St. (☎ **970/945-7317**).

Sunlight's Cross-Country and Nordic Center has 16 kilometers of groomed Nordic trails, available free, with rentals and lessons available. Also see "Snowmobiling," below. Information and equipment are also available at **Summit Canyon Mountaineering,** 732 Grand Ave. (☎ **800/360-6994** or 970/945-6994).

SNOWMOBILING The Sunlight to Powderhorn Trail, running 120 miles from Glenwood's local ski area to Grand Junction's, on the Grand Mesa, is the longest multi-use winter recreational trail in Colorado, traversing White River and Grand Mesa National Forests. It is fully marked and continuously groomed. Other trails can be accessed from the end of County Road 11, 2 miles beyond Sunlight Mountain Resort and 12 miles south of Glenwood Springs. For information and rentals, contact **Rocky Mountain Sports,** 2177 300th Rd. (☎ **970/945-8885**).

TAKING THE WATERS

There may be no better or more luxurious way to rejuvenate the dusty, tired traveler than a soak in a natural hot spring. In Glenwood Springs, there are two places to experience this ancient therapy.

Glenwood Hot Springs Pool. 401 N. River Rd. ☎ **800/537-7946** or 970/945-6571. Admission $7.25 adults, $4.75 children 3 to 12, free for children 2 and under. Reduced night rates available. Water slide, $3 for four rides or $4 for eight rides. Summer, daily 7:30am–10pm; rest of year, daily 9am–10pm.

Named Yampah Springs—meaning "Big Medicine"—by the Utes, this pool was created in 1888 when enterprising developers diverted the course of the Colorado River and built a stone bathhouse. The springs flow at a rate of 3.5 million gallons per day, and, with a temperature of 122°F, they're one of the world's hottest springs. The content is predominantly sodium chloride, but there are significant quantities of calcium sulfate, potassium sulfate, calcium bicarbonate, and magnesium bicarbonate, plus traces of other therapeutic minerals.

The two open-air pools together are nearly 2 city blocks in length. The larger pool, 405 by 100 feet, holds more than a million gallons of water, and is maintained at 90°F. The smaller pool, 100 feet square, is kept at 104°F. There's also a children's pool with a water slide, plus a restaurant, sport shop, and miniature golf course. The red-sandstone administration building overlooking the pools was the Hot Springs Lodge from 1890 until 1986, when a new hotel (see "Where to Stay," below) and bathhouse complex were built, and an athletic club opened (day passes are $12.50, which includes pool).

Suit and towel rentals and coin-operated lockers are available, as are Swedish, Thai, and other types of massages, starting at $35 for a half hour.

Yampah Spa and Vapor Caves. 709 E. Sixth St. ☎ **970/945-0667.** Admission to caves $8.75, spa treatments start at $32. Daily 9am–9pm.

The hot Yampah Spring water flows through the floor of nearby caves, creating natural underground steam baths. Once used by Utes for their curative powers, today the cave has an adjacent spa where such treatments as massages, facials, herbal wraps, and body muds are offered. There's also a full-service beauty salon on the premises.

EXPLORING GLENWOOD SPRINGS' FRONTIER PAST

Although most Colorado visitors tend to think of Telluride or Cripple Creek when the subject of the Wild West comes up, Glenwood Springs had its share of desperados and frontier justice. The Ute tribe first inhabited the area, using it as a base for hunting and fishing, and also making use of its mineral hot springs. When whites finally arrived in the mid- to late 1800s, the growing community—then called Defiance—was little more than a muddy street lined with saloons, brothels, and boardinghouses, where miners from nearby Aspen and Leadville could be relieved of their new-found wealth. The hot springs began to attract mine owners and other prominent businessmen to Defiance, and in 1885, the town's name was changed to the more refined Glenwood Springs. However, it wasn't until 1886 that civilization finally arrived, along with the railroad. The following year notorious gunfighter Doc Holliday arrived, and although he is said to have practiced his card-playing skills (and even a bit of dentistry), there is no record that he was involved in any gunplay in the town. By 1888, the lavish Hot Springs Pool and Hotel Colorado opened, and Glenwood Springs—now dubbed the "Spa in the Rockies"—began to attract the rich and famous, and numerous impressive hotels and other buildings were constructed.

Much of the grandeur of Glenwood Springs in the late 19th and early 20th centuries remains, and can be seen on a walk through the downtown area. The self-guided **Historic Walking Tour** guide and map is available ($1) at the Chamber Resort Association's visitor center (see above) and the Frontier Historical Museum (see below), describing more than 40 historic buildings and sites. These include the 1884 Mirror Saloon, the oldest existing building in downtown Glenwood Springs; the site of the 1884 Hotel Glenwood (only a small portion remains), where Doc Holliday died; the 1893 Hotel Colorado, which was used by President Theodore Roosevelt as his "Western White House" in the early 1900s; and the 1885 Kamm Building, where gangster Al Capone is said to have been a jewelry customer in the 1920s.

The Frontier Historical Society also offers **guided walking tours** of Glenwood Springs by reservation. Inquire at the museum (☎ **970/945-4448**).

Doc Holliday's Grave. Linwood Cemetery.

After the famous shoot-out at the OK Corral, Doc Holliday began a final search for relief from his advanced tuberculosis. But even the mineral-rich waters of Glenwood Springs could not dissipate the ravages of hard drinking and disease, and Doc died in 1887 at the Hotel Glenwood. Although the exact location of Doc's grave is not known, it is believed he was buried in or near the Linwood Cemetery, on Lookout Mountain overlooking the city. Also in the cemetery are the graves of other early citizens of Glenwood. Train robber Harvey Logan, alias Kid Curry, was shot dead while pursuing his chosen profession; he was originally buried here, but his body was later moved to an unmarked grave in another area cemetery.

From the chamber office on Grand Avenue, walk or drive uphill on 11th to Bennett and turn right. Not far on the left is the sign marking the trail to the cemetery. The trail is a half-mile uphill hike, and you'll have a grand view of the city as you climb it. In the cemetery, near the flagpole, is a tombstone with the inscription, "Doc Holliday 1852–1887 He Died in Bed," and in front of it is another monument that reads, "This Memorial Dedicated to Doc Holliday who is Buried Someplace in the Cemetery."

Frontier Historical Museum. 1001 Colorado Ave. ☎ **970/945-4448.** Admission $3 adults, $2 seniors 60 and older, free for children 12 and under. May–Sept, Mon–Sat 11am–4pm; Oct–Apr, Mon, Thurs–Sat 1–4pm.

The highlight of this museum, which occupies a late Victorian home, is the original bedroom furniture of Colorado legends Horace and Baby Doe Tabor, brought here from Leadville. The collection also includes other pioneer home furnishings, including a complete kitchen, plus antique dolls and toys, historic photos and maps, American Indian artifacts, and a mining and minerals display. The museum also contains an extensive archive of documents on the history of the West.

WHERE TO STAY

Rates are usually highest in summer, although busy ski times, such as Christmas week, can also be high. You can book a wide variety of lodgings throughout the area with **Glenwood Springs Central Reservations** (☎ **888/445-3696**). Room tax adds a bit under 9% to lodging bills.

Among the reliable moderately priced chains and franchises are the **Best Western Caravan Inn,** 1826 Grand Ave. (☎ 800/945-5495 or 970/945-7451), with rates for two of $59 to $91; the brand-new **Hampton Inn,** 401 W. First St. (☎ 800/426-7866 or 970/947-9400), with rates for two of $79 to $109; the **Holiday Inn Express** (also new), 501 W. First St. (☎ 800/465-4329 or 970/928-7800), with rates for two from $69 to $99; and **Ramada Inn,** 124 W. Sixth St. (☎ 800/332-1472 or 970/945-2500), with rates for two of $52 to $109.

MODERATE

Back in Time. 927 Cooper Ave., Glenwood Springs, CO 81601. ☎ **888/854-7733** or 970/945-6183. Fax 970/947-1324. E-mail: bitnb@sprynet.com. 3 units. AC. $85 double. AE, DISC, MC, V.

This cozy two-story 1903 Victorian, completely refurbished and restored in the early 1990s, offers personal service in a homelike setting. Guests share the living room, where they'll find a TV, VCR, and a good selection of movies, plus a stereo, a variety of CDs, board games, and books. Guests also have use of a small fridge and microwave. At the top of the stairs you'll meet Charlie, a three-quarters-size suit of armor, and throughout the house are antique clocks of every description—some functioning and some awaiting repair by clock expert Ron Robinson, who with his wife, June, owns Back in Time. Rooms are furnished with antiques from the late 1800s and early 1900s, and each is unique. For instance, the Oldie Room, which contains one queen-sized bed, is decorated with old family photos. There are two average-size rooms, each with private bathroom with shower only; one tiny room has a single bed for one person only (call for rates) and a private bathroom across the hall with a large footed tub with shower. Breakfasts include fresh fruit and baked goods, homemade granola, and a hot entree such as apple pancakes or quiche; a breakfast meat is sometimes served on the side. Afternoon snacks often include June's locally famous chocolate-chip cookies.

Hotel Colorado. 526 Pine St., Glenwood Springs, CO 81601. ☎ **800/544-3998** or 970/945-6511. Fax 970/945-7030. 126 units. TV TEL. $70–$98 double; $110–$295 suite. Children under 18 stay free in parents' room. AE, CB, DC, DISC, MC, V. Pets accepted with a $25 deposit.

The stately Hotel Colorado, constructed of sandstone and Roman brick in 1893, was modeled after Italy's Villa de Medici, and is a registered National Historic Landmark. Two American presidents—William Howard Taft and Theodore Roosevelt—spoke to crowds gathered beneath the orators' balcony in a lovely landscaped fountain piazza. In fact, this is reportedly the birthplace of the Teddy bear: One story has it that when a disappointed Roosevelt returned to the hotel in May 1905 after an unsuccessful bear hunt, hotel maids made him a small bear from scraps of cloth, inspiring a reporter to coin the phrase.

The attractive guest rooms are individually decorated, most with firm double beds and the usual hotel furnishings; suites are more spacious, with upgraded decor and period antiques. Fifth-floor penthouse suites also have wet bars and refrigerators, as well as outstanding views. Two bell-tower suites, reached by stairs only, have double Jacuzzis and private dining balconies. They also have private staircases into the ancient bell towers, where 19th-century graffiti can still be deciphered.

Hotel restaurants serve three meals daily. There's a full bar and a large outdoor dining and cocktail area, with gardens and a fountain for summer use. Amenities include valet laundry; 24-hour concierge; a European-style health spa with sauna, whirlpool, massage, and Nautilus and free weights; chiropractor; gift shop; and meeting space for up to 200.

Hot Springs Lodge & Pool. 415 Sixth St. (P.O. Box 308), Glenwood Springs, CO 81602. ☎ **800/537-7946** or 970/945-6571. Fax 970/947-2950. www.hotspringspool.com. 107 units. A/C TV TEL. Mid-March to Sept and Christmas, $84–$105 double; rest of year, $63–$80. AE, CB, DC, DISC, MC, V.

Heated by the springs that bubble through the hillside beneath it, this handsome modern motel overlooks the Glenwood Hot Springs Pool complex. Three-quarters of the rooms have private balconies or patios. Rooms are spacious, with one king or two queen beds, cherry or light-wood furnishings, coffeemakers, hair dryers, and safes; some have hide-a-beds, refrigerators, and double vanities. Facilities include a poolside restaurant that serves coffee shop–style meals, a small lounge, and a shop with swimwear and other merchandise. The hotel also offers guests discounts for the hot springs pools and athletic club (see "Taking the Waters," above), plus a whirlpool, video arcade, guest laundry, and meeting space for 50.

The Kaiser House. 932 Cooper Ave. (at Tenth St.), Glenwood Springs, CO 81601. ☎ **888/456-7366** or 970/928-0101. Fax 970/928-0101. E-mail: kaiser@sopris.net. 7 units. AC. $80–$180 double. MC, V.

Built in 1902, this handsome four-story Queen Anne–style home was meticulously and beautifully restored in the late 1980s to become a charming B&B that remains rich in history while providing today's level of comfort and amenities. Rooms are decorated with antiques—most from the early 1900s—and have functioning transoms, good lighting, and either queen- or king-sized beds. The honeymoon suite is decorated with white wicker furnishings and romantic touches such as heart-shaped pillows. All rooms have private bathrooms with showers only. Phones and TVs are available on request. Guests have use of the parlor, with fireplace; the living room, with TV and stereo; and an outdoor patio, with gas barbecue grill. Other facilities include a year-round outdoor whirlpool tub for four, exercise equipment, a massage table (massages can be arranged), and a self-serve laundry. Breakfasts feature homemade entrees such as waffles, eggs Benedict, or an egg souffle; afternoon refreshments are served.

INEXPENSIVE

Glenwood Springs Hostel. 1021 Grand Ave., Glenwood Springs, CO 81601. ☎ **800/ 946-7835** or 970/945-8545. www.rof.net/yp/gwshostel. E-mail: gshostel@rof.net. 42 beds including dorm and 5 private rooms. $12 per person per night, $39 per person for four nights; $19 single, $26 double in private rooms. No private bathrooms. AE, MC, V.

Active travelers will find the bargain sports packages this hostel offers a real plus. Activities featured include downhill and cross-country skiing, rafting, kayaking, mountain biking, and caving. There's a large record library, free coffee or tea in the mornings, and two fully equipped kitchens for guests' use. Like most hostels, there are dormitory bunks, common toilets and showers, guest laundry, and other common areas. Linen is available ($1), and it's just a 5-minute walk from the train and bus. The individual rooms are great for couples and others who prefer more privacy, although they will still share bathrooms.

Red Mountain Inn. 51637 U.S. 6 and 24, Glenwood Springs, CO 81601. ☎ **800/ 748-2565** or 970/945-6353. Fax 970/928-9432. www.redmountaininn.com. E-mail: redmtnin@rof.net. 40 units. AC TV TEL. $46–$87 motel units, $62–$192 cabins. AE, DISC, MC, V. On I-70 north frontage road between exits 114 and 116. Pets accepted with a $100 deposit.

This bright, cheery, modern motel lives up to its advertising as "Glenwood's best value." Rooms are spacious, decorated with light earth tones, and have better-than-average lighting, firm mattresses, and comfortable seating. Most rooms have 10-foot ceilings. The dozen cabins are essentially larger motel units, with sleeping for two to eight, plus complete kitchens. Some cabins have fireplaces, while a few have private patios with picnic tables. All guests share the nicely landscaped heated outdoor pool (open in summer) and the year-round outdoor hot tub, plus a delightful shaded grassy picnic area back from the road. Facilities include a coin-op laundry and meeting facilities for up to 45; several restaurants and a miniature golf course are within easy walking distance.

CAMPING

Rock Gardens Camper Park. 1308 County Rd. 129 (I-70 exit 119), Glenwood Springs, CO 81601. ☎ **970/945-6737.** Fax 970/945-2413. www.rockgardens.com. E-mail: the-rock@sopris.net. 75 sites. $19 tent sites; $23 RV sites, with electric-and-water hookups. MC, V. Closed Nov to mid-Apr.

On the banks of the Colorado River in beautiful Glenwood Canyon, this campground is a great home base for those exploring this scenic wonderland. The Glenwood Canyon Recreational Trail passes the campground on its way into Glenwood Springs, and hiking trails into the White River National Forest are nearby. Bathhouses are clean, showers are hot, and there's a dump station, although no sewer hookups. A store sells groceries, firewood, and ice, and bike rentals and raft trips are also offered (see "Sports & Outdoor Activities," above).

WHERE TO DINE

✪ **The Bayou.** 52103 U.S. 6, West Glenwood Springs. ☎ **970/945-1047.** www. glenwoodguide.com/bayou. Main courses $6–$15. AE, DC, DISC, MC, V. Daily 4–10pm. CAJUN/CREOLE.

Western Colorado's classic New Orleans–style eatery can't be mistaken: Frog eyes bulge from the green awning over its deck, which looks toward I-70 near exit 114. Harlequin masks hang on the walls and zydeco music filters through this rustic and often entertaining restaurant. In nice weather there's also dining on the outdoor deck. Come for down-home Cajun cuisine—including sautéed frogs' legs, deep-fried catfish, shrimp lagniappe, chicken étouffée, or swamp and moo (redfish and rib eye)—and stay for the staff-provided entertainment, including "dumb server tricks," birthday specials (ask if you dare), and the Frog Leg Revue. They have the largest selection of hot sauces in the valley, and on summer Sunday afternoons there's live music on the deck.

✪ **Daily Bread Cafe & Bakery.** 729 Grand Ave. ☎ **970/945-6253**. $3–$7. DISC, MC, V. Mon–Fri 7am–2pm, Sat 8am–2pm, Sun 8am–noon. CAFE/BAKERY.

Try not to be in a hurry when you go to the Daily Bread—it's not because service is slow, but because this is such a popular breakfast and lunch spot that you're likely to find yourself waiting behind a line of locals for your table or booth. Decor here is strictly American cafe: storefront windows with lace curtains, a high ceiling, oak floor, and local art on the walls. For breakfast you might try one of the many egg dishes, such as Terry's Delight—an English muffin topped with eggs, shaved ham, and melted cheese—or perhaps the wonderful (and extra healthy) Fresh Fruit Special, which consists of a carved-out half cantaloupe melon stuffed with fresh fruit, covered with fat-free vanilla yogurt and granola, and served with a fat-free muffin. The lunch menu lists dozens of sandwiches, burgers, and salads, including a number of low-fat offerings. Favorites include the Grand Avenue Deli—roast beef, turkey breast, Swiss cheese, lettuce, tomato, sprouts, and thousand island dressing on your choice of the bakery's own bread. Portions for both breakfast and lunch are more than generous, and half portions of many items are offered.

Delice. 1512 Grand Ave. ☎ **970/945-9424.** $2.75–$6.20. No credit cards. Mon–Fri 10am–3pm. SANDWICH/PASTRY SHOP.

This busy bakery and sandwich shop in Glenwood Springs' Executive Plaza is especially popular with area office workers, who like the friendly, casual atmosphere and completely-from-scratch European-style pastries. The Swiss Huber family serves a different homemade soup each day, and there are a variety of sandwiches, prepared with the bakery's French or whole wheat bread, or a croissant. A house specialty is the Swiss sausage platter, served with potato salad, sauerkraut, bread, and butter. Whole cakes, such as the decadent Black Forest cake, are available to go, as are pies, apple strudel, pastries, breads, rolls, homemade jams, and honey. Delice often closes for one week each spring and fall.

Glenwood Canyon Brewing Company. 402 Seventh St. (in the Hotel Denver). ☎ **970/945-1276**. $6–$17. AE, MC, V. Daily 11am–10pm (bar open later). BREW PUB.

There are two dining rooms in this busy and popular brew pub—one that's particularly noisy with a long bar and an under-30 crowd, and the other one, slightly more sedate, for the rest of us. Both are what we expect in a brew pub: brick walls, historic photos, wood tables, TVs with sporting events, and a view of the brewing equipment. Served at all times are a selection of half-pound burgers, several sandwiches (such as a reuben on German rye or blackened chicken on a kaiser roll), salads, pasta, and bread bowls (filled with soup or stew). Entrees (served after 5pm) are a bit more elaborate, and include a tasty steak-and-potato pie, simmered in a brown sauce and served inside a large plate of garlic mashers; and soft tacos made of Maine lobster, chopped spinach, Monterey jack cheese, and salsa. There are usually at least a half-dozen fresh ales on tap, and half-gallon growler jugs are available for takeout.

✪ Italian Underground. 715 Grand Ave. ☎ **970/945-6422.** Reservations not accepted. Main courses $8.25–$9.50; pizzas $8–$14. AE, DISC, MC, V. Daily 5–10pm. ITALIAN.

Get here early and expect to wait. A favorite of locals, the Italian Underground offers good Italian food at excellent prices. Located in a basement along busy Grand Avenue, the restaurant has stone walls, brick floors, red-and-white checked tablecloths, candlelight, and exceedingly generous portions of fine food. Try the lasagna, linguine with pesto, or spaghetti with tomato and basil sauce. All entrees come with salad, bread, and ice cream. Smaller portions of most items are available at 15% off the regular price. There's an excellent selection of Italian wines by the glass, as well as a full bar; espresso and cappuccino are also served. Smoking is not permitted.

Sopris. 7215 Colo. 82, 5 miles south of Glenwood Springs. ☎ **970/945-7771.** Reservations recommended. Main courses $9–$34. AE, DISC, MC, V. Daily 5–10pm. CONTINENTAL.

Luzern, Switzerland, native Kurt Wigger spent 17 years as chef at Aspen's Red Onion before opening the Sopris in 1974. Amid red-lit Victorian decor, accented by reproductions of classic oil paintings, Wigger serves up generous portions of veal-and-seafood dishes, as well as steaks and other meats. House specialties include the pepper steak flambe—New York strip with cracked pepper, shallots, and red-wine sauce; and Swiss veal—minced veal and mushrooms served in a cream sauce. There's an extensive wine list and full bar.

Wild Rose Bakery. 310 7th St. ☎ **970/928-8973**. $2–$3.50. AE, DISC, MC, V. Mon–Fri 7am–5:30pm, Sat 7am–5pm. BAKERY.

Take a walk down Seventh Street and the aroma of fresh-baked breads, cakes, and pastries will pull you in the door of this small neighborhood bakery, where locals line up for goodies-to-go or sit at one of the dining area's four tables sipping organic coffee and gorging on a huge cinnamon roll. The list of made-from-scratch baked goods is extensive, ranging from breads, cookies, and muffins to elaborately decorated pies and cakes—the three-layer iced carrot cake is stupendous. There are also several lunch specials each day, including a soup, salad, and quiche, and often something from the bakery, such as a spinach-ricotta turnover.

3 Montrose & Black Canyon of the Gunnison National Monument

61 miles S of Grand Junction, 108 miles N of Durango

A ranching and farming center, this quiet city of just under 10,000 has an ideal location that is quickly being discovered by hikers, mountain bikers, anglers, and others who want to explore western Colorado. Surrounded by the Uncompahgre, Gunnison, and Grand Mesa national forests, and within a short drive of Black Canyon of the Gunnison National Monument and Curecanti National Recreation Area, it's becoming a major outdoor recreation center.

Ute Chief Ouray and his wife, Chipeta, ranched in the Uncompahgre Valley here until the government forced the tribe to migrate to Utah in 1881. Once the Utes were gone, settlers founded the town of Pomona, named for the Roman goddess of fruit. Later the town's name was changed to Montrose, for a character in a Sir Walter Scott novel. The railroad arrived in 1882, providing relatively reliable transportation and a means to ship out potatoes, beets, and other crops; and Montrose began in earnest its role as one of Colorado's major food producers, which continues today.

ESSENTIALS

GETTING THERE   By Car   Montrose is an hour's drive southeast of Grand Junction via U.S. 50, a 2½-hour drive north of Durango via U.S. 550, and a 5½-hour drive west of Colorado Springs via U.S. 50 through Salida and Gunnison.

By Plane   The **Montrose Regional Airport,** 2100 Airport Rd. (☎ **970/249-3203**), is off U.S. 50 2 miles northwest of town. Regional airlines serving the town include **Air West** (☎ **970/249-7660**).

GETTING AROUND   Montrose lies along the east bank of the Uncompahgre River. Townsend Avenue (U.S. 50 and U.S. 550) parallels the stream; Main Street (U.S. 50 and Colo. 90) crosses Townsend in the center of town. Numbered streets extend north and south from Main.

   Western Express Taxi (☎ 970/249-8880) provides local cab service. Car-rental agencies include **Budget** (☎ 970/249-6083), **Dollar** (☎ 970/249-3770), **Enterprise** (☎ 970/240-3835), **Hertz** (☎ 970/249-9447), and **Thrifty** (☎ 970/249-8741).

VISITOR INFORMATION   Contact the **Montrose Visitors & Convention Bureau,** 433 S. First St. (P.O. Box 335), Montrose, CO 81402 (☎ **800/873-0244** or 970/240-1413; www.montrose.org), or stop at the **Visitor Center** (☎ **970/249-1726**) in the ✪ **Ute Indian Museum,** 17253 Chipeta Dr., on the south side of town off U.S. 550. Information is also available from the **Montrose Chamber of Commerce,** 1519 E. Main St., Montrose, CO 81401 (☎ **800/923-5515** or 970/249-5000).

FAST FACTS   Montrose Memorial Hospital, with a 24-hour emergency room, is at 800 S. Third St. (☎ **970/249-2211**). The **post office** is at 321 S. First St. Call the U.S. Postal Service (☎ **800/275-8777**) for hours and other information. For **road conditions,** call ☎ 970/249-9363.

SPECIAL EVENTS   Lighter Than Air Balloon Affaire, early July; Montrose County Fair, early August; Chocolate Lovers' Affaire and Parade of Lights, early December.

✪ BLACK CANYON OF THE GUNNISON
NATIONAL MONUMENT

"No other canyon in North America combines the depth, narrowness, sheerness, and somber countenance of the Black Canyon." So said geologist Wallace Hansen, who mapped the canyon in the 1950s and probably knew it better than anyone else. It was avoided by early American Indians and later Utes and Anglo explorers, who believed that no human could survive a trip to its depths. Today, the deepest and most spectacular 12 miles of the 53-mile canyon comprise this national monument.

   Located on Colo. 347, 6 miles north of U.S. 50, the Black Canyon ranges in depth from 1,730 to 2,700 feet. Its width at its narrowest point (cleverly called "The Narrows") is only 1,100 feet at the rim and 40 feet at the river. This deep slash in the earth was created by two million years of erosion, a process that's still going on—albeit slowed by the damming of the Gunnison River above the monument.

   Accessible only in summer, a road winds to the bottom of the canyon at the East Portal dam in the adjoining Curecanti National Recreation Area, but the only access to this part of the canyon floor is by hiking down steep side canyons. Few visitors make that trek. Most view the canyon from the South Rim Road, site of a **visitor center** (☎ **970/249-1915**), or the lesser-used North Rim Road. Short paths branching off both roads lead to splendid viewpoints with signs explaining the canyon's unique geology. Brochures describe several hikes, and the sheer canyon walls are popular with rock climbers.

Trails on the monument's rims range from short, easy nature walks to moderate-to-strenuous hikes of several miles. Permits are not needed, and leashed pets are allowed on some of the trails (check with rangers). On the south rim, the moderately difficult **Rim Rock Nature Trail** follows the rim along a relatively flat path to an overlook, providing good views of the Gunnison River and the canyon's sheer rock walls. A pamphlet available at the trailhead describes plant life along the half-mile (one-way) trail. A longer south rim hike is the 2-mile (round-trip) **Oak Flat Loop Trail,** rated moderate to strenuous, which drops slightly below the rim, offering excellent views into the canyon. Be aware that the trail is narrow in spots, and a bit close to steep drop-offs. On the monument's north rim, the **North Vista Trail** offers some of the best scenic views in the Black Canyon, and a good chance of seeing red-tailed hawks, white-throated swifts, Clark's nutcrackers, and ravens. You might also be lucky enough to see the rare peregrine falcon. The trail goes through a piñon-juniper forest along the canyon's rim about 1½ miles to **Exclamation Point,** which offers one of the best views into the canyon. Up to this point the trail is rated moderate, but it continues another 2 miles (rated strenuous) to Green Mountain, where you'll find broad, panoramic vistas.

Experienced hikers in excellent physical condition may want to hike down into the canyon. Although there are no maintained or marked trails, there are several routes that rangers can help you find. It usually takes from 4½ to 8 hours to get down to the river and back up, and free permits are required. There are also a limited number of campsites available for backpackers.

Fishermen occasionally make their way to the bottom in a quest for brown and rainbow trout; only artificial lures are permitted. In winter, the monument is popular with cross-country skiers. See "Sports & Outdoor Activities," below.

The monument is home to a variety of wildlife, and you're likely to see chipmunks, ground squirrels, badgers, marmots, and mule deer. Although not frequently seen, there are also black bear, cougars, and bobcats, and you'll probably hear the lonesome high-pitched call of coyotes at night. The peregrine falcon can sometimes be spotted along the cliffs, and you may also see red-tailed hawks, turkey vultures, golden eagles, and white-throated swifts.

There are **campgrounds** on both rims, usually open from May through October, with a limited water supply hauled in by truck. They have pit toilets, but no showers or RV hookups. Sites are available on a first-come, first-served basis, and the cost is $8 per site. The south rim campground, which rarely fills up, has 102 sites, but the north rim campground, with only 13 sites, does occasionally fill up. Campgrounds with hot showers and RV hookups are available in Montrose. See "Camping," below.

Pets must be leashed at all times and are not allowed in the inner canyon or in wilderness areas, and bicycles are not permitted on hiking trails. Visitors are also warned to not throw anything from the rim into the canyon, since even a single small stone thrown or kicked from the rim could be fatal to people below and to supervise children very carefully because many sections of the rim have no guard rails or fences.

To reach the south rim, travel east 6 miles from Montrose on U.S. 50 to the well-marked turnoff. To reach the north rim from Montrose, drive north 21 miles on U.S. 50 to Delta, east 31 miles on Colo. 92 to Crawford, then south on a 13-mile access road.

Admission is $4 per vehicle. The visitor center is open daily from 8am to 6pm in summer, with intermittent hours the rest of the year. The road to the south rim is open 24 hours a day year-round; the north rim road is open 24 hours except when closed by snow, usually between December and March. For a brochure and other information, contact Superintendent, **Black Canyon of the Gunnison National Monument,** 102 Elk Creek, Gunnison, CO 81230 (☎ **970/641-2337,** ext. 205); or if you have specific questions, call the visitor center (☎ **970/249-1914,** ext. 23).

MORE TO SEE & DO

Those wanting to step back into Montrose's past should ask at the visitor center for a free copy of the self-guided **Historic Montrose Downtown Walking Tour** brochure. It contains a map to help you locate numerous historic buildings and interpretative signs.

Montrose County Historical Museum. W. Main St. and Rio Grande Ave. ☎ **970/ 249-2085** or 970/249-6135. E-mail: stepbackintime@Montrose.com. Admission $2.50 adults, $2 seniors over 55, 50¢ children 5–12, free for children under 5. Mid-May to Sept, Mon–Sat 9am–5pm.

Pioneer life of western Colorado is highlighted at this museum, housed in a historic Denver & Rio Grande Railroad Depot. The museum features an 1890s homesteader's cabin, railroad memorabilia including a Union Pacific caboose, farm equipment, antique dolls and toys, old musical instruments, a country store, and American Indian artifacts. At the museum's library you'll find historical photos and publications, plus a complete set of Montrose newspapers from 1896 to 1940. The museum usually schedules historical programs the first Wednesday evening of each month, as well as occasional tours and day trips. Call for details.

Fort Uncompahgre. 205 Gunnison River Dr. (in Confluence Park), Delta. ☎ **970/ 874-8349**. Admission $3.50 adults, $2.50 youths 6 to 16 and seniors 65 and older, free for children under 6. June–Aug, Tues–Sat 10am to 5pm; Mar–May and Sept to mid-Dec, Tues–Sat 10am–4pm. Just north of Delta, about 20 miles north of Montrose on U.S. 50.

The original fort was built in 1828 at the confluence of the Gunnison and Uncompahgre Rivers as a small fur-trading post, and abandoned in 1844 after an attack by Utes. Today it has been replicated as a living-history museum, with hand-hewn log buildings facing a courtyard. Costumed traders, trappers, and laborers describe their lives and guide visitors to the trade room, hide room, kitchen, and' other areas of the fort.

✪ **Ute Indian Museum.** 17253 Chipeta Dr. ☎ **970/249-3098.** Admission $2.50 adults, $2 seniors over 65, $1.50 children 6–16, free for children under 6. May 15–Sept, Mon–Sat 9am–5pm, Sun 11am–4pm; shorter hours the rest of the year. Located 2 miles south of downtown Montrose off U.S. 550.

Located on the site of the final residence of southern Ute chief Ouray and his wife, Chipeta, the Ute Indian Museum offers one of Colorado's most complete exhibitions of Ute traditional and ceremonial artifacts, including clothing, baskets, and household items. Several dioramas depict mid-19th-century lifestyles, and historic photos are displayed. Also on the grounds are Chipeta's grave, bubbling Ouray Springs, a native plants garden, and an outdoor display on Spanish explorers who passed this way in 1776. The museum also houses the Montrose Visitor Center.

SPORTS & OUTDOOR ACTIVITIES

In addition to boating and other outdoor recreational activities available in Black Canyon of the Gunnison National Monument (see above) and nearby Curecanti National Recreation Area (see "Gunnison & Curecanti National Recreation Area," in chapter 14), there are plenty of opportunities for hiking, mountain biking, horseback riding, off-roading, fishing, camping, cross-country skiing, and snow-

Sweets for the Sweet & a Touch of the Grape

Chocolate lovers can't leave Montrose without a stop at the **Russell Stover Candies Factory Outlet,** 2200 Stover Ave., just off Townsend Avenue on the south side of town (☎ **970/249-6681**), for bargain prices on holiday candy (after the holiday) and boxes of chocolates that may not look quite right but taste great nonetheless. **Rocky Hill Winery** (☎ **970/249-3765**), is a fun place to stop and sample some locally produced wines. Grapes are Colorado grown, and free tastings are offered. The wines sell for $8 to $14 per bottle, and in the tasting room you'll also find a wide variety of Colorado-made gifts and food items. At press time, the winery was planning to move, so call for its new location.

---

mobiling on other federal lands in the area. Information is available at the **Public Lands Center,** 2505 S. Townsend Ave. (☎ **970/240-5300**).

BIKING   There are more than 9 miles of paved off-street walking and biking trails in Montrose, plus numerous areas for mountain biking in nearby lands administered by the National Forest Service and Bureau of Land Management. A free map of **city trails** is available at the visitor center, chamber of commerce, and city hall (433 S. First St.); stop at the Public Lands Center (see above) for information on where to ride on BLM and Forest Service lands. You can also obtain maps, information, bike repairs, and accessories at **Cascade Bicycles,** 25 N. Cascade Ave. (☎ **970/249-7375**); and **Grand Mesa Cyclery,** 2015 S. Townsend Ave. (☎ **970/ 249-7515**), which also has rentals ($25 per day).

The Tabeguache Trail—142 miles from Shavano Valley near Montrose, to No Thoroughfare Canyon near the Colorado National Monument west of Grand Junction—is a popular and challenging route for mountain bikers. Send a self-addressed, stamped envelope for a free trail map to the **Colorado Plateau Mountain-Bike Trail Association,** P.O. Box 4602, Grand Junction, CO 81502. Bikers can also use the Uncompahgre Riverway; it is scheduled to eventually connect Montrose with Delta (21 miles north) and Ouray (37 miles south).

FISHING   For starters, you can drop a line into the Uncompahgre River from Riverbottom Park, reached via Apollo Road off Rio Grande Avenue. Most anglers seek rainbow trout here and at Chipeta Lake, behind the Ute Indian Museum, south of Montrose. About 20 miles east via U.S. 50 is the Gunnison River, which produces trophy-class brown and rainbow trout.

GOLF   The 18-hole **Montrose Golf Course,** 1350 Birch St. (☎ **970/ 249-8551**), is open year-round, weather permitting. Greens fees are $14 for 9 holes and $20 for 18 holes.

HIKING   The best hiking in the area is in the Black Canyon of the Gunnison National Monument (see above), but there are also paved paths in town (see "Biking," above) and plenty of trails on nearby national forest and BLM lands. These include the 4½-mile Ute Trail along the Gunnison River, 20 miles northeast of Montrose; and the 17-mile Alpine Trail from Silver Jack Reservoir in Uncompahgre National Forest, 35 miles southeast of Montrose via Cimarron on U.S. 50. Contact the Public Lands Center (see above) for information.

WHERE TO STAY

Rates here are usually highest in July and August, and lowest from November through April. Room tax is just under 9%. In addition to the properties discussed below, Montrose also has a **Comfort Inn,** 2100 E. Main St. (☎ 800/228-5151 or

970/240-8000), with rates for two of $45 to $73; **Days Inn,** 1655 E. Main St. (☎ 800/329-7466 or 970/249-3411), with double rates from $40 to $65; **Holiday Inn Express,** 1391 S. Townsend Ave. (☎ 800/465-4329 or 970/240-1800), with rates for two from $79 to $149; and **Super 8,** 1705 E. Main St. (☎ 800/800-8000 or 970/249-9294), with double rates from $40 to $59.

Best Western Red Arrow Motor Inn. 1702 E. Main St. (P.O. Box 236), Montrose, CO 81402. ☎ **800/468-9323** or 970/249-9641. Fax 970/249-8380. E-mail: redarrow@gwe.net. 60 units. A/C TV TEL. $76–$109. Children under 12 stay free in parents' room. Rates include continental breakfast. AE, CB, DC, DISC, MC, V.

The Red Arrow is a large two-story building near the east end of town. Spacious rooms, most with firm queen beds, have coffeemakers, bathrobes, and hair dryers. A handful of "spa rooms" have large whirlpool tubs. Amenities include a solarium with a hot tub and fitness center, outdoor pool, playground and picnic area, guest laundry, conference space for 360, and courtesy transportation. The adjoining restaurant serves three meals daily.

Western Motel. 1200 E. Main St. (at Stough Ave.), Montrose, CO 81401. ☎ **800/ 445-7301** or 970/249-3481. Fax 970/249-3471. 28 units. A/C TV TEL. Memorial Day–Labor Day, $48–$58 double; Labor Day to mid-Nov, $40–$46 double; Mid-Nov to Memorial Day, $36–$45 double. Family units $52–$90. AE, DC, DISC, MC, V.

A one-story redbrick building with a two-story annex, this pleasant motel offers cozy, clean, and comfortable rooms with good-size desks. A few family rooms and waterbed rooms are available, and most units have door-front parking. VCRs are available to rent, and there's free coffee in the lobby. Facilities include a heated outdoor pool, open in summer.

CAMPING

In addition to the campgrounds in Black Canyon of the Gunnison National Monument mentioned above, we recommend the following.

The Hangin' Tree R.V. Park. 17250 U.S. 550 S., Montrose, CO 81401. ☎ **970/249-9966.** 25 sites. $13–$19.50. AE, DISC, MC, V.

A conveniently located campground, open year-round, the Hangin' Tree has tent sites and large pull-through RV sites. Bathhouses are exceptionally clean, but there are no private dressing areas. There's also a self-service laundry, convenience store, and 24-hour gas station. The campground is just a short walk from Chipeta Lakes, with excellent trout fishing.

WHERE TO DINE

A good bet for those seeking groceries, deli sandwiches, a bakery, or a buy-by-the-pound salad bar is one of the two **City Market** grocery stores in Montrose, at 128 S. Townsend Ave., and 16400 S. Townsend Ave. For information call ☎ **970/ 249-3405**.

Glenn Eyrie Restaurant. 2351 S. Townsend Ave. ☎ **970/249-9263.** Reservations recommended. Main courses $9.75–$24. AE, CB, DC, DISC, MC, V. Tues–Sat 5–9pm. CONTINENTAL/AMERICAN.

This small, cozy restaurant is lodged in a colonial farmhouse on the south end of town. In summer, guests can dine outdoors in the garden; in winter, folks seek tables near the large central fireplace. Just about everything is made in-house, including rolls, jams, and sauces. Many items, such as fruits, herbs, and greens, are grown on the grounds. Owner/chef Steve Schwathe changes the menu frequently to reflect the seasons and availability of fresh ingredients, but choices might include whole rack of lamb, which is grilled, then slow-baked, and served with a sauce of tomato, rosemary, and garlic; or steak Diane, a butterflied beef tenderloin steak that is flamed tableside in a mustard, applejack brandy, and cream sauce, and served with mushrooms and artichoke hearts. There are also fresh seafood selections, vegetarian dishes, and a children's menu.

The Whole Enchilada. 44 S. Grand Ave., near W. Main St. ☎ **970/249-1881.** Main courses $3–$6 lunch, $3–$12 dinner. AE, MC, V. Mon–Sat 11am–10pm, Sun noon–9pm. Closes 1 hour earlier in winter. MEXICAN.

Come to this local favorite for well-prepared standard Mexican fare, such as burritos, tostadas, fajitas, and tacos. Those seeking a bit more adventure might opt for enchiladas Acapulco (corn tortillas stuffed with chicken, black olives, almonds, and cheese), or from the "Not for Gringos" section of the menu, the El Paso chimichanga (a fried flour tortilla filled with beef and jalapeños, and smothered in green chile sauce). Also available are a variety of burgers and a children's menu. The restaurant is locally famous for its margaritas, and a delightful outdoor patio is open in summer.

13 Southwestern Colorado

A land apart from the rest of the state, Southwestern Colorado is set off by the spectacular mountain wall of the San Juan Range. The ancestral Puebloans (also called Anasazi) who once lived here created cliff dwellings that more closely resemble structures found in New Mexico and Arizona than anything you might expect to see in Colorado. The ancient cliff dwellings of Mesa Verde National Park are a case in point, and there are similar but less well-known sites throughout the area, primarily around Cortez.

Durango is the area's major city. Its vintage main street (circa 1880) and narrow-gauge railroad hearken back to the Old West days of the late 19th century, when it boomed as a transportation center for the region's silver and gold mines. Telluride, at the end of a box canyon surrounded by 14,000-foot peaks, has capitalized on its highly evident mining heritage in its evolution as a major ski and summer resort. And those who drive the Million Dollar Highway—down U.S. 550 from Ouray, over 11,008-foot Red Mountain Pass through Silverton, and on past the Purgatory Resort to Durango—can't miss the remains of turn-of-the-century mines scattered over the mountainsides.

1 Durango

332 miles SW of Denver, 169 miles S of Grand Junction, 50 miles N of Farmington, New Mexico

Born as a railroad town more than a century ago, Durango remains a railroad town to this day, as thousands of visitors take a journey back in time aboard the Durango & Silverton Narrow Gauge Railroad. Durango was founded in 1880 when the Denver & Rio Grande Railroad line was extended to Silverton to haul precious metals from high-country mines. Within a year, 2,000 new residents had turned the town into a smelting and transportation center. Although more than $300 million worth of silver, gold, and other minerals rode along the route over the years, the unstable nature of the mining business gave the town many ups and downs. One of the "ups" occurred in 1915, when southern Colorado boy Jack Dempsey, then 20, won $50 in a 10-round boxing match at the Central Hotel. Dempsey went on to become the world heavyweight champion.

Durango remained a small center for ranching and mining into the 1960s. In 1965, with the opening of the Purgatory ski resort,

25 miles north of Durango, a tourism boom began. When the railroad abandoned its tracks from Antonito, Colorado, to Durango in the late 1960s, leaving only the Durango–Silverton spur, the town panicked. But from that potential economic disaster blossomed a savior. The Durango & Silverton Narrow Gauge Railroad is now Durango's biggest attraction, hauling more than 200,000 passengers each summer. Durango also attracts mountain-biking enthusiasts from all over the country—in fact, opportunities abound for outdoor activities of all kinds, from river rafting to trout fishing.

ESSENTIALS

GETTING THERE   By Car   Durango is located at the crossroads of east–west U.S. 160 and north-south U.S. 550.

By Plane   Durango/La Plata County Airport, 14 miles southeast of Durango off Colo. 172 (☎ **970/247-8143**), has direct daily nonstop service from Denver, Phoenix, and in winter, Dallas/Fort Worth, with connections to cities throughout North America. The airport is served by **America West Express** (☎ **800/ 247-5692**) and **United Express** (☎ **800/241-6522** or 970/259-5178).

VISITOR INFORMATION   Contact the **Durango Area Chamber Resort Association,** 111 S. Camino del Rio (P.O. Box 2587), Durango, CO 81302 (☎ **800/525-8855** or 970/247-0312; www.durango.org; e-mail: durango@ frontier.net). The chamber's **visitor center** is just south of downtown, on U.S. 160/550 opposite the intersection of East Eighth Avenue. From June through October, it's open Monday through Friday from 8am to 7pm, Saturday from 10am to 7pm, and Sunday from noon to 7pm; the rest of the year, from 8am to 5pm daily.

GETTING AROUND   The city is situated on the banks of the south-flowing Animas River. U.S. 160 lies along the southern edge, and is joined by U.S. 550 about 5 miles east of Durango. U.S. 550 branches north at the river as Camino del Rio, and junctions with Main Avenue at 14th Street. Downtown Durango is built around Main Avenue from 14th Street south to Fifth Street. College Drive (Sixth Street) is the principal downtown cross street.

Transportation throughout Durango is provided by **The Durango Lift** (☎ **970/ 259-5438**). The **city bus** has three fixed-route loops that operate weekdays, from about 7am to 7pm, year-round (closed major public holidays). The fare is 50¢ per ride one-way. Also part of the Durango Lift is the **Durango Trolley** (☎ **970/ 259-5438**), which runs up and down Main Avenue every 30 minutes, seven days a week, year-round. In summer it operates from 6am to 10pm; winter hours are 7am to 7pm. Cost is 25¢. Bus and trolley schedules and route maps are available at the visitor center (see above).

Taxi service is provided 24 hours a day by **Durango Transportation** (☎ 970/ 259-4818). Car-rental agencies include **Avis** (☎ 970/247-9761), **Dollar** (☎ 970/ 259-3012), **Enterprise** (☎ 970/259-8570), and **National** (☎ 970/259-0068).

FAST FACTS   There's a 24-hour emergency room at **Centura Health–Mercy Medical Center,** 375 E. Park Ave. (☎ **970/247-4311**). For **winter driving conditions,** call ☎ 970/247-3355, and for a **weather forecast** and ski conditions, call ☎ 970/247-0930.

SPECIAL EVENTS   Snowdown!, late January; Iron Horse Bicycle Classic, Memorial Day weekend; Animas River Days, last weekend in June; Music in the Mountains, in Purgatory, July; La Plata County Fair, August; the Durango Cowboy Gathering, October; and the Durango Choral Society Christmas Program, December.

Southwestern Colorado

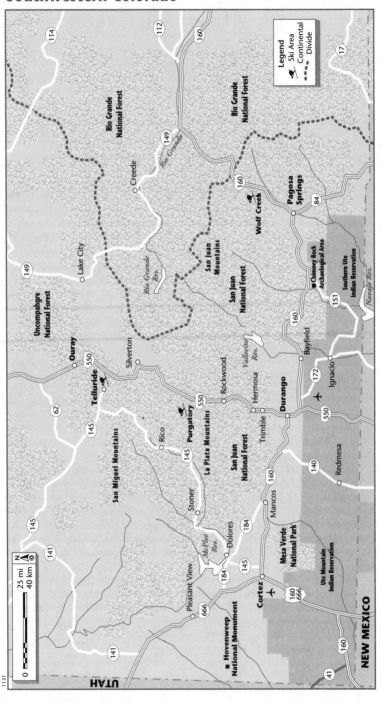

THE TOP ATTRACTION

✪ **The Durango & Silverton Narrow Gauge Railroad.** 479 Main Ave., Durango, CO 81301. ☎ **888/872-4607** or 970/247-2733. www.durango.com/train. Advance reservations strongly advised. Summer, round-trip fare $49.10 adults, $24.65 children 5–11; $84.50 for the parlor car (minimum age 21). Winter Train, round-trip fare $41.55 adults, $20.80 children 5–11; $69.45 for the parlor car. Parking $7 per day per car, $9 for RVs and buses.

Colorado's most famous train has been in continual operation since 1881. In all that time, its route has never varied: up the *Rio de las Animas Perdidas* (River of Lost Souls), through 45 miles of mountain and San Juan National Forest wilderness to the historic mining town of Silverton, and back. The coal-fired steam locomotives pull strings of gold-colored Victorian coaches on the 3,000-foot climb, past relics of mining and railroad activity from the last century.

The trip takes 3¼ hours each way, with a 2-hour stopover in the picturesque town of Silverton before the return trip. You can also overnight in Silverton and return to Durango the following day. (For information on what to see and do during your layover, see "A Side Trip to Silverton," below). Stops are made for water, and also for hikers and fishermen at trailheads inaccessible by road. Refreshments and snacks are available on all trains; the first-class Parlor Car has a bar. Several private cars are available for charter, including an 1886 caboose and the 1878 *Nomad*—believed to be the oldest operating private car in the world, host of U.S. presidents from Taft to Ford.

The summer schedule runs from early May through October, making the full trip to Silverton and back to Durango, with several trains daily during the peak season, from early June through mid-August, and fewer trains at other times. What's called the Winter Train runs to Cascade Canyon and back to Durango (52 miles round-trip) for several days around Thanksgiving and from mid-December through early May (except Christmas), leaving at 10am.

OTHER DURANGO HIGHLIGHTS

While taking a steam-train trip on the Durango & Silverton Narrow Gauge Railroad is undeniably the area's top attraction, it is by far not the only thing to do here. Those interested in a close-up view of the city's numerous historic buildings will want to pick up free copies of several **Walking Tour** brochures from the visitor center (see above) or Animas Museum (see below). Along Main Avenue you'll see the handsome **Strater Hotel,** the building that housed the region's first bank, and the sites of saloons and other businesses of the late 1800s and early 1900s; while walking down Third Avenue you'll pass several stone churches and some of the finest homes in Durango from the same period, including the house where silent movie star Harold Lloyd lived during part of his childhood.

Animas Museum. 31st St. and W. Second Ave. ☎ **970/259-2402.** Admission $2 adults, free for children under 12. May–Oct, Mon–Sat 10am–6pm; call for winter hours.

An old stone schoolhouse in north Durango is the home of the La Plata County Historical Society museum, so it's appropriate that a turn-of-the-century classroom is one of its central displays. There is also a restored 1870s log cabin from the early days of Animas City, the town that predated Durango, as well as exhibits depicting local history, American Indians (including a display of Navajo weavings), and the American West. The museum shop has a good selection of new and used books on regional history and culture, Indian arts and crafts, and unique gifts.

Children's Museum of Durango. 802 E. Second Ave., upstairs at the Arts Center. ☎ **970/259-9234**. Admission $1 adults, $2 children, free for seniors. Wed, Thurs, Sat 10am–2pm.

Southwestern Colorado on the Silver Screen

This area is John Wayne country, where the Duke slugged it out, shot it out, and sometimes yelled it out as he tamed the West on American movie screens from the late 1920s through the 1970s. It was also the location shoot for the multi-Oscar–winning 1969 hit, *Butch Cassidy and the Sundance Kid,* starring Robert Redford and Paul Newman. More recently, it hosted *City Slickers,* the 1991 comedy starring Billy Crystal as a hapless city dweller on an Old West–style cattle drive.

Movie critics may argue the point, but to many Americans, the king of them all was the Duke—none other than John Wayne. This bigger-than-life symbol of American manhood made numerous films in and around Gunnison, Ridgway, Delta, Durango, and Pagosa Springs, where you can still find the exact spots certain scenes were filmed.

The classic, if bleak, 1956 John Ford film *The Searchers,* with Wayne, Jeffrey Hunter, Vera Miles, and Ward Bond, used a ranch near Gunnison as a military outpost. To reach the ranch, go north from Gunnison for 3 miles on Colo. 135, then turn left onto Ohio Creek Road and drive for about 8 miles, where you'll see a barn and several other buildings off to the left. Ford's later western *How the West Was Won* (which, to the great disappointment of Wayne fans, didn't include the Duke) shows a wagon train crossing the Gunnison River west of Delta along 1800 Road, as well as scenes of the Durango & Silverton Narrow Gauge Railroad.

As real John Wayne aficionados know, in 1969 he teamed with Glen Campbell and Kim Darby to make one of his most famous films, *True Grit.* The town of Ridgway becomes Fort Smith in the movie, and nearby is the ranch where Wayne jumps his horse over a river. (Contact the Montrose Chamber of Commerce for directions if you'd like to find it.) *The Cowboys,* filmed in 1972 outside Pagosa Springs, finds Wayne as a cattleman who hires a group of schoolboys to drive his

---

Hands-on activities for children from pre-school through pre-teen make a nice break for vacationing kids who have seen too many Victorian homes. Parents stay with and supervise their children while the kids enjoy the wood shop, mini-grocery store, puppet theater, dress-up area, and physics demonstrations including magnets and optical illusions. One of the most popular activities is the watershed, where children see how water rushing downhill creates channels and floods—the best part about this supposedly educational activity is that the kids are encouraged to play in the muck! There are also computer games, arts and crafts, and an archeology section; various workshops and special events are planned.

Durango & Silverton Narrow Gauge Railroad Museum. 479 Main Ave. ☎ **888/872-4607** or 970/247-2733. Admission $5 adults ($4 with a train ticket), $2.50 children under 12 ($2 with a train ticket). Yard tours (including museum admission) $7.50 adults, $3.75 children 5–11. Daily 7am–8pm; tours daily at 3pm.

The glory days of steam trains come alive here, where you can climb up into a full-size locomotive, a caboose, parlor car, and other rolling stock to get a close-up view. The large and well-lit museum also houses a vast amount of railroad memorabilia, from conductors' uniforms, watches, and belt buckles to lanterns, railroad art, and historic photos. Located in the Durango & Silverton rail yard, the museum is also the starting point for 1-hour guided yard tours that provide a behind-the-scenes look at a working railroad, with stops in the round house, machine shop, rail car restoration areas, yard, and museum.

herd of 1,500 cattle after the gold rush lures away his crew. There are two location shoots from this film in the area. From the Pagosa Springs Chamber of Commerce, take U.S. 160 west about 3½ miles to Upper Piedra Road. Turn right and travel about 10 miles to Jack Pasture Road; then turn left and go about 2 miles, where filming was done on both sides of the road. After returning to Upper Piedra Road, turn left and go about 5½ miles; scenes were shot along the left side of the road.

But Wayne wasn't the only one shooting up Colorado's southwest corner. Several movie companies have made use of the area, particularly the classic Durango & Silverton Narrow Gauge Railroad. The best train scene has to be the one in *Butch Cassidy and the Sundance Kid,* where Butch, Sundance, and their gang attempt to blow open the train's safe and instead blow up the entire mail car, sending money flying in all directions. Reportedly the extent of this explosion was a surprise to everyone, even the special-effects technicians who apparently were a bit too liberal with their use of black powder. You can see the train at the depot at 479 Main Ave. in Durango, or in summer hop aboard for a ride to Silverton and back. There's a plaque commemorating the filming about 10 miles east of Durango; ask at the chamber of commerce for directions. The chamber can also give directions to two area ranches used in *City Slickers.*

Some of these locations are on private property, and some are difficult to find. For details, contact the chambers of commerce or visitor information centers in each of the communities. And, if you're interested in being in a film yourself, the **Colorado Film Commission** in Denver operates a recorded bulletin board that lists film projects underway in the state that may be hiring crew members (☎ **303/ 620-4567**; www.coloradofilm.org).

The Grand Motorcar & Piano Collection. 586 Animas View Dr. ☎ **970/247-1250.** www.grandmotorcar.com. Admission $6 adults, $4 children 14 and under, $5 seniors. May–Oct, daily 9am–7pm; slightly shorter hours in winter.

This museum and auto showroom houses about 30 fine classic cars, including exotic luxury models and independents such as Hudson, Hupmobile, and Nash. Most cars here are from the 1930s and 1940s, although there are also some more recent classics. The cars are all in pristine condition—many with very low original mileage—and all are ready to drive coast to coast at the turn of an ignition key. They're all for sale (don't forget your checkbook), so the selection is constantly changing, but you're likely to see a Packard convertible, an early 1930s Hudson coupe, a pre–World War II Buick, or possibly an early 1950s DeSoto. The museum also has several grand pianos on display, and a shop sells rare old automobile magazines and other literature.

SPORTS & OUTDOOR ACTIVITIES

In addition to contacting the various companies listed below, you can arrange for most activities through the **Durango Area Chamber Resort Association** (☎ **800/ 525-8855** or 970/247-0312). The **Durango Parks and Recreation Department** (☎ **970/385-2950**) operates about 20 parks throughout the city, where you'll find picnic areas, free tennis courts, a swimming pool, and other facilities.

ALPINE SLIDE The **Purgatory Alpine Slide** (☎ 970/247-9000) is open from Memorial Day to Labor Day, weather permitting (call for hours). You ride the chairlift up, then come down the mountain in a chute on a self-controlled sled. Cost is $8 per ride or $35 for an all-day pass.

BOATING Lakes in the Durango area include 6-mile-long Vallecito Lake, 22 miles east via County Roads 240 and 501. Among marinas where you can rent boats and fishing equipment is **Angler's Wharf,** 17250 County Rd. 501 (☎ 970/884-9477), on the lake's west shore. Small fishing boats with outboard motors cost $40 for 4 hours or $60 for 8 hours; large pontoon boats rent for $35 per hour or $150 for an 8-hour day. The marina also has moorings, a tackle shop, and a snack bar. For additional information about activities at the lake, contact the **Vallecito Lake Chamber of Commerce** (☎ 970/884-9782).

Forty miles southeast of Durango on Colo. 151, the village of Arboles is the northern gateway to Navajo State Park, a 37-mile-long reservoir that spans the Colorado–New Mexico border. **San Juan Marina** (☎ 970/883-2343) has rental boats, supplies, fuel, a launch ramp, Colorado and New Mexico fishing licenses, and a cafe. Fishing boats with small outboards cost $35 for 4 hours or $60 for 8 hours; runabouts with 120-horsepower motors and 24-foot pontoon boats are $90 for 4 hours or $140 for 8 hours. The marina also rents fully equipped houseboats from 36 to 50 feet, with prices from $302 to $829 for 3 days and 2 nights.

FISHING Vallecito Lake (see "Boating," above) is a prime spot for rainbow trout, brown trout, kokanee salmon, and northern pike. Navajo State Park (see "Boating," above) also has good fishing, especially for huge northern pike and catfish, but although the park is in Colorado, much of the lake is in New Mexico, thus a New Mexico fishing license is required.

To buy Colorado fishing licenses and supplies, get information on the best areas to fish, or arrange for a guided fly-fishing trip, stop in at **Duranglers,** 801-B Main Ave. (☎ 970/385-4081; www.duranglers.com), or **Durango Fly Goods,** 139 E. Fifth St. (☎ 970/259-0999; fax 970/259-8426; www.durangoflygoods.com). Full-day float trips for two people cost about $300; wading trips for two cost about $275. Lunch is included.

GLIDER RIDES For a quiet, airborne look at Durango and the San Juan Mountains, take a glider ride with **Durango Soaring Club** (☎ 970/247-9037), located 3 miles north of Durango on U.S. 550. Rides are given daily from May 15 through September; 1998 rates were $75 for 25 minutes and $135 for 50-minutes.

GOLF Two public 18-hole golf courses open in April, weather permitting. In Durango, there's **Hillcrest Golf Course,** 2300 Rim Dr., adjacent to Fort Lewis College (☎ 970/247-1499), with greens fees of $10 for 9 holes and $17 for 18 holes; and **Dalton Ranch and Golf Club,** 589 Trimble Lane (County Rd. 252), 6 miles north of Durango via U.S. 550 (☎ 970/247-8774), charging $25 for 9 holes and $45 for 18 holes.

HIKING & BACKPACKING Durango is at the western end of the 500-mile Colorado Trail to Denver. The trailhead is 3½ miles up Junction Creek Road, an extension of 25th Street west of Main Avenue. There are numerous other trails in the Durango area, including paths into the Weminuche Wilderness Area reached via the Durango & Silverton railroad. For information, contact the Animas Ranger District, San Juan National Forest (☎ 970/247-4874), or the Bureau of Land Management (☎ 970/247-4082), both at 701 Camino del Rio.

HORSEBACK RIDING To see this spectacular country as the pioneers did, arrange for a short horseback ride or a 2- to 6-day expedition into the San Juan

National Forest or Weminuche Wilderness. Licensed outfitters include **Southfork Riding Stables and Outfitters, Inc.,** 5 miles south of Durango at 28481 U.S. 160 E. (☎ **970/259-4871**), which provides year-round horseback rides lasting from an hour to multi-day wilderness pack trips. Prices start at $18 for a 1-hour ride; a full day in the saddle costs about $85. You can also join in a cattle drive for a little under $200 per day, and breakfast rides and sunset supper rides are offered as well.

LLAMA TREKKING   Guided llama trips, overnight pack trips, and llama leasing are the specialty of **Buckhorn Llama Co.** (☎ **800/318-9454** or 970/667-7411; www.llamapack.com). Pack trips start at $150 per person per day; call for rates for shorter trips and additional information.

MOUNTAIN BIKING   The varied terrain and myriad trails of San Juan National Forest have made Durango a nationally known mountain-biking center. The Colorado Trail (see "Hiking & Backpacking," above), Hermosa Creek Trail (beginning 11 miles north of Durango off U.S. 550), and La Plata Canyon Road (beginning 11 miles west of Durango off U.S. 160) are among favorite jaunts. For information on mountain-biking trails in the area, contact the Animas Ranger District, San Juan National Forest, or the Bureau of Land Management (see above).

You can also get information and rent mountain bikes at **Southwest Adventures,** 12th Street and Camino del Rio (☎ **800/642-5389** or 970/259-0370; www.frontier.net/~mtnguide). Bike rentals cost $15 for a half day or $25 for a full day. Southwest also offers guided and unguided tours, both downhill and traditional, starting at $38 unguided and $45 guided for a half day. Guided trips include bike, transportation, and guide; unguided rides include bike, transportation, and a map. Southwest Adventures also offers shuttle services. Bike rentals and related services are also provided, at about the same rates, from **Mountain Bike Specialists,** 949 Main Ave. (☎ **970/247-4066**), and **Hassle Free Sports,** 2615 Main Ave. (☎ **800/835-3800** or 970/259-3874; www.hasslefreesports.com).

MOUNTAINEERING & ROCK CLIMBING   A variety of terrain offers mountaineering and rock- and ice-climbing opportunities for beginners as well as advanced climbers. Guided tours and instruction are offered by **Southwest Adventures** (see above), with rates starting at $50 for a half-day rock-climbing course, and $190 for the first person ($45 for each additional person) per day for a 3-day mountaineering course.

RIVER RAFTING   The three stages of the Animas River provide excitement for rafters of all experience and ability levels. The churning Class IV and V rapids of the upper Animas mark its rapid descent from the San Juan Range. The 6 miles from Trimble Hot Springs into downtown Durango are an easy, gently rolling rush. Downstream from Durango, the river is mainly Classes II and III, promising a few thrills but mostly relaxation.

Most of the many outfitters in Durango offer a wide variety, such as 1- and 2-hour raft trips that cost $10 to $30 for adults and $5 to $15 for kids, full-day river trips costing $55 to $65 for adults and $50 to $55 for kids, and overnight guided excursions starting at about $200 per person. Local rafting companies include **Durango Rivertrippers** (☎ 800/292-2885 or 970/259-0289; www.durangorivertrippers.com), **Flexible Flyers** (☎ 970/247-4628), **Mild to Wild Rafting** (☎ 800/567-6745 or 970/247-4789; www.mild2wildrafting.com), **Rivers West** (☎ 800/622-0852 or 970/259-5077), and **Southwest Whitewater** (☎ 800/989-9792 or 970/259-8313), which offers both raft and kayak trips. Also providing trips down the Animas River in an inflatable kayak is **Mountain Waters Rafting** (☎ 800/748-2507 or 970/259-4191), which offers kayak trips at $38 for a half day.

RODEO　From early June through the third week of August, the **Durango Pro Rodeo** series takes place every Tuesday and Wednesday night starting at 7:30pm at the La Plata County Fairgrounds, Main Avenue and 25th Street (☎ **970/ 247-1666**). Admission costs $12 for adults and $5 for kids 12 and under. The **All-Women Rodeo,** billed as the only all-women rodeo in Colorado, takes place on Fourth of July weekend; the **All-Indian Rodeo** is planned on Labor Day weekend.

SWIMMING & MINERAL BATHS　**Trimble Hot Springs,** 6 miles north of Durango just off U.S. 550 (☎ **970/247-0111**), at the junction of County Road 203 and Trimble Lane, is a national historic site dating back more than 100 years, where you'll often find Mom and Dad relaxing in the soothing mineral pools or getting a massage while the kids have fun in the adjacent swimming pool. Facilities include two natural hot-springs therapy pools, a separate Olympic-size swimming pool (heated by the hot springs but not containing hot-springs water), massage and therapy rooms, a snack bar, picnic area, and gardens. Water from the natural hot springs comes out of the ground at 118 to 120 degrees Fahrenheit, and the therapy pools are kept at a more comfortable temperature of 102 to 108 degrees. The swimming pool is usually about 85 degrees. The complex is open daily from 8am to 11pm in summer, from 9am to 10pm in winter. Day passes cost $7 for adults and $5 for children 12 and younger, which covers use of the therapy mineral pools and the swimming pool. Rates for therapeutic massage start at $35 for a half hour; also available are herbal oil wraps, face and scalp treatments, dry body brush, and radiant salt glow (call for rates).

WINTER SPORTS　Some 25 miles north of Durango on U.S. 550, ✪ **Purgatory Resort,** 1 Skier Place, Durango, CO 81301 (☎ **800/525-0892** or 970/ 247-9000; fax 970/385-2131; www.ski-purg.com), has a reputation of getting more sunshine than any other Colorado resort. Surprisingly, the sun doesn't come at the expense of snow: Average annual snowfall is 240 inches. There are 1,200 acres of skiable terrain (745 groomed acres), with 75 trails rated 23% beginner, 51% intermediate, and 26% advanced, and eleven lifts (one high-speed quad, four triples, four doubles, one surface lift, and one Magic Carpet). The mountain has a vertical drop of 2,029 feet from a summit elevation of 10,822 feet.

Snowboarders are welcome on all lifts and trails, and a snowboard park offers jumps, slides, and a quarter-pipe. The Purgatory Cross-Country Ski Center offers 16 kilometers (10 miles) of trails for Nordic skiers.

Three on-mountain restaurants complement the facilities of Purgatory Village, which include a hotel, condominiums, several restaurants and taverns, shops, and equipment rentals. All-day lift tickets (1998–99 rates) are $43 for adults, $21 for children 6 to 12, $25 for seniors 62 to 69, and free for kids 5 and younger and seniors 70 and older. Purgatory is usually open from Thanksgiving to mid-April, daily from 9am to 4pm.

SHOPPING

You'll find some of your best shopping opportunities in southwest Colorado in downtown Durango, along Main Avenue from the Durango & Silverton Railroad Depot north to 10th Street. Here, interspersed among restaurants and historic hotels, are shops selling a wide variety of items—ranging from custom-made western hats to kitchen gizmos to fine porcelain and imported gifts. And yes, there are plenty of tacky T-shirts, as well.

One of our favorite shops is the **Durango Cat Company,** 600 Main Ave., #208, at College Drive (☎ **970/247-4045**), where everything is cat-related. You can easily find the perfect (or is that purr-fect?) gift for the cat-fancier in your life. Those seeking the region's premier art gallery will have to leave Main Avenue, but it's not far to **Toh-Atin Gallery,** 145 W. Ninth St. (☎ **800/525-0384** or 970/247-8277). Specializing in original southwestern and American Indian art, the gallery stocks Navajo weavings, bronze and alabaster sculptures, original paintings, pueblo pottery, and handcrafted jewelry.

WHERE TO STAY

Durango has a definite lodging season. When the Durango & Silverton Narrow Gauge Railroad runs most of its trains in mid-summer, expect to pay top dollar for your room, and expect higher rates during the Christmas holidays and in peak ski seasons as well. But go in the off-season—late spring and fall—and you'll find much more reasonable rates.

Among chain and franchise motels offering moderately priced rooms are the **Best Western Mountain Shadows,** 3255 N. Main Ave. (☎ 800/521-5218 or 970/247-5200), charging $57 to $105 double; the **Comfort Inn,** 2930 N. Main Ave. (☎ 800/228-5150 or 970/259-5373), with rates for two of $46 to $105; **Days Inn,** 1700 County Rd. 203 (☎ 800/329-7466 or 970/259-5741), with rates for two of $54 to $99; **Econo Lodge,** 2002 Main Ave. (☎ 800/553-2666 or 970/247-4242), charging $32 to $96 double; **Rodeway Inn,** 2701 Main Ave. (☎ 800/752-6072 or 970/259-2540), with rates for two of $40 to $94; and **Super 8,** 20 Stewart Dr. (☎ 800/800/8000 or 970/259-0590), with rates for two of $40 to $80.

An easy way to book accommodations is to contact the **Durango Area Chamber Resort Association** (☎ **800/525-8855** or 970/247-0312). Room taxes add about 9% to lodging bills.

VERY EXPENSIVE

The Wit's End Guest Ranch & Resort. 254 County Rd. 500, Bayfield, CO 81122. ☎ **970/884-4113.** Fax 970/884-3261. 34 cabins. TV TEL. From $3,990 per week for two guests. Extra person $1,795. Rates include all meals and activities. These rates effective Memorial Day–Labor Day, with 7-day minimum stay. Off-season cabin-only rates available. AE, DISC, MC, V.

A delightful dude ranch encompassing 550 acres in a narrow valley at the head of Vallecito Lake, surrounded by the 12,000- to 14,000-foot peaks of the Weminuche Wilderness, the Wit's End offers guests a unique combination of rustic outdoors and sophisticated luxury. Riding opportunities, other activities, and sports facilities are numerous. The main focus is a beautiful three-story log hunting lodge, dating from the 1870s, with a huge stone fireplace and walls mirrored with cut glass from London's 1853 Crystal Palace.

Log cabins, some dating to the 1870s, have retained their rustic outer appearance, but the knotty-pine interiors have been fully renovated. All have full kitchens, stone fireplaces, queen beds, full bathrooms, porches, and striking views.

Dining/Diversions: Dinner and drinks are served in the Old Lodge at the Lake Restaurant and Colorado Tavern. All meals are included in the full American plan package for resort guests, and are not open to the general public. Filet mignon, roast duckling, chicken Culbertson, and other hearty American dishes are served, with fine dining three evenings each week and outdoor western cookouts the other nights. The Game Room, on the second floor, has an antique billiards table.

Amenities: Room service, pool (summer only), several spas, tennis courts, volleyball, horseshoes, mountain bikes, children's programs, trout-fishing and fly-fishing instruction (five spring-fed ponds), winter sports equipment. Additional charge for hunting and fishing packages, snowmobile rental, private horseback-riding lessons, private boat rentals, trap shooting, massages, and airport transportation. Guided hiking, horseback riding, and motor-touring are also available.

EXPENSIVE

Purgatory Village Hotel. Purgatory Resort, 5 Skier Place, Durango, CO 81301. ☎ **800/ 693-0175** or 970/383-2100. Fax 970/382-2248. www.ski-purg.com. 155 units. TV TEL. Summer $65–$75 double; $85–$290 condo. Winter $90–$125 double; $100–$585 condo; higher for holidays. Weekly rates available Apr–Nov. AE, DISC, MC, V.

This ski-in/ski-out hotel at Purgatory Resort, 25 miles north of Durango, is located at the base of the mountain, surrounded by a village offering shops, bars, restaurants, and just about everything skiers want.

A variety of room types are available, both in the hotel building itself and in adjacent condominiums. Most rooms, regardless of size, have a kitchen, fireplace, and private deck, as well as a "snow room" with a ski locker. Standard one- and two-bedroom condominiums have whirlpool baths and/or steam showers, classic furnishings, and full kitchens. Efficiency units make ultimate use of space with a Murphy bed that doubles as a dining table.

The hotel restaurant offers continental dining, evenings during the winter and summer seasons. A cafeteria and lounge serves three meals daily. The pub adjacent to the hotel offers pizza and live music for dancing. Baby-sitting can be arranged; amenities include a concierge, activities desk, sports shop, rental shop, indoor/outdoor pool (summer only), several hot tubs, and guest laundry.

✪ **Rochester Hotel.** 726 E. Second Ave. (write to 721 E. Second Ave.), Durango, CO 81301. ☎ **800/664-1920** or 970/385-1920. Fax 970/385-1967. www.creativelinks.com/rochester. E-mail: leland@frontier.net. 15 units. AC TV TEL. $125–$195 double. Rates include full breakfast. AE, CB, DC, DISC, MC, V. Pets accepted in two units.

The Old West, and especially our memories of the Old West from Hollywood movies, lives here at the Rochester. Built in 1892, the hotel had become a flophouse by the early 1990s when the Komick family bought and restored the Leland House directly across the street and opened it as a bed-and-breakfast (see below). As they were completing work on the Leland House, the Komicks took a good look at the Rochester and realized it would scare off potential B&B guests. So they bought the property and began the difficult task of restoration, changing a dilapidated disgrace of 33 small rooms and three bathrooms into an elegant western hotel.

Now listed on the National Register of Historic Places, the Rochester retains the feel of an Old West hotel, with high ceilings, the original trim and hardware, many antiques, historic photos and original western art, and 1890s-style furnishings. But instead of 33 small rooms, there are now 15 spacious rooms, each with its own bathroom (two have whirlpool tubs, one has a tub/shower combo, and the rest have large walk-in showers). Rooms have good, firm queen or king beds; one unit has a king bed and a kitchen. With a decor that might be called "cowboy Victoriana," the hotel's hallways are lined with posters and photos from many of the films shot in the area, including *City Slickers, Support Your Local Gunfighter, Butch Cassidy and the Sundance Kid, How the West Was Won,* and *The Cowboys.*

Although technically a hotel, the Rochester is run more like a large bed-and-breakfast inn, with an innkeeper on hand to act as concierge. Breakfasts include fresh-baked muffins, scones, or breads, a selection of fruit, oatmeal, cold cereals, yogurt, and beverages, plus a hot entree such as pumpkin pancakes with honey butter, huevos rancheros, or multi-grain waffles with cream and berries. Fresh-baked cookies and other refreshments are also provided in the evening. Smoking is not permitted.

✪ **Strater Hotel.** 699 Main Ave. (P.O. Drawer E), Durango, CO 81302. ☎ **800/247-4431** or 970/247-4431. Fax 970/259-2208. www.strater.com. 93 units. AC TV TEL. Mid-May–mid-Oct and Christmas holidays $159–$195 double; mid-Oct–mid-May $94–$149 double. Rates include full breakfast. AE, DC, DISC, MC, V.

Durango's most famous hotel, the four-story red-brick Strater is an exceptional example of American Victorian architecture. Built in 1887 by Henry H. Strater, a prominent druggist of the mining-boom era, the hotel boasts its original ornamental brickwork and white-stone cornices. Crystal chandeliers and a variety of ornate woodworking styles grace the public areas, along with intricately carved columns and anaglyphic ceiling designs. It has been in the Barker family (Rod Barker is the current CEO) since 1926.

Spread throughout the guest rooms is one of the world's largest collections of American Victorian walnut antiques, and even the wallpaper is authentic to the 1880s. One of the most popular units is Room 222, a corner room directly over the Diamond Belle Saloon, where prolific author Louis L'Amour gave life to his western heroes. The modern bathrooms all have hair dryers; 77 have tub/shower combos and 16 have showers only.

Employees—many who have been with the Strater for years—seem to take a personal interest in the happiness of each guest, and manage to be attentive and friendly without falling into the trap of becoming too chummy. Amenities include a concierge, limited room service, valet laundry, complimentary newspaper delivery, complimentary airport transportation, valet parking, and a business center. The hotel also offers a Victorian-style hot tub, by reservation only. Guests of the Strater from Thanksgiving through New Year's are treated to a display of Victorian Christmas decorations, plus complimentary homemade cookies. Henry's restaurant serves three meals daily in an elegant atmosphere (see "Where to Dine," below). The Diamond Belle Saloon has live ragtime piano, and the hotel's theater presents summer melodrama (see "Durango After Dark," below).

MODERATE

The Leland House Bed & Breakfast Suites. 721 E. Second Ave., Durango, CO 81301. ☎ 800/664-1920 or 970/385-1920. Fax 970/385-1967. www.creativelinks.com/rochester. E-mail: leland@frontier.net. 10 units. AC TV TEL. $95–$155. Rates include full breakfast. AE, CB, DC, DISC, MC, V.

Built as an apartment house in 1927 and restored in 1993, the Leland House offers an intriguing mix of lodging types—a comfy bed-and-breakfast inn with early-20th-century decor. Owned by the Komick family, who also own the historic Rochester Hotel across the street (see above), the Leland House contains six suites with sitting rooms and full kitchens, plus four mini-suites with kitchenettes. All have private bathrooms with walk-in showers (no tubs), and are decorated with a compatible combination of good-quality beds, antiques, near-antiques, and contemporary furniture. Rooms are named for historic figures associated with the Leland House and its neighbors, such as Max Baer, world heavyweight boxing champion in the 1930s. Throughout the house are photos, memorabilia, and framed biographies of these individuals, many of whom played significant roles in the development of early Durango.

In the B&B style, you'll find the friendly staff to be service oriented. Breakfasts, which are served across the street at the Rochester, include a selection of fresh-baked goods, fruit, cereals, juice and coffee, plus a hot entree such as orange pancakes, an herb-and-cheese frittata with hash browns and toast, or multi-grain waffles with cream and berries. Fresh-baked cookies and other refreshments are served in the evening. Smoking is not permitted.

Silver Spur Inn & Suites. 3416 Main Ave., Durango, CO 81301. ☎ **800/748-1715** or 970/247-5552. 37 units. A/C TV TEL. May–Oct $79–$89 double, $120 suite; Nov–Apr $38–$40 double, $70 suite. Rates include continental breakfast. AE, CB, DC, DISC, MC, V.

Surrounded by junipers and pine trees, the Silver Spur is one of Durango's older motels, and was a favorite of actor John Wayne, who stayed in room no. 104 while in town filming *True Grit* and several other movies. A recent extensive renovation combined with reasonable rates make it a good choice for value-minded travelers. All units are clean and comfortable, with modern western decor, including posters from Wayne's movies. Rooms have good-quality beds, fridges, and microwaves; VCRs are available. Seven units have showers only; the rest have shower/tub combos. Amenities include a family restaurant, lounge, limited room service, heated outdoor pool (summer only), and sundeck. Dry-cleaning and in-room massage are available.

WHERE TO DINE
EXPENSIVE

Henry's on Main. In the Strater Hotel, 699 Main Ave. ☎ **970/247-4431.** Reservations recommended. Main courses $13–$29. AE, CB, DC, DISC, MC, V. May–Sept Mon–Sat 6–11am and 11:30am–1:30pm, Sun 6am–1pm; daily 5–9:30pm; slightly shorter hours Oct–Apr. CHOP & STEAK HOUSE.

This elegant restaurant, which continues the Victorian theme of the 1887 Strater Hotel with fine antiques, rich wood trim, and a large stained-glass ceiling, is just as popular with locals as with hotel guests. The breakfast buffet (complimentary for hotel guests, $9.95 for others), which includes cooked-to-order omelets plus an extensive buffet, is the best in the area. The menu offers a good variety, including a number of creative twists on basic American cuisine, and portions are generous. Beef is top-of-the-line midwestern corn fed, and includes the cowboy rib chop (grilled with wild mushrooms, garlic, and sun-dried tomatoes), and a New York steak (prepared with a five-pepper rub and served with a garlic-butter wine sauce). Lamb chops are served with a rosemary and burgundy wine sauce, and the pan-seared duck breast comes with a cherry teriyaki glaze. There's also seafood, such as the Atlantic salmon, wrapped in smoked bacon, oven-roasted, and served with tomato-basil wine sauce; and pasta dishes such as the walnut chicken fettuccine, with tomatoes, chives, and artichoke hearts in walnut creme. The atmosphere is upscale casual and the restaurant is kid-friendly.

MODERATE

Cyprus Cafe. 725 E. Second Ave. ☎ **970/385-6884.** Reservations not accepted. Lunch $6.25–$9.25; dinner $7–$15. AE, DISC, MC, V. Mid-May–Sept, daily 11:30am–3pm and 5–10pm; Oct–mid-May, daily 11:30am–2:30pm and 5–9pm. MEDITERRANEAN.

This tiny restaurant a block from Durango's busy Main Avenue offers a delightful alternative to the basic American and southwestern cuisine that dominates this part of Colorado. Located in what was once the living room of a modest home, the dining room has a simple cafe atmosphere, with ten wood tables, a stained-glass window, and a few pieces of original art. In summer, there's also outdoor patio seating, which more than doubles the restaurant's capacity, with live music usually four evenings a week. Waits of up to a half hour are not uncommon on weekends year-round, so arrive early.

The emphasis is on fresh, with produce from local farms when available, and a menu that is mostly Greek but includes a few other Mediterranean selections. Dinner entrees include spanakopita, kota lemoni (a chargrilled half chicken marinated in lemon and herbs), and Colorado leg of lamb, rolled with herbs and garlic. Those new to Mediterranean cuisine might try the combination appetizer plate that includes hummus, tzajiki, baba ganoush, olives, feta, spanakopita, and grilled pita, and can easily serve several people as an appetizer or one for dinner.

Francisco's Restaurante y Cantina. 619 Main Ave. ☎ **970/247-4098.** Reservations not accepted. Lunch $5.50–$10; dinner $7–$22. AE, CB, DC, DISC, MC, V. Daily 11am–10pm; Sun breakfast 9am. MEXICAN/STEAK/SEAFOOD.

This large come-as-you-are family restaurant, with seating for 250, maintains a festive Mexican atmosphere in an adobe-style building with carved wood and a traditional *viga-y-latilla* ceiling. The menu ranges from south-of-the-border specialties such as enchiladas Durango (two blue-corn tortillas over a bed of beef and green chiles) and carne adovada burritos (marinated pork in a hot chile Caribe sauce) to aged Colorado beef, a good variety of fresh seafood, specialty salads, and a number of pasta and chicken dishes. There's a children's menu, and the bar mixes a killer margarita.

The Palace Restaurant. 505 Main Ave. ☎ **970/247-2018.** Main courses $7–$9 lunch, $14–$24 dinner. AE, MC, V. Daily 11:30am–10:30pm. STEAK/SEAFOOD/PASTA.

Adjacent to the Durango & Silverton Narrow Gauge Railroad terminal, the Palace has a Victorian drawing-room atmosphere, with Tiffany lamps hanging over the tables, historical photos and classic oil paintings on the walls, and a large fireplace. House specialties include the duck, slow roasted with a honey-and-almond sauce; and steak McMahon, a 12-ounce Kansas City cut steak served on hash browns with a roasted garlic sauce and sautéed onions. Locally popular is the chicken and dumplings, served with cranberry compote; and a variety of seafood and pasta dishes are also offered. The Quiet Lady Tavern, named for the headless female sculpture at its entrance, is a beautiful lounge, complete with library.

Steamworks Brewing Co. 801 E. Second Ave. at Eighth St. ☎ **970/259-9200.** Main courses $6–$16; pizza $7–$9 (serves one or two). MC, V. Daily 11am–10pm, pizza served until 11pm. BREWPUB.

Situated in a 1918 building, formerly a car dealership, this brewpub has made the most of the funky, warehouse-like structure. During a renovation, removal of a suspended ceiling exposed huge wooden rafters—there's a 1950s bicycle perched on one of the massive beams—and pipes of all sizes running in all directions. The brewing vats are in the middle of everything, behind glass, and visible from every seat in the house. There's lots of wood—floor, tables, chairs, and a long bar—and booths line a wall that looks out over a patio dining area. The food matches the decor: large, substantial portions to satisfy any appetite. Half-pound burgers come in a variety of choices, such as southwestern, with green chile, Monterey Jack, and a chipotle sauce. There's also a marinated grilled chicken sandwich, grilled reuben, and a veggie sandwich, plus soups and salads. Entrees include enchiladas and burritos, pork chops and ribs, pasta, steak, and chicken. The tasty side salad with Italian vinaigrette dressing practically overflows the plate, and along with a pepperoni pizza was a perfect dinner for two. About a half-dozen of the brewer's beers are usually on tap, including a delightfully bitter pale ale, a light ale, and a mind-clearing stout.

INEXPENSIVE

Carver's Brewing Co. 1022 Main Ave. ☎ **970/259-2545.** Main courses $5.25–$8. Mon–Sat 6:30am–10pm, Sun 6:30am–1pm. AMERICAN.

Carver's was a popular breakfast spot for years, in large part because of its wonderful baked goods; it jumped into another niche in the restaurant world when it opened Durango's first brewpub. Breakfast selections include French toast, prepared with the bakery's own cinnamon bread; lunch specialties include burgers made from locally raised beef, and either beef or vegetarian-style shepherd's pie. On the dinner menu you'll find flatbread pizzas, cheese-filled baked tortellini, and fresh-baked bread bowls filled with soups, stews, or salads. The brewery produces a variety of beers, ranging from fairly light lagers to hearty stouts.

Olde Tymer's Cafe. 10th St. and Main Ave. ☎ **970/259-2990.** Reservations not accepted. Most items $3.50–$9. AE, DISC, MC, V. Daily 11am–10pm. AMERICAN.

This popular local hangout is located in a historic building with the original tin ceiling and antique bottles and tins from the early-20th-century Wall Drugstore once located here. We think its hamburgers—seven ounces of beef in an onion roll—are among the best in Durango. The menu also features homemade chile, a variety of sandwiches, and hearty salads such as the Chinese chicken salad. There are also daily specials, including burger and pasta nights and Mexican meals on weekends. There's patio dining in warm weather.

DURANGO AFTER DARK

During the summer season, the highly acclaimed **Diamond Circle Melodrama,** in the Strater Hotel, 699 Main Ave. (☎ 970/247-3400), presents turn-of-the-century melodrama and professional vaudeville. Tickets are $15 for adults, $12 for children under 12.

For a multimedia production that brings the fascinating history, geology, and scenery of the region to life, drop in for a showing of **Spirit of the Southwest,** in the Abbey Theater, 128 College Dr. (☎ 970/385-1711), with several shows nightly year-round (call for times). Admission costs $5 for adults, $3.50 for seniors and children under 12.

You'll get a tasty meal and a live western stage show at **Bar D Chuckwagon Suppers,** 8080 County Road 250 (☎ 888/800-5753 or 970/247-5753), 9 miles north of Durango via U.S. 550 and Trimble Lane (County Road 252). Open from Memorial Day weekend to mid-September, Bar D offers a choice of roast beef or chicken breast in barbecue sauce, served with baked potato, beans, biscuits, dessert, and coffee or lemonade, served cafeteria-style. The complex, which includes an Old West town of shops and a miniature train, opens at 5:30pm, with supper at 7:30pm, followed by a western show of music and comedy. Reservations are required; cost (including supper and show) is $14 for those 9 and older, and $7 for children under 9.

A SIDE TRIP TO SILVERTON

Silverton calls itself "the mining town that never quit." At an altitude of 9,318 feet at the northern terminus of the Durango & Silverton Narrow Gauge Railroad, the town has a year-round population of about 500. Founded on silver production in 1871, today the entire town is a National Historic Landmark District. In its heyday, Blair Street was such a notorious area of saloons and brothels that no less a character than Bat Masterson, fresh from taming Dodge City, Kansas, was imported to subdue the criminal elements. Today the original false-fronted buildings remain, but they now house restaurants and galleries, and are frequently used as Old West movie sets.

The **San Juan County Historical Society Museum,** in the turn-of-the-century jail on Greene Street at 15th Street (☎ 970/387-5838), displays memorabilia of Silverton's boom days, including mining equipment and minerals, a collection of Derringer handguns, and railroad collectibles. Altogether, there are three floors of historic displays, including the original jail cells, and the gift shop has a variety of books on area history. The museum is open daily, Memorial Day weekend through mid-September from 9am to 5pm, and mid-September through mid-October from 10am to 3pm. Admission is $2.50 for adults and free for children 12 and under. The adjacent San Juan County Courthouse has a gold-domed clock tower, and the restoration of the Town Hall, at 14th and Greene Streets, after a devastating 1993 fire, has won national recognition.

Two guided tours provide a look at the area's mining history. The **Old Hundred Gold Mine** (☎ **800/872-3009** or 970/387-5444; www.minetour.com) is located about 5 miles east of Silverton via Colo. 110, offering an underground tour that starts with a ride 1,600 feet underground in an electric mine train, and continues with a walk through lighted tunnels where you see drilling and mucking demonstrations. There's also gold panning aboveground, plus a gift shop, snack bar, and picnic area. Cost is $11.95 for adults 13 to 60, $5.95 for children 5 to 12 (children under 5 held on a lap are free), and $10.95 for seniors 60 and older. The mine is open mid-May through early October, daily from 10am to 4pm.

The **Mayflower Gold Mill Tour** (☎ **970/387-0294**) takes place in the old Sunnyside Mill, about 2 miles northeast of Silverton via Colo. 110. Former miners demonstrate the process of milling, and you can see the historic mill and its original milling equipment, much of it still operational. A video explains the mill's history. There's also gold panning, a rock and mineral shop, and gift shop. Cost is $8.50 for adults 17 to 59, $4.50 for children 11 to 16, $7.50 for seniors 60 and over, and free for children 10 and younger. Tours are offered daily from 10am to 3:30pm, from Memorial Day into September (call for exact end of season).

In the historic buildings of Silverton's downtown are a host of shops, galleries, restaurants, and hotels. Among the top art galleries are **Silverton Artworks,** 1028 Blair St. (☎ **970/387-5823**), featuring baskets, weavings, and pottery by local artist Ruth Ann Caitland; and the **Silver San Juan Gallery,** 1309 Greene St. (☎ **970/387-0210**), showing watercolors, photographs, and prints by Michael Darr and other local artists, as well as handcrafted guitars, mandolins, and other musical instruments.

You can get walking-tour maps of the historic downtown area; information on local shops, restaurants, and lodgings; plus details on the numerous outdoor activities in the surrounding mountains from the **Silverton Chamber of Commerce,** Greene Street (Colo. 110) off U.S. 550 (P.O. Box 565), Silverton, CO 81433 (☎ **800/752-4494** or 970/387-5654).

WHERE TO STAY

Wyman Hotel & Inn. 1371 Greene St, Silverton, CO 81433. ☎ **800/609-7845** or 970/387-5372. Fax 970/387-5745. 17 units. TV TEL. $90–$170 double. AE, DISC, MC, V. Rates include full breakfast. Closed mid-Nov–mid-Jan and mid-Feb–Apr. Pets accepted ($12 per night per pet) in ground-floor rooms.

Our choice for overnight lodging in Silverton, the Wyman fits in beautifully with the historic ambiance of this Old West mining town, but then it ought to—the hotel's been here almost as long as the town. Built in 1902 and now listed on the National Register of Historic Places, this handsome red-sandstone building has arched windows, high ceilings, Victorian-style wallpaper, and rooms and common areas furnished with antiques dating from the 1870s to the early 1900s—mostly Renaissance and East Lake styles.

Each room is different, ranging in size from small to large, and including a very large family room, a two-room suite, and a three-room suite. Unlike hotels of the early 20th century, all rooms now have private bathrooms—the six downstairs rooms have tub/shower combos (including two suites with whirlpool tubs), ten second-floor rooms have walk-in showers only, and there's one whirlpool suite upstairs. All rooms have VCRs, hair dryers, and top-quality king- or queen-size beds. Breakfasts include fresh-baked muffins, fresh fruit, the usual beverages, and an entree such as quiche with rosemary potatoes. Afternoon tea with homemade cookies is provided, and honeymoon packages are available. The entire hotel is nonsmoking.

2 A Spectacular Drive Along the San Juan Skyway

The ✪ San Juan Skyway, a 236-mile circuit that crosses five mountain passes, takes in the magnificent San Juan Mountains, as well as the cities and towns of the region. It can be accomplished in a single all-day drive from Durango or divided into several days, incorporating stops in Cortez, Telluride, and Ouray—all of which are discussed later in this chapter. Check for closed passes in winter and early spring.

The route can be driven either clockwise (heading west from Durango on U.S. 160) or counterclockwise (heading north from Durango on U.S. 550). We'll describe the clockwise route.

Leaving Durango, 11 miles west you'll pass through the village of Hesperus, from which a county road runs 10 miles north into **La Plata Canyon,** with its mining ruins and ghost towns.

Farther west, U.S. 160 passes the entrance road to **Mesa Verde National Park.** About 45 miles west of Durango, just before Cortez, turn north on Colo. 145, which traverses the historic town of Dolores, site of the **Anasazi Heritage Center** (see section 4 of this chapter), then proceeds up the Dolores River Valley, a favorite of trout fishermen.

Sixty miles from Cortez, the route crosses 10,222-foot **Lizard Head Pass,** named for a startling rock spire looming above the roadside alpine meadows. It then descends 13 miles to the resort town of **Telluride,** set in a beautiful box canyon 4 miles off the main road.

Follow Colo. 145 west from Telluride down the San Miguel River valley to **Placerville,** then turn north on Colo. 62, across 8,970-foot Dallas Divide, to Ridgway, a historic railroad town and home of **Ridgway State Park** (☎ **970/626-5822**), with a sparkling mountain reservoir, trout fishing, boating (there's a full-service marina), swimming, hiking, mountain biking, horseback riding, and camping.

From Ridgway, turn south, and follow U.S. 550 to the scenic and historic town of **Ouray.** Here begins the remarkable **Million Dollar Highway,** so named for all the mineral wealth that passed over it.

The 23 miles from Ouray over 11,008-foot **Red Mountain Pass** to Silverton is an unforgettable drive. It shimmies up the sheer sides of the Uncompahgre Gorge, through tunnels and past cascading waterfalls, then follows a historic toll road built in the 19th century. Mining equipment and log cabins are in evidence on the slopes of the iron-colored mountains, many of them over 14,000 feet in elevation. Along this route you'll pass a monument to the snowplow operators who died trying to keep the road open during winter storms.

From Silverton, U.S. 550 climbs over the Molas Divide (elevation 10,910 feet), then more or less parallels the track of the Durango & Silverton Narrow Gauge Railroad as it follows the Animas River south to Durango, passing en route the **Purgatory/Durango** ski resort (see section 1, above).

3 Mesa Verde National Park

10 miles E of Cortez

Mesa Verde is the largest archaeological preserve in the United States, with some 4,000 known sites dating from A.D. 600 to 1300, including the most impressive cliff dwellings in the Southwest.

The area was little known until ranchers Charles and Richard Wetherill chanced upon it in 1888. Looting of artifacts followed their discovery until a Denver newspaper reporter's stories aroused national interest in protecting the site. The 52,000-

acre site was declared a national park in 1906—it's the only U.S. national park devoted entirely to the works of humans.

The earliest known inhabitants of Mesa Verde (Spanish for "green table") built subterranean pit houses on the mesa tops. During the 13th century they moved into shallow caves and constructed complex cliff dwellings. Although a massive construction project, these homes were only occupied for about a century; their residents left in about 1300 for reasons as yet undetermined.

The **Cliff Palace,** the park's largest and best-known site, is a four-story apartment complex with stepped-back roofs forming porches for the dwellings above. Accessible by guided tour only, it is reached by a quarter-mile downhill path. Its towers, walls, and kivas (large circular rooms used for ceremonies) are all set back beneath the rim of a cliff. Another ranger-led tour takes visitors up a 32-foot ladder to explore the interior of **Balcony House.** Each of these tours are given only in summer and into fall (call for exact dates).

Two more important sites—**Step House** and **Long House,** both on Wetherill Mesa—can be visited in summer only. Rangers lead free tours to **Spruce Tree House,** another of the major cliff-dwelling complexes, only in winter, when other park facilities are closed. Visitors can also explore Spruce Tree House on their own at any time. Three-hour ($16) and 6-hour ($21) guided park tours are offered from Far View Lodge (see below) during the summer.

Although none of the trails to the Mesa Verde sites are strenuous, the 7,000-foot elevation can make the treks tiring for visitors who aren't used to the altitude. For those who want to avoid hiking and climbing, the 12-mile **Mesa Top Road** makes a number of pit houses and cliffside overlooks easily accessible by car.

In addition to the hidden cliffside villages, the park's **Chapin Mesa Museum,** open daily year-round, houses artifacts and specimens related to the history of the area, including other nearby sites.

Chapin Mesa, site of the park headquarters, museum, and a post office, is 21 miles from the park entrance on U.S. 160. **Morefield Village,** site of Mesa Verde's 477-site campground, is 4 miles in from U.S. 160. The **Far View Visitor Center,** site of Far View Lodge (see below), a restaurant, gift shop, and other facilities, is 15 miles off U.S. 160. In summer, rangers give nightly campfire programs. In winter, the Mesa Top Road and museum remain open, but many other facilities are closed.

Although this is not an outdoor recreation park per se—the reason to come here is to see the ancient cliff dwellings and other archaeological sites—you'll find yourself hiking and climbing to get to the sites. Several longer **hikes** into scenic Spruce Canyon let you stretch your legs and get away from the crowds. Hikers must register at the ranger's office before setting out. Open from mid-April to mid-October, **Morefield Campground** (☎ **970/533-7731**), 4 miles south of the park entrance, has almost 500 sites, including 15 with full RV hookups. Facilities include modern rest rooms, showers, picnic tables, grills, and an RV dump station. Reservations are not accepted. Cost is $10, $17 with hookups.

Admission to the park costs $10 per vehicle. Tours of Cliff Palace and Balcony House are $1.75. The cliff dwellings can be viewed daily from 9am to 5pm; the Far View Visitor Center is open in summer only, from 8am to 5pm. The park museum is open daily from 8am to 6:30pm in summer, daily from 8am to 5pm the rest of the year. Food, gas, and lodging are available in the park from May to October only; full interpretive services are available from mid-June to Labor Day.

For a park brochure, contact Superintendent, P.O. Box 8, Mesa Verde National Park, CO 81330 (☎ **970/529-4461;** www.nps.gov/meve). For information on camping, lodging, and dining, call park concessionaire Mesa Verde Company (☎ **970/533-7731**).

WHERE TO STAY & DINE

Far View Lodge. Mesa Verde National Park (P.O. Box 277, Mancos, CO 81328). ☎ **800/ 449-2288** or 970/529-4421. Fax 970/529-4411. www.visitmesaverde.com. E-mail: judithswain@ world.att.net. 150 units. Open late April to late Oct only. $94 double mid-June to early Oct, $86 double at other times. AE, DISC, MC, V. Pets accepted with a deposit.

Located in the heart of Mesa Verde National Park, Far View Lodge offers not only the most convenient location for visiting the park, but also the best views of any accommodations in the area. The facility lodges guests in 17 separate buildings spread across a hilltop. Rooms aren't fancy, but they are cozy, with one queen-sized bed or two doubles, and southwestern decor including American Indian sand paintings. There's no TV or phone, but each unit has a private balcony, and the views are magnificent in all directions.

The lodge serves three meals daily, with two restaurants and a bar. Amenities include a 24-hour front desk, complimentary morning coffee and newspaper, and gift shop. Half-day guided tours of the park leave the lodge daily at 9am and 1pm, and full-day tours leave at 9:30am.

4 Cortez: Gateway to the Archaeological Sites of the Four Corners Region

45 miles W of Durango, 203 miles S of Grand Junction

An important archaeological center, Cortez is surrounded by a vast complex of ancient villages that dominated the Four Corners region—where Colorado, New Mexico, Arizona, and Utah's borders meet—1,000 years ago. The inhabitants of those ancient villages, called ancestral Puebloans or ancient Pueblo people, have long been known as the Anasazi. That term is being phased out, however, because modern American Indians who trace their roots to the ancestral Puebloans consider the term demeaning. "Anasazi" is a Navajo word meaning "enemy of my people," as the Navajos considered the ancestral Puebloans their enemies.

Mesa Verde National Park, 10 miles east, is certainly the most prominent nearby attraction, drawing hundreds of thousands of visitors annually. (See section 3 of this chapter, above.) In addition, archaeological sites such as those at Hovenweep National Monument, Lowry Pueblo, and Ute Mountain Tribal Park are an easy drive from the city. San Juan National Forest, just to the north, offers a wide variety of recreational opportunities.

ESSENTIALS

GETTING THERE   By Car   Cortez is located at the junction of north–south U.S. 666 and east-west U.S. 160.

As it enters Cortez from the east, U.S. 160 crosses Dolores Road (Colo. 145, which goes north to Telluride and Grand Junction), then runs due west through town for about 2 miles as Main Street. The city's main thoroughfare, Main Street eventually intersects U.S. 666 (Broadway) at the west end of town.

By Plane   Cortez Airport, off U.S. 160 and 666, southwest of town (☎ **970/ 565-7458**), is served by **United Express Airlines** (☎ **800/241-6522** or 970/565-9510), with direct daily flights to Denver.

U-Save (☎ **970/565-9168**) provides car rentals at the airport as well as free delivery in Cortez.

VISITOR INFORMATION   Stop at the **Colorado Welcome Center at Cortez,** Cortez City Park, 928 E. Main St. (☎ **800/253-1616** or 970/565-3414); or contact the **Mesa Verde Country Visitor Information Bureau,** P.O. Box HH, Cortez,

CO 81321 (also ☎ **800/253-1616**); or the **Cortez Area Chamber of Commerce,** P.O. Box 968, Cortez, CO 81321 (☎ **970/565-3414**).

FAST FACTS   The local hospital is **Southwest Memorial Hospital,** 1311 N. Mildred Rd. (☎ **970/565-6666**), which has a 24-hour emergency room. The **post office** is at 35 S. Beech St.; contact the U.S. Postal Service (☎ **800/275-8777**) for hours and additional information.

SPECIAL EVENTS   Indian Dances, Memorial Day to Labor Day; Mountain Roundup Rodeo, mid-June; Montezuma County Fair, early August.

THE MAJOR ARCHAEOLOGICAL SITES
HOVENWEEP NATIONAL MONUMENT

Preserving some of the most striking and isolated archaeological sites in the Four Corners area, this national monument straddles the Colorado–Utah border, 40 miles west of Cortez. Take U.S. 160 south about 2 miles to County Rd. G, and follow signs into Utah and the monument.

Hovenweep is the Ute word for "deserted valley." Its inhabitants apparently left the area around 1300, and even today it's often overlooked by tourists, who instead flock to the more famous Mesa Verde (see section 3 of this chapter, above). The monument contains six separate sites, and is noted for mysterious, 20-foot-high sandstone towers, some of them square, others oval, circular, or D-shaped. The towers have small windows up and down their masonry sides, and remain very solid today. Archaeologists have suggested their possible function as everything from guard or signal towers, celestial observatories, and ceremonial structures to water towers or granaries.

A ranger station, with exhibits, rest rooms, and drinking water, is located at the **Square Tower Site,** in the Utah section of the monument, the most impressive and best preserved of the sites. The **Tower Point Loop Trail** here winds among the stone structures and identifies desert plants used for food, clothing, medicine, and other purposes. The other five sites are difficult to find, and you'll need to obtain detailed driving directions and check on current road conditions before setting out.

The **Hovenweep Campground,** with 30 sites, is open year-round. It has flush toilets, drinking water, picnic tables, and fire pits, but no showers or RV hookups. Cost is $10 per night; reservations are not accepted, but the campground rarely fills up, even during the peak summer season.

Regulations are much the same here as at most National Park Service properties, with an emphasis on taking care not to damage archaeological sites. Summer temperatures can reach over 100° Fahrenheit, and water supplies are limited—so take your own and carry a canteen, even on short walks. Bug repellent is advised, as gnats can be a nuisance in late May. Dogs must be leashed but are permitted on trails.

The ranger station is open daily from 8am to 4:30pm year-round, but may be closed for short periods while the ranger is on patrol. Admission costs $6 per vehicle. For advance information, contact Hovenweep National Monument, McElmo Route, Cortez, CO 81321 (☎ **970/749-0510** or 970/529-4461; www. nps.gov/hove).

ANASAZI HERITAGE CENTER

When the Dolores River was dammed and McPhee Reservoir created in 1985, some 1,600 ancient archaeological sites were threatened. Four percent of the project costs were set aside for archaeological work, and over two million artifacts and other prehistoric items were rescued. The largest share are displayed in this museum. Located 10 miles north of Cortez, it is set into a hillside near the remains of 12th-century sites.

Operated by the Bureau of Land Management, the center emphasizes visitor involvement. Children and adults are invited to examine corn-grinding implements, a loom and other weaving materials, and a re-created pit house. You can touch artifacts 1,000 to 2,000 years old, examine samples through microscopes, use interactive computer programs, and engage in video lessons in archaeological techniques.

A half-mile trail leads from the museum to the **Dominguez and Escalante Ruins,** atop a low hill, with a beautiful view across the Montezuma Valley.

The center is located at 27501 Colo. 184, Dolores (☎ **970/882-4811;** www.co.blm.gov/ahchmepge.htm). It's open March through October, daily from 9am to 5pm; November through February, daily from 9am to 4pm; and closed Thanksgiving, Christmas, and New Year's Day. Admission is $3 for adults, free for those 17 and under.

CORTEZ COLORADO UNIVERSITY CENTER & MUSEUM

The center, at 25 N. Market St., Cortez (☎ 970/565-1151; www.fone.net/ ~cucenter), is a clearinghouse for information on various ancestral Puebloan sites and related activities in southwestern Colorado, and the museum features interpretive exhibits from the sites as well as on the nearby Ute, Navajo, and Pueblo peoples. Evening programs, including American Indian dances and cultural programs, are presented Monday through Saturday in summer, and about once a week the rest of the year. There's also a small gift shop and bookstore. Admission is free, though donations are welcome. The center is open June through August, Monday through Saturday from 10am to 9pm; in May, September, and October, Monday through Saturday from 10am to 6pm; and November through April, Monday through Saturday from 10am to 5pm.

LOWRY PUEBLO

An excavated 12th-century village, 26 miles from Cortez via U.S. 666, on County Road CC, 9 miles west of Pleasant View (☎ 970/247-4874), Lowry Pueblo may have been a ritual center. Though believed to have been abandoned by 1200, during its heyday the 42-room pueblo was home to about 100 people. A short, self-guided interpretive trail leads past a kiva (circular underground ceremonial chamber) decorated with geometric designs. It then continues to the remains of a great kiva, which, at 54 feet in diameter, is among the largest ever found. The Bureau of Land Management, which maintains this designated National Historic Landmark, also maintains a picnic area and rest room facilities. Admission is free. The site is open daily from 8am to sunset, year-round (except when winter weather conditions close the gravel access road).

✪ UTE MOUNTAIN TRIBAL PARK

If you liked Mesa Verde, but would have enjoyed it more without the company of so many fellow tourists, you'll *love* the Ute Mountain Tribal Park, in Towaoc (☎ 800/847-5485 or 970/565-3751, ext. 282). Set aside by the Ute Mountain tribe to preserve its heritage, the 125,000-acre park—which abuts Mesa Verde National Park—includes hundreds of surface sites and cliff dwellings that compare in size and complexity with those in Mesa Verde, as well as wall paintings and ancient petroglyphs.

Accessibility to the park is strictly limited to guided tours, which are offered from April through October. Full- and half-day tours begin at the Ute Mountain Museum and Visitor Center at the junction of U.S. 666 and U.S. 160, 19 miles south of Cortez. Mountain-biking and backpacking trips are also offered. No food, lodging, gasoline, or other services are available within the park. Some climbing is necessary. There's one primitive **campground** ($10 per vehicle).

Charges for tours in your vehicle start at $20 per person for a half day, $30 for a full day; it's $5 extra to go in the tour guide's vehicle. Reservations are required.

OTHER NEARBY HIGHLIGHTS
FOUR CORNERS MONUMENT

This is the only place in the United States where you can stand, or sit if you prefer, in four states at once. Operated by the Navajo Parks and Recreation Department (☎ 520/871-6647), there's a flat monument marking the spot where Utah, Colorado, New Mexico, and Arizona meet, and visitors perch for photos. Official seals of the four states are displayed, along with the motto, "Four states here meet in freedom under God." Surrounding the monument are the states' flags, flags of the Navajo Nation and Ute tribe, and the U.S. flag.

There are rows of booths where vendors sell traditional Navajo food, such as fry bread, along with traditional American snack food. There are often crafts demonstrations, and an abundance of jewelry, pottery, sand paintings, and other crafts for sale, plus T-shirts, postcards, and souvenirs. The monument is located half a mile northwest of U.S. 160, about 38 miles southwest of Cortez. It's open daily from 7am to 8pm in summer, with shorter hours in winter. Admission costs $1.50 per person.

Ute Mountain Casino. Towaoc (11 miles south of Cortez on U.S. 160/666). ☎ **800/ 258-8007** or 970/565-8800. Free admission. Daily 8am–4am.

Colorado's first tribal gaming facility has slot machines, blackjack and poker tables, and high-stakes bingo. As with all Colorado gambling, bets are limited to $5 and gamblers must be at least 21 years old, except for bingo where the minimum age is 18. The casino has a full-service restaurant offering southwestern cuisine. No alcoholic beverages are served or permitted in the building or on the grounds.

WHERE TO STAY

Summer is the busy season here, and that's when you'll pay the highest lodging rates. Among the major chains providing comfortable, reasonably priced lodging in Cortez are **Best Western Turquoise Inn & Suites,** 536 E. Main St. (☎ 800/ 547-3376 or 970/565-3778), with rates for two ranging from $45 to $150; **Comfort Inn,** 2308 E. Main St. (☎ 800/228-5150 or 970/565-3400), which charges $59 to $96 for two; **Days Inn,** 430 N. Colo. 145 (☎ 800/329-7466 or 970/ 565-8577), with double occupancy rates of $44 to $56; **Super 8,** 505 E. Main St. (☎ 800/800-8000 or 970/565-8888), with rates of $40 to $74 double; and **Econo Lodge,** 2020 E. Main St. (☎ 800/553-2666 or 970/565-3474), with rates of $40 to $85 double. Room tax adds about 8% to lodging bills.

✪ **Arrow Motel.** 440 S. Broadway, Cortez, CO 81321. ☎ **800/727-7692** or 970/ 565-7778. Fax 970/565-7214. 42 units. A/C TV TEL. Memorial Day–Labor Day $48–$59 double; Labor Day–Memorial Day $34–$48 double. Children under 12 stay free in parents' room, $4 charge for children 12 and over. AE, DISC, MC, V. Small pets accepted with $25 deposit.

A small mom-and-pop–style motel affiliated with National 9 Inns, the Arrow is perfect for travelers on a budget. Flower boxes decorate the buildings, and facilities include a small heated outdoor swimming pool, whirlpool, and guest laundry. Ten rooms have fridges and microwaves. Most of the attractive units have good-quality queen beds; a few have kings. You'll find tub/shower combos in 31 rooms, showers only in the rest.

WHERE TO DINE

Homesteaders Restaurant. 45 E. Main St. ☎ **970/565-6253.** Breakfast $2.50–$6; main courses $3–$6.50 lunch, $4–$14 dinner. AE, DISC, MC, V. Mon–Sat 7am–3pm; daily 5–9:30pm. AMERICAN/MEXICAN.

A rustic barn provides the atmosphere for this popular family restaurant. A big waterwheel greets guests at the entrance, while throughout the dining room hang harnesses, skillets, and other pioneer artifacts. The menu ranges from tacos to chicken-fried steak, rainbow trout to barbecued spareribs. We recommend the omelets to start your day right. Smoking is not permitted.

Millwood Junction. U.S. 160 and Main St., Mancos. ☎ **970/533-7338.** Main courses $7–$18.50. MC, V. Daily 4–10:30pm. STEAK/SEAFOOD.

The atmosphere at this restaurant, 7 miles east of Mesa Verde National Park, recalls the timber industry that supported this area 100 years ago, but the food is decidedly modern. House specialties include steak Diane and blackened catfish; you can also get pastas, pork ribs, and a variety of other steaks and seafood. Especially popular are the homemade ice creams and desserts.

✪ **Nero's.** 303 W. Main St. ☎ **970/565-7366.** Reservations recommended. Entrees $6–$18. AE, MC, V. Daily 5–10pm. Closed Sun in winter. ITALIAN/AMERICAN.

A small, homey restaurant with a southwestern art-gallery decor, Nero's doubles its capacity in summer with an outdoor patio. The innovatively prepared entrees include an excellent selection of beef, such as grilled beef tenderloin medallions in a Chianti wine sauce, plus seafood, chicken, veal, and homemade pasta. House specialties include shrimp Alfredo and sirloin—sautéed shrimp with Alfredo sauce served over fettuccine with a 6-ounce charbroiled sirloin steak.

5 Telluride

126 miles N of Durango, 127 miles S of Grand Junction

This was one seriously rowdy town a century ago—in fact, this is where Butch Cassidy robbed his first bank, in 1889. Incorporated with the boring name of Columbia in 1878, the mining town assumed its present name the following decade. Some say the name came from tellurium, a gold-bearing ore, while others insist the name really means "to hell you ride," referring to the town's boisterous nature.

Telluride became a National Historic District in 1964, and in 1968 entrepreneur Joe Zoline set to work on a "winter recreation area second to none." The Telluride Ski Company opened its first runs in 1972, and Telluride was a boom town again. Telluride's first summer festivals (bluegrass in June, film in September) were celebrated the following year. Today, the resort, at 8,745 feet elevation, is a year-round destination for mountain bikers, skiers, anglers, and hikers.

ESSENTIALS

GETTING THERE   By Car   Telluride is located on Colo. 145. From Cortez, follow Colo. 145 northeast for 73 miles. From the north (Montrose), turn west off U.S. 550 at Ridgway, onto Colo. 62. Proceed 25 miles to Placerville, and turn left (southeast) onto Colo. 145. Thirteen miles ahead is a junction—a right turn will take you to Cortez, but for Telluride, continue straight ahead 4 miles to the end of a box canyon. From Durango, in summer take U.S. 550 north to Colo. 62, and follow the directions above; in winter it's best to take the route through Cortez and avoid Red Mountain Pass above Silverton.

By Plane   Telluride Regional Airport (☎ **970/728-5313**), atop a plateau at 9,078-feet elevation 5 miles west of Telluride, is served by **United Express** (☎ **800/ 241-6522** or 970/728-4868) from Denver, and **America West** (☎ **800/235-9292** or 970/728-4868) from Phoenix.

VISITOR INFORMATION   Contact **Telluride Visitor Services/Telluride Central Reservations,** 666 W. Colorado Ave. (P.O. Box 653), Telluride, CO 81435 (☎ **800/525-3455**). The **Telluride Visitor Information Center** can be found with the visitor services and central reservations offices, located above Rose's Food Mart.

GETTING AROUND   The city is located on the San Miguel River where it flows out of a box canyon formed by the 14,000-foot peaks of the San Juan Mountains. Colo. 145 enters town from the west and becomes Colorado Avenue, the main street.

With restaurants, shops, and attractions within easy walking distance of most lodging facilities, many visitors leave their cars parked and take to their feet. However, if you do want to ride, **Telluride Shuttle & Taxi** (☎ **888/212-8294** or 970/728-6667) provides taxi service. There's a free town shuttle in winter. Telluride Mountain Village, at 9,500 feet, can be reached by a free gondola, which operates year-round, daily from 7am to 11pm. Motorists can take Mountain Village Boulevard off Colo. 145, a mile south of the Telluride junction.

Budget (☎ **800/221-2419** or 970/728-4642), at the airport, and **Thrifty** (☎ **800/367-2277** or 970/728-3266), in town, provide car rentals, including vans and four-wheel-drive vehicles.

FAST FACTS   The hospital, **Telluride Medical Center,** with a 24-hour emergency room, is at 500 W. Pacific Ave. (☎ **970/728-3848**). The **post office** is at 101 E. Colorado Ave; call the U.S. Postal Service (☎ **800/275-8777**) for hours and other information. For **road conditions,** call ☎ **970/249-9363.**

SPECIAL EVENTS   Telluride Wine Festival, late June; Melee in the Mines Mountain Bike Race, July; World Aerobatic Hang Gliding Championships, August; the Chamber Music Festival, August; Mushroom Festival, fourth weekend in August; Imogene Pass Run, early September. See also "The Festival Scene," below.

SKIING & SNOWBOARDING

The elegant European-style Mountain Village, built in 1987, offers a fascinating contrast to the laid-back community of artists, shopkeepers, and drop-outs in the 1870s Victorian mining town of Telluride below. Located mid-mountain at an elevation of 9,450 feet, the Mountain Village offers ski-in/ski-out accommodations; eight slopeside restaurants including Gorrono Ranch, a historic homestead; spectacular scenery; and—of course—great skiing.

The mountain's **South Face,** which drops sharply from the summit to the town of Telluride, is characterized by steep moguls, tree-and-glade skiing, and challenging groomed pitches for experts and advanced intermediates. **Gorrono Basin,** which rises from the Mountain Village Resort, caters to intermediate skiers. The broad, gentle slopes of the **Meadows** stretch beneath Gorrono Basin to the foot of Sunshine Peak. This part of the mountain, with trails over 2½ miles long devoted entirely to novice skiers, is served by a high-speed quad chair. Average annual snowfall is 300 inches (25 feet).

In all, Telluride offers 1,050 acres of skiable terrain. The lift-served vertical drop is an impressive 3,165 feet from the 11,890-foot summit. The mountain has 64 trails served by 10 lifts (two high-speed quads, two triples, five doubles, and a Poma) and a gondola. Twenty-one percent of the trails are rated for beginners, 47% for intermediates, and 32% for experts. Helicopter skiing is also available (☎ **970/ 728-4904**).

The Mountain Village has 30 kilometers (18.6 miles) of **Nordic trails**, which connect with 20 kilometers of groomed trails at Town Park and River Corridor Trail, giving cross-country skiers a total of 50 kilometers (31 miles). For Nordic skiers who really want to put some miles behind them, there's the ✪ **San Juan Hut System** (☎ **970/728-6935**), providing backcountry huts with bunks, wood stoves and wood, and kitchens (see "Mountain Biking," below). The Mountain Village also has one of the top **snowboarding parks** in Colorado, offering more than 13 acres of terrain.

Full-day lift tickets (1998–99 season) are $53 for adults, $26 for children 6 to 12, $31 for seniors 65 to 69, and free for children under 6 and seniors over 69. Rates over the Christmas holidays are $2 more, and there are discounts for early season skiing. Ski and snowboarding lessons are offered, as well as child care. The resort is open daily from Thanksgiving to mid-April.

Call ☎ **800/728-7425** for snow reports, and for additional information, contact Telluride Ski and Golf Company, P.O. Box 11155, Telluride, CO 81435 (☎ **800/801-4832** or 970/728-7533; www.telski.com).

OTHER WINTER ACTIVITIES

In addition to skiing at Telluride Ski Resort, virtually every cold-weather activity imaginable is available in the Telluride area. Much of it takes place at **Town Park,** at the east end of town (☎ **970/728-3071**), where there are groomed cross-country trails, daytime sledding and tubing at Firecracker Hill, and ice-skating (see below). The **River Corridor Trail** follows the San Miguel River from Town Park to the valley floor. Popular with bikers and hikers in warm weather, it's perfect for cross-country skiing and skate-skiing after the snow falls.

The major outfitter and arranger of outdoor activities here is the versatile and dependable **Telluride Outside,** 1982 W. Colo. 145 (☎ **800/831-6230** or 970/728-3895; fax 970/728-2062; www.tellurideoutside.com), which seems to be involved in every form of outdoor recreation except skiing.

ICE-SKATING   There's free ice-skating in winter at Town Park (☎ **970/728-3071**), and also at the outdoor rink in the Mountain Village (☎ **970/729-2555**). Skate rentals are available at local sporting-goods stores.

SLEIGH & DOGSLED RIDES   Both dogsled (starting at $130 for a half day) and old-fashioned horse-drawn sleigh rides (about $60 for adults and $35 for children 3 to 12, including dinner), can be arranged with **Telluride Outside.**

SNOWMOBILING   Tours are offered by **Telluride Outside,** starting at about $120 for one person for a 2-hour ride, $175 for two people on one machine for 2 hours.

WARM-WEATHER & YEAR-ROUND ACTIVITIES

Telluride isn't just a ski town—there's a wide variety of year-round outdoor activities. **Town Park,** at the east end of town (☎ **970/728-3071** or 970/728-2173), is home to the community's various festivals. It also has a public outdoor pool, open in summer, plus tennis courts, sand volleyball courts, small outdoor basketball court, skateboarding ramp, playing fields, picnic area, and fishing pond (see "Fishing," below). A campground for tent and car campers, open May 15 to October 15, has showers ($1.50) but no RV hookups, and costs $9 to $11 per night.

As with winter activities, the major outfitter and guide service here is **Telluride Outside** (see above).

FISHING   There's excellent fishing in the San Miguel River through Telluride, but it's even better in nearby alpine lakes, including Silver Lake, reached by foot in Bridal Veil Basin, and Trout and Priest Lakes, about 12 miles south via Colo. 145. At Town Park there's the Kids Fishin' Pond for children 12 and under, which is stocked from Memorial Day to Labor Day.

Equipment, licenses, and fly-fishing instruction are offered by **Telluride Outside,** with a walk-and-wade trip for two costing about $200 for a half day and $260 for a full day. Similar services at similar rates are offered by **Telluride Angler,** 121 W. Colorado Ave. (☎ **970/728-0773**), and **Telluride Flyfishing & Rafting Expeditions**, 150 W. Colorado Ave. (☎ **800/297-4441** or 970/728-4440).

FOUR-WHEELING   To see old ghost towns, mining camps, and spectacular mountain scenery from the relative comfort of a bouncing four-wheel-drive vehicle, join **Telluride Outside** for a full-day trip ($85) over the 14,114-foot Imogene Pass jeep road. Also offering guided four-wheel-drive excursions at similar rates are **Dave's Jeep Tours** (☎ 970/728-6265) and **Telluride Shuttle & Taxi** (☎ **888/ 212-8294** or 970/728-6667). To rent your own 4×4, contact **Telluride Outside** or the car-rental companies mentioned in "Getting Around," above.

GOLF   The 18-hole par-71 **Telluride Golf Course** is located at Telluride Mountain Village (☎ **970/728-6366** or 970/728-6157). Greens fees with the required cart are $120 July through Labor Day, $100 at other times.

HIKING & MOUNTAINEERING   Sporting-goods stores and the visitor center have maps of trails in the Telluride area. Especially popular are the easy 4-mile (round-trip) ✪ **Bear Creek Canyon Trail,** which starts at the end of S. Pine Street and leads to a picturesque waterfall; the **Jud Wiebe Trail** that begins at the north end of Aspen Street and does a 2.7-mile loop above the town, offering views of Bridel Veil Falls, the town, and ski area; and the 1.8-mile (one-way) hike to the top of **Bridal Veil Falls,** which starts at the east end of Telluride Canyon.

A variety of guided hikes and mountain expeditions can be arranged through **Telluride Outside,** at a cost of $50 for a half day and $80 for a full day (including lunch). Guided hikes are also offered by **Lizard Head Mountain Guides** (☎ 970/ 728-4904) and **Fantasy Ridge Alpinism** (☎ 970/728-3546), which also offers mountaineering instruction. **Herb Walker Tours** (☎ 970/728-4538) leads herb/nature hikes for those interested in learning about local plants, identifying mushrooms, and the uses of plants. Cost for a 3-hour hike with two to four people is $40 per person.

HORSEBACK RIDING   One of the best ways to see this spectacular country is by horse. **Telluride Horseback Adventures** (☎ 800/828-7547 through Telluride Sports, or 970/728-9611), has "gentle horses for gentle people and fast horses for fast people, and for people who don't like to ride, horses that don't like to be rode." Operating year-round, the company offers 1-hour rides for $25, 2-hour rides for $40, and all-day rides for $100. There are also breakfast ($55) and dinner ($65) rides; ask about multi-day pack trips in September and private rides for small groups of experienced riders.

MOUNTAIN BIKING   Telluride is a major mountain-biking center. The **San Juan Hut System** links Telluride with Moab, Utah, via a 206-mile-long network of backcountry dirt roads. Every 35 miles is a primitive cabin, with bunks, a wood stove, propane cooking stove, and cooking gear. The route is appropriate for intermediate level riders in good physical condition, and an advanced technical single track is found near the huts for more experienced cyclists. Cost for riders who plan to make the whole trip is about $450, which includes use of the six huts, three meals daily, sleeping bags at each hut, and maps and trail descriptions. Shorter trips, guide services, and vehicle shuttles are also available. Trail system offices are at 117 N. Willow St. (☎ **970/728-6935**). For a brochure write to P.O. Box 1663, Telluride, CO 81435.

Telluride Outside (see above) and **Back Country Biking** (☎ **970/728-0861**) offer guided downhill tours, with rates starting at $55 per person, including a bike. Mountain-bike rentals are available from **Telluride Outside, Telluride Sports** (☎ **800/828-7547** or 970/728-4477), and **Paragon Ski & Sport** (☎ **800/903-4525** or 970/728-4525). Rates start at about $20 per day for basic 21-speed bikes, going up to about $40 per day for full-suspension and racing bikes.

RIVER RAFTING   Those wanting to run the local rivers can hop in a raft with **Telluride Outside, Telluride Sports** (☎ **800/828-7547** or 970/728-4477), or **Telluride Flyfishing & Rafting Expeditions** (☎ **800/297-4441** or 970/728-4440). Rates start at $60 for a half-day trip. Do-it-yourselfers can rent inflatable kayaks from **Telluride Sports,** at $45 per day for a two-person kayak.

SEEING THE SIGHTS

The best way to see the Telluride National Historic District and get a feel for the West of the late 1800s is to take to the streets, following the excellent **walking tour** described in the *Telluride Visitor's Guide,* available at the Visitor Information Center (☎ **888/355-8743**). Among the buildings you'll see are the **San Miguel County Courthouse,** Colorado Avenue at Oak Street, built in 1887 and still in use today. A block north and west, at Columbia Avenue and Aspen Street, is the **L. L. Nunn House,** home of the late-19th-century mining engineer who created the first high-voltage alternating-current power plant in the world. Two blocks east of Fir Street, on Galena Avenue at Spruce Street, is **St. Patrick's Catholic Church,** built in 1895, whose wooden Stations of the Cross figures were carved in Austria's Tyrol region. Perhaps Telluride's most famous landmark is the **New Sheridan Hotel** and the **Sheridan Opera House,** opposite the County Courthouse at Colorado and Oak. The hotel, built in 1895, in its early days rivaled Denver's famed Brown Palace Hotel in service and cuisine. The exquisite Opera House, added in 1914, boasts a Venetian scene painted on its roll curtain.

Colorado's highest waterfall (365 feet) can be seen from the east end of Colorado Avenue. **Bridal Veil Falls** freeze in winter, then slowly melt in early spring, creating a dramatic effect. Perched at the top edge of the falls is a National Historic Landmark, a hydroelectric power plant that served area mines in the late 1800s. It has been recently restored and is once again supplying power to the community. It is accessible by hiking or driving a switchback, four-wheel-drive road.

Telluride Historical Museum. 317 N. Fir St. ☎ **970/728-3344.** Admission $7 adults; $5 seniors, children 5 and over, and high school and college students with ID; free for children under 5. Wed–Mon 10am–4pm.

Built in 1893 as the community hospital, at press time this historic building was undergoing major renovation and the museum was closed. It's expected to reopen during the summer of 1999. The museum has some 9,000 artifacts and 1,400 historic photos that show what Telluride was like in its Wild West days, when the likes of Butch Cassidy stalked the streets. There are exhibits on the area's Indian heritage, mining memorabilia, a turn-of-the-century schoolroom display, antique toys, and exhibits on Telluride's ski boom of the 1970s. There's also a furnished hospital room from the late 1800s that tells the story of a doctor of that era who removed his own appendix, using an experimental local anesthetic.

THE FESTIVAL SCENE

Telluride must be the most festival-happy town in the West, and visitors come from around the world to see the finest new films, hear the best musicians, and even pick the most exotic mushrooms. In addition to the phone numbers listed, you can get additional details and often tickets from **Telluride Visitor Services** (☎ **800/ 525-3455**).

✪ **Telluride Film Festival**, an influential festival within the film industry that takes place over Labor Day weekend, has premiered some of the finest films produced in recent years (*The Crying Game, The Piano,* and *Sling Blade* are just a few examples). What truly sets it apart, however, is the casual interaction between stars and attendees. Open-air films and seminars are free to all. Contact the National Film Preserve (☎ **603/643-1255**) for further information.

MountainFilm, which takes place every Memorial Day weekend, brings together filmmakers, writers, and outdoor enthusiasts to celebrate mountains, adventure, and the environment. Four days are filled with films, seminars, and presentations; recent guests have included Sir Edmund Hillary. Call ☎ **970/728-4123** for tickets and information.

Telluride Bluegrass Festival is one of the most intense and renowned bluegrass, folk, and country jam sessions in the United States. Held over four days during late June in conjunction with the Bluegrass Academy, recent lineups have featured Mary Chapin Carpenter, Shawn Colvin, and James Taylor. Call ☎ **800/624-2422** for further information.

Telluride Jazz Celebration, a 2-day event the first week in August, is marked by day concerts in Town Park and evening happenings in downtown saloons. Recent performers have included Marleena Shaw, Stanley Jordan, and Terence Blanchard.

Mushroom Fest draws fungophiles for a weekend of wild mushroom forays into the surrounding forests, plus lectures on edible, psychoactive, and poisonous mushrooms. Held in late August, there's also a parade and plenty of mushroom tasting.

Nothing Fest, a non-event begun in the early 1990s, is just that—nothing special happens, and it doesn't happen all over town. It's usually scheduled in mid- to late July. When founder Dennis Wrestler was asked how long the festival would continue, he responded, "How can you cancel something that doesn't happen?" Admission is free.

WHERE TO STAY

Telluride's lodging rates probably have more different "seasons" than anywhere else in Colorado. Generally speaking, you'll pay top dollar for a room over the Christmas holidays, during the film and bluegrass festivals, and at certain other peak times. Non-holiday skiing is a bit cheaper, summertime lodging (except for festival times) is cheaper yet, and you may find some real bargains in spring and fall. The key to finding inexpensive lodging and avoiding crowds is timing; unless you particularly want to attend the Bluegrass Festival, plan your trip another time. You're also much more likely to find attractive package deals on skiing and other activities if you can go during quieter times, and not on weekends.

Many of the lodging properties in Telluride (there are beds for approximately 4,000 visitors) are condominiums, managed by **Telluride Resort Accommodations** (☎ **800/538-7754** or 970/728-6621; fax 970/728-6160; www.telluridelodging. com). There's also a **Telluride Visitor's Guide Online** (www.telluridemm.com), where you can research accommodations and make your own reservations, as well as get other information on Telluride. Perhaps the best way to book lodging, however, is with **Telluride Visitor Services** (☎ **800/525-3455** or 888/355-8743), which represents practically all accommodations in the area.

EXPENSIVE

Camel's Garden Hotel. 250 W. San Juan Ave. (P.O. Box 4145), Telluride, CO 81435. ☎ **888/772-2635** or 970/728-9300. Fax 970/728-0433. E-mail: camelsgarden@infozone. org. 39 units. TV TEL. Ski season $210–$585 double; rest of year $120–$310. Rates include continental breakfast. AE, CB, DC, DISC, MC, V. Free underground heated parking, height limit 6 ft. 10 in. (outside parking available for larger vehicles).

This luxury property, with 31 rooms and suites plus eight condo units, has a perfect location—it's ski-in/ski-out—and only steps from the town gondola, and also within 2 short blocks of the main shopping and dining section of historic Telluride. Brand new (it opened in the fall of 1997), the hotel rooms—even the smallest, least expensive ones—are spacious, with the feel of upscale condo units. All units have cherry-oak furnishings, Italian marble bathrooms with oversized tubs, CD players (bring your own CDs), TV/VCRs, and gas fireplaces. All the condos and suites and all but four of the hotel rooms have balconies, with views of either the town or mountains. Rooms have quality beds (mostly kings) on pedestals (step stools available on request), hair dryers, and several phones, with dataports and voice mail. The simple but tasteful decor includes nature prints and black-and-white photos of the area. Condos are huge, with complete kitchens, washer/dryers, jetted tubs and showers, and heated towel racks. Safe deposit boxes are available on request.

The continental breakfast includes the usual fresh fruit, juices, coffee, tea, and cereals, plus excellent baked goods from an on-site bakery. Afternoon refreshments are served during ski season. Other amenities include a 25-foot outdoor jetted hot tub that offers great views of the nearby mountains, a steam room, ski storage and ski valet services, laundry, in-room massage, and conference facilities. On the premises are a deli/bakery (serving three meals daily) and a sporting-goods store that stocks a good selection of recreation equipment and clothing, and rents skis and mountain bikes as well. The entire property is nonsmoking.

The Peaks Resort & Spa. 136 Country Club Dr. (P.O. Box 2702), Telluride, CO 81435. ☎ **800/789-2220** or 970/728-6800. Fax 970/728-6175. 181 units. MINIBAR TV TEL. $150–$595 double; $235–$1,295 suite. AE, MC, V.

Set on 6 acres in the Mountain Village above Telluride, this luxury resort is surrounded by 8,000- to 14,000-foot peaks. The lofty lobby is elegantly decorated in southwestern style with beautiful leather couches, wooden tables and chairs, and handwoven rugs centered on a grand floor-to-ceiling fireplace.

Many rooms have a balcony or terrace offering breathtaking views of the mountains. The southwestern decor is luxurious and comfortable, and all units have coffee makers and hairdryers. There's ski-in/ski-out access to the slopes, in-room massage, dry cleaning, and valet parking. Thirteen spa rooms offer individual spa services.

The hotel restaurant serves three meals daily. A concierge, room service, and tennis and ski valet services are available. Facilities include North America's highest championship 18-hole golf course, a 42,000-square-foot spa with fitness center, several heated pools, sauna, whirlpool, steam room, rock-climbing wall, KidSpa for ages 2½ to 11, day-care center, beauty salon, shops, five tennis courts, mountain-bike rentals, and conference facilities.

MODERATE

Ice House Lodge and Condominiums. 310 S. Fir St. (P.O. Box 2909), Telluride, CO 81435. ☎ **800/544-3436** or 970/728-6300. Fax 970/728-6358. E-mail: icehouse@infozone.org. 42 units. MINIBAR TV TEL. Summer $145–$260 double; Feb–Mar $195–$305 double; Christmas holidays $250–$405 double; rest of ski season $175–$285 double. Higher rates on some festival weekends. Rates include continental breakfast and afternoon refreshments. AE, CB, DC, DISC, MC, V.

A full-service lodging just half a block from the Oak Street chairlift, the Ice House offers casual and comfortable accommodations in a European alpine style. Stairs and an elevator ascend from the ground-floor entrance to the lobby, furnished with simple southwestern pieces. The decor carries to the guest rooms, which contain a king bed and sleeper sofa or two full-size beds, European comforters, custom-made light wood furniture, and great mountain views from private decks. Thirty-nine of the rooms have shower/tub combos with oversized tubs; three rooms have showers only. Limited room service is available, along with laundry service and in-room massage. Facilities include a swimming pool (half indoors, half outdoors), hot tub, steam room, and conference facilities. VCRs are available on request.

New Sheridan Hotel. 231 W. Colorado Ave. (P.O. Box 980), Telluride, CO 81435. ☎ **800/ 200-1891** or 970/728-4351. Fax 970/728-5024. 38 units (24 with private bathroom). TV TEL. $70–$200 double; $160–$400 suite. Rates include full breakfast. AE, DC, MC, V.

The pride of Telluride when it was built in 1895, the New Sheridan reached the peak of its fame in 1902 when presidential candidate William Jennings Bryan delivered a speech from a platform outside. Decor is Victorian; roll-aways or day beds are available; and some units have whirlpool tubs. The suites, in a separate building, are condominium-style units, with full kitchen, bedrooms, and living room. The Sheridan lounge, with an Austrian-made cherry-wood bar, is on the hotel's first floor. Smoking is not permitted.

Pennington's Mountain Village Inn. 100 Pennington Court (P.O. Box 2428), Mountain Village Resort, Telluride, CO 81435. ☎ **800/543-1437** or 970/728-5337. Fax 970/ 728-5338. 12 units. TV TEL. $140–$300. Rates include full breakfast. AE, DISC, MC, V.

Located just off Colo. 145 at the entrance to Telluride Mountain Village, Pennington's is a luxurious getaway, the ultimate in bed-and-breakfasts, with French-country decor throughout. Every room has top quality king or queen beds, private decks, and refrigerators stocked with beverages (included in the price of the room); some have hot tubs. Amenities include afternoon refreshments; a library lounge with books, games, and a large fireplace; a billiards room; an indoor whirlpool and sauna; complimentary guest laundry facilities; and lockers for ski and golf equipment.

INEXPENSIVE

The Victorian Inn. 401 W. Pacific Ave. (P.O. Box 217), Telluride, CO 81435. ☎ **970/ 728-6601.** Fax 970/728-3233. www.telluridemm.com/victorin.html. 26 units (20 with private bathroom). TV TEL. $67–$155 double with private bathroom; $55–$123 double with shared bathroom. Rates include continental breakfast. AE, CB, DC, DISC, MC, V.

Built in 1976 in keeping with the turn-of-the-century flavor of the town of Telluride, the Victorian offers a pleasant alternative to the seemingly hundreds of condos that populate this town. The spacious and recently renovated rooms, decorated with Victorian-style furnishings, are fully carpeted and have individually controlled heating, one or two queen beds, and refrigerators. Two units have kitchenettes. Guests have use of a sauna and hot tub; the continental breakfast includes fresh-baked muffins, coffee, and tea. Smoking is not permitted.

WHERE TO DINE
EXPENSIVE

Campagna. 435 W. Pacific Ave. ☎ **970/728-6190.** Reservations recommended. Main courses $16–$32. MC, V. Mid-June–early Oct and late Nov–early Apr, daily from 6pm. TUSCAN.

Chef Vincent Esposito has converted an old miner's house into a friendly, country-style Italian restaurant, with an open kitchen and sepia-toned photographs of

Italian scenes. A third-generation chef, Esposito was in Italy studying art history when he fell in love with Tuscan food. The menu changes nightly, but might include wild game, such as grilled wild boar sausages with broccoli rabe, served over grilled polenta; rabbit braised with white wine, artichokes, carrots, and tarragon; fresh black sea bass grilled whole with fennel and garlic; or fresh hand-shucked sea scallops and Gulf shrimp sautéed in a tomato wine sauce with fresh herbs and served over spaghettini. Desserts include a hazelnut tart covered with Belgian chocolate and served with hazelnut ice cream. The restaurant also offers an excellent selection of Italian dinner and dessert wines.

Cosmopolitan. 300 W. San Juan Ave. ☎ **970/728-292.** Reservations recommended. Dinner main courses $18–$24. AE, MC, V. Summer, daily 11:30am–10:30pm; ski season, daily 7:30am–10pm. CREATIVE AMERICAN.

A high-class restaurant offering fine dining, the Cosmopolitan is also casual enough for a relaxing meal after a hard day on the slopes. Decor is tastefully simple—sort of upscale cafe—and there's an outdoor patio for warm-weather dining. The dinner menu includes a variety of dishes—beef, fish, lamb, duck, and vegetarian—all prepared with an innovative flair by chef/owner Chad Scothorn. Among recommended dishes are coriander-crusted halibut with lobster sorrel potato salad, and the grilled dry-aged rib-eye. Those feeling adventurous might start their meal with some barbecued eel.

La Marmotte. 150 W. San Juan Ave. ☎ **970/728-6232.** Reservations recommended. Main courses $17–$28. AE, CB, DC, DISC, MC, V. Daily 6–10pm (closed Tues in summer). Closed mid-April–mid-June and mid-Oct–Nov. FRENCH.

In a tiny house of exposed brick and weathered wood beside the Ice House Lodge—in fact, this building was Telluride's icehouse at the turn of the century—Bertrand and Noëlle Lepel-Cointet have fashioned a memorable dining experience of country-style French cuisine. The menu changes seasonally, but you might begin with an hors d'oeuvre such as baked escargots with sautéed Belgian endives in tomato and garlic sauce, and then move on to an entree such as roasted Colorado rack of lamb with fresh green beans and garlic cream sauce. The restaurant often offers innovative variations of grilled salmon or beef, plus sautéed sea bass or venison.

MODERATE

Fat Alley. 122 S. Oak St. ☎ **970/728-3985.** Reservations not accepted. $5.75–$15.25. AE, MC, V. Daily 11am–10pm. BARBECUE.

A favorite of local ski bums with big appetites and near-empty wallets, Fat Alley offers a variety of hickory smoked meats, sandwiches, and even a few vegetarian items. In a small, simply-decorated, cafe-style restaurant, it delivers spicy pork spare ribs or beef ribs by the rack or half rack, and whole, half, or quarter roast chicken. Sandwiches include smoked brisket, chicken, or pork shoulder; and vegetarian entrees include a ziti and black bean plate. Free in-town delivery is available.

Maggie's Bakery & Cafe. 217 E. Colorado Ave. ☎ **970/728-3334.** Reservations not accepted. Breakfast and lunch $2.75–$6.75. No credit cards. Daily 7am–4pm. AMERICAN.

The atmosphere here is simple, with oak tables and antique cookie jars, and the cuisine is geared toward those who appreciate home-baked breads and pastries and hearty sandwiches. Breakfast dishes include traditional bacon and eggs with potatoes and fresh-baked bread, pancakes, biscuits with sausage gravy, and fresh fruit. Lunch possibilities include half-pound burgers on home-baked buns, a variety of deli and vegetarian sandwiches, pizzas, and soups. Smoking is not permitted.

6 Ouray

73 miles N of Durango, 96 miles S of Grand Junction

Named for the greatest chief of the southern Ute tribe, whose homeland was in this area, Ouray, at an elevation of 7,760 feet, got its start in 1876 as a gold- and silver-mining camp, but within 10 years had 1,200 residents, a school, several churches, a hospital, and dozens of saloons and brothels. Today Ouray retains much of its 19th-century charm, with many of its original buildings still standing. It offers visitors a restful getaway while serving as home base for exploring the beautiful San Juan Mountains, with peaks rising to over 14,000 feet.

ESSENTIALS

GETTING THERE   By Car   U.S. 550 runs through the heart of Ouray, paralleling the Uncompahgre River, and connecting it with Durango to the south and Montrose to the north.

As you enter from the north, the highway passes the Ouray Hot Springs Pool and becomes Main Street. Above Third Avenue, U.S. 550 begins its climb up switchbacks to the Million Dollar Highway.

VISITOR INFORMATION   Stop in the **Ouray Visitor Center** beside the Hot Springs Pool, on U.S. 550 at the north end of town, or contact the **Ouray Chamber Resort Association,** P.O. Box 145, Ouray, CO 81427 (☎ **800/ 228-1876** or 970/325-4746; www.ouraycolorado.com; e-mail:ouray@rmii.com). If you're planning a winter visit, be sure to ask about half-price skiing at Telluride when you stay in Ouray.

FAST FACTS   The **Ouray Medical Center** (call for hours) is on the south side of town at 302 Second Ave. (☎ **970/626-5123**). The **post office** is at 620 Main St.; contact the U.S. Postal Service (☎ **800/275-8777**) for hours and additional information.

SPECIAL EVENTS   Cabin Fever Days, mid-February; Music in Ouray, June; the Artists' Alpine Holiday, July; Ouray County Fair, early September.

WHAT TO SEE & DO

The main summertime outdoor activity here is exploring the spectacularly beautiful mountains and forests, by foot, mountain bike, horse, or four-wheel-drive vehicle. Local outfitters include **San Juan Scenic Jeep Tours,** 824 Main St. (☎ **877/ 325-4385** or 970/325-4444), which has been offering off-road tours since 1946. Half-day tours start at $30 for adults and $15 for children 5 to 12 (free for kids under 5), and full-day tours start at $60 and $30, respectively. Another is **Switzerland of America,** 226 Seventh Ave. (☎ **800/432-5337** or 970/325-4484; www. soajeep.com; e-mail: soajeep@independence.net), which rents four-wheel-drive jeeps, leads jeep tours into the high country, and arranges horseback rides, fishing trips, raft rides, and balloon rides.

At the southwest corner of Ouray, at Oak Street above Third Avenue, the ✪ **Box Canyon Falls** (☎ **970/325-4464**) are among the most impressive in the Rockies. The Uncompahgre River tumbles 285 feet through—not over, *through*—a cliff: It's easy to get a feeling of vertigo as you study the spectacle. The trail to the bottom of the falls is easy; to the top it is moderate to strenuous. Admission to the area is $2 for adults, $1.50 for seniors, and $1 for children 5 to 12. It's open daily from 8am to dusk.

✪ **Bachelor-Syracuse Mine Tour.** 2 miles from Ouray via County Rd. 14. ☎ **970/ 325-0220.** Fax 970/325-4500. www.ouraycolorado.com/activits.html. Admission $10.95 adults, $9.95 seniors 62 and over, $5.95 children 3–12, free for children under 3. Mid-May to mid-Sept, 9am–5pm; shorter hours at the beginning and end of this period. Closed July 4. Reservations recommended, especially July–Aug.

A mine train takes visitors 3,350 feet inside Gold Hill, to see where some $8 million in gold, $90 million in silver, and $5 million in other minerals have been mined since the first silver strike was made by three men in 1884. Guides, many of them former miners, explain the mining process and equipment and recite the various legends of the mine. Also on the property is an operating blacksmith shop, plus streams where you can learn the technique of gold-panning ($5.95 extra). An outdoor cafe serves an all-you-can-eat breakfast until noon and Texas-style barbecue all day. The mine temperature is a cool 50°, so jackets are recommended, even in summer.

Ouray County Historical Museum. 420 Sixth Ave. ☎ **970/325-4576.** Admission $3 adults, $1 children 6–12. June–mid-Sept, daily 9am–4pm; Mid-Sept to May, Sat and Mon 10am–4pm, Sun 1–4pm.

Lodged in the original Miners' Hospital, completed in 1887 and operated by the Sisters of Mercy, this three-story museum is packed to the rafters with fascinating exhibits from Ouray's past. Displays include pioneer and mining-era relics, items relating to railroad and other transportation modes of the 19th century, memorabilia of Chief Ouray and the Utes, early hospital equipment including some scary-looking medical devices, Victorian artifacts, and historic photos. Ask here for a walking-tour guide to the town's many historic buildings.

Ouray Hot Springs Pool. U.S. 550, at the north end of Ouray. ☎ **970/325-4638.** Admission $6 adults, $5 students 7–17, $3 children 3–6, and $5 seniors 65 and over. June–Aug, daily 10am–10pm; Sept–May, daily noon–9pm.

This oval outdoor pool, 250 feet by 150 feet, holds nearly a million gallons of odorless mineral water. Spring water is cooled from 150°F; the pool is normally 80°F, but there's a hot soak of 105°F. Also on the property is a fitness center, with exercise equipment and aerobics classes (call for rates); there's a picnic area and playground in an adjacent municipal park.

WHERE TO STAY

Columbus House Bed & Breakfast. 746 Main St. (P.O. Box 31), Ouray, CO 81427. ☎ **970/325-4551.** Fax 970/325-7388. 6 units (all share bathroom with shower only). $59–$69 double. Rates include full breakfast. DC, MC, V. Closed mid-Oct to mid-May. Children over 12 accepted.

This handsome Victorian building was constructed in 1898 as a saloon with what was then called a "female rooming attachment" on the second floor, and almost immediately neighboring businesses and citizens began complaining about the women's line of work. Things have changed, and today this former house of sin is a well-kept budget bed-and-breakfast inn, where those who don't mind sharing a bathroom can spend the night in a small but delightfully-decorated room, with a good firm queen bed and Victorian-style wallpaper and furnishings, including some genuine antiques. Guests share a sitting room with a TV, and breakfast is served downstairs at the Silver Nugget Cafe (see "Where to Dine," below). All rooms are on the second floor, accessible by stairs only. Smoking is not permitted.

Ouray Victorian Inn. 50 Third Ave. (P.O. Box 1812), Ouray, CO 81427. ☎ **800/846-8729** or 970/325-7222. Fax 970/325-7225. www.ouraylodging.com. E-mail: info@ouraylodging. com. 48 units. TV TEL. $49–$95 double; $64–$180 townhomes (up to four persons);

$100–$180 cabins (up to six persons). Rates include buffet breakfast October through the third week in May. AE, DC, DISC, MC, V. Pets allowed in some units with $50 deposit.

Located in Ouray's National Historic District, this Victorian-style inn offers spacious rooms with outstanding views, in-room coffee, a sundeck, playground, and two outdoor hot tubs. There's a variety of choices, including rooms with one king-size bed and a sofa, units with two queen beds and a table and chairs, suites with kitchenettes and balconies, town homes with full kitchens, and cabins with full kitchens.

St. Elmo Hotel. 426 Main St. (P.O. Box 667), Ouray, CO 81427. ☎ **970/325-4951.** Fax 970/325-0348. www.colorado-bnb.com/stelmo. E-mail: steh@rmi.net. 9 units. Summer and Christmas holidays $92–$102 double; winter $65–$94 double. Rates include full breakfast and afternoon refreshments. AE, DISC, MC, V.

An 1898 town landmark, restored to Victorian splendor, the St. Elmo has an old-fashioned lobby that's a meeting place for locals and guests alike. Its rooms contain many original furnishings. Throughout are stained glass, polished wood, and brass trim. There's a TV in the parlor, plus an outdoor hot tub and sauna. On the premises is the Bon Ton Restaurant (see "Where to Dine," below). Smoking is not permitted.

Wiesbaden Hot Springs Spa & Lodgings. Sixth Ave. and Fifth St. (P.O. Box 349), Ouray, CO 81427. ☎ **970/325-4347.** Fax 970/325-4358. E-mail: wiesbaden@gwe.net. 24 units. TV TEL. $85–$100 double; $120–$150 suite and cottage. DISC, MC, V.

Built over a continually flowing hot-springs vapor cave, the Wiesbaden need never worry about artificial heating. Included in the rates are use of the vapor cave and its 108°F to 110°F soaking pool plus the swimming pool, which, though outdoors, is open year-round and heated to between 100°F and 103°F. Guests also have free use of the spa's exercise equipment, and receive discounts on services such as therapeutic massage, facials, aromatherapy wraps, and acupressure. There's also an outdoor flowing hot springs spa. Units include standard rooms with a variety of bed choices; suites with a living room, bedroom, and sitting area; small apartments with kitchen facilities; and a cottage with a wood stove. The original structure was built in 1879, and today's rooms have an "old-country" ambiance with historic photographs on the walls. Smoking is not permitted.

WHERE TO DINE

Bon Ton Restaurant. In the St. Elmo Hotel, 426 Main St. ☎ **970/325-4951.** Reservations recommended. Main courses $9–$24. AE, DISC, MC, V. Daily 5–9pm, plus Sun 9:30am–1pm. ITALIAN.

A fixture in Ouray for more than a century—it had another location before moving into the St. Elmo Hotel basement in 1898—the Bon Ton is Ouray's finest. With stone outer walls, hardwood floors, and reproduction antique furnishings, it carries a western Victorian appeal. The menu, which varies nightly, includes a variety of pasta dishes, from tortellini carbonara to ravioli pesto; a "miner's medley" of sautéed veal, sausage, and chicken on fettuccine; and various beef, veal, chicken, and fresh seafood dishes. There's an exceptionally good wine list, a children's menu, and an elaborate brunch offered each Sunday.

Silver Nugget Cafe. 740 Main St. ☎ **970/325-4100.** Lunch $4.25–$7; dinner $5–$17. DC, MC, V. Daily 7am–9pm. Closed mid-Oct–Apr. AMERICAN.

A busy, contemporary eatery, the Silver Nugget occupies a historic building at the north end of Ouray. You can get a Denver omelet or huevos rancheros for breakfast, and a wide variety of deli-style sandwiches for lunch. The dinner menu runs the gamut from liver and onions and spaghetti with meat sauce to deep-fried

Rocky Mountain rainbow trout and top sirloin steak, with most dinner choices under $10.

7 Wolf Creek Ski Area

75 miles E of Durango, 65 miles W of Alamosa

Wolf Creek is famous throughout Colorado as the area that consistently has the most snow in the state—an annual average of 465 inches (almost 39 feet).

One of the state's oldest ski areas, Wolf Creek has terrain for skiers of all ability levels, but especially intermediates. Expert skiers often leave the lift-served slopes to dive down the powder of the Water Fall Area, then await pickup by a snowcat shuttle that returns them to the base area. The Alberta Peak area offers extremely steep skiing and one of the most spectacular views of the peaks and pristine wilderness. Slopes are rated 20% beginner, 35% intermediate, 25% advanced, and 20% expert. Snowboarders are welcome in all areas of the resort.

In all, the area has 1,000 acres of terrain with 30 miles of trails, and a vertical drop of 1,604 feet from the 11,904-foot summit. The mountain has 50 trails served by five lifts (two triple chairs, two doubles, and a Magic Carpet rolling conveyor) plus a snowcat shuttle. Wolf Creek Lodge is a day lodge with restaurant and bar service, where you'll also find ski sales and rentals.

Contact **Wolf Creek Ski Area,** P.O. Box 2800, Pagosa Springs, CO 81147 (☎ **970/264-5639** for information or 970/264-5629 for a ski report; fax 970/264-5732; www.wolfcreekski.com; e-mail: wolfcreekski@wolfcreekski.com). Lift tickets (1998–99 season) cost $36 for adults, $23 for children 12 and under and seniors 65 and over. Full-day ski and snowboard class lessons start at $34; rental packages begin at $13 for adults and $10 for children. The resort is open early November through mid-April, daily from 9am to 4pm.

WHERE TO STAY & DINE   Among nearby communities with lodging, dining, and other services is Pagosa Springs, 25 miles southwest of the ski area via U.S. 160.

Lodging choices here include the **Spring Inn,** 165 Hot Springs Blvd. (☎ **800/225-0934** or 970/264-4168), which has six outdoor hot tubs with therapeutic mineral water from the nearby hot springs, and rates for two of $64 to $90 in standard rooms and $79 to $135 in suites and one cabin. Among chain properties in Pagosa Springs are **Best Western Oak Ridge Lodge,** 158 Hot Springs Blvd. (☎ **800/528-1234** or 970/264-4173), with rates of $53 to $84 double; and **Super 8,** 34 Piedra Rd. (☎ **800/800-8000** or 970/731-4005), with double rates of $48 to $64.

Recommended restaurants in Pagosa Springs include **Greenhouse Restaurant & Bar**, 505 Piedra Rd. (☎ **970/731-2021**), which serves dinner nightly, offering New American cuisine with organically produced beef and poultry and lots of fresh herbs, and main courses in the $10 to $20 range; and the **Rolling Pin Bakery & Cafe,** 214 Pagosa St. (☎ **970/264-2255**), which is open daily for breakfast and lunch, serving lots of fresh-baked goods plus burgers, sandwiches, and quiche, with prices in the $3 to $6 range.

Pagosa Springs is also a good base for hiking, camping, and fishing during the summer months; it has hot mineral baths and more than a dozen historic buildings and sites. For information, consult the **Pagosa Springs Chamber of Commerce,** P.O. Box 787, Pagosa Springs, CO 81147 (☎ **800/252-2204** or 970/264-2360; www.pagosa-springs.com; e-mail: chamber@pagosa-springs.com). The chamber operates a **visitor center** on the south bank of the San Juan River at Hot Springs Boulevard, across from Town Park, which has picnic tables and a river walk.

The Southern Rockies   14

If Colorado is the rooftop of America, then the southern Rockies are the peak of that roof. Some 30 of Colorado's fourteeners—14,000-plus-foot peaks—ring the area, and from Monarch Pass, at 11,312 feet, rivers flow in three directions.

Isolated from the rest of Colorado by its high mountains and rugged canyons, this region has historically bred proud, independent-minded people. In the 18th century, settlers came from Taos, New Mexico, and built some of the region's striking Spanish architecture. To this day, the influence of these Spanish settlers remains strong, particularly in the San Luis Valley and Colorado's oldest town of San Luis, incorporated in 1851.

Today these mountain and river towns have earned a reputation as recreational capitals: Gunnison for fishing and hunting, Crested Butte for skiing and mountain biking, and Salida and Buena Vista for white-water rafting. Alamosa is within easy reach of numerous scenic attractions, including the remarkable Great Sand Dunes National Monument. In the foothills of the San Juan Range are the historic mining towns of Creede and Lake City, and in the tiny community of Antonito you can hop a narrow-gauge steam train for a trip back to a simpler but smokier time. This is a rugged and sparsely populated land, with numerous opportunities for seeing the wilds of mountain America at their best.

1 Gunnison & Curecanti National Recreation Area

196 miles SW of Denver, 161 miles W of Pueblo, 65 miles E of Montrose

A rough-and-ready western town, Gunnison is where you go to get a hot shower and a good meal after a week of camping, hiking, boating, or hunting in the rugged mountains and canyons in the surrounding area.

Utes began hunting here about 1650, and although Spanish explorers probably never penetrated this isolated region, mountain men, pursuing pelts, arrived by the 1830s. First mapped by U.S. Army captain John Gunnison in 1853, the town was established in 1874, soon growing into a ranching center and transportation hub for nearby silver and gold mines. Western State College was established in 1911; now with an enrollment of 2,500, it is the only college in the United States with a certified technical-evacuation mountain-rescue team.

The Southern Rockies

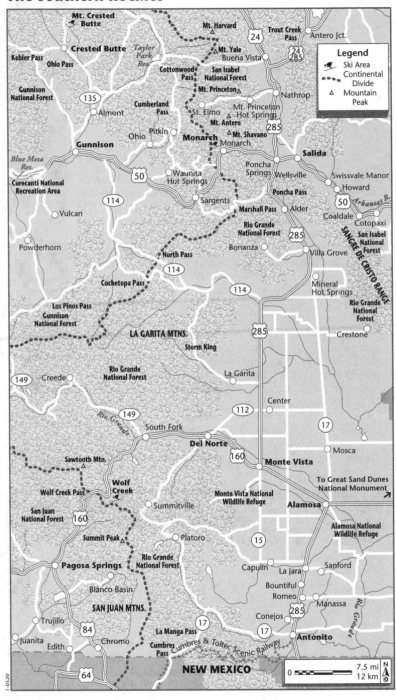

Mt. Crested Butte

Mt. Harvard △

Trout Creek Pass

Antero Jct.

24

Crested Butte

△ Mt. Yale
Buena Vista

Legend

Ski Area

Continental Divide

△ Mountain Peak

Kebler Pass

Ohio Pass

Taylor Park Res.

Cottonwood Pass

San Isabel National Forest

24
285

Gunnison National Forest

135

Cumberland Pass

Mt. Princeton △

Nathrop

Almont

St. Elmo

Mt. Princeton Hot Springs

Ohio

Pitkin

Mt. Antero △

285

Gunnison

Monarch

△ Mt. Shavano

Monarch

Salida

Blue Mesa Res.

50

Waunita Hot Springs

Poncha Springs

Wellsville

Swissvale Manor

Curecanti National Recreation Area

114

Sargents

Poncha Pass

Alder

Howard

50

Arkansas R.

Vulcan

Marshall Pass

Coaldale

Cotopaxi

Powderhorn

Rio Grande National Forest

Bonanza

Villa Grove

San Isabel National Forest

North Pass

114

Mineral Hot Springs

Rio Grande National Forest

Cochetopa Pass

114

285

SANGRE DE CRISTO RANGE

Los Pinos Pass

Gunnison National Forest

LA GARITA MTNS.

285

Crestone

Storm King

149

Creede

Rio Grande National Forest

La Garita

Center

Rio Grande

149

112

17

South Fork

Del Norte

Mosca

Sawtooth Mtn. △

160

Monte Vista

Wolf Creek Pass

Wolf Creek

Summitville

Monte Vista National Wildlife Refuge

Alamosa

To Great Sand Dunes National Monument

San Juan National Forest

160

Summit Peak △

Platoro

15

Alamosa National Wildlife Refuge

Pagosa Springs

Rio Grande National Forest

Capulin

La Jara

Sanford

Blanco Basin

Bountiful

Romeo

SAN JUAN MTNS.

Manassa

Trujillo

84

Conejos

285

Juanita

Edith

Chromo

La Manga Pass

17

17

Antonito

Cumbres Pass

Cumbres & Toltec Scenic Railway

64

NEW MEXICO

Rio Grande

0   7.5 mi
    12 km

N

1-0520

370

ESSENTIALS

GETTING THERE   By Car   Gunnison is located on U.S. 50, midway between Montrose and Salida. From Denver, the most direct route is U.S. 285 southwest to Poncha Springs, then west on U.S. 50. From Grand Junction, follow U.S. 50 through Montrose.

By Plane   The **Gunnison County Airport,** 711 Rio Grande Ave. (☎ 970/ 641-2304), is just off U.S. 50, a few blocks south of downtown Gunnison. **United Express** (☎ 800/241-6522 or 970/641-0111) provides daily year-round service from Denver; **America West Express** (☎ 800/235-9292) offers daily year-round service from Phoenix. During nearby Crested Butte's winter ski season, air service is also provided by **Delta** (☎ 800/221-1212) and **American Airlines** (☎ 800/ 433-7300); **Adventure Tours USA** (☎ 214/360-5050) provides twice-weekly ski packages from Dallas.

    Alpine Express (☎ 800/822-4844 or 970/641-5074) provides shuttle service from Gunnison County Airport to Crested Butte and Telluride. It runs frequently during ski season, but call for availability at other times.

VISITOR INFORMATION   Contact the **Gunnison Country Chamber of Commerce,** 500 E. Tomichi Ave. (P.O. Box 36), Gunnison, CO 81230 (☎ 800/ 274-7580 or 970/641-1501; www.gunnison-co.com; e-mail: guncham@ rmii. com), which operates a visitor center.

GETTING AROUND   The town lies along the southeast bank of the west-flowing Gunnison River. Tomichi Avenue (U.S. 50) runs east-west through town. Main Street (Colo. 135) intersects Tomichi Avenue in the center of town and proceeds north to Crested Butte.

    Car-rental agencies at Gunnison County Airport include **Avis** (☎ 970/ 641-0263), **Budget** (☎ 970/641-4403), and **Hertz** (☎ 970/641-2881).

FAST FACTS   Gunnison Valley Hospital, with a 24-hour emergency room, is at 214 E. Denver Ave. (☎ **970/641-1456**), 2 blocks east of Main Street and 6 blocks north of U.S. 50. The **post office** is at Virginia Avenue and Wisconsin Street; for hours and other information contact the U.S. Postal Service (☎ **800/ 275-8777**). For **road conditions,** call ☎ **970/249-9363**.

SPECIAL EVENTS   Gunnison County Airshow, mid-June; Cattlemen's Days, Colorado's oldest continually held rodeo, third week in July; and the Parade of Lights, early December.

CURECANTI NATIONAL RECREATION AREA

Dams on the Gunnison River, just below Gunnison, have created a series of three very different reservoirs, extending 35 miles to the mouth of the Black Canyon of the Gunnison (see "Montrose & Black Canyon of the Gunnison National Monument," in chapter 12). **Blue Mesa Lake** (elevation 7,519 feet), the easternmost (beginning 9 miles west of Gunnison), is the largest lake in Colorado when filled to capacity, and a water-sports paradise popular for fishing, motorboating, sailboating, board sailing, and other activities. Fjord-like **Morrow Point Lake** (elevation 7,160 feet) and **Crystal Lake** (elevation 6,755 feet) fill long, serpentine canyons accessible only by precipitous trails and thus are limited to use by hand-carried boats.

    These lakes offer some of Colorado's best boating. Daily boating permits cost $4. Call ☎ 970/641-2337 for information. Boat rentals can be arranged at **Elk Creek Marina** on Blue Mesa Lake, 16 miles west of Gunnison off U.S. 50 (☎ **970/ 641-0707**). Rates are about $10 per hour or $50 per day for small fishing boats with outboard motors, and about $25 to $27 per hour or $125 to $135 per day for pontoon boats. There's a second marina at Lake Fork, 25 miles west of Gunnison, at the reservoir's west end (☎ 970/641-3084), with similar rates. A boat tour, offered by Elk Creek Marina, leaves the Pine Creek Trail boat dock on Morrow Point Lake daily, Memorial Day through Labor Day, to explore the Upper Black Canyon of the Gunnison. Rates are $8.50 for adults, $8 for youths 13 to 17, $7.50 for seniors 62 and older, and $5 for children under 13. Reservations are required (☎ 970/641-0402).

Hikers find a variety of trails, often with splendid views of the lakes. Those who want to see birds can't go wrong with the **Neversink Trail,** a 1½-mile round-trip hike on the north shore of the Gunnison River, near a great blue heron rookery. Also watch for warblers, red-wing blackbirds, and great horned owls, plus an occasional mule deer among the cottonwoods and willows that shade the river. The trail is flat and relatively easy, and also provides fishing access. A moderately strenuous hike where you might see a golden eagle or two, and possibly some bighorn sheep, is the 4-mile round-trip **Dillon Pinnacles Trail,** which is open to horseback riders as well as hikers. It provides spectacular views of the strangely eroded volcanic formations called the Dillon Pinnacles. The visitor center has a free brochure that describes these and several other hikes.

Anglers visit Curecanti year-round—there's ice-fishing in winter—but the main season is May to October, when rainbow, brown, and Mackinaw trout and kokanee salmon are caught in large numbers. **Hunting,** especially for elk and deer, is popular in the adjacent West Elk Mountains.

The recreation area has four major **campgrounds,** with almost 350 sites, plus several smaller campgrounds. Campgrounds with showers cost $9 per night, while most of those without showers cost $8 per night. Several have marinas, boat ramps, and RV dump stations, but there are no RV hookups. Campgrounds remain open until blocked by snow, and there are usually sites available in at least one campground year-round, although water is available only from late May to mid-September. Backcountry and boat-in camping is also permitted, at no charge; check with rangers.

The **Elk Creek Visitor Center,** 15 miles west of Gunnison off U.S. 50, has exhibits and audiovisual programs, as well as maps and publications. It's open daily from mid-May through September and weekends the rest of the year. Nature hikes and evening campground programs are presented throughout the summer. At **Cimarron,** 45 miles west of Gunnison, there's a visitor center open daily from Memorial Day to Labor Day, with a historic train exhibit and a road to **Morrow Point Dam** power plant. For a brochure and other information before your trip, contact Superintendent, Curecanti National Recreation Area, 102 Elk Creek, Gunnison, CO 81230 (☎ 970/641-2337; www.nps.gov/cure).

OTHER SPORTS & OUTDOOR ACTIVITIES

In addition to activities in Curecanti National Recreation Area, there are opportunities for hiking, mountain biking, hunting, fishing, camping, and four-wheeling on other nearby public lands. For maps and other information, contact offices of the **Gunnison National Forest** and **Bureau of Land Management** at 216 N. Colorado St. (☎ 970/641-0471), open Monday through Friday year-round. A good base for exploring this area is **Three Rivers Resort and Outfitting,** 11 miles north of Gunnison on Taylor Canyon Road (P.O. Box 339), Almont, CO 81210 (☎ 888/761-3474 or 970/641-1303; www.3riversresort.com). Located between Gunnison and Crested Butte, close to the national forest, Three Rivers offers fishing and rafting trips (see below), and also has fully equipped and furnished cabins ($35 and up) and an RV park ($18 including hookups). Your best bet for sporting goods, including hiking boots, cross-country and downhill ski rentals, fishing and hunting gear, licenses, maps, and information is **Gene Taylor's Sporting Goods,** 201 W. Tomichi Ave. (☎ **970/641-1845**).

FISHING   The Gunnison River, both above and below town, and the tributary Taylor River, which joins the Gunnison at Almont, 11 miles north of town, are outstanding trout streams. In addition, the region's lakes are also rich in fish. **Willowfly Anglers,** at Three Rivers Resort, Almont (☎ **970/641-1303**), offers fly-fishing instruction, rentals, and guide service. Full-day float fishing trips cost $200 for one person and $230 for two, and walking trips are also available.

GOLF   The 18-hole **Dos Rios Golf Club,** off U.S. 50 southwest of town (☎ **970/641-1482**), charges $25 for 9 holes and $40 for 18 holes.

HORSEBACK RIDING   **Ferro's Trading Post,** P.O. Box 853, Gunnison, CO 81230 (☎ **970/641-4671**), offers horseback rides, with rates of $15 per hour or $45 for a half day. Pack trips are also available, starting at $100 per day. Ferro's is located on Soap Creek Road, about 26 miles west of Gunnison, overlooking Blue Mesa Reservoir. In addition to horseback rides, Ferro's has a general store with fishing licenses and supplies, plus six cabins, including several historic cabins (call for rental information).

RIVER RAFTING & KAYAKING   For trips on the Taylor and other rivers, check with **Three Rivers Resort and Outfitting** (see above). Rates for 2-hour raft trips over relatively calm stretches are $20 for adults and $14 for children under 12. Three Rivers also offers guided white-water trips in inflatable kayaks called "duckies," with rates of $35 for 2 hours and $75 for a full day, which includes lunch. Full-day trips are usually available only in spring, when water is highest.

SKIING   The two major winter-sports centers in the area are **Crested Butte,** 32 miles north on Colo. 135 (see section 2 of this chapter) and **Monarch,** 44 miles east on U.S. 50 (see section 3 of this chapter).

DISCOVERING GUNNISON'S PAST

Founded in the 1870s, the town of Gunnison has a number of historic buildings, ranging from log cabins to fancy 1880s homes—many in Gothic revival and Italianate styles—plus the 1882 stone Episcopal Church and various businesses. A free walking-tour brochure is available at the chamber of commerce visitor center (see above).

Gunnison Pioneer Museum. East U.S. 50. ☎ **970/641-4530** or 970/641-0740. Admission (1998 rates) $5 adults, $1 children 6–12, free for children under 6. Memorial Day–Labor Day, Mon–Sat 9am–5pm.

A Denver & Rio Grande narrow-gauge steam train, depot, and water tank are highlights at this local historical society museum, which includes eight buildings from the area's past. Among its other exhibits are a rural schoolhouse (circa 1905), a home with 19th-century furnishings, a dairy barn (circa 1880), minerals and arrowheads, antique cars and wagons, dolls, toys, and Gunnison's first post office (1876).

WHERE TO STAY

Highest lodging rates in Gunnison are in summer and during the Christmas holidays. You'll usually find the lowest rates in late winter and early spring. Major chain and franchise motels that provide reasonably priced lodging in Gunnison include the **Best Western Tomichi Village Inn,** on U.S. 50, 1 mile east of Gunnison (☎ 800/641-1131 or 970/641-1131), charging double rates of $76 to $100 in summer and $46 to $90 the rest of the year; **Econo Lodge,** 37760 U.S. 50

The Bizarre Tale of Alferd Packer

The winter of 1873 to 1874 was bad in southwest Colorado's San Juan Mountains—deep snow, staggeringly strong winds, and below-zero temperatures. But among the many miners who found themselves there, drawn by the hope of staking a claim among the region's newly discovered silver deposits, the temptation to change their fortunes in a day was just too powerful to resist. In February, six eager miners, led by Alferd Packer, set out from a Ute encampment near the present-day town of Delta, ignoring warnings from Ouray, chief of the Ute people. They took only 10 days' worth of food and weren't heard from for over 2 months, until Packer arrived alone at Los Piños Indian Agency, about 25 miles south of the present town of Gunnison.

Packer told Indian Agency officials that after he became ill, his companions abandoned him, and he survived on roots and bushes while making his way through the mountains. Curiously, he refused food upon his arrival. After resting, Packer traveled to the nearby community of Saguache, where he went on a drinking binge, paying with money from several wallets.

Since Packer had claimed to be penniless when the six men left the Ute encampment, and because Packer was the only one to return, Indian Agency officials became suspicious. Then, strips of what appeared to be human flesh were discovered along the path Packer had taken to the agency. Under questioning, Packer changed his story, claiming that others in the party had killed their companions, one by one, as they traveled, until only Packer and fellow miner Wilson Bell remained, and Packer was forced to kill Bell in self-defense. Packer admitted eating the remains of his companions and was arrested and jailed.

That August, Packer escaped from jail, just about the time that five partially decomposed bodies were discovered along the northeast side of Lake San

(☎ 800/553-2666 or 970/641-1000), with rates for two of $74 in summer and $42 to $56 at other times; **Ramada Limited**, 1011 W. Rio Grande Ave. (☎ 800/272-6232 or 970/641-2804), charging for two people $69 to $89 in summer and $58 to $74 at other times; and **Super 8,** 411 E. Tomichi Ave. (☎ 800/800-8000 or 970/641-3068), with rates for two from $70 to $77 in summer and $47 to $63 at other times. Room tax adds just under 9% to lodging bills.

Mary Lawrence Inn. 601 N. Taylor St., Gunnison, CO 81230. ☎ 970/641-3343. www.gunnison-co.com/main/lodging/maryl.htm. 7 units. $69–$85 double; from $99 suite. Rates include full breakfast. MC, V.

Built in 1885 in Italianate style, the house was purchased in 1908 by Illinois widow Mary Axtell Lawrence, who operated a boardinghouse in the home while serving as teacher and school administrator in Gunnison. Now owned and operated by Doug and Beth Parker, the inn is located in a quiet neighborhood near Western State College. Rooms are individually decorated with antique furnishings, some four-poster beds, colorful quilts, sponge-painted and stenciled walls, and original artwork. Five units have shower/tub combos and two have showers only; two suites have TVs. The shared parlor contains a TV, fireplace, games, and an over-stuffed leather couch. There's a large outdoor deck, gazebo, and hot tub, as well as a cozy sunroom. Creative country-style breakfasts are served, with an assortment of juices, hot teas, and gourmet coffees; fresh-baked snacks are available throughout the day. Smoking is not permitted.

Cristobal, a few miles south of the present town of Lake City. Four of the men had apparently been murdered in their sleep, their heads split open with an ax, while a fifth had been shot. Chunks of flesh had been cut from at least two of the men's chests and thighs, and one was decapitated.

The search for Packer was now on in earnest, but he was nowhere to be found. Finally, about 9 years later, Packer was discovered living in Wyoming, using the name John Schwartz. Packer was arrested, and in April 1883, tried on a charge of premeditated murder, convicted, and sentenced to hang. That would have been the end of Packer, but the trial was declared unconstitutional on a technicality.

Packer was retried in 1886, convicted on five counts of manslaughter, and sentenced to 45 years in prison. However, due to poor health, he was pardoned by Governor Charles Thomas after only 5 years behind bars. Packer died of natural causes in the Denver area in 1907, at the age of 64, and was buried in the Littleton Cemetery. As an interesting aside, all through his life Packer's first name, Alferd, had been misspelled. Apparently, it was a problem that followed him into death, since today the name "Alfred" is prominently displayed on his tombstone.

Though many at the time considered it an open-and-shut case, some have questioned whether Packer was really guilty of murder, or if he was simply convicted because of the public's revulsion at his admission of cannibalism. In 1989, the bodies were exhumed, and it was determined that they had likely been victims of cannibalism—but no evidence has shown definitively that Packer killed them. The site where the bodies were found, near the town of Lake City (see "A Side Trip to Lake City," below) is now known as Cannibal Plateau.

Wildwood Motel. 1312 W. Tomichi Ave., Gunnison, CO 81230. ☎ **970/641-1663.** www.gunnison-co.com/main/lodging/wildwood.htm. E-mail: wldwdmtl@rmi.net. 18 units. TV TEL. $50–$57 double. Fishing, hunting, and ski packages available. Campsites $16 including RV hookups. DISC, MC, V. From downtown, continue straight on Tomichi Ave. when U.S. 50 curves to the left and you see the motel's billboard; from the west turn left on New York Ave. (the first traffic light), then right on 8th and left onto Tomichi. The motel is ahead on the right.

Built in 1928 as a summer refuge for members of the Chicago underworld, the Wildwood today is a favorite hideaway for budget-conscious outdoor sports lovers. Rooms here aren't fancy, but they're quiet, very clean, and well maintained, and all include a full kitchen, including coffeemakers (some also have microwaves). Five units have shower/tub combos and the rest have showers only. The attractive grounds contain a playground, swings, horseshoe pits, a beach volleyball court, badminton court, shady picnic tables, a fish cleaning station, and two duck ponds, where Tasmanian rainbow trout are raised for release into the Gunnison River. A half-size basketball court is planned for 1999.

Also on the property is a campground for fully self-contained RVs (no tents). Open from May through September, weather permitting, it has 16 large sites, with complete hookups including cable TV. Reservations are recommended.

CAMPING

In addition to the campgrounds in Curecanti National Recreation Area (see above), you'll find dozens of sites scattered throughout the Gunnison National Forest and lands administered by the Bureau of Land Management (☎ **970/641-0471**), with fees ranging from nothing to $12, depending on facilities. Wildwood Motel (see above) also offers RV sites.

Mesa Campground. 36128 W. U.S. 50, Gunnison, CO 81230. ☎ **800/482-8384** or 970/641-3186. 135 sites. $16–$22. DISC, MC, V. Closed Nov–Apr. Located 3 miles west of Gunnison.

A good base camp for fishing, hunting, or sightseeing trips, this campground caters mostly to RVs but does accept tenters. The campground has increased its number of large pull-through sites to accommodate big RVs, and 50 amp electric service is available. Facilities include clean bathhouses with plenty of hot water, a self-service laundry, gas pumps, and a store with propane and a limited selection of groceries and RV supplies.

WHERE TO DINE

Blue Iguana. 303 E. Tomichi Ave. ☎ **970/641-3403.** Reservations not accepted. $2–$6.25. DISC, MC, V. Summer, Mon–Sat 11am–9pm; shorter hours in winter. MEXICAN.

Homemade Sonoran-style Mexican fast food is the fare at the Blue Iguana, a somewhat hard-to-find storefront in the Elk Horn Building, 2 blocks east of Main Street—look for the big chrome sculpture of an elk out front. The restaurant decor is simple: picnic tables with red plastic coverings, and light-colored walls with bright red trim and red chile designs. In fast-food style, you order at the counter and pick up your taco, burrito, enchilada, or combo plate when your name is called, and either eat there or haul it away. House specialty is the chimichanga—a deep-fried flour tortilla stuffed with your choice of five fillings (shredded beef, beans, chicken, rice, green chile, red chile, and on and on), and topped with sour cream and guacamole. Okay, maybe it isn't health food, but it tastes great and the price is right. Delivery service is available (☎ **970/641-9546**).

Cattlemen Inn. 301 W. Tomichi Ave. ☎ **970/641-1061.** Reservations not accepted. Lunch $3–$7; dinner $6–$23. AE, CB, DC, MC, V. Upstairs dining room, daily 6:30am–3pm and 5–9pm; downstairs dining room, daily 5–11pm. AMERICAN.

Essentially there are two restaurants here: the downstairs one with attached bar has the look of a western steak house, with lots of rough wood, while the upstairs is more family-oriented. At the downstairs dining room—called the Beef & Barrel— it's no surprise to find that beef is the specialty, and only the best hand-cut steer beef, so you can bet you'll thoroughly enjoy your steak, prime rib, or burger. Upstairs, you'll find a basic American menu, with all the standard breakfast selections, plus southwest variations. Lunches include lots of sandwiches, fish-and-chips, burritos, pinto-bean soup, and a salad bar. Dinner is served upstairs as well as downstairs. In addition to the great steaks, you can get many of the lunch items, plus trout, broiled chicken breast, and deep-fried breaded shrimp.

Josef's Restaurant. U.S. 50, 1½ miles east of Gunnison. ☎ **970/641-5032.** Main courses $6–$18. AE, CB, DC, DISC, MC, V. Daily 5–9pm. EUROPEAN/AMERICAN.

An Old World atmosphere pervades this fine restaurant adjacent to the Best Western Tomichi Village. The menu features a variety of charbroiled steaks, poultry, pasta, and fresh seafood, but the house specialties are true European favorites, including traditional Wiener schnitzel, Hungarian-style goulash (slowly braised beef tips with onions, mushrooms, paprika, and cabernet sauvignon demi-glace sauce), and rack of lamb with kiwi mint sauce. A special treat is Josef's fresh-baked pastries.

✪ A SIDE TRIP TO LAKE CITY

The historic mining town of Lake City is 55 miles southwest via Colo. 149 (turn south off U.S. 50, 9 miles west of Gunnison). Founded in 1874, this former silver and gold town is set against a backdrop of 14,000-plus-foot peaks in three different national forests—the Gunnison, Uncompahgre, and Rio Grande.

One of Colorado's largest national historic districts, Lake City has more than 75 buildings that date from the 19th century. Visit the recently renovated **Hinsdale County Courthouse,** 317 N. Henson St., built in 1877 and still the home of county government. You'll see exhibits on the trial of the notorious Alferd Packer and the courtroom where the trial took place (see "The Bizarre Tale of Alferd Packer," above). History buffs will also enjoy the **Hinsdale County Museum,** corner of Second and Silver streets (☎ 970/944-9515), with exhibits about the Packer trial, of course, plus the area's silver-mining heritage. Next door is the 1880s Smith-Grantham House, a small, furnished Victorian home where you can see how people here lived in the late 1800s. The museum is open Memorial Day through September; admission costs $2 for adults and 50¢ for children. The Hinsdale County Historical Society guides tours into some of the town's historic homes regularly throughout the summer. Check with the chamber of commerce (see below).

Surrounded by some 600,000 acres of public land, Lake City is an important recreational center, offering hiking, mountain biking, horseback riding, jeep rides, camping, and fishing in summer; and ice-fishing, cross-country skiing, snowshoeing, and snowmobiling in winter. Lake San Cristobal, just south of town via County Road 30, is Colorado's second-largest natural lake and particularly popular with fishermen. Also nearby you'll find several ghost towns and historic sites, most of which will require a four-wheel-drive vehicle, horse, mountain bike, or a good pair of hiking boots.

For information, including lists of boat and jeep rentals, outfitters, stables, accommodations, and restaurants, contact the **Lake City/Hinsdale County Chamber of Commerce,** P.O. Box 430, Lake City, CO 81235 (☎ **800/569-1874** or 970/944-2527; www.hinsdale-county.com; e-mail: chamber@pcrs.net). The chamber operates a visitor information center on Silver Street, in the middle of town.

2 Crested Butte

28 miles N of Gunnison, 224 miles SW of Denver

The town of Crested Butte was born in 1880 as the Denver & Rio Grande line laid a narrow-gauge rail track from Gunnison to serve the gold and silver mines in the area. But coal, not the more precious minerals, sustained the town from the late 1880s until 1952, when the last of the mines closed. The economy then languished until Mt. Crested Butte ski area was developed in 1961.

An influx of newcomers began renovating the old buildings in the 1970s, and in 1974 the entire town was designated a National Historic District. An architectural review board requires all new construction to be true to the town's heritage, ensuring that Crested Butte stays a cute little Victorian town—some would say it's almost *too* cute.

Today Crested Butte is known for skiing in winter, and hiking, bicycling, and other outdoor recreational activities in warmer weather. It has the best mountain biking in the state, and many Coloradans claim it's the best place to see fields of wildflowers.

ESSENTIALS

GETTING THERE   By Car   Crested Butte is 28 miles north of Gunnison on Colo. 135, the only year-round access. In summer, the gravel-surface Kebler Pass Road links Crested Butte with Colo. 133 at Paonia Reservoir, to the west; and four-wheel-drive vehicles can negotiate a difficult route south from Aspen, around the Maroon Bells.

By Plane   The **Gunnison County Airport** serves Crested Butte (see section 1 of this chapter). **Alpine Express** (☎ **800/822-4844** or **970/641-5074**) provides shuttle service from Gunnison County Airport to Crested Butte. It runs frequently during ski season, but call for availability at other times.

VISITOR INFORMATION   Consult the **Crested Butte–Mt. Crested Butte Chamber of Commerce,** P.O. Box 1288, Crested Butte, CO 81224 (☎ **800/ 545-4505** or 970/349-6438; fax 970/349-1023; www.cbinteractive.com). An **Information Center** is located downtown at the four-way stop at the corner of Elk Avenue and Sixth Street.

GETTING AROUND   There are actually two separate communities here: the old mining town of Crested Butte and the modern resort village of Mt. Crested Butte, 3½ miles away. Colo. 135 enters Crested Butte from the south and is intersected by Elk Avenue, which runs west-east as the town's main street.

Mountain Express (☎ **970/349-7318**) provides free shuttle-bus service between Crested Butte, Mt. Crested Butte, and area condominiums. Call for schedules. Local taxi service is available from **Town Taxi** (☎ **970/349-5543**).

FAST FACTS   The **Crested Butte Medical Center,** in the Ore Bucket Building in downtown Crested Butte (☎ **970/349-0321**), can handle most health needs; call 24 hours a day for urgent care. The **post office** is on the north side of Elk Avenue between Second and Third streets; contact the U.S. Postal Service (☎ **800/ 275-8777**) for hours and other information. For local **road conditions,** call ☎ 970/641-8008.

SPECIAL EVENTS   Fat Tire Bike Week, late June; Wildflower Festival, early July; Mountain Man Rendezvous, early August; the Arts Festival, August; Vinotok Slavic Fall Festival, mid-September.

SKIING & OTHER WINTER SPORTS

Crested Butte may be Colorado's best-kept secret. Situated at the intersection of two overlapping winter storm tracks, it's guaranteed to have outstanding snow. Offering abundant opportunities for beginners and intermediate skiers, Crested Butte has what many experts consider the most challenging runs—extreme-limits skiing—in the Rockies.

The resort has 1,160 acres of skiable terrain, including 550 acres of extreme limits, double black diamond ungroomed terrain for experts only. Altogether, trails are rated 13% beginner, 29% intermediate, 11% advanced, and 47% expert. Vertical drop is 3,062 feet from a summit of 12,162 feet. There are 85 trails served by 13 lifts (three high-speed quads, three triples, three doubles, and four surface lifts). Average annual snowfall is 229 inches, and there's snowmaking on trails served by all but two of the resort's lifts.

Crested Butte offers a ski program for the physically challenged, with specially trained and certified instructors; the children's ski center provides lessons, rental equipment, day care, and nursery services. The resort also has a designated snowboarding area as well as snowboard rentals and lessons.

For more information, contact **Crested Butte Mountain Resort,** 500 Gothic Rd. (P.O. Box A), Mt. Crested Butte, CO 81225 (☎ **800/544-8448** or 970/ 349-2222; 888/867-6933 or 970/349-2323 for snow reports; fax 970/349-2250; www.cbinteractive.com). Lift tickets (1998–99 season) are $49 for adults; children 12 and under pay their age. The resort offers free skiing from opening until the week before Christmas, and for several weeks in April (call for exact dates). It's usually open from just before Thanksgiving to mid-April, daily from 9am to 4pm.

CROSS-COUNTRY SKIING, SNOWSHOEING & ICE-SKATING The **Crested Butte Nordic Center,** based at Big Mine Park, Second Street and Whiterock Avenue in downtown Crested Butte (P.O. Box 1269), Crested Butte, CO 81224 (☎ **970/349-1707**), maintains 35 kilometers of groomed trails and organizes backcountry tours over more than 100 miles of wilderness trails. It's open in winter daily from 9am to 4pm. Cost is $7 for adults and $3.50 for children. The center also maintains a lighted ice-skating rink and offers skate rentals, plus snowshoe tours and rentals.

SNOWMOBILING Local companies that lead snowmobile tours through Gunnison National Forest include **Action Adventures Snowmobiling** (☎ 800/ 383-1974 or 970/349-5909; www.actionadventures.com), **Alpine Expeditions** (☎ 800/833-8052 or 970/349-5011), and **Burt Rentals** (☎ 970/349-2441). A wide variety of trips are available, at a wide range of prices.

WARM-WEATHER SPORTS & OUTDOOR ACTIVITIES

This is rugged country, surrounded by **Gunnison National Forest.** For maps and tips on the many activities available, contact the forest service office at 216 N. Colorado St. in Gunnison (☎ **970/641-0471**). The chairlifts at Crested Butte Mountain Resort don't stop just because the snow's gone, but operate daily from late June through August for hikers, mountain bikers, or those who simply want to enjoy this beautiful mountain scenery without hiking or biking. Single trips cost $13 for adults, $6 for children 6 to 12 and seniors 65 and older; all-day passes cost $15 and $7, respectively. Kids 5 and younger ride free (one per paying adult).

FOUR-WHEELING There are plenty of opportunities here to use your four-wheel-drive rig on old mining and logging roads. For maps, check at the Crested Butte Information Center or with the forest service (see above). Jeep Wranglers are rented by **Flatiron Sports,** Treasury Center, 10 Crested Butte Way, Mt. Crested Butte (☎ **800/821-4331** or 970/349-6656), for about $90 per day.

GOLF The 18-hole course at **Crested Butte Country Club,** 2 miles south of Crested Butte off Colo. 135 (☎ **970/349-6131**), is one of Colorado's best mountain courses. It's usually open from mid-May through October. The fee for 18 holes, including the mandatory cart, is $95 in summer, lower in the off-seasons.

HIKING There are practically unlimited opportunities for hiking and backpacking in the Crested Butte area. Ask the chamber of commerce for trail suggestions, or contact the Gunnison National Forest office.

HORSEBACK RIDING Guided rides are offered from June to mid-October by **Fantasy Ranch** (☎ **888/688-3488** or 970/349-5425), ranging from rides lasting several hours to week-long pack trips. Trips go into three different mountain wilderness areas, at elevations from 7,000 feet to 12,700 feet, including the incredibly scenic Maroon Bells. Prices are about $65 for rides of 3 to 4 hours, and start at $115 per person per day for overnight pack trips. Fantasy Ranch also offers supper barbecue rides and hunting trips, and has lodging available as well.

MOUNTAIN BIKING ✪ **Crested Butte** has established a firm reputation as the place to mountain bike in Colorado. From jeep roads to hiking trails, there's something here to please every ability level. Popular choices include the challenging 25-mile ride over 10,707-foot Schofield Pass to the village of Marble, off Colo. 133; and the shorter Cement Creek Trail to the base of Italian Mountain. You can get information from the Crested Butte Information Center or the forest service (see above).

For trail information, maps, and mountain-bike rentals, stop at **Flatiron Sports** in the Treasury Center at Mt. Crested Butte (☎ 800/821-4331 or 970/349-6656); **Christy Sports,** in the Treasury Center in Mt. Crested Butte (☎ 970/349-6601); or **Pinnacle Cycles,** in the Gothic Building at Mt. Crested Butte (☎ 970/349-2237). Bike rentals start at about $22 per day. To schedule a guided mountain-bike tour, contact **Pioneer Guide Service** (☎ 970/349-5517; e-mail: pioneer@crestedbutte.net), which offers half-day, full-day, and multi-day trips for individuals and small groups. The rate for a half-day tour for one person is $60, or $75 for two or three people. Four-day/three-night trips are $525 per person. Bike rentals are extra.

OTHER HIGHLIGHTS

The Crested Butte–Mt. Crested Butte Chamber of Commerce provides a free brochure on a **self-guided walking tour** of more than three dozen historic buildings in Crested Butte, including the picturesque 1883 Town Hall, 1881 railroad depot, numerous saloons and homes, and a unique two-story outhouse.

Downtown Crested Butte is home to about 10 **art galleries,** mostly along or just off Elk Avenue. These include **Paragon Galley,** at the corner of Second Street and Elk Avenue (☎ 970/349-6484), which is a cooperative gallery displaying the works of more than a dozen local artists and craftsworkers. A free brochure and map, *The Art Galleries of Crested Butte,* is available at the visitor center.

Crested Butte Mountain Heritage Museum. 200 Sopris Ave. ☎ **970/349-1880.** Call for hours and fees.

This museum concentrates on the area's mining and ranching heritage, with a wide array of memorabilia from local settlers' cabins. Exhibits also include a 1920 fire truck, used by the Crested Butte Fire Department, and vintage mountain bikes. You can pick up a free copy of the Crested Butte walking-tour map here.

WHERE TO STAY

Rates are highest in ski season. Area lodging reservations can be made with **Central Reservations** (☎ 800/215-2226). Room tax adds just under 10% to lodging bills.

The Claim Jumper. 704 Whiterock Ave. (P.O. Box 1181), Crested Butte, CO 81224. ☎ **970/349-6471.** 7 units. TV. $99–$149 double. Rates include full breakfast. DISC, MC, V. Dogs and well-behaved children over 10 are welcome.

A huge log home packed with antiques and family heirlooms, this B&B easily qualifies as Crested Butte's most unique accommodation. Each guest room has a particular theme: The Rough and Ready Room is dedicated to cowboys; Prospector's Gulch, to miners; and Commodore Corrigan's Cabin, to seafarers. Ethyl's Room, complete with restored gas pump, appeals to 1950s nostalgia buffs; and the Sports Room contains a putting range built into the floor. Rooms contain VCRs, with several hundred movies available. One unit has a claw-foot tub only, two have showers only, and four have shower/tub combos. The inn also features a redwood hot tub, sauna, and antique gaming parlor. Hearty five-course breakfasts include fresh fruit, fresh-baked items, and entrees such as bacon and eggs and pancakes.

Crested Butte International Hostel. 615 Teocalli Ave. (P.O. Box 1332), Crested Butte, CO 81224. ☎ **888/389-0588** or 970/349-0588. Fax 970/349-0586. www.gunnison.com/~hostel. E-mail: hostel@crestedbutte.net. 52 beds. All share bathrooms. Summer $18 per bed; winter $26 per bed. $3 discounts for Hostelling International members. DISC, MC, V.

This handsome, three-story hostel, which opened in late 1997, is among the nicest you'll find in Colorado. The 11 rooms have four, six, or eight single beds, so a family can have a private room by renting all its beds. Of course, in the hostelling tradition, they'll share the large bathrooms and other facilities. Each bunk has its own reading light and a lockable drawer, and most rooms have a desk. Each individual should bring a sleeping bag or sheets and a towel, although these are also available for rent. The large shared living room has mountain-lodge decor, with a stone fireplace and comfortable sitting areas; guests also have use of a fully equipped kitchen. All three meals are available ($3.50 to $8). Smoking and alcoholic beverages are not permitted.

Elk Mountain Lodge. Second and Gothic sts. (P.O. Box 148), Crested Butte, CO 81224. ☎ **800/374-6521** or 970/349-7533. Fax 970/349-5114. E-mail: elkmtn@crestedbutte.net. 17 units. TV TEL. Summer $69–$95 double; winter $88–$118 double. Rates include full breakfast. AE, DISC, MC, V.

Built in 1919 as a miners' hotel, this historic three-story lodge has been beautifully renovated. Located near the center of town, it offers rooms with twin, queen, or king beds. Third-floor units have spectacular views of the town and surrounding mountains, and many have balconies. There's also an indoor hot tub, lobby bar, and ski storage.

The Nordic Inn. 14 Treasury Rd. (P.O. Box 939, Crested Butte, CO 81224), Mt. Crested Butte, CO 81225. ☎ **970/349-5542.** Fax 970/349-6487. E-mail: acox@csn.com. 28 units. TV TEL. Winter, $95–$175 room, $125–$315 suite or chalet; summer, $72–$116 room, $107–$160 suite or chalet. Rates include continental breakfast. AE, MC, V. Closed from the end of ski season through May.

Among the first lodges built at the foot of the Crested Butte ski slopes, this well-kept, family-owned inn is still going strong. The big fireplace in the lobby is the focus of attention at breakfast, and the whirlpool tub on the sundeck is open year-round. Guest rooms have Scandinavian decor and hair dryers; most have two double beds, although a few contain either one king- or two queen-sized beds. Some kitchenette and full-kitchen units are available, especially good for families.

WHERE TO DINE

The Bakery Cafe. 401 Elk Ave., at Fourth St. ☎ **970/349-7280.** Reservations not accepted. $3–$6. DISC, MC, V. Daily 7am–9pm; may close slightly earlier spring and fall. DELI/BAKERY.

Large picture windows and a sunroom give this cafe, located in a big red building, a bright, spacious atmosphere. All food is made fresh daily, including savory pastries, overstuffed deli-style sandwiches, soups, and desserts. There's a salad bar with greens plus homemade prepared salads such as seafood, cucumber and lentil, and potato salad. All the traditional American breakfasts are offered, with an emphasis on fresh-baked goods. Patio dining is available in summer.

Le Bosquet. Sixth St. at Belleview Ave. (in Majestic Plaza). ☎ **970/349-5808.** Reservations recommended. Entrees $13–$37. AE, DISC, MC, V. Winter, daily 5:30–10pm; summer, daily 6–10pm. FRENCH.

Green plants are glimpsed through the lace curtains of this popular garden-style restaurant, operated by the same owners since 1978. The menu changes weekly, but usually includes fresh seafood, beef, lamb, and vegetarian entrees. Typical selections might include a roast Colorado rack of lamb in a red wine and garlic butter sauce, or salmon in a puff pastry with fresh asparagus and Parmesan hollandaise sauce. There's also an excellent wine list. Smoking is not permitted.

Attached to the restaurant is an upscale take-out service called **Why Cook?** (☎ 970/349-5858). Call for current selections and prices.

The Slogar Bar & Restaurant. Second St. at Whiterock Ave. ☎ **970/349-5765.** Reservations recommended. Fixed-price dinner $12–$20. AE, MC, V. Daily 5–9pm. AMERICAN.

If you do something right, why mess around with anything else? That's the way the Slogar feels about its skillet-fried chicken. The fixed-price menu offers chicken every night, accompanied by tangy coleslaw, mashed potatoes and gravy, biscuits with honey butter, creamed corn, and ice cream. Also available is a family-style steak dinner. The atmosphere here, incidentally, is 1880s Victorian. The Slogar was the Slogar then, too, but nowhere near as elegant as it is today.

3 Salida: White-Water Rafting Center of the Rockies

138 miles SW of Denver, 96 miles W of Pueblo, 82 miles N of Alamosa

With a strategic location on the upper Arkansas River, near the headwaters of the Colorado River and Rio Grande tributaries, it was natural that Salida (elevation 7,038 feet) should become an important farming and transportation center in its early days, and a major river-rafting center today. Zebulon Pike opened the area for Americans in the 19th century; he was followed by trappers, then miners after the discovery of gold in 1859. When Leadville boomed on silver in the late 1870s, the Denver & Rio Grande Railroad built a line up the Arkansas from Pueblo, and the town of Salida was founded at a key point on the line. The downtown core has kept its historic ambiance alive, and although the railway no longer carries passengers, it still operates as a freight line.

ESSENTIALS

GETTING THERE   By Car   U.S. 50 connects Salida with Gunnison, 66 miles west, and Pueblo, 96 miles east on I-25. U.S. 285 runs north-south 5 miles west of Salida (through Poncha Springs). Colo. 291 heads north from Salida, providing a vital 9-mile link between the two U.S. highways.

By Plane   The nearest airport with commercial service is at **Gunnison,** 65 miles west (see section 1 of this chapter).

By Van   Chaffee Transit, 132 W. First St. (☎ **800/288-1375** or 719/539-3935), provides charter van service to and from Denver, Colorado Springs, Pueblo, and Albuquerque, New Mexico, airports.

VISITOR INFORMATION   Consult the **Heart of the Rockies Chamber of Commerce,** 406 W. Rainbow Blvd. (U.S. 50), Salida, CO 81201 (☎ **719/ 539-2068**; www.colorado.com/chaffee), which operates an information center.

GETTING AROUND   Salida sits on the southwestern bank of the Arkansas River, just above its confluence with the South Arkansas. U.S. 50 (Rainbow Boulevard), which follows the north bank of the South Arkansas, marks the southern edge of the town. At the eastern city limit, Colo. 291 (Oak Street) turns north off U.S. 50, and 6 blocks later, turns northwest as First Street through the historic downtown area.

Chaffee County Transit, 132 W. First St. (☎ **800/288-1375** or 719/539-3935), provides charter van service throughout the Salida/Buena Vista/Monarch area.

FAST FACTS   The **Heart of the Rockies Regional Medical Center,** 448 E. First St. (☎ **719/539-6661**), has a 24-hour emergency room. The **post office** is at

310 D St. Contact the U.S. Postal Service (☎ 800/275-8777) for hours and other information. For **road conditions,** call ☎ 719/539-6688.

SPECIAL EVENTS   FIBArk Festival ("First in Boating on the Arkansas"), mid-June; and the Chaffee County Fair, late July or early August.

RIVER RAFTING

Considered the white-water rafting center of the Rockies, Salida is the perfect base for enjoying the **Arkansas Headwaters Recreation Area,** a 148-mile stretch of river from Leadville to Pueblo Reservoir. With headquarters off Colo. 291, in downtown Salida at 307 W. Sackett St. (P.O. Box 126), Salida, CO 81201 (☎ 719/ 539-7289), the recreation area includes more than a dozen developed sites along the river, offering raft and kayak access, fishing, hiking, camping, and picnicking. There are also undeveloped areas that offer access to the river, but be careful to avoid trespassing on private property.

The busiest stretch of the river is Browns Canyon, a granite wilderness between Buena Vista and Salida, with Class III and IV rapids (moderately difficult to difficult) along a 10-mile stretch of river from Nathrop to Stone Bridge. User fees are $2 per person per day (free for kids 15 and under), plus $7 per night for camping.

Most people explore Colorado's rivers with experienced rafting companies, which provide trips on stretches of river that range from practically calm and suitable for everyone, to extremely difficult, with long, violent rapids that are recommended only for skilled white-water boaters. For a full listing of more than 60 rafting companies approved to run the Arkansas, contact the recreation area office (see above). Leading outfitters include ✪ **Dvorak's Kayak & Rafting Expeditions** (☎ 800/ 824-3795 or 719/539-6851; fax 719/539-3378; www.vtinet.com/ dvorak; e-mail: dvorakex@ amigo.net), which offers half- and full-day trips, multi-day excursions, plus a week-long trip with a chamber music group that performs live concerts among the canyons and forests. Other major rafting companies include **Four Corners Rafting** (☎ 800/ 332-7238 or 719/395-4137; fax 719/396-8949; www.pikes-peak.com/ fourcorners; e-mail: dils@usa.net), **Mild to Wild River Rafting** (☎ 800/288-0675 or 719/539-4680; www.americanadventure. com), and **River Runners, Ltd.** (☎ 888/ 236-6716; www.riverrunnersltd. com). Generally, adult rates for half-day raft trips are $30 to $35, full-day trips are in the $50 to $75 range, and multi-day excursions start at about $200. Prices for children are 10% to 20% less, and trips through Royal Gorge are usually higher.

OTHER SPORTS & OUTDOOR ACTIVITIES

FISHING   The Arkansas River is considered by many to be the finest fishing river in Colorado. There's also trout fishing in numerous alpine lakes, including Cottonwood Lake, Twin Lakes, Rainbow Lake, and O'Haver Lake. You can get licenses, supplies, and equipment in Salida at **Arkansas River Fly Shop,** 7500 U.S. 50 (☎ 970/539-3474), which also rents rods and reels, and offers a guide service ($235 for two anglers for a full-day walk and wade trip) and fly-fishing and fly-tying lessons. Similar services are available from **Browner's Guide Service,** 228 F St. (☎ 800/288-0675 or 719/539-4506).

GOLF   The **Salida Golf Club,** a municipal course that opened in 1926, is at Crestone Avenue and Grant Street (☎ 719/539-1060). Greens fees are $15 for 9 holes and $25 for 18 holes.

HIKING   There are outstanding trails for all experience levels throughout the region, particularly in the San Isabel National Forest, along the eastern slope of the Continental Divide west of Salida. Of particular interest are hikes into the

Collegiate Range (Mounts Harvard, Columbia, Yale, Princeton, and Oxford) off Cottonwood Creek Road west of Buena Vista, and trips from the ghost town of St. Elmo up Chalk Creek Road from Mt. Princeton Hot Springs.

For maps and other information, stop at the **U.S. Forest Service,** 325 W. Rainbow Blvd. (☎ **719/539-3591**).

HORSEBACK RIDING   Those who want to explore the backcountry on horseback can contact **Brown's Canyon Horse Leasing** (☎ 719/539-2095), **High Country Trail Rides** (☎ 719/539-9819), or **Mt. Princeton Riding Stables** (☎ 719/395-6498). Cost for a one-hour ride is $15 to $18, while full-day rides with lunch are about $95; overnight pack trips start at about $250 per person.

MOUNTAIN BIKING   There are numerous trails suitable for mountain biking throughout the area, and many provide stupendous views of the surrounding 14,000-plus-foot peaks. **Otero Cyclery,** 108 F St. (☎ **719/539-6704**), sells and services mountain bikes, offers rentals, and can provide information on nearby trails. Ask for a free copy of the *Mountain Bike Guide,* which gives details, including maps, for 15 area rides. Rentals of both dual and front suspension mountain bikes are available, priced from $25 per day.

ROCKHOUNDING   The richest mineral and gem beds in Colorado are found in the upper Arkansas River valley and the eastern slope of the Continental Divide, just west of Salida. For a free brochure on rockhounding locations, stop at the Chamber of Commerce office. Those wanting hammers, eye protection, and other equipment will find it at **Homestead Sport & Ski,** 444 U.S. 50, Poncha Springs (☎ **800/ 539-7507** or 719/539-7507; www.homesteadsports.com), 5 miles west of Salida.

SKIING & SNOWBOARDING   Among the finest of Colorado's small ski resorts, **Monarch Ski & Snowboard Area,** 20 miles west of Salida at Monarch Pass on U.S. 50, serves all levels of ability with 54 trails covering 670 acres, plus more than 900 additional acres accessible by snowcat.

Monarch's four chairlifts serve distinctly different terrain. The short Tumbelina Lift is ideal for beginners and early intermediates, and Breeze Way provides access to predominantly intermediate runs. The Garfield Lift is popular among advanced skiers, who can tango down the Kanonen and Cleanzer runs, while the long, winding Sleepy Hollow and Roundabout trails are ideal for novices. Less experienced skiers can also take Panorama Lift to the mountaintop (at the Continental Divide) and ski to the bottom via Ticaboo or Sky Walker. This lift also takes experts to runs like High Anxiety, and a recent expansion has added 30 acres of upper-level glade and powder skiing in the Curecanti Bowl.

All-day tickets (1998–99 rates) are $32 for adults, $14 for juniors ages 7 to 12, $18 for seniors ages 62 to 69, and free for all those under 7 or over 69. Group ski lessons cost $27 for adults, $22 for juniors. The area is open mid-November through mid-April, daily from 9am to 4pm. For information, contact the resort at 1 Powder Place, Monarch, CO 81227 (☎ **888/996-7669** or 719/539-3573; fax 719/539-7652; www.skimonarch.com). You'll find comfortable and affordable accommodations and dining at the 100-room **Monarch Mountain Lodge** (☎ **800/332-3668** or 719/539-2581), at the above address, with rates for doubles in the $79 to $119 range. Rates are higher during holiday periods and considerably less during the summer; a variety of packages are available.

SEEING THE SIGHTS

Salida Hot Springs. 410 W. Rainbow Blvd. (U.S. 50). ☎ **719/539-6738.** Admission $5 adults, $3 seniors 60 and over, $3 students 6–17, $2 children 5 and under. Memorial

Day–Labor Day daily 1–9pm (adult lap swimming noon–1pm Mon–Sat); Labor Day–Memorial Day Tues–Thurs 4–9pm, Fri–Sun 1–9pm.

Colorado's largest indoor hot springs have been in commercial operation since 1937, when the Works Progress Administration built the pools as a Depression-era project. Ute tribes considered the mineral waters, rich in bicarbonate, sodium, and sulfate, to be sacred and medicinal. Today, the main 25-meter (27.3-yard) pool, with two lap lanes available at all times, is kept at about 90°, a shallow pool about 100°, and wading pool about 96°. European-style private hot baths, at 114° to 120°, are available for adults only ($5 per person per hour). Also available are aqua-size, arthritis classes, and lessons for all ages. Adjacent Centennial Park has a picnic area, playground, and tennis and volleyball courts.

Salida Museum. 406½ W. Rainbow Blvd. (U.S. 50). ☎ **719/539-4602** for information. Admission 50¢ ages 6 and over, free for kids under 6. Memorial Day to mid-Sept, Mon–Sat 9am–5pm. Located just behind the Chamber of Commerce.

The Salida Museum provides a look back into the history of this part of Colorado, with a wide selection of pioneer, mining, and railroad exhibits, plus displays on the lives of the American Indians who lived here. You'll see lots of arrowheads, plus exhibits that explain how baskets and pots were made. The museum also contains rocks, fossils, and shells of the area, plus petrified wood and dinosaur bones and teeth. You can learn about Laura Evans, a local madam who operated a brothel in Salida from the late 1800s until 1953, and see a complete pioneer kitchen, a replica of a lady's bedroom of the late 1800s, a general store, bizarre-looking medical equipment, and bone baskets—used to transport corpses in the early 1800s.

Monarch Scenic Tram. Monarch Pass, U.S. 50, 22 miles west of Salida. ☎ **719/539-4789.** Admission $6 adults, $5 seniors 65 and over, $3 children 12 and under. Mid-May to Oct, weather permitting, daily 8am–6:30pm.

Climbing from 11,312-foot Monarch Pass to the Continental Divide at an altitude of 12,012 feet, this tram offers views of five mountain ranges—up to 150 miles away when skies are clear. The tram includes six four-passenger gondolas. At the top is a large gift shop.

Mt. Shavano Trout Rearing Unit. 7725 County Road 154. ☎ **719/539-6877.** Free admission. Daily 7:30am–4pm.

This state-run fish hatchery, about a half mile northwest of town, produces some four million trout each year, used to stock Colorado's numerous streams and lakes. Visitors can see how the hatchery operates, walk among the fish raceways and ponds, and feed the fish (food provided from coin-operated machines).

WHERE TO STAY

Highest lodging rates here are during summer, with lowest rates in late winter and early spring (before rafting season begins). Among reliable chain motels are **Days Inn,** 407 E. U.S. 50 (☎ 800/329-7466 or 719/539-6651), with double rates of $38 to $70; **Econo Lodge,** 1310 E. U.S. 50 (☎ 800/553-2666 or 719/539-2895), with rates for two of $35 to $85; and **Super 8,** 525 W. U.S. 50 (☎ 800/800-8000 or 719/539-6689), with rates for two of $40 to $67. Room tax adds just under 9% to lodging bills.

Aspen Leaf Lodge. 7350 W. U.S. 50, Salida, CO 81201. ☎ **800/759-0338** for reservations only, or 719/539-6733. Fax 719/539-6304. 18 units. A/C TV TEL. June–Sept and holidays $40–$60 double; spring and fall $30–$50 double. Children under 12 stay free in parents' room. AE, DC, DISC, MC, V. Pets accepted.

This small family-owned and -operated motel has a friendly feel, from the forest of small evergreens and aspens around a hot-tub pavilion to the coffeepot that's on in the office each morning. Single rooms have a king-size bed, desk, and a table. The more spacious doubles contain two queen beds. Two rooms have refrigerators and microwaves, and rollaways and cribs are available.

Redwood Lodge. 7310 U.S. 50, Salida, CO 81201. ☎ **800/234-1077** or 719/539-2528. Fax 719/539-2528. 27 units. A/C TV TEL. May–Sept and holidays $59–$75 double, $66–$86 mini-suite; rest of year $45–$52 double, $52–$72 mini-suite. Rates include continental breakfast. AE, DC, DISC, MC, V.

Red cedar is used throughout this attractive property, from construction to custom furnishings to the two outdoor hot tubs. Every room is unique, but each typically has king or queen beds, original artwork, and pedestal sinks; some have whirlpool tubs. Ten units have showers only; the rest have shower/tub combos. Mini-suites have two full bedrooms and kitchenettes. The heated outdoor pool is open in summer.

River Run Inn. 8495 County Rd. 160, Salida, CO 81201. ☎ **800/385-6925** or 719/ 539-3818. Fax 719/539-3818. www.riverruninn.com. E-mail: riverrun@amigo.net. 7 units (3 with private bathroom), plus 13 dormitory beds, with shared bath, for groups of five or more. $60–$65 double with shared bathroom, $80 double with private bathroom; $30 dorm bed. Rates include full breakfast. AE, MC, V. Children over 12 welcome.

Built by Chaffee County in 1895 as a home for the indigent, this building—about 2 miles northwest of town—served that purpose for half a century. Since 1983, however, it has functioned as a charming bed-and-breakfast, listed on the National Register of Historic Places. The grounds cover 11 acres, including a quarter-mile section of the Arkansas River. A wide front porch leads into a large sitting room and library, and the back porch looks out over a pond. The seven guest rooms have antique poster beds—two twins in one, one king in another, and queens in the rest—and most have mountain views. Smoking is not allowed.

WHERE TO DINE

Country Bounty Restaurant & Gift Shoppe. 413 W. U.S. 50. ☎ **719/539-3546.** Lunch $4–$9; dinner $7.50–$13. DISC, MC, V. Summer, daily 6:30am–9pm; winter, daily 7am–8pm. AMERICAN

This combination gift shop and restaurant gives diners plenty to look at while waiting for their mesquite-broiled tuna, hot beef sandwich, or country-fried chicken. The gift shop seems to spill over into the restaurant with all manner of country-style crafts, southwestern jewelry, and other items. Breakfast selections include hotcakes and eggs Benedict; the lunch menu offers cheeseburgers, smoked turkey and avocado on rye, and homemade soup; and for dinner, there's chicken-fried steak, pork chops, lemon-herb chicken breast, and Rocky Mountain trout. There's also a Mexican menu and a variety of salads, plus locally famous pies and cobblers. The entire restaurant is smoke-free.

✪ **First St. Cafe.** 137 E. First St. ☎ **719/539-4759.** Lunch $4.25–$8; dinner $7.25–$16. AE, DISC, MC, V. May–Oct, Mon–Sat 8am–10pm, Sun brunch 10am–3pm. Nov–Apr, Mon–Thurs 8am–8pm, Fri–Sat 8am–9pm. AMERICAN/MEXICAN.

In the heart of historic downtown Salida, First St. Cafe occupies a two-story brick building dating from 1890, with hardwood floors and regional paintings that give the cafe a gallery feel. Among the town's most popular restaurants, it's a focal point for artists, musicians, and other creative types. Breakfast is served any time, and the kitchen turns out gourmet home cooking such as French toast stuffed with cream cheese and walnuts vegetarian casseroles and a variety of sandwiches for lunch and steak, barbecued ribs, and charbroiled halibut steak for dinner. You'll also find innovative Mexican selections, a salad bar, and daily specials.

4 Alamosa & Great Sand Dunes National Monument

212 miles SW of Denver, 149 miles E of Durango, 173 miles N of Santa Fe, New Mexico

If you're looking for Colorado's largest sandbox, here it is: Just 38 miles from Alamosa are the tallest sand dunes in North America.

Founded in 1878 with the extension of the Denver & Rio Grande Railroad into the San Luis Valley, the town was named for the cottonwood (*alamosa*) trees that lined the banks of the Rio Grande. Soon rails spread out in all directions from the community, and it became a thriving transportation center for farmers and a supply depot for miners. Today this town of 9,500 remains a center for farming, especially vegetables. It is also an educational center with Adams State College, a 4-year institution founded in 1921, and a good home base for southern Colorado visitors.

ESSENTIALS

GETTING THERE   By Car   Alamosa is at the junction of U.S. 160, which runs east 73 miles to I-25 at Walsenburg and west to Durango; and U.S. 285, which extends south to Santa Fe, New Mexico, and north to Denver. Because of a jog in U.S. 285, however, a more direct route into the city from the north is to take Colo. 17 the last 50 miles.

By Plane   The **Alamosa Municipal Airport** (☎ **719/589-6444**), 3 miles off U.S. 285 South, has service to and from Denver with **United Express** (☎ **800/ 241-6522** or 719/589-9446).

VISITOR INFORMATION   The **Alamosa County Chamber of Commerce,** Cole Park (Chamber Drive at Third Street), Alamosa, CO 81101 (☎ **800/ 258-7597** or 719/589-3681; www.alamosa.org; e-mail:bluskys@rmii.net), operates a visitor information center.

FAST FACTS   The **San Luis Valley Regional Medical Center**, with a 24-hour emergency room, is at 106 Blanca Ave. (☎ **719/589-2511**). The **post office** is at 505 Third St., off State Avenue. Contact the U.S. Postal Service (☎ **800/ 275-8777**) for hours and other information.

SPECIAL EVENTS   Crane Festival, mid-March, in Monte Vista; Pro Rodeo, Dance, and Parade, June; Colorado State Mining Championships, Fourth of July weekend, in Creede.

✪ GREAT SAND DUNES NATIONAL MONUMENT

Just 38 miles northeast of Alamosa, on Colo. 150, you'll come to a startling sight—a 39-square-mile expanse of sand, piled nearly 750 feet high against the western edge of the Sangre de Cristo Mountains. The tallest sand dunes on the continent, they seem incongruous here, far from any sea or major desert.

The dunes were created over thousands of years by southwesterly winds blowing across the valley. They began forming at the end of the last ice age, when streams of water from melting glaciers carried rocks, gravel, and silt down from the mountains. In addition, as the Rio Grande changed its course, it left behind sand, silt, and debris.

Even today the winds are changing the face of the dunes. So-called "reversing winds" from the mountains pile the dunes back upon themselves, building them higher and higher. Though it's physically impossible for sand to be piled steeper than 34°, the dunes often appear more sheer because of deceptive shadows and colors that change with the light: gold, pink, tan, sometimes even bluish. Climbing dunes is fun, but it can be tiring at this 8,200-foot altitude. *Beware:* The sand's surface can reach 140°F in summer.

Among the specialized animals that survive in this weird environment are the Ord's kangaroo rat, a creature that never drinks water, plus four insects found nowhere else on earth: the Great Sand Dunes tiger beetle and three other beetle varieties. These animals and the flora of the adjacent mountain foothills are discussed in evening programs and guided walks during summer.

For orientation, walk the easy half-mile self-guided nature trail that begins at the visitor center. If you want more of a challenge, hike the dunes—you can get to the top of a 750-foot dune and back in about 90 minutes. Those who make it all the way to the end are rewarded with spectacular views of the dunes and the surrounding mountains.

Pinyon Flats Campground, with 88 sites, is open year-round. It has flush toilets and drinking water, but no showers or RV hookups. Campsites are assigned on a first-come, first-served basis, and cost $10 per night. Admission to the monument is $3 per person (free for those under 17). The **visitor center** is open from 8am to 6pm daily in summer, with shorter hours at other times. For further information, contact Great Sand Dunes National Monument, 11999 Colo. 150, Mosca, CO 81146 (☎ **719/378-2312;** www.nps.gov/grsa).

From Alamosa, there are two main routes to Great Sand Dunes: east 14 miles on U.S. 160, then north on Colo. 150; or north 14 miles on Colo. 17 to Mosca, then east on Six Mile Lane to the junction of Colo. 150.

SPORTS & OUTDOOR ACTIVITIES

Many of the best outdoor activities in this part of the state take place in the **Rio Grande National Forest,** with the Supervisor's Office at 1803 West U.S. 160, Monte Vista, CO 81144 (☎ **970/852-5941**).

FISHING   The Rio Grande is an outstanding stream for trout, walleye, and catfish; and there are numerous high mountain lakes and streams throughout the Rio Grande National Forest where you're apt to catch rainbow, brown, brook, cutthroat, and Rio Grande cutthroat trout. For information, contact the forest service office (see above). You can get licenses, tackle, and advice in Alamosa from **Spencer Sporting Goods,** 616 Main St. (☎ **719/589-4361**), or **Alamosa Sporting Goods,** 1114 Main St. (☎ **719/589-3006**).

GOLF   The **Cattails Golf Club,** 6615 N. River Rd. (☎ **719/589-9515**), is an 18-hole course along the Rio Grande on the north side of Alamosa. Generally open March through November, the cost is $16 for 9 holes and $25 for 18 holes. The **Great Sand Dunes Golf Course,** 5303 Colo. 150 (☎ **800/284-9213** or 719/378-2357), is a championship 18-hole course, 26 miles northeast of Alamosa at Zapata Ranch (see "Where to Stay," below). The course is usually open from mid-April to mid-November. Greens fees are $35 for all day. The 9-hole **Monte Vista Golf Club,** at 101 Country Club in the town of Monte Vista (☎ **719/852-4906**), 17 miles west of Alamosa, is a particularly challenging course due to its small greens. Open April through October, the course is on the migratory path of sandhill and whooping cranes. Fees are $10 for 9 holes and $15 for 18 holes.

HIKING   The best opportunities in the region are found in the surrounding **Rio Grande National Forest,** with nearly two million acres. One of the most popular hikes, with easy access, is **Zapata Falls,** reached off Colo. 150 about 20 miles northeast of Alamosa and south of Great Sand Dunes. This cavernous waterfall on the northwest flank of 14,345-foot Mt. Blanca freezes in winter, turning its cave into a natural icebox that often remains frozen well into summer. More challenging hikes

The Cumbres & Toltec Scenic Railroad

Born in 1880 to serve remote mining camps, the Cumbres & Toltec Scenic Railroad follows a spectacular 64-mile path through the San Juan Mountains from Antonito, Colorado, to Chama, New Mexico. This narrow-gauge steam railroad weaves through groves of pine and aspen, and past strange rock formations, before ascending through the spectacular Toltec Gorge of the Los Piños River. At the rail-junction community of Osier, passengers picnic or enjoy a catered lunch while the *Colorado Limited* exchanges engines with the *New Mexico Express*. Round-trip passengers return to their starting point in Antonito, while onward passengers continue a climb through tunnels and trestles to the summit of 10,015-foot Cumbres Pass, then drop down a precipitous 4% grade to Chama. A joint venture by the states of Colorado and New Mexico, the train is a registered National Historic Site.

A through-trip from Antonito to Chama (or vice versa), traveling one-way by van, runs $52 for adults, $27 for children 11 and under. A regular round-trip, without transfers, is $34 for adults and $17 for children 11 and under, but this omits either the gorge or the pass. Either way, it's an all-day adventure, leaving between 8 and 10:30am, and returning between 4:30 and 6:30pm. The train operates daily from Memorial Day weekend to mid-October. For reservations and information, contact the Cumbres & Toltec Scenic Railroad, P.O. Box 668, Antonito, CO 81120 (☎ **800/724-5451** or 719/376-5483). The depot is 28 miles south of Alamosa, just off U.S. 285.

include trails into the **Wheeler Geologic Area,** set aside by President Theodore Roosevelt in 1911 because of its unique rock formations. Obtain directions from the forest service.

MOUNTAIN BIKING   There are plenty of opportunities for mountain biking on local federal lands. Get information from the forest service (see above), or stop at **Kristi Mountain Sports,** Villa Mall, on West U.S. 160 (☎ **719/589-9759**), for information on the best places to go, rentals ($15 per day), repairs, and accessories. A *Mountain Bike Guide* is available for $2.50 from the visitor center.

SWIMMING   **Splashland Hot Springs,** Colo. 17 (☎ **719/589-6307** in summer, 719/589-5772 in winter), 1 mile north of Alamosa via U.S. 160, has a geothermally heated outdoor pool (94°F average temperature) measuring 150 feet by 60 feet, with both high dive and low dive, and a popular mini-waterslide. There's also an 18-inch-deep wading pool. Bathing suits, towels, flippers, goggles, and other pool paraphernalia can be rented. Facilities include a snack bar and public showers ($1 for non-swimmers). It's open Memorial Day to Labor Day, Thursday through Tuesday. Weekday hours are 10am to 6:30pm; Saturdays and Sundays, from noon to 6pm. All-day pool passes cost $4 for adults, $3 for children 3 to 12, $1.50 for babies, and $2.50 for seniors 60 and older. Non-swimmers are charged $1.

OTHER HIGHLIGHTS

Adams State College–Luther Bean Museum. 208 Edgemont Blvd. ☎ **719/587-7121.** Free admission. Mon–Fri 1–4:30pm. Closed Dec 23–Jan 1.

Located on the second floor of Richardson Hall, this museum has one of the Southwest's most complete collections of Hispanic *santos* (carved or painted images of saints), plus ancestral Puebloan artifacts, Rio Grande weavings, western art, and a priceless collection of European porcelains and furniture.

✪ **San Luis Valley Alligator Farm.** Two Mile Creek. ☎ **719/589-3032** or 719/ 378-2612. www.rmii.com/~gatorfrm. Admission $4 adults, $2 children 6–12, free for children under 6 and seniors over 80. June–Aug, daily 7am–7pm; Sept–May, daily 10am–3pm.

Geothermal wells keep the temperature a cozy 87° at this alligator farm and wildlife habitat, located 18 miles north of Alamosa off Colo. 17. There are more than 100 alligators at the farm, and you can watch them being fed several times each day. In addition to the alligators, the farm raises fish—in particular the Rocky Mountain white tilapia—plus desert tortoises, turtles, and iguanas.

NATURAL HIGHLIGHTS

The **Alamosa–Monte Vista National Wildlife Refuge Complex,** 6 miles southeast of Alamosa via U.S. 160 (☎ 719/589-4021), has preserved nearly 25,000 acres of vital land for a variety of marsh birds and waterfowl, including many migrating and wintering species. Sandhill and whooping cranes visit in October and March; at other times of the year there may be egrets, herons, avocets, bitterns, and other avian species. A wide variety of ducks are year-round residents. Check at the refuge office about the best spots from which to see wildlife, hiking and biking trails, and a driving tour. Admission to the refuge is free. It's open daily from sunrise to sunset; the office is open Monday through Friday from 7:30am to 4pm.

WHERE TO STAY

Among chain lodging in Alamosa is **Super 8,** W. 2505 Main St. (☎ 800/ 800-8000 or 719/589-6447), with rates for two of $47 to $64. Room tax adds just over 9% to lodging bills.

EXPENSIVE

Inn at Zapata Ranch. 5303 Colo. 150, Mosca, CO 81146. ☎ **800/284-9213** or 719/ 378-2356. Fax 719/378-2428. www.greatsanddunes.com. E-mail: zapatainn@greatsand-dunes. com. 15 units. July–Oct $150–$180 double, $200–$250 suite; Mar–June $100–$120 double, $150–$170 suite. Closed Nov–Feb. Rates include breakfast. Golf packages available. AE, DC, DISC, MC, V. Located 26 miles northeast of Alamosa. Take U.S. 160 east 14 miles; turn north on Colo. 150 toward Great Sand Dunes National Monument; 4 miles before the monument gate, turn onto a gravel road (signposted Zapata Ranch) and proceed three-quarters of a mile to the inn. Children 10 and older are welcome.

Beautiful cottonwood trees surround and shade this resort, located on a former cattle ranch established by Spanish land grant in the early 19th century. The cattle are gone, but buffalo are raised on the ranch, and mule deer frequently browse the fairways of the 18-hole championship golf course (see "Golf," above). Guest rooms are intentionally rustic, with furnishings made by hand right on the ranch, but they do include private bathrooms, individually controlled heating, and quilted comforters. This is a getaway spot: no TVs or phones in the rooms, but plenty of great views. A gourmet restaurant (see "Where to Dine," below) specializes in contemporary American cuisine. Besides the golf course, facilities include a pool, sauna, hot tub, exercise and massage room, mountain-bike rentals, and horseback-riding stables.

INEXPENSIVE

Best Western Alamosa Inn. 1919 Main St., Alamosa, CO 81101. ☎ **800/459-5123,** 800/528-1234 or 719/589-2567. Fax 719/589-0767. 120 units. AC TV TEL. $72–$82 double; $125 suite. Rates slightly lower in winter. Children under 12 stay free in parents' room. AE, CB, DC, DISC, MC, V. Pets under 25 pounds permitted.

This comfortable, modern motel has clean, quiet rooms and an enclosed heated pool and whirlpool. Guests also have use of a full-service health club, courtesy transportation, and conference rooms. The restaurant serves three meals daily.

✪ **The Cottonwood Inn & Gallery.** 123 San Juan Ave., Alamosa, CO 81101. ☎ **800/ 955-2623** or 719/589-3882. Fax 719/589-6437. www.cottonwoodinn.com. E-mail: julie@ cottonwoodinn.com. 9 units (7 with private bathroom). TEL. $52–$95 double. Rates include full breakfast. AE, DISC, MC, V. Located 3 blocks north of Main St. Pets accepted in 2 apartment suites with $50 deposit.

This delightful bed-and-breakfast has a distinctly artsy orientation. Innkeeper Julie Mordecai has decorated the common areas and bedrooms as a gallery of regional art, much of which is for sale. The Cottonwood is composed of two buildings. The 1908 neo-colonial two-story bungalow has five guest rooms, furnished largely in Arts and Crafts style. Each room is unique: The Rosa Room has queen and single beds to accommodate small families, along with children's books and stuffed animals, while the Blanca Room weds southwestern decor with art deco motifs. Three of these five units have private bathrooms with showers only; the other two share a bathroom with a shower/tub combo. A TV and video library are in the living room. Adjacent to the bungalow is a 1920s fourplex with four apartment suites, each with a kitchen and claw-foot tub with shower conversion. Nostalgia buffs will especially appreciate the apartment suite with a complete 1940s-era kitchen. Full homemade breakfasts often feature regional specialties, such as fresh fruit crepes with Mexican chocolate and whipped cream. Smoking is not permitted.

WHERE TO DINE

Inn at Zapata Ranch. 5303 Colo. 150, Mosca, CO 81146. ☎ **800/284-9213** or 719/ 378-2356. Reservations required for dinner. Main courses $4–$7 lunch, $9–$25 dinner. AE, DISC, MC, V. Summer, daily 11:30am–3pm and 6–9pm. Call for winter hours. Children 10 and older are welcome. CONTEMPORARY AMERICAN.

While breakfast is served to guests only (see "Where to Stay," above), the restaurant is open to the public daily for lunch and dinner, with outdoor seating in warm weather. The hearty cuisine includes entrees such as grilled porterhouse, lemon-sage grilled chicken breast, and five-bean cassoulet. There's a good selection of American wines and an excellent selection of microbrewed beers.

St. Ives Pub & Eatery. 719 Main St. ☎ **719/589-0711.** $3–$7. DISC, MC, V. Mon–Sat 11am–midnight. AMERICAN/MEXICAN.

You'll find the eatery in front, with plants and large sidewalk windows, and the pub in the rear, with a sports TV, pool table, pinball machine, and video games. The fare focuses on both hot and cold New York–style deli sandwiches, burgers, and salads, as well as a number of Mexican dishes—try the nachos either as an appetizer or a full meal.

5 A Side Trip to Creede: A Slice of Colorado's Mining History

Among the best preserved of all 19th-century Colorado mining towns, Creede had a population of 10,000 in 1892 when a balladeer wrote, "It's day all day in the daytime, and there is no night in Creede." Over $1 million in silver was mined every day, but the Silver Panic of 1893 eclipsed Creede's rising star. For most of the next century, area mines produced just enough silver and other minerals to sustain the community until the 1960s, when tourism and outdoor recreation became paramount. Today, this mountain town, at an elevation of 8,852 feet, has a population of about 300.

From Alamosa, drive west on U.S. 160 about 48 miles to South Fork, and turn north on Colo. 149, which follows the Rio Grande about 23 miles to Creede.

WHAT TO SEE & DO   You can obtain information from the **Creede–Mineral County Chamber of Commerce,** north of the county courthouse at the north end of Main Street (P.O. Box 580), Creede, CO 81130 (☎ **800/327-2102** or 719/ 658-2374; fax 719/658-2717; www.creede.com; e-mail: creede@rmii.com). The chamber will also provide directions to the **Wheeler Geologic Area,** a region of volcanic rock formations accessible only by jeep, horseback, or 5-hour hike; and **North Creede Canyon,** where remnants of the old town of Creede still stand near the **Commodore Mine,** whose workings seem to keep a ghostly vigil over the canyon.

The former Denver & Rio Grande Railroad depot is now the **Creede Museum,** behind City Park, which tells the story of the town's wild-and-woolly heyday. There were dozens of saloons and gambling tables, and shoot-outs were not uncommon. Bob Ford, the killer of Jesse James, was murdered in his own saloon, and Bat Masterson and "Poker Alice" Tubbs were other notorious residents. Photographs and exhibits on gambling and other activities are among the museum's collection, and you can obtain a walking-tour map of the town here. It's usually open daily from 10am to 4pm in summer. Check at the museum or Chamber of Commerce for hours for the **Creede Firehouse,** hewn out of solid rock, and next door, the **Underground Mining Museum,** where you can go on a winding trip through a 250-foot tunnel to explore the history of mining.

The **Creede Repertory Theatre,** P.O. Box 269, Creede, CO 81130 (☎ **719/ 658-2540**; www.creederep.com), was established in 1966 by a small troupe of young actors from the University of Kansas. Now nationally acclaimed, it has matinee and evening performances from mid-June to late September in its 243-seat theater at 124 North Main St. It usually presents four full-length productions, a children's show, historical show, and a one-act play, in repertory. Productions vary, but include musicals, comedies, and contemporary and classic dramas. Tickets for full-length productions run $13 to $16, the one-act play is about $8, and the children's production costs about $5. Advance reservations are strongly recommended.

The 17-mile **Bachelor Historic Tour** is described in a booklet available from the Chamber of Commerce ($1). The route follows a forest service road through the mountains, past abandoned mines, mining equipment, the original Creede cemetery, and 19th-century town sites. The road is fine for passenger cars in dry weather, but may be closed by winter snow.

WHERE TO STAY & DINE   Next door to the Rep Theatre is the **Creede Hotel & Restaurant,** 120 Main St. (☎ **719/658-2608**). Located in a restored 1892 hotel, this bed-and-breakfast inn is fully open in summer, with limited availability at other times. There are four rooms in the hotel, each with private bathroom, plus three additional rooms in an adjoining building. Rates run $69 to $89 double, with full breakfast included; discounts in the off-season are available. The restaurant also serves lunch and dinner, with entrees such as lasagna, Rocky Mountain trout, charbroiled steak, and vegetarian dishes, in the $10 to $20 range.

Wason Ranch, a good choice for hunters, fishermen, and others seeking a secluded mountain getaway, is 2 miles southeast of Creede on Colo. 149 (☎ **719/ 658-2413**). The ranch has modern, two-bedroom log cabins for $58 per day, for up to four people; and three-bedroom cottages for $149 (3-day minimum). There is one large 100-year-old colonial home, starting at $169, which will accommodate four to ten people. All units have fully equipped kitchenettes. The ranch can provide guided fishing and hunting trips, and guests also have opportunities to see eagles, elk, moose, mountain sheep, deer, and other wildlife.

Southeastern Colorado

Colorado's southeastern quadrant owes its life to the Arkansas River. This mighty stream forges one of the world's most spectacular canyons—the deep, narrow Royal Gorge—as it wends its way down from the Rocky Mountain foothills. On its trek through Pueblo it supplies water for a major steel industry. Then it rolls across the Great Plains, providing life-giving water to an arid but soil-rich region that produces a wide variety of vegetables and fruits. Bent's Old Fort, a national historic site that has re-created one of the West's most important frontier trading posts, also rests beside the river, east of the community of La Junta. South of Pueblo, the town of Trinidad is the center of a century-old coal-mining district.

1 Pueblo

111 miles S of Denver, 42 miles S of Colorado Springs, 317 miles N of Albuquerque, New Mexico

Don't trust your first impressions. As you drive through Pueblo along the interstate, it might appear that this bland but industrious city—with its railroad tracks, warehouses, and factories—doesn't warrant a stop. But take the time to get off the superslab and discover the real Pueblo. You'll find handsome historic homes, fine western art, a well-run zoo, and a surprising number of outdoor recreational opportunities.

Although Zebulon Pike and his U.S. Army exploratory expedition camped at the future site of Pueblo in 1806, there were no white settlements here until 1842, when El Pueblo Fort was constructed as a fur-trading outpost. It was abandoned following a Ute massacre in late 1854, but when the Colorado gold rush began five years later, the town of Pueblo was born on the site of the former fort. Other towns were platted nearby, and eventually four of them grew together, each with its own street system, to become the Pueblo of today.

In the early 20th century, the city grew as a major center for coal mining and steel production. Job opportunities attracted large numbers of immigrants, especially from Mexico and eastern Europe. Pueblo today is home to high-tech industries as well as the University of Southern Colorado. As the largest city (population 100,000) in southeastern Colorado, it is the market center for a 15-county region extending to the borders of New Mexico, Oklahoma, and Kansas.

ESSENTIALS

GETTING THERE   By Car   I-25 links Pueblo directly with Colorado Springs, Denver, and points north; and Santa Fe, Albuquerque, and other New Mexico cities to the south. U.S. 50 runs east to La Junta and west to Cañon City, Gunnison, and Montrose.

By Plane   Pueblo Memorial Airport, Keeler Parkway off U.S. 50 East (☎ 719/948-3355), is served daily by **Great Lakes Aviation** (☎ 719/948-9462), flying for **United Airlines,** with daily flights to Denver and other locations. Several companies offer air charter, air ambulance, and other services, including **Flower Aviation** (☎ 719/948-2447), **Peak Aviation** (☎ 719/948-4560), and **Travelaire Aviation** (☎ 719/948-4181).

Agencies providing rental cars at the airport include **Avis** (☎ 800/831-2847 or 719/948-9665) and **Hertz** (☎ 800/654-3131 or 719/948-3345).

By Bus   Buses of TNM&O (Texas, New Mexico, and Oklahoma) serve Pueblo with more than a dozen buses daily, including connections with Greyhound buses. The station is located at 703 U.S. 50 West (☎ **719/544-6295**).

VISITOR INFORMATION   Contact the **Greater Pueblo Chamber of Commerce,** 302 N. Santa Fe Ave. (P.O. Box 697), Pueblo, CO 81002 (☎ **800/233-3446** or 719/542-1704; www.pueblo.org), for most travel-related needs. A **Visitor Information Center** is located in a modular unit adjacent to the caboose off I-25 exit 101, in the K-Mart parking lot on Elizabeth Street at U.S. 50 West (☎ **719/543-1742**); it's open daily from 8am to 6pm in summer, from 8am to 4pm in winter.

GETTING AROUND   Pueblo lies on the eastward-flowing Arkansas River at its confluence with Fountain Creek. The downtown core is located north of the Arkansas and west of the Fountain, immediately west of I-25. Santa Fe Avenue and Main Street, one block west, are the principal north–south thoroughfares; the cross streets are numbered (counting northward), with Fourth and Eighth Streets the most important. Pueblo Boulevard circles the city on the south and west, with spurs leading to the Nature Center and Lake Pueblo State Park.

Public transportation is provided by **City Bus** (☎ **719/542-4306**). For taxi service, call **City Cab** (☎ **719/543-2525**). In addition to the rental-car agencies at the airport (see above), there is also an outlet for **Enterprise Rent-A-Car** in Pueblo (☎ **800/325-8007** or 719/542-6100).

FAST FACTS   Medical services are provided downtown by **Parkview Episcopal Medical Center,** 400 W. 16th St. (☎ **719/584-4000**), or on the south side by **St. Mary–Corwin Regional Medical Center,** 1008 Minnequa Ave. (☎ **719/560-4000**). The main post office is downtown at 420 N. Main St.; call the U.S. Postal Service (☎ **800/275-8777**) for hours and locations of other post offices. For road conditions, call ☎ **719/545-8520.** For time, temperature, and weather, call ☎ **719/542-4444.**

SPECIAL EVENTS   Bluegrass on the River, at the Greenway and Nature Center, May; the Governor's Cup Regatta, at Lake Pueblo State Park, May; the Pueblo Chamber Golf Tournament, June; the Rolling River Raft Race, July; the Colorado State Fair, late August; the Chile and Frijole Festival, September; Parade of Lights, November; and the Christmas Posada, December. The chamber of commerce offers a recorded listing of weekly events (☎ **719/542-1776**).

WHAT TO SEE & DO

Historic Pueblo runs along Union Avenue north from the Arkansas River to First Street, a distance of about five blocks. More than 40 buildings here are listed on the National Register of Historic Places, including the Vail Hotel, headquarters of the **Pueblo County Historical Society** museum and library (☎ 719/543-6772), with railroad memorabilia, locally made saddles, and some 4,500 books, historical maps, and photographs depicting Pueblo's history. **Union Depot,** with its mosaic tile floors and beautiful stained-glass windows, still serves rail freight lines. **Walking-tour maps** can be obtained from the Greater Pueblo Chamber of Commerce, 302 N. Santa Fe Ave. (☎ **719/542-1704**), as well as from Union Avenue businesses. Those visiting in mid- to late August and early September will be just in time for the **Colorado State Fair** (☎ **800/444-3247**), which includes a professional rodeo, carnival rides, food booths, industrial displays, horse shows, animal exhibits, and top-name entertainers.

El Pueblo Museum. 324 W. First St. ☎ **719/583-0453.** Admission $2.50 adults, $2 children 6–16 and seniors over 65, free for children under 6. Mon–Sat 10am–4:30pm, Sun noon–3pm.

This downtown museum presents colorful exhibits of American Indian, Mexican, and American cultures. Named for the site's original trading post, the museum also has displays on frontier trapping, ranching, and agriculture, as well as the coming of industry to southwestern Colorado. The Chile and Frijole Festival in September features live music, traditional dances, and food.

Fred E. Weisbrod/International B-24 Memorial Museum. 31001 Magnuson Ave. ☎ **719/948-9219.** www.pueblo.org/phas. Free admission, donations welcome. Mon–Fri 10am–4pm, Sat 10am–2pm, Sun 1–4pm. Six miles east of Pueblo via U.S. 50.

About two dozen historic aircraft—from World War II and earlier—are on display, as well as numerous exhibits and photographs depicting the B-24 bomber and its role in World War II. There's also a souvenir shop containing military and general aviation-related items.

✪ The Greenway & Nature Center. 5200 Nature Center Rd. ☎ **719/549-2414.** www.uscolo.edu/gnc. Free admission, but donations welcome. Grounds open daily dawn–10pm. Raptor Center, Tues–Sat 11am–4pm. Interpretive Center and nature shop, Tues–Sun 9am–5pm.

A major recreation and education center, this area provides access to more than 36 miles of biking and hiking trails along the Arkansas River. There's also a fishing dock, volleyball courts, horseshoe pits, amphitheater, and nature trails. An interpretive center displays exhibits on the flora and fauna of the area, and the Cafe del Rio serves American and southwestern dishes. At the Raptor Center, injured eagles, owls, hawks, and other birds of prey are nursed back to health and released to the wild. The center also houses exhibits and several resident birds of prey.

Pueblo Zoo. City Park, 3455 Nuckolls Ave. ☎ **719/561-9664.** Admission $4 adults, $2 youths 13–18, $1 children 3–12, free for children 2 and under. Summer daily 10am–5pm (until 8pm Fri); winter daily 9am–4pm.

More than 300 animals reside in this 30-acre zoo, which includes a tropical rain forest and the only underwater viewing of penguins in Colorado. You'll find all sorts of cold-blooded creatures in the herpetarium, including reptiles and insects; kangaroos and emus in the Australia Station; an excellent lion exhibit; endangered species such as cottontop tamarins, black-and-white ruffed lemurs, and rusty spotted cats. The Asian Adventure contains sun bears and black-crested Macaque monkeys. In the Pioneer Ranch-at-the-Zoo, visitors can feed a variety of rare domesticated animals, and the Discovery Room features hands-on exhibits for all ages. The zoo is listed on the National Register of Historic Places for several buildings and other structures (including a moat) that were constructed of native sandstone during the Depression. Also at the zoo are a snack bar and gift shop, with a better-than-average selection of animal-related items.

✪ **Rosemount Museum.** 419 W. 14th St. ☎ 719/545-5290. Admission $5 adults, $4 seniors 60 and over, $3 youths 13–18, $2 children 6–12, free for children 5 and under. June–Aug Tues–Sat 10am–4pm, Sun 2–4pm; Sept–Dec and Feb–May Tues–Sat 1–4pm, Sun 2–4pm. Last tour begins at 3:30pm.

Pueblo's most important historic attraction is this 37-room mansion, built in 1891 for the pioneer Thatcher family. Considered one of the finest surviving examples of late-19th-century architecture and decoration in North America, the three-story, 24,000-square-foot home was constructed entirely of pink rhyolite stone. Inside you'll find handsome oak, maple, and mahogany woodwork; remarkable works of stained glass; hand-decorated ceilings; exquisite Tiffany lighting fixtures; and 10 fireplaces. About 85% of the furnishings were in the original mansion.

Sangre de Cristo Arts & Conference Center. 210 N. Santa Fe Ave. ☎ **719/543-0130.** Free admission to galleries; children's museum, $1 adults, 50¢ children. Children's museum, Mon–Sat 11am–5pm; arts center, Mon–Sat 9am–5pm; galleries, Mon–Sat 11am–4pm.

Pueblo's cultural hub is a two-building complex that houses a 500-seat theater, two dance studios, several art galleries (including one with a fine collection of western art), a conference room, gift shop, and hands-on children's museum with arts and science exhibits. A new, larger children's museum is under construction and is scheduled to open in late 1999. The center also hosts outdoor summer concerts (call for details).

OUTDOOR ACTIVITIES

Lake Pueblo State Park (also called Pueblo Reservoir) is undoubtedly the water-sports capital of southern Colorado. The 17,000-acre park, with 4,600 acres of water and 60 miles of shoreline, is open to boating of all kinds, swimming, hiking, biking, and horseback riding. From Pueblo, take U.S. 50 west for 4 miles, turn south onto Pueblo Boulevard and go another 4 miles to Thatcher Avenue, turn west and go 6 miles to the park.

BICYCLING   The Greenway & Nature Center (see above) includes more than 20 miles of bicycle paths along the Arkansas River. The Pueblo Chamber of Commerce can provide maps of the 35-mile River Trail System that stretches from Lake Pueblo State Park to the University of Southern Colorado, where bicyclists and in-line skaters are welcome.

BOATING   Lake Pueblo State Park (see above) is one of Colorado's most popular water-sports areas. The park's **North Marina** (☎ 719/547-3880) provides a gas dock, boating and fishing supplies, groceries, a restaurant, and boat rentals ($10 to $15 per hour; $50 to $75 per day for fishing boats). The marina is open year-round, but boats are available only from April through October. Boats and canoes can also be put into the Arkansas River at the Greenway & Nature Center (see above).

FISHING   Within the Greenway & Nature Center (see above) is a 150-foot fishing dock on the Arkansas River. Angling for rainbow trout, brown trout, crappie, black bass, and channel catfish is popular from shore or boat at Lake Pueblo State Park (see above), where you'll also find a fish cleaning station.

GOLF   Local courses open to the public include **Walking Stick,** 4300 Walking Stick Blvd. (☎ **719/584-3400**), at the northwest corner of the University of Southern Colorado. Rated among Colorado's best courses and best values, this 18-hole course has a driving range and charges green fees of $22 weekdays and $24 weekends for 18 holes. Other local courses include **City Park,** 3900 Thatcher Ave. (☎ **719/561-4946**), with an 18-hole regulation course plus executive 9-hole course. Greens fees for 18 holes are $17 weekdays and $18 weekends; for 9 holes, $9 at any time. **Los Verdes at Pueblo West,** 251 McCulloch Blvd. (☎ **719/547-2280**), is an 18-hole regulation course with greens fees for 18 holes, including cart, of $25 to $28 weekdays and $32 weekends.

HIKING   Pueblo is the headquarters of the Pike and San Isabel National Forests, and Comanche and Cimarron National Grasslands, 1920 Valley Dr. (☎ **719/545-8737**), with information on hiking and backpacking opportunities throughout central and southern Colorado and southwestern Kansas. Lake Pueblo State Park (see above) is also popular among hikers, with 18 miles of trails.

ICE-SKATING   Public skating, lessons, hockey, and figure skating take place at **Pueblo Plaza Ice Arena,** 100 N. Grand Ave. (☎ **719/542-8784**). Admission is $2 for adults, $1.50 for children 12 and under. In summer, the rink is usually open for public skating Monday and Wednesday from 1 to 3pm, Tuesday and Thursday from 1 to 5pm, and Friday from 1 to 3pm and 7:30 to 9:30pm. From mid-September through May, school groups use the rink, but it is open most afternoons and some evenings for public skating. Call for specific times. Skate rentals ($1) and sharpening are available.

SWIMMING   The most popular local swimming hole is the **Rock Canyon Swim Beach** at the east end of Lake Pueblo State Park (see above). The area has a beach ($1 admission), a water slide ($7 for all day), and bumper boats ($1 for 5 minutes); lifeguards are on duty in the summer.

There are also several public swimming pools in Pueblo, administered by the City of Pueblo Parks and Recreation Department (☎ **719/566-1745**).

SPECTATOR SPORTS

AUTOMOBILE RACING   Top stock-car races are held from mid-April through September on the quarter-mile paved oval track at **Beacon Hill Speedway,** 400 Gobatti Place (☎ **719/545-6105**). Nationally sanctioned drag racing, motocross, quarter scale, quarter-midget racing, and Sports Car Club of America competitions take place April through September at the **Pueblo Motor Sports Park,** U.S. 50 and Pueblo Boulevard in Pueblo West (☎ **719/543-7747**).

DOG RACING   There's live and simulcast dog racing and simulcast horse racing at **Pueblo Greyhound Park,** Colorado's oldest dog track, Lake Avenue at Pueblo Boulevard, I-25 exit 94 (☎ **719/566-0370**).

WHERE TO STAY

There are numerous lodging possibilities in Pueblo, with many of the national franchises and chains represented. Rates are highest in summer, and most motels in Pueblo also charge higher rates during the State Fair (mid-August to early September). Among reliable major chains are **Ramada Inn,** 2001 N. Hudson St. (☎ 800/272-6232 or 719/542-3750), which charges $60 to $90 double; **Best Western Inn at Pueblo West,** 201 S. McCulloch Blvd. (☎ 800/448-1972 or

719/547-2111), charging $70 to $94 double in summer and $54 to $74 double in winter; **Hampton Inn,** 4703 N. Freeway, just west of I-25 exit 102 (☎ 800/ 972-0165 or 800/HAMPTON or 719/544-4700), with rates for two, including continental breakfast, of $79 to $99 in summer and $65 to $75 the rest of the year; **Econo Lodge,** 4615 N. Elizabeth St. (☎ 800/553-2666 or 719/539-2895), with rates for two of $45 to $75 from May through September and $30 to $55 from October through May; and **Super 8,** 1100 U.S. 50 West (☎ 800/800-8000 or 719/545-4104), with rates for two of $51 to $62 in summer and $41 to $50 at other times.

An alternative to calling individual properties is to contact the **Pueblo central reservation service,** which represents most area accommodations (☎ 800/ 781-2200). State and local taxes on accommodations total almost 12%.

Abriendo Inn. 300 W. Abriendo Ave., Pueblo, CO 81004. ☎ **719/544-2703.** Fax 719/ 542-6544. E-mail: abriendo@rmi.net. 10 units. A/C TV TEL. $59–$115 double. Rates include full breakfast. AE, DC, MC, V.

Built in 1906 as a mansion for brewing magnate Martin Walter, his wife, and their eight children, this traditional Foursquare-style house is listed on the National Register of Historic Places. It is also one of Pueblo's finest B&Bs. Guest rooms are decorated with antique furniture and period reproductions, plus king- or queen-size brass or four-poster beds. All rooms have phones with modem jacks. Four units have shower only; six have shower/tub combos; and three contain whirlpool tubs. Breakfasts, which might include egg-sausage soufflé or baked apricot French toast, are served in the oak-wainscoted dining room or on the outdoor patio. Complimentary refreshments are served each evening. The inn offers golf packages Sunday through Thursday. Smoking is permitted on the veranda only.

CAMPING

There are 401 campsites spread across Lake Pueblo State Park (see "Outdoor Activities," above). A dump station and showers are available, as well as hookups at some sites. Sites cost from $7 to $12.

WHERE TO DINE

Irish Brewpub & Grille. 108 W. Third St. ☎ **719/542-9974.** Main courses $6–$18. AE, CB, DC, DISC, MC, V. Mon–Sat 9am–11pm (bar open until 2am). IRISH/ITALIAN/AMERICAN.

If you want to meet everybody who's anybody in Pueblo, squeeze into this busy brewpub—Pueblo's only microbrewery—any evening after work. Have a drink, hobnob with the locals, then head to a table for a great meal. The Calantino family, which opened the pub in 1944, is still there, serving everything from traditional bar food such as Philly cheese steak, buffalo burgers, and chicken club, to exotic pasta dishes, lamb, chicken, beef, and wild game, as well as some Irish specialties. Brewed in-house are a golden ale, lager, brown ale, porter, wheat beer, and, for the adventurous, a chili beer.

Ianne's Whiskey Ridge. 4333 Thatcher Ave. ☎ **719/564-8551.** Reservations recommended. Main courses $7–$21. AE, DISC, MC, V. Mon–Sat 4–10pm, Sun 11am–9pm. ITALIAN/STEAK/SEAFOOD.

Serving Pueblo for more than 50 years, this family-owned and -operated restaurant prepares everything from scratch and warns evening diners that because each meal is cooked to order, they may have to wait. Pasta dishes are a specialty; our favorites are the lasagna and ravioli. There's also a large selection of fresh seafood, chicken, veal, and certified Angus steaks.

La Renaissance. 217 E. Routt Ave., Mesa Junction. ☎ **719/543-6367.** Reservations recommended. Three-course lunch $5–$10; five-course dinner $9.75–$29. AE, CB, DC, DISC, MC, V. Mon–Fri 11am–2pm; Mon–Sat 5–9pm. STEAK/SEAFOOD. From I-25 exit 97B, take Abriendo Ave. northwest for 4 blocks, turn left onto Michigan St., and go 2 blocks to the restaurant.

Housed in an historic 1880s Presbyterian church, La Renaissance offers casual dining in a unique atmosphere, with stained-glass windows, high vaulted ceilings, and oak pews providing some of the seating. Complete lunches and dinners begin with a tureen of soup and finish with dessert, served at the table from a wooden cart. Broiled salmon fillet and baked asparagus Virginia (wrapped in ham) are popular lunches. Slow-roasted prime rib, New Zealand deep sea fillet, and breast of chicken stuffed with broccoli and cheese are among dinner favorites. There's a wide variety of domestic and imported wine and beer.

2 Royal Gorge & Cañon City

Royal Gorge, among the most impressive natural attractions in the state and spanned by what is said to be the world's highest suspension bridge, lies 8 miles west of Cañon City off U.S. 50, at the head of the Arkansas River valley.

This narrow canyon, 1,053 feet deep, was cut through solid granite by 3 million years of water and wind erosion. When Zebulon Pike saw the gorge in 1806, he predicted that man would never conquer it—but by 1877 the Denver & Rio Grande Railroad had laid a route through the canyon, and it soon became a major tourist attraction.

The gorge is spanned by the bridge and an aerial tramway, built for no other reason than to thrill tourists. The quarter-mile-long bridge was constructed in 1929, suspended from two 300-ton cables, and reinforced in 1983. An incline railway, believed to be the world's steepest, was completed in 1931; it plunges from the rim of the gorge 1,550 feet to the floor at a 45° angle, giving passengers the view from the bottom as well as the top. Added in 1969, the 35-passenger tram provides views of the gorge and the bridge from a height of 1,178 feet above the Arkansas River.

Owned by Cañon City, the park also includes a 260-seat multimedia theater, where visitors can see a video presentation on the area's history and construction of the bridge. There's also live entertainment, a miniature railway, a trolley, a beautiful old-fashioned carousel, restaurants, gift shops, and herds of tame mule deer.

The park is open year-round, daily from dawn to dusk. Admission is $12 for adults, $9 for children 4 to 11, and free for children under 4, and includes crossing the bridge and all other park attractions. For information, contact Royal Gorge Bridge, P.O. Box 549, Cañon City, CO 81215 (☎ **888/333-5597** or 719/275-7507).

To see this beautiful gorge from the river, while also enjoying some thrills, consider a raft trip. Rates for adults run $80 to $90 for a full-day trip, including lunch; a half-day trip is about $50. Most Royal Gorge raft trips include rough white-water stretches of the river, but those preferring calmer sections should inquire about such excursions with local rafting companies. Major outfitters include **Arkansas River Tours** (☎ 800/321-4352), **Echo Canyon River Expeditions** (☎ 800/748-2953), and **Royal Gorge Rafting** (☎ 800/758-5161).

OTHER AREA ATTRACTIONS

Cañon City was a popular setting for filmmaking during the industry's early days, and it was a special favorite of silent screen actor Tom Mix, who reputedly worked as a cowboy in the area before becoming a film star. The drowning death of a prominent actress discouraged film companies from coming here for a time, but the area's beautiful scenery and Old West heritage lured the industry back in the late 1950s with the creation of Buckskin Joe, a western theme park and movie set where dozens of films have been shot, including *How the West Was Won, True Grit,* and *Cat Ballou.*

Now called **Royal Gorge Frontier Town & Railway,** this popular attraction is about 8 miles west of Cañon City on U.S. 50. Royal Gorge Frontier Town (☎ 719/ 275-5149) is an authentic-looking Old West town, created from genuine 19th-century buildings relocated from around the state. Visitors can watch gunfights, pan for gold, see a musical revue and medicine-man show, ride horseback (or in a horse-drawn trolley), and wander around a western maze. The Scenic Railway (☎ 719/275-5485) offers a 30-minute trip through rugged Royal Gorge country, where you're likely to see deer and other wildlife, to the rim of the Royal Gorge for a panoramic view of the gorge and bridge.

Frontier Town is open from May through September. Hours from Memorial Day to Labor Day are 9am to 6pm; call for hours at other times. The Railway runs from March through December. Hours from Memorial Day to Labor Day are 8am to 8pm; call for hours at other times. Combination admission tickets, which include the Scenic Railway, horse-drawn trolley, and all the attractions and entertainment in Frontier Town, are $13 for adults, $11 for children 4 to 11, and free for children under 4. Separate tickets are also available.

Other Cañon City attractions include the ✪ **Colorado Territorial Prison Museum and Park,** 201 N. First St. (☎ 719/269-3015). Housed in the state's former women's prison, just outside the walls of the original 1871 territorial prison, the museum contains an actual gas chamber, historic photos of life behind bars, weapons confiscated from inmates, the last hangman's noose used legally in the state, a simulation of a lethal injection system, a simulation of the "Old Gray Mare" (a cruel apparatus used to punish misbehaving prisoners), and other exhibits showing what prison life was like in the Old West and even in more modern times. A gift shop sells arts and crafts made by inmates housed at a medium-security prison next door. The museum is open May through September, daily from 8:30am to 6pm; and October through April, Friday through Sunday from 10am to 5pm. Admission is $4 for adults, $3.50 for seniors, $2.50 for children 6 to 12, and free for children 5 and under.

The **Cañon City Municipal Museum,** U.S. 50 (Royal Gorge Boulevard) at Sixth Street (☎ 719/269-9018), displays American Indian artifacts, guns, gems and minerals, wild game trophies, historic photos, old dolls, and pioneer household items and other memorabilia. Behind the main museum building you'll find the renovated and furnished 1860 log cabin built by Anson Rudd, local blacksmith and first warden of the Colorado Territorial Prison, as well as the Rudd family's three-story stone house built in 1881, which contains a collection of Victorian furniture and western artifacts. The museum is open Tuesday through Sunday from early May to Labor Day, and Tuesday through Saturday the rest of the year. It is closed Christmas Eve plus all state and federal holidays. Hours are 10am to 4pm. Admission is $1.50 for adults, $1 for children 6 to 12, and free for children 5 and under.

For information on where to stay and eat, a walking tour of historic downtown Cañon City, and other attractions, contact the **Cañon City Chamber of Commerce,** P.O. Bin 749, Cañon City, CO 81215 (☎ 800/876-7922 or 719/ 275-2331).

3 Trinidad

197 miles S of Denver, 247 miles N of Albuquerque, New Mexico

History and art are two reasons to stop in Trinidad when traveling along I-25 through southern Colorado. Bat Masterson was sheriff in the 1880s, Wyatt Earp drove the stage, Kit Carson helped open the trade routes, and even Billy the Kid passed through. Many historic buildings—handsome structures of brick and sandstone—survive from this era. Plains tribes roamed the area for centuries before the first 17th- and 18th-century forays by Spanish explorers and settlers. Later, traders and trappers made this an important stop on the northern branch of the Santa Fe Trail.

German, Irish, Italian, Jewish, Polish, and Slavic immigrants were drawn to the area starting in the late 1800s for jobs at area coal mines and cattle ranches, and agriculture and railroading were also important economic factors. Ranching remains a cornerstone of the economy today, and the tourism industry is growing.

ESSENTIALS

GETTING THERE   By Car   If you're traveling from north or south, take I-25: Trinidad straddles the interstate, halfway between Denver and Santa Fe, New Mexico. From the east, take U.S. 50 into La Junta, then turn southwest for 80 miles on U.S. 350. From Durango and points west, follow U.S. 160 to Walsenburg, then travel south 37 miles on I-25.

By Plane   Pueblo has the nearest commercial airport (see section 1, earlier in this chapter).

By Train   The **Amtrak** *Southwest Chief* passes through Trinidad twice daily—once eastbound, once westbound—on a run between Chicago and Los Angeles. The depot is on Nevada Street north of College Street, beneath I-25 (☎ **800/872-7245**).

VISITOR INFORMATION   The **Colorado Welcome Center,** 309 N. Nevada Ave. (I-25 exit 14A), Trinidad, CO 81082 (☎ **719/846-9512**), open daily from 8am to 5pm in winter and 8am to 6pm in summer, has information not only on Trinidad and southeastern Colorado, but also on the entire state. The **Trinidad–Las Animas County Chamber of Commerce** is in the same building (☎ **719/846-9285;** www.trinidadco.com).

GETTING AROUND   Main Street (U.S. 160/350) parallels El Rio de Las Animas en Purgatorio ("the river of lost souls in purgatory"), better known as the Purgatoire River, which flows south to north through the center of town. The historic downtown area is focused around Main and Commercial Streets on the south side of the river. Main joins I-25 on the west side of downtown.

Car rentals are available from **Hadad Motor Sales** (☎ 719/846-3318) or **Circle Chevrolet** (☎ 719/846-9805). Taxi service is provided by **Your Ride Taxi Company** (☎ 719/859-3344).

The **Trinidad Trolley,** operating from Memorial Day to Labor Day, provides an excellent—and free—way to see this historic city. Running daily from 10am to 5pm, you can board the trolley at the Colorado Welcome Center (see above), and get on and off at the various museums and other attractions. Pick up a schedule at the Welcome Center.

FAST FACTS   Medical services, including a 24-hour emergency room, are provided at **Mt. San Rafael Hospital,** 410 Benedicta Avenue off Main Street

(☎ 719/ 846-9213). The **post office** is at 301 E. Main St. Contact the U.S. Postal Service (☎ 800/275-8777) for hours and other information. For **road conditions,** call ☎ 719/846-9262.

SPECIAL EVENTS   Santa Fe Trail Festival, second weekend in June; fireworks display over Trinidad Lake on the Fourth of July; the Trinidad Roundup and Las Animas County Fair, late August; Labor Day parade, early September; Fallfest, October; and Las Posadas, Los Pastores, and other Christmas events in December.

WHAT TO SEE & DO

Main Street was once part of the Mountain Route of the Santa Fe Trail, and many of the streets that cross it are paved with locally made red brick. The Trinidad Historical Society distributes a booklet titled *A Walk Through the History of Trinidad* ($2), available at local museums. Among the buildings it singles out for special attention are the Trinidad Opera House (1883) and Columbian Hotel (1879), which are across from each other on Main Street, as well as the Trinidad Water Works (1879), on Cedar Street at the Purgatoire River.

✪ **A. R. Mitchell Memorial Museum of Western Art.** 150 E. Main St. ☎ 719/ 846-4224. Free admission. Mid-Apr–Sept Mon–Sat 10am–4pm; off-season by appointment.

More than 250 paintings and illustrations by western artist Arthur Roy Mitchell (1889–1977) are displayed here, along with works by other nationally recognized artists and a collection of early Hispanic religious folk art. The museum also contains the Aultman collection of photographs, taken by Oliver E. Aultman and his son Glenn from the late 1800s through much of the 20th century, a photographic time line from the early 1600s to the present, plus early cameras, darkroom equipment, and studio props. The huge building, originally a department store, is a 1906 western-style structure with the original pressed-tin ceiling, wood floors, and a horseshoe-shaped mezzanine.

Louden-Henritze Archaeology Museum. Freudenthal Memorial Library, Trinidad State Junior College, near the intersection of Park and Prospect Streets. ☎ 719/846-5508. Free admission. May–Sept, Mon–Fri 10am–4pm; winter by appointment.

Millions of years of history are displayed here, including fossils, casts of dinosaur tracks, arrowheads, pottery, petroglyphs, and other artifacts from prehistoric man discovered during area excavations. Watch for the fossilized partial skeleton of a mosasaur (a sea reptile) that lived in the area some 80 million years ago.

Old Firehouse No. 1 Children's Museum. 314 N. Commercial St. ☎ 719/846-8220 or 719/846-2024. Free admission. June–Aug, Mon–Sat noon–4pm. Closed July 4.

On exhibit here are a historic fire truck, Trinidad's original 1930s-era alarm system, a model train diorama, and a restored turn-of-the-century schoolroom. Kids will enjoy the hands-on displays, including Grandma's trunk for dress-up.

✪ **Trinidad History Museum.** 300 E. Main St. ☎ 719/846-7217. Admission $5 adults, $2.50 children 6–16, $4.50 seniors, free for children under 6. May–Sept daily 10am–4pm; off-season by appointment.

Together, the Baca House, Bloom Mansion, and Santa Fe Trail Museum rank as Trinidad's principal attraction. The 1870 Baca House, along the Mountain Route of the Santa Fe Trail, is a two-story Greek Revival–style adobe. Originally owned by sheep rancher Felipe Baca, the house contains some of the Baca family's original furnishings. Nearby stands the 1882 Bloom Mansion, a Second Empire–style Victorian manor embellished with fancy wood carving and ornate ironwork. The

Colorado Historical Society operates both homes as well as the Santa Fe Trail Museum, located behind the homes in a building that was originally living quarters for Baca's hired help. Both the Baca House and Santa Fe Trail Museum are Certified Sites on the Santa Fe National Historic Trail.

SPORTS & OUTDOOR ACTIVITIES

Located 3 miles west of town on Colo. 12, ✪ **Trinidad Lake State Park** (☎ 719/846-6951) is the place to go for all sorts of outdoor recreation possibilities, and is also a good base camp for exploring southern Colorado and northern New Mexico. Its 700-acre reservoir on the Purgatoire River is popular for powerboating, waterskiing, sailboating, and sailboarding. Swimming is prohibited, however. There's a boat ramp and dock, but no boat rentals or supplies. Fishermen go after largemouth bass, rainbow and brown trout, channel catfish, walleye, crappie, and bluegills. Ten miles of hiking and mountain-biking trails here include the Levsa Canyon Trail, a 1-mile self-guided loop that also branches off for another 4 miles to the historic town of Cokedale. For those who thought to bring a horse, there are 4 miles of equestrian trails on the south side of the lake. The Long's Canyon Watchable Wildlife Area offers viewing blinds in a wetlands area. Commonly seen in the park are great blue herons, Canada geese, red-tailed hawks, great horned owls, hummingbirds, mule deer, cottontail rabbits, and ground squirrels. An attractive 62-unit campground, with fees of $9 to $12, has electric hookups, a dump station, and showers. During the winter there's cross-country skiing, ice-skating, and ice-fishing.

GOLF   The 9-hole **Trinidad Golf Course,** off the Santa Fe Trail adjacent to I-25 at exit 13A (☎ 719/846-4015), is considered among the best 9-hole courses in the state, with weekend fees of $13 for 9 holes, $17 for 18 holes ($1 less for each on weekdays).

SKIING   **Cuchara Mountain Resort,** 946 Panadero Ave., Cuchara, CO 81055 (☎ 888/282-4272 or 719/742-3163; www.cuchara.com), is a family-oriented ski area with more than two dozen runs covering some 230 acres, and it claims to never have a lift line. Located 60 miles west of Trinidad on Colo. 12, the ski area has a vertical drop of 1,562 feet from the summit of 10,810-foot Baker Mountain. There are four lifts, including three double chairs and one triple chair, and trails are rated 40% beginner, 40% intermediate, and 20% advanced. Facilities include a ski school, day lodge with fast food, restaurant, equipment rentals, and a kids' program for children 5 to 12 years old. A Snowboard Park was recently added. The resort also offers snowshoeing, ice-skating, tubing, dogsled rides, and sleigh rides, and cross-country skiing trails are nearby. Full-day rates (1998–1999 season) are $31 for adults, $20 for youths 7 to 19, and free for kids under 7 and seniors 65 and over. When the ski season ends, the resort is open for mountain biking, hiking, horseback riding, and art and music festivals.

WHERE TO STAY

Several national chains and franchises provide lodging in Trinidad. Rates here are for two people in summer; rates at other times are usually 10% to 20% lower. Among your choices are **Best Western Trinidad Inn,** 900 W. Adams St., I-25 exit 13A (☎ 800/955-2215 or 719/846-2215), with rates of $79 to $99; **Holiday Inn,** 9995 County Rd. 69.1, just off I-25 exit 11 (☎ 800-HOLIDAY or 719/846-4491), with rates of $89 to $119; and **Days Inn,** 702 W. Main St. (☎ 800/DAYS INN or 719/846-2271), charging $57 to $82. State and city sales taxes of about 8% are added to lodging bills.

WHERE TO DINE

El Capitan Restaurant & Lounge. 321 State St. ☎ **719/846-9903.** Sandwiches and à la carte Mexican items $2–$5.50; dinners $3–$10. AE, DISC, MC, V. Mon–Fri 11am–9pm, Sat 4:30–10pm. MEXICAN/ITALIAN/AMERICAN.

This attractive restaurant, with a relaxing, comfortable atmosphere, serves some of the best margaritas in southern Colorado. It's known for its Mexican and Italian dishes, although you can also get steaks, seafood, barbecued ribs, burgers, and sandwiches. Mexican items include green or red chile, bean or beef burritos, enchiladas, chimichangas, and a vegetable quesadilla. On the Italian side of the menu you'll find gnocchi, beef ravioli, and spaghetti with meatballs, meat sauce, or sausage. Desserts include fried ice cream.

Nana & Nano's Pasta House. 415 University St. (I-25 exit 14A). ☎ **719/846-2696.** Main courses $5.50–$12.50; deli sandwiches $2.50–$3.50. AE, DISC, MC, V. Restaurant: Memorial Day–Labor Day, Tues–Fri 4:30–8:30pm, Sat 4:30–9pm; closes half an hour earlier in winter. Deli: year-round, Tues–Fri 10am–5pm, Sat 9am–1pm. ITALIAN.

The Monteleone family takes pride in the Italian specialties served here, each cooked to order (expect a 20-minute wait), and served with salad, bread, and butter. Daily specials include rigatoni, mostaccioli, and lasagna, and the regular menu offers a good selection of pasta, sandwiches, fish, or a rib-eye steak. Many pasta selections are available with a choice of meatballs or Italian sausage, and there is also a "Smaller Appetite" menu for all ages starting at $6.25. Monteleone's Deli, next to the restaurant, offers Italian and you-choose-it sandwiches, plus deli meats and cheeses.

4 A Drive Along the Scenic Highway of Legends

Unquestionably the most fascinating day trip from Trinidad is the appropriately named Scenic Highway of Legends, which runs some 80 miles west, north, then northeast, mostly on Colo. 12, from Trinidad to Walsenburg.

Traveling west about 7 miles from Trinidad, past Trinidad Lake State Park, the first site of special note is **Cokedale,** just north of the highway. The best existing example of a coal camp in Colorado, **Cokedale** was founded in 1906 by the American Smelting and Refining Co. as a self-contained company town, and by 1909 was a thriving community of 1,500. When the mine closed in 1947, residents were offered the company-owned homes at $100 per room and $50 per lot. Some stayed, incorporating in 1948, and in 1984 Cokedale was placed on the National Register of Historic Places. Many of today's 120 or so residents are descendants of those miners, or retired miners themselves. As you drive in you'll see some of the 350 coke ovens, used to convert coal to hotter-burning coke, for which the town was named. Walking through the community, you'll see the icehouse, schoolhouse, mining office, Sacred Heart of Jesus and Mary Church, Gottlieb Mercantile Company, and other buildings, including a boardinghouse where bachelors could get room and board for $25 a month.

Proceeding west, you'll pass several old coal towns, including Segundo, Weston, and Vigil, and two coal mines—the Golden Eagle, where underground mining is still done, and New Elk Mine, now a processing plant—before entering **Stonewall Valley,** 33 miles west of Trinidad. Named for a striking rock formation, a vertical bed of lithified sandstone, Stonewall is both the site of a small timber industry and the location of many vacation homes.

From Stonewall, Colo. 12 turns north past **Monument Lake,** a resort and water supply for the city of Trinidad, named for a rock formation in the middle of the lake that some say resembles two American Indian chiefs. Several miles past Monument Lake is **North Lake,** a state wildlife area and home to rainbow, cutthroat, kokanee, and brown trout.

The highway continues north across 9,941-foot **Cucharas Pass.** Overlooking the pass are the **Spanish Peaks,** eroded remnants of a 20-million-year-old volcano. The native Arapahoe believed them to be the home of the gods, and they served as guideposts to early travelers. Legends persist about the existence of a treasure of gold in this area, but none has been found. Several miles north of Cucharas Pass is **Cucharas River Recreation Area,** home of Blue Lake, named for its spectacular color.

Numerous geologic features become prominent as the road descends toward Walsenburg. Among them are the **Devil's Stairsteps,** one of a series of erosion-resistant igneous dikes that radiate out like spokes from the Spanish Peaks; **Dakota Wall,** a layer of pressed sandstone thrust vertically from the earth; and **Goemmer Butte,** sometimes called "Sore Thumb Butte," a volcanic plug rising 500 feet from the valley floor.

At this point, about 65 miles from Trinidad, is the foothills village of **La Veta** (population 750), founded in 1862 by Colonel John M. Francisco, who reportedly said after seeing the pretty valley, "This is paradise enough for me." Continuing east, Colo. 12 joins U.S. 160, which goes by **Lathrop State Park** (☎ **719/ 738-2376**), the state's oldest state park, with two lakes for boating (no rentals), swimming, and fishing; camping ($7 to $12); a 2-mile hiking and mountain-biking trail; and cross-country skiing and ice-skating. There's also a 9-hole golf course (☎ 719/ 738-2739), with fees of $11 to $13 for 9 holes.

From the park it's about 2 miles to Walsenburg on U.S. 160, and then just under 40 miles south down I-25 to return to Trinidad.

5 La Junta

81 miles NE of Trinidad, 64 miles E of Pueblo, 274 miles NW of Amarillo, Texas

One of Colorado's pockets of fruit growing, this busy little town has several surprises for visitors, including some of the best American Indian art in the country, and nearby a handsome reconstruction of an historic fort.

Once the hunting and fishing grounds of the Arapahoe, Cheyenne, and Ute tribes, and visited briefly by Spanish soldiers in the 17th and 18th centuries, it was not until Zebulon Pike led his exploratory expedition into the Arkansas River valley in 1806 that the area became known to white Americans. Trappers and traders followed, creating the Santa Fe Trail; brothers William and Charles Bent then built Bent's Fort in 1833 as a trading post and the first American settlement in the region.

La Junta was founded in 1875 as a railroad camp. First called Manzaneras, then Otero, it was renamed La Junta—Spanish for "the junction"—on completion of rail links to Pueblo and Trinidad in 1877. The town flourished as a farming and ranching center. Today, with a population of about 8,500, its highly irrigated land produces a wide variety of fruits, vegetables, and wheat.

ESSENTIALS

GETTING THERE   By Car   La Junta is easily reached via U.S. 50, which comes into town from Kansas in the east, and continues west to I-25 at Pueblo. From New Mexico, exit I-25 at Trinidad and take U.S. 350; from Durango and southwestern Colorado, take U.S. 160 to Walsenburg, and continue on Colo. 10 to La Junta.

By Plane Pueblo has the nearest commercial airport (see section 1 of this chapter).

By Train Passenger service is available aboard **Amtrak,** with a depot on First Street at Colorado Avenue (☎ **800/872-7245**). The *Southwest Chief* passes through twice daily (once in each direction) on the main line between Chicago and Los Angeles.

VISITOR INFORMATION Contact the **La Junta Chamber of Commerce,** 110 Santa Fe Ave., La Junta, CO 81050 (☎ **719/384-7411**; fax 719/384-2217; www.coloplains.com/lajunta).

GETTING AROUND La Junta is located on the Arkansas River at an elevation of 4,100 feet. U.S. 50, which runs through town as First Street, follows the river's south bank. Highways from Trinidad and Walsenburg join it just west of town. The downtown core focuses on First, Second, and Third Streets, crossed by north–south Colorado and Santa Fe Avenues. At the east edge of town, Colo. 109 (Adams Avenue) crosses the Arkansas into North La Junta (where it becomes Main Street); six blocks past the river, Colo. 194 (Trail Road) forks to the right and leads 5 miles to Bent's Old Fort.

FAST FACTS Health services are provided by the **Arkansas Valley Regional Medical Center,** 1100 Carson Ave. at 10th Street (☎ **719/384-5412**), which has a 24-hour emergency room. The **post office** is located at Fourth Street and Colorado Avenue; contact the U.S. Postal Service (☎ **800/275-8777**) for hours and other information. For **road conditions,** call ☎ **303/639-1111** (toll call).

SPECIAL EVENTS Fur Trade Encampment, at Bent's Old Fort, July; Kid's Rodeo, August; Early Settlers Day, Saturday after Labor Day; and 1846 Christmas, at Bent's Old Fort, mid-December.

WHAT TO SEE & DO

To see a number of buildings from the late 1800s and early 1900s listed on the National Register of Historic Places, take the self-guided *Historic Homes of La Junta* walking/driving tour, described in a free brochure available from the La Junta Chamber of Commerce.

✪ **Bent's Old Fort National Historic Site.** 35110 Colo. 194 E. ☎ **719/383-5010.** www.nps.gov/beol. Admission $2 per person 17 and older June–Aug, free Sept–May. June–Aug, daily 8am–5:30pm; Sept–May, daily 9am–4pm. Closed Thanksgiving, Christmas, and New Year's Day.

Once the most important settlement on the Santa Fe Trail between Missouri and New Mexico, Bent's Old Fort has been reconstructed as it was during its reign as a major trading post, from 1833 to 1849. Located 7 miles east of modern La Junta, this adobe fort on the Arkansas River was built by brothers Charles and William Bent and partner Ceran St. Vrain. It was the hub of trade for eastern U.S. merchants, Rocky Mountain fur trappers, and Plains tribes (mainly Cheyenne, but also Arapahoe, Ute, Apache, Kiowa, and Comanche).

As American settlement increased, driving off the buffalo that were the lifeblood of the tribes, the Bents were caught between two cultures. Serious hostilities began in 1847, and trade rapidly declined during a cholera epidemic in 1849. Part of the fort burned that year, and was not rebuilt until modern times. Reproductions furnish the 33 rooms, which include a kitchen with an adjoining pantry, a cook's room, and a dining room; a trade room with robes, pelts, and blankets; blacksmith and carpenter shops; William Bent's office and bedroom; quarters for Mexican

In Search of Dinosaur Tracks

Dinosaur tracks from the Jurassic period, about 150 million years ago, are a highlight of ✪ **Comanche National Grassland,** a 435,000-acre area south of La Junta that also draws bird-watchers, hunters, anglers, and hikers. Access to Picket Wire Canyonlands, where the dinosaur tracks are located, is limited to those hiking or on mountain bikes or horseback.

The tracks are believed to be from dinosaurs in the Sauropodmorpha "lizard feet" and Theropoda "beast feet" families, who lived here when the area was a savannah—a tropical grassland with a few scattered trees. There was plenty of food for the Sauropods, who were plant-eaters, making them all the more tempting to their enemies, the meat-eating Theropods. The Sauropods, particularly the Brontosaurus, grew to about 14 feet tall and weighed up to 33 tons. Theropods grew to about 16 feet tall, but were not as long, and weighed only about one ton. Still, with their sharp claws, they would attack the Sauropods whenever given the chance.

From the Withers Canyon Trailhead, there's a 10.6-mile round-trip hike to the dinosaur tracks. Visitors should be prepared for temperature extremes (summer temperatures can exceed 100°F), carry lots of drinking water, and watch for flash floods, biting insects, and snakes. Maps to the area are available from the **Comanche National Grassland office,** 1420 E. Third St., La Junta, CO 81050 (☎ **719/384-2181**). The office also offers a variety of guided auto, hiking, and mountain-biking tours into Picket Wire Canyonlands (including stops at the dinosaur tracks) for a fee, with reservations available after January 1 for that summer. Also contact the office for information on other attractions in the grasslands, including its wildlife—such as the lesser prairie chicken, a threatened species—and rock art that's hundreds of years old.

laborers, trappers, and soldiers; a billiards room; and the quarters of a merchant's wife (who kept a meticulous diary).

It's a quarter-mile walk on a paved path from the historic site's entry station to the fort itself, where hosts in period costume greet visitors during the summer. You'll see demonstrations of frontier life, such as blacksmithing, adobe-making, trapping, cooking, and medical and survival skills. In summer, 45-minute guided tours begin on the hour daily; a 20-minute film on the fort is shown year-round. There's also a gift and book shop.

✪ **Koshare Indian Museum and Kiva.** Otero Junior College, 115 W. 18th St. ☎ **800/693-5482** or 719/384-4411. www.ruralnet.net/koshare. Admission $2 adults, $1 students and seniors; free the first Sun of each month; dances $5 adults, $3 students and youth. Daily 10am–5pm, extended hours during ceremonials and other special events. Dancers perform June–mid-Aug, Fri–Sat 8pm; call for additional times. Located 1 block west of Colorado Ave.

More than $10 million worth of American Indian art—featuring tribal members both as artists and subjects—is the focus of this excellent museum. On display are authentic clothing, jewelry, and baskets, along with western paintings and sculptures. One of the finest collections of works by early Taos, New Mexico, artists is presented as well, including what is considered one of Bert Phillips's best works, *Relics of His Ancestors.* The museum itself is an adobe-style building resembling a northern New Mexico pueblo and is on the Colorado Register of Historic Sites.

The Koshare Dancers, a nationally acclaimed troop of Boy Scout Explorers, perform an average of 60 times a year, primarily in their own great *kiva,* a circular chamber traditionally used for religious rites by southwestern tribes. Dances are held at least weekly in summer, and the Koshare Winter Ceremonials are a December tradition.

Otero Museum. Third and Anderson sts. ☎ **719/384-7500** or 719/384-7406. Free admission, donations welcome. June–Sept, Mon–Sat 1–5pm; off-season tours by appointment.

This museum provides a look at what life was like in eastern Colorado between the 1870s and 1940s. There's a genuine 1876 stage coach, a complete well-stocked grocery store from the early 20th century, several early La Junta homes, a replica of the community's first school, a doctor's office, railroad equipment and memorabilia, items from both world wars, and restored classic motorcars displayed in an early-20th-century gas station.

WHERE TO STAY

Among the national chain motels in La Junta is **Quality Inn,** 1325 E. Third St. (☎ **800/221-2222** or 719/384-2571), with summer rates for two of $59 to $89, and lower rates the rest of the year. The motel's restaurant is a good breakfast spot. La Junta also has a **Super 8,** 27882 Frontage Rd., on the west side of La Junta along U.S. 50 (☎ **800/800-8000** or 719/384-4408), charging $55 to $59 for two people from April through September, and lower rates the rest of the year. Room tax of just over 7% is added to lodging bills.

✪ **Mid-Town Motel.** 215 E. Third St., La Junta, CO 81050. ☎ **719/384-7741.** Fax 719/384-7323. E-mail: pjnjack@ria.net. 26 units. A/C TV TEL. $32–$38 double. AE, CB, DC, DISC, MC, V. Pets accepted.

A great little mom-and-pop motel off the main highway, the Mid-Town offers clean, quiet, and comfortable rooms with good-quality beds and linens. Rooms have desks and one or two beds; several have couches or loveseats, and the one-bedrooms also have recliners. Owners Jack and P. J. Culp are an invaluable source of information for area visitors. Free morning coffee is served in the lobby.

WHERE TO DINE

Chiaramonte's Restaurant and Lounge. 208 Santa Fe Ave. ☎ **719/384-8909.** Lunch $4.75–$7.95; dinner $4.75–$27.50. DISC, MC, V. Mon–Sat 11am–2pm and 5–9pm. STEAK/SEAFOOD.

This casually elegant basement restaurant, with polished wood walls, looks fancy but welcomes everyone. A local favorite for its pepper steak, green-chile burger, and daily luncheon specials, it's also the place to come for a wide variety of charbroiled steaks, chicken Alfredo, halibut, salmon, or shrimp, plus the Friday- and Saturday-night prime-rib specials.

Appendix: Useful Toll-Free Numbers & Web Sites

AIRLINES

Air Canada
☎ 800/776-3000
www.aircanada.ca

American Airlines
☎ 800/433-7300
www.americanair.com

America West Airlines
☎ 800/235-9292
www.americawest.com

Aspen Mountain Air
☎ 800/877-3932
www.aspenmountainair.com

British Airways
☎ 800/247-9297
☎ 0345/222-111 in Britain
www.british-airways.com

**Canadian Airlines
International**
☎ 800/426-7000
www.cdnair.ca

Continental Airlines
☎ 800/525-0280
www.flycontinental.com

Delta Air Lines
☎ 800/221-1212
www.delta-air.com

Frontier Airlines
☎ 800/432-1359
www.frontierairlines.com

Korean Air
☎ 800/438-5000
www.koreanair.com

Martinair
☎ 800/366-4655
www.martinair.com

Mesa Air
☎ 800/637-2247
www.mesa-air.com

Mexicana Airlines
☎ 800/531-7921
www.mexicana.com

Midwest Express Airlines
☎ 800/452-2022
www.midwestexpress.com

Northwest Airlines
☎ 800/225-2525
www.nwa.com

Reno Air
☎ 800/736-6247
www.renoair.com

Sun Country Airlines
☎ 800/359-5786
www.suncountry.com

Trans World Airlines (TWA)
☎ 800/221-2000
www.twa.com

United Airlines
☎ 800/241-6522
www.ual.com

US Airways
☎ 800/428-4322
www.usair.com

Vanguard Airlines
☎ 800/826-4827
www.flyvanguard.com

CAR-RENTAL AGENCIES

Advantage
☎800/777-5500
www.arac.com

Alamo
☎800/327-9633
www.goalamo.com

Avis
☎800/331-1212 in Continental U.S.
☎800/TRY-AVIS in Canada
www.avis.com

Budget
☎800/527-0700
www.budgetrentacar.com

Cruise America
☎800/327-7778
www.cruiseamerica.com

Dollar
☎800/800-4000
www.dollarcar.com

Enterprise
☎800/325-8007
www.pickenterprise.com

Hertz
☎800/654-3131
www.hertz.com

Kemwel Holiday Auto (KHA)
☎800/678-0678
www.kemwel.com

National
☎800/CAR-RENT
www.nationalcar.com

Thrifty
☎800/367-2277
www.thrifty.com

MAJOR HOTEL & MOTEL CHAINS

Best Western International
☎800/528-1234
www.bestwestern.com

Clarion Hotels
☎800/CLARION
www.hotelchoice.com/cgi-bin/res/webres?
    clarion.html

Comfort Inns
☎800/228-5150
www.hotelchoice.com/cgi-bin/res/webres?
    comfort.html

Courtyard by Marriott
☎800/321-2211
www.courtyard.com

Days Inn
☎800/325-2525
www.daysinn.com

Doubletree Hotels
☎800/222-TREE
www.doubletreehotels.com

Econo Lodges
☎800/55-ECONO
www.hotelchoice.com/cgi-bin/res/webres?
    econo.html

Fairfield Inn by Marriott
☎800/228-2800
www.fairfieldinn.com

Hampton Inn
☎800/HAMPTON
www.hampton-inn.com

Hilton Hotels
☎800/HILTONS
www.hilton.com

Holiday Inn
☎800/HOLIDAY
www.holiday-inn.com

Howard Johnson
☎800/654-2000
www.hojo.com/hojo.html

Hyatt Hotels & Resorts
☎800/228-9000
www.hyatt.com

ITT Sheraton
☎800/325-3535
www.sheraton.com

La Quinta Motor Inns
☎800/531-5900
www.laquinta.com

Marriott Hotels
☎800/228-9290
www.marriott.com

Motel 6
☎800/4-MOTEL6 (800/466-8536)

Quality Inns
☎800/228-5151
www.hotelchoice.com/cgi-bin/res/webres?
   quality.html

Radisson Hotels International
☎800/333-3333
www.radisson.com

Ramada Inns
☎800/2-RAMADA
www.ramada.com

Red Carpet Inns
☎800/251-1962

Red Lion Hotels & Inns
☎800/547-8010
www.travelweb.com

Red Roof Inns
☎800/843-7663
www.redroof.com

Residence Inn by Marriott
☎800/331-3131
www.residenceinn.com

Rodeway Inns
☎800/228-2000
www.hotelchoice.com/cgi-bin/res/webres?
   rodeway.html

Super 8 Motels
☎800/800-8000
www.super8motels.com

Travelodge
☎800/255-3050

Vagabond Inns
☎800/522-1555
www.vagabondinns.com

Wyndham Hotels and Resorts
☎800/822-4200 in Continental U.S.
   and Canada
www.wyndham.com

Index

FROMMER'S® COMPLETE TRAVEL GUIDES

Alaska
Amsterdam
Arizona
Atlanta
Australia
Austria
Bahamas
Barcelona, Madrid & Seville
Belgium, Holland & Luxembourg
Bermuda
Boston
Budapest & the Best of Hungary
California
Canada
Cancún, Cozumel & the Yucatán
Cape Cod, Nantucket & Martha's Vineyard
Caribbean
Caribbean Cruises & Ports of Call
Caribbean Ports of Call
Carolinas & Georgia
Chicago
China
Colorado
Costa Rica
Denver, Boulder & Colorado Springs
England
Europe
Florida

France
Germany
Greece
Greek Islands
Hawaii
Hong Kong
Honolulu, Waikiki & Oahu
Ireland
Israel
Italy
Jamaica & Barbados
Japan
Las Vegas
London
Los Angeles
Maryland & Delaware
Maui
Mexico
Miami & the Keys
Montana & Wyoming
Montréal & Québec City
Munich & the Bavarian Alps
Nashville & Memphis
Nepal
New England
New Mexico
New Orleans
New York City
Nova Scotia, New Brunswick & Prince Edward Island
Oregon
Paris
Philadelphia & the Amish Country

Portugal
Prague & the Best of the Czech Republic
Provence & the Riviera
Puerto Rico
Rome
San Antonio & Austin
San Diego
San Francisco
Santa Fe, Taos & Albuquerque
Scandinavia
Scotland
Seattle & Portland
Singapore & Malaysia
South Pacific
Spain
Switzerland
Thailand
Tokyo
Toronto
Tuscany & Umbria
USA
Utah
Vancouver & Victoria
Vermont, New Hampshire & Maine
Vienna & the Danube Valley
Virgin Islands
Virginia
Walt Disney World & Orlando
Washington, D.C.
Washington State

FROMMER'S® DOLLAR-A-DAY GUIDES

Australia from $50 a Day
California from $60 a Day
Caribbean from $60 a Day
England from $60 a Day
Europe from $50 a Day
Florida from $60 a Day

Greece from $50 a Day
Hawaii from $60 a Day
Ireland from $50 a Day
Israel from $45 a Day
Italy from $50 a Day
London from $75 a Day

New York from $75 a Day
New Zealand from $50 a Day
Paris from $70 a Day
San Francisco from $60 a Day
Washington, D.C., from $60 a Day

FROMMER'S® PORTABLE GUIDES

Acapulco, Ixtapa & Zihuatanejo
Alaska Cruises & Ports of Call
Bahamas
California Wine Country
Charleston & Savannah
Chicago

Dublin
Las Vegas
London
Maine Coast
New Orleans
New York City
Paris

Puerto Vallarta, Manzanillo & Guadalajara
San Francisco
Sydney
Tampa & St. Petersburg
Venice
Washington, D.C.

Frommer's® National Park Guides

Family Vacations in the
National Parks
Grand Canyon

National Parks of the
American West
Yellowstone & Grand Teton

Yosemite & Sequoia/
Kings Canyon
Zion & Bryce Canyon

Frommer's® Great Outdoor Guides

New England
Northern California

Southern California & Baja
Pacific Northwest

Frommer's® Memorable Walks

Chicago
London

New York
Paris

San Francisco
Washington D.C.

Frommer's® Irreverent Guides

Amsterdam
Boston
Chicago

London
Manhattan

New Orleans
Paris

San Francisco
Walt Disney World
Washington, D.C.

Frommer's® Best-Loved Driving Tours

America
Britain
California

Florida
France
Germany

Ireland
Italy
New England

Scotland
Spain
Western Europe

The Complete Idiot's Travel Guides

Boston
Cruise Vacations
Planning Your Trip to Europe
Hawaii

Las Vegas
London
Mexico's Beach Resorts
New Orleans

New York City
San Francisco
Walt Disney World
Washington D.C.

The Unofficial Guides®

Branson, Missouri
California with Kids
Chicago
Cruises
Disney Companion

Florida with Kids
The Great Smoky &
Blue Ridge
Mountains

Las Vegas
Miami & the Keys
Mini-Mickey
New Orleans

New York City
San Francisco
Skiing in the West
Walt Disney World
Washington, D.C.

Special-Interest Titles

Born to Shop: Caribbean Ports of Call
Born to Shop: France
Born to Shop: Hong Kong
Born to Shop: Italy
Born to Shop: New York
Born to Shop: Paris
Frommer's Britain's Best Bike Rides
The Civil War Trust's Official Guide
   to the Civil War Discovery Trail
Frommer's Caribbean Hideaways
Frommer's Europe's Greatest Driving Tours
Frommer's Food Lover's Companion to France
Frommer's Food Lover's Companion to Italy
Frommer's Gay & Lesbian Europe

Israel Past & Present
Monks' Guide to California
Monks' Guide to New York City
New York City with Kids
New York Times Weekends
Outside Magazine's Guide
   to Family Vacations
Places Rated Almanac
Retirement Places Rated
Washington, D.C., with Kids
Wonderful Weekends from Boston
Wonderful Weekends from New York City
Wonderful Weekends from San Francisco
Wonderful Weekends from Los Angeles